Brief Version of

STARTING OUT WITH

C++

4th Edition Update

Tony Gaddis
Barret Krupnow

PEARSON
Addison
Wesley

Boston San Francisco New York
London Toronto Sydney Tokyo Singapore Madrid
Mexico City Munich Paris Cape Town Hong Kong Montreal

Publisher	Greg Tobin
Senior Acquisitions Editor	Michael Hirsch
Editorial Assistant	Lindsey Triebel
Managing Editor	Patty Mahtani
Cover Designer	Nicole Clayton, Joyce Wells
Supplements Supervisor	Jason Miranda
Media Producer	Bethany Tidd
Senior Marketing Manager	Michelle Brown
Marketing assistant	Dana Lopreato
Senior Manufacturing Buyer	Caroline Fell
Text Design, Composition	Stephen Adams
Proofreader	Kristin Furino
Production Coordination	Mario M. Rodriguez

Access the latest information about Addison-Wesley titles from our World Wide Web site:
http://www.aw-bc.com/computing

Many of the designations used by manufacturers and sellers to distinguish their products are claimed as trademarks. Where those designations appear in this book, and Addison-Wesley was aware of a trademark claim, the designations have been printed in initial caps or all caps.

The programs and applications presented in this book have been included for their instructional value. They have been tested with care but are not guaranteed for any particular purpose. The published does not offer any warranties or representations, nor does it accept any liabilities with respect to the programs or applications.

Library of Congress Cataloging-in-Publication Data

Gaddis, Tony.
   Starting Out with C++ / Tony Gaddis and Barret Krupnow.-- Brief version, 4th ed. Update
      p. cm.

   ISBN 0-321-38766-X

   1. C++ (Computer program language) I. Krupnow, Barret. II. Title.

   QA76.73.C153G33 2005

   005.13'3--dc22

                                                                    2005016015

ISBN 0-321-38766-X
 2 3 4 5 6 7 8 9 10—CRS—09 08 07 06 05

Preface

The Brief Version of *Starting Out with C++, Fourth Edition Update,* is intended for use in a one-semester C++ programming course, or a two-quarter C++ programming sequence. Students who are new to programming, as well those with prior course work in other languages, will find this text beneficial. The fundamentals of programming are covered for the novice, while the details, pitfalls, and nuances of the C++ language are explored in-depth for both the beginner and more experienced student. The book is written in clear, easy-to-understand language. At the same time, it covers all the necessary topics of an introductory computer science course. The text is rich in example programs that are concise, practical, and real world oriented. This approach is used so the student not only learns how to implement the features and constructs of C++, but why and when to use them.

Organization of the Text

This text teaches C++ in a step-by-step fashion. Each chapter covers a major set of topics and builds knowledge as the student progresses through the book. Although the chapters can be easily taught in their existing sequence, some flexibility is provided. The following diagram suggests possible sequences of instruction.

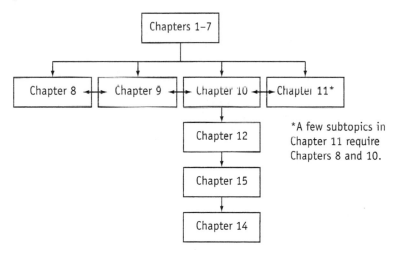

Chapters 1–7 cover the fundamentals of design, flow control, modular programming, and an introduction to arrays. Then, the professor may choose to continue to Chapter 8, 9, 10 or 11. Chapters 12–14 should be covered after Chapter 10.

The approach taken in this text is to start with a firm foundation in structured, procedural programming. Only then does the text delve fully into object-oriented programming and advanced data structures.

Global Changes in the Fourth Edition Update

◆ Previously, this book had a lot of programs using variables of the `float` data type. Most of these have been changed to use the `double` data type.

◆ Previously, named constants were sometimes written in camel-casing, just like a regular variable name. Here is an example of how a named constant definition might appear in previous printings:

```
const double interestRate = 0.03;
```

In this edition, all named constants are written in uppercase characters. Here is an example of how a named constant definition now appears:

```
const double INTEREST_RATE = 0.03;
```

◆ Previous editions and printings had a lot of programs that used literal values as array size declarators. In this edition, named constants are consistently used as array size declarators.

◆ The truth tables in Chapter 4 have been improved for readability.

◆ In previous editions and printings, the `eof` member function was introduced in Chapter 5 for detecting the end of a file. Now the student is shown the more reliable technique of testing the return value of the stream extraction operator. The `eof` member function is still discussed in Chapter 11, however.

◆ Enumerated data types (`enum`) are now discussed in-depth in Chapter 10.

◆ The appendices on the Student CD have been reorganized. Now each appendix is stored in its own PDF file. This should make it easier for students to locate specific appendices. There is also a `ReadMe.html` file on the CD that will help students navigate to the appendices.

◆ A new appendix on using the Unified Modeling Language (UML) in class design has been added to the Student CD. The UML icon 🔧 appears throughout Chapters 12, 13, and 14 alerting the student to the contents of the appendix.

◆ A new appendix on the .NET Framework and managed C++ has been added to the Student CD. The .NET icon . net appears at various locations alerting the student to the contents of the appendix.

The following overview details the changes that were made to the individual chapters.

Brief Overview of Each Chapter

Chapter 1: Introduction to Computers and Programming. This chapter provides an introduction to the field of computer science, and covers the fundamentals of programming, problem solving, and software engineering. The components of programs, such as key words, variables, operators, and punctuation are covered. The tools of the trade, such as hierarchy charts, flow charts and pseudocode are also presented.

Chapter 2: Introduction to C++. This chapter gets the student started in C++ by introducing data types, identifiers, variable declarations, constants, comments, program output, and simple arithmetic operations. The conventions of programming style are also introduced.

Chapter 3: Expressions and Interactivity. In this chapter, the student learns to write programs that allow numeric, character, and C-string input. The creation of mathematical expressions is also taught. These topics include operators, conversion and promotion, typecasting, and library functions for working with numbers.

Chapter 4: Making Decisions. Here the student learns about relational operators, relational expressions and how to control the flow of a program with the if, if/else, and if/else if statements. The conditional operator and the switch statement are also covered. Crucial applications of these constructs are covered, such as menu-driven programs and the validation of input.

Chapter 5: Looping. This chapter covers C++'s repetition control structures. The while loop, do-while loop, and for loop are taught, along with common uses for these devices. Counters, accumulators, running totals, sentinels, and other application-related topics are discussed.

Changes in Chapter 5 for the Fourth Edition Update

The section on using a loop to read data from a file has been modified. The section now uses the stream extraction operator's return value to detect the end of the file.

Chapter 6: Functions. The student learns how and why to modularize programs. Arguments, parameters, return values, local, and global variables are taught. Overloaded functions are also discussed and demonstrated.

Chapter 7: Arrays. Here the student learns to create and work with single and multi-dimensional arrays. Programming techniques using parallel arrays are also discussed and demonstrated. The STL vector is also introduced in this chapter.

Chapter 8: Pointers. This chapter explains how to use pointers. The topics include pointer arithmetic, initialization of pointers, comparison of pointers, pointers and arrays, pointers and functions, dynamic memory allocation, and more.

Chapter 9: Characters C-strings, and the Standard string Class. This chapter focuses on library functions that manipulate or test characters or strings. A review of the internal storage of strings is given. An extensive discussion of the standard string class is also presented. Coverage of the string class in each subsequent chapter is optional. Exercises in each subsequent chapter assume students have become familiar with C style strings, but can easily be adapted for string class objects.

Changes in Chapter 10 for the Fourth Edition Update

In the Fourth Edition Update, a new section discussing enumerated data types in detail has been added.

Chapter 10: Structured Data. In this chapter, the student is introduced to enumerated data types and abstract data types. The student will learn how to implement abstract data types through the use of C++ structures and unions. Discussion and examples include using `enum`, pointers to structures, passing structures to functions, and returning structures from functions.

Chapter 11: Advanced File Operations. This chapter discusses advanced techniques for working with sequential access, random access, text, and binary files. The various modes for opening files are discussed, as well as the many methods for reading and writing file contents.

Chapter 12: Introduction to Classes. The student now shifts focus to the object-oriented paradigm. This chapter covers the fundamental concepts of classes. Member variables and functions are discussed. The student learns about private and public access specifications, and reasons to use each. The topics of constructors, overloaded constructors, and destructors are also presented.

Changes in Chapter 12 for the Fourth Edition Update

In the Fourth Edition Update, UML icons are inserted alerting the student to the contents of the new UML appendix.

Chapter 13: More About Classes. This chapter continues the study of classes. Static members, friends, memberwise assignment, and copy constructors are discussed. The chapter also includes in-depth sections on operator overloading, object conversion, and object composition.

Changes in Chapter 13 for the Fourth Edition Update

In the Fourth Edition Update, UML icons are inserted alerting the student to the contents of the new UML appendix.

Chapter 14: Inheritance and Polymorphism. The study of classes concludes in this chapter with the subjects of inheritance and polymorphism. The topics covered include base and derived class constructors and destructors, virtual member functions, base class pointers, multiple inheritance, and layers of inheritance.

Changes in Chapter 14 for the Fourth Edition Update

In the Fourth Edition Update, UML icons are inserted alerting the student to the contents of the new UML appendix.

The following appendices are on the accompanying Student CD:

Appendix A: ASCII Chart. Lists the ASCII and Extended ASCII characters and their codes.

Appendix B: Operator Precedence. Lists the C++ operators and their precedence.

Appendix C: Introduction to Flowcharting. A brief introduction to flowcharting. This tutorial discusses sequence, selection, case, repetition, and module structures. Sample flowcharts for several of the book's example programs are presented.

Appendix D: New in the Fourth Edition Update

Appendix D: Using UML in Class Design. This appendix shows the student how to use the Unified Modeling Language to design classes. Notation for showing access specification, data types, parameters, return values, overloaded functions, composition, and inheritance are included.

Appendix E: Namespaces. This appendix explains namespaces and their purpose. Examples showing how to define a namespace and access its members are given.

Appendix F: New in the Fourth Edition Update

Appendix F: .NET and Managed C++. This appendix introduces the student to the concepts surrounding managed C++ in Microsoft's .NET environment.

Appendix G: Passing Command-Line Arguments. Teaches the student how to write a C++ program that accepts arguments from the command line. This appendix will be useful to students working in a command line environment, such Unix, Linux, or the Windows MS-DOS prompt console.

Appendix H: Header File and Function Reference. This appendix provides a reference for the C++ library functions and header files discussed in the book.

Appendix I: Binary Numbers and Bitwise Operations. A guide to the C++ bitwise operators, as well as a tutorial on the internal storage of integers.

Appendix J: Multi Source File Programs. Provides a tutorial on creating programs that consist of multiple source files. Function header files, class specification files, and class implementation files are discussed.

Appendix K: Introduction to Microsoft Visual C++ 6.0. A tutorial on how to start a project in Microsoft Visual C++ 6.0, compile a program, save source files, and more.

Appendix L: Introduction to Borland C++ Builder 5. A tutorial on how to start a Borland C++ Builder 5 project, compile a program, save source files, and more.

Appendix M: Introduction to Microsoft Visual C++ .NET. This appendix shows the student how to start a project, compile and run, save, and reopen files. It also explains how to set up a multifile project. (The appendix on Visual C++ 6.0 is still with the book.)

Appendix N: Stream Member Functions for Formatting. Because the book now focuses on stream manipulators, the material on stream member functions for formatting (such as `setf`) has been moved to this appendix.

Appendix O: Linked Lists. This appendix covers linked list operations such as creating a linked list, appending a node, traversing the list, searching for a node, inserting a node, deleting a node, and destroying the list.

Appendix P: Recursion. Recursion is defined and demonstrated. This appendix discusses recursive applications and demonstrates a recursive factorial function.

Appendix Q: Searching and Sorting Arrays, This appendix discusses the basics of sorting arrays and searching for data stored in them. It covers the bubble sort, selection sort, linear search, and binary search algorithms.

Appendix R: Answers to Checkpoints. Students may test their own progress by comparing their answers to the checkpoint exercises against this appendix. The answers to all Checkpoints are included.

Appendix S: Answers to Odd-Numbered Review Questions. Another tool that students can use to gauge their progress.

Features of the Text

CONCEPT	*Concept Statements* Each major section of the text starts with a concept statement. This statement concisely summarizes the meaning of the section.

Example Programs The text has an abundant number of complete and partial example programs, each designed to highlight the topic currently being studied. In most cases, the programs are practical, real-world examples.

Program Output

After each example program is a sample of its screen output. This immediately shows the student how the program functions.

 ## Checkpoints

Checkpoints are questions placed at intervals throughout each chapter. They are designed to query the student's knowledge quickly after learning a new topic.

 Note: Notes appear throughout the text. They are short explanations of interesting or often misunderstood points relevant to the topic at hand.

 WARNING! Warnings are notes that caution the student about certain C++ features, programming techniques, or practices that can lead to malfunctioning programs or lost data.

Case Studies Case studies that simulate real-world business applications are placed throughout the text. These case studies are designed to highlight the major topics of each chapter they appear in.

Review Questions Each chapter presents a thorough and diverse set of review questions. The format of these includes fill-in-the-blank, true–false, multiple choice, short answer, and find the error.

Programming Challenges Each chapter offers a pool of programming exercises designed to solidify the student's knowledge of topics at hand. In most cases the assignments present real-world problems to be solved. When applicable, these exercises also include input validation rules.

Group Projects There are several group programming projects throughout the text, which can be constructed by a team of students. One student might build the program's user interface, while another student writes the mathematical code, and another designs the file I/O. This process is similar to the way many professional programs are written and encourages teamwork within the classroom.

MyCodeMate The Online Tutorial and Homework Resource

Addison-Wesley's MyCodeMate is a book-specific resource that provides tutorial help and evaluation of student work on programming challenges. The code displays and selected programming challenges in this book have been fully integrated into MyCodeMate. Using MyCodeMate, a student can get hints on programming challenges, write and compile the project, and receive feedback on how to address compiler error messages, all over any computer with Internet access. Instructors can track each student's progress on many of the books programming challenges, and can develop projects of their own. A complimentary subscription is offered when an access code is ordered packaged with a new copy of this text. Subscriptions may also be purchased online. For more information visit www.MyCodeMate.com, or contact your campus Addison-Wesley representative.

Supplements

A variety of supplemental materials are available for this text. The following resources are available for all students on a CD in this book, as well as at www.aw.com/cssupport:

- ◆ Source Code for all the example programs in this book;
- ◆ A collection of valuable C++ programming appendices;
- ◆ A Flowcharting tutorial;

The CDs also include a variety of C++ programming environments.

In addition, the following supplements are available to qualified instructors. Visit our Instructor Resource Center (www.aw.com/irc) or send email to computing@aw.com for information on how to access them:

- ◆ Answers to Review Questions;
- ◆ Solutions for Programming Challenges;
- ◆ PowerPoint presentation slides for each chapter;
- ◆ Test Bank in powerful test generator software -- includes a wealth of free response, multiple choice, and true/false type questions;

A Lab Manual (along with Instructors supplements) is available as a stand-alone item, or packaged with this book. Contact your local Addison-Wesley representative for more information or visit www.aw.com/computing.

◆ *Starting Out Quickly with Visual C++ 6.0* by Doug White. Northern Colorado University, a brief introduction to the rudiments of the Visual C++ 6.0 Development Environment

Web Resources

The web site for the *Starting Out with C++* series of books is located at the following URL:

`http://www.aw.com/gaddisbooks`

Versions of This Book

Anyone who has ever taught out of a book that tried to be "all things to all people" knows that the book probably didn't work very well. Accordingly, this book appears in two additional formats, for classes with alternate objectives and preferences. The differences among these formats are summarized below:

	Standard Version (late objects)	This Book	Alternate Version (early objects)
Use of C-strings and the C++ string Class	Null-terminated C-strings are fully covered throughout the text. The C++ string class is introduced in Chapter 10.	Null-terminated C-strings are fully covered throughout the text. The C++ string class is introduced in Chapter 9.	C++ string class objects used throughout with information on C-strings covered in Chapters 3 and 12.
File Operations	File operations are introduced in Chapters 3, 4, and 5. Chapter 12 presents advanced file operations.	File operations are introduced in Chapters 3, 4, and 5. Chapter 11 presents advanced file operations.	File operations are introduced in Chapters 3 and 5. Chapter 14 provides presents advanced file operations.
Data structures and advanced programming	Includes chapters on exceptions, templates, the Standard Template Library (STL), linked lists, stacks, queues, recursion, and binary trees.	Includes appendices on sorting and searching arrays, linked lists, recursion, and binary numbers.	Includes chapters on exceptions, templates, the Standard Template Library (STL), linked lists, stacks, queues, recursion, and binary trees.

	Standard Version (late objects)	This Book	Alternate Version (early objects)
Introduction to classes and object-oriented programming	Classes are introduced in Chapter 13, after control structures, arrays, and functions. Advanced class topics, inheritance, and polymorphism are covered in Chapters 14 and 15.	Classes are introduced in Chapter 11, after control structures, arrays, and functions. Advanced class topics, inheritance, and polymorphism are covered in Chapters 12 and 13.	Classes are introduced in Chapter 7, after control structures and functions, but before arrays. The use of classes and objects is discussed throughout the remainder of the text. Advanced class topics, inheritance, and polymorphism are covered in Chapters 11 and 13.

Acknowledgments

There have been many helping hands in the development and publication of this text. We would like to thank the following faculty reviewers for their helpful suggestions and expertise during the production of this manuscript:

Reviewers for the Fourth Edition Update

Karen M. Arlien
Bismark State College

Joseph DeLibero
Arizona State University

Michael Dowell
Augusta State U

Ranette Halverson, Ph.D.
Midwestern State University

Ric Heishman
Northern Virgina Community College

Ilga Higbee
Black Hawk College

A.J. Krygeris
Houston Community College

Jennifer Li
Augusta State University

Norman H. Liebling
San Jacinto College

Rick Matzen
Northeastern State University

Dean Mellas
Cerritos College

Frederick Pratter
Eastern Oregon University

Dale Suggs
Campbell University–Pope Air Force Base

David Topham
Ohlone College

Reviewers for the Previous Edition

Ahmad Abuhejleh
University of Wisconsin, River Falls

David Akins
El Camino College

Steve Allan
Utah State University

Vicki Allan
Utah State University

Jaz A. Awan
Savannah State University

Robert Baird
Salt Lake Community College

Don Biggerstaff
Fayetteville Technical Community College

Michael Bolton
Northeastern Oklahoma State University

Bill Brown
Pikes Peak Community College

Charles Cadenhead
Richland Community College

Randall Campbell
Morningside College

Randolph Campbell
Morningside College

Wayne Caruolo
Red Rocks Community College

Cathi Chambley-Miller
Aiken Technical College

C.C. Chao
Jacksonville State University

Joseph Chao
Bowling Green State University

Royce Curtis
Western Wisconsin Technical College

Jeanne Douglas
University of Vermont

Judy Etchison
University of Texas at Dallas

Dennis Fairclough
Utah Valley State College

Richard Flint
North Central College

James Gifford
University of Wisconsin, Stevens Point

Leon Gleiberman
Touro College

Carol Hannahs
University of Kentucky

Dennis Heckman
Portland Community College

Ric Heishman
Northern Virginia Community College–Manassas Campus

Michael Hennessy
University of Oregon

Patricia Hines
Brookdale Community College

Mike Holland
Northern Virginia Community College

Mary Hovik
Lehigh Carbon Community College

Richard Hull
Lenoir-Rhyne College

Chris Kardaras
North Central College

Willard Keeling
Blue Ridge Community College

Ray Larson
Inver Hills Community College

Zhu-qu Lu
University of Maine, Presque Isle

Heidar Malki
University of Houston

Debbie Mathews
J. Sargeant Reynolds

Robert McDonald
East Stroudsburg University

James McGuffee
Austin Community College

Dean Mellas
Cerritos College

Lisa Milkowski
Milwaukee School of Engineering

Marguerite Nedreberg
Youngstown State University

Lynne O'Hanlon
Los Angeles Pierce College

Frank Paiano
Southwestern Community College

Theresa Park
Texas State Technical College

Mark Parker
Shoreline Community College

Tino Posillico
SUNY Farmingdale

Susan L. Quick
Penn State University

Alberto Ramón
Diablo Valley College

Bazlur Rasheed
*Sault College of Applied Arts
and Technology*

Dolly Samson
Weber State University

Dr. Sung Shin
South Dakota State University

Ruth Sapir
SUNY Farmingdale

Bari Siddique
University of Texas at Brownsville

Shep Smithline
University of Minnesota

Caroline St. Claire
North Central College

Kirk Stephens
Southwestern Community College

Cherie Stevens
South Florida Community College

Mark Swanson
Red Wing Technical College

Dale A. Suggs
Campbell University

Martha Tillman
College of San Mateo

Ralph Tomlinson
Iowa State University

David Topham
Ohlone College

Rober Tureman
Paul D. Camp Community College

Arisa K. Ude
Richland College

Stewart Venit
California State University, Los Angeles

Judy Walters
North Central College

Vida Winans
Illinois Institute of Technology

John H. Whipple
Northampton Community College

The authors would like to thank their families for their tremendous support throughout this project. We would also like to thank the entire computer science team at Addison-Wesley, especially Michael Hirsch and Michelle Brown, for their commitment to this book. We also want to thank our long-time friend and mentor Richard Jones for his guidance and expertise. In addition, Mario Rodriguez, Stephen Adams, Kristin Furino and Nicole Clayton worked tirelessly to bring this book into production. Thanks to you all! Of course, we thank our students at Haywood Community College for inspiring us to write student-friendly textbooks.

About the Authors

Tony Gaddis is the principal author of the "Starting Out with" series of textbooks. Tony teaches computer science courses at Haywood Community College in North Carolina. He is a highly acclaimed instructor who was previously selected as the North Carolina Community College "Teacher of the Year," and has received the Teaching Excellence award from the National Institute for Staff and Organizational Development. Besides C++ books, the "Starting Out with" series includes introductory books using the Java™ programming language, Microsoft® Visual Basic® .NET, and Microsoft® C#®, all published by Addison-Wesley.

Barret Krupnow teaches computer science, electronic engineering, and telecommunications courses at Haywood Community College in North Carolina. He has also worked as an engineering consultant and software developer in North Carolina's Research Triangle Park.

Contents at a Glance

Contents

The following appendices are on the accompanying student CD:

1

Introduction to Computers
and Programming

- ## Topics in this Chapter

1.1   Why Program?

CONCEPT Computers can do many different jobs because they are programmable.

Every profession has tools that make its job easier to do. Carpenters use hammers, saws, and measuring tapes. Mechanics use wrenches, screwdrivers, and ratchets. Electronics technicians use probes, scopes, and meters. Some tools are unique and can be categorized as belonging to a single profession. For example, surgeons have certain tools that are designed specifically for surgical operations. Those tools probably aren't used by anyone other than surgeons. There are some tools, however, that are used in several professions. Screwdrivers, for instance, are used by mechanics, carpenters, and many others.

The computer is a tool that is used by so many professions, it cannot be easily categorized. It can perform so many different jobs that it is perhaps the most versatile tool ever made. To the accountant, computers balance books, analyze profits and losses, and prepare tax reports. To the factory worker, computers control manufacturing machines and track production. To

- 1

the mechanic, computers analyze the various systems in an automobile and pinpoint hard-to-find problems.

What makes the computer so useful? Quite simply, the computer can do such a wide variety of tasks because it can be *programmed*. It is a machine specifically designed to follow instructions.

Because of the computer's programmability, it doesn't belong to any single profession. Computers are designed to do whatever job their programs, or *software*, tell them to do.

Computer programmers do a very important job. They create software that transforms computers into the specialized tools of many trades. Without programmers, the users of computers would have no software, and without software, computers would not be able to do anything.

Computer programming is both an art and a science. It is an art because every aspect of a program should be carefully designed. Listed below are a few of the things that must be designed for any real-world computer program:

- ◆ The logical flow of the instructions

- ◆ The mathematical procedures

- ◆ The appearance of the screens

- ◆ The way information is presented to the user

- ◆ The program's "user-friendliness"

- ◆ Manuals and other forms of written documentation

There is also a scientific, or engineering side to programming. Because programs rarely work right the first time they are written, a lot of experimentation, correction, and redesigning is required. This demands patience and persistence of the programmer. Writing software demands discipline as well. Programmers must learn special languages like C++ because computers do not understand English or other human languages. Languages such as C++ have strict rules that must be carefully followed.

Both the artistic and scientific nature of programming makes writing computer software like designing a car: Both cars and programs should be functional, efficient, powerful, easy to use, and pleasing to look at.

1.2 Computer Systems: Hardware and Software

CONCEPT All computer systems consist of similar hardware devices and software components. This section provides an overview of standard computer hardware and software organization.

Hardware

Hardware refers to the physical components that a computer is made of. A computer, as we generally think of it, is not an individual device, but a system of devices. Like the instruments in a symphony orchestra, each device plays its own part. A typical computer system consists of the following major components:

1. The central processing unit (CPU)
2. Main memory
3. Secondary storage devices
4. Input devices
5. Output devices

The organization of a computer system is depicted in Figure 1-1.

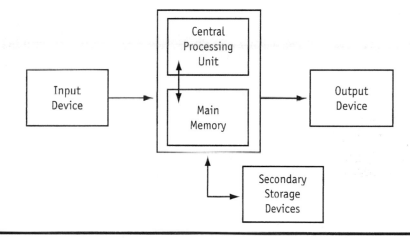

Figure 1-1

The CPU

At the heart of a computer is its *central processing unit,* or *CPU.* The CPU's job is to fetch instructions, follow the instructions, and produce some result or resultant information. Internally, the central processing unit consists of two parts: the *control unit* and the *arithmetic and logic unit* *(ALU).* The control unit coordinates all of the computer's operations. It is responsible for determining where to get the next instruction and regulating the other major components of the computer with control signals. The arithmetic and logic unit, as its name suggests, is designed to perform mathematical operations. The organization of the CPU is shown in Figure 1-2.

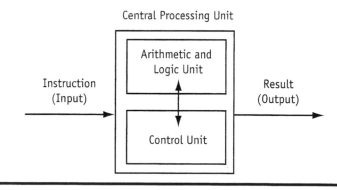

Figure 1-2

A program is a sequence of instructions stored in the computer's memory. When a computer is running a program, the CPU is engaged in a process known formally as the *fetch/decode/execute cycle*. The steps in the fetch/decode/execute cycle are as follows:

Fetch   The CPU's control unit fetches, from main memory, the next instruction in the sequence of program instructions.

Decode   The instruction is encoded in the form of a number. The control unit decodes the instruction and generates an electronic signal.

Execute   The signal is routed to the appropriate component of the computer (such as the ALU, a disk drive, or some other device). The signal causes the component to perform an operation.

These steps are repeated as long as there are instructions to perform.

Main Memory

Commonly known as *random-access memory*, or *RAM*, the computer's main memory is a device that holds information. Specifically, RAM holds the sequences of instructions in the programs that are running and the data those programs are using.

Memory is divided into sections, or cells, that each holds an equal amount of data. Each cell is made of eight "switches" that may be either on or off. A switch that is in the on position usually represents the number 1, while a switch in the off position usually represents the number 0. The computer stores data by setting the switches in a memory cell to a pattern that represents a character of information. Each of these switches is known as a *bit*, which stands for *binary digit*. Each cell, which is a collection of eight bits, is known as a *byte*. Each byte is assigned a unique number known as an *address*. The addresses are ordered from lowest to highest. A byte is identified by its address in much the same way a post office box is identified by an address. Figure 1-3 shows a group of memory cells with their addresses. In the illustration, sample data is stored in memory. The number 149 is stored in the cell with the address 16, and the number 72 is stored at address 23.

0	1	2	3	4	5	6	7	8	9
10	11	12	13	14	15	16 149	17	18	19
20	21	22	23 72	24	25	26	27	28	29

Figure 1-3

RAM is usually a volatile type of memory, used only for temporary storage. When the computer is turned off, the contents of RAM are erased.

Secondary Storage

Secondary storage is a type of memory that can hold data for long periods of time—even when there is no power to the computer. Frequently used programs are stored in secondary memory and loaded into main memory as needed. Important information, such as word processing documents, payroll data, and inventory figures, is saved to secondary storage as well.

The most common type of secondary storage device is the *disk drive*. A disk drive stores data by magnetically encoding it onto a circular disk. There are several different types of disks, each with advantages and disadvantages. The most common types are hard disks, floppy disks, and Zip disks. Hard disks are capable of storing very large amounts of data and can access data quickly. Hard disks are not usually portable, however. Floppy disks are small and portable, but hold only a small amount of data. Also, a floppy disk drive's access speed is considerably slower than that of a hard disk. A Zip disk is a small portable device that holds much more data than a floppy disk.

Optical devices such as the compact disc (CD) are also popular for data storage. Data is not recorded magnetically on a CD, but is encoded as a series of pits on the disc surface. The CD drive uses a laser to detect the pits and thus reads the encoded data. CDs hold large amounts of data, and because recordable CD drives are now commonplace, they make a suitable backup medium.

Input Devices

Input is any information the computer collects from the outside world. The device that collects the information and sends it to the computer is called an *input device*. Common input devices are the keyboard, mouse, scanner, digital camera, and microphone. Disk drives and CD drives can also be considered input devices because programs and information are retrieved from them and loaded into the computer's memory.

Output Devices

Output is any information the computer sends to the outside world. It might be a sales report, a list of names, or a graphic image. The information is sent to an *output device*, which formats and presents it. Common output devices are monitors, printers and speakers. Output sent to a monitor is sometimes called "softcopy," while output sent to a printer is called "hardcopy." Disk drives and CD recorders can also be considered output devices because the CPU sends information to them in order to be saved.

Software

As previously mentioned, software refers to the programs that run on a computer. There are two general categories of software: *operating systems* and *application software*. An operating system is a set of programs that manages the computer's hardware devices and controls their processes. Operating systems fall into one of the following categories.

Single tasking A single tasking operating system is capable of running only one program at a time. The computer devotes all its hardware resources and CPU time to each program as it executes. MS-DOS is an example of a single tasking operating system.

Multitasking   A multitasking operating system is capable of running multiple programs
                     at once. Through a technique called *time sharing*, the system divides the
                     allocation of hardware resources and the attention of the CPU among all
                     the executing programs. UNIX, Windows 2000, and Windows XP are
                     multitasking operating systems.

In addition, operating systems fall into one of the following categories, which describe the number of users they can accommodate.

Single user   This type of system allows only one user to operate the computer at a time.
                     MS-DOS and Windows 9X are single user operating systems.

Multiuser   Multiuser systems allow several users to run programs and operate the
                     computer at once. Most variations of the UNIX operating system are
                     multiuser systems.

Application software refers to programs that make the computer useful to the user. These programs solve specific problems or perform general operations that satisfy the needs of the user. Word processing, spreadsheet, and database packages are all examples of application software.

 ## Checkpoint   [1.1–1.2]

1.1   Why is the computer used by so many different people, in so many different professions?

1.2   List the five major hardware components of a computer system.

1.3   Internally, the CPU consists of what two units?

1.4   Describe the steps in the fetch/decode/execute cycle.

1.5   What is a memory address? What is its purpose?

1.6   Explain why computers have both main memory and secondary storage.

1.7   What are the two general categories of software?

1.8   What is the difference between a single tasking system and a multitasking system?

1.9   What is the difference between a single user system and a multiuser system?

1.3   Programs and Programming Languages

 A program is a set of instructions a computer follows in order to perform a task. A programming language is a special language used to write computer programs.

What Is a Program?

Computers are designed to follow instructions. A computer program is a set of instructions that tells the computer how to solve a problem or perform a task. For example, suppose we want the computer to calculate someone's gross pay. Here is a list of things the computer should do:

1. Display a message on the screen asking "How many hours did you work?"
2. Wait for the user to enter the number of hours worked. Once the user enters a number, store it in memory.
3. Display a message on the screen asking "How much do you get paid per hour?"
4. Wait for the user to enter an hourly pay rate. Once the user enters a number, store it in memory.
5. Multiply the number of hours by the amount paid per hour, and store the result in memory.
6. Display a message on the screen that tells the amount of money earned. The message must include the result of the calculation performed in Step 5.

Collectively, these instructions are called an *algorithm*. An algorithm is a set of well-defined steps for performing a task or solving a problem. Notice these steps are sequentially ordered. Step 1 should be performed before Step 2, and so forth. It is important that these instructions be performed in their proper sequence.

In order for a computer to perform instructions such as the pay-calculating algorithm, the steps must be converted to a form the computer can process. In reality, the CPU only processes instructions written in *machine language*. If you were to look at a machine language program, you would only see a stream of numbers. The CPU interprets these numbers as commands. As you might imagine, the process of encoding an algorithm in machine language is very tedious and difficult. *Computer programming languages*, which use words instead of numbers, were invented to ease this task. Programmers can write their programs in a language such as C++, and then use special software to convert the program into machine language.

Program 1-1 shows how the pay-calculating algorithm might be written in C++.

Program 1-1

```
// This program calculates the user's pay.

#include <iostream>
using namespace std;

int main()
{
    double hours, rate, pay;

    cout << "How many hours did you work? ";
    cin >> hours;
    cout << "How much do you get paid per hour? ";
    cin >> rate;
    pay = hours * rate;
    cout << "You have earned $" << pay << endl;
    return 0;
}
```

Program Output with Example Input Shown in Bold
```
How many hours did you work? 10 [Enter]
How much do you get paid per hour? 15 [Enter]
You have earned $150
```

The "Program Output with Example Input" shows what the program will display on the screen when it is running. In the example, the user enters 10 for the number of hours worked and 15 for the hourly pay rate. The program displays the earnings, which are $150.

Programming Languages

In a broad sense, there are two categories of programming languages: low-level and high-level. A low-level language is close to the level of the computer, which means it resembles the numeric machine language of the computer more than the natural language of humans. The easiest languages for people to learn are *high-level languages*. They are called "high-level" because they are closer to the level of human-readability than computer-readability. Figure 1-4 illustrates the concept of language levels.

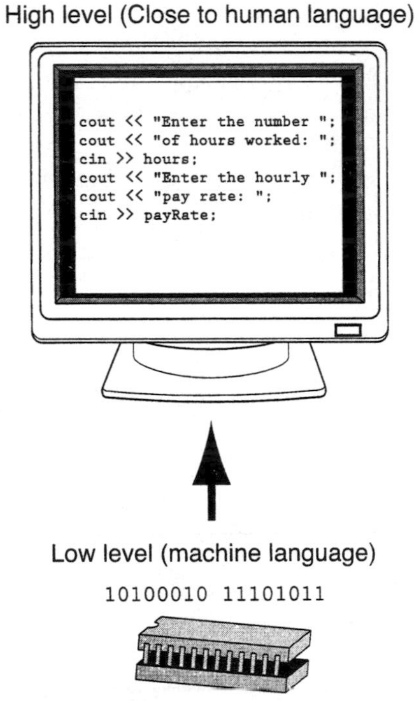

High level (Close to human language)

```
cout << "Enter the number ";
cout << "of hours worked: ";
cin >> hours;
cout << "Enter the hourly ";
cout << "pay rate: ";
cin >> payRate;
```

Low level (machine language)

10100010 11101011

Figure 1-4

Many high-level languages have been created. Table 1-1 lists a few of the well-known ones.

In addition to the high-level features necessary for writing applications such as payroll systems and inventory programs, C++ also has many low-level features. C++ is based on the C language, which was invented for purposes such as writing operating systems and compilers. Since C++ evolved from C, it carries all of C's low-level capabilities with it.

C++ is popular not only because of its mixture of low and high-level features, but also because of its *portability*. This means that a C++ program can be written on one type of computer and then run on many other types of systems. This usually requires the program to be re-compiled on each type of system, but the program itself may need little or no change.

Table 1-1

Language	Description
BASIC	Beginners All-purpose Symbolic Instruction Code. A general programming language originally designed to be simple enough for beginners to learn.
FORTRAN	Formula Translator. A language designed for programming complex mathematical algorithms.
COBOL	Common Business-Oriented Language. A language designed for business applications.
Pascal	A structured, general-purpose language designed primarily for teaching programming.
C	A structured, general-purpose language developed at Bell Laboratories. C offers both high-level and low-level features.
C++	Based on the C language, C++ offers object-oriented features not found in C. Also invented at Bell Laboratories.
C#	Pronounced "C sharp." A language invented by Microsoft for developing applications based on the Microsoft .NET platform.
Java	An object-oriented language invented at Sun Microsystems. Java may be used to develop programs that run over the Internet, in a Web browser.
Visual Basic	A Microsoft programming language and software development environment that allows programmers to quickly create Windows-based applications.

Note: Programs written for specific graphical environments often require significant changes when moved to a different type of system. Examples of such graphical environments are Windows, the X-Window System, and the Macintosh operating system.

Source Code, Object Code, and Executable Code

When a C++ program is written, it must be typed into the computer and saved to a file. A *text editor*, which is similar to a word processing program, is used for this task. The statements written by the programmer are called *source code*, and the file they are saved in is called the *source file*.

After the source code is saved to a file, the process of translating it to machine language can begin. During the first phase of this process, a program called the *preprocessor* reads the source code. The preprocessor searches for special lines that begin with the # symbol. These lines contain commands that cause the preprocessor to modify the source code in some way. During the next phase the *compiler* steps through the preprocessed source code, translating each source code instruction into the appropriate machine language instruction. This process will uncover any *syntax errors* that may be in the program. Syntax errors are illegal uses of key words, operators, punctuation, and other language elements. If the program is free of syntax errors, the compiler stores the translated machine language instructions, which are called *object code*, in an *object file*.

Although an object file contains machine language instructions, it is not a complete program. Here is why: C++ is conveniently equipped with a library of prewritten code for performing common operations or sometimes-difficult tasks. For example, the library contains hardware-specific code for displaying messages on the screen and reading input from the keyboard. It also provides routines for mathematical functions, such as calculating the square root of a number. This collection of code, called the *run-time library,* is extensive. Programs almost always use some part of it. When the compiler generates an object file, however, it does not include machine code for any runtime library routines the programmer might have used. During the last phase of the translation process, another program called the *linker* combines the object file with the necessary library routines. Once the linker has finished with this step, an *executable file* is created. The executable file contains machine language instructions, or *executable code,* and is ready to run on the computer.

Figure 1-5 illustrates the process of translating a source file into an executable file.

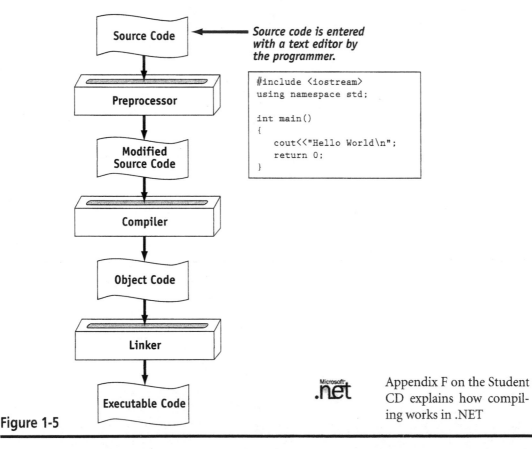

Figure 1-5

Appendix F on the Student CD explains how compiling works in .NET

The entire process of invoking the preprocessor, compiler, and linker can be initiated with a single action. For example, on a Linux system, the following command causes the C++ program named hello.cpp to be preprocessed, compiled, and linked. The executable code is stored in a file named hello.

```
g++ -o hello hello.cpp
```

Many development systems, particularly those on personal computers, have *integrated development environments (IDEs)*. These environments consist of a text editor, compiler, debugger, and other utilities integrated into a package with a single set of menus. Preprocessing, compiling, linking, and even executing a program is done with a single click of a button, or by selecting a single item from a menu. Figure 1-6 shows a screen from the Microsoft Visual C++ 6.0 IDE.

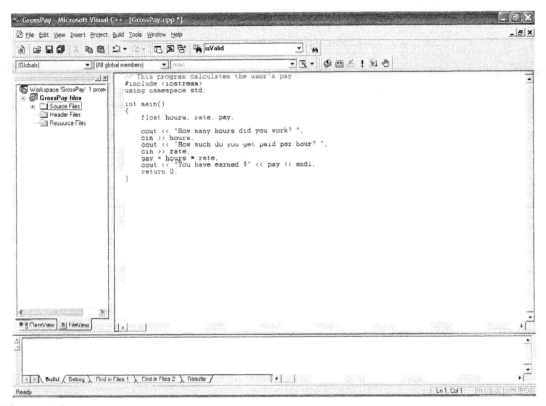

Figure 1-6

Checkpoint [1.3]

1.10 What is an algorithm?

1.11 Why were computer programming languages invented?

1.12 What is the difference between a high-level language and a low-level language?

1.13 What does *portability* mean?

1.14 Explain the operations carried out by the preprocessor, compiler, and linker.

1.15 Explain what is stored in a source file, an object file, and an executable file.

1.16 What is an integrated development environment?

1.4 What Is a Program Made of?

> **CONCEPT** There are certain elements that are common to all programming languages.

Language Elements

All programming languages have a few things in common. Table 1-2 lists the common elements you will find in almost every language.

Table 1-2

Language Element	Description
Key Words	Words that have a special meaning. Key words may only be used for their intended purpose. Key words are also known as reserved words.
Programmer-Defined Identifiers	Words or names defined by the programmer. They are symbolic names that refer to variables or programming routines.
Operators	Operators perform operations on one or more operands. An operand is usually a piece of data, like a number.
Punctuation	Punctuation characters that mark the beginning or ending of a statement, or separate items in a list.
Syntax	Rules that must be followed when constructing a program. Syntax dictates how key words and operators may be used, and where punctuation symbols must appear.

Let's look at some specific parts of Program 1-1 (the pay-calculating program) to see examples of each element listed in the table above. For your convenience, Program 1-1 is listed again, this time with each line numbered.

 Note: The line numbers are NOT part of the program. They are included to help point out specific parts of the program.

Key Words (reserved words)

Four of C++'s key words appear on lines 4 and 6: using, namespace, int, and main. The word double, which appears on line 8, is also a C++ key word. These words, which are always written in lowercase, each have a special meaning in C++ and can only be used for their intended purposes. As you will see, the programmer is allowed to make up his or her own names for certain things in a program. Key words, however, are reserved and cannot be used for anything other than their designated purposes. Part of learning a programming language is learning what the key words are, what they mean, and how to use them.

Program 1-1 (With Line Numbers)

```
1:  // This program calculates the user's pay.
2:
3:  #include <iostream>
4:  using namespace std;
5:
6:  int main()
7:  {
8:      double hours, rate, pay;
9:
10:     cout << "How many hours did you work? ";
11:     cin >> hours;
12:     cout << "How much do you get paid per hour? ";
13:     cin >> rate;
14:     pay = hours * rate;
15:     cout << "You have earned $" << pay << endl;
16:     return 0;
17: }
```

Note: The #include <iostream> statement in line 3 is a preprocessor directive.

Note: In C++, key words are written in all lowercase.

Programmer-Defined Identifiers

The words hours, rate, and pay that appear in the program on lines 8, 11, 13, 14, and 15 are programmer-defined identifiers. They are not part of the C++ language but rather are names made up by the programmer. In this particular program, these are the names of variables. As you will learn later in this chapter, variables are the names of memory locations that may hold data.

Operators

On line 14 the following line appears:

```
pay = hours * rate;
```

The = and * symbols are both operators. They perform operations on pieces of data, known as operands. The * operator multiplies its two operands, which in this example are the variables hours and rate. The = symbol is called the assignment operator. It takes the value of the expression on the right and stores it in the variable whose name appears on the left. In this example, the = operator stores in the pay variable the result of the hours variable multiplied by the rate variable. In other words, the statement says, "Make the pay variable equal to hours times rate, or "pay is assigned the value of hours times rate."

Punctuation

Notice that lines 4, 8, and 10 through 16 end with a semicolon. A semicolon in C++ is similar to a period in English: It marks the end of a complete sentence (or statement, as it is called in programming jargon). Semicolons do not appear at the end of every line in a C++ program, however. There are rules that govern where semicolons are required and where they are not. Part of learning C++ is learning where to place semicolons and other punctuation symbols.

Lines and Statements

Often, the contents of a program are thought of in terms of lines and statements. A "line" is just that—a single line as it appears in the body of a program. Program 1-1 is shown with each of its lines numbered. Most of the lines contain something meaningful; however, some of the lines are empty. The blank lines are only there to make the program more readable.

A statement is a complete instruction that causes the computer to perform some action. Here is the statement that appears in line 10 of Program 1-1:

```
cout << "How many hours did you work? ";
```

This statement causes the computer to display the message "How many hours did you work?" on the screen. Statements can be a combination of key words, operators, and programmer-defined symbols. Statements often occupy only one line in a program, but sometimes they are spread out over more than one line.

Variables

A variable is a named storage location in the computer's memory for holding a piece of information. The information stored in variables may change while the program is running (hence the name "variable"). Notice that in Program 1-1 the words hours, rate, and pay appear in several places. All three of these are the names of variables. The hours variable is used to store the number of hours the user has worked. The rate variable stores the user's hourly pay rate. The pay variable holds the result of hours multiplied by rate, which is the user's gross pay.

 Note: Notice the variables in Program 1-1 have names that reflect their purpose. In fact, it would be easy to guess what the variables were used for just by reading their names. This is discussed further in Chapter 2.

Variables are symbolic names that represent locations in the computer's random-access memory (RAM). When information is stored in a variable, it is actually stored in RAM. Assume a program has a variable named length. Figure 1-7 illustrates the way the variable name represents a memory location.

In Figure 1-7, the variable length is holding the value 7. The number 7 is actually stored in RAM at address 112, but the name length symbolically represents this storage location. If it helps, you can think of a variable as a box that holds information. In Figure 1-7, the number 7 is

100	101	102	103	104	105	106	107	108	109
110	111	112	113	114	115	116	117	118	119

Figure 1-7

length

stored in the box named length. Only one item may be stored in the box at any given time. If the program stores another value in the box, it will take the place of the number 7.

Variable Definitions

In programming, there are two general types of data: numbers and characters. Numbers are used to perform mathematical operations and characters are used to print data on the screen or on paper.

Numeric data can be categorized even further. For instance, the following are all whole numbers, or integers:

```
5
7
-129
32154
```

The following are real, or floating point numbers:

```
3.14159
6.7
1.0002
```

When creating a variable in a C++ program, you must know what type of data the program will be storing in it. Look at line 8 of Program 1-1:

```
double hours, rate, pay;
```

The word double in this statement indicates that the variables hours, rate, and pay will be used to hold double precision floating-point numbers. This statement is called a *variable definition*. It is used to *define* one or more variables that will be used in the program, and indicate the type of data they will hold. The variable definition causes the variables to be created in memory, so all variables must be defined before they can be used. If you review the listing of Program 1-1, you will see that the variable definitions come before any other statements using those variables.

Note: Programmers often use the term "variable declaration" to mean the same thing as "variable definition." Strictly speaking, there is a difference between the two terms. A definition statement always causes a variable to be created in memory. Some types of declaration statements, however, do not cause a variable to be created in memory. You will learn more about declarations later in this book.

1.5 Input, Processing, and Output

> **CONCEPT** The three primary activities of a program are input, processing, and output.

Computer programs typically perform a three-step process of gathering input, performing some process on the information gathered, and then producing output. Input is information a program collects from the outside world. It can be sent to the program from the user, who is entering data at the keyboard or using the mouse. It can also be read from disk files or hardware devices connected to the computer. Program 1-1 allows the user to enter two items of information: the number of hours worked and the hourly pay rate. Lines 11 and 13, use the cin (pronounced "see in") object to perform these input operations:

```
cin >> hours;
cin >> rate;
```

Once information is gathered from the outside world, a program usually processes it in some manner. In Program 1-1, the hours worked and hourly pay rate are multiplied in line 14 and the result is assigned to the pay variable:

```
pay = hours * rate;
```

Output is information that a program sends to the outside world. It can be words or graphics displayed on a screen, a report sent to the printer, data stored in a file, or information sent to any device connected to the computer. Lines 10, 12, and 15 in Program 1-1 all perform output:

```
cout << "How many hours did you work? ";
cout << "How much do you get paid per hour? ";
cout << "You have earned $" << pay << endl;
```

These lines use the cout (pronounced "see out") object to display messages on the computer's screen. You will learn more details about the cin and cout objects in Chapter 2.

Checkpoint   [1.4–1.5]

1.17 Describe the difference between a key word and a programmer-defined symbol.

1.18 Describe the difference between operators and punctuation symbols.

1.19 Describe the difference between a program line and a statement.

1.20 Why are variables called "variable"?

1.21 What happens to a variable's current contents when a new value is stored there?

1.22 What must take place in a program before a variable is used?

1.23 What are the three primary activities of a program?

1.6 The Programming Process

CONCEPT The programming process consists of several steps, which include design, creation, testing, and debugging activities.

Designing and Creating a Program

Now that you have been introduced to what a program is, it's time to consider the process of creating a program. Quite often, when inexperienced students are given programming assignments, they have trouble getting started because they don't know what to do first. If you find yourself in this dilemma, the steps listed in Figure 1-8 may help. These are the steps recommended for the process of writing a program.

1. Clearly define what the program is to do.
2. Visualize the program running on the computer.
3. Use design tools such as a hierarchy chart, flowcharts, or pseudocode to create a model of the program.
4. Check the model for logical errors.
5. Type the code, save it, and compile it.
6. Correct any errors found during compilation. Repeat steps 5 and 6 as many times as necessary.
7. Run the program with test data for input.
8. Correct any errors found while running the program. Repeat steps 5 through 8 as many times as necessary.
9. Validate the results of the program.

Figure 1-8

The steps listed in Figure 1-8 emphasize the importance of planning. Just as there are good ways and bad ways to paint a house, there are good ways and bad ways to create a program. A good program always begins with planning.

With the pay-calculating program as our example, let's look at each of the steps in more detail.

1. Clearly define what the program is to do.

This step requires that you identify the purpose of the program, the information that is to be input, the processing that is to take place, and the desired output. Let's examine each of these requirements for the example program:

Purpose   To calculate the user's gross pay.

Input   Number of hours worked, hourly pay rate.

Process   Multiply number of hours worked by hourly pay rate. The result is the user's gross pay.

Output   Display a message indicating the user's gross pay.

2. Visualize the program running on the computer.

Before you create a program on the computer, you should first create it in your mind. Step 2 is the visualization of the program. Try to imagine what the computer screen looks like while the program is running. If it helps, draw pictures of the screen, with sample input and output, at various points in the program. For instance, here is the screen produced by the pay-calculating program:

```
How many hours did you work? 10
How much do you get paid per hour? 15
You earned $150
```

In this step, you must put yourself in the shoes of the user. What messages should the program display? What questions should it ask? By addressing these concerns, you will have already determined most of the program's output.

3. Use design tools such as a hierarchy chart, flowcharts, or pseudocode to create a model of the program.

While planning a program, the programmer uses one or more design tools to create a model of the program. Three common design tools are hierarchy charts, flowcharts, and pseudocode. A *hierarchy chart* is a diagram that graphically depicts the structure of a program. It has boxes that represent each step in the program. The boxes are connected in a way that illustrates their relationship to one another. Figure 1-9 shows a hierarchy chart for the pay-calculating program.

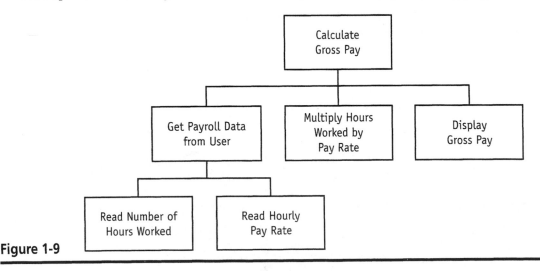

Figure 1-9

A hierarchy chart begins with the overall task, and then refines it into smaller subtasks. Each of the subtasks are then refined into even smaller sets of subtasks, until each are small enough to be easily performed. For instance, in Figure 1-9, the overall task "Calculate Gross Pay" is listed in the top-level box. That task is broken into three subtasks. The first subtask, "Get Payroll Data from User," is broken further into two subtasks. This process of "divide and conquer" is known as *top-down design*.

A *flowchart* is a diagram that shows the logical flow of a program. It is a useful tool for planning each operation a program performs, and the order in which the operations are to occur. For more information see Appendix C, Introduction to Flowcharting.

Pseudocode is a cross between human language and a programming language. Although the computer can't understand pseudocode, programmers often find it helpful to write an algorithm in a language that's "almost" a programming language, but still very similar to natural language. For example, here is pseudocode that describes the pay-calculating program:

> *Get payroll data.*
> *Calculate gross pay.*
> *Display gross pay.*

Although the pseudocode above gives a broad view of the program, it doesn't reveal all the program's details. A more detailed version of the pseudocode follows.

> *Display "How many hours did you work?".*
> *Input hours.*
> *Display "How much do you get paid per hour?".*
> *Input rate.*
> *Store the value of hours times rate in the pay variable.*
> *Display the value in the pay variable.*

Notice the pseudocode contains statements that look more like commands than the English statements that describe the algorithm in section 1.3 (What Is a Program?). The pseudocode even names variables and describes mathematical operations.

4. Check the model for logical errors.

Logical errors are mistakes that cause the program to produce erroneous results. Once a hierarchy chart, flowchart, or pseudocode model of the program is assembled, it should be checked for these errors. The programmer should trace through the charts or pseudocode, checking the logic of each step. If an error is found, the model can be corrected before the next step is attempted.

5. Type the code, save it, and compile it.

Once a model of the program (hierarchy chart, flowchart, or pseudocode) has been created, checked, and corrected, the programmer is ready to write source code on the computer. The programmer saves the source code to a file, and begins the process of translating it to machine language. During this step the compiler will find any syntax errors that may exist in the program.

6. Correct any errors found during compilation. Repeat steps 5 and 6 as many times as necessary.

If the compiler reports any errors, they must be corrected. Steps 5 and 6 must be repeated until the program is free of compile-time errors.

7. Run the program with test data for input.

Once an executable file is generated, the program is ready to be tested for run-time errors. A run-time error is an error that occurs while the program is running. These are usually logical errors, such as mathematical mistakes.

Testing for run-time errors requires that the program be executed with sample data or sample input. The sample data should be such that the correct output can be predicted. If the program does not produce the correct output, a logical error is present in the program.

8. Correct any run-time errors found while running the program. Repeat steps 5 through 8 as many times as necessary.

When run-time errors are found in a program, they must be corrected. You must identify the step where the error occurred and determine the cause. Desk-checking is a process that can help locate run-time errors. The term *desk-checking* means the programmer starts reading the program, or a portion of the program, and steps through each statement. A sheet of paper is often used in this process to jot down the current contents of all variables and sketch what the screen looks like after each output operation. When a variable's contents change, or information is displayed on the screen, this is noted. By stepping through each statement, many errors can be located and corrected. If an error is a result of incorrect logic (such as an improperly stated math formula), you must correct the statement or statements involved in the logic. If an error is due to an incomplete understanding of the program requirements, then you must restate the program purpose, modify the hierarchy and/or flowcharts, pseudocode, and source code. The program must then be saved, re-compiled and re-tested. This means steps 5 through 8 must be repeated until the program reliably produces satisfactory results.

9. Validate the results of the program.

When you believe you have corrected all the run-time errors, enter test data and determine if the program solves the original problem.

What Is Software Engineering?

The field of software engineering encompasses the whole process of crafting computer software. It includes designing, writing, testing, debugging, documenting, modifying, and maintaining complex software development projects. Like traditional engineers, software engineers use a number of tools in their craft. Here are a few examples:

◆ Program specifications

◆ Charts and diagrams of screen output

◆ Hierarchy charts and flowcharts

◆ Pseudocode

◆ Examples of expected input and desired output

◆ Special software designed for testing programs

Most commercial software applications are very large. In many instances one or more teams of programmers, not a single individual, develop them. It is important that the program requirements be thoroughly analyzed and divided into subtasks that are handled by individual teams, or individuals within a team.

In step 3 of the programming process, you were introduced to the hierarchy chart as a tool for top-down design. The subtasks that are identified in a top-down design can easily become modules, or separate components of a program. If the program is very large or complex, a team of software engineers can be assigned to work on the individual modules. As the project develops, the modules are coordinated to finally become a single software application.

1.7 Procedural and Object-Oriented Programming

CONCEPT Procedural programming and object-oriented programming are two ways of thinking about software development and program design.

C++ is a language that can be used for two methods of writing computer programs: *procedural programming* and *object-oriented programming*. This book is designed to teach you some of both.

In procedural programming, the programmer constructs procedures (or functions, as they are called in C++). The procedures are collections of programming statements that perform a specific task. The procedures each contain their own variables and commonly share variables with other procedures. This is illustrated by Figure 1-10.

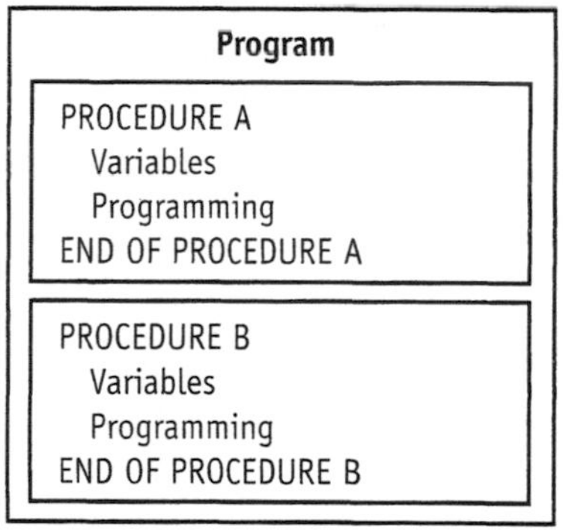

Program

PROCEDURE A
  Variables
  Programming
END OF PROCEDURE A

PROCEDURE B
  Variables
  Programming
END OF PROCEDURE B

Figure 1-10

Procedural programming is centered on the procedure, or function. Object-oriented programming (OOP), on the other hand, is centered on the object. An object is a programming element that contains data and the procedures that operate on the data. It is a self-contained unit. This is illustrated in Figure 1-11.

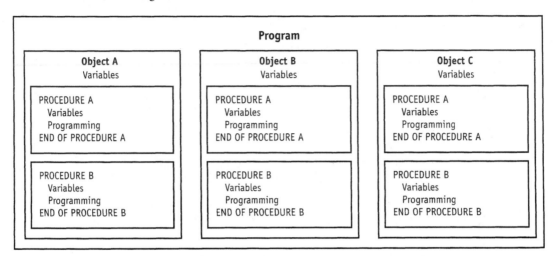

Figure 1-11

The objects contain, within themselves, both information and the ability to manipulate the information. Operations are carried out on the information in an object by sending the object a *message*. When an object receives a message instructing it to perform some operation, it carries out the instruction. As you study this text, you will encounter many other aspects of object-oriented programming.

 ## Checkpoint [1.6–1.7]

1.24 What four items should you identify when defining what a program is to do?

1.25 What does it mean to "visualize a program running"? What is the value of such an activity?

1.26 What is a hierarchy chart?

1.27 Describe the process of desk-checking.

1.28 Describe what a compiler does with a program's source code.

1.29 What is a run-time error?

1.30 Is a syntax error (such as misspelling a key word) found by the compiler or when the program is running?

1.31 What is the purpose of testing a program with sample data or input?

1.32 Briefly describe the difference between procedural and object-oriented programming.

Review Questions and Exercises

Short Answer

1. Both main memory and secondary storage are types of memory. Describe the difference between the two.
2. What is the difference between operating system software and application software?
3. Indicate all the categories that the following operating systems belong to.

   System A   This system allows multiple users to run multiple programs simultaneously.

   System B   Only one user may access the system at a time, but multiple programs can be run simultaneously.

   System C   Only one user may access the system at a time, and only one program can be run on the system at a time.

4. Why must programs written in a high-level language be translated into machine language before they can be run?
5. Why is it easier to write a program in a high-level language than in machine language?
6. Explain the difference between an object file and an executable file.
7. What is the difference between a syntax error and a logical error?

Algorithm Workbench

Draw hierarchy charts or flowcharts that depict the programs described below. (See Appendix C for instructions on creating flowcharts.)

8. Available Credit

   The following steps should be followed in a program that calculates a customer's available credit:

   1. Display the message "Enter the customer's maximum credit."
   2. Wait for the user to enter the customer's maximum credit.
   3. Display the message "Enter the amount of credit used by the customer."
   4. Wait for the user to enter the customer's credit used.
   5. Subtract the used credit from the maximum credit to get the customer's available credit.
   6. Display a message that shows the customer's available credit.

9. Sales Tax

   Design a hierarchy chart or flowchart for a program that calculates the total of a retail sale. The program should ask the user for:

• The retail price of the item being purchased

• The sales tax rate

Once these items have been entered, the program should calculate and display:

• The sales tax for the purchase

• The total of the sale

10. Account Balance

Design a hierarchy chart or flowchart for a program that calculates the current balance in a savings account. The program must ask the user for:

• The starting balance

• The total dollar amount of deposits made

• The total dollar amount of withdrawals made

• The monthly interest rate

Once the program calculates the current balance, it should be displayed on the screen.

Predict the Result

Questions 11–12 are programs expressed as English statements. What would each display on the screen if they were actual programs?

11. The variable j starts with the value 10.
    The variable k starts with the value 2.
    The variable 1 starts with the value 4.
    Store the value of j times k in j.
    Store the value of k times 1 in 1.
    Add j and 1, and store the result in k.
    Display the value in k on the screen.

12. The variable a starts with the value 1.
    The variable b starts with the value 10.
    The variable c starts with the value 100.
    The variable x starts with the value 0.
    Store the value of c times 3 in x.
    Add the value of b times 6 to the value already in x.
    Add the value of a times 5 to the value already in x.
    Display the value in x on the screen.

Find the Error

13. The following *pseudocode algorithm* has an error. The program is supposed to ask the user for the length and width of a rectangular room, and then display the room's area. The program must multiply the width by the length in order to determine the area. Find the error.

> *area = width × length.*
> *Display "What is the room's width?".*
> *Input width.*
> *Display "What is the room's length?".*
> *Input length.*
> *Display area.*

2

Introduction to C++

■ Topics in this Chapter

2.1 The Parts of a C++ Program

> **CONCEPT** C++ programs have parts and components that serve specific purposes.

Every C++ program has an anatomy. Unlike human anatomy, the parts of C++ programs are not always in the same place. Nevertheless, the parts are there and your first step in learning C++ is to learn what they are. We will begin by looking at a simple example:

Program 2-1

```cpp
// A simple C++ program
#include <iostream>
using namespace std;

int main()
{
    cout << "Programming is great fun!";
    return 0;
}
```

The output of the program is shown below. This is what appears on the screen when the program runs.

Program Output

```
Programming is great fun!
```

Let's examine the program line by line. Here's the first line:

```
// A simple C++ program
```

The // marks the beginning of a *comment*. The compiler ignores everything from the double-slash to the end of the line. That means you can type anything you want on that line and the compiler will never complain! Although comments are not required, they are very important to programmers. Real programs are much more complicated than the example in Program 2-1, and comments help explain what's going on.

The next line looks like this:

```
#include <iostream>
```

Because this line starts with a #, it is called a *preprocessor directive*. The preprocessor reads your program before it is compiled and only executes those lines beginning with a # symbol. Think of the preprocessor as a program that "sets up" your source code for the compiler.

The #include directive causes the preprocessor to include the contents of another file in the program. The word inside the brackets, iostream, is the name of the file that is to be included. The iostream file contains code that allows a C++ program to display output on the screen and read input from the keyboard. Because this program uses cout to display screen output, the iostream file must be included. The contents of the iostream file are included in the program at the point the #include statement appears. The iostream file is called a *header file,* so it should be included at the head, or top, of the program.

The next line reads:

```
using namespace std;
```

Programs usually contain several items with unique names. In this chapter you will learn to create variables. In Chapter 6 you will learn to create functions. In Chapter 13 you will learn to create objects. Variables, functions, and objects are examples of program entities that must have names. C++ uses *namespaces* to organize the names of program entities. The statement using namespace std; declares that the program will be accessing entities whose names are part of the namespace called std. (Yes, even namespaces have names.) The reason the program needs access to the std namespace is because every name created by the iostream file is part of that namespace. In order for a program to use the entities in iostream, it must have access to the std namespace.

The next line reads:

```
int main()
```

This marks the beginning of a *function*. A function can be thought of as a group of one or more programming statements that collectively has a name. The name of this function is *main*, and the set of parentheses that follows the name indicate that it is a function. The word int stands for "integer." It indicates that the function sends an integer value back to the operating system when it is finished executing.

Although most C++ programs have more than one function, every C++ program must have a function called main. It is the starting point of the program. If you are ever reading someone else's C++ program and want to find where it starts, just look for the function named main.

 Note: C++ is a case-sensitive language. That means it regards uppercase letters as being entirely different characters than their lowercase counterparts. In C++, the name of the function main must be written in all lowercase letters. C++ doesn't see "Main" the same as "main," or "INT" the same as "int." This is true for all the C++ key words.

The next line of our program contains a single, solitary character:

```
{
```

This is called a left-brace, or an opening brace, and it is associated with the beginning of the function main. All the statements that make up a function are enclosed in a set of braces. If you look at the third line down from the opening brace you'll see the closing brace. Everything between the two braces is the contents of the function main.

 WARNING! Make sure you have a closing brace for every opening brace in your program!

After the opening brace you see the following line:

```
cout << "Programming is great fun!";
```

To put it simply, this line displays a message on the screen. You will read more about cout and the << operator later in this chapter. The message "Programming is great fun!" is printed without the quotation marks. In programming terms, the group of characters inside the quotation marks is called a *string literal* or *string constant*.

Note: This is the only line in the program that causes anything to be printed on the screen. The other lines, like #include <iostream> and int main(), are necessary for the framework of your program, but they do not cause any screen output. Remember, a program is a set of instructions for the computer. If something is to be displayed on the screen, you must use a programming statement for that purpose.

At the end of the line is a semicolon. Just as a period marks the end of a sentence, a semicolon marks the end of a complete statement in C++. Comments are ignored by the compiler, so the semicolon isn't required at the end of a comment. Preprocessor directives, like #include statements, simply end at the end of the line and never require semicolons.* The beginning of a function, like int main(), is not a complete statement, so you don't place a semicolon there either.

It might seem that the rules for where to put a semicolon are not clear at all. Rather than worry about it now, just concentrate on learning the parts of a program. You'll soon get a feel for where you should and should not use semicolons.

The next line in the program reads:

```
return 0;
```

This sends the integer value 0 back to the operating system upon the program's completion. The value 0 usually indicates that a program executed successfully.

The last line of the program contains the closing brace:

```
}
```

This brace marks the end of the main function. Since main is the only function in this program, it also marks the end of the program.

In the sample program you encountered several sets of special characters. Table 2-1 provides a short summary of how they were used.

 # Checkpoint   [2.1]

2.1   The following C++ program will not compile because the lines have been mixed up.

```
int main()
}
// A crazy mixed up program
return 0;
#include <iostream>
cout << "In 1492 Columbus sailed the ocean blue.";
{
using namespace std;
```

---

* Some compilers do not allow you to terminate a preprocessor directive with a semicolon.

Table 2-1 Special Characters

Character	Name	Description
/ /	Double slash	Marks the beginning of a comment.
#	Pound sign	Marks the beginning of a preprocessor directive.
⟨ ⟩	Opening and closing brackets	Encloses a filename when used with the #include directive.
( )	Opening and closing parentheses	Used in naming a function, as in int main()
{ }	Opening and closing braces	Encloses a group of statements, such as the contents of a function.
" "	Opening and closing quotation marks	Encloses a string of characters, such as a message that is to be printed on the screen.
;	Semicolon	Marks the end of a complete programming statement.

When the lines are properly arranged the program should display the following on the screen:

```
In 1492 Columbus sailed the ocean blue.
```

Rearrange the lines in the correct order. Test the program by entering it on the computer, compiling it, and running it.

2.2 The cout Object

CONCEPT Use the cout object to display information on the computer's screen.

One of the primary jobs of a computer is to produce output. When a program is ready to send information to the outside world, it must have a way to transmit that information to an output device. The *console* is normally considered the standard output device. The word *console* might make you think of a vinyl-covered dashboard, but it simply refers to your monitor and keyboard.

The cout object is referred to as the *standard output object*. Its job is to output information using the standard output device. (Think of the word cout as meaning *console output*.)

cout is classified as a *stream object*, which means it works with streams of data. To print a message on the screen, you send a stream of characters to cout. Let's look at a line from Program 2-1:

```
cout << "Programming is great fun!";
```

Notice that the << operator is used to send the string "Programming is great fun!" to cout. When the << symbol is used this way, it is called the *stream insertion operator*. The information immediately to the right of the operator is sent to cout and then displayed on the screen.

The stream insertion operator is always written as two less-than signs with no space between them. Because you are using it to send a stream of data to the cout object, you can think of the stream insertion operator as an arrow that must point toward cout. This is illustrated in Figure 2-1.

```
cout << "Programming is great fun!";
```
Think of the stream insertion operator as
an arrow that points toward cout.
```
cout ← "Programming is great fun!";
```

Figure 2-1

Let's look at another way to write the same program.

Program 2-2

```
// A simple C++ program
#include <iostream>
using namespace std;

int main()
{
    cout << "Programming is " << "great fun!";
    return 0;
}
```

Program Output
```
Programming is great fun!
```

As you can see, the stream-insertion operator can be used to send more than one item to cout. The output of this program is identical to Program 2-1. The following statements show yet another way to accomplish the same thing.

```
cout << "Programming is ";
cout << "great fun!";
```

An important concept to understand about these statements is that, although the output is broken up into two programming statements, it will still display the message on a single line. Unless you specify otherwise, the information you send to cout is displayed in a continuous stream. Sometimes this can produce less-than-desirable results. Program 2-3 is an example.

The layout of the actual output looks nothing like the arrangement of the strings in the source code. First, notice there is no space displayed between the words "sellers" and "during," or between "June:" and "Computer." cout displays messages exactly as they are sent. If spaces are to be displayed, they must appear in the strings.

Program 2-3

```
// An unruly printing program
#include <iostream>
using namespace std;

int main()
{
    cout << "The following items were top sellers";
    cout << "during the month of June:";
    cout << "Computer games";
    cout << "Coffee";
    cout << "Aspirin";
    return 0;
}
```

Program Output

```
The following items were top sellersduring the month of June:Computer gamesCoff
eeAspirin
```

Second, even though the output is broken into five lines in the source code, it comes out as one long line of output. Because the output is too long to fit on one line on the screen, it wraps around to a second line when displayed. The reason the output comes out as one long line is because cout does not start a new line unless told to do so. There are two ways to instruct cout to start a new line. The first is to send cout a *stream manipulator* called end1 (which is pronounced "end-line" or "end-L"). Program 2-4 is an example.

Program 2-4

```
// A well-adjusted printing program
#include <iostream>
using namespace std;

int main()
{
    cout << "The following items were top sellers" << endl;
    cout << "during the month of June:" << endl;
    cout << "Computer games" << endl;
    cout << "Coffee" << endl;
    cout << "Aspirin" << endl;
    return 0;
}
```

Program Output

```
The following items were top sellers
during the month of June:
Computer games
Coffee
Aspirin
```

Every time cout encounters an endl stream manipulator it advances the output to the beginning of the next line for subsequent printing. The manipulator can be inserted anywhere in the stream of characters sent to cout, outside the double quotes. The following statements show an example.

```
cout << "My pets are" << endl << "dog";
cout << endl << "cat" << endl << "bird" << endl;
```

Another way to cause cout to go to a new line is to insert an *escape sequence* in the string itself. An escape sequence starts with the backslash character (\), and is followed by one or more control characters. It allows you to control the way output is displayed by embedding commands within the string itself. Program 2-5 is an example.

Program 2-5

```
// Yet another well-adjusted printing program
#include <iostream>
using namespace std;

int main()
{
    cout << "The following items were top sellers\n";
    cout << "during the month of June:\n";
    cout << "Computer games\nCoffee";
    cout << "\nAspirin\n";
    return 0;
}
```

Program Output
```
The following items were top sellers
during the month of June:
Computer games
Coffee
Aspirin
```

The *newline escape sequence* is \n. When cout encounters \n in a string, it doesn't print it on the screen, but interprets it as a special command to advance the output cursor to the next line. You have probably noticed inserting the escape sequence requires less typing than inserting endl. That's why many programmers prefer it.

 WARNING! Do not confuse the backslash (\) with the forward slash (/). An escape sequence will not work if you accidentally start it with a forward slash. Also, do not put a space between the backslash and the control character.

There are many escape sequences in C++. They give you the ability to exercise greater control over the way information is output by your program. Table 2-2 lists a few of them.

Table 2-2 Common Escape Sequences

Escape Sequence	Name	Description
\n	Newline	Causes the cursor to go to the next line for subsequent printing.
\t	Horizontal tab	Causes the cursor to skip over to the next tab stop.
\a	Alarm	Causes the computer to beep.
\b	Backspace	Causes the cursor to back up, or move left one position.
\r	Return	Causes the cursor to go to the beginning of the current line, not the next line.
\\	Backslash	Causes a backslash to be printed.
\'	Single quote	Causes a single quotation mark to be printed.
\"	Double quote	Causes a double quotation mark to be printed.

2.3 The #include Directive

 CONCEPT The #include directive causes the contents of another file to be inserted into the program.

Now is a good time to expand our discussion of the #include directive. The following line has appeared near the top of every example program.

```
#include <iostream>
```

The header file iostream must be included in any program that uses the cout object. This is because cout is not part of the "core" of the C++ language. Specifically, it is part of the *input-output stream library*. The header file, iostream, contains information describing iostream objects. Without it, the compiler will not know how to properly compile a program that uses cout.

Preprocessor directives are not C++ statements. They are signals to the preprocessor, which runs prior to the compiler (hence the name "preprocessor"). The preprocessor's job is to set programs up in a way that makes life easier for the programmer.

For example, any program that uses the cout object must contain the extensive setup information found in iostream. The programmer could type all this information into the program, but it would be too time consuming. An alternative would be to use an editor to "cut and paste" the information into the program, but that would quickly become tiring as well. The solution is to let the preprocessor insert the contents of iostream automatically.

WARNING! Do not put semicolons at the end of processor directives. Because preprocessor directives are not C++ statements, they do not require them. In many cases an error will result from a preprocessor directive terminated with a semicolon.

An #include directive must always contain the name of a file. The preprocessor inserts the entire contents of the file into the program at the point it encounters the #include directive. The compiler doesn't actually see the #include directive. Instead it sees the information that was inserted by the preprocessor, just as if the programmer had typed it there.

The information contained in header files is C++ code. Typically it describes complex objects like cout. Later you will learn to create your own header files.

 ## Checkpoint [2.2–2.3]

2.2   The following C++ program will not compile because the lines have been mixed up.

```cpp
cout << "Success\n";
cout << " Success\n\n";
int main()
cout << "Success";
}
using namespace std;
// It's a mad, mad program
#include <iostream>
cout << "Success\n";
{
return 0;
```

When the lines are properly arranged the program should display the following on the screen:

Program Output

```
Success
Success Success

Success
```

Rearrange the lines in the correct order. Test the program by entering it on the computer, compiling it, and running it.

2.3 Study the following program and show what it will print on the screen.

```cpp
// The Works of Wolfgang
#include <iostream>
using namespace std;

int main()
{
    cout << "The works of Wolfgang\ninclude the following";
    cout << "\nThe Turkish March" << endl;
    cout << "and Symphony No. 40 ";
    cout << "in G minor." << endl;
    return 0;
}
```

2.4 On paper, write a program that will display your name on the first line, your street address on the second line, your city, state, and ZIP code on the third line, and your telephone number on the fourth line. Place a comment with today's date at the top of the program. Test your program by entering, compiling, and running it.

2.4 Variables and Literals

 CONCEPT Variables represent storage locations in the computer's memory. Literals are constant values that are assigned to variables.

As you discovered in Chapter 1, variables allow you to store and work with data in the computer's memory. They provide an "interface" to RAM. Part of the job of programming is to determine how many variables a program will need and what types of information they will hold. Program 2-6 is an example of a C++ program with a variable.

Let's look more closely at this program. Here is the first line in the function main.

```cpp
int number;
```

This is called a *variable definition*. It tells the compiler the variable's name and the type of data it will hold. This line indicates the variable's name is number. The word int stands for integer, so number will only be used to hold integer numbers. Later in this chapter you will learn all the types of data that C++ allows.

Program 2-6

```
// This program has a variable.
#include <iostream>
using namespace std;

int main()
{
    int number;

    number = 5;
    cout << "The value in number is " << number << endl;
    return 0;
}
```

Program Output
```
The value in number is 5
```

 Note: You must have a definition for every variable you intend to use in a program. In C++, variable definitions can appear at any point in the program. Later in this chapter, and throughout the book, you will learn the best places to define variables.

Notice that variable definitions end with a semicolon. Here is the next line.

```
    number = 5;
```

This is called an *assignment*. The equal sign is an operator that copies the value on its right (5) into the variable named on its left (number). After this line executes, number will be set to 5.

 Note: This line does not print anything on the computer's screen. It runs silently behind the scenes, storing a value in RAM.

Look at the next line.

```
    cout << "The value in number is " << number << endl;
```

The second item sent to cout is the variable name number. When you send a variable name to cout it prints the variable's contents. Notice there are no quotation marks around number. Look at what happens in Program 2-7.

When double quotation marks are placed around the word number it becomes a string literal, and is no longer a variable name. When string literals are sent to cout they are printed exactly as they appear inside the quotation marks. You've probably noticed by now the endl stream manipulator has no quotation marks around it for the same reason.

Program 2-7

```cpp
// This program has a variable.
#include <iostream>
using namespace std;

int main()
{
    int number;

    number = 5;
    cout << "The value in number is " << "number" << endl;
    return 0;
}
```

Program Output
```
The value in number is number
```

Not All Data Are Created Equally

As shown in Program 2-7, just placing quotation marks around a variable name changes the program's results. In fact, placing double quotation marks around anything that is not intended to be a string literal will create an error of some type. For example, in Program 2-7 the number 5 was assigned to the variable number. It would have been incorrect to perform the assignment this way:

```cpp
number = "5";
```

In this line, 5 is no longer an integer, but a string literal. Because number was defined as an integer variable, you can only store integers in it. The integer 5 and the string literal "5" are not the same thing.

The fact that numbers can be represented as strings frequently confuses students who are new to programming. Just remember that strings are intended for humans to read. They are to be printed on computer screens or paper. Numbers, however, are intended primarily for mathematical operations. You cannot perform math on strings. Before numbers can be displayed on the screen, they must first be converted to strings. (Fortunately, cout handles the conversion automatically when you send a number to it.)

Literals

A variable is called a "variable" because its value may be changed. A literal, on the other hand, is a value that does not change during the program's execution. Program 2-8 contains both literals and a variable.

Program 2-8

```cpp
// This program has literals and a variable.
#include <iostream>
using namespace std;

int main()
{
    int apples;

    apples = 20;
    cout << "Today we sold " << apples << " bushels of apples.\n";
    return 0;
}
```

Program Output

```
Today we sold 20 bushels of apples.
```

Of course, the variable is apples. It is defined as an integer. Table 2-3 lists the literals found in the program.

Table 2-3

Literal	Type of Literal
20	Integer literal
"Today we sold "	String literal
"bushels of apples.\n"	String literal

What are literals used for? As you can see from this program, they are commonly used to store known values in variables and display messages on the screen or a printout.

 Note: Literals are also called constants.

 # Checkpoint [2.5]

2.5 Examine the following program.

```cpp
// This program uses variables and literals.
#include <iostream>
using namespace std;

int main()
{
    int little;
    int big;
```

```
        little = 2;
        big = 2000;
        cout << "The little number is " << little << endl;
        cout << "The big number is " << big << endl;
        return 0;
    }
```

List all the variables and literals that appear in the program.

2.6   What will the following set of statements display on the screen?

```
int number;
number = 712;
cout << "The value is " << "number" << endl;
```

2.5 Identifiers

Choose variable names that indicate what the variables are used for.

An *identifier* is a programmer-defined name that represents some element of a program. Variable names are examples of identifiers. You may choose your own variable names in C++, as long as you do not use any of the C++ *key words*. The key words make up the "core" of the language and have specific purposes. Table 2-4 shows a complete list of the C++ key words. Note that they are all lowercase.

Table 2-4   The C++ Key Words

asm	auto	break	bool	case
catch	char	class	const	const_cast
continue	default	delete	do	double
dynamic_cast	else	enum	explicit	extern
false	float	for	friend	goto
if	inline	int	long	mutable
namespace	new	operator	private	protected
public	register	reinterpret_cast	return	short
signed	sizeof	static	static_cast	struct
switch	template	this	throw	true
try	typedef	typeid	typename	union
unsigned	using	virtual	void	volatile
wchar_t	while			

You should always choose names for your variables that give an indication of what the variables are used for. You may be tempted to define variables with names like this:

```
int x;
```

The rather nondescript name, x, gives no clue as to the variable's purpose. Here is a better example.

```
int itemsOrdered;
```

The name itemsOrdered gives anyone reading the program an idea of the variable's use. This way of coding helps produce self-documenting programs, which means you get an understanding of what the program is doing just by reading its code. Because real-world programs usually have thousands of lines, it is important that they be as self-documenting as possible.

You probably have noticed the mixture of uppercase and lowercase letters in the name itemsOrdered. Although all of C++'s key words must be written in lowercase, you may use uppercase letters in variable names.

The reason the O in itemsOrdered is capitalized is to improve readability. Normally "items ordered" is two words. Unfortunately you cannot have spaces in a variable name, so the two words must be combined into one. When "items" and "ordered" are stuck together you get a variable definition like this:

```
int itemsordered;
```

Capitalization of the second word and succeeding words makes itemsOrdered easier to read. It should be mentioned that this style of coding is not required. You are free to use all lowercase letters, all uppercase letters, or any combination of both. In fact, some programmers use the underscore character to separate words in a variable name, as in the following.

```
int items_ordered;
```

Legal Identifiers

Regardless of which style you adopt, be consistent and make your variable names as sensible as possible. Here are some specific rules that must be followed with all identifiers.

- ◆ The first character must be one of the letters a through z, A through Z, or an underscore character (_).
- ◆ After the first character you may use the letters a through z or A through Z, the digits 0 through 9, or underscores.
- ◆ Uppercase and lowercase characters are distinct, This means ItemsOrdered is not the same as itemsordered.

Table 2-5 lists variable names and tells whether each is legal or illegal in C++.

Table 2-5 Some Variable Names

Variable Name	Legal or Illegal?
dayOfWeek	Legal.
3dGraph	Illegal. Variable names cannot begin with a digit.
_employee_num	Legal.
June1997	Legal.
Mixture#3	Illegal. Variable names may only use letters, digits, or underscores.

2.6 Integer Data Types

 CONCEPT There are many different types of data. Variables are classified according to their data type, which determines the kind of information that may be stored in them. Integer variables can only hold whole numbers.

Computer programs collect pieces of data from the real world and manipulate them in various ways. There are many different types of data. In the realm of numeric information, for example, there are whole numbers and fractional numbers. There are negative numbers and positive numbers. And there are numbers so large, and others so small, that they don't even have a name. Then there is textual information. Names and addresses, for instance, are stored as groups of characters. When you write a program you must determine what types of information it will be likely to encounter.

If you are writing a program to calculate the number of miles to a distant star, you'll need variables that can hold very large numbers. If you are designing software to record microscopic dimensions, you'll need to store very small and precise numbers. Additionally, if you are writing a program that must perform thousands of intensive calculations, you'll want variables that can be processed quickly. The data type of a variable determines all of these factors.

Although C++ offers many data types, in the very broadest sense there are only two: numeric and character. Numeric data types are broken into two additional categories: integer and floating point. Integers are whole numbers like 12, 157, −34, and 2. Floating point numbers have a decimal point, like 23.7, 189.0231, and 0.987. Additionally, the integer and floating point data types are broken into even more classifications. Before we discuss the character data type, let's carefully examine the variations of numeric data.

Your primary considerations for selecting a numeric data type are:

◆ The largest and smallest numbers that may be stored in the variable

◆ How much memory the variable uses

◆ Whether the variable stores signed or unsigned numbers

◆ The number of decimal places of precision the variable has

The size of a variable is the number of bytes of memory it uses. Typically, the larger a variable is, the greater the range it can hold.

Table 2-6 shows the C++ integer data types with their typical sizes and ranges.

Table 2-6   Integer Data Types, Sizes and Ranges

Data Type	Size	Range
short	2 bytes	−32,768 to +32,767
unsigned short	2 bytes	0 to +65,535
int	4 bytes	−2,147,483,648 to +2,147,483,647
unsigned int	4 bytes	0 to 4,294,967,295
long	4 bytes	−2,147,483,648 to +2,147,483,647
unsigned long	4 bytes	0 to 4,294,967,295

Note: The data type sizes and ranges shown in Table 2-6 are typical on Windows systems. If you are using a different operating system, the sizes and ranges may be different.

Here are some examples of variable definitions:

```
int days;
unsigned speed;
short month;
unsigned short amount;
long deficit;
unsigned long insects;
```

Unsigned data types can only store non-negative values. They can be used when you know your program will not encounter negative values. For example, variables that hold ages or weights would rarely hold numbers less than 0.

Note: An `unsigned int` variable can also be defined using only the word `unsigned`. For example, the following variable definitions are equivalent.

```
unsigned int days;
unsigned days;
```

Notice in Table 2-6 that the int and long data types have the same sizes and ranges, and that the unsigned int data type has the same size and range as the unsigned long data type. This is not always true because the size of integers is dependent on the type of system you are using. Here are the only guarantees:

- ◆ Integers are at least as big as short integers.

- ◆ Long integers are at least as big as integers.

- ◆ Unsigned short integers are the same size as short integers.

- ◆ Unsigned integers are the same size as integers.

- ◆ Unsigned long integers are the same size as long integers.

Later in this chapter you will learn to use the sizeof operator to determine how large all the data types are on your computer.

As mentioned before, variables are defined by stating the data type key word followed by the name of the variable. Program 2-9 defines three integers, an unsigned integer, and a long integer.

Program 2-9

```
//This program uses some of the different integer type variables.
#include <iostream>
using namespace std;

int main()
{
    int length, width, height;
    unsigned int area;
    long volume;

    length = 100;
    width = 100;
    height = 100;
    area = 10000;
    volume = 1000000;

    cout << "A perfect cube has a length = " << length << " inches," << endl;
    cout << "width = " << width << " inches," << endl;
    cout << "height = " << height << " inches." << endl;
    cout << "The area = " << area << " square inches." << endl;
    cout << "The volume = " << volume << " cubic inches" << endl;
    return 0;
}
```

Program Output
```
A perfect cube has a length = 100 inches,
width = 100 inches,
height = 100 inches.
The area = 10000 square inches.
The volume = 1000000 cubic inches.
```

Program 2-9 illustrates how variables of the different types must be defined on their own line. Variables of the same type can be defined on different lines, like this:

```
int length;
int width;
int height;
```

However, as shown in Program 2-9, variables of the same type can be defined on same line with the key word proceeding the variable list and a comma separating the variable names.

```
int length, width, height;
```

Integer and Long Integer Literals

Look at the following lines from Program 2-9:

```
length = 100;
width = 100;
height = 100;
```

Each of these lines contains an integer literal. In C++, integer literals are normally stored in memory just as an `int`. On a system that uses 2 byte integers and 4 byte longs, the literal 50000 is too large to be stored as an `int`, so it is stored as a `long`.

One of the pleasing characteristics of the C++ language is that it allows you to control almost every aspect of your program. If you need to change the way something is stored in memory, the tools are provided to do that. For example, what if you are in a situation where you have an integer literal, but you need it to be stored in memory as a long integer? (Rest assured, this is a situation that does arise.) C++ allows you to force an integer literal to be stored as a long integer by placing the letter L at the end of the number. Here is an example:

```
32L
```

On a computer that uses 2-byte integers and 4-byte long integers, this literal will use 4 bytes. This is called a long integer literal.

 Note: You can use either an uppercase or lowercase L. The lowercase l looks too much like the number 1, so you should always use the uppercase L.

If You Plan to Continue in Computer Science: Hexadecimal and Octal Literals

Programmers sometimes express values in numbering systems other than decimal (or base 10). Hexadecimal (base 16) and octal (base 8) are popular because they make certain programming tasks more convenient than decimal numbers do.

By default, C++ assumes that all integer literals are expressed in decimal. You express hexadecimal numbers by placing 0x in front of them. (This is zero-x, not oh-x.) Here is how the hexadecimal number F4 would be expressed in C++:

```
0xF4
```

Octal numbers must be preceded by a 0 (zero, not oh). For example, the octal 31 would be written

```
031
```

 Note: You will not be writing programs for some time that require this type of manipulation. It is important, however, that you understand this material. Good programmers should develop the skills for reading other people's source code. You may find yourself reading programs that use items like long integer, hexadecimal, or octal literals.

 ## Checkpoint [2.5–2.6]

2.7 Which of the following are illegal variable names, and why?

```
x
99bottles
july97
theSalesFigureForFiscalYear98
r&d
grade_report
```

2.8 Is the variable name `Sales` the same as `sales`? Why or why not?

2.9 Refer to the data types listed in Table 2-6 for these questions.

A) If a variable needs to hold numbers in the range 32 to 6,000, what data type would be best?

B) If a variable needs to hold numbers in the range –40,000 to +40,000, what data type would be best?

C) Which of the following literals use more memory? 20 or 20L

2.10 On any computer, which data type uses more memory, an integer or an unsigned integer?

2.7 The `char` Data Type

You might be wondering why there isn't a 1-byte integer data type. Actually there is. It is called the `char` data type, which gets its name from the word "character." As its name suggests, it is primarily for storing characters, but strictly speaking, it is an integer data type.

 Note: On some systems the char data type is larger than 1 byte.

The reason an integer data type is used to store characters is because characters are internally represented by numbers. Each printable character, as well as many nonprintable characters, are assigned a unique number. The most commonly used method for encoding characters is ASCII, which stands for the American Standard Code for Information Interchange. (There are other codes, such as EBCDIC, which is used by many IBM mainframes.)

When a character is stored in memory, it is actually the numeric code that is stored. When the computer is instructed to print the value on the screen, it displays the character that corresponds with the numeric code.

You may want to refer to Appendix A, which shows the ASCII character set. Notice that the number 65 is the code for A, 66 is the code for B, and so on. Program 2-10 demonstrates that when you work with characters, you are actually working with numbers.

Program 2-10

```
// This program demonstrates the close relationship between
// characters and integers.
#include <iostream>
using namespace std;

int main()
{
    char letter;

    letter = 65;
    cout << letter << endl;
    letter = 66;
    cout << letter << endl;
    return 0;
}
```

Program Output

```
A
B
```

Figure 2-2 illustrates that when you think of characters, such as A, B, and C, being stored in memory, it is really the numbers 65, 66, and 67 that are stored.

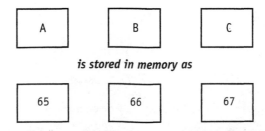

Figure 2-2

Character Literals

Although Program 2-10 nicely illustrates the way characters are represented by numbers, it isn't necessary to work with the ASCII codes themselves. Program 2-11 is another version that works that same way.

Program 2-11 assigns character literals to the variable letter. Anytime a program works with a character, it internally works with the code that represents that character, so this program is still assigning the values 65 and 66 to letter.

Program 2-11

```
// This program uses character literals
#include <iostream>
using namespace std;

int main()
{
    char letter;

    letter = 'A';
    cout << letter << endl;
    letter = 'B';
    cout << letter << endl;
    return 0;
}
```

Program Output

```
A
B
```

Notice that the character literals are enclosed in single quotation marks. It is important that you do not confuse character literals with string literals, which are enclosed in double quotation marks. String literals cannot be assigned to standard char variables. The reason is because of the way string literals are stored internally.

Strings are a series of characters stored in consecutive memory locations. The problem with strings is that they can be virtually any length. This means that there must be some way for the program to know how long the string is. In C++ an extra byte is appended to the end of most strings. In this last byte, the number 0 is stored. This *null terminator* or *null character* marks the end of the string. Strings that are stored in memory in this fashion, with the null terminator appended to their end, are called *C-strings*. They are called C-strings because this storage technique was initially used in the C programming language.

Don't confuse the null terminator with the character '0'. If you look at Appendix A you will see that ASCII code 48 corresponds to the character '0', whereas the null terminator is the same as the ASCII code 0. If you want to print the character 0 on the screen, you use ASCII code 48. If you want to mark the end of a string, however, you use ASCII code 0.

Let's look at an example of how a string is stored in memory. Figure 2-3 depicts the way the string "Sebastian" would be stored.

Figure 2-3

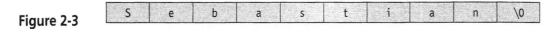

First, notice the quotation marks are not stored with the string. They are simply a way of marking the beginning and end of the string in your source code. Second, notice the very last byte of the string. It contains the null terminator, which is represented by the \0 character. The addition of this last byte means that although the string "Sebastian" is 9 characters long, it occupies 10 bytes of memory.

The null terminator is another example of something that sits quietly in the background. It doesn't print on the screen when you display a string, but nevertheless, it is there silently doing its job.

 Note: C++ automatically places the null terminator at the end of string literals.

Now let's compare the way a string and a char are stored. Suppose you have the literals 'A' and "A" in a program. Figure 2-4 depicts their internal storage.

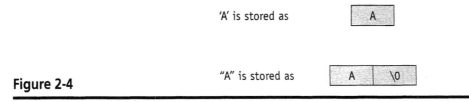

Figure 2-4

As you can see, 'A' is a 1-byte element and "A" is a 2-byte element. Since characters are really stored as ASCII codes, Figure 2-5 shows what is actually being stored in memory.

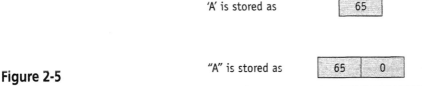

Figure 2-5

Because char variables are only large enough to hold one character, you cannot assign string literals to them. For example, the following code defines a char variable named letter. The character literal 'A' can be assigned to the variable, but the string literal "A" cannot.

```
char letter;
letter = 'A'; // This will work.
letter = "A"; // This will not work!
```

You are probably wondering what kind of variable is used to hold strings in C++. You must define a variable that is made of several 1-byte elements, enough for the entire string and its null terminator. We will discuss this in Chapter 3.

One final topic about characters should be discussed. You have learned that some strings look like a single character but really aren't. It is also possible to have a character that looks like a string. A good example is the newline character, \n. Although it is represented by two characters, a slash and an n, it is internally represented as one character. In fact, all escape sequences, internally, are just 1 byte.

Program 2-12 shows the use of \n as a character literal, enclosed in single quotation marks. If you refer to the ASCII chart in Appendix A, you will see that ASCII code 10 is the linefeed character. This is the code C++ uses for the newline character.

Program 2-12

```
// This program uses character literals.
#include <iostream>
using namespace std;

int main()
{
    char letter;

    letter = 'A';
    cout << letter << '\n';
    letter = 'B';
    cout << letter << '\n';
    return 0;
}
```

Program Output
```
A
B
```

Let's review some important points regarding characters and strings:

◆ Printable characters are internally represented by numeric codes. Most computers use ASCII codes for this purpose.

◆ Characters normally occupy a single byte of memory.

◆ Strings are consecutive sequences of characters that occupy consecutive bytes of memory.

◆ C-strings always have a null terminator at the end. This marks the end of the string.

◆ Character literals are enclosed in single quotation marks.

◆ String literals are enclosed in double quotation marks.

◆ Escape sequences are stored internally as a single character.

Checkpoint [2.7]

2.11 What are the ASCII codes for the following characters? (Refer to Appendix A)

C
F
W

2.12 Which of the following is a character literal?

'B'
"B"

2.13 Assuming the char data type uses 1 byte of memory, how many bytes do the following literals use?

'Q'
"Q"
"Sales"
'\n'

2.14 Write a program that has the following character variables: first, middle, and last. Store your initials in these variables and then display them on the screen.

2.8 Floating-Point Data Types

CONCEPT Floating-point data types are used to define variables that can hold real numbers.

Whole numbers are not adequate for many jobs. If you are writing a program that works with dollar amounts or precise measurements, you need a data type that allows fractional values. In programming terms, these are called *floating-point* numbers.

Internally, floating-point numbers are stored in a manner similar to *scientific notation*. Take the number 47,281.97. In scientific notation this number is 4.728197×10^4. (10^4 is equal to 10,000, and $4.728197 \times 10,000$ is 47,281.97.) The first part of the number, 4.728197, is called the *mantissa*. The mantissa is multiplied by a power of ten.

Computers typically use *E notation* to represent floating-point values. In E notation, the number 47,281.97 would be 4.728197E4. The part of the number before the E is the mantissa, and the part after the E is the power of 10. When a floating point number is stored in memory, it is stored as the mantissa and the power of 10.

Table 2-7 shows other numbers represented in scientific and E notation.

Table 2-7 Floating Point Representations

Decimal Notation	Scientific Notation	E Notation
247.91	2.4791×10^2	2.4791E2
0.00072	7.2×10^{-4}	7.2E–4
2,900,000	2.9×10^6	2.9E6

In C++ there are three data types that can represent floating-point numbers. They are

```
float
double
long double
```

The float data type is considered *single precision*. The double data type is usually twice as big as float, so it is considered *double precision*. As you've probably guessed, the long double is intended to be larger than the double. Of course, the exact sizes of these data types is dependent on the computer you are using. The only guarantees are:

◆ A double is at least as big as a float.

◆ A long double is at least as big as a double.

Table 2-8 shows the sizes and ranges of floating-point data types usually found on PCs.

Table 2-8 Floating Point Data Types on PCs

Data Type	Key Word	Description
Single precision	float	4 bytes. Numbers between ±3.4E-38 and ±3.4E38
Double precision	double	8 bytes. Numbers between ±1.7E-308 and ±1.7E308
Long double precision	long double*	8 bytes. Numbers between ±1.7E-308 and ±1.7E308

*Some compilers use 10 bytes for long doubles. This allows a range of ±3.4E-4932 to ±1.1E4832

You will notice there are no unsigned floating point data types. On all machines, variables of the float, double, and long double data types can store positive or negative numbers.

Floating Point Literals

Floating point literals may be expressed in a variety of ways. As shown in Program 2-13, E notation is one method. When you are writing numbers that are extremely large or extremely small, this will probably be the easiest way. E notation numbers may be expressed with an uppercase E or a lowercase e. Notice in the source code the literals were written as 1.49598E11 and 1.989E30, but the program printed them as 1.4958e+011 and 1.989e+30. The two sets of numbers are equivalent. (The plus sign in front of the exponent is also optional.) In Chapter 3 you will learn to control the way cout displays E notation numbers.

Program 2-13

```cpp
// This program uses floating point data types
#include <iostream>
using namespace std;

int main()
{
    float distance;
    double mass;

    distance = 1.49598E11;
    mass = 1.989E30;
    cout << "The Sun is " << distance << " kilometers away.\n";
    cout << "The Sun\'s mass is " << mass << " kilograms.\n";
    return 0;
}
```

Program Output
```
The Sun is 1.49598e+011 kilometers away.
The Sun's mass is 1.989e+030 kilograms.
```

You can also express floating-point literals in decimal notation. The liteal 1.49598E11 could have been written as

```
149598000000.00
```

Obviously the E notation is more convenient for lengthy numbers, but for numbers like 47.39, decimal notation is preferable to 4.739E1.

All of the following floating-point literals are equivalent:

```
1.4959E11
1.4959e11
1.4959E+11
1.4959e+11
149590000000.00
```

Floating-point literals are normally stored in memory as `doubles`. But remember, C++ provides tools for handling just about any situation. Just in case you need to force a literal to be stored as a `float`, you can append the letter F or f to the end of it. For example, the following literals would be stored as `floats`:

```
1.2F
45.907f
```

 Note: Because floating-point literals are normally stored in memory as `doubles`, many compilers issue a warning message when you assign a floating-point literal

to a `float` variable. For example, assuming `num` is a `float`, the following statement might cause the compiler to generate a warning message:

```
num = 14.725;
```

You can suppress the warning message by appending the f suffix to the floating-point literal, as shown below:

```
num = 14.725f;
```

If you want to force a value to be stored as a `long double`, append an L or 1 to it, as in the following examples:

```
1034.56L
89.21
```

The compiler won't confuse these with long integers because they have decimal points. (Remember, the lowercase L looks so much like the number 1 that you should always use the uppercase L when suffixing literals.)

Assigning Floating-Point Values to Integer Variables

When a floating-point value is assigned to an integer variable, the fractional part of the value (the part after the decimal point) is discarded. For example, look at the following code.

```
int number;
number = 7.5;  // Assigns 7 to number
```

This code attempts to assign the floating-point value 7.5 to the integer variable `number`. As a result, the value 7 will be assigned to `number`, with the fractional part discarded. When part of a value is discarded, it is said to be *truncated*.

Assigning a floating-point variable to an integer variable has the same effect. For example, look at the following code.

```
int i;
float f;
f = 7.5;
i = f;        // Assigns 7 to i.
```

When the `float` variable f is assigned to the `int` variable i, the value being assigned (7.5) is truncated. After this code executes i will hold the value 7 and f will hold the value 7.5.

 Note: When a floating-point value is truncated, it is not rounded. Assigning the value 7.9 to an `int` variable will result in the value 7 being stored in the variable.

WARNING! Floating-point variables can hold a much larger range of values than integer variables can. If a floating-point value is being stored in an integer variable, and the whole part of the value (the part before the decimal point) is too large for the integer variable, an invalid value will be stored in the integer variable.

2.9 The `bool` Data Type

CONCEPT	Boolean variables are set to either `true` or `false`.

Expressions that have a `true` or `false` value are called *Boolean* expressions, named in honor of English mathematician George Boole (1815–1864).

The `bool` data type allows you to create small integer variables that are suitable for holding `true` or `false` values. Program 2-14 demonstrates the defintion and assignment of a `bool` variable.

Program 2-14

```
// A program for demonstrating boolean variables
#include <iostream>
using namespace std;

int main()
{
    bool boolValue;

    boolValue = true;
    cout << boolValue << endl;
    boolValue = false;
    cout << boolValue << endl;
    return 0;
}
```

Program Output

```
1
0
```

As you can see from the program output, the value `true` is represented in memory by the number 1, and `false` is represented by 0. You will not be using `bool` variables until Chapter 4, however, so just remember they are useful for evaluating conditions that are either true or false.

2.10   Determining the Size of a Data Type

CONCEPT   The sizeof operator may be used to determine the size of a data type on any system.

Chapter 1 discussed the portability of the C++ language. As you have seen in this chapter, one of the problems of portability is the lack of common sizes of data types on all machines. If you are not sure what the sizes of data types are on your computer, C++ provides a way to find out.

A special operator called sizeof will report the number of bytes of memory used by any data type or variable. Program 2-15 illustrates its use. The first line that uses the operator reads

```
cout << "The size of an integer is " << sizeof(int);
```

The name of the data type or variable is placed inside the parentheses that follow the operator. The operator "returns" the number of bytes used by that item. This operator can be invoked anywhere you can use an unsigned integer, including in mathematical operations.

Program 2-15

```
// This program determines the size of integers, long
// integers, and long doubles.
#include <iostream>
using namespace std;

int main()
{
    long double apple;

    cout << "The size of an integer is " << sizeof(int);
    cout << " bytes.\n";
    cout << "The size of a long integer is " << sizeof(long);
    cout << " bytes.\n";
    cout << "An apple can be eaten in " << sizeof(apple);
    cout << " bytes!\n";
    return 0;
}
```

Program Output
```
The size of an integer is 4 bytes.
The size of a long integer is 4 bytes.
An apple can be eaten in 8 bytes!
```

Checkpoint [2.8–2.10]

2.15 Yes or No: Is there an unsigned floating-point data type? If so, what is it?

2.16 How would the following number in scientific notation be represented in E notation?

$$6.31 \times 10^{17}$$

2.17 Write a program that defines an integer variable named `age` and a `float` variable named `weight`. Store your age and weight, as literals, in the variables. The program should display these values on the screen in a manner similar to the following:

Program Output
My age is 26 and my weight is 180 pounds.

(Feel free to lie to the computer about your age and your weight—it'll never know!)

2.11 Variable Assignments and Initialization

> **CONCEPT** An assignment operation assigns, or copies, a value into a variable. When a value is assigned to a variable as part of the variable's definition, it is called an initialization.

As you have already seen in several examples, a value is stored in a variable with an *assignment statement*. For example, the following statement copies the value 12 into the variable `unitsSold`.

```
unitsSold = 12;
```

The = symbol is called the *assignment operator*. Operators perform operations on data. The data that operators work with are called *operands*. The assignment operator has two operands. In the previous statement, the operands are `unitsSold` and 12.

In an assignment statement, C++ requires the name of the variable receiving the assignment to appear on the left side of the operator. The following statement is incorrect.

```
12 = unitsSold;      // Incorrect!
```

In C++ terminology, the operand on the left side of the = symbol must be an *lvalue*. It is called an lvalue because it is a value that may appear on the left side of an assignment operator. An lvalue is something that identifies a place in memory whose contents may be changed. Most of the time this will be a variable name. The operand on the right side of the = symbol must be an *rvalue*. An rvalue is any expression that has a value. The assignment statement takes the value of the rvalue and puts it in the memory location of the object identified by the lvalue.

You may also assign values to variables as part of the definition. This is called *initialization*. Program 2-16 shows how it is done.

Program 2-16

```
// This program shows variable initialization.
#include <iostream>
using namespace std;

int main()
{
    int month = 2, days = 28;

    cout << "Month " << month << " has " << days << " days.\n";
    return 0;
}
```

Program Output
```
Month 2 has 28 days.
```

As you can see, this simplifies the program and reduces the number of statements that must be typed by the programmer. Here are examples of other definition statements that perform initialization.

```
double interestRate = 12.9;
char stockode = 'D';
long customerNum = 459L;
```

Of course, there are always variations on a theme. C++ allows you to define several variables and only initialize part of them. Here is an example of such a definition:

```
int flightNum = 89, travelTime, departure = 10, distance;
```

The variable `flightNum` is initialized to 89 and `departure` is initialized to 10. `travelTime` and `distance` remain uninitialized.

2.12 Scope

CONCEPT A variable's scope is the part of the program that has access to the variable.

Every variable has a *scope*. The scope of a variable is the part of the program where the variable may be used. The rules that define a variable's scope are complex, and you will only be introduced to the concept here. In other sections of the book we will revisit this topic and expand on it.

The first rule of scope you should learn is that a variable cannot be used in any part of the program before the definition. Program 2-17 illustrates this.

Program 2-17

```
// This program can't find its variable.
#include <iostream>
using namespace std;

int main()
{
    cout << value; // ERROR! value not defined yet!

    int value = 100;
    return 0;
}
```

The program will not work because it attempts to send the contents of the variable value to cout before the variable is defined. The compiler reads your program from top to bottom. If it encounters a statement that uses a variable before the variable is defined, an error will result. To correct the program, the variable definition must be put before any statement that uses it.

2.13 Arithmetic Operators

CONCEPT There are many operators for manipulating numeric values and performing arithmetic operations.

C++ offers a multitude of operators for manipulating data. Generally, there are three types of operators: *unary*, *binary*, and *ternary*. These terms reflect the number of operands an operator requires.

Unary operators only require a single operand. For example, consider the following expression:

```
-5
```

Of course, we understand this represents the value negative five. The literal 5 is preceded by the minus sign. The minus sign, when used this way, is called the *negation operator*. Since it only requires one operand, it is a unary operator.

Binary operators work with two operands. The assignment operator is in this category. Ternary operators, as you may have guessed, require three operands. C++ only has one ternary operator, which will be discussed in Chapter 4.

Arithmetic operations are very common in programming. Table 2-9 shows the common arithmetic operators in C++.

Each of these operators work as you probably expect. The addition operator returns the sum of its two operands. In the following assignment statement, the variable amount will be assigned the value 12:

```
amount = 4 + 8;
```

Table 2-9   Fundamental Arithmetic Operators

Operator	Meaning	Type	Example
+	Addition	Binary	`total = cost + tax;`
−	Subtraction	Binary	`cost = total - tax;`
*	Multiplication	Binary	`tax = cost * rate;`
/	Division	Binary	`salePrice = original / 2;`
%	Modulus	Binary	`remainder = value % 3;`

The subtraction operator returns the value of its right operand subtracted from its left operand. This statement will assign the value 98 to `temperature`:

```
temperature = 112 - 14;
```

The multiplication operator returns the product of its two operands. In the following statement, `markUp` is assigned the value 3:

```
markUp = 12 * 0.25;
```

The division operator returns the quotient of its left operand divided by its right operand. In the next statement, `points` is assigned the value 5:

```
points = 100 / 20;
```

 WARNING! When both operands of a division statement are integers, the statement will perform integer division. This means the result of the division will be an integer as well. If there is a remainder, it will be discarded. For example, in the following statement, `parts` is assigned the value 5:

```
parts = 17 / 3;
```

This may seem like an annoyance, but it can actually be useful in some programs. Remember, C++ gives you the tools to solve just about any problem! If you want to make sure a statement, like the one shown above, performs regular division, express one of the numbers as a floating point. Here is an example:

```
parts = 17.0 / 3;
```

In the statement above, since 17.0 is interpreted as a floating point number, the division operation will return a floating-point number. The result of the division is 5.66667.

The modulus operator, which only works with integer operands, returns the remainder of an integer division. The following statement assigns 2 to leftOver:

```
leftOver = 17 % 3;
```

In Chapter 3 you will learn how to use these operators in more complex mathematical formulas. For now we will concentrate on their basic usage, as illustrated in Program 2-18.

Program 2-18

```
// This program calculates hourly wages

#include <iostream>
using namespace std;

int main()
{
    double regWages,        // calculated regular wages
           basePay = 18.25, // base pay rate
           regHours = 40.0, // hours worked less overtime
           otWages,         // overtime wages
           otPay = 27.78,   // overtime pay rate
           otHours = 10,    // overtime hours worked
           totalWages;      // total wages

    regWages = basePay * regHours;
    otWages = otPay * otHours;
    totalWages = regWages + otWages;
    cout << "Wages for this week are $" << totalWages << endl;
    return 0;
}
```

Program Output
```
Wages for this week are $1007.8
```

Program 2-18 calculates the total wages an hourly paid worker earned in one week. As mentioned in the comments, there are variables for regular wages, base payrate, regulars hours worked, overtime wages, overtime payrate, overtime hours worked, and total wages.

The following line from the program multiplies basePay times regHours and stores the result, which is 730, in regWages:

```
regWages = basePay * regHours;
```

The next line multiplies otPay times otHours and stores the result, which is 277.8, in otWages:

```
otWages = otPay * otHours;
```

The following line adds the regular wages and the overtime wages and stores the result, 1007.8, in totalWages:

```
totalWages = regWages + otWages;
```

The last line displays the message on the screen reporting the week's wages.

Checkpoint   [2.11 –2.13]

2.18 Is the following assignment statement valid or invalid? If it is invalid, why?

```
72 = amount;
```

2.19 How would you consolidate the following definitions into one statement?

```
int x = 7;
int y = 16;
int z = 28;
```

2.20 What is wrong with the following program? How would you correct it?

```
#include <iostream>
using namespace std;

int main()
{
    number = 62.7;
    float number;
    cout << number << endl;
    return 0;
}
```

2.21 Is the following an example of integer division or floating-point division? What value will be stored in portion?

```
portion = 70 / 3;
```

2.14 Comments

CONCEPT Comments are notes of explanation that document lines or sections of a program. Comments are part of the program, but the compiler ignores them. They are intended for people who may be reading the source code.

It may surprise you that one of the most important parts of a program has absolutely no impact on the way it runs. In fact, the compiler pretends this part of a program doesn't even exist. Of course, I'm speaking of the comments.

If you are like most programmers, you will be resistant to putting more than just a few comments in your source code. After all, it's painful enough typing the parts of the program that actually do something. It is crucial, however, that you develop the habit of thoroughly annotating your code with descriptive comments. It might take extra time now, but it will almost certainly save time in the future.

Imagine writing a program of medium complexity with about 8,000 to 10,000 lines of C++ code. Once you have written the code and satisfactorily debugged it, you happily put it away and move on to the next project. Ten months later you are asked to make a modification to the program (or worse, track down and fix an elusive bug). You pull out the massive pile of paper that contains your source code and stare at thousands of statements that now make no sense at all. You find variables with names like z2, and you can't remember what they are for. If only you had left some notes to yourself explaining all the program's nuances and oddities. Of course it's too late now. All that's left to do is decide what will take less time: figuring out the old program or completely rewriting it!

This scenario might sound extreme, but it's one you don't want to happen to you. Real world programs are big and complex. Thoroughly documented programs will make your life easier, not to mention the other poor souls who may have to read your code in the future.

Commenting the C++ Way

You have already seen one way to place comments in a C++ program. You simply place two forward slashes (//) where you want the comment to begin. The compiler ignores everything from that point to the end of the line. Program 2-19 shows that comments may be placed liberally throughout a program.

In addition to telling who wrote the program and describing the purpose of variables, comments can also be used to explain complex procedures in your code.

Just in case you are one of those who believes "if a little of something is good then a whole lot of it must be better," let me caution you about putting too many comments in your programs. Comments should explain the aspects of your code that are not evident. They do not have to explain every little detail, however.

Program 2-19

```
// PROGRAM: PAYROLL.CPP
// Written by Herbert Dorfmann
// This program calculates company payroll
// Last modification: 3/30/2005
#include <iostream>
using namespace std;

int main()
{
    double payRate;    // holds the hourly pay rate
    double hours;      // holds the hours worked
    int empNum;        // holds the employee number
```

(The remainder of this program is left out.)

Commenting the C Way

Recall from Chapter 1 that C++ is a descendent of the C language. Comments in C start with /* (a forward slash followed by an asterisk) and end with */ (an asterisk followed by a forward slash). Everything between these markers is ignored. Program 2-20 illustrates how C style comments may be used in a C++ program.

Program 2-20

```
/*
    PROGRAM: PAYROLL.CPP
    Written by Herbert Dorfmann
    This program calculates company payroll
    Last modification: 3/30/2005
*/

#include <iostream>
using namespace std;

int main()
{
    double payRate;    /* payRate holds hourly pay rate */
    double hours;      /* hours holds hours worked      */
    int empNum;        /* empNum holds employee number  */
```

(The remainder of this program is left out.)

Unlike a C++ style comment, a C style comment can span several lines. This makes it more convenient to write large, multiline comments because you do not have to mark every line. Consequently, the C style is inconvenient for single-line comments because you must type both a beginning and ending comment symbol.

Many programmers prefer to use a combination of both styles, using the C style for multiline comments and the C++ style for single line comments.*

There are two pitfalls to avoid when using C style comments:

◆ Be careful not to reverse the beginning symbol with the ending symbol.

◆ Be sure not to forget the ending symbol.

Both of these mistakes can be difficult to track down and will prevent the program from compiling correctly.

2.15 Focus on Software Engineering: *Programming Style*

CONCEPT Programming style refers to the way a programmer uses identifiers, spaces, tabs, blank lines, and punctuation characters to visually arrange a program's source code. These are some, but not all, of the elements of programming style.

In Chapter 1 you learned that syntax rules govern the way a language may be used. The syntax rules of C++ dictate how and where to place key words, semicolons, commas, braces, and other components of the language. The compiler's job is to check for syntax errors, and if there are none, generate object code.

When the compiler reads a program it processes it as one long stream of characters. The compiler doesn't care that each statement is on a separate line, or that spaces separate operators from operands. Humans, on the other hand, find it difficult to read programs that aren't written in a visually pleasing manner. Consider Program 2-21 for example.

Program 2-21

```
#include <iostream>
using namespace std;int main(){double shares=220.0;
double avgPrice=14.67;cout<<"There were "<<shares
<<" shares sold at $"<<avgPrice<<" per share.\n";
return 0;}
```

Program Output
```
There were 220 shares sold at $14.67 per share.
```

---

* There is anecdotal evidence that some compilers determine whether you are programming in C or C++ by detecting the style of comment being used. If a C++ program contains both C and C++ style comments, such a compiler might mistakenly interpret it as a C program, and expect it to follow the syntax of that language.

Although the program is syntactically correct (it doesn't violate any rules of C++), it is very difficult to read. The same program is shown in Program 2-22, written in a more reasonable style.

Program 2-22

```
// This example is much more readable than Program 2-21.

#include <iostream>
using namespace std;

int main()
{
    double shares = 220.0;
    double avgPrice = 14.67;

    cout << "There were " << shares << " shares sold at $";
    cout << avgPrice << " per share.\n";
    return 0;
}
```

Program Output
```
There were 220 shares sold at $14.67 per share.
```

Programming style refers to the way source code is visually arranged. Ideally, it is a consistent method of putting spaces and indentions in a program so visual cues are created. These cues quickly tell a programmer important information about a program.

For example, notice in Program 2-22 that inside the function main's braces each line is indented. It is a common C++ style to indent all the lines inside a set of braces. You will also notice the blank line between the variable definitions and the cout statements. This is intended to visually separate the definitions from the executable statements.

 Note: Although you are free to develop your own style, you should adhere to common programming practices. By doing so, you will write programs that visually make sense to other programmers.

Another aspect of programming style is how to handle statements that are too long to fit on one line. Because C++ is a free-flowing language, it is usually possible to spread a statement over several lines. For example, here is a cout statement that uses five lines:

```
cout << "The fahrenheit temperature is "
     << fahrenheit
     << " and the centigrade temperature is "
     << centigrade
     << endl;
```

This statement will work just as if it were typed on one line. Here is an example of variable definitions treated similarly:

```
int fahrenheit,
    centigrade,
    kelvin;
```

There are many other issues related to programming style. They will be presented throughout the book.

2.16   If You Plan to Continue in Computer Science: *Standard and Prestandard C++*

CONCEPT   C++ programs written before the language became standardized may appear slightly different from programs written today.

C++ is now a standardized programming language, but it hasn't always been. The language has evolved over the years and, as a result, there is a "newer style" and an "older style" of writing C++ code. The newer style is the way programs are written with standard C++, while the older style is the way programs were typically written using prestandard C++. Although the differences between the older and newer styles are subtle, it is important that you recognize them. When you go to work as a computer science professional, it is likely that you will see programs written in the older style. It is also possible that your workplace's programming tools only support the older conventions, and you may need to write programs using the older style.

Older Style Header Files

In older style C++, all header files end with the ".h" extension. For example, in a pre-standard C++ program the statement that includes the `iostream.h` header file is written as:

```
#include <iostream.h>
```

Absence of using namespace std;

Another difference between the newer and older styles is that older style programs typically do not use the `using namespace std;` statement. In fact, some older compilers do not support namespaces at all, and will produce an error message if a program has that statement.

An Older Style Program

To illustrate these differences, look at the program below. It is a modification of Program 2-1, written in the older style.

```cpp
// A simple C++ program
#include <iostream.h>

int main()
{
    cout << "Programming is great fun!";
    return 0;
}
```

Most standard C++ compilers support programs written in the older style. Prestandard compilers, however, may not support programs written in the newer style.

Review Questions and Exercises

Short Answer

1. How many operands do each of the following types of operators require?

    _____ Unary
    _____ Binary
    _____ Ternary

2. How may the float variables temp, weight, and age be defined in one statement?

3. How may the int variables months, days, and years be defined in one statement, with months initialized to 2 and years initialized to 3?

4. Write assignment statements that perform the following operations with the variables a, b, and c.

    A) Adds 2 to a and stores the result in b.
    B) Multiplies b times 4 and stores the result in a.
    C) Divides a by 3.14 and stores the result in b.
    D) Subtracts 8 from b and stores the result in a.
    E) Stores the value 27 in a.
    F) Stores the character 'K' in c.
    G) Stores the ASCII code for 'B' in c.

5. Is the following comment a C style comment, or a C++ style comment?

    ```cpp
    /* This program was written by M. A. Codewriter*/
    ```

6. Is the following comment a C style comment, or a C++ style comment?

    ```cpp
    // This program was written by M. A. Codewriter
    ```

7. Modify the following program so it prints two blank lines between each line of text.

```
#include <iostream>
using namespace std;

int main()
{
    cout << "Two mandolins like creatures in the";
    cout << "dark";
    cout << "Creating the agony of ecstasy.";
    cout << "                  - George Barker";
    return 0;
}
```

8. What will the following program segments print on the screen?

A)
```
int freeze = 32, boil = 212;
freeze = 0;
boil = 100;
cout << freeze << endl << boil << endl;
return 0;
```

B)
```
int x = 0, y = 2;
x = y * 4;
cout << x << endl << y << endl;
```

C)
```
cout << "I am the incredible";
cout << "computing\nmachine";
cout << "\nand I will\namaze\n";
cout << "you.";
```

D)
```
cout << "Be careful\n";
cout << "This might/n be a trick ";
cout << "question\n";
```

Multiple Choice

9. Every complete statement ends with a

A) period
B) # symbol
C) semicolon
D) ending brace

10. Which of the following statements is correct?

    A) `#include (iostream)`
    B) `#include {iostream}`
    C) `#include <iostream>`
    D) `#include [iostream]`
    E) All of the above

11. Every C++ program must have a

    A) `cout` statement.
    B) function `main`.
    C) `#include` statement.
    D) All of the above

12. Preprocessor directives begin with a

    A) `#`
    B) `!`
    C) `<`
    D) `*`
    E) None of the above

13. The following data

```
72
'A'
"Hello World"
2.8712
```

are all examples of

    A) Variables
    B) Literals or constants
    C) Strings
    D) None of the above

14. A group of statements, such as the contents of a function, are enclosed in

    A) Braces `{ }`
    B) Parentheses `( )`
    C) Brackets `< >`
    D) All of the above will do

15. Which of the following are *not* a valid assignment statements? (Circle all that apply.)

    A) `total = 9;`
    B) `72 = amount;`
    C) `profit = 129`
    D) `letter = 'W';`

16. Which of the following are *not* valid `cout` statements? (Circle all that apply.)

    A) `cout << "Hello World";`
    B) `cout << "Have a nice day"\n;`
    C) `cout < value;`
    D) `cout << Programming is great fun;`

17. Assume $w = 5$, $x = 4$, $y = 8$, and $z = 2$. What value will be stored in `result` in each of the following statements?

    A) `result = x + y;`
    B) `result = z * 2;`
    C) `result = y / x;`
    D) `result = y - z;`
    E) `result = w % 2;`

18. How would each of the following numbers be represented in E notation?

    A) 3.287×10^6
    B) -978.65×10^{12}
    C) 7.65491×10^{-3}
    D) -58710.23×10^{-4}

19. The negation operator is

    A) Unary
    B) Binary
    C) Ternary
    D) None of the above

20. When do preprocessor directives execute?

    A) Before the compiler compiles your program
    B) After the compiler compiles your program
    C) At the same time as the compiler compiles your program
    D) None of the above

True or False

21. T F A variable must be defined before it can be used.

22. T F Variable names may begin with a number.

23. T F Variable names may be up to 31 characters long.

24. T F A left brace in a C++ program should always be followed by a right brace later in the program.

Algorithm Workbench

25. Convert the following pseudocode to C++ code. Be sure to define the appropriate variables.

    Store 20 in the speed *variable.*
    Store 10 in the time *variable.*
    Multiply speed *by* time *and store the result in the* distance *variable.*
    Display the contents of the distance *variable.*

26. Convert the following pseudocode to C++ code. Be sure to define the appropriate variables.

   Store 172.5 in the force *variable.*
   Store 27.5 in the area *variable.*
   Divide area *by* force *and store the result in the* pressure *variable.*
   Display the contents of the pressure *variable.*

Find the Error

27. There are a number of syntax errors in the following program. Locate as many as you can.

```
*/ What's wrong with this program? /*
#include iostream
using namespace std;

int main();
}
    int a, b, c\\ Three integers
    a = 3
    b - 4
    c = a + b
    Cout < "The value of c is %d" < C;
    return 0;
{
```

Programming Challenges

1. Sum of Two Numbers

Write a program that stores the integers 62 and 99 in variables, and stores the sum of these two in a variable named total.

2. Sales Prediction

The East Coast sales division of a company generates 62 percent of total sales. Based on that percentage, write a program that will predict how much the East Coast division will generate if the company has $4.6 million in sales this year.

3. Sales Tax

Write a program that will compute the total sales tax on a $52 purchase. Assume the state sales tax is 4 percent and the county sales tax is 2 percent.

4. Cyborg Data Type Sizes

You have been given a job as a programmer on a Cyborg supercomputer. In order to accomplish some calculations, you need to know how many bytes the following data types use: char, int, float, and double. You do not have any manuals, so you can't look this information up. Write a C++ program that will determine the amount of memory used by these types and display the information on the screen.

5. Miles Per Gallon

A car holds 12 gallons of gasoline and can travel 350 miles before refueling. Write a program that calculates the number of miles per gallon the car gets. Display the result on the screen.

6. Land Calculation

One acre of land is equivalent to 43,560 square feet. Write a program that calculates the number of acres in a tract of land with 389,767 square feet.

7. Circuit Board Price

An electronics company sells circuit boards at a 40 percent profit. Write a program that will calculate the selling price of a circuit board that costs $12.67. Display the result on the screen.

8. Personal Information

Write a program that displays the following information, each on a separate line:

    Your name
    Your address, with city, state, and ZIP
    Your telephone number
    Your college major

Use only a single cout statement to display all of this information.

9. Star Pattern

Write a program that displays the following pattern:

```
     *
    ***
   *****
  *******
   *****
    ***
     *
```

10. Test Average

Write a program that holds five test scores in five variables. Display each test score, as well as the average of the scores.

3

Expressions and Interactivity

■ **Topics in this Chapter**

3.1 The cin Object

CONCEPT The cin object can be used to read data typed at the keyboard.

So far you have written programs with built-in data. Without giving the user an opportunity to enter his or her own data, you have initialized the variables with the necessary starting values. These types of programs are limited to performing their task with only a single set of starting data. If you decide to change the initial value of any variable, the program must be modified and recompiled.

In reality, most programs ask for values that will be assigned to variables. This means the program does not have to be modified if the user wants to run it several times with different sets of data. For example, a program that calculates payroll for a small business might ask the user to enter the name of the employee, the hours worked, and the hourly pay rate. When the paycheck for that employee has been printed, the program could start over again with the name, hours worked, and hourly payrate of the next employee.

Just as cout is C++'s standard output object, cin is the standard input object. It reads input from the console (or keyboard) as shown in Program 3-1.

Program 3-1

```
// This program asks the user to enter the length and width of
// a rectangle. It calculates the rectangle's area and displays
// the value on the screen.
#include <iostream>
using namespace std;

int main()
{
    int length, width, area;
    cout << "This program calculates the area of a ";
    cout << "rectangle.\n";
    cout << "What is the length of the rectangle? ";
    cin >> length;
    cout << "What is the width of the rectangle? ";
    cin >> width;
    area = length * width;
    cout << "The area of the rectangle is " << area << ".\n";
    return 0;
}
```

Program Output with Example Input Shown in Bold
```
This program calculates the area of a rectangle.
What is the length of the rectangle? 10 [Enter]
What is the width of the rectangle? 20 [Enter]
The area of the rectangle is 200.
```

Instead of calculating the area of one rectangle, this program can be used to get the area of any rectangle. The values that are stored in the length and width variables are entered by the user when the program is running. Look at the following lines:

```
cout << "What is the length of the rectangle? ";
cin >> length;
```

In the first line, the cout object is used to display the question "What is the length of the rectangle?" This question is known as a *prompt,* and it tells the user what data he or she should enter. Your program should always display a prompt before it uses cin to read input. This way, the user will know that he or she must type a value at the keyboard.

The next line uses the cin object to read a value from the keyboard. The >> symbol is the *stream extraction operator.* It gets characters from the stream object on its left and stores them in the variable whose name appears on its right. In this line, characters are taken from the cin object (which gets them from the keyboard) and are stored in the length variable.

Note: Notice the >> and << operators appear to point in the direction data is flowing. The >> operator indicates data flows from cin to a variable, and the << operator shows that data flows from a variable (or literal) to cout.

The cin object causes a program to wait until data is typed at the keyboard and the **[Enter]** key is pressed. No other lines in the program will be executed until cin gets its input.

cin automatically converts the data read from the keyboard to the data type of the variable used to store it. If the user types 10, it is read as the characters '1' and '0'. cin is smart enough to know this will have to be converted to an int value before it is stored in length. cin is also smart enough to know a value like 10.7 cannot be stored in an integer variable. If the user enters a floating-point value for an integer variable, cin will not read the part of the number after the decimal point.

Note: You must include the iostream file in any program that uses cin.

Entering Multiple Values

The cin object may be used to gather multiple values at once. Look at Program 3-2, which is a modified version of Program 3-1.

Program 3-2

```
// This program asks the user to enter the length and width of
// a rectangle. It calculates the rectangle's area and displays
// the value on the screen.
#include <iostream>
using namespace std;

int main()
{
    int length, width, area;

    cout << "This program calculates the area of a ";
    cout << "rectangle.\n";
    cout << "Enter the length and width of the rectangle ";
    cout << "separated by a space.\n";
    cin >> length >> width;
    area = length * width;
    cout << "The area of the rectangle is " << area << endl;
    return 0;
}
```

Program Output with Example Input Shown in Bold
```
This program calculates the area of a rectangle.
Enter the length and width of the rectangle separated by a space.
```
10 20 [Enter]
```
The area of the rectangle is 200
```

The following line waits for the user to enter two values. The first is assigned to length and the second to width.

```
cin >> length >> width;
```

In the example output, the user entered 10 and 20, so 10 is stored in length and 20 is stored in width.

Notice the user separates the numbers by spaces as they are entered. This is how cin knows where each number begins and ends. It doesn't matter how many spaces are entered between the individual numbers. For example, the user could have entered

```
10            20
```

 Note: The [Enter] key is pressed after the last number is entered.

cin will also read multiple values of different data types. This is shown in Program 3-3.

Program 3-3

```
// This program demonstrates how cin can read multiple values
// of different data types.
#include <iostream>
using namespace std;

int main()
{
    int whole;
    double fractional;
    char letter;

    cout << "Enter an integer, a double, and a character: ";
    cin >> whole >> fractional >> letter;
    cout << "Whole: " << whole << endl;
    cout << "Fractional: " << fractional << endl;
    cout << "Letter: " << letter << endl;
    return 0;
}
```

Program Output with Example Input Shown in Bold
```
Enter an integer, a double, and a character: 4 5.7 b [Enter]
Whole: 4
Fractional: 5.7
Letter: b
```

As you can see in the example output, the values are stored in their respective variables. But what if the user had responded in the following way?

Enter an integer, a double, and a character: **5.7 4 b [Enter]**

When the user types values at the keyboard, those values are first stored in an area of memory known as the *keyboard buffer*. So, when the user enters the values 5.7, 4, and b, they are stored in the keyboard buffer as shown in Figure 3-1.

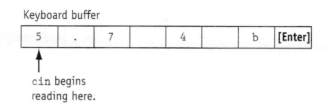

Keyboard buffer

| 5 | . | 7 | | 4 | | b | [Enter] |

cin begins
reading here.

Figure 3-1

When the user presses the **[Enter]** key, cin reads the value 5 into the variable whole. It does not read the decimal point because whole is an integer variable. Next it reads .7 and stores that value in the double variable fractional. The space is skipped and 4 is the next value read. It is stored in the char variable letter. (Recall that char variables actually hold integer values.) Because this cin statement reads only three values, the b is left in the keyboard buffer. So, in this situation the program would have stored 5 in whole, 0.7 in fractional, and the number 4 in letter. It is important that the user enters values in the correct order.

Reading Strings

cin can read a string as input and store it as a C-string. In C++, C-strings are commonly stored in *character arrays*. An array is like a group of variables with a single name, located together in memory. Here is an example of a character array definition:

    char company[12];

The number inside the brackets indicates the size of the array. The name of the array is company, and it is large enough to hold 12 characters. Remember, however, that C-strings have the null terminator at the end, so this array is large enough to hold a C-string that is 11 characters long.

 Note: If a character array is intended to hold strings, it must be at least one character larger than the largest string that will be stored in it. This extra character is for the null terminator.

Program 3-4 shows how cin may be used to read a string into a character array.

Program 3-4

```cpp
// This program demonstrates how cin can read a string into
// a character array.
#include <iostream>
using namespace std;

int main()
{
    char name[21];

    cout << "What is your name? ";
    cin >> name;
    cout << "Good morning " << name << endl;
    return 0;
}
```

Program Output with Example Input Shown in Bold
What is your name? **Charlie [Enter]**
Good morning Charlie

Let's examine the array definition:

```cpp
char name[21];
```

The name of the array is name and it is large enough to hold 21 characters. The null terminator at the end of a C-string is a character, so the longest string that may be stored in this array is 20 characters.

 WARNING! The user can enter a string larger than the array can hold. If this happens, the string will overflow the array's boundaries and destroy other data in memory.

Notice in the following lines the brackets and the size indicator are left out.

```cpp
cin >> name;
cout << "Good morning " << name << endl;
```

When reading a string into an array, you use the name of the array only. You would not get the desired result if you wrote these lines as:

```cpp
cin >> name[21];  //Incorrect!
cout << "Good morning " << name[21] << endl;  //Incorrect!
```

Program 3-5 shows another example of using character arrays in a program.

The arrays, first and last, are large enough to hold strings of 15 characters. The following line reads a string into each array:

```cpp
cin >> first >> last;
```

Program 3-5

```cpp
// This program reads two strings into two character arrays.
#include <iostream>
using namespace std;

int main()
{
    char first[16], last[16];

    cout << "Enter your first and last names and I will\n";
    cout << "reverse them.\n";
    cin >> first >> last;
    cout << last << ", " << first << endl;
    return 0;
}
```

Program Output with Example Input Shown in Bold
Enter your first and last names and I will
reverse them.
Johnny Jones [Enter]
Jones, Johnny

Just as before, spaces separate the two items.

> **Note:** If you wish the user to enter a string that has spaces in it, you cannot use this input method. Later in this chapter you will learn how to accomplish this.

Checkpoint [3.1]

3.1 What header file must be included in programs using cin?

3.2 What type of variable is used to hold a C-string?

3.3 Write a definition statement for a character array named customer. It should be large enough to hold a string 52 characters in length.

3.4 TRUE or FALSE: cin requires the user to press the **[Enter]** key when finished entering data.

3.5 Assume value is an integer variable. If the user enters 3.14 in response to the following programming statement, what will be stored in value?

    cin >> value;

A) 3.14
B) 3
C) 0
D) Nothing. An error message is displayed.

3.6 A program has the following variable definitions.

```
long miles;
int feet;
double inches;
```

Write one `cin` statement that reads a value into each of these variables.

3.7 The following program will run, but the user will have difficulty understanding what to do. How would you improve the program? Also, allow the user to input a value for a second without adding another `cin` object.

```
int main()
{
    double first, second, product;
    second = 10.5;
    cin >> first;
    product = first * second;
    cout << product;
    return 0;
}
```

3.2 Mathematical Expressions

CONCEPT C++ allows you to construct complex mathematical expressions using multiple operators and grouping symbols.

In Chapter 2 you were introduced to the basic mathematical operators, which are used to build mathematical expressions. An *expression* is a programming statement that has a value. Usually, an expression consists of an operator and its operands. Look at the following statement:

```
sum = 21 + 3;
```

Since 21 + 3 has a value, it is an expression. Its value, 24, is stored in the variable sum. Expressions do not have to be in the form of mathematical operations. In the following statement, 3 is an expression.

```
number = 3;
```

Here are some programming statements where the variable result is being assigned the value of an expression:

```
result = x;
result = 4;
result = 15 / 3;
result = 22 * number;
result = sizeof(int);
result = a + b + c;
```

In each of these statements, a number, variable name, or mathematical expression appears on the right side of the = symbol. A value is obtained from each of these and stored in the variable result. These are all examples of a variable being assigned the value of an expression.

Program 3-6 shows how mathematical expressions can be used with the cout object.

Program 3-6

```cpp
// This program asks the user to enter the numerator
// and denominator of a fraction and it displays the
// decimal value.
#include <iostream>
using namespace std;

int main()
{
    double numerator, denominator;

    cout << "This program shows the decimal value of ";
    cout << "a fraction.\n";
    cout << "Enter the numerator: ";
    cin >> numerator;
    cout << "Enter the denominator: ";
    cin >> denominator;
    cout << "The decimal value is ";
    cout << (numerator / denominator) << endl;
    return 0;
}
```

Program Output with Example Input Shown in Bold
```
This program shows the decimal value of a fraction.
Enter the numerator: 3 [Enter]
Enter the denominator: 16 [Enter]
The decimal value is 0.1875
```

The cout object will display the value of any legal expression in C++. In the program above, the value of the expression numerator / denominator is displayed.

 Note: The example input above shows the user entering 3 and 16. Since these values are assigned to double variables, they are stored as the double values 3.0 and 16.0.

 Note: When sending an expression that consists of an operator to cout, it is always a good idea to put parentheses around the expression. Some advanced operators will yield unexpected results otherwise.

Operator Precedence

It is possible to build mathematical expressions with several operators. The following statement assigns the sum of 17, x, 21, and y to the variable answer.

```
answer = 17 + x + 21 + y;
```

Some expressions are not that straightforward, however. Consider the following statement:

```
outcome = 12 + 6 / 3;
```

What value will be stored in outcome? 6 is used as an operand for both the addition and division operators. outcome could be assigned either 6 or 14, depending on whether the addition operation or the division operator takes place first. The answer is 14 because the division operator has higher *precedence* than the addition operator.

Mathematical expressions are evaluated from left to right. When two operators share an operand, the operator with the highest precedence works first. Multiplication and division have higher precedence than addition and subtraction, so the statement above works like this:

A) 6 is divided by 3, yielding a result of 2
B) 12 is added to 2, yielding a result of 14

It could be diagrammed in the following way:

```
outcome = 12 + 6 / 3
               \ /
outcome = 12 +   2

outcome = 14
```

Table 3-1 shows the precedence of the arithmetic operators. The operators at the top of the table have higher precedence than the ones below it

Table 3-1   Precedence of Arithmetic Operators (Highest to Lowest)

(unary negation)   -
* / %
+   -

The multiplication, division, and modulus operators have the same precedence. This is also true of the addition and subtraction operators. Table 3-2 shows some expressions with their values.

Table 3-2 Some Expressions with Their Values

Expression	Value
5 + 2 * 4	13
10 / 2 - 3	2
8 + 12 * 2 - 4	28
4 + 17 % 2 - 1	4
6 - 3 * 2 + 7 - 1	6

Associativity

If two operators sharing an operand have the same precedence, they work according to their *associativity*. Associativity is either *left to right* or *right to left*. It is the order in which an operator works with its operands. The associativity of the division operator is left to right, so it divides the operand on its left by the operand on its right. Table 3-3 shows the arithmetic operators and their associativity.

Table 3-3 Associativity of Arithmetic Operators

Operator	Associativity
(unary negation) -	Right to left
* / %	Left to right
+ -	Left to right

Grouping with Parentheses

Parts of a mathematical expression may be grouped with parentheses to force some operations to be performed before others. In the following statement, the sum of a, b, c, and d is divided by 4.

```
average = (a + b + c + d) / 4;
```

Without the parentheses, however, d would be divided by 4 and the result added to a, b, and c. Table 3-4 shows more expressions and their values.

Converting Algebraic Expressions to Programming Statements

In algebra it is not always necessary to use an operator for multiplication. C++, however, requires an operator for any mathematical operation. Table 3-5 shows some algebraic expressions that perform multiplication and the equivalent C++ expressions.

Table 3-4 More Expressions

Expression	Value
(5 + 2) * 4	28
10 / (5 - 3)	5
8 + 12 * (6 - 2)	56
(4 + 17) % 2 - 1	0
(6 - 3) * (2 + 7) / 3	9

Table 3-5 Algebraic and C++ Multiplication Expressions

Algebraic Expression	Operation	C++ Equivalent
6B	6 times B	6 * B
(3)(12)	3 times 12	3 * 12
4xy	4 times x times y	4 * x * y

When converting some algebraic expressions to C++, you may have to insert parentheses that do not appear in the algebraic expression. For example, look at the following expression:

$$x = \frac{a + b}{c}$$

To convert this to a C++ statement, $a + b$ will have to be enclosed in parentheses:

```
x = (a + b) / c;
```

Table 3-6 shows more algebraic expressions and their C++ equivalents.

Table 3-6 Algebraic and C++ Expressions

Algebraic Expression	C++ Expression
$y = 3\frac{x}{2}$	y = x / 2 * 3;
$z = 3bc + 4$	z = 3 * b * c + 4;
$a = \dfrac{3x + 2}{4a - 1}$	a = (3 * x + 2) / (4 * a - 1)

No Exponents Please!

Unlike many programming languages, C++ does not have an exponent operator. Raising a number to a power requires the use of a *library function*. The C++ library isn't a place where you check out books, but a collection of specialized functions. Think of a library function as a "routine" that performs a specific operation. One of the library functions is called pow, and its purpose is to raise a number to a power. Here is an example of how it's used:

```
area = pow(4.0, 2.0);
```

This statement contains a *call* to the pow function. The numbers inside the parentheses are *arguments*. Arguments are data being sent to the function. pow always raises the first argument to the power of the second argument. In this example, 4 is raised to the power of 2. The result is *returned* from the function and used in the statement where the function call appears. In this case, the value 16 is returned from pow and assigned to the variable area. This is illustrated in Figure 3-2.

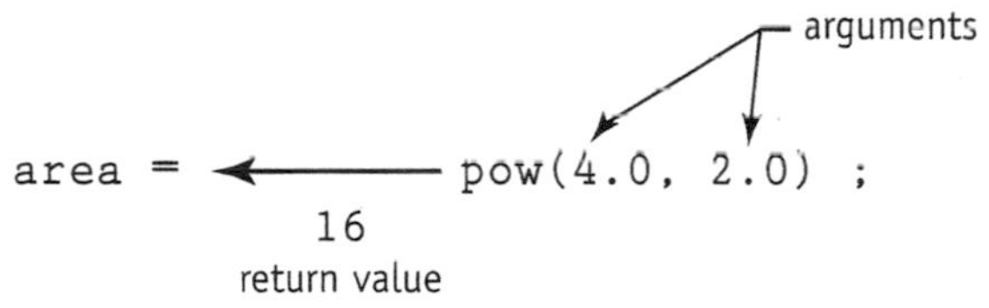

arguments

$$area = \longleftarrow \overset{}{\underset{16}{\text{—}}} pow(4.0,\ 2.0)\ ;$$

return value

Figure 3-2

The statement area = pow(4.0,2.0) is equivalent to the following algebraic statement:

$$area = 4^2$$

Here is another example of a statement using the pow function. It assigns 3 times 6^3 to x:

```
x = 3 * pow(6.0, 3.0);
```

And the following statement displays the value of 5 raised to the power of 4:

```
cout << pow(5.0, 4.0);
```

It might be helpful to think of pow as a "black box" that you plug two numbers into, which then sends a third number out. The number that comes out has the value of the first number raised to the power of the second number, as illustrated in Figure 3-3:

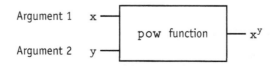

Argument 1 x —[pow function]— x^y

Argument 2 y —

Figure 3-3

There are some rules that must be followed when the pow function is used. First, the program must include the cmath header file. Second, the variable used to store pow's return value should be defined as a `double`. For example, in the following statement the variable `area` should be a `double`:

```
area = pow(4.0, 2.0);
```

 Note: The `pow` function is designed to return a `double`. Remember that a `double` value will fit in a `float` variable only if the value is small enough. If the arguments of the `pow` function are large enough to cause `pow` to produce a value outside the range of a `float`, a `double` variable should be used to store the return value.

Program 3-7 solves a simple algebraic problem. It asks the user to enter the radius of a circle and then calculates the area of the circle. The formula is

$$\text{Area} = \pi r^2$$

which is expressed in the program as

```
area = 3.14159 * pow(radius, 2.0);
```

Program 3-7

```cpp
//   This program calculates the area of a circle.
//   The formula for the area of a circle is Pi times
//   the radius squared. Pi is 3.14159.
#include <iostream>
#include <cmath>    // needed for pow function
using namespace std;

int main()
{
    double area, radius;

    cout << "This program calculates the area of a circle.\n";
    cout << "What is the radius of the circle? ";
    cin >> radius;
    area = 3.14159 * pow(radius, 2.0);
    cout << "The area is " << area << endl;
    return 0;
}
```

Program Output with Example Input Shown in Bold
```
This program calculates the area of a circle.
What is the radius of the circle? 10 [Enter]
The area is 314.159
```

Note: Program 3-7 is presented as a demonstration of the pow function. In reality, there is no reason to use the pow function in such a simple operation. The math statement could just as easily be written as

```
area = 3.14159 * radius * radius;
```

The pow function is useful, however, in operations that involve larger exponents.

 ## Checkpoint [3.2]

3.8 Complete the table below by writing the value of each expression in the "Value" column.

Expression	Value
6 + 3 * 5	
12 / 2 - 4	
9 + 14 * 2 - 6	
5 + 19 % 3 - 1	
(6 + 2) * 3	

3.9 Write C++ expressions for the following algebraic expressions:

$$y = 6x$$

$$a = 2b + 4c$$

$$y = x^2$$

$$g = \frac{x + 2}{z^2}$$

3.10 Study the following program segment and complete the table.

```
double value1, value2, value3;
cout << "Enter a number: ";
cin >> value1;
value2 = 2 * pow(value1, 2.0);
value3 = 3 + value2 / 2 - 1;
cout << value3 << endl;
```

If the User Enters...	The Program Segment Will Display What Number (Stored in `value3`)?
2	
5	
4.3	
6	

3.3 When You Mix Apples and Oranges: *Type Conversion*

> **CONCEPT** When an operator's operands are of different data types, C++ will automatically convert them to the same data type. This can affect the results of mathematical expressions.

If an `int` is multiplied by a `float`, what data type will the result be? What if a `double` is divided by an `unsigned int`? Is there any way of predicting what will happen in these instances? The answer is yes. C++ follows a set of rules when performing mathematical operations on variables of different data types. It's helpful to understand these rules to prevent subtle errors from creeping into your programs.

Just like officers in the military, data types are ranked. One data type outranks another if it can hold a larger number. For example, a `float` outranks an `int`. Table 3-7 lists the data types in order of their rank, from highest to lowest.

Table 3-7   Data Type Ranking

```
long double
double
float
unsigned long
long
unsigned int
int
```

One exception to the ranking in Table 3-7 is when an `int` and a `long` are the same size. In that case, an `unsigned int` outranks `long` because it can hold a higher value.

When C++ is working with an operator, it strives to convert the operands to the same type. This automatic conversion is known as *type coercion*. When a value is converted to a higher data type, it is said to be *promoted*. To *demote* a value means to convert it to a lower data type. Let's look at the specific rules that govern the evaluation of mathematical expressions.

Rule 1: chars, shorts, and unsigned shorts are automatically promoted to int.

You will notice that char, short, and unsigned short do not appear in Table 3-7. That's because anytime they are used in a mathematical expression, they are automatically promoted to an int. The only exception to this rule is when an unsigned short holds a value larger than can be held by an int. This can happen on systems where shorts are the same size as ints. In this case, the unsigned short is promoted to unsigned int.

Rule 2: When an operator works with two values of different data types, the lower-ranking value is promoted to the type of the higher-ranking value.

In the following expression, assume that years is an int and interestRate is a float:

```
years * interestRate
```

Before the multiplication takes place, years will be promoted to a float.

Rule 3: When the final value of an expression is assigned to a variable, it will be converted to the data type of that variable.

In the following statement, assume that area is a long int, while length and width are both ints:

```
area = length * width;
```

Since length and width are both ints, they will not be converted to any other data type. The result of the multiplication, however, will be converted to long so it can be stored in area.

 WARNING! Remember, when both operands of a division are integers, the fractional part will be truncated, or thrown away.

Watch out for situations where an expression results in a fractional value being assigned to an integer variable. Here is an example:

```
int x, y = 4;
float z = 2.7;
x = y * z;
```

In the expression y * z, y will be promoted to float and 10.8 will result from the multiplication. Since x is an integer, however, 10.8 will be truncated and 10 will be stored in x.

3.4 Overflow and Underflow

> **CONCEPT** When a variable is assigned a value that is too large or too small in range for that variable's data type, the variable overflows or underflows.

Trouble can arise when a variable is being assigned a value that is too large for its type. Here is a statement where a, b, and c are all short integers:

```
a = b * c;
```

If b and c are set to values large enough, the multiplication will produce a number too big to be stored in a. To prepare for this, a should have been defined as an int, or a long int.

When a variable is assigned a number that is too large for its data type, it *overflows*. Likewise, assigning a value that is too small for a variable causes it to *underflow*. Program 3-8 shows what happens when an integer overflows or underflows. (The output shown is from a system with two-byte short integers.)

Program 3-8

```cpp
// This program demonstrates integer overflow and underflow.
#include <iostream>
using namespace std;

int main()
{
    short testVar = 32767;

    cout << testVar << endl;
    testVar = testVar + 1;
    cout << testVar << endl;
    testVar = testVar - 1;
    cout << testVar << endl;
    return 0;
}
```

Program Output
```
32767
-32768
32767
```

Typically, when an integer overflows, its contents wrap around to that data type's lowest possible value. In Program 3-8, testVar wrapped around from 32,767 to –32,768 when 1 was added to it. When 1 was subtracted from testVar, it underflowed, which caused its contents to wrap back around to 32,767. No warning or error message is given, so be careful when working with numbers close to the maximum or minimum range of an integer. If an overflow or underflow occurs, the program will use the incorrect number, and therefore produce incorrect results.

When floating-point variables overflow or underflow, the results depend upon which compiler is being used. Your system may produce programs that do any of the following:

♦ Produces an incorrect result and continues running.

♦ Prints an error message and immediately stops when either floating point overflow or underflow occurs.

♦ Prints an error message and immediately stops when floating point overflow occurs, but stores a 0 in the variable when it underflows.

♦ Gives you a choice of behaviors when overflow or underflow occurs.

You can find out how your system reacts by compiling and running Program 3-9.

Program 3-9

```
// This program can be used to see how your system handles
// floating point overflow and underflow.
#include <iostream>
using namespace std;

int main()
{
    float test;

    test = 2.0e38 * 1000;          // Should overflow test.
    cout << test << endl;
    test = 2.0e-38 / 2.0e38;       // Should underflow test.
    cout << test << endl;
    return 0;
}
```

3.5 Type Casting

CONCEPT Type casting allows you to perform manual data type conversion.

A *type cast expression* lets you manually promote or demote a value in the same way automatic conversion takes place. The general format of a type cast expression is

```
static_cast<DataType>(Value)
```

where *Value* is a variable or literal value that you wish to convert and *DataType* is the data type you wish to convert *Value* to. Here is an example of code that uses a type cast expression:

```
double number = 3.7;
int val;
val = static_cast<int>(number);
```

This code defines two variables: number, a double, and val, an int. The type cast expression in the third statement returns a copy of the value in number, converted to an int. When a double is converted to an int, the fractional part is truncated so this statement stores 3 in val. The original value in number is not changed, however.

Type cast expressions are useful in situations where C++ will not perform the desired conversion automatically. Program 3-10 shows an example where a type cast expression is used to prevent integer division from taking place. The statement that uses the type cast expression is

Program 3-10

```
// This program uses the type cast expression to avoid integer division.
#include <iostream>
using namespace std;

int main()
{
    int months, books;
    double perMonth;

    cout << "How many books do you plan to read? ";
    cin >> books;
    cout << "How many months will it take you to read them? ";
    cin >> months;
    perMonth = static_cast<double>(books) / months;
    cout << "That is " << perMonth << " books per month.\n";
    return 0;
}
```

Program Output with Example Input Shown in Bold
How many books do you plan to read? **30 [Enter]**
How many months will it take you to read them? **7 [Enter]**
That is 4.28571 books per month.

```
perMonth = static_cast<double>(books) / months;
```

The variable books is an integer, but its value is converted to a double before the division takes place. Without the type cast expression, integer division would have been performed resulting in an incorrect answer.

WARNING! In Program 3-10, the following statement would still have resulted in integer division:

```
perMonth = static_cast<double>(books / months);
```

The result of the expression `books / months` is 4. When 4 is converted to a `double`, it is 4.0. To prevent the integer division from taking place, one of the operands should be converted to a `double` prior to the division operation. This forces C++ to automatically convert the value of the other operand to a `double`.

The following program segment shows another use of the type cast expression.

```
int number = 65;
cout << number << endl;
cout << static_cast<char>(number) << endl;
```

Program Output
```
65
A
```

`cout` normally displays variable contents in a format suitable for the variable's native data type. If you want to change this, as in the previous program segment, you can use a type cast.

 Note: C++ provides several different type cast expressions. `static_cast` is the most commonly used type cast expression, so we will primarily use it in this book.

If You Plan to Continue in Computer Science: C-style and Prestandard Type Cast Expressions

C++ also supports two other methods of creating type cast expressions: the C-style form and the prestandard C++ form. The C-style cast is the name of a data type enclosed in parentheses, preceding the value that is to be converted. For example, the following statement converts the value in number to an `int`.

```
val = (int)number;
```

The following statement shows another example.

```
perMonth = (double)books / months;
```

In this statement the value in the `books` variable is converted to a `double` before the division takes place.

The prestandard C++ form of the type cast expression appears as a data type name followed by a value inside a set of parentheses. Here is an example:

```
val = int(number);
```

The type cast in this statement returns a copy of the value in number, converted to an int. Here is another example:

```
perMonth = double(books) / months;
```

Although the static_cast expression is preferable to either the C-style or the prestandard C++ form of the type cast expression, you will probably see code in the workplace that uses these older styles.

 ## Checkpoint [3.3–3.5]

3.11 Assume the following variable definitions:

```
int a = 5, b = 12;
double x = 3.4, z = 9.1;
```

What are the values of the following expressions?

```
A)  b / a
B)  static_cast<double>(b / a)
C)  static_cast<double>(b) / a
D)  b / static_cast<double>(a)
E)  b / static_cast<int>(x)
F)  static_cast<int>(x) * static_cast<int>(z)
G)  static_cast<int>(x * z)
```

3.12 What will the following program segment display?

```
int integer1, integer2;
float float1;
integer1 = 19;
integer2 = 2;
float1 = integer1 / integer2;
cout << float1 << endl;
float1 = static_cast<float>(integer1) / integer2;
cout << float1 << endl;
float1 = static_cast<float>(integer1 / integer2);
cout << float1 << endl;
```

3.6 Named Constants

CONCEPT Literals may be given names that symbolically represent them in a program.

In Chapter 2 you learned about numbers and strings being expressed as literals. For example, the following statement contains the numeric literal 0.129:

```
amount2 = amount1 * 0.129;
```

Let's assume this statement appears in a banking program that calculates data pertaining to loans. In such a program, two potential problems arise. First, it is not clear to anyone other than the original programmer what 0.129 is. It appears to be an interest rate, but in some situations there are fees associated with loan payments. How can the purpose of this statement be determined without painstakingly checking the rest of the program?

The second problem occurs if this number is used in other calculations throughout the program and must be changed periodically. Assuming the number is an interest rate, what if the rate changes from 12.9 percent to 13.2 percent? The programmer will have to search through the source code for every occurrence of the number.

Both of these problems can be addressed by using named constants. A *named constant* is really a variable whose content is read-only, and cannot be changed while the program is running. Here is a definition of a named constant:

```
const double INTEREST_RATE = 0.129;
```

It looks just like a regular variable definition except that the word const appears before the data type name, and the name of the variable is written in all uppercase characters. The key word const is a qualifier that tells the compiler to make the variable read-only. Its value will remain constant throughout the program's execution. It is not required that the variable name be written in all uppercase characters, but many programmers prefer to write them this way so they are easily distinguishable from regular variable names.

An initialization value must be given when defining a variable with the const qualifier, or an error will result when the program is compiled. A compiler error will also result if there are any statements in the program that attempt to change the contents of a named constant.

An advantage of using named constants is that they make programs more self-documenting. The following statement

```
amount2 = amount1 * 0.129;
```

can be changed to read

```
amount2 = amount1 * INTEREST_RATE;
```

A new programmer can read the second statement and know what is happening. It is evident that amount1 is being multiplied by the interest rate. Another advantage to this approach is that widespread changes can easily be made to the program. Let's say the interest rate appears in a dozen different statements throughout the program. When the rate changes, the initialization value in the definition of the named constant is the only value that needs to be modified. If the rate increases to 13.2% the definition is changed to the following:

```
const double INTEREST_RATE = 0.132;
```

The program is then ready to be recompiled. Every statement that uses INTEREST_RATE will be updated with the new value.

It is also useful to define named constants for common values that are difficult to remember. For example, Program 3-7 calculated the area of a circle. The number 3.14159 is used for pi in the formula. This value could easily be defined as a named constant, as shown in Program 3-11.

Program 3-11

```
//   This program calculates the area of a circle.
#include <iostream>
#include <cmath>   // needed for pow function
using namespace std;

int main()
{
    const double PI = 3.14159;
    double area, radius;

    cout << "This program calculates the area of a circle.\n";
    cout << "What is the radius of the circle? ";
    cin >> radius;
    area = PI * pow(radius, 2);
    cout << "The area is " << area << endl;
    return 0;
}
```

The #define Directive

The older C-style method of creating named constants is with the #define preprocessor directive. Although it is preferable to use the const modifier, there are programs with the #define directive still in use. In addition, Chapter 13 teaches other uses of the #define directive, so it is important to understand.

In Chapter 2 you learned that the #include directive causes the preprocessor to include the contents of another file in your program. Program 3-12 shows how the preprocessor can be used to create a named constant.

Remember, the preprocessor scans your program before it is compiled. It looks for directives, which are lines that begin with the # symbol. Preprocessor directives cause your source code to be modified prior to being compiled. The #define statement in Program 3-12 reads

```
#define PI 3.14159
```

The word PI is a named constant and 3.14159 is its value. Anytime PI is used in the program, it will be replaced by the value 3.14159. The line that reads

```
area = PI * pow(radius, 2);
```

Program 3-12

```
//   This program calculates the area of a circle.
#include <iostream>
#include <cmath>    // needed for pow function
using namespace std;

#define PI 3.14159

int main()
{
    double area, radius;

    cout << "This program calculates the area of a circle.\n";
    cout << "What is the radius of the circle? ";
    cin >> radius;
    area = PI * pow(radius, 2);
    cout << "The area is " << area << endl;
    return 0;
}
```

will be modified by the preprocessor to read

```
    area = 3.14159 * pow(radius, 2);
```

If there had been a line that read

```
    cout << PI << endl;
```

it would have been modified to read

```
    cout << 3.14159 << endl;
```

It is important to realize the difference between constant variables and constants created with the #define directive. Constant variables are defined like regular variables. They have a data type and a specific storage location in memory. They are like regular variables in every way except that you cannot change their value while the program is running. Constants created with the #define directive, however, are not variables at all, but textual substitutions. Each occurrence of the named constant in your source code is removed and the value of the constant is written in its place.

 Note: It is not required that constants created with the #define directive be named with uppercase letters. Most programmers do this so they can tell the difference between constants and variable names in later sections of the program.

Be careful not to put a semicolon at the end of a #define directive. The semicolon will actually become part of the value of the constant. If the #define directive in Program 3-12 had read like this:

```
#define PI 3.14159;
```

The mathematical statement

```
area = PI * pow(radius, 2);
```

would have been modified to read

```
area = 3.14159; * pow(radius, 2);
```

Because of the semicolon, the preprocessor would have created a syntax error in the statement above and the compiler would have given an error message when trying to process this statement.

 Note: #define directives are intended for the preprocessor and C++ statements are intended for the compiler. The preprocessor does not look for semicolons to terminate directives.

 # Checkpoint [3.6]

3.13 Write statements using the const qualifier to create named constants for the following literal values:

Literal Value	Description
2.71828	Euler's number (known in mathematics as e)
5.26E5	Number of seconds in a year
32.2	The gravitational acceleration constant (in feet per second^2)
9.8	The gravitational acceleration constant (in meters per second^2)
1609	Number of meters in a mile

3.14 Write #define directives for the literal values listed in question 3.13.

3.15 Assuming the user enters 6 in response to the question, what will the following program display on the screen?

```
#include <iostream>
using namespace std;

#define GREETING1 "This program calculates the number "
#define GREETING2 "of candy pieces sold."
#define QUESTION "How many jars of candy have you sold? "
#define RESULTS "The number of pieces sold: "
```

```
#define YOUR_COMMISSION "Candy pieces you get for commission: "
#define COMMISSION_RATE .20

int main()
{
    const int perJar = 1860;
    int jars, pieces;
    double commission;

    cout << GREETING1;
    cout << GREETING2 << endl;
    cout << QUESTION;
    cin >> jars;
    pieces = jars * perJar;
    cout << RESULTS << pieces << endl;
    commission = pieces * COMMISSION_RATE;
    cout << YOUR_COMMISSION << commission << endl;
    return 0;
}
```

3.7 Multiple Assignment and Combined Assignment

CONCEPT Multiple assignment means to assign the same value to several variables with one statement.

C++ allows you to assign a value to multiple variables at once. If a program has several variables, such as a, b, c, and d, and each variable needs to be assigned a value, such as 12, the following statement may be constructed:

```
a = b = c = d = 12;
```

The value 12 will be copied to each variable listed in the statement.*

Combined Assignment Operators

Quite often, programs have assignment statements of the following form:

```
number = number + 1;
```

---

* The assignment operator works from right to left. 12 is first assigned to d, then to c, then to b, then to a.

On the right-hand side of the assignment operator, 1 is added to `number`. The result is then assigned to `number`, replacing the value that was previously stored there. Effectively, this statement adds 1 to `number`. In a similar fashion, the following statement subtracts 5 from `number`.

```
number = number - 5;
```

If you have never seen this type of statement before, it might cause some initial confusion because the same variable name appears on both sides of the assignment operator. Table 3-8 shows other examples of statements written this way.

Table 3-8   (Assume x = 6)

Statement	What It Does	Value of x after the Statement
x = x + 4;	Adds 4 to x	10
x = x - 3;	Subtracts 3 from x	3
x = x * 10;	Multiplies x by 10	60
x = x / 2;	Divides x by 2	3
x = x % 4	Makes x the remainder of x / 4	2

These types of operations are very common in programming. For convenience, C++ offers a special set of operators designed specifically for these jobs. Table 3-9 shows the *combined assignment operators*, also known as *compound operators*, and *arithmetic assignment operators*.

Table 3-9

Operator	Example Usage	Equivalent To
+=	x += 5;	x = x + 5;
-=	y -= 2;	y = y - 2;
*=	z *= 10;	z = z * 10;
/=	a /= b;	a = a / b;
%=	c %= 3;	c = c % 3;

As you can see, the combined assignment operators do not require the programmer to type the variable name twice. Also, they give a clearer indication of what is happening in the statement. Program 3-13 uses combined assignment operators.

Program 3-13

```cpp
// This program tracks the inventory of three widget stores that opened at the
// same time. Each store started with the same number of widgets in inventory. By
// subtracting the number of widgets each store has sold from its inventory, the
// current inventory can be calculated.

#include <iostream>
using namespace std;

int main()
{
    int begInv, sold, store1, store2, store3;

    cout << "One week ago, 3 new widget stores opened\n";
    cout << "at the same time with the same beginning\n";
    cout << "inventory. What was the beginning inventory?\n";
    cin >> begInv;
    store1 = store2 = store3 = begInv;
    cout << "How many widgets has store 1 sold? ";
    cin >> sold;
    store1 -= sold; // Subtract sold from store1
    cout << "How many widgets has store 2 sold? ";
    cin >> sold;
    store2 -= sold; // Subtract sold from store2
    cout << "How many widgets has store 3 sold? ";
    cin >> sold;
    store3 -= sold; // Subtract sold from store3
    cout << "\nThe current inventory of each store:\n";
    cout << "Store 1: " << store1 << endl;
    cout << "Store 2: " << store2 << endl;
    cout << "Store 3: " << store3 << endl;
    return 0;
}
```

Program Output with Example Input Shown in Bold
```
One week ago, 3 new widget stores opened
at the same time with the same beginning
inventory. What was the beginning inventory? 100 [Enter]
How many widgets has store 1 sold? 25 [Enter]
How many widgets has store 2 sold? 15 [Enter]
How many widgets has store 3 sold? 45 [Enter]

The current inventory of each store:
Store 1: 75
Store 2: 85
Store 3: 55
```

More elaborate statements may be expressed with the combined assignment operators. Here is an example:

```
result *= a + 5;
```

In this statement, `result` is multiplied by the sum of `a + 5`. When constructing such statements, you must realize the precedence of the combined assignment operators is lower than that of the regular math operators. The statement above is equivalent to

```
result = result * (a + 5);
```

Which is different from

```
result = result * a + 5;
```

Table 3-10 shows other examples of such statements and their assignment statement equivalencies.

Table 3-10

Example Usage	Equivalent To
x += b + 5;	x = x + (b + 5);
y -= a * 2;	y = y - (a * 2);
z *= 10 - c;	z = z * (10 - c);
a /= b + c;	a = a / (b + c);
c %= d - 3;	c = c % (d - 3);

Checkpoint [3.7]

3.16 Write a multiple assignment statement that assigns 0 to the variables `total`, `subtotal`, `tax`, and `shipping`.

3.17 Write statements using combined assignment operators to perform the following:

A) Add 6 to `x`.
B) Subtract 4 from `amount`.
C) Multiply `y` by 4.
D) Divide `total` by 27.
E) Store in `x` the remainder of `x` divided by 7.
F) Add `y * 5` to `x`.
G) Subtract `discount` times 4 from `total`.
H) Multiply `increase` by `salesRep` times 5.
I) Divide `profit` by `shares` minus 1000.

3.18 What will the following program segment display?

```
int unus, duo, tres;
unus = duo = tres = 5;
unus += 4;
duo *= 2;
tres -= 4;
unus /= 3;
duo += tres;
cout << unus << endl;
cout << duo << endl;
cout << tres << endl;
```

3.8 Formatting Output

CONCEPT The cout object provides ways to format data as it is being displayed. This affects the way data appears on the screen.

The same data can be printed or displayed in several different ways. For example, all of the following numbers have the same value, although they look different:

```
720
720.0
720.00000000
            720
7.2e+2
+720.0
```

The way a value is printed is called its *formatting*. The cout object has a standard way of formatting variables of each data type. Sometimes, however, you need more control over the way data is displayed. Consider Program 3-14, for example, which displays three rows of numbers with spaces between each one.

Program 3-14

```
// This program displays three rows of numbers.
#include <iostream>
using namespace std;

int main()
{
    int num1 = 2897, num2 = 5,    num3 = 837,
        num4 = 34,   num5 = 7,    num6 = 1623,
        num7 = 390,  num8 = 3456, num9 = 12;
```

(program continues)

Program 3-14 *(continued)*

```
// Display the first row of numbers
cout << num1 << "   " << num2 << "   " << num3 << endl;

// Display the second row of numbers
cout << num4 << "   " << num5 << "   " << num6 << endl;

// Display the third row of numbers
cout << num7 << "   " << num8 << "   " << num9 << endl;

return 0;
}
```

Program Output
```
2897  5   837
34  7   1623
390  3456  12
```

Unfortunately, the numbers do not line up in columns. This is because some of the numbers, such as 5 and 7, occupy one position on the screen, while others occupy two or three positions. cout uses just the number of spaces needed to print each number.

To remedy this, cout offers a way of specifying the minimum number of spaces to use for each number. A stream manipulator, setw, can be used to establish print fields of a specified width. Here is an example of how it is used:

```
value = 23;
cout << setw(5) << value;
```

The number inside the parentheses after the word setw specifies the *field width* for the value immediately following it. The field width is the minimum number of character positions, or spaces, on the screen to print the value in. In the example above, the number 23 will be displayed in a field of 5 spaces. Since 23 only occupies 2 positions on the screen, 3 blanks spaces will be printed before it. To further clarify how this works, look at the following statements:

```
value = 23;
cout << "(" << setw(5) << value << ")";
```

This will cause the following output:

```
(   23)
```

Notice that the number occupies the last two positions in the field. Since the number did not use the entire field, cout filled the extra 3 positions with blank spaces. Because the number appears on the right side of the field with blank spaces "padding" it in front, it is said to be *right-justified*.

Program 3-15 shows how the numbers in Program 3-15 can be printed in columns that line up perfectly by using setw.

Program 3-15

```cpp
// This program displays three rows of numbers.
#include <iostream>
#include <iomanip>        // Required for setw
using namespace std;

int main()
{
    int num1 = 2897, num2 = 5,     num3 = 837,
        num4 = 34,    num5 = 7,     num6 = 1623,
        num7 = 390,   num8 = 3456, num9 = 12;

    // Display the first row of numbers
    cout << setw(6) << num1 << setw(6)
         << num2 << setw(6) << num3 << endl;

    // Display the second row of numbers
    cout << setw(6) << num4 << setw(6)
         << num5 << setw(6) << num6 << endl;

    // Display the third row of numbers
    cout << setw(6) << num7 << setw(6)
         << num8 << setw(6) << num9 << endl;

    return 0;
}
```

Program Output
```
2897     5    837
  34     7   1623
 390  3456     12
```

By printing each number in a field of 6 positions, they are displayed in perfect columns.

 Note: A new header file, iomanip, is included in Program 3-15. It must be used in any program that uses setw.

Notice how a setw manipulator is used with each value because setw only establishes a field width for the value immediately following it. After that value is printed, cout goes back to its default method of printing.

You might wonder what will happen if the number is too large to fit in the field, as in the following statement:

```cpp
value = 18397;
cout << setw(2) << value;
```

In cases like this, cout will print the entire number. setw only specifies the minimum number of positions in the print field. Any number larger than the minimum will cause cout to override the setw value.

You may specify the field width of any type of data. Program 3-16 shows setw being used with an integer, a floating-point number, and a string.

Program 3-16

```cpp
// This program demonstrates the setw manipulator being
// used with values of various data types.
#include <iostream>
#include <iomanip>
using namespace std;

int main()
{
    int intValue = 3928;
    double doubleValue = 91.5;
    const int ARRAY_SIZE = 14;
    char cStringValue[ARRAY_SIZE] = "John J. Smith";

    cout << "(" << setw(5) << intValue << ")" << endl;
    cout << "(" << setw(8) << doubleValue << ")" << endl;
    cout << "(" << setw(16) << cStringValue << ")" << endl;
    return 0;
}
```

Program Output
```
( 3928)
(    91.5)
(   John J. Smith)
```

Program 3-16 can be used to illustrate the following points:

   ♦ The field width of a floating-point number includes a position for the decimal point.

   ♦ The field width of a string includes all characters in the string, including spaces.

   ♦ The values printed in the field are right-justified by default. This means they are aligned with the right side of the print field, and any blanks that must be used to pad it are inserted in front of the value.

The setprecision Manipulator

Floating-point values may be rounded to a number of *significant digits*, or *precision*, which is the total number of digits that appear before and after the decimal point. You can control the number of significant digits with which floating-point values are displayed by using the setprecision manipulator. Program 3-17 shows the results of a division operation displayed with different numbers of significant digits.

Program 3-17

```cpp
// This program demonstrates how setprecision rounds a floating point value.
#include <iostream>
#include <iomanip>
using namespace std;

int main()
{
    double quotient, number1 = 132.364, number2 = 26.91;
    quotient = number1 / number2;
    cout << setw(8) << quotient;
    cout << setw(8) << setprecision(4) << quotient;
    cout << setw(8) << setprecision(2) << quotient;
    cout << setw(8) << setprecision(1) << quotient;
    return 0;
}
```

Program Output
```
4.91877   4.919    4.9        5
```

 Note: With prestandard compilers, your output may be different than shown in Program 3-17.

The first value is displayed without the setprecision manipulator. (By default, the system in the illustration displays floating-point values with 6 significant digits.) The subsequent cout statements print the same value, but rounded to 4, 2, and 1 significant digits.

If the value of a number is expressed in fewer digits of precision than specified by setprecision, the manipulator will have no effect. In the following statements, the value of dollars only has four digits of precision, so the number printed by both cout statements is 24.51.

```cpp
double dollars = 24.51;
cout << dollars << endl;                         // Displays 24.51
cout << setprecision(5) << dollars << endl;      // Displays 24.51
```

Table 3-11 shows how setprecision affects the way various values are displayed.

Table 3-11

Number	Manipulator	Value Displayed
28.92786	setprecision(3)	28.9
21	setprecision(5)	21
109.5	setprecision(4)	109.5
34.28596	setprecision(2)	34

Unlike field width, the precision setting remains in effect until it is changed to some other value. As with all formatting manipulators, you must include the header file iomanip to use setprecision.

Program 3-18 shows how the setw and setprecision manipulators may be combined to fully control the way floating point numbers are displayed.

Program 3-18

```
// This program asks for sales figures for 3 days. The total
// sales are calculated and displayed in a table.
#include <iostream>
#include <iomanip>
using namespace std;

int main()
{
    double day1, day2, day3, total;

    cout << "Enter the sales for day 1: ";
    cin >> day1;
    cout << "Enter the sales for day 2: ";
    cin >> day2;
    cout << "Enter the sales for day 3: ";
    cin >> day3;
    total = day1 + day2 + day3;
    cout << "\nSales Figures\n";
    cout << "-------------\n";
    cout << setprecision(5);
    cout << "Day 1: " << setw(8) << day1 << endl;
    cout << "Day 2: " << setw(8) << day2 << endl;
    cout << "Day 3: " << setw(8) << day3 << endl;
    cout << "Total: " << setw(8) << total << endl;
    return 0;
}
```

Program Output with Example Input Shown in Bold
```
Enter the sales for day 1: 321.57 [Enter]
Enter the sales for day 2: 269.62 [Enter]
Enter the sales for day 3: 307.77 [Enter]

Sales Figures
-------------
Day 1:   321.57
Day 2:   269.62
Day 3:   307.77
Total:   898.96
```

The `fixed` Manipulator

The `setprecision` manipulator can sometimes surprise you in an undesirable way. When the precision of a number is set to a lower value, numbers tend to be printed in scientific notation. For example, here is the output of Program 3-18 with larger numbers being input:

Program Output with Example Input Shown in Bold
```
Enter the sales for day 1: 145678.99 [Enter]
Enter the sales for day 2: 205614.85 [Enter]
Enter the sales for day 3: 198645.22 [Enter]

Sales Figures
-------------
Day 1: 1.4568e+005
Day 2: 2.0561e+005
Day 3: 1.9865e+005
Total: 5.4994e+005
```

Another stream manipulator, `fixed`, forces `cout` to print the digits in *fixed-point notation*, or decimal. The following program segment shows how the `fixed` manipulator could be used in Program 3-18.

```
cout << "\nSales Figures\n";
cout << "-------------\n";
cout << setprecision(2) << fixed;
cout << "Day 1:  " << setw(8) << day1 << endl;
cout << "Day 2:  " << setw(8) << day2 << endl;
cout << "Day 3:  " << setw(8) << day3 << endl;
cout << "Total:  " << setw(8) << total<< endl;
```

The program segment would produce the following output.

Program Output with Example Input Shown in Bold
```
Enter the sales for day 1:  1321.87 [Enter]
Enter the sales for day 2:  1869.26 [Enter]
Enter the sales for day 3:  1403.77 [Enter]

Sales Figures
-------------
Day 1:   1321.87
Day 2:   1869.26
Day 3:   1403.77
Total:   4594.90
```

Here is the statement from the program segment that uses the `fixed` manipulator:

```
cout << setprecision(2) << fixed;
```

When the `fixed` manipulator is used, all floating point numbers that are subsequently printed will be displayed in fixed point notation, with the number of digits to the right of the decimal point specified by the `setprecision` manipulator.

When the `fixed` and `setprecision` manipulators are used together, the value specified by the `setprecision` manipulator will be the number of digits to appear after the decimal point, not the number of significant digits. For example, look at the following code.

```
double x = 123.4567;
cout << setprecision(2) << fixed << x << endl;
```

Because the `fixed` manipulator is used, the `setprecision` manipulator will cause the number to be displayed with two digits after the decimal point. The value will be displayed as 123.46.

The `showpoint` Manipulator

By default, floating-point numbers are not displayed with trailing zeroes, and floating-point numbers that do not have a fractional part are not displayed with a decimal point. For example, look at the following code.

```
double x = 123.4,
       y = 456.0;
cout << setprecision(6) << x << endl;
cout << y << endl;
```

The `cout` statements will produce the following output.

```
123.4
456
```

Although six significant digits are specified for both numbers, neither number is displayed with trailing zeroes. If we want the numbers padded with trailing zeroes, we must use the `showpoint` manipulator as shown in the following code.

```
double x = 123.4,
       y = 456.0;
cout << setprecision(6) << showpoint << x << endl;
cout << y << endl;
```

These `cout` statements will produce the following output.

```
123.400
456.000
```

 Note: With most compilers, trailing zeroes are displayed when the `setprecision` and `fixed` manipulators are used together.

The left and right Manipulators

Normally output is right-justified. For example, look at the following code.

```
double x = 146.789, y = 24.2, z = 1.783;
cout << setw(10) << x << endl;
cout << setw(10) << y << endl;
cout << setw(10) << z << endl;
```

Each of the variables, x, y, and z, are displayed in a print field of 10 spaces. The output of the cout statements is

```
   146.789
      24.2
     1.783
```

Notice that each value is right-justified, or aligned to the right of its print field. You can cause the values to be left-justified by using the left manipulator, as shown in the following code.

```
double x = 146.789, y = 24.2, z = 1.783;
cout << left << setw(10) << x << endl;
cout << setw(10) << y << endl;
cout << setw(10) << z << endl;
```

The output of these cout statements is

```
146.789
24.2
1.783
```

In this case, the numbers are aligned to the left of their print fields. The left manipulator remains in effect until you use the right manipulator, which causes all subsequent output to be right-justified.

Table 3-12 summarizes the manipulators we have discussed.

Table 3-12

Stream Manipulator	Description
setw(n)	Establishes a print field of n spaces.
fixed	Displays floating-point numbers in fixed point notation.
showpoint	Causes a decimal point and trailing zeroes to be displayed, even if there is no fractional part.
setprecision(n)	Sets the precision of floating-point numbers.
left	Causes subsequent output to be left-justified.
right	Causes subsequent output to be right-justified.

Checkpoint [3.8]

3.19 Write cout statements with stream manipulators that perform the following:

A) Display the number 34.789 in a field of nine spaces with two decimal places of precision.

B) Display the number 7.0 in a field of five spaces with three decimal places of precision. The decimal point and any trailing zeroes should be displayed.

C) Display the number 5.789e+12 in fixed point notation.

D) Display the number 67 left justified in a field of seven spaces.

3.20 The following program will not compile because the lines have been mixed up.

```cpp
#include <iomanip>
}
cout << person << endl;
char person[15] = "Wolfgang Smith";
int main()
cout << person << endl;
{
#include <iostream>
return 0;
cout << left;
using namespace std;
cout << setw(20);
cout << right;
```

When the lines are properly arranged the program should display the following:

```
        Wolfgang Smith
Wolfgang Smith
```

Rearrange the lines in the correct order. Test the program by entering it on the computer, compiling it, and running it.

3.21 The following program skeleton asks for an angle in degrees and converts it to radians. The formatting of the final output is left to you.

```cpp
#include <iostream>
#include <iomanip>
using namespace std;

int main()
{
    const double PI = 3.14159;
    double degrees, radians;

    cout << "Enter an angle in degrees and I will convert it\n";
    cout << "to radians for you: ";
```

```
      cin >> degrees;
      radians = degrees * PI / 180;
      // Display the value in Radians left justified, in fixed
      // point notation, with 4 places of precision, in a field
      // 5 spaces wide, making sure the decimal point is always
      // displayed.
      return 0;
   }
```

3.9 Formatted Input

CONCEPT The cin object provides ways of controlling string and character input.

The cin object has formatting tools similar to those of cout. For instance, an input field width may be set with the setw manipulator. This is most helpful when cin is reading a string and storing it in a character array. You may recall that cin has no way of knowing how large the array is. If the user types more characters than the array will hold, cin will store the string in the array anyway, overwriting whatever is in memory next to the array. An input field width solves this problem by telling cin how many characters to read.

Here is a statement defining an array of 10 characters and a cin statement reading no more characters than the array will hold:

```
      char word[10];
      cin >> setw(10) >> word;
```

The field width specified is 10. cin will read one character less than this, leaving room for the null character at the end. Program 3-19 illustrates the use of the setw manipulator with cin.

Program 3-19

```
// This program uses setw with the cin object.
#include <iostream>
#include <iomanip>
using namespace std;

int main()
{
   const int SIZE = 5;
   char word[SIZE];

   cout << "Enter a word: ";
   cin >> setw(SIZE) >> word;
   cout << "You entered " << word << endl;
   return 0;
}
```

Program 3-19 *(continued)*

Program Output with Example Input Shown in Bold
Enter a word: **Eureka [Enter]**
You entered Eure

In this program, cin only reads 4 characters into the word array. Without the field width, cin would have written the entire word "Eureka" into the array, overflowing it. Figure 3-4 illustrates the way memory would have been affected by this. The shaded area is the 5 bytes of memory used by the string array. The word "Eureka" with its null terminator would spill over into the adjacent memory. Anything that was stored there would be destroyed.

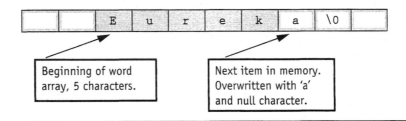

Figure 3-4

There are two important points to remember about the way cin handles field widths:

- ◆ The field width only pertains to the very next item entered by the user.

- ◆ cin stops reading input when it encounters a *whitespace* character. Whitespace characters include the **[Enter]** key, space, and tab.

Reading a "Line" of Input

cin provides a member function to read a string containing spaces. The function is called getline, and its purpose is to read an entire "line" of text, until the **[Enter]** key is pressed. Here is an example of how it is used:

```
cin.getline(sentence, 20);
```

The getline function takes two arguments separated by a comma. The first argument is the name of the array that the string is to be stored in. In the statement above, the name of the array is sentence. The second argument is the size of the array. cin will read up to one character less than this number, leaving room for the null terminator. This eliminates the need for using the setw manipulator. The statement above will read up to 19 characters and the null terminator will automatically be placed in the array, after the last character. Program 3-20 shows the getline member function being used to read a sentence of up to 80 characters.

Program 3-20

```cpp
// This program demonstrates cin's getline member function.
#include <iostream>
using namespace std;

int main()
{
    const int SIZE = 81;
    char sentence[SIZE];

    cout << "Enter a sentence: ";
    cin.getline(sentence, SIZE);
    cout << "You entered " << sentence << endl;
    return 0;
}
```

Program Output with Example Input Shown in Bold
Enter a sentence: **To be, or not to be, that is the question. [Enter]**
You entered To be, or not to be, that is the question.

Reading a Character

Quite often a program will ask the user to "press any key to continue." This can be useful in a program that displays more data than will fit on the screen. The program can keep track of how many lines of text it has displayed and when the screen is filled, it will wait for the user to press a key before displaying more data.

Another instance when it is convenient to read a single character is when a menu of items is displayed for the user to choose from. Often the selections will be denoted by the letters A, B, C, and so forth. The user chooses an item from the menu by typing a character. The simplest way to read a single character is with the >> operator, as shown in the following code.

```cpp
char ch;        // Define a character variable.
cout << "Type a character and press Enter: ";
cin >> ch;      // Read a character.
cout << "You entered " << ch << endl;
```

If the user types the character A and presses **[Enter]**, cin will store the character 'A' in the variable ch. Remember, cin is smart enough to know the data type of the variable it is storing data into. Since ch is a char variable, it will only store the single character 'A' there. If ch had been a char array, cin would have stored the string "A" with its null terminator there.

Using cin.get

A limiting characteristic of the >> operator with char variables is that it requires a character to be entered and it ignores all leading whitespace characters. This means the program will not continue past the cin statement until some character other than the spacebar, the **[tab]** key, or the **[Enter]** key has been pressed. (The **[Enter]** key must still be pressed after the character has been typed.) Programs that ask the user to "press the enter key to continue" cannot use the >> operator to read only the pressing of the **[Enter]** key.

In those situations another of cin's member functions, get, becomes useful. The get function reads a single character including any whitespace character. Here is an example:

```
char ch;      // Define a character variable.
cout << "Type a character and press Enter: ";
cin.get(ch);  // Read a character.
cout << "You entered " << ch << endl;
```

If the user types the character A and presses Enter, the cin.get function will store the character 'A' in the variable ch. Program 3-21 shows the function being used to pause a program.

Program 3-21

```
#include <iostream>
using namespace std;

int main()
{
    char ch;

    cout << "This program has paused. Press enter to continue.";
    cin.get(ch);
    cout << "Thank you!" << endl;
    return 0;
}
```

Program Output
```
This program has paused. Press Enter to continue. [Enter]
Thank you!
```

The only difference between the get function and the >> operator is that get reads the first character typed, even if it is a space, **[tab]**, or the **[Enter]** key.

Mixing `cin >>` and `cin.get`

Mixing cin.get with cin >> can cause an annoying and hard-to-find problem. For example, look at the following statements:

```
char ch;      // Define a character variable.
int number;   // Define an integer variable.
cout << "Enter a number: ";
cin >> number;        // Read an integer.
cout << "Enter a character: ";
cin.get(ch);          // Read a character.
cout << "Thank You!\n";
```

These statements may allow the user to enter a number, but not a character. It will appear that the `cin.get` statement is skipped. This happens because both `cin >>` and `cin.get` read the user's keystrokes from the keyboard buffer. After the user enters a number, in response to the first prompt, he or she presses the **[Enter]** key. Pressing the **[Enter]** key causes a newline ('\n') character to be stored in the keyboard buffer. For example, suppose the user enters 100 and presses **[Enter]**. The input will be stored in the keyboard buffer as shown in Figure 3-5.

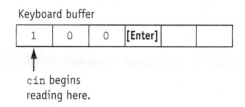

Figure 3-5

When the `cin >>` statement reads data from the keyboard buffer, it stops reading at the newline character that was generated by the **[Enter]** key. This newline character is left in the keyboard buffer. That means the first character read by `cin.get` will be the newline character. So, the `cin.get` statement will read only the newline character left in the keyboard buffer, and it will appear that the `cin.get` statement did not execute. You can remedy this situation by using the `cin.ignore` function, described in the following section.

Using `cin.ignore`

To solve the problem previously described, the `cin.ignore` member function can be used. `cin.ignore` tells the `cin` object to skip characters in the keyboard buffer. Here is its general form:

```
cin.ignore(n, c);
```

The arguments shown in the parentheses are optional. If they are used, *n* is an integer and *c* is a character. They tell `cin` to skip *n* number of characters, or until the character *c* is encountered. For example, the following statement causes `cin` to skip the next 20 characters, or until a newline is encountered, whichever comes first:

```
cin.ignore(20, '\n');
```

If no arguments are used, `cin` will only skip the very next character. Here's an example:

```
cin.ignore();
```

The previous statements that mix `cin >>` and `cin.get` can be repaired by inserting a `cin.ignore` statement after the `cin >>` statement:

```
char ch;        // Define a character variable.
int number;     // Define an integer variable.
cout << "Enter a number: ";
```

```
cin >> number;         // Read an integer.
cin.ignore();          // Skip the newline character.
cout << "Enter a character: ";
cin.get(ch);           // Read a character.
cout << "Thank You!" << endl;
```

3.10 Focus on Object-Oriented Programming: *More About Member Functions*

> **CONCEPT** A member function is a procedure, written in C++ code, that is part of an object. A member function causes the object it is a member of to perform an action.

The concept of object-oriented programming (OOP) was introduced in Chapter 1, section 1.7 (*Procedural and Object-Oriented Programming*). Recall from that section that objects are programming elements containing both data and procedures that operate on the data. The packaging together of data and the data's related procedures within an object is known as *encapsulation*.

In C++, the procedures that are part of an object are known as *member functions*. They are called member functions because they are functions that are members of, or belong to, an object. The use of member functions simplifies programming and reduces errors. Anywhere an object is used, it not only contains data, but also the correct algorithms and operations for working with the data. If you are the user of an object (as you are the user of cout and cin) you do not need to write your own code to manipulate the object's data. All that is necessary is that you learn the object's member functions and how to use them.

In this chapter you have used the following member functions of the cin object:

- ◆ getline
- ◆ get
- ◆ ignore

Calling an object's member function causes the object to perform some operation. For example, calling cin's getline member function causes cin to read a line of input from the keyboard.

In OOP terminology, calling a member function is also described as *passing a message* to the object. For example, you can think of the following statement as sending a message to the cin object, instructing it to read a character from the keyboard and then store the character in the ch variable.

```
cin.get(ch);
```

All of cin's member functions are written in C++ code. In Chapter 13 you will learn to design your own objects, complete with member functions.

3.11 More Mathematical Library Functions

CONCEPT	The C++ runtime library provides several functions for performing complex mathematical operations.

Earlier in this chapter you learned to use the pow function to raise a number to a power. The C++ library has numerous other functions that perform specialized mathematical operations. These functions are useful in scientific and special purpose programs. Table 3-13 shows several of these, each of which requires the cmath header file.

Table 3-13

Function	Example	Description
abs	y = abs(x);	Returns the absolute value of the argument. The argument and the return value are integers.
cos	y = cos(x);	Returns the cosine of the argument. The argument should be an angle expressed in radians. The return type and the argument are doubles.
exp	y = exp(x);	Computes the exponential function of the argument, which is x. The return type and the argument are doubles.
fmod	y = fmod(x, z);	Returns, as a double, the remainder of the first argument divided by the second argument. Works like the modulus operator, but the arguments are doubles. (The modulus operator only works with integers.) Take care not to pass zero as the second argument. Doing so would cause division by zero.
log	y = log(x);	Returns the natural logarithm of the argument. The return type and the argument are doubles.
log10	y = log10(x);	Returns the base-10 logarithm of the argument. The return type and the argument are doubles.
sin	y = sin(x);	Returns the sine of the argument. The argument should be an angle expressed in radians. The return type and the argument are doubles.
sqrt	y = sqrt(x);	Returns the square root of the argument. The return type and argument are doubles.
tan	y = tan(x);	Returns the tangent of the argument. The argument should be an angle expressed in radians. The return type and the argument are doubles.

Each of these functions is as simple to use as the pow function. The following program segment demonstrates the sqrt function, which returns the square root of a number:

```
cout << "Enter a number: ";
cin >> num;
s = sqrt(num);
cout << "The square root of " << num << " is " << s << endl;
```

Here is the output of the program segment, with 25 as the number entered by the user:

```
Enter a number: 25
The square root of 25 is 5
```

Program 3-22 shows the sqrt function being used to find the hypotenuse of a right triangle. The program uses the following formula, taken from the Pythagorean theorem:

$$c = \sqrt{a^2 + b^2}$$

In the formula, c is the length of the hypotenuse, and a and b are the lengths of the other sides of the triangle.

Program 3-22

```
// This program asks for the lengths of the two sides of a
// right triangle. The length of the hypotenuse is then
// calculated and displayed.
#include <iostream>
#include <iomanip>      // For setprecision
#include <cmath>        // For the sqrt and pow functions
using namespace std;

int main()
{
    double a, b, c;

    cout << "Enter the length of side a: ";
    cin >> a;
    cout << "Enter the length of side b: ";
    cin >> b;
    c = sqrt(pow(a, 2.0) + pow(b, 2.0));
    cout << "The length of the hypotenuse is ";
    cout << setprecision(2) << c << endl;
    return 0;
}
```

Program Output with Example Input Shown in Bold
```
Enter the length of side a: 5.0 [Enter]
Enter the length of side b: 12.0 [Enter]
The length of the hypotenuse is 13
```

The following statement, taken from Program 3-22, calculates the square root of the sum of the squares of the triangle's two sides:

```
c = sqrt(pow(a, 2.0) + pow(b, 2.0));
```

Notice that the following mathematical expression is used as the sqrt function's argument:

```
pow(a, 2.0) + pow(b, 2.0)
```

This expression calls the pow function twice: once to calculate the square of a and again to calculate the square of b. These two squares are then added together, and the sum is sent to the sqrt function.

Random Numbers

Some programming techniques require the use of randomly generated numbers. The C++ library has a function, rand(), for this purpose. (rand() requires the header file cstdlib.) The number returned by the function is an int. Here is an example of its usage:

```
y = rand();
```

After this statement executes, the variable y will contain a random number. In actuality, the numbers produced by rand() are pseudorandom. The function uses an algorithm that produces the same sequence of numbers each time the program is repeated on the same system. For example, suppose the following statements are executed.

```
cout << rand() << endl;
cout << rand() << endl;
cout << rand() << endl;
```

The three numbers displayed will appear to be random, but each time the program runs, the same three values will be generated. In order to randomize the results of rand(), the srand() function must be used. srand() accepts an unsigned int argument, which acts as a seed value for the algorithm. By specifying different seed values, rand() will generate different sequences of random numbers. Program 3-23 demonstrates the two functions.

 Note: If you wish to limit the range of the random number, use the following formula.

```
y = 1 + rand() % maxRange;
```

The maxRange value is the upper limit of the range. For example, if you wish to generate a random number in the range of 1 through 100, use the following statement.

```
y = 1 + rand() % 100;
```

This is how the statement works: Look at the following expression.

```
rand() % 100
```

Assuming `rand()` returns 37894, the value of the expression above is 94. That is because 37894 divided by 100 is 378 with a remainder of 94. (The modulus operator returns the remaider.) But, what if `rand()` returns a number that is evenly divisible by 100, such as 500? The expression above will return a 0. If we want a number in the range 1 - 100, we must add 1 to the result. That is why we use the expression `1 + rand() % 100`.

Program 3-23

```
// This program demonstrates random numbers.
#include <iostream>
#include <cstdlib>
using namespace std;

int main()
{
    unsigned seed;

    cout << "Enter a seed value: ";
    cin >> seed;
    srand(seed);
    cout << rand() << ", " << rand() << ", " << rand() << endl;
    return 0;
}
```

Program Output with Example Input Shown in Bold
```
Enter a seed value: 5 [Enter]
1731, 32036, 21622
```

Program Output with Other Example Input Shown in Bold
```
Enter a seed value: 16 [Enter]
5540, 29663, 9920
```

Checkpoint [3.11]

3.22 Write a short description of each of the following functions:

cos	log	sin
exp	log10	sqrt
fmod	pow	tan

3.23 Assume the variables angle1 and angle2 hold angles stored in radians. Write a statement that adds the sine of angle1 to the cosine of angle2, and stores the result in the variable x.

3.24 To find the cube root (the third root) of a number, raise it to the power of $1/3$. To find the fourth root of a number, raise it to the power of $1/4$. Write a statement that will find the fifth root of the variable x and store the result in the variable y.

3.25 The cosecant of the angle a is:

$$\frac{1}{\sin a}$$

Write a statement that calculates the cosecant of the angle stored in the variable a, and stores it in the variable y.

See the CaseStudies.pdf file on the accompanying CD for this chapter's case studies.

3.12 Introduction to File Input and Output

CONCEPT This section discusses simple techniques to write input and output operations with files.

The programs you have written so far require you to re-enter data each time the program runs. This is because the data stored in RAM disappears once the program stops running or the computer is shut down. If a program is to retain data between the times it runs, it must have a way of saving it. Data is saved in a file, which is usually stored on a computer's disk. Once the data is saved in a file, it will remain there after the program stops running. The data can then be retrieved and used at a later time.

There are always three steps that must be taken when a file is used by a program:

1. The file must be *opened*. If the file does not yet exist, opening it means creating it.

2. Data is then saved to the file, read from the file, or both.

3. When the program is finished using the file, the file must be *closed*.

When a program is actively working with data, the data is located in random-access memory, usually in variables. When data is written into a file, it is copied from the variables. This is illustrated in Figure 3-6.

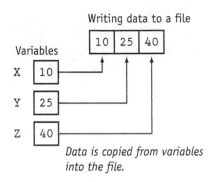

Figure 3-6

When data is read from a file, it is copied from the file into variables. Figure 3-7 illustrates this.

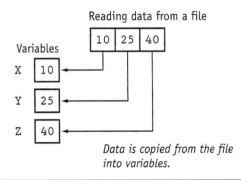

Figure 3-7

Setting Up a Program for File Input/Output

Just as `cin` and `cout` require the `iostream` file to be included in the program, C++ file access requires another header file. The file *fstream* contains all the declarations necessary for file operations. It is included with the following statement:

```
#include <fstream>
```

The next step in setting up a program to perform file I/O is to define one or more *file stream objects.* They are called "stream" objects because a file can be thought of as a stream of data. File stream objects work very much like the `cin` and `cout` objects. A stream of data may be sent to `cout`, which causes values to be displayed on the screen. A stream of data may be read from the keyboard by `cin`, and stored in variables. Likewise, streams of data may be sent to a file stream object, which writes the data to a file. Data that is read from a file flows from a file stream object into other variables.

The `fstream` header file defines the data types *ofstream*, *ifstream*, and *fstream*. Before a C++ program can work with a file, it must define an object of one of these data types. The object will be "linked" with an actual file on the computer's disk, and the operations that may be performed on the file depend on which of these three data types you pick for the file stream object. Table 3-14 lists and describes the file stream data types.

Table 3-14

File Stream Data Type	Description
ofstream	Output file stream. This data type can be used to create files and write data to them. With the ofstream data type, data may only be copied from variables to the file, but not vice-versa.
ifstream	Input file stream. This data type can be used to open existing files and read data from them into memory. With the ifstream data type, data may only be copied from the file into variables, not but vice-versa.
fstream	File stream. This data type can be used to create files, write data to them, and read data from them. With the fstream data type, data may be copied from variables into a file, or from a file into variables.

Note: In this section we only discuss the *ofstream* and *ifstream* types. The *fstream* type is covered in Chapter 12.

Here are example statements that define ofstream and ifstream objects:

```
ofstream outputFile;
ifstream inputFile
```

The statements above define the objects outputFile and inputFile. outputFile is of the ofstream type, so data can be written to any file associated with it. inputFile is of the ifstream type, so data can be read from any file it is associated with.

Opening a File

Before data can be written to or read from a file, the file must be opened. Outside of the C++ program, a file is identified by its name. Inside a C++ program, however, a file stream object identifies a file. The object and the file name are linked when the file is opened.

Files are opened through the open member function of a file stream object. Assume inputFile is an ifstream object, defined as:

```
ifstream inputFile;
```

For example, the following statement uses inputFile to open a file named customer.dat:

```
inputFile.open("customer.dat");
```

The argument to the open function in this statement is the name of the file. This links the file customer.dat with the stream object inputFile. Until inputFile is associated with another file, any operations performed with it will be carried out on the file customer.dat. (Remember, ifstream objects can only perform input operations with files. This means data may only be read from the customer.dat file using the inputFile stream object.)

Often, when opening a file, you will need to specify its location as well as its name. For example, if you were attempting to open a file on the A: drive of a DOS or Windows computer, you would need to specify the file's drive designator and path. Here is an example of a statement that opens a file located on a PC's floppy drive:

```
outputFile.open("a:\\invtry.dat");
```

In this statement, the file a:\invtry.dat is opened and linked with outputFile.

Note: Notice the use of two backslashes in the file's path. As mentioned before in this text, two backslashes are needed to represent one backslash in a string literal.

You may also use a character array as an argument to the open function. For example, the following program segment defines an ifstream object and a 20-element character array. The user is asked to enter the name of the file, which is passed to the open function.

```
ifstream inputFile;
char fileName[20];
cout << "Enter the name of the file: ";
cin >> filename;
inputFile.open(fileName);
```

Closing a File

The opposite of opening a file is closing it. Although a program's files are automatically closed when the program shuts down, it is a good programming practice to write statements that close them. Here are two reasons a program should close files when it is finished using them:

◆ Most operating systems temporarily store data in a *file buffer* before it is written to a file. A file buffer is a small "holding section" of memory that file-bound data is first written to. When the buffer is filled, all the data stored there is written to the file. This technique improves the system's performance. Closing a file causes any unsaved data that may still be held in a buffer to be saved to its file. This means the data will be in the file if you need to read it later in the same program.

◆ Some operating systems limit the number of files that may be open at one time. When a program closes files that are no longer being used, it will not deplete more of the operating system's resources than necessary.

Calling the file stream object's close member function closes a file. Here is an example:

```
outputFile.close();
```

Writing Data to a File

You already know how to use the stream insertion operator (<<) with the cout object to write data to the screen. It can also be used with file stream objects to write data to a file. Assuming outputFile is a file stream object, the following statement demonstrates using the << operator to write a string to a file:

```
outputFile << "I love C++ programming";
```

This statement writes the string "I love C++ programming" to the file that is associated with outputFile. As you can see, the statement looks like a cout statement, except the file stream object name replaces cout. Here is a statement that writes both a string and the contents of a variable to a file:

```
outputFile << "Price: " << price;
```

The statement above writes the stream of data to outputFile exactly as cout would write it to the screen.

Program 3-24 demonstrates opening a file, writing data to the file, and closing the file.

Program 3-24

```cpp
// This program uses the << operator to write data to a file.
#include <iostream>
#include <fstream>
using namespace std;

int main()
{
    ofstream outputFile;

    outputFile.open("demofile.txt");
    cout << "Now writing data to the file.\n";

    // Write 4 great names to the file
    outputFile << "Bach\n";
    outputFile << "Beethoven\n";
    outputFile << "Mozart\n";
    outputFile << "Schubert\n";

    // Close the file
    outputFile.close();
    cout << "Done.\n";
    return 0;
}
```

Program Screen Output
```
Now writing data to the file.
Done.
```

Program 3-24 *(continued)*

Output to File `demofile.txt`

```
Bach
Beethoven
Mozart
Schubert
```

Reading Data from a File

The >> operator not only reads user input from the `cin` object, but it can also read data from a file. Assuming `inFile` is a file stream object, the following statement shows the >> operator reading data from the file into the variable name:

```
inFile >> name;
```

In Program 3-24, the file demofile.txt was created and the following list of names was stored there.

```
Bach
Beethoven
Mozart
Schubert
```

Program 3-25 demonstrates the use of the >> operator to read the names from the file and store them in a variable.

Program 3-25

```
// This program uses the >> operator to read data
// from a file.
#include <iostream>
#include <fstream>
using namespace std;

int main()
{
    ifstream inFile;
    const int SIZE = 81;
    char name[SIZE];

    inFile.open("demofile.txt");
    cout << "Reading data from the file.\n\n";
```

(program continues)

Program 3-25 *(continued)*

```
    inFile >> name;          // Read name 1 from the file
    cout << name << endl;    // Display name 1

    inFile >> name;          // Read name 2 from the file
    cout << name << endl;    // Display name 2

    inFile >> name;          // Read name 3 from the file
    cout << name << endl;    // Display name 3

    inFile >> name;          // Read name 4 from the file
    cout << name << endl;    // Display name 4

    inFile.close();          // Close the file
    cout << "\nDone.\n";
    return 0;
}
```

Program Screen Output
```
Reading data from the file.

Bach
Beethoven
Mozart
Schubert

Done.
```

Data is read from files in a sequential manner. When a file is first opened, the file stream object's *read position* is at the first byte of the file. The first read operation extracts data starting at the first byte. As data is read, the file stream object's read position advances through the file.

When the >> operator extracts data from a file, it expects to read pieces of data that are separated by whitespace characters (spaces, tabs, or newlines). In Program 3-25, the following statement reads a string from the file:

```
    inFile >> name;
```

In the statement above, the >> operator extracts a string because name is a character array. Figure 3-8 shows the first 5 bytes in the file:

Figure 3-8

B	a	c	h	\n	...

The >> operator will extract all of the characters up to the newline, so "Bach" is the first string read from the file. After "Bach" is extracted, the file stream object will be positioned so the following read operation would extract the string "Beethoven." This procedure is followed until all four strings have been read from the file.

Sometimes, when a program has a substantial amount of input, it is preferable to read the input from a file instead of the keyboard. For example, consider Program 3-26. It reads the length and width of five rectangles from a file and displays the area of each rectangle on the screen.

Program 3-26

```cpp
// This program uses the >> operator to read data from a file.
#include <iostream>
#include <fstream>
using namespace std;

int main()
{
    ifstream inFile;
    int length, width, area;

    inFile.open("dimensions.txt");
    cout << "Reading dimensions of 5 rectangles from the file.\n\n";

    // Process rectangle 1
    inFile >> length;
    inFile >> width;
    area = length * width;
    cout << "Area of rectangle 1: " << area << endl;

    // Process rectangle 2
    inFile >> length;
    inFile >> width;
    area = length * width;
    cout << "Area of rectangle 2: " << area << endl;

    // Process rectangle 3
    inFile >> length;
    inFile >> width;
    area = length * width;
    cout << "Area of rectangle 3: " << area << endl;

    // Process rectangle 4
    inFile >> length;
    inFile >> width;
    area = length * width;
    cout << "Area of rectangle 4: " << area << endl;
```

(program continues)

Program 3-26   *(continued)*

```
        // Process rectangle 5
        inFile >> length;
        inFile >> width;
        area = length * width;
        cout << "Area of rectangle 5: " << area << endl;

        // Close the file
        inFile.close();
        cout << "\nDone.\n";
        return 0;
}
```

Before this program is executed, the file dimensions.txt must be created with a text editor (such as Windows Notepad). Here is an example of the file's contents:

```
10 2
5 7
18 9
6 20
8 3
```

Notice that the program first reads a value into length, and then reads a value into width. It then multiplies length by width to get the rectangle's area. So, these file contents specify the following dimensions:

```
Rectangle 1: length = 10, width = 2
Rectangle 2: length = 5, width = 7
Rectangle 3: length = 18, width = 9
Rectangle 4: length = 6, width = 20
Rectangle 5: length = 8, width = 3
```

The program's output follows.

Program 3-26   *(continued)*

Program Output

```
Reading dimensions of 5 rectangles from the file.

Area of rectangle 1: 20
Area of rectangle 2: 35
Area of rectangle 3: 162
Area of rectangle 4: 120
Area of rectangle 5: 24

Done.
```

Review Questions and Exercises

Short Answer

1. Assuming the array `description` is defined as follows:

   ```
   char description[40];
   ```
   A) How many characters *total* can the array hold?

   B) What is the length of the largest string that may be stored in the array?

   C) Will the following `cin` statement automatically stop reading input when the array is filled?

   ```
   cin >> description;
   ```

2. Write a definition statement for a character array large enough to hold any of the following strings:

   ```
   "Billy Bob's Pizza"
   "Downtown Auto Supplies"
   "Betty Smith School of Architecture"
   "ABC Cabinet Company"
   ```

3. Assume the array `name` is defined as follows:

   ```
   char name[25];
   ```

   A) Using a stream manipulator, write a `cin` statement that will read a string into `name`, but will read no more characters than `name` can hold.

   B) Using the `getline` member function, write a `cin` statement that will read a string into `name`, but will read no more characters than `name` can hold.

4. Assuming the following variables are defined:

   ```
   int age;
   float pay;
   char section;
   ```

   Write a single `cin` statement that will read input into each of these variables.

5. What header files must be included in the following program?

   ```
   int main()
   {
       double amount = 89.7;
       cout << showpoint << fixed;
       cout << setw(8) << amount << endl;
       return 0;
   }
   ```

6. Write a definition statement for a character array named `city`. It should be large enough to hold a string 30 characters in length.

7. Assume the following preprocessor directive appears in a program:

   ```
   #define SIZE 12
   ```

How will the preprocessor rewrite the following lines?

A) `price = SIZE * unitCost;`
B) `cout << setw(SIZE) << 98.7;`
C) `cout << SIZE;`

8. Complete the following table by writing the value of each expression in the Value column.

Expression	Value
28 / 4 - 2	
6 + 12 * 2 - 8	
6 + 17 % 3 - 2	
2 + 22 * (9 - 7)	
(8 + 7) * 2	
12 / (10 - 6)	

9. Write C++ expressions for the following algebraic expressions:

$a = 12x$

$z = 5x + 14y + 6k$

$y = x^4$

$g = \dfrac{h + 12}{4k}$

10. Assume a program has the following variable definitions:

```
int units;
float mass;
double weight;
```

and the following statement:

```
weight = mass * units;
```

Which automatic data type conversion will take place?

A) `mass` is demoted to an `int`, `units` remains an `int`, and the result of `mass * units` is an `int`.

B) `units` is promoted to a `float`, `mass` remains a `float`, and the result of `mass * units` is a `float`.

C) `units` is promoted to a `float`, `mass` remains a `float`, and the result of `mass * units` is a `double`.

11. Assume a program has the following variable definitions:

```
int a, b = 2;
float c = 4.2;
```

and the following statement:

```
a = b * c;
```

What value will be stored in a?

A) 8.4   B) 8   C) 0   D) None these

12. Assume that qty and salesReps are both integers. Use a type cast expression to rewrite the following statement so it will no longer perform integer division.

```
unitsEach = qty / salesReps;
```

13. Rewrite the following variable definition so the variable is a named constant.

```
int rate;
```

14. Complete the folowing table by writing statements with combined assignment operators in the right-hand column. The statements should be equivalent to the statements in the left-hand column.

Statements with Assignment Operator	Statements with Combined Assignment Operator

`x = x + 5;`
`total = total + subtotal;`
`dist = dist / rep;`
`ppl = ppl * period;`
`inv = inv - shrinkage;`
`num = num % 2;`	

15. Write a multiple assignment statement that can be used instead of the following group of assignment statements:

```
east = 1;
west = 1;
north = 1;
south = 1;
```

16. Write a cout statement so the variable divSales is displayed in a field of 8 spaces, in fixed point notation, with a precision of 2 decimal places. The decimal point should always be displayed.

17. Write a cout statement so the variable totalAge is displayed in a field of 12 spaces, in fixed point notation, with a precision of 4 decimal places.

18. Write a cout statement so the variable population is displayed in a field of 12 spaces, left-justified, with a precision of 8 decimal places. The decimal point should always be displayed.

Algorithm Workbench

19. A retail store grants its customers a maximum amount of credit. Each customer's available credit is his or her maximum amount of credit minus the amount of credit used. Write a pseudocode algorithm for a program that asks for a customer's maximum amount of credit and amount of credit used. The program should then display the customer's available credit.

    After you write the pseudocode algorithm, convert it to a complete C++ program.

20. Write a pseudocode algorithm for a program that calculates the total of a retail sale. The program should ask for the amount of the sale and the sales tax rate. The sales tax rate should be entered as a floating-point number. For example, if the sales tax rate is 6 percent, the user should enter 0.06. The program should display the amount of sales tax and the total of the sale.

    After you write the pseudocode algorithm, convert it to a complete C++ program.

Find the Errors

Each of the following programs has some errors. Locate as many as you can.

21.
```cpp
#include <iostream>
using namespace std;

int main()
{
    int number1, number2;
    float quotient;
    cout << "Enter two numbers and I will divide\n";
    cout << "the first by the second for you.\n";
    cin >> number1, number2;
    quotient = float<static_cast>(number1) / number2;
    cout << quotient
    return 0;
}
```

22.
```cpp
#include <iostream>;
using namespace std;

main
{
    float number, half;

    cout << "Enter a number and I will divide it\n"
    cout << "in half for you.\n"
    cin >> number1;
    half =/ 2;
    cout << fixedpoint << showpoint << half << endl;
    return 0;
}
```

23.
```
#include <iostream>;
using namespace std;

int main()
{
    char name, go;

    cout << "Enter your name: ";
    cin >> setw(20);
    cin.getline >> name;
    cout << "Hi " << name << endl;
    cout "Press the ENTER key to end this program.";
    cin >> go;
    return 0;
}
```

Predict the Output

What will each of the following program segments display? (Some should be hand traced, and require a calculator.)

24. *(Assume the user enters 38700. Use a calculator.)*
```
double salary, monthly;
cout << "What is your annual salary? ";
cin >> salary;
monthly = static_cast<int>(salary) / 12;
cout << "Your monthly wages are " << monthly << endl;
```

25.
```
long x, y, z;
x = y = z = 4;
x += 2;
y -= 1;
z *= 3;
cout << x << " " << y << " " << z << endl;
```

26. *(Assume the user enters George Washington.)*
```
const int SIZE = 20;
char userInput[SIZE];
cout << "What is your name? ";
cin >> setw(SIZE) >> userInput;
cout << "Hello " << userInput << endl;
```

27. *(Assume the user enters George Washington.)*
```
const int SIZE = 20;
char userInput[SIZE];
cout << "What is your name? ";
cin.getline(userInput, SIZE);
cout << "Hello " << userInput << endl;
```

Programming Challenges

1. Miles Per Gallon

Write a program that calculates a car's gas mileage. The program should ask the user to enter the number of gallons of gas the car can hold, and the number of miles it can be driven on a full tank. It should then display the number of miles that may be driven per gallon of gas.

2. Stadium Seating

There are three seating categories at a stadium. For a softball game, Class A seats cost $15, Class B seats cost $12, and Class C seats cost $9. Write a program that asks how many tickets for each class of seats were sold, then displays the amount of income generated from ticket sales. Format your dollar amount in fixed-point notation, with two decimal places of precision, and be sure the decimal point is always displayed.

3. Test Average

Write a program that asks for five test scores. The program should calculate the average test score and display it. The number displayed should be formatted in fixed-point notation, with one decimal point of precision.

4. Average Rainfall

Write a program that calculates the average rainfall for three months. The program should ask the user to enter the name of each month, such as June or July, and the amount of rain (in inches) that fell each month. The program should display a message similar to the following:

The average rainfall for June, July, and August is 6.72 inches.

5. Box Office

A movie theater only keeps a percentage of the revenue earned from ticket sales. The remainder goes to the movie distributor. Write a program that calculates a theater's gross and net box office profit for a night. The program should ask for the name of the movie, and how many adult and child tickets were sold. (The price of an adult ticket is $6.00 and a child's ticket is $3.00.) It should display a report similar to

Movie Name:	"Wheels of Fury"
Adult Tickets Sold:	382
Child Tickets Sold:	127
Gross Box Office Profit:	$ 2673.00
Net Box Office Profit:	$ 534.60
Amount Paid to Distributor:	$ 2138.40

 Note: Assume the theater keeps 20 percent of the gross box office profit.

6. How Many Widgets?

The Yukon Widget Company manufactures widgets that weigh 9.2 pounds each. Write a program that calculates how many widgets are stacked on a pallet, based on the total weight of the pallet.

The program should ask the user how much the pallet weighs by itself and with the widgets stacked on it. It should then calculate and display the number of widgets stacked on the pallet.

7. Centigrade to Fahrenheit

Write a program that converts centigrade temperatures to Fahrenheit temperatures. The formula is

$$F = \frac{9}{5}C + 32$$

F is the Fahrenheit temperature and C is the centigrade temperature.

8. Currency

Write a program that will convert US dollar amounts to Japanese Yen and to Euros. The conversion factors to use are:

1 Dollar = 134.33 yen
1 Dollar = 1.1644 euros

Format your currency amounts in fixed-point notation, with two decimal places of precision, and be sure the decimal point is always displayed.

9. Monthly Sales Tax

A retail company must file a monthly sales tax report listing the sales for the month and the amount of sales tax collected. Write a program that asks for the month, the year, and the total amount collected at the cash register (that is, sales plus sales tax). Assume the state sales tax is 4 percent and the county sales tax is 2 percent.

If the total amount collected is known and the total sales tax is 6 percent, the amount of product sales may be calculated as:

$$S = \frac{T}{1.06}$$

S is the product sales and T is the total income (product sales plus sales tax).

The program should display a report similar to

```
Month: October 2005
--------------------
Total Collected:    $ 26572.89
Sales:              $ 25068.76
County Sales Tax:   $   501.38
State Sales Tax:    $  1002.75
Total Sales Tax:    $  1504.13
```

10. Property Tax

A county collects property taxes on the assessment value of property, which is 60 percent of the property's actual value. If an acre of land is valued at $10,000, its assessment value is $6,000. The property tax is then 64¢ for each $100 of the assessment value. The tax for the acre assessed at $6,000 will be $38.40. Write a program that asks for the actual value of a piece of property and displays the assessment value and property tax.

11. Math Tutor

Write a program that can be used as a math tutor for a young student. The program should display two random numbers to be added, such as:

```
  247
+ 129
```

The program should then pause while the student works on the problem. When the student is ready to check the answer, he or she can press a key and the program will display the correct solution.

```
  247
+ 129
  376
```

12. Interest Earned

Assuming there are no deposits other than the original investment, the balance in a savings account after one year may be calculated as:

$$\text{Amount} = \text{Principal} * \left(1 + \frac{\text{Rate}}{\text{T}}\right)^{\text{T}}$$

Principal is the balance in the savings account, Rate is the interest rate, and T is the number of times the interest is compounded during a year (T is 4 if the interest is compounded quarterly).

Write a program that asks for the principal, the interest rate, and the number of times the interest is compounded. It should display a report similar to

```
Interest Rate:           4.25%
Times Compounded:          12
Principal:         $ 1000.00
Interest:          $   43.34
Amount in Savings: $ 1043.34
```

13. Monthly Payments

The monthly payment on a loan may be calculated by the following formula:

$$\text{Payment} = \frac{\text{Rate} * (1 + \text{Rate})^N}{((1 + \text{Rate})^N - 1)} * L$$

Rate is the monthly interest rate, which is the annual interest rate divided by 12. (12% annual interest would be 1 percent monthly interest.) N is the number of payments and L is the amount of the loan. Write a program that asks for these values and displays a report similar to

```
Loan Amount:                 $ 10000.00
Monthly Interest Rate:               1%
Number of Payments:                  36
Monthly Payment:             $    332.14
Amount Paid Back:            $ 11957.15
Interest Paid:               $  1957.15
```

14. Pizza Pi

Joe's Pizza Palace needs a program to calculate the number of slices a pizza of any size can be divided into. The program should perform the following steps:

A) Ask the user for the diameter of the pizza in inches.

B) Calculate the number of slices that may be taken from a pizza of that size.

C) Display a message telling the number of slices.

To calculate the number of slices that may be taken from the pizza, you must know the following facts:

♦ Each slice should have an area of 14.125 inches.

♦ To calculate the number of slices, simply divide the area of the pizza by 14.125.

♦ The area of the pizza is calculated with this formula:

Area = πr^2

 Note: π is the Greek letter pi. 3.14159 can be used as its value. The variable r is the radius of the pizza. Divide the diameter by 2 to get the radius.

Make sure the output of the program displays the number of slices in fixed-point notation, rounded to one decimal point of precision. Use a named constant for pi.

15. Angle Calculator

Write a program that asks the user for an angle, entered in radians. The program should then display the sine, cosine, and tangent of the angle. (Use the sin, cos, and tan library functions to determine these values.) The output should be displayed in fixed-point notation, rounded to four decimal places of precision.

16. Saving Numbers to a File

For this assignment you will write two programs:

Program 1   Write a program that asks the user to enter five numbers. Use a floating-point data type to hold the numbers. The program should create a file and save all five numbers to the file.

Program 2   Write a program that opens the file created by Program 1, reads the five numbers, and displays them. The program should also calculate and display the sum of the five numbers.

17. Monthly Sales Tax Modification

Modify the program you wrote for Programming Challenge 9 (Monthly Sales Tax) so it writes its output to a file instead of the screen.

18. Average Rainfall Modification

Modify the program you wrote for Programming Challenge 4 (Average Rainfall) so it reads its input from a file instead of the keyboard.

4

Making Decisions

■ Topics in this Chapter

4.1 Relational Operators

CONCEPT Relational operators allow you to compare numeric* values and determine if one is greater than, less than, equal to, or not equal to another.

*chars are also considered numeric values.

So far, the programs you have written follow this simple scheme:

◆ Gather input from the user.

◆ Perform one or more calculations.

◆ Display the results on the screen.

Computers are good at performing calculations, but they are also quite adept at comparing values to determine if one is greater than, less than, or equal to, the other. These types of operations are valuable for tasks such as examining sales figures, determining profit and loss, checking a number to ensure it is within an acceptable range, and validating the input given by a user.

Numeric data is compared in C++ by using relational operators. Each relational operator determines if a specific relationship exists between two values. For example, the greater-than operator (>) determines if a value is greater than another. The equality operator (==) determines if two values are equal. Table 4-1 lists all of C++'s relational operators.

Table 4-1

Relational Operators	Meaning
>	Greater than
<	Less than
>=	Greater than or equal to
<=	Less than or equal to
==	Equal to
!=	Not equal to

All of the relational operators are binary, which means they use two operands. Here is an example of an expression using the greater-than operator:

```
x > y
```

This expression is called a *relational expression*. It is used to determine if x is greater than y. The following expression determines if x is less than y:

```
x < y
```

Table 4-2 shows examples of several relational expressions that compare the variables x and y.

Table 4-2

Expression	What the Expression Means
x > y	Is x greater than y?
x < y	Is x less than y?
x >= y	Is x greater than or equal to y?
x <= y	Is x less than or equal to y?
x == y	Is x equal to y?
x != y	Is x not equal to y?

Note: All the relational operators have left-to-right associativity. Recall that associativity is the order on which an operator works with its operands.

The Value of a Relationship

So, how are relational expressions used in a program? Remember, all expressions have a value. Relational expressions are also known as Boolean expressions, which means their value can only be *true* or *false*. If **x** is greater than y, the expression **x** > y will be true, while the expression y == x will be false.

The == operator determines if the operand on its left is equal to the operand on its right. If both operands have the same value, the expression is true. Assuming that a is 4, the following expression is true:

```
a == 4
```

But the following is false:

```
a == 2
```

WARNING! Notice the equality operator is two = symbols together. Don't confuse this operator with the assignment operator, which is one = symbol. The == operator determines if a variable is equal to another value, but the = operator assigns the value on the operator's right to the variable on its left. There will be more about this later in the chapter.

A couple of the relational operators actually test for two relationships. The >= operator determines if the operand on its left is greater than *or* equal to the operand on the right. Assuming that a is 4, b is 6, and c is 4, both of the following expressions are true:

```
b >= a
a >= c
```

But the following is false:

```
a >= 5
```

The <= operator determines if the operand on its left is less than *or* equal to the operand on its right. Once again, assuming that a is 4, b is 6, and c is 4, both of the following expressions are true:

```
a <= c
b <= 10
```

But the following is false:

```
b <= a
```

The last relational operator is !=, which is the not-equal operator. It determines if the operand on its left is not equal to the operand on its right, which is the opposite of the == operator. As before, assuming a is 4, b is 6, and c is 4, both of the following expressions are true:

```
a != b
b != c
```

These expressions are true because a is *not* equal to b and b is *not* equal to c. But the following expression is false because a *is* equal to c:

```
a != c
```

Table 4-3 shows other relational expressions and their true or false values.

Table 4-3 (Assume x is 10 and y is 7.)

Expression	Value
x < y	False, because x is not less than y.
x > y	True, because x is greater than y.
x >= y	True, because x is greater than or equal to y.
x <= y	False, because x is not less than or equal to y.
y != x	True, because y is not equal to x.

What Is Truth?

The question "what is truth?" is one you would expect to find in a philosophy book, not a C++ programming text. It's a good question for us to consider, though. If a relational expression can be either true or false, how are those values represented internally in a program? How does a computer store *true* in memory? How does it store *false*?

As you saw in Program 2-16, those two abstract states are converted to numbers. In C++, relational expressions represent true states with the number 1 and false states with the number 0.

 Note: As you will see later in this chapter, 1 is not the only value regarded as true.

To illustrate this more fully, look at Program 4-1.

Program 4-1

```
// This program displays the values of true and false states.
#include <iostream>
using namespace std;
```

(program continues)

Program 4-1 *(continued)*

```
int main()
{
    bool trueValue, falseValue;
    int x = 5, y = 10;

    trueValue = x < y;
    falseValue = y == x;

    cout << "True is  " << trueValue << endl;
    cout << "False is  " << falseValue << endl;
    return 0;
}
```

Program Output
True is 1
False is 0

Let's examine the statements containing the relational expressions a little closer:

```
trueValue = x < y;
falseValue = y == x;
```

These statements may seem odd because they are assigning the value of a comparison to a variable. In the first statement, the variable trueValue is being assigned the result of x < y. Since x is less than y, the expression is true, and the variable trueValue is assigned the value 1. In the second statement the expression y == x is false, so the variable falseValue is set to 0. Table 4-4 shows examples of other statements using relational expressions and their outcomes.

Table 4-4 **(Assume** x **is 10,** y **is 7, and z, a, and b are** ints **or** bools**)**

Statement	Outcome
z = x < y	z is assigned 0 because x is not less than y.
cout << (x > y);	Displays 1 because x is greater than y.
a = x >= y;	a is assigned 1 because x is greater than or equal to y.
cout << (x <= y);	Displays 0 because x is not less than or equal to y.
b = y != x;	b is assigned 1 because y is not equal to x.

Note: Relational expressions have a higher precedence than the assignment operator. In the statement

```
z = x < y;
```

the expression x < y is evaluated first, and then its value is assigned to z.

As interesting as relational expressions are, we've only scratched the surface of how to use them. In this chapter's remaining sections you will see how to get the most from relational expressions by using them in statements that take action based on the results of the comparison.

Checkpoint [4.1]

4.1 Assuming x is 5, y is 6, and z is 8, indicate by circling the T or F if each of the following relational expressions is true or false:

A)	x == 5	T	F
B)	7 <= (x + 2)	T	F
C)	z < 4	T	F
D)	(2 + x) != y	T	F
E)	x <= (y * 2)	T	F

4.2 Indicate whether the following statements about relational expressions are correct or incorrect.

A) x <= y is the same as y > x.

B) If it is true that x >= y and it is also true that z == x, then z == y?

C) If it is true that x != y and it is also true that x != z, then z != y?

4.3 What will the following code display?

```
int a = 0, b = 2, x = 4, y = 0;
cout << (a == b) << endl;
cout << (a != y) << endl;
cout << (b <= x) << endl;
cout << (y > a) << endl;
```

4.2 The if Statement

> **CONCEPT** The if statement can cause other statements to execute only under certain conditions.

You might think of the statements in a procedural program as individual steps taken as you are walking down a road. To reach the destination, you must start at the beginning and take each step, one after the other, until you reach the destination. The programs you have written so far are like a "path" of execution for the program to follow.

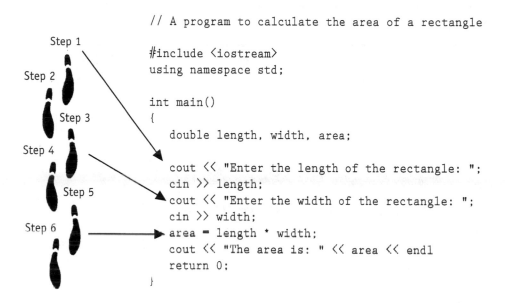

```
// A program to calculate the area of a rectangle

#include <iostream>
using namespace std;

int main()
{
    double length, width, area;

    cout << "Enter the length of the rectangle: ";
    cin >> length;
    cout << "Enter the width of the rectangle: ";
    cin >> width;
    area = length * width;
    cout << "The area is: " << area << endl
    return 0;
}
```

Figure 4-1

As shown in Figure 4-1, the program's execution flows sequentially from one statement to the next. This type of program is sometimes called an *straight-line program*, because the statements are executed in a straight "line," without branching off in another direction.

Wouldn't it be useful, though, if a program could have more than one "path" of execution? What if the program could execute some statements only under certain circumstances? That can be accomplished with the if statement, as illustrated by Program 4-2. The user enters three test scores and the program calculates their average. If the average is greater than 95, the program congratulates the user on obtaining a high score.

Program 4-2

```
// This program averages 3 test scores.
#include <iostream>
#include <iomanip>
using namespace std;
```

(program continues)

Program 4-2 *(continued)*

```
int main()
{
    int score1, score2, score3;
    double average;

    cout << "Enter 3 test scores and I will average them: ";
    cin >> score1 >> score2 >> score3;
    average = (score1 + score2 + score3) / 3.0;
    cout << fixed << showpoint << setprecision(1);
    cout << "Your average is " << average << endl;
    if (average > 95)
        cout << "Congratulations! That's a high score!\n";
    return 0;
}
```

Program Output with Example Input Shown in Bold
```
Enter 3 test scores and I will average them: 80 90 70 [Enter]
Your average is 80.0
```

Program Output with Other Example Input Shown in Bold
```
Enter 3 test scores and I will average them: 100 100 100 [Enter]
Your average is 100.0
Congratulations! That's a high score!
```

The last two lines of the program cause the congratulatory message to be printed:

```
if (average > 95)
    cout << "Congratulations! That's a high score!\n";
```

Here is the general format of the if statement:

```
if (expression)
    statement;
```

The if statement is simple in the way it works: If the expression inside the parentheses is true, the very next statement is executed. Otherwise, it is skipped. The statement is *conditionally executed* because it only executes under the condition that the expression in parentheses is true. In Program 4-2, the cout statement is only executed under the condition that average **is greater than 95**. If average **is not greater than 95**, the cout statement is skipped. This is similar to the way we mentally test conditions every day:

If the car is low on gas, stop at a service station and get gas.

If it's raining outside, go inside.

If you're hungry, get something to eat.

The if statement in Program 4-2 is saying the following:

If the average score is greater than 95, congratulate the user on obtaining a high test score average.

Table 4-5 shows other examples of if statements and their outcomes.

Table 4-5

Statements	Outcome
`if (hours > 40)` `    overTime = true;`	Assigns true to the bool variableoverTime only when hours is greater than 40
`if (value > 32)` `    cout << "Invalid number\n";`	Displays the message "Invalid number" only when value is greater than 32
`if (overTime == true)` `    payRate *= 2;`	Multiplies payRate by 2 only when overTime is equal to true

Be Careful with Semicolons

Semicolons do not mark the end of a line, but the end of a complete C++ statement. The if statement isn't complete without the conditionally executed statement that comes after it. So, you must not put a semicolon after the if (*expression*) portion of an if statement.

No semicolon goes here.

```
if (expression)
    statement;
```

Semicolon goes here.

If you inadvertently put a semicolon after the if part, the compiler will assume you are placing a null statement there. The *null statement* is an empty statement that does nothing. This will prematurely terminate the if statement, which disconnects it from the statement that follows it. The statement following the if will always execute, as shown in the following program segment.

```
int x = 0, y = 10;
cout << "x is " << x << " and y is " << y << endl;
if (x > y);    //misplaced semicolon;
    cout << "x is greater than y\n"; // This statement is always executed.
```

Program Output
```
x is 0 and y is 10
x is greater than y
```

Programming Style and the `if` Statement

Even though `if` statements usually span more than one line, they are technically one long statement. For instance, the following `if` statements are identical except in style:
```
if (a >= 100)
    cout << "The number is out of range.\n";
if (a >= 100) cout << "The number is out of range.\n";
```
In both the examples above, the compiler considers the `if` part and the `cout` statement as one unit, with a semicolon properly placed at the end. Indentions and spacing are for the human readers of a program, not the compiler. Here are two important style rules you should adopt for writing `if` statements:

◆ The conditionally executed statement should appear on the line after the `if` statement.

◆ The conditionally executed statement should be indented one "level" from the `if` statement.

 Note: In most editors, each time you press the **[tab]** key, you are indenting one level.

By indenting the conditionally executed statement you are causing it to stand out visually. This is so you can tell at a glance what part of the program the `if` statement executes. This is a standard way of writing `if` statements and is the method you should use.

 Note: Indentation and spacing are for the human readers of a program, not the compiler. Even though the `cout` statement following the `if` statement in the previous program segment is indented, the semicolon still terminates the `if` statement.

Comparing Floating-Point Numbers

Because of the way that floating-point numbers are stored in memory, rounding errors sometimes occur. This is because some fractional numbers cannot be exactly represented using binary. So, you should be careful when using the equality operator (`==`) to compare floating point numbers. For example, the following program segment uses two `double` variables, a and b. Both variables are initialized to the value 1.5. Then, the value 0.0000000000000001 is added to a. This should make a's contents different than b's contents. Because of a round-off error, however, the two variables are still the same.

```
double a = 1.5,          // a is 1.5.
b = 1.5;                 // b is 1.5.
a += 0.0000000000000001;                          // Add a little to a.
if (a == b)
    cout << "Both a and b are the same.\n";
else
    cout << "a and b are not the same.\n";
```

Program Output

```
Both a and b are the same.
```

To prevent round-off errors from causing this type of problem, you should stick with greater-than and less-than comparisons with floating-point numbers.

And Now Back to Truth

Now that you've gotten your feet wet with relational expressions and if statements, let's look at the subject of truth again. You have seen that a relational expression has the value 1 when it is true and 0 when false. In the world of the if statement, however, the concept of truth is expanded. 0 is still false, but all values other than 0 are considered true. This means that any value, even a negative number, represents true as long as it is not 0.

Just as in real life, truth is a complicated thing. Here is a summary of the rules you have seen so far:

♦ When a relational expression is true it has the value 1.

♦ When a relational expression is false it has the value 0.

♦ An expression that has the value 0 is considered false by the if statement. This includes the bool value false, which is equivalent to 0.

♦ An expression that has any value other than 0 is considered true by the if statement. This includes the bool value true, which is equivalent to 1.

The fact that the if statement considers any nonzero value as true opens many possibilities. Relational expressions are not the only conditions that may be tested. For example, the following is a legal if statement in C++:

```
if (value)
    cout << "It is True!";
```

The if statement above does not test a relational expression, but rather the contents of a variable. If the variable, value, contains any number other than 0, the message "It is True!" will be displayed. If value is set to 0, however, the cout statement will be skipped. Here is another example:

```
if (x + y)
    cout << "It is True!";
```

In this statement the sum of x and y is tested like any other value in an if statement: 0 is false and all other values are true. You may also use the return value of function calls as conditional expressions. Here is an example that uses the pow function:

```
if (pow(a, b))
    cout << "It is True!";
```

This if statement uses the pow function to raise a to the power of b. If the result is anything other than 0, the cout statement is executed. This is a powerful programming technique that you will learn more about in Chapter 6.

Not All Operators Are "Equal"

Earlier you saw a warning not to confuse the equality operator (==) with the assignment operator (=), as in the following statement:

```
if (x = 2)  // Caution here!
    cout << "It is True!";
```

The statement above does not determine if x is equal to 2, it assigns x the value 2! Furthermore, the cout statement will *always* be executed because the expression x = 2 is always true.

This occurs because the value of an assignment expression is the value being assigned to the variable on the left side of the = operator. That means the value of the expression x = 2 is 2. Since 2 is a nonzero value, it represents a true condition. Program 4-3 is a version of Program 4-2 that attempts to test for a perfect average of 100. The = operator, however, was mistakenly used in the if statement.

Program 4-3

```
// This program averages 3 test scores. The if statement
// uses the = operator, but the == operator was intended.
#include <iostream>
#include <iomanip>
using namespace std;

int main()
{
    int score1, score2, score3;
    double average;

    cout << "Enter 3 test scores and I will average them: ";
    cin >> score1 >> score2 >> score3;
    average = (score1 + score2 + score3) / 3.0;
    cout << fixed << showpoint << setprecision(1);
    cout << "Your average is " << average << endl;
    if (average = 100)          // WRONG! This is an assignment
        cout << "Congratulations! That's a perfect score!\n";
    return 0;
}
```

Program Output with Example Input Shown in Bold
```
Enter 3 test scores and I will average them: 80 90 70 [Enter]
Your average is 80.0
Congratulations! That's a perfect score!
```

Regardless of the average score, this program will print the message congratulating the user on a perfect score.

4.3 Flags

A flag is a Boolean variable that signals when a condition exists.

Flag variables are meant to signal that some condition exists in the program. When the flag contains a 0 (false), it indicates the condition does not yet exist. When the flag contains a nonzero value (true), it means the condition does exist. The following program segment is the test-averaging program modified to use a flag variable, `highScore`.

```
int score1, score2, score3;
bool highScore = false;
double average;
cout << "Enter your 3 test scores and I will average them: ";
cin >> score1 >> score2 >> score3;
average = (score1 + score2 + score3) / 3.0;
if (average > 95)
    highScore = true;          // Set the flag variable
cout << fixed << showpoint << setprecision(1);
cout << "Your average is " << average << endl;
if (highScore)
    cout << "Congratulations! That's a high score!\n";
```

Program Output with Example Input Shown in Bold
Enter your 3 test scores and I will average them: **100 100 100 [Enter]**
Your average is 100.0
Congratulations! That's a high score!

 Note: The two `if` statements in the previous program segment are redundant. However, the program is presented to demonstrate a flag variable. Similar programs follow in this chapter.

Notice the flag variable, `highScore`, is initialized to `false`. The first `if` statement changes `highScore`'s value to `true` (1) if the average is greater than 95. Otherwise, `highScore` keeps its value of `false` (0). The last `if` statement only prints the message of congratulations if `highScore` is set to `true`. You will find flag variables useful in many circumstances, and we will come back to them in Chapter 5.

 Note: Variables that are created inside a function, like `main`, are not automatically initialized. If you need a variable to start with a particular value, you should initialize it to that value.

4.4 Expanding the `if` Statement

CONCEPT The `if` statement can conditionally execute a block of statements enclosed in braces.

What if you want an `if` statement to conditionally execute a group of statements, not just one line? For instance, what if the test averaging program needed to use several `cout` statements when a high score was reached? The answer is to enclose all of the conditionally executed statements inside a set of braces. Here is the format:

```
if (expression)
{
    statement;
    statement;
    // Place as many statements here as necessary.
}
```

Program 4-4, another modification of the test-averaging program, demonstrates this type of `if` statement.

Program 4-4

```
// This program averages 3 test scores.
// It demonstrates an if statement executing
// a block of statements.
#include <iostream>
#include <iomanip>
using namespace std;

int main()
{
    int score1, score2, score3;
    double average;

    cout << "Enter 3 test scores and I will average them: ";
    cin >> score1 >> score2 >> score3;
    average = (score1 + score2 + score3) / 3.0;
    cout << fixed << showpoint << setprecision(1);
    cout << "Your average is " << average << endl;
```

(program continues)

Program 4-4 *(continued)*

```
    if (average > 95)
    {
        cout << "Congratulations!\n";
        cout << "That's a high score.\n";
        cout << "You deserve a pat on the back!\n";
    }
    return 0;
}
```

Program Output with Example Input Shown in Bold
```
Enter 3 test scores and I will average them: 100 100 100 [Enter]
Your average is 100.0
Congratulations!
That's a high score.
You deserve a pat on the back!
```

Program Output with Different Example Input Shown in Bold
```
Enter 3 test scores and I will average them: 80 90 70 [Enter]
Your average is 80.0
```

Program 4-4 prints a more elaborate message when the average score is greater than 95. The if statement was expanded to execute 3 cout statements when highScore is set to true. Enclosing a group of statements inside a set of braces creates a *block* of code. The if statement will execute all the statements in the block, in the order they appear, only when average is greater than 95. If average is less than 96, the block will be skipped.

Notice all the statements inside the braces are indented. As before, this visually separates the statements from lines that are not indented, making it more obvious they are part of the if statement.

 Note: Anytime your program has a block of code, all the statements inside the braces should be indented.

Don't Forget the Braces!

If you intend to couple a block of statements with an if statement, don't forget the braces. Remember, without a set of braces, the if statement only executes the very next statement. Using the previous code segment, let's examine the effects of leaving off the set of braces in the if statement. The if statement becomes:

```
    if (average > 95)
        cout << "Congratulations!\n";
        cout << "That's a high score.\n";
        cout << "You deserve a pat on the back!\n";
```

The output of the code with the missing if braces is as follows:

Program Output with Example Input Shown in Bold
```
Enter 3 test scores and I will average them: 80 90 70 [Enter]
Your average is 80
That's a high score.
You deserve a pat on the back!
```

The last two `cout` statements are always executed, even when `average` is less than 96. Because all three `cout` statements are no longer inside braces, the `if` statement only controls execution of the first one.

Checkpoint [4.2–4.4]

4.4   TRUE or FALSE: Both of the following `if` statements perform the same operation.
```
if (sales > 10000)
    commissionRate = 0.15;
```
```
if (sales > 10000) commissionRate = 0.15;
```

4.5   TRUE or FALSE: Both of the following `if` statements perform the same operation.
```
if (calls == 20)
    rate *= 0.5;
```
```
if (calls = 20)
    rate *= 0.5;
```

4.6   Although the following code segments are syntactically correct, each contains an error. Locate the error.

A)
```
hours = 12;
if (hours > 40);
cout << hours << "hours qualifies for over-time.\n";
```

B)
```
interestRate = .05;
balance = 1000;
if (interestRate > .07)
        cout << "This account earns a $10 bonus.\n";
balance += 10.0;
balance *= interestRate;
cout << "The new balance is " << balance << endl;
```

4.7   Write an `if` statement that multiplies `payRate` by 1.5 when `hours` is greater than 40.

4.8   Write an `if` statement that assigns .20 to `commission` when `sales` is greater than or equal to 10000.00.

4.9   Write an `if` statement that sets the variable `fees` to 50 when the flag variable `max` is set to `true`.

4.5 The if/else Statement

CONCEPT The if/else statement will execute one group of statements if the expression is true, or another group of statements if the expression is false.

The if/else statement is an expansion of the if statement. Here is its format:

```
if (expression)
    statement or block
else
    statement or block
```

Like the if statement, an expression is evaluated. If the expression is true, a statement or block of statements is executed. If the expression is false, however, a separate group of statements is executed. Program 4-5 uses the if/else statement along with the modulus operator to determine if a number is odd or even.

Program 4-5

```cpp
// This program uses the modulus operator to determine
// if a number is odd or even. If the number is evenly divisible
// by 2, it is an even number. A remainder indicates it is odd.
#include <iostream>
using namespace std;

int main()
{
    int number;

    cout << "Enter an integer and I will tell you if it\n";
    cout << "is odd or even. ";
    cin >> number;
    if (number % 2 == 0)
        cout << number << " is even.\n";
    else
        cout << number << " is odd.\n";
    return 0;
}
```

Program Output with Example Input Shown in Bold
```
Enter an integer and I will tell you if it
is odd or even. 17 [Enter]
17 is odd.
```

The else part at the end of the if statement specifies a statement that is to be executed when the expression is false. When number % 2 does not equal 0, a message is printed indicating the number is odd. Note that the program will only take one of the two paths in the if/else statement. If you think of the statements in a computer program as steps taken down a road, consider the if/else statement as a fork in the road. Instead of being a momentary detour, like an if statement, the if/else statement causes program execution to follow one of two exclusive paths.

Notice the programming style used to construct the if/else statement. The word else is at the same level of indention as if. The statement whose execution is controlled by else is indented one level. This visually depicts the two paths of execution that may be followed.

Like the if part, the else part controls a single statement. If you wish to control more than one statement with the else part, create a block by writing the lines inside a set of braces. Program 4-6 shows this as a way of handling a classic programming problem: *division by zero*.

Division by zero is mathematically impossible to perform and it normally causes a program to crash. This means the program will prematurely stop running, sometimes with an error message. Program 4-6 shows a way to test the value of a divisor before the division takes place.

Program 4-6

```cpp
// This program asks the user for two numbers, num1 and num2.
// num1 is divided by num2 and the result is displayed.
// Before the division operation, however, num2 is tested
// for the value 0. If it contains 0, the division does not
// take place.
#include <iostream>
using namespace std;

int main()
{
    double num1, num2, quotient;

    cout << "Enter a number: ";
    cin >> num1;
    cout << "Enter another number: ";
    cin >> num2;
    if (num2 == 0)
    {
        cout << "Division by zero is not possible.\n";
        cout << "Please run the program again and enter\n";
        cout << "a number other than zero.\n";
    }
    else
    {
        quotient = num1 / num2;
        cout << "The quotient of " << num1 << " divided by ";
        cout<< num2 << " is " << quotient << ".\n";
    }
    return 0;
}
```

Program 4-6 *(continued)*

Program Output with Example Input Shown in Bold
(When the user enters 0 for num2)
```
Enter a number: 10 [Enter]
Enter another number: 0 [Enter]
Division by zero is not possible.
Please run the program again and enter
a number other than zero.
```

The value of num2 is tested before the division is performed. If the user enters 0, the lines controlled by the if part execute, displaying a message which indicates the program cannot perform a division by zero. Otherwise, the else part takes control, which divides num1 by num2 and displays the result.

Checkpoint [4.5]

4.10 TRUE or FALSE: The following if/else statements cause the same output to display.

```
A)  if (x > y)
        cout << "x is the greater.\n";
    else
        cout << "x is not the greater.\n";
```

```
B)  if (y <= x)
        cout << "x is not the greater.\n";
    else
        cout << "x is the greater.\n";
```

4.11 Write an if/else statement that assigns 0.10 to commission unless sales is greater than or equal to 50000.00, in which case it assigns 0.20 to commission.

4.12 Write a complete program so that it computes the correct sales tax. If the customer is an in-state resident, taxRate should be set to .05. If the customer is an out-of-state resident, taxRate should be set to 0. Use the following program segment as a starting point.

```
double taxRate, saleAmount;
char residence;

cout << "Enter the amount of the sale: ";
cin >> saleAmount;
cout << "Enter I for in-state residence or O for out-of-\n";
cout <<"state: ";
cin.get(residence);

// Write code here that assigns 0 to taxRate if residence
// is set to 'O' or .05 to taxRate if residence is set
// to 'I'

saleAmount += saleAmount * taxRate;
cout << "The total is " << saleAmount;
```

4.6 The `if/else if` Statement

We make certain mental decisions by using sets of different but related rules. For example, we might decide the type of coat or jacket to wear by consulting the following rules:

```
if it is very cold, wear a heavy coat,
else, if it is chilly, wear a light jacket,
else, if it is windy wear a windbreaker,
else, if it is hot, wear no jacket.
```

The purpose of these rules is to decide on one type of outer garment to wear. If it is cold, the first rule dictates that a heavy coat must be worn. All the other rules are then ignored. If the first rule doesn't apply, however (if it isn't cold), then the second rule is consulted. If that rule doesn't apply, the third rule is consulted, and so forth.

The way these rules are connected is very important. If they were consulted individually, we might go out of the house wearing the wrong jacket or, possibly, more than one jacket. For instance, if it is windy, the third rule says to wear a windbreaker. What if it is both windy and very cold? Will we wear a windbreaker? A heavy coat? Both? Because of the order that the rules are consulted in, the first rule will determine that a heavy coat is needed. The third rule will not be consulted, and we will go outside wearing the most appropriate garment.

This type of decision making is also very common in programming. In C++ it is accomplished through the `if/else if` statement. Here is its format:

```
if (expression)
    statement or block
else if (expression)
    statement or block
//
// Put as many else if's as needed here
//
else if (expression)
    statement or block
```

This construction is like a chain of `if/else` statements. The `else` part of one statement is linked to the `if` part of another. When put together this way, the chain of `if/else`'s becomes one long statement. Program 4-7 shows an example. The user is asked to enter a numeric test score and the program displays the letter grade earned.

The `if/else if` statement has a number of notable characteristics. Let's analyze how it works in Program 4-7. First, the relational expression `testScore < 60` is tested.

Program 4-7

```cpp
// This program uses an if/else if statement to assign a
// letter grade (A, B, C, D, or F) to a numeric test score.
#include <iostream>
using namespace std;

int main()
{
    int testScore;
    char grade;

    cout << "Enter your numeric test score and I will\n";
    cout << "tell you the letter grade you earned: ";
    cin >> testScore;
    if (testScore < 60)
        grade = 'F';
    else if (testScore < 70)
        grade = 'D';
    else if (testScore < 80)
        grade = 'C';
    else if (testScore < 90)
        grade = 'B';
    else if (testScore <= 100)
        grade = 'A';
    cout << "Your grade is " << grade << ".\n";
    return 0;
}
```

Program Output with Example Input Shown in Bold

```
Enter your numeric test score and I will
tell you the letter grade you earned: 88 [Enter]
Your grade is B.
```

```cpp
→   if (testScore < 60)
        grade = 'F';
    else if (testScore < 70)
        grade = 'D';
    else if (testScore < 80)
        grade = 'C';
    else if (testScore < 90)
        grade = 'B';
    else if (testScore <= 100)
        grade = 'A';
```

If `testScore` is less than 60, the letter 'F' is assigned to `grade` and the rest of the linked `if` statements are skipped.

If testScore is not less than 60, the else part takes over and causes the next if statement to be executed.

```
    if (testScore < 60)
        grade = 'F';
→   else if (testScore < 70)
        grade = 'D';
    else if (testScore < 80)
        grade = 'C';
    else if (testScore < 90)
        grade = 'B';
    else if (testScore <= 100)
        grade = 'A';
```

The first if statement filtered out all of the grades less than 60, so when this if statement executes, testScore will have a value of 60 or greater. If testScore is less than 70, the letter 'D' is assigned to grade and the rest of the if/else if statement is ignored. This chain of events continues until one of the conditional expressions is found true, or the end of the statement is encountered. In either case, the program resumes at the statement immediately following the if/else if statement, which is the cout statement that prints the grade. Figure 4-2 shows a flowchart for the if/else if statement.

Each if statement in the structure depends on all the if statements before it being false. The statements following a particular else if are executed when the conditional expression following the else if is true and all previous conditional expressions are false. To demonstrate how this interconnection works, let's look at Program 4-8, which uses independent if statements instead of an if/else if statement.

In Program 4-8, all the if statements execute because they are individual statements. In the example output, testScore is assigned the value 40, yet the student recieves an A. Because testScore is less than 60, the first if statement causes 'F' to be assigned to grade.

```
→   if (testScore < 60)
        grade = 'F';
    if (testScore < 70)
        grade = 'D';
    if (testScore < 80)
        grade = 'C';
    if (testScore < 90)
        grade = 'B';
    if (testScore <= 100)
        grade = 'A';
```

However, because the next if statement is not connected to the first through an else, it executes as well. testScore is also less than 70, so it causes 'D' to be assigned to grade. The character 'D' overwrites the 'F' that was previously stored there.

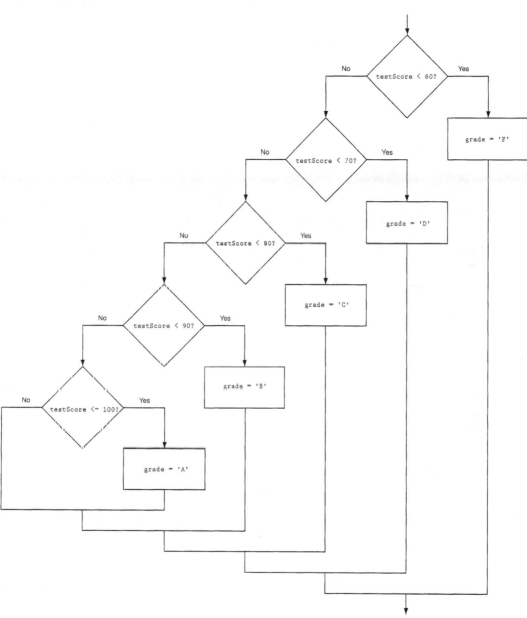

Figure 4-2

Program 4-8

```cpp
// This program uses independent if/else statements to assign a
// letter grade (A, B, C, D, or F) to a numeric test score.
// Do you think it will work?
#include <iostream>
using namespace std;

int main()
{
    int testScore;
    char grade;

    cout << "Enter your test score and I will tell you\n";
    cout << "the letter grade you earned: ";
    cin >> testScore;
    if (testScore < 60)
        grade = 'F';
    if (testScore < 70)
        grade = 'D';
    if (testScore < 80)
        grade = 'C';
    if (testScore < 90)
        grade = 'B';
    if (testScore <= 100)
        grade = 'A';
    cout << "Your grade is " << grade << ".\n";
    return 0;
}
```

Program Output with Example Input Shown in Bold
```
Enter your test score and I will tell you
the letter grade you earned: 40 [Enter]
Your grade is A.
```

```
        if (testScore < 60)
            grade = 'F';
    →   if (testScore < 70)
            grade = 'D';
        if (testScore < 80)
            grade = 'C';
        if (testScore < 90)
            grade = 'B';
        if (testScore <= 100)
            grade = 'A';
```

This will continue until all the if statements have executed. The last one will cause 'A' to be assigned to grade. (Most students prefer this method since 'A' is the only grade it gives out!)

4.7 Using a Trailing else

CONCEPT A trailing else, placed at the end of an if/else if statement, provides default action when none of the if's have true expressions.

There is one minor problem with the test score examples shown so far. What if the user enters a test score greater than 100? The if/else if statement handles all scores through 100, but none greater.

If the user enters a value greater than 100, the programs do not give a letter grade because there is no code to handle a score greater than 100. Assuming that any grade over 100 is invalid, we can fix the program by placing an else at the end of the if/else if statement. This is shown in the following program segment.

```cpp
int testScore;
char grade;
cout << "Enter your numeric test score and I will\n";
cout << "tell you the letter grade you earned: ";
cin >> testScore;
if (testScore < 60)
    cout << "Your grade is F.\n";
else if (testScore < 70)
    cout << "Your grade is D.\n";
else if (testScore < 80)
    cout << "Your grade is C.\n";
else if (testScore < 90)
    cout << "Your grade is B.\n";
else if (testScore <= 100)
    cout << "Your grade is A.\n";
else
    cout << testScore << " is an invalid score.\n";
```

Program Output with Example Input Shown in Bold
```
Enter your numeric test score and I will
tell you the letter grade you earned: 104 [Enter]
104 is an invalid score.
```

The trailing else catches any value that "falls through the cracks." It provides a default response when none of the if's find a true condition.

4.8 Menus

CONCEPT You can use the `if/else if` statement to create menu-driven programs. A *menu-driven* program allows the user to determine the course of action by selecting it from a list of actions.

A menu is a screen displaying a set of choices the user selects from. For example, a program that keeps a mailing list might give you the following menu:

1. Add a name to the list.

2. Remove a name from the list.

3. Change a name in the list.

4. Print the list.

5. Quit the program.

The user selects one of the operations by entering its number. Entering 4, for example, causes the mailing list to be printed, and entering 5 causes the program to end. The `if/else if` structure can be used to set up such a menu. After the user enters a number, it compares the number to the available selections and executes the statements that perform that operation.

Program 4-9 calculates the charges for membership in a health club. The club has three membership packages to choose from: standard adult membership, child membership, and senior citizen membership. The program presents a menu that allows the user to choose the desired package and then calculates the cost of the membership.

Program 4-9

```
// This program displays a menu and asks the user to make a
// selection. An if/else if statement determines which item
// the user has chosen.
#include <iostream>
#include<iomanip>
using namespace std;
int main()
{
    int choice, months;
    double charges;
    cout << "\t\tHealth Club Membership Menu\n\n";
    cout << "1. Standard Adult Membership\n";
    cout << "2. Child Membership\n";
    cout << "3. Senior Citizen Membership\n";
    cout << "4. Quit the Program\n\n";
    cout << "Enter your choice: ";
    cin >> choice;
    cout << fixed << showpoint << setprecision(2);
```

(program continues)

Program 4-9 *(continued)*

```cpp
    if (choice == 1)
    {
        cout << "For how many months? ";
        cin >> months;
        charges = months * 40.00;
        cout << "The total charges are $" << charges << endl;
    }
    else if (choice == 2)
    {
        cout << "For how many months? ";
        cin >> months;
        charges = months * 20.00;
        cout << "The total charges are $" << charges << endl;
    }
    else if (choice == 3)
    {
        cout << "For how many months? ";
        cin >> months;
        charges = months * 30.00;
        cout << "The total charges are $" << charges << endl;
    }

    else if (choice != 4)
    {
        cout << "The valid choices are 1 through 4. Run the\n";
        cout << "program again and select one of those.\n";
    }
    return 0;
}
```

Program Output with Example Input Shown in Bold
```
    Health Club Membership Menu

1. Standard Adult Membership
2. Child Membership
3. Senior Citizen Membership
4. Quit the Program

Enter your choice: 3 [Enter]
For how many months? 6 [Enter]
The total charges are $180.00
```

Notice the program also lets the user know when an invalid choice is made. If a number other than 1, 2, 3, or 4 is entered, an error message is printed. This is known as *input validation*.

4.9 Focus on Software Engineering: *Nested* `if` *Statements*

CONCEPT A nested `if` statement is an `if` statement in the conditionally executed code of another `if` statement.

Anytime an `if` statement appears inside another `if` statement, it is considered "nested." In actuality, the `if`/`else if` structure is a nested `if` statement. Each `if` (after the first one) is nested in the `else` part of the previous `if`.

You may also nest `if`s inside the `if` part, as shown in Program 4-10. Suppose the program is used to determine if a bank customer qualifies for a special interest rate on loans, intended for people who recently graduated from college and are employed.

Program 4-10

```cpp
// This program demonstrates the nested if statement.
#include <iostream>
using namespace std;

int main()
{
    char employed, recentGrad;

    cout << "Answer the following questions\n";
    cout << "with either Y for Yes or ";
    cout << "N for No.\n";
    cout << "Are you employed? ";
    cin >> employed;
    cout << "Have you graduated from college ";
    cout << "in the past two years? ";
    cin >> recentGrad;
    if (employed == 'Y')
    {
        if (recentGrad == 'Y') //Nested if
        {
            cout << "You qualify for the special ";
            cout << "interest rate.\n";
        }
    }
    return 0;
}
```

Program 4-10 *(continued)*

Program Output with Example Input Shown in Bold
```
Answer the following questions
with either Y for Yes or N for No.
Are you employed? Y [Enter]
Have you graduated from college in the past two years? Y [Enter]
You qualify for the special interest rate.
```

Program Output with Other Example Input Shown in Bold
```
Answer the following questions
with either Y for Yes or N for No.
Are you employed? Y [Enter]
Have you graduated from college in the past two years? N [Enter]
```

Because the first if statement conditionally executes the second one, both the employed and recentGrad variables must be set to 'Y' for the message to be printed informing the user he or she qualifies for the special interest rate. This type of nested if statement is good for narrowing choices down and categorizing data. The only way the program will execute the second if statement is for the conditional expression of the first one to be true.

There is an undesirable feature (otherwise known as a bug) in Program 4-10. If the user enters an 'N' (or any character other than 'Y') for employed or recentGrad, the program does not print a message letting them know they do not qualify. An else statement should be able to remedy this, as illustrated by the following program segment.

```cpp
if (employed == 'Y')
{
    if (recentGrad == 'Y')   // Nested if
    {
        cout << "You qualify for the special ";
        cout << "interest rate.\n";
    }
    else   // Not a recent grad, but employed
    {
        cout << "You must have graduated from ";
        cout << "college in the past two\n";
        cout << "years to qualify.\n";
    }
}
else          // Not employed
{
    cout << "You must be employed to qualify.\n";
}
```

Program Output with Example Input Shown in Bold
```
Answer the following questions
with either Y for Yes or N for No.
Are you employed? N [Enter]
Have you graduated from college in the past two years? Y [Enter]
You must be employed to qualify.
```

Program Output with Other Example Input Shown in Bold
```
Answer the following questions
with either Y for Yes or N for No.
Are you employed? Y [Enter]
Have you graduated from college in the past two years? N [Enter]
You must have graduated from college in the past two
years to qualify.
```

Program Output with Example Input Shown in Bold
```
Answer the following questions
with either Y for Yes or N for No.
Are you employed? Y [Enter]
Have you graduated from college in the past two years? Y [Enter]
You qualify for the special interest rate.
```

Note: When you are debugging a program with nested `if`/`else` statements, it's important to know which `if` statement each `else` belongs to. The rule for matching `else`s with `if`s is that an `else` goes with the last `if` statement that doesn't have its own `else`. This is easier to see when the `if` statements are properly indented. Each `else` should line up with the `if` it belongs to. These visual cues are important because nested `if` statements can be very long and complex.

Checkpoint [4.6–4.9]

4.13 Program 4-8 asks the user for a numeric test score and displays the letter grade for that score. Modify it so an error message is displayed if the user enters a test score less than 0.

4.14 What will the following program segment display?

```
int funny = 7, serious = 15;
funny = serious % 2;
if (funny != 1)
{
    funny = 0;
    serious = 0;
}
else if (funny == 2)
{
    funny = 10;
    serious = 10;
}
```

```
else
{
    funny = 1;
    serious = 1;
}
cout << funny << " " << serious << endl;
```

4.15 Write nested if statements that perform the following test: If amount1 is greater than 10 and amount2 is less than 100, display the greater of the two.

4.10 Logical Operators

CONCEPT Logical operators connect two or more relational expressions into one or reverse the logic of an expression.

In the previous section you saw how a program tests two conditions with two if statements. In this section you will see how to use logical operators to combine two or more relational expressions into one. Table 4-6 lists C++'s logical operators.

Table 4-6

Operator	Meaning	Effect
&&	AND	Connects two expressions into one. Both expressions must be true for the overall expression to be true.
||	OR	Connects two expressions into one. One or both expressions must be true for the overall expression to be true. It is only necessary for one to be true, and it does not matter which.
!	NOT	The ! operator reverses the "truth" of an expression. It makes a true expression false, and a false expression true.

The && Operator

The && operator is known as the logical AND operator. It takes two expressions as operands and creates an expression that is true only when both sub-expressions are true. Here is an example of an if statement that uses the && operator:

```
if (temperature < 20 && minutes > 12)
    cout << "The temperature is in the danger zone.";
```

In the statement above the two relational expressions are combined into a single expression. The cout statement will only be executed if temperature is less than 20 AND minutes is greater than 12. If either relational test is false, the entire expression is false and the cout statement is not executed.

Tip: You must provide complete expressions on both sides of the && operator. For example, the following is not correct because the condition on the right side of the && operator is not a complete expression.

```
temperature > 0 && < 100
```

The expression must be rewritten as

```
temperature > 0 && temperature < 100
```

Table 4-7 shows a truth table for the && operator. The truth table lists all the possible combinations of values that two expressions may have, and the resulting value returned by the && operator connecting the two expressions.

Table 4-7

Expression	Value of the Expression
true && false	false (0)
false && true	false (0)
false && false	false (0)
true && true	true (1)

As the table shows, both sub-expressions must be true for the && operator to return a true value.

Note: If the sub-expression on the left side of an && operator is false, the expression on the right side will not be checked. Since the entire expression is false if only one of the sub-expressions is false, it would waste CPU time to check the remaining expression. This is called *short circuit evaluation*.

The && operator can be used to simplify programs that otherwise would use nested if statements. The following program segment uses the logical operator of a nested if statement.

```
if (employed == 'Y' && recentGrad == 'Y')   //&& logical operator
{
    cout << "You qualify for the special ";
    cout << "interest rate.\n";
}
else
{
    cout << "You must be employed and have\n";
    cout << "graduated from college in the\n";
    cout << "past two years to qualify.\n";
}
```

Program Output with Example Input Shown in Bold
```
Answer the following questions
with either Y for Yes or N for No.
```

```
Are you employed? Y [Enter]
Have you graduated from college in the past two years? N [Enter]
You must be employed and have
graduated from college in the
past two years to qualify.
```

Program Output with Example Input Shown in Bold
```
Answer the following questions
with either Y for Yes or N for No.
Are you employed? N [Enter]
Have you graduated from college in the past two years? Y [Enter]
You must be employed and have
graduated from college in the
past two years to qualify.
```

Program Output with Example Input Shown in Bold
```
Answer the following questions
with either Y for Yes or N for No.
Are you employed? Y [Enter]
Have you graduated from college in the past two years? Y [Enter]
You qualify for the special interest rate.
```

The message "You qualify for the special interest rate" is only displayed when both the expressions employed == 'Y' and recentGrad == 'Y' are true. If either of these are false, the message "You must be employed and have graduated from college in the past two years to qualify." is printed.

Note: Although the two program segments are similar, they are not logically equivalent. For example, the later dosen't display the message "You must be employed to qualify."

The || Operator

The || operator is known as the logical OR operator. It takes two expressions as operands and creates an expression that is true when either of the sub-expressions are true. Here is an example of an if statement that uses the || operator:

```
if (temperature < 20 || temperature > 100)
    cout << "The temperature is in the danger zone.";
```

The cout statement will be executed if temperature is less than 20 OR temperature is greater than 100. If either relational test is true, the entire expression is true and the cout statement is executed.

Tip: You must provide complete expressions on both sides of the || operator. For example, the following is not correct because the condition on the right side of the || operator is not a complete expression.

```
temperature < 0 || > 100
```

The expression must be rewritten as

```
temperature < 0 || temperature > 100
```

Table 4-8 shows a truth table for the || operator.

Table 4-8

Expression	Value of the Expression
true || false	true (1)
false || true	true (1)
false || false	false (0)
true || true	true (1)

All it takes for an OR expression to be true is for one of the sub-expressions to be true. It doesn't matter if the other sub-expression is false or true.

 Note: If the sub-expression on the left side of an || operator is true, the expression on the right side will not be checked. Since it's only necessary for one of the sub-expressions to be true, it would waste CPU time to check the remaining expression.

Program 4-11 performs different tests to qualify a person for a loan. This one determines if the customer earns at least $35,000 per year, or has been employed for more than five years.

Program 4-11

```
// This program asks the user for annual income and
// the number of years of employment at the current
// job. The || operator is used in a if statement that
// determines if the income is at least $35,000 or the time
// on the job is more than five years.
#include <iostream>
using namespace std;

int main()
{
    double income;
    int years;
```

(program continues)

Program 4-11 *(continued)*

```
        cout << "What is your annual income? ";
        cin >> income;
        cout << "How many years have you worked at "
             << "your current job? ";
        cin >> years;
        if (income >= 35000 || years > 5)  //Uses || logical operator
            cout << "You qualify.\n";
        else
        {
            cout << "You must earn at least $35,000 or have\n";
            cout << "been employed for more than 5 years.\n";
        }
        return 0;
}
```

Program Output with Example Input Shown in Bold

```
What is your annual income? 40000 [Enter]
How many years have you worked at your current job? 2 [Enter]
You qualify.
```

Program Output with Example Input Shown in Bold

```
What is your annual income? 20000 [Enter]
How many years have you worked at your current job? 7 [Enter]
You qualify.
```

Program Output with Example Input Shown in Bold

```
What is your annual income? 30000 [Enter]
How many years have you worked at your current job? 3 [Enter]
You must earn at least $35,000 or have
been employed for more than 5 years.
```

The message "You qualify\n." is displayed when either or both the expressions income >= 35000 or years > 5 are true. If both of these are false, the disqualifying message is printed.

The ! Operator

The ! operator performs a logical NOT operation. It takes an operand and reverses its truth or falsehood. In other words, if the expression is true, the ! operator returns false, and if the expression is false, it returns true. Here is an if statement using the ! operator:

```
if (!(temperature > 100))
    cout << "You are below the maximum temperature.\n";
```

First, the expression (temperature > 100) is tested to be true or false. Then the ! operator is applied to that value. If the expression (temperature > 100) is true, the ! operator returns false. If it is false, the ! operator returns true. In the example, it is equivalent to asking "is the temperature not greater than 100?"

Table 4-9 shows a truth table for the ! operator.

Table 4-9

Expression	Value of the Expression
!true	false (0)
!false	true (1)

The following program segment performs the same task as Program 4-11. The if statement, however, uses the ! operator to determine if the user does *not* make at least $35,000 or has *not* been on the job more than 5 years.

```
double income;
int years;
cout << "What is your annual income? ";
cin >> income;
cout << "How many years have you worked at "
     << "your current job? ";
cin >> years;
if (!(income >= 35000 || years > 5))   // Uses ! logical operator
{
    cout << "You must earn at least $35,000 or have\n";
    cout << "been employed for more than 5 years.\n";
}
else
    cout << "You qualify.\n";
```

The output is the same as Program 4-11.

Precedence and Associativity of Logical Operators

Table 4-10 shows the precedence of C++'s logical operators, from highest to lowest.

Table 4-10

Logical Operators in Order of Precedence
!
&&

The ! operator has a higher precedence than many of the C++ operators. To avoid an error, you should always enclose its operand in parentheses unless you intend to apply it to a variable or a simple expression with no other operators. For example, consider the following expressions:

```
!(x > 2)
!x > 2
```

The first expression applies the ! operator to the expression x > 2. It is asking "is x not greater than 2?" The second expression, however, applies the ! operator to x only. It is asking "is the logical negation of x greater than 2?" Suppose x is set to 5. Since 5 is nonzero, it would be considered true, so the ! operator would reverse it to false, which is 0. The > operator would then determine if 0 is greater than 2. To avoid a catastrophe like this, always use parentheses!

The && and ⵏ operators rank lower in precedence than the relational operators, so precedence problems are less likely to occur. If you feel unsure, however, it doesn't hurt to use parentheses anyway.

```
(a > b) && (x < y)     is the same as   a > b && x < y
(x == y) || (b > a)    is the same as   x == y || b > a
```

The logical operators have left to right associativity. In the following expression, a < b is evaluated before y == z.

```
a < b || y == z
```

In the following expression, y == z is evaluated first, however, because the && operator has higher precedence than ||.

```
a < b || y == z && m > j
```

The expression is equivalent to:

```
(a < b) || ((y == z) && (m > j))
```

4.11   Checking Numeric Ranges with Logical Operators

CONCEPT Logical operators are effective for determining if a number is in or out of a range.

When determining if a number is inside a numeric range, it's best to use the && operator. For example, the following if statement checks the value in x to determine if it is in the range of 20 through 40:

```
if (x >= 20 && x <= 40)
    cout << x << " is in the acceptable range.\n";
```

The expression in the if statement will be true only when x is both greater than or equal to 20 AND less than or equal to 40. x must be within the range of 20 through 40 for this expression to be true.

When determining if a number is outside a range, the || operator is best to use. The following statement determines if x is outside the range of 20 to 40:

```
if (x < 20 || x > 40)
    cout << x << " is outside the acceptable range.\n";
```

It's important not to get the logic of these logical operators confused. For example, the following `if` statement would never test true:

```
if (x < 20 && x > 40)
    cout << x << " is outside the acceptable range.\n";
```

Obviously, x cannot be less than 20 and at the same time greater than 40.

 Note: C++ does not allow you to check numeric ranges with expressions such as 5 < x < 20. Instead, you must use a logical operator to connect two relational expressions, as previously discussed.

 ## Checkpoint [4.10–4.11]

4.16 Assume the variables a = 2, b = 4, and c = 6. Indicate by circling the T or F if each of the following conditions is true or false:

```
a == 4 || b > 2      T    F
6 <= c && a > 3      T    F
1 != b && c != 3     T    F
a >= -1 || a <= b    T    F
!(a > 2)             T    F
```

4.17 Write an `if` statement that prints the message "The number is valid" if the variable speed is within the range 0 through 200.

4.18 Write an `if` statement that prints the message "The number is not valid" if the variable speed is outside the range 0 through 200.

4.12 Focus on Software Engineering: *Validating User Input*

CONCEPT	As long as the user of a program enters bad input, the program will produce bad output. Programs should be written to filter out bad input.

Perhaps the most famous saying of the computer world is "garbage in, garbage out." The integrity of a program's output is only as good as its input, so you should try to make sure garbage does not go into your programs. *Input validation* is the process of inspecting data given to a program by the user and determining if it is valid. A good program should give clear instructions about the kind of input that is acceptable, and not assume the user has followed those instructions. Here are just a few examples of input validations performed by programs:

♦ Numbers are checked to ensure they are within a range of possible values. For example, there are 168 hours in a week. It is not possible for a person to be at work longer than 168 hours in one week.

◆ Values are checked for their "reasonableness." Although it might be possible for a person to be at work for 168 hours per week, it is not probable.

◆ Items selected from a menu or other sets of choices are checked to ensure they are available options.

◆ Variables are checked for values that might cause problems, such as division by zero.

Program 4-12 is a modification of Program 4-7, the test scoring program. It rejects any test score less than 0 or greater than 100.

Program 4-12

```cpp
// This program uses an if/else if statement to assign a
// letter grade (A, B, C, D, or F) to a numeric test score.
#include <iostream>
using namespace std;

int main()
{
    int testScore;
    char grade;

    cout << "Enter your test score and I will tell you\n";
    cout << "the letter grade you earned: ";
    cin >> testScore;
    if (testScore < 0 || testScore > 100)  //Input validation
    {
        cout << testScore << " is an invalid score.\n";
        cout << "Run the program again and enter a value\n";
        cout << "in the range of 0 to 100.\n";
    }

    else
    {
        if (testScore < 60)
            grade = 'F';
        else if (testScore < 70)
            grade = 'D';
        else if (testScore < 80)
            grade = 'C';
        else if (testScore < 90)
            grade = 'B';
        else if (testScore <= 100)
            grade = 'A';
        cout << "Your grade is " << grade << endl;
    }
    return 0;
}
```

Program 4-12   *(continued)*

Program Output with Example Input Shown in Bold
```
Enter your test score and I will tell you
the letter grade you earned: -12 [Enter]
-12 is an invalid score.
Run the program again and enter a value
in the range of 0 to 100.
```

Program Output with Example Input Shown in Bold
```
Enter your test score and I will tell you
the letter grade you earned: 81 [Enter]
Your grade is B
```

4.13   More About Variable Definitions and Scope

CONCEPT   The scope of a variable is limited to the block in which it is defined.

C++ allows you to create variables almost anywhere in a program. Program 4-13A is a modification of Program 4-11, which determines if the user qualifies for a loan. The definitions of the variables income and years have been moved to later points in the program.

Program 4-13A

```cpp
// This program demonstrates late variable definition
#include <iostream>
using namespace std;

int main()
{
    cout << "What is your annual income? ";
    double income;    // Variable definition
    cin >> income;
    cout << "How many years have you worked at "
        << "your current job? ";
    int years;        // Variable definition
    cin >> years;
    if (income >= 35000 || years > 5)
        cout << "You qualify.\n";
    else
    {
        cout << "You must earn at least $35,000 or have\n";
        cout << "been employed for more than 5 years.\n";
    }
    return 0;
}
```

It is a common practice to define all of a function's variables at the top of the function. Sometimes, especially in longer programs, it's a good idea to define variables near the part of the program where they are used. This makes the purpose of the variable more evident.

Recall from Chapter 2 that the scope of a variable is defined as the part of the program where the variable may be used. Program 4-13B shows the scope of the variable income as a shaded area.

Program 4-13B

```cpp
// This program demonstrates late variable definition.
#include <iostream>
using namespace std;

int main()
{
    cout << "What is your annual income? ";

    double income;     // variable definition
    cin >> income;
    cout << "How many years have you worked at "
        << "your current job? ";
    int years;         // variable definition
    cin >> years;
    if (income >= 35000 || years > 5)
        cout << "You qualify.\n";
    else
    {
        cout << "You must earn at least $35,000 or have\n";
        cout << "been employed for more than 5 years.\n";
    }
    return 0;
}
```

The shaded area shows the part of the program in which income is visible. Program 4-13C highlights the scope of the variable years.

Program 4-13C

```cpp
// This program demonstrates late variable definition.
#include <iostream>
using namespace std;

int main()
{
    cout << "What is your annual income? ";
    double income;     //variable definition
    cin >> income;
```

(program continues)

Program 4-13C *(continued)*

```
    int years;        //variable definition
    cout << "How many years have you worked at "
         << "your current job? ";
    cin >> years;
    if (income >= 35000 || years > 5)
        cout << "You qualify.\n";
    else
    {
        cout << "You must earn at least $35,000 or have\n";
        cout << "been employed for more than 5 years.\n";
    }
    return 0;
}
```

The variables income and years are defined inside function main's braces. Variables defined inside a set of braces have *local scope* or *block scope*. They may only be used in the part of the program between their definition and the block's closing brace.

You may define variables inside any block. For example, look at Program 4-14. This version of the loan program has the variable years defined inside the block of the if statement. The scope of years is shaded.

Program 4-14

```
// This program demonstrates a variable defined in an inner block.
#include <iostream>
using namespace std;

int main()
{
    cout << "What is your annual income? ";
    double income;      //variable definition
    cin >> income;
    if (income >= 35000)
    {
        int years;        //variable definition
        cout << "How many years have you worked at "
             << "your current job? ";
        cin >> years;
        if (years > 5)
            cout << "You qualify.\n";
        else
        {
            cout << "You must have been employed for\n";
            cout << "more than 5 years to qualify.\n";
        }
    }
}
```

(program continues)

Program 4-14 *(continued)*

```
else
{
    cout << "You must earn at least $35,000 to\n";
    cout << "qualify.\n";
}
return 0;
}
```

Notice the scope of years is only within the block where it is defined. The variable is not visible before its definition or after the closing brace of the block. This is true of any variable defined inside a set of braces.

 Note: When a program is running and it enters the section of code that constitutes a variable's scope, it is said that the variable *comes into scope*. This simply means the variable is now visible and the program may reference it. Likewise, when a variable *leaves scope*, it may no longer be used.

Variables with the Same Name

When a block is nested inside another block, a variable defined in the inner block may have the same name as a variable defined in the outer block. As long as the variable in the inner block is visible, however, the variable in the outer block will be hidden. This is illustrated by the following program segment.

```
int number;
cout << "Enter a number greater than 0: ";
cin >> number;
if (number > 0)
{
    int number;
    cout << "Now enter another number: ";
    cin >> number;
    cout << "The second number you entered was ";
    cout << number << endl;
}
cout << "Your first number was " << number << endl;
```

Program Output with Example Input Shown in Bold
```
Enter a number greater than 0: 2 [Enter]
Now enter another number: 7 [Enter]
The second number you entered was 7
Your first number was 2
```

The program segment has two separate variables named number. The cin and cout statements in the inner block (belonging to the if statement) can only work with the number variable defined in that block. As soon as the program leaves that block, the inner number goes out of scope, revealing the outer number variable.

 WARNING! Although it's perfectly acceptable to define variables inside nested blocks, you should avoid giving them the same names as variables in the outer blocks. It's too easy to confuse one variable with another.

 # Checkpoint   [4.12–4.13]

4.19 The following program segment asks the user for two numbers and then multiplies them. The first should be negative and the second should be positive. Write the input validation code for both numbers.

```
int first, second, result;
cout << "Enter a negative integer: ";
cin >> first;
cout << "Now enter a positive integer: ";
cin >> second;
//
// Write input validation code
//
result = first * second;
cout << first << " times " << second << " is "
     << result << endl;
```

4.20 What will the following program segment display if the user enters 40 for test1 and 30 for test2?

```
cout << "Enter your first test score: ";
int test1;
cin >> test1;
cout << "Enter your second test score: ";
int test2;
cin >> test2;
int sum = test1 + test2;
if (sum > 50)
{
    test1 += 10;
    test2 += 10;
    int sum = test1 + test2;
}
cout << "test 1: " << test1 << endl;
cout << "test 2: " << test2 << endl;
cout << "sum    : " << sum << endl;
```

4.14 Comparing Strings

CONCEPT You must use the `strcmp` library function to compare C-strings.

The relational operators can be used to compare numbers, but not C-strings. Program 4-15 asks the user to enter two strings, stores them in arrays as C-strings, and incorrectly tries to compare them using the equality operator.

Program 4-15

```cpp
// This program illustrates that you cannot compare C-strings
// with relational operators. Although it appears to test the
// strings for equality, that is NOT what happens.
#include <iostream>
using namespace std;

int main()
{
    const int SIZE = 40;
    char firstString[SIZE], secondString[SIZE];

    cout << "Enter a string: ";
    cin.getline(firstString, SIZE);
    cout << "Enter another string: ";
    cin.getline(secondString, SIZE);
    if (firstString == secondString)
        cout << "You entered the same string twice.\n";
    else
        cout << "The strings are not the same.\n";
    return 0;
}
```

Program Output with Example Input Shown in Bold
```
Enter a string: Alfonso [Enter]
Enter another string: Alfonso [Enter]
The strings are not the same.
```

Although two identical strings may be entered, the program will always report they are not the same. This is because of the way C++ handles C-strings. When you use the name of an array or a string literal, you are actually working with the *memory address* of the array or literal. In Program 4-15, the following statement is comparing the memory addresses of `firstString` and `secondString`:

```cpp
    if (firstString == secondString)
```

Because the addresses of firstString and secondString are not the same (the two arrays are not located in the same place in memory), the comparison will always be false.

The strcmp Function

In C++, C-string comparisons are done with the library function strcmp. To use the strcmp function, you must include the cstring header file. Here is the function's format:

```
strcmp(string1, string2);
```

The function compares the contents of string1 with that of string2 and returns one of the following values:

♦ If the two strings are identical, strcmp returns 0.

♦ If string1 < string2, strcmp returns a negative number.

♦ If string1 > string2, strcmp returns a positive number.

In general, strcmp compares the ASCII codes of each character in the two strings. If it goes all the way through both strings finding no characters different, it returns 0. As soon as it finds two corresponding characters that have different codes, however, it stops the comparison. If the ASCII code for the character in string2 is higher than the code in string1, it returns a negative number. But, if the code in string2 is lower than the code in string1, a positive number is returned. Here is the format of an if/else statement using strcmp to determine if two strings are equal:

```
if (strcmp(string1, string2) == 0)
    statement; // The strings are the same
else
    statement; // The strings are NOT the same
```

Tip: It might help you to think of strcmp as using inverted logic: If the two strings are equal, strcmp returns false (zero). If the two strings are not equal, strcmp returns true (a nonzero value).

Program 4-15, which incorrectly tested two C-strings with a relational operator, can be correctly rewritten with the strcmp function, as shown in Program 4-16.

Program 4-16

```
// This program correctly tests two C-strings for equality
// with the strcmp function.
#include <iostream>
#include <cstring>
using namespace std;
```

(program continues)

Program 4-16 *(continued)*

```
int main()
{
    const int SIZE = 40;
    char firstString[SIZE], secondString[SIZE];

    cout << "Enter a string: ";
    cin.getline(firstString, SIZE);
    cout << "Enter another string: ";
    cin.getline(secondString, SIZE);
    if (strcmp(firstString, secondString) == 0)
        cout << "You entered the same string twice.\n";
    else
        cout << "The strings are not the same.\n";
    return 0;
}
```

Program Output with Example Input Shown in Bold
```
Enter a string: Alfonso [Enter]
Enter another string: Alfonso [Enter]
You entered the same string twice.
```

The function strcmp is case-sensitive when it compares the two strings. If the user enters "Dog" and "dog" in Program 4-16, it will report they are not the same. Most compilers provide non-standard versions of strcmp that perform case-insensitive comparisons. For instance, Borland C++ has the stricmp function. It works identically to strcmp except the case of the characters is ignored.

Program 4-17 is a more practical example of how strcmp can be used. It asks the user to enter the part number of the stereo they wish to purchase. The part number contains numbers, letters, and a hyphen, so it must be stored as a string. Once the user enters the part number, the program displays the price of the stereo.

Program 4-17

```
int main()
{
    const double APRICE = 249.0, BPRICE = 299.0;
    const int SIZE = 9;
    char partNum[SIZE];
```

(program continues)

Program 4-17   *(continued)*

```
    cout << "The stereo part numbers are:\n";
    cout << "\tBoom Box, part number S147-29A\n";
    cout << "\tShelf Model, part number S147-29B\n";
    cout << "Enter the part number of the stereo you\n";
    cout << "wish to purchase: ";
    cin.width(SIZE);// Restrict input.
    cin >> partNum;
    cout << fixed << showpoint << setprecision(2);
    if (strcmp(partNum, "S147-29A") == 0)
        cout << "The price is $" << APRICE << endl;
    else if (strcmp(partNum, "S147-29B") == 0)
        cout << "The price is $" << BPRICE << endl;
    else
        cout << partNum << " is not a valid part number.\n";
    return 0;
}
```

Program Output with Example Input Shown in Bold
```
The stereo part numbers are:
    Boom Box, part number S147-29A
    Shelf Model, part number S147-29B
Enter the part number of the stereo you
wish to purchase: S147-29B [Enter]
The price is $299.00
```

Using ! With `strcmp`

Some programmers prefer to use the logical NOT operator with `strcmp` when testing strings for equality. Because 0 is considered logically false, the ! operator converts that value to true. The expression `!strcmp(string1, string2)` will return true when both strings are the same, and false when they are different. The two following statements perform the same operation:

```
    if (strcmp(firstString, secondString) == 0)
    if (!strcmp(firstString, secondString))
```

Sorting Strings

Programs are frequently written to print alphabetically sorted lists of items. For example, consider a department store computer system that keeps customer's names and addresses in a file. The names do not appear in the file alphabetically, but in the order the operator entered them. If a list were to be printed in this order, it would be very difficult to locate any specific name. The list would have to be sorted before it was printed.

Because strcmp's return value indicates which of the two strings is higher on the ASCII chart, it can be used in programs that sort strings. Program 4-18 asks the user to enter two names. Then it prints the names alphabetically.

Program 4-18

```cpp
// This program uses the return value of strcmp to alphabetically
// sort two strings entered by the user.
#include <iostream>
#include <cstring>
using namespace std;

int main()
{
    const int SIZE = 30;
    char name1[SIZE], name2[SIZE];

    cout << "Enter a name (last name first): ";
    cin.getline(name1, SIZE);
    cout << "Enter another name: ";
    cin.getline(name2, SIZE);
    cout << "Here are the names sorted alphabetically:\n";
    if (strcmp(name1, name2) < 0)
        cout << name1 << endl << name2 << endl;
    else if (strcmp(name1, name2) > 0)
        cout << name2 << endl << name1 << endl;
    else
        cout << "You entered the same name twice!\n";
    return 0;
}
```

Program Output with Example Input Shown in Bold
```
Enter a name (last name first): Smith, Richard [Enter]
Enter another name: Jones, John [Enter]
Here are the names sorted alphabetically:
Jones, John
Smith, Richard
```

 Checkpoint [4.14]

4.21 Indicate whether the following strcmp function calls will return 0, a negative number, or a positive number. Refer to the ASCII table in Appendix A if necessary.

A) strcmp("ABC", "abc");
B) strcmp("Jill", "Jim");
C) strcmp("123", "ABC");
D) strcmp("Sammy", "Sally");

4.22 Complete the `if` statements in following program skeleton.

```cpp
#include <iostream>
#include <cstring>
using namespace std;

int main()
{
    const int SIZE = 20;
    char iceCream[SIZE];

    cout << "What flavor of ice cream do you like best? ";
    cout << "Chocolate, Vanilla, or Pralines and Pecan? ";
    cin.getline(iceCream, SIZE);
    cout << "Here is the number of fat grams for a half ";
    cout << "cup serving:\n";
    //
    // Finish the following if/else if statement
    // so the program will select the ice cream entered
    // by the user.
    //
    if (/* insert your code here */)
        cout << "Chocolate: 9 fat grams.\n";
    else if (/* insert your code here */)
        cout << "Vanilla: 10 fat grams.\n";
    else if (/* insert your code here */)
        cout << "Pralines & Pecan: 14 fat grams.\n";
    else
        cout << "That's not one of our flavors!\n";
    return 0;
}
```

4.15 The Conditional Operator

CONCEPT You can use the conditional operator to create short expressions that work like `if/else` statements.

The conditional operator is powerful and unique. It provides a shorthand method of expressing a simple `if/else` statement. The operator consists of the questionmark (?) and the colon(:). Its format is:

```
expression ? expression : expression;
```

Here is an example of a statement using the conditional operator:

```
x < 0 ? y = 10 : z = 20;
```

The statement above is called a *conditional expression* and consists of three sub-expressions separated by the ? and : symbols. The expressions are x < 0, y = 10, and z = 20, as illustrated here:

```
x < 0        ?          y = 10     :          z = 20;
```

 Note: Since it takes three operands, the conditional operator is considered a *ternary* operator.

The conditional expression above performs the same operation as the following if/else statement:

```
if (x < 0)
    y = 10;
else
    z = 20;
```

The part of the conditional expression that comes before the question mark is the expression to be tested. It's like the expression in the parentheses of an if statement. If the expression is true, the part of the statement between the ? and the : is executed. Otherwise, the part after the : is executed. Figure 4-3 illustrates the roles played by the three sub-expressions.

Figure 4-3

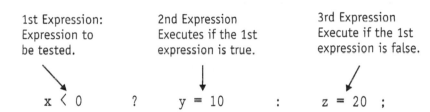

1st Expression: Expression to be tested.

2nd Expression Executes if the 1st expression is true.

3rd Expression Execute if the 1st expression is false.

x < 0   ?   y = 10   :   z = 20 ;

If it helps, you can put parentheses around the sub-expressions, as in the following:

```
(x < 0) ? (y = 10) : (z = 20);
```

Using the Value of a Conditional Expression

Remember, in C++ all expressions have a value, and this includes the conditional expression. If the first sub-expression is true, the value of the conditional expression is the value of the second sub-expression. Otherwise it is the value of the third sub-expression. Here is an example of an assignment statement using the value of a conditional expression:

```
a = x > 100 ? 0 : 1;
```

The value assigned to a will be either 0 or 1, depending upon whether x is greater than 100. This statement could be expressed as the following if/else statement:

```
if (x > 100)
    a = 0;
else
    a = 1;
```

The following program segment can be used to help a consultant calculate her charges. Her rate is $50.00 per hour, but her minimum charge is for 5 hours. The conditional operator is used in a statement that ensures the number of hours does not go below 5.

```
const double PAY_RATE = 50.0;
double hours, charges;
cout << "How many hours were worked? ";
cin >> hours;
hours = hours < 5 ? 5 : hours;   //conditional operator
charges = PAY_RATE * hours;
cout << fixed << showpoint << setprecision(2);
cout << "The charges are $" << charges << endl;
```

Program Output with Example Input Shown in Bold
How many hours were worked? **10 [Enter]**
The charges are $500.00

Program Output with Example Input Shown in Bold
How many hours were worked? **2 [Enter]**
The charges are $250.00

Here is the statement with the conditional expression:

```
hours = hours < 5 ? 5 : hours;
```

If the value in hours is less than 5, then 5 is stored in hours. Otherwise hours is assigned the value it already has. hours will not have a value less than 5 when it is used in the next statement, which calculates the consultant's charges.

As you can see, the conditional operator gives you the ability to pack decision-making power into a concise line of code. With a little imagination it can be applied to many other programming problems. For instance, consider the following statement:

```
cout << "Your grade is: " << (score < 60 ? "Fail." : "Pass.");
```

If you were to use an if/else statement, the statement above would be written as follows:

```
if (score < 60)
    cout << "Your grade is: Fail.";
else
    cout << "Your grade is: Pass.";
```

Note: The parentheses are placed around the conditional expression because the << operator has higher precedence than the ? : operator. Without the parentheses, just the value of the expression score < 60 would be sent to cout.

Checkpoint [4.15]

4.23 Rewrite the following if/else statements as conditional expressions:

A) ```
    if (hours > 40)
        wages *= 1.5;
    else
        wages *= 1;
    ```

B)  ```
    if (result >= 0)
        cout << "The result is positive\n";
    else
        cout << "The result is negative.\n";
    ```

4.24 Rewrite the following conditional expressions as if/else statements:

A) ```
    j = k > 90 ? 57 : 12;
    ```

B)  ```
    cout << (((num % 2) == 0) ? "Even\n" : "Odd\n");
    ```

4.16 The switch **Statement**

> **CONCEPT** The switch statement lets the value of a variable or expression determine where the
> program will branch.

A branch occurs when one part of a program causes another part to execute. The if/else if
statement allows your program to branch into one of several possible paths. It performs a series of
tests (usually relational) and branches when one of these tests is true. The switch statement is a
similar mechanism. It, however, tests the value of an integer expression and then uses that value
to determine which set of statements to branch to. Here is the format of the switch statement:

```
switch (integer expression)
{
    case constant-expression:    // place one or more
                                 // statements here
    case constant-expression:    // place one or more
                                 // statements here
        // case statements may be repeated as many
        // times as necessary

        case constant-expression:    // place one or more
                                     // statements here
        default:    // place one or more
                    // statements here
}
```

The first line of the statement starts with the word `switch`, followed by an integer expression inside parentheses. This can be either of the following:

♦ a variable of any of the integer data types (including `char`)

♦ an expression whose value is of any of the integer data types

On the next line is the beginning of a block containing several `case` statements. Each `case` statement is formatted in the following manner:

```
case constant-expression:    // place one or more
                             // statements here
```

After the word `case` is a constant expression (which must be of an integer type), followed by a colon. The constant expression may be an integer literal or an integer named constant. The `case` statement marks the beginning of a section of statements. These statements are branched to if the value of the `switch` expression matches that of the `case` expression.

 WARNING! The expressions of each `case` statement in the block must be unique.

 Note: The expression following the word case must be an integer literal or constant. It cannot be a variable, and it cannot be an expression such as `x < 22` or `n == 50`.

An optional `default` section comes after all the `case` statements. This section is branched to if none of the `case` expressions match the switch expression. So, it functions like a trailing `else` in an `if/else if` statement.

Program 4-19 shows how a simple `switch` statement works.

Program 4-19

```cpp
// The switch statement in this program tells the user something
// he or she already knows: what they just entered!
#include <iostream>
using namespace std;

int main()
{
    char choice;

    cout << "Enter A, B, or C: ";
    cin >> choice;
```

(program continues)

Program 4-19 *(continued)*

```cpp
switch (choice)
{
    case 'A':  cout << "You entered A.\n";
               break;
    case 'B':  cout << "You entered B.\n";
               break;
    case 'C':  cout << "You entered C.\n";
               break;
    default:   cout << "You did not enter A, B, or C!\n";
}
    return 0;
}
```

Program Output with Example Input Shown in Bold
Enter A, B, or C: **B [Enter]**
You entered B.

Program Output with Example Input Shown in Bold
Enter A, B, or C: **F [Enter]**
You did not enter A, B, or C!

The first case statement is case 'A':, the second is case 'B':, and the third is case 'C':. These statements mark where the program is to branch to if the variable choice contains the values 'A', 'B', or 'C'. (Remember, character variables and literals are considered integers.) The default section is branched to if the user enters anything other than A, B, or C.

Notice the break statements that are in the case 'A', case 'B', and case 'C' sections.

```cpp
switch (choice)
{
    case 'A':cout << "You entered A.\n";
            break;   ◄──────
    case 'B':cout << "You entered B.\n";
            break;   ◄──────
    case 'C':cout << "You entered C.\n";
            break;   ◄──────
    default:cout << "You did not enter A, B, or C!\n";
}
```

The case statements show the program where to start executing in the block and the break statements show the program where to stop. Without the break statements, the program would execute all of the lines from the matching case statement to the end of the block.

Note: The default section (or the last case section, if there is no default) does not need a break statement. Some programmers prefer to put one there anyway, for consistency.

The following program segment is a modification of Program 4-19, without the `break` statements.

```cpp
// The following switch is
// missing its break statements!
switch (choice)
{
    case 'A':  cout << "You entered A.\n";
    case 'B':  cout << "You entered B.\n";
    case 'C':  cout << "You entered C.\n";
    default:   cout << "You did not enter A, B, or C!\n";
}
```

Program Output with Example Input Shown in Bold
```
Enter A, B, or C: A [Enter]
You entered A.
You entered B.
You entered C.
You did not enter A, B, or C!
```

Program Output with Example Input Shown in Bold
```
Enter a A, B, or C: C [Enter]
You entered C.
You did not enter A, B, or C!
```

Without the `break` statement, the program "falls through" all of the statements below the one with the matching `case` expression. Sometimes this is what you want. Program 4-20 lists the features of three TV models a customer may choose from. The model 100 has remote control. The model 200 has remote control and stereo sound. The model 300 has remote control, stereo sound, and picture-in-a-picture capability. The program uses a `switch` statement with carefully omitted `break`s to print the features of the selected model.

Program 4-20

```cpp
// This program is carefully constructed to use the "fall through"
// feature of the switch statement.
#include <iostream>
using namespace std;

int main()
{

    int modelNum;

    cout << "Our TVs come in three models:\n";
    cout << "The 100, 200, and 300. Which do you want? ";
    cin >> modelNum;
    cout << "That model has the following features:\n";
```

(program continues)

Program 4-20 *(continued)*

```
    switch (modelNum)
    {
        case 300:cout << "\tPicture-in-a-picture.\n";
        case 200:cout << "\tStereo sound.\n";
        case 100:cout << "\tRemote control.\n";
                 break;
        default:cout << "You can only choose the 100,";
                cout << "200, or 300.\n";
    }
    return 0;
}
```

Program Output with Example Input Shown in Bold
```
    Our TVs come in three models:
    The 100, 200, and 300. Which do you want? 100 [Enter]
    That model has the following features:
        Remote control.
```

Program Output with Example Input Shown in Bold
```
    Our TVs come in three models:
    The 100, 200, and 300. Which do you want? 200 [Enter]
    That model has the following features:
        Stereo sound.
        Remote control.
```

Program Output with Example Input Shown in Bold
```
    Our TVs come in three models:
    The 100, 200, and 300. Which do you want? 300 [Enter]
    That model has the following features:
        Picture-in-a-picture.
        Stereo sound.
        Remote control.
```

Program Output with Example Input Shown in Bold
```
    Our TVs come in three models:
    The 100, 200, and 300. Which do you want? 500 [Enter]
    That model has the following features:
    You can only choose the 100,200, or 300.
```

Another example of how useful this "fall through" capability can be is when you want the program to branch to the same set of statements for multiple case expressions. For instance, Program 4-21 asks the user to select a grade of dog food. The available choices are A, B, and C. The switch statement will recognize either upper or lowercase letters.

Program 4-21

```cpp
// The switch statement in this program uses the "fall through"
// feature to catch both uppercase and lowercase letters entered
// by the user.
#include <iostream>
using namespace std;

int main()
{
    char feedGrade;

    cout << "Our dog food is available in three grades:\n";
    cout << "A, B, and C. Which do you want pricing for? ";
    cin >> feedGrade;
    switch(feedGrade)
    {
        case 'a':
        case 'A':  cout << "30 cents per pound.\n";
                   break;
        case 'b':
        case 'B':  cout << "20 cents per pound.\n";
                   break;
        case 'c':
        case 'C':  cout << "15 cents per pound.\n";
                   break;
        default:   cout << "That is an invalid choice.\n";
    }
    return 0;
}
```

Program Output with Example Input Shown in Bold
```
Our dog food is available in three grades:
A, B, and C. Which do you want pricing for? b [Enter]
20 cents per pound.
```

Program Output with Example Input Shown in Bold
```
Our dog food is available in three grades:
A, B, and C. Which do you want pricing for? B [Enter]
20 cents per pound.
```

When the user enters 'a' the corresponding case has no statements associated with it, so the program falls through to the next case, which corresponds with 'A'.

```cpp
        case 'a':
        case 'A':  cout << "30 cents per pound.\n";
                   break;
```

The same is technique is used for 'b' and 'c'.

Using switch in Menu Systems

The switch statement is a natural mechanism for building menu systems. Recall that Program 4-14 gives a menu to select which health club package the user wishes to purchase. The program uses if/else if statements to determine which package the user has selected and displays the calculated charges. Program 4-22 is a modification of that program, using a switch statement instead of if/else if.

Program 4-22

```cpp
// This program displays a menu and asks the user to make a
// selection. A switch statement determines which item
// the user has chosen.
#include <iostream>
#include <iomanip>
using namespace std;

int main()
{
    int choice. months;
    double charges;

    cout << "\t\tHealth Club Membership Menu\n\n";
    cout << "1. Standard Adult Membership\n";
    cout << "2. Child Membership\n";
    cout << "3. Senior Citizen Membership\n";
    cout << "4. Quit the Program\n\n";
    cout << "Enter your choice: ";
    cin >> choice;
    if (choice >= 1 && choice <= 3)
    {
        cout << "For how many months? ";
        cin >> months;
        cout << fixed << showpoint << setprecision(2);
        switch (choice)
        {
            case 1:charges = months * 40.0;
                    break;
            case 2:charges = months * 20.0;
                    break;
            case 3:charges = months * 30.0;
        }
        // Display the monthly charges.
        cout << "The total charges are $";
        cout << charges << endl;
    }
```

(program continues)

Program 4-22   *(continued)*

```
    else if (choice != 4)
    {
        cout << "The valid choices are 1 through 4. Run the\n";
        cout << "program again and select one of those.\n";
    }
    return 0;
}
```

Program Output with Example Input Shown in Bold
```
        Health Club Membership Menu

1. Standard Adult Membership
2. Child Membership
3. Senior Citizen Membership
4. Quit the Program

Enter your choice: 2 [Enter]
For how many months? 6 [Enter]
The total charges are $120.00
```

 Checkpoint   [4.16]

4.25   Explain why you cannot convert the following if/else if statement into a switch statement.

```
if (temp == 100)
    x = 0;
else if (population > 1000)
    x = 1;
else if  (rate < .1)
    x = -1;
```

4.26   What is wrong with the following switch statement?

```
switch (temp)
{
    case temp < 0 :    cout << "Temp is negative.\n";
                       break;
    case temp == 0:    cout << "Temp is zero.\n";
                       break;
    case temp > 0 :    cout << "Temp is positive.\n";
                       break;
}
```

Testing for File Open Errors ■ 205

4.27 What will the following program segment display?

```
int funny = 7, serious = 15;

funny = serious * 2;
switch (funny)
{   case 0 :   cout << "That is funny.\n";
               break;
    case 30:   cout << "That is serious.\n";
               break;
    case 32:   cout << "That is seriously funny.\n";
               break;
    default:   cout << funny << endl;
}
```

4.28 Write a complete program using the provided program segment by writing a switch state-ment that displays "one" if the user has entered 1, "two" if the user has entered 2, and "three" if the user has entered 3. If a number other than 1, 2, or 3 is entered, the program should display an error message.

```
int userNum;
cout << "Enter one of the numbers 1, 2, or 3: ";
cin >> userNum;
//
// Write the switch statement here.
```

4.17   Testing for File Open Errors

CONCEPT When opening a file you can test the file stream object to determine if an error occurred.

In Chapter 3 you were introduced to file operations and saw that the file stream member function open is used to open a file. Sometimes the open member function will not work. For example, the following code will fail if the file info.txt does not exist:

```
ifstream inputFile;
inputFile.open("info.txt");
```

You can determine when the open function has failed by testing the value of the file stream object with the ! operator. The following program segment attempts to open the file customers.txt. If the file cannot be opened, an error message is displayed:

```
ifstream inputFile;
inputFile.open("customers.txt");
if (!inputFile)
{
    cout << "Error opening file.\n";
}
```

Another way to detect a failed attempt to open a file is with the `fail` member function, as shown in the following code:

```
ifstream inputFile;
inputFile.open("customers.txt");
if (inputFile.fail())
{
    cout << "Error opening file.\n";
}
```

The `fail` member function returns true when an attempted file operation is unsuccessful. When using file I/O, you should always test the file stream object to make sure the file was opened successfully. If the file could not be opened, the user should be informed and appropriate action taken by the program. For instance, the following program segment attempts to open the file customer.txt for output. In the event the file cannot be opened, the user is informed and given some clue as to why.

```
ofstream outputFile;
outputFile.open("customer.txt");
if (outputFile.fail())
{
    cout << "The customer.txt file could not be opened.\n";
    cout << "Perhaps the disk is full or you do not have\n";
    cout << "sufficient privileges. Contact your system\n";
    cout << "manager for assistance.\n";
}
```

 See the CaseStudies.pdf file on the accompanying CD for this chapter's case studies.

Review Questions and Exercises

Short Answer

1. Describe the difference between the `if`/`else if` statement and a series of `if` statements.
2. In an `if`/`else if` statement, what is the purpose of a trailing `else`?
3. What is a flag and how does it work?
4. Can an `if` statement test expressions other than relational expressions? Explain.

5. Briefly describe how the && operator works.

6. Briefly describe how the ‖ operator works.

7. Why are the relational operators called relational?

8. Why do most programmers indent the conditionally executed statements in a decision structure?

Algorithm Workbench

9. Write an if statement that assigns 100 to x when y is equal to 0.

10. Write an if/else statement that assigns 0 to x when y is equal to 10. Otherwise it should assign 1 to x.

11. Using the following chart, write an if/else if statement that assigns .10, .15, or .20 to commission, depending on the value in sales.

Sales	Commission Rate
Up to $10,000	10%
$10,000 to $15,000	15%
Over $15,000	20%

12. Write an if statement that sets the variable hours to 10 when the flag variable minimum is set.

13. Write nested if statements that perform the following tests: If amount1 is greater than 10 and amount2 is less than 100, display the greater of the two.

14. Write an if statement that prints the message "The number is valid" if the variable grade is within the range 0 through 100.

15. Write an if statement that prints the message "The number is valid" if the variable temperature is within the range −50 through 150.

16. Write an if statement that prints the message "The number is not valid" if the variable hours is outside the range 0 through 80.

17. Write an if/else statement that displays the strings in the arrays title1 and title2 in alphabetical order.

18. Convert the following if/else if statement into a switch statement:

```
if (choice == 1)
{
     cout << fixed << showpoint << setprecision(2);
}
else if (choice == 2 ‖ choice == 3)
{
     cout << fixed << showpoint << setprecision(4);
}
```

```
else if (choice == 4)
{
      cout << fixed << showpoint << setprecision(6);
}
else
{
      cout << fixed << showpoint << setprecision(8);
}
```

19. Match the conditional expression with the if/else statement that performs the same operation.

    A) `q = x < y ? a + b : x * 2;`

    B) `q = x < y ? x * 2 : a + b;`

    C) `x < y ? q = 0 : q = 1;`

    ```
    _____ if (x < y)
              q = 0;
          else
              q = 1;
    _____ if (x < y)
              q = a + b;
          else
              q = x * 2;
    _____ if (x < y)
              q = x * 2;
          else
              q = a + b;
    ```

True or False

20. T F The = operator and the == operator perform the same operation.

21. T F A variable defined in an inner block may not have the same name as a variable defined in the outer block.

22. T F A conditionally executed statement should be indented one level from the if statement.

23. T F All lines in a block should be indented one level.

24. T F It's safe to assume that all uninitialized variables automatically start with 0 as their value.

25. T F When an if statement is nested in the if part of another statement, the only time the inner if is executed is when the expression of the outer if is true.

26. T F When an if statement is nested in the else part of another statement, as in an if/else if, the only time the inner if is executed is when the expression of the outer if is true.

27. T F The scope of a variable is limited to the block in which it is defined.

28. T F Strings may be directly compared with the == operator.

29. T F x != y is the same as (x > y || x < y)

30. T F y < x is the same as x >= y

31. T F x >= y is the same as (x > y && x = y)

Assume the variables x = 5, y = 6, and z = 8. Indicate by circling the T or F if each of the following conditions is true or false:

32. T F x == 5 || y > 3

33. T F 7 <= x && z > 4

34. T F 2 != y && z != 4

35. T F x >= 0 || x <= y

Find the Errors

Each of the following programs has errors. Find as many as you can.

36.
```cpp
// This program divides a user-supplied number by another
// user-supplied number. It checks for division by zero.
#include <iostream>
using namespace std;

int main()
{
    double num1, num2, quotient;

    cout << "Enter a number: ";
    cin >> num1;
    cout << "Enter another number: ";
    cin >> num2;
    if (num2 == 0)
        cout << "Division by zero is not possible.\n";
        cout << "Please run the program again ";
        cout << "and enter a number besides zero.\n";
    else
        quotient = num1 / num2;
        cout << "The quotient of " << num1 <<
        cout << " divided by " << num2 << " is ";
        cout << quotient << endl;
    return 0;
}
```

37.
```cpp
// This program uses a switch-case statement to assign a
// letter grade (A, B, C, D, or F) to a numeric test score.
#include <iostream>
using namespace std;
```

```
int main()
{
    double testScore;
    cout << "Enter your test score and I will tell you\n";
    cout << "the letter grade you earned: ";
    cin >> testScore;
    switch (testScore)
    {
        case (testScore < 60.0):
                cout << "Your grade is F.\n";
                break;
        case (testScore < 70.0):
                cout << "Your grade is D.\n";
                break;
        case (testScore < 80.0):
                cout << "Your grade is C.\n";
                break;
        case (testScore < 90.0):
                cout << "Your grade is B.\n";
                break;
        case (testScore <= 100.0):
                cout << "Your grade is A.\n";
                break;
        default:
                cout << "That score isn't valid\n"; }
    return 0;
}
```

38. The following statement should determine if **x** is not greater than 20. What is wrong with it?

    ```
    if (!x > 20)
    ```

39. The following statement should determine if count is within the range of 0 through 100. What is wrong with it?

    ```
    if (count >= 0 || count <= 100)
    ```

40. The following statement should determine if count is outside the range of 0 through 100. What is wrong with it?

    ```
    if (count < 0 && count > 100)
    ```

41. The following statement should assign 0 to z if a is less than 10, otherwise it should assign 7 to z. What is wrong with it?

    ```
    z = (a < 10) : 0 ? 7;
    ```

Programming Challenges

1. Minimum/Maximum

Write a program that asks the user to enter two numbers. The program should use the conditional operator to determine which number is the smaller and which is the larger.

2. Roman Numeral Converter

Write a program that asks the user to enter a number within the range of 1 through 10. Use a switch statement to display the Roman numeral version of that number.

> *Input Validation: Do not accept a number less than 1 or greater than 10.*

3. State Abbreviations

Write a program that asks the user to enter one of the following state abbreviations: NC, SC, GA, FL, or AL. The program should then display the name of the state that corresponds with the abbreviation entered (North Carolina, South Carolina, Georgia, Florida, or Alabama.)

> *Input Validation: Accept abbreviations with both letters in uppercase or both in lowercase. Display an error message if an abbreviation other than what is listed is entered.*

4. Math Tutor

This is a modification of problem 11 from Chapter 3. Write a program that can be used as a math tutor for a young student. The program should display two random numbers that are to be added, such as:

```
  247
+ 129
-----
```

The program should wait for the student to enter the answer. If the answer is correct, a message of congratulations should be printed. If the answer is incorrect, a message should be printed showing the correct answer.

5. Software Sales

A software company sells a package that retails for $99. Quantity discounts are given according to the following table.

Quantity	Discount
10–19	20%
20–49	30%
50–99	40%
100 or more	50%

Write a program that asks for the number of units sold and computes the total cost of the purchase.

Input Validation: Make sure the number of units is greater than 0.

6. Bank Charges

A bank charges $10 per month plus the following check fees for a commercial checking account:

$.10 each for less than 20 checks
$.08 each for 20–39 checks
$.06 each for 40–59 checks
$.04 each for 60 or more checks

The bank also charges an extra $15 if the balance of the account falls below $400 (before any check fees are applied). Write a program that asks for the beginning balance and the number of checks written. Compute and display the bank's service fees for the month.

Input Validation: Do not accept a negative value for the number of checks written. If a negative value is given for the beginning balance, display an urgent message indicating the account is overdrawn.

7. Shipping Charges

The Fast Freight Shipping Company charges the following rates:

Write a program that asks for the weight of the package and the distance it is to be shipped, and then displays the charges.

Weight of Package (in kilograms)	Rate Per 500 Miles Shipped
2 Kg or less	$1.10
Over 2 Kg but not more than 6 Kg	$2.20
Over 6 Kg but not more than 10 Kg	$3.70
Over 10 Kg but not more than 20 Kg	$4.80

Input Validation: Do not accept values of 0 or less for the weight of the package. Do not accept weights of more than 20 Kg (this is the maximum weight the company will ship). Do not accept distances of less than 10 miles or more than 3,000 miles. These are the company's minimum and maximum shipping distances.

8. Fat Gram Calculator

Write a program that asks for the number of calories and fat grams in a food. The program should display the percentage of calories that come from fat. If the calories from fat are less than 30% of the total calories of the food, it should also display a message indicating the food is low in fat.

One gram of fat has 9 calories, so:

```
Calories from fat = fat grams * 9
```

The percentage of calories from fat can be calculated as

```
Calories from fat ÷ total calories
```

Input Validation: Make sure the number of calories and fat grams are not less than 0. Also, the number of calories from fat cannot be greater than the total number of calories. If that happens display an error message indicating that either the calories or fat grams were Incorrectly entered.

9. Running the Race

Write a program that asks for the names of three runners and the time it took each of them to finish a race. The program should display who came in first, second, and third place.

Input Validation: Be sure the names do not overflow the arrays. Only accept positive numbers for the times.

10. Spectral Analysis

If a scientist knows the wavelength of an electromagnetic wave she can determine what type of radiation it is. Write a program that asks for the wavelength of an electromagnetic wave and then displays what that wave is according to the chart below. (For example, a wave with a wavelength of 1E-10 would be an X-ray.)

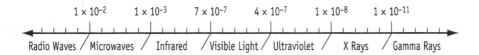

11. Geometry Calculator

Write a program that displays the following menu:

```
Geometry Calculator

    1. Calculate the Area of a Circle
    2. Calculate the Area of a Rectangle
    3. Calculate the Area of a Triangle
    4. Quit

Enter your choice (1-4):
```

If the user enters 1, the program should ask for the radius of the circle and then display its area. Use the following formula:

$$Area = \pi r^2$$

Use 3.14159 for π and the radius of the circle for r. If the user enters 2, the program should ask for the length and width of the rectangle and then display the rectangle's area. Use the following formula:

```
area = length * width
```

If the user enters 3 the program should ask for the length of the triangle's base and its height, and then display its area. Use the following formula:

```
area = base * height * .5
```

If the user enters 4, the program should end.

Input Validation: Display an error message if the user enters a number outside the range of 1 through 4 when selecting an item from the menu. Do not accept negative values for the circle's radius, the rectangles length or width, or the triangle's base or height.

12. The Speed of Sound

The following table shows the approximate speed of sound in air, water, and steel.

Medium	Speed
Air	1100 feet per second
Water	4900 feet per second
Steel	16,400 feet per second

Write a program that displays a menu allowing the user to select air, water, or steel. After the user has made a selection, he or she should be asked to enter the distance a sound wave will travel in the selected medium. The program will then display the amount of time it will take. (Round the answer to 4 decimal places.)

Input Validation: Check that the user has selected one of the available choices from the menu. Do not accept distances less than 0.

13. Freezing and Boiling Points

The following table lists the freezing and boiling points of several substances. Write a program that asks the user to enter a temperature, and then shows all the substances that will freeze at that temperature and all that will boil at that temperature. For example, if the user enters –20 the program should report that water will freeze and oxygen will boil at that temperature.

Substance	Freezing Point (°F)	Boiling Point (°F)
Ethyl alcohol	–173	172
Mercury	–38	676
Oxygen	–362	–306
Water	32	212

14. Long-Distance Calls

A long-distance carrier charges the following rates for telephone calls:

Starting Time of Call	Rate Per Minute
00:00–06:59	0.12
07:00–19:00	0.55
19:01–23:59	0.35

Write a program that asks for the starting time and the number of minutes of call, and displays the charges. The program should ask for the time to be entered as a floating point number in the form HH.MM. For example, 07:00 hours will be entered as 07.00, and 16:28 hours will be entered as 16.28.

Input Validation: The program should not accept times that are greater than 23:59. Also, no number whose last two digits are greater than 59 should be accepted. Hint: Assuming num is a floating-point variable, the following expression will give you its fractional part:

```
num - static_cast<int>(num)
```

15. Internet Service Provider

An Internet service provider has three different subscription packages for its customers:

Package A: For $9.95 per month 10 hours of access are provided. Additional hours are $2.00 per hour.

Package B: For $14.95 per month 20 hours of access are provided. Additional hours are $1.00 per hour.

Package C: For $19.95 per month unlimited access is provided.

Write a program that calculates a customer's monthly bill. It should ask which package the customer has purchased and how many hours were used. It should then display the total amount due.

Input Validation: Be sure the user only selects package A, B, or C. Also, the number of hours used in a month cannot exceed 744.

16. Internet Service Provider, Part 2

Modify the program in problem 15 so it also displays how much money Package A customers would save if they purchased packages B or C, and how much money package B customers would save if they purchased package C. If there would be no savings, no message should be printed.

17. Internet Service Provider, Part 3

Months with 30 days have 720 hours, and months with 31 days have 744 hours. February, with 28 days, has 672 hours. Enhance the input validation of the Internet Service Provider program by asking the user for the month (by name), and validating that the number of hours entered is not more than the maximum for the entire month. Here is a table of the months, their days, and number of hours in each.

Month	Days	Hours
January	31	744
February	28	672
March	31	744
April	30	720
May	31	744
June	30	720
July	31	744
August	31	744
September	30	720
October	31	744
November	30	720
December	31	744

18. File Input (Freezing and Boiling Points Modification)

Modify the program that you wrote for Programming Challenge 13 (Freezing and Boiling Points) so it reads its input from a file instead of the keyboard. Perform the necessary test to determine if an error occurs when the file is opened. If an error occurs, display a message informing the user.

5

Looping

■ Topics in this Chapter

5.1 The Increment and Decrement Operators

CONCEPT ++ and - - are operators that add and subtract 1 from their operands.

To *increment* a value means to increase it by one, and to *decrement* a value means to decrease it by one. Both of the following statements increment the variable num:

```
num = num + 1;
num += 1;
```

And num is decremented in both of the following statements:

```
num = num - 1;
num -= 1;
```

■ **219**

C++ provides a set of simple unary operators designed just for incrementing and decrementing variables. The increment operator is ++ and the decrement operator is --. The following statement uses the ++ operator to increment num:

```
num++;
```

And the following statement decrements num:

```
num--;
```

 Note: The expression num++ is pronounced "num plus plus," and num-- is pronounced "num minus minus."

Our examples so far show the increment and decrement operators used in *postfix mode*, which means the operator is placed after the variable. The operators also work in *prefix mode*, where the operator is placed before the variable name:

```
++num;
--num;
```

In both postfix and prefix mode, these operators add 1 to or subtract 1 from their operand. Program 5-1 shows how they work.

Program 5-1

```cpp
// This program demonstrates the increment and decrement operators.
#include <iostream>
using namespace std;

int main()
{
    int bigVal = 10, smallVal = 1;

    cout << "bigVal is " << bigVal
         << " and smallVal is " << smallVal << endl;
    smallVal++;
    bigVal--;
    cout << "bigVal is " << bigVal
         << " and smallVal is " << smallVal << endl;
    ++smallVal;
    --bigVal;
    cout << "bigVal is " << bigVal
         << " and smallVal is " << smallVal << endl;
    return 0;
}
```

Program Output
```
bigVal is 10 and smallVal is 1
bigVal is 9 and smallVal is 2
bigVal is 8 and smallVal is 3
```

The Difference Between Postfix and Prefix Modes

In the simple statements used in Program 5-1, it doesn't matter if the operator is used in postfix or prefix mode. The difference is important, however, when these operators are used in statements that do more than just incrementing or decrementing. For example, look at the following lines:

```
num = 4;
cout << num++;
```

This cout statement is doing two things: (1) displaying the value of num, and (2) incrementing num. But which happens first? cout will display a different value if num is incremented first than if num is incremented last. The answer depends on the mode of the increment operator.

Postfix mode causes the increment to happen after the value of the variable is used in the expression. In the example, cout will display 4, then num will be incremented to 5. Prefix mode, however, causes the increment to happen first. In the following statements, num will be incremented to 5, then cout will display 5:

```
num = 4;
cout << ++num;
```

The following program segment illustrates these dynamics further:

```
int bigVal = 10, smallVal = 1;
cout << "bigVal starts as " << bigVal;
cout << " and smallVal starts as " << smallVal << endl;
cout << "bigVal--: " << bigVal-- << endl;
cout << "smallVal++: " << smallVal++ << endl;
cout << "Now bigVal is: " << bigVal << endl;
cout << "Now smallVal is: " << smallVal << endl;
cout << "--bigVal: " << --bigVal << endl;
cout << "++smallVal: " << ++smallVal << endl;
```

Program Output
```
bigVal starts as 10 and smallVal starts as 1
bigVal--: 10
smallVal++: 1
Now bigVal is: 9
Now smallVal is: 2
--bigVal: 8
++smallVal: 3
```

Let's analyze the statements in this program segment. bigVal starts with the value 10. The following statement displays the value in bigVal and then decrements bigVal. The decrement happens last because it is used in postfix mode:

```
cout << "bigVal--: " << bigVal-- << endl;
```

Although this statement displays 10 as the value in `bigVal`, it will be 9 after the statement executes.

`smallVal` starts with the value 1. The following statement displays the number in `smallVal`, then uses the increment operator to add one to it. Because the increment operator is used in post-fix mode, it works after the value is displayed:

```
cout << "smallVal++: " << smallVal++ << endl;
```

This statement displays 1 as the value in `smallVal`, then increments `smallVal`, making it 2.

The last two statements in Program 5-2 use the increment and decrement operators in prefix mode. This means they work on their operands before the values are displayed on the screen.

```
cout << "--bigVal: " << --bigVal << endl;
cout << "++smallVal: " << ++smallVal << endl;
```

In these two statements, `bigVal` is decremented (making it 8) before its value is displayed on the screen. `smallVal` is incremented (making it 3), before its value is displayed.

Using ++ and -- in Mathematical Expressions

The increment and decrement operators can also be used on variables in mathematical expressions. Consider the following program segment:

```
a = 2;
b = 5;
c = a * b++;
cout << a << " " << b << " " << c;
```

In the statement `c = a * b++`, c is assigned the value of a times b, which is 10. The variable b is then incremented. The `cout` statement will display

```
2 6 10
```

If the statement were changed to read

```
c = a * ++b;
```

The variable b would be incremented before it was multiplied by a. In this case c would be assigned the value of 2 times 6, so the `cout` statement would display

```
2 6 12
```

You can pack a lot of action into a single statement using the increment and decrement operators, but don't get too tricky with them. You might be tempted to try something like the following, thinking that c will be assigned 11:

```
a = 2;
b = 5;
c = ++(a * b);        // Error!
```

But this assignment statement simply will not work because the operand of the increment and decrement operators must be an lvalue. Recall from Chapter 2 that an lvalue identifies a place in memory whose contents may be changed. The increment and decrement operators usually have variables for their operands, but generally speaking, anything that can go on the left side of an = operator is legal.

Using ++ and -- in Relational Expressions

As you'll see later in this chapter, the ++ and -- operators are sometimes used in relational expressions. Just as in mathematical expressions, the difference between postfix and prefix mode is critical. Consider the following program segment:

```
x = 10;
if (x++ > 10)
    cout << "x is greater than 10.\n";
```

Two operations are happening in this if statement: (1) The value in x is tested to determine if it is greater than 10, and (2) x is incremented. Because the increment operator is used in postfix mode, the comparison happens first. Since 10 is not greater than 10, the cout statement won't execute. If the mode of the increment operator is changed, however, the if statement will compare 11 to 10 and the cout statement will execute:

```
x = 10;
if (++x > 10)
    cout << "x is greater than 10.\n";
```

Checkpoint [5.1]

5.1   What will the following program segments display?

A)
```
x = 2;
y = 4;
cout << x++ << --y;
```
B)
```
x = 2;
y = 2 * x++;
cout << x << y;
```
C)
```
x = 99;
if (x++ < 100)
    cout "It is true!\n";
else
    cout << "It is false!\n";
```
D)
```
x = 0;
if (++x)
    cout << "It is true!\n";
else
    cout << "It is false!\n";
```

5.2 Introduction to Loops: The `while` Loop

CONCEPT A loop is part of a program that repeats.

Chapter 4 introduced the concept of control structures, which direct the flow of a program. A *loop* is a control structure that causes a statement or group of statements to repeat. C++ has three looping control structures: the `while` loop, the `do-while` loop, and the `for` loop. The difference between each of these is how they control the repetition.

The `while` Loop

The `while` loop has two important parts: (1) an expression that is tested for a true or false value, and (2) a statement or block that is repeated as long as the expression is true. Here is the general format of the while loop:

```
while (expression)
    statement;
```

Notice there is no semicolon after the expression in parentheses. Like the `if` statement, the `while` loop is not complete without the statement that follows it.

If you wish the `while` loop to repeat a block of statements, its format is

```
while (expression)
{
    statement;
    statement;
    // Place as many statements here
    // as necessary.
}
```

The expression inside parentheses is tested and if it has a true value, the next statement or block is executed. (The statement or block that is repeated is known as the *body* of the loop.) This cycle is repeated until the expression in parentheses is false.

The `while` loop works like an `if` statement that executes over and over. As long as the expression in the parentheses is true, the conditionally-executed statement or block will repeat. Program 5-2 shows a `cin` statement inside a loop.

Program 5-2

```
// This program demonstrates a simple while loop.
#include <iostream>
using namespace std;
```

(program continues)

Program 5-2   *(continued)*

```cpp
int main()
{
    int number = 0;

    cout << "This program will let you enter number after\n";
    cout << "number. Enter 99 when you want to quit the ";
    cout << "program.\n";
    while (number != 99)
        cin >> number;
    cout << "Done.\n";
    return 0;
}
```

Program Output with Example Input Shown in Bold
```
This program will let you enter number after
number. Enter 99 when you want to quit the program.
 1 [Enter]
 2 [Enter]
30 [Enter]
75 [Enter]
99 [Enter]
Done.
```

This program repeatedly reads values from the keyboard until the user enters 99. The loop controls this action by testing the variable number. As long as number does not equal 99, the loop repeats. The cin statement, inside the loop, puts the user's input into number, where, at the beginning of the next cycle, it will be tested again. (Figure 5-1 illustrates the role of the test expression and the body of the loop.) Each repetition is known as an *iteration*.

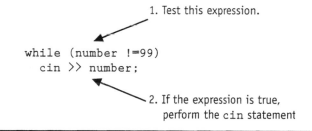

Figure 5-1

 Note: Many programmers choose to enclose the body of a loop in braces, even if it only has one statement:

```cpp
while (number != 99)
{
    cin >> number;
}
```

This is a good programming practice since the braces visually offset the body of the loop. The braces are not required for only one statement, however, so the choice of using them in this manner is yours.

while Is a Pretest Loop

The while loop is known as a *pretest* loop, which means it tests its expression before each iteration. Notice the variable definition of number in Program 5-2:

```
int number = 0;
```

number is initialized to 0. If number had been initialized to 99, as shown in the following program segment, the loop would never execute the cin statement:

```
int number = 99;
while (number != 99)
    cin >> number;
```

An important characteristic of the while loop is that the loop will never iterate if the test expression is false to start with. If you want to be sure a while loop executes the first time, you must initialize the relevant data in such a way that the test expression starts out as true.

Terminating a Loop

In all but rare cases, loops must contain within themselves a way to terminate. This means that something inside the loop must eventually make the test expression false. The loop in Program 5-2 stops when the user enters 99 at the keyboard, which is subsequently stored in the variable number by the cin object.

If a loop does not have a way of stopping, it is called an *infinite loop*. Infinite loops keep repeating until the program is interrupted. Here is an example:

```
int test = 0;
while (test < 10)
    cout << "Hello\n";
```

This loop will execute forever because it does not contain a statement that changes test. Each time the test expression is evaluated, test will still be equal to 0. Here is another version of the loop. This one will stop after it has executed 10 times:

```
int test = 0;
while (test < 10)
{
    cout << "Hello\n";
    test++;
}
```

This loop increments test after each time it prints "Hello\n". When test reaches 10, the expression test < 10 is no longer true, so the loop will stop.

It's also possible to create an infinite loop by accidentally placing a semicolon after the test expression. Here is an example:

```cpp
int test = 0;
while (test < 10);   // Error: Notice the semicolon here.
{
    cout << "Hello\n";
    test++;
}
```

The semicolon after the test expression is assumed to be a null statement and disconnects the `while` statement from the block that comes after it. To the compiler, the loop looks like this:

```cpp
while (test < 10);
```

This `while` loop will forever execute the null statement, which does nothing. The program will appear to have "hung," or "gone into space" because there is nothing to display screen output or show activity.

Another common pitfall with loops is accidentally using the `=` operator when you intend to use the `==` operator. The following is an infinite loop because the test expression assigns 1 to `remainder` each time it is evaluated instead of testing whether `remainder` is equal to 1.

```cpp
while (remainder = 1)   // Error: Notice the assignment
{
    cout << "Enter a number: ";
    cin >> num;
    remainder = num % 2;
}
```

Remember, any nonzero value is evaluated as true.

Programming Style and the `while` Loop

It's possible to create loops that look like this:

```cpp
while (number != 99) cin >> number;
```

as well as this:

```cpp
while (test < 10) { cout << "Hello\n"; test++; }
```

Avoid this style of programming, however. The programming style you should use with the `while` loop is similar to that of the `if` statement:

♦ If there is only one statement repeated by the loop, it should appear on the line after the `while` statement and be indented one additional level.

♦ If the loop repeats a block, the block should begin on the line after the `while` statement and each line inside the braces should be indented.

In general, you'll find a similar style being used with the other types of loops presented in this chapter.

5.3   Counters

CONCEPT A counter is a variable that is regularly incremented or decremented each time a loop iterates.

Sometimes it's important for a program to control or keep track of the number of iterations a loop performs. For example, Program 5-3 displays a table consisting of the numbers 1 through 10 and their squares, so its loop must iterate 10 times.

Program 5-3

```cpp
// This program displays the numbers 1 through 10 and
// their squares.
#include <iostream>
using namespace std;

int main()
{
    int num = 1;   //Initialize counter.

    cout << "Number     Number Squared\n";
    cout << "------------------------\n";
    while (num <= 10)
    {
        cout << num << "\t\t" << (num * num) << endl;
        num++;   //Increment counter.
    }
    return 0;
}
```

Program Output

```
Number     Number Squared
------------------------
1               1
2               4
3               9
4               16
5               25
6               36
7               49
8               64
9               81
10              100
```

In Program 5-3, the variable num, which starts at 1, is incremented each time through the loop. When num reaches 11 the loop stops. num is used as a *counter* variable, which means it is regularly incremented in each iteration of the loop. In essence, num keeps count of the number of iterations the loop has performed.

Note: It's important that num be properly initialized. Remember, variables defined inside a function have no guaranteed starting value.

In Program 5-3, num is incremented in the last statement of the loop. Another approach is to combine the increment operation with the relational test, as shown in the follwoing program segment. The output is the same as Program 5-3.

```cpp
int num = 0;
cout << "Number     Number Squared\n";
cout << "-------------------------\n";
while (num++ < 10)
    cout << num << "\t\t" << (num * num) << endl;
```

Notice that num is now initialized to 0, rather than 1, and the relational expression uses the < operator instead of <=. This is because of the way the increment operator works when combined with the relational expression.

The increment operator is used in postfix mode, which means it adds one to num after the relational test. When the loop first executes, num is set to 0, so 0 is compared to 10. The ++ operator then increments num immediately after the comparison. When the cout statement executes, num has the value 1.

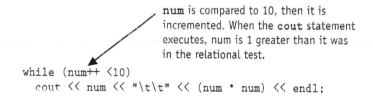

Figure 5-2

Inside the loop, num always has a value of 1 greater than the value previously compared to 10. That's why the relational operator is < instead of <=. When num is 9 in the relational test, it will be 10 in the cout statement.

5.4   Letting the User Control the Loop

CONCEPT	We can let the user indicate the number of times a loop should iterate.

Sometimes the user has to decide how many times a loop should iterate. Program 5-4 averages a series of three test scores for any number of students. The program asks the user how many students he or she wishes to enter scores for. This number is stored in numStudents. The while statement increments a counter variable up to this number, causing the loop to iterate once for each student.

Program 5-4

```cpp
// This program averages a set of test scores for multiple
// students. It lets the user decide how many.
#include <iostream>
#include <iomanip>
using namespace std;

int main()
{
    int numStudents, count;

    cout << "This program will give you the average of three\n";
    cout << "test scores per student.\n";
    cout << "How many students do you have test scores for? ";
    cin >> numStudents;
    cout << "Enter the scores for each of the students.\n";
    cout << fixed << showpoint << setprecision(2);

    count = 1;     // Initialize the counter variable.
    while (count <= numStudents)
    {
        int score1, score2, score3;
        float average;
        cout << "\nStudent " << count << ": ";
        cin >> score1 >> score2 >> score3;
        average = (score1 + score2 + score3) / 3.0;
        cout << "The average is " << average << ".\n";
        count++;   // Increment the counter variable.
    }
    return 0;
}
```

Program 5-4   *(continued)*

Program Output with Example Input Shown in Bold
```
This program will give you the average of three
test scores per student.
How many students do you have test scores for? 3 [Enter]
Enter the scores for each of the students.

Student 1: 75 80 82 [Enter]
The average is 79.00.

Student 2: 85 85 90 [Enter]
The average is 86.67.

Student 3: 60 75 88 [Enter]
The average is 74.33.
```

5.5   Keeping a Running Total

CONCEPT   A *running total* is a sum of numbers that accumulates with each iteration of a loop. The variable used to keep the running total is called an *accumulator*.

Some programming tasks require a running total to be kept. Program 5-5, for example, calculates a company's total sales over a period of time by taking daily sales figures as input and keeping a running total of them as they are gathered.

Program 5-5

```cpp
// This program takes daily sales figures over a period of time
// and calculates their total.
#include <iostream>
#include <iomanip>
using namespace std;

int main()
{
    int days, count = 1;    // Initialize the counter.
    double total = 0.0;     // Initialize the accumulator.

    cout << "For how many days do you have sales figures? ";
    cin >> days;
```

(program continues)

Program 5-5   *(continued)*

```
    while (count <= days)
    {
        float sales;
        cout << "Enter the sales for day " << count << ": ";
        cin >> sales;
        total += sales;    // Accumulate the running total.
        count++;           // Increment the counter.
    }
    cout << fixed << showpoint << setprecision(2);
    cout << "The total sales are $" << total << endl;
    return 0;
}
```

Program Output with Example Input Shown in Bold

```
For how many days do you have sales figures? 5 [Enter]
Enter the sales for day 1: 489.32 [Enter]
Enter the sales for day 2: 421.65 [Enter]
Enter the sales for day 3: 497.89 [Enter]
Enter the sales for day 4: 532.37 [Enter]
Enter the sales for day 5: 506.92 [Enter]
The total sales are $2448.15
```

The daily sales figures are stored in `sales` (a variable defined inside the body of the `while` loop). The contents of `sales` is then added to `total`. The variable `total` was initialized to 0, so the first time through the loop it will be set to the same value as `sales`. During each iteration after the first, `total` will be increased by the amount in `sales`. After the loop has finished, `total` will contain the total of all the daily sales figures entered.

5.6   Sentinels

CONCEPT   A *sentinel* is a special value that marks the end of a list of values.

Program 5-5, in the previous section, requires the user to know in advance the number of days he or she wishes to enter sales figures for. Sometimes the user has a list that is very long and doesn't know how many items there are. In other cases, the user might be entering several lists and it is impractical to require that every item in every list be counted.

A technique that can be used in these situations is to ask the user to enter a sentinel at the end of the list. A *sentinel* is a special value that cannot be mistaken as a member of the list and signals that there are no more values to be entered. When the user enters the sentinel, the loop terminates.

Program 5-6 calculates the total points earned by a soccer team over a series of games. It allows the user to enter the series of game points, then −1 to signal the end of the list.

Program 5-6

```cpp
// This program calculates the total number of points a
// soccer team has earned over a series of games. The user
// enters a series of point values, then -1 when finished.
#include <iostream>
using namespace std;

int main()
{
    int game = 1, points, total = 0;

    cout << "Enter the number of points your team has earned\n";
    cout << "so far in the season, then enter -1 when finished.\n\n";
    cout << "Enter the points for game " << game << ": ";
    cin >> points;

    while (points != -1)
    {
        total += points;
        cout << "Enter the points for game " << ++game << ": ";
        cin >> points;
    }
    cout << "\nThe total points are " << total << endl;
    return 0;
}
```

Program Output with Example Input Shown in Bold
```
Enter the number of points your team has earned
so far in the season, then enter -1 when finished.

Enter the points for game 1: 7 [Enter]
Enter the points for game 2: 9 [Enter]
Enter the points for game 3: 4 [Enter]
Enter the points for game 4: 6 [Enter]
Enter the points for game 5: 8 [Enter]
Enter the points for game 6: -1 [Enter]

The total points are 34
```

Notice that a `cin` statement reads a value into the `points` variable before the loop begins. This is to ensure that `points` contains a value the first time the loop tests it. The value −1 was chosen for the sentinel because it is not possible for a team to score negative points.

5.7   Using a Loop to Read Data from a File

CONCEPT	When reading a value from a file with the stream extraction operator, the operator returns a true or false value indicating whether the value was successfully read. This return value can be used to detect when the end of a file has been reached.

A loop can be used to read the items stored in a file. For example, suppose the file numbers.txt exists with the following contents.

```
8
7
3
9
12
```

As you can see, there are five numbers stored in the file. Program 5-7 uses a loop to read the five numbers and display them on the screen.

Program 5-7

```cpp
// This program displays five numbers in a file.
#include <iostream>
#include <fstream>
using namespace std;

int main()
{
    int number, count = 1;          // Initialize the loop counter.
    ifstream inputFile;

    inputFile.open("numbers.txt");  // Open the file.
    if (!inputFile)                 // Test for errors.
       cout << "Error opening file.\n";
    else
    {
       while (count <= 5)
       {
          inputFile >> number;      // Read a number.
          cout << number << endl;   // Display the number.
          count++;                  // Increment the counter.
       }
       inputFile.close();           // Close the file.
    }
    return 0;
}
```

This program is limited, however, because it depends on the file having five numbers stored in it. If the file contains less than five numbers, an error will occur because the program will attempt to read beyond the end of the file. If the file has more than five numbers stored in it, the program will only display the first five. In many cases the exact number of items stored in a file is unknown and the program must have a way of detecting the end of the file. Fortunately, you can use the >> operator to do this.

The stream extraction operator (>>) not only reads data from a file, but it also returns a value indicating whether the data was successfully read or not. If the operator returns `true`, then a value was successfully read. If the operator returns `false`, it means that no value was read from the file. For example, look at the following code.

```
if (inputFile >> number)
{
    // Data was successfully read from the file.
    cout << "The data read from the file is " << number << endl;
}
else
{
    // No data was read from the file.
    cout << "Could not read an item from the file.\n";
}
```

Notice that the statement that reads an item from the file is also used as the conditional expression in the `if` statement:

```
if (inputFile >> number)
```

This statement does two things:

1. It uses the expression `inputFile >> number` to read an item from the file and stores the item in the `number` variable. The >> operator returns `true` if the item was successfully read, or `false` otherwise.

2. It tests the value returned by the stream extraction operator.

You can use the stream extraction operator's return value in a loop to determine when the end of the file has been reached. Here is an example:

```
    while (inputFile >> number)
{
    cout << number << endl;
}
```

Because the value returned from the >> operator controls the loop, it will read items from the file until the end of the file has been reached.

The following program segment is a modification of Program 5-7. Instead of reading the first five items in the file, however, this program reads all of the items in the file regardless of how many there are.

```
int number;
ifstream inputFile;
inputFile.open("numbers.txt");          // Open the file.
if (!inputFile)                          // Test for errors.
    cout << "Error opening file.\n";
```

```
    else
    {
        inputFile >> number;                    // Read the first number.
        while (!inputFile.eof())
        {
            cout << number << endl;             // Display the number.
            inputFile >> number;                // Read the next number.
        }
        inputFile.close();                      // Close the file.
    }
```

Checkpoint   [5.2–5.7]

5.2   How many times will "Hello World\n" be printed in the following program segment?

```
int count = 10;
while (count < 1)
{
    cout << "Hello World\n";
    count++;
}
```

5.3   In the following program segment, which variable is the counter and which is the accumulator?

```
int x = 0, y = 0, z;
cout << "How many numbers do you wish to enter? ";
cin >> z;

while (x++ < z)
{
    int a;
    cout << "Enter a number: ";
    cin >> a;
    y += a;
}
cout << "The sum of those numbers is " << y << endl;
```

5.4   Modify Program 5-8 so any negative number is a sentinel.

5.8   The do-while and for Loops

In addition to the while loop, C++ also offers the do-while and for loops. Each loop is appropriate for different programming problems.

The do-while loop looks similar to a while loop turned upside down. Here is its format when a single statement is to be repeated:

```
do
    statement;
while (expression);
```

Here is the format of the do-while loop when repeating a block of statements:

```
do
{
    statement;
    statement;
    // Place as many statements here
    // as necessary.
} while (expression);
```

 Note: The do-while loop must be terminated with a semicolon after the closing parenthesis of the test expression.

Besides the way it looks, the difference between the do-while loop and the while loop is that do-while is a *posttest* loop. It tests its expression after each iteration is complete. This means do-while always performs at least one iteration, even if the test expression is false from the start. For example, in the following while loop the cout statement will not execute at all:

```
int x = 1;
while (x < 0)
    cout << x << endl;
```

But the cout statement in the following do-while loop will execute once because the do-while loop does not evaluate the expression x < 0 until the end of the iteration.

```
int x = 1;
do
    cout << x << endl;
while (x < 0);
```

You should use do-while when you want to make sure the loop executes at least once. Program 5-8, another version of the test averaging program, uses a do-while loop to repeat as long as the user wishes.

Program 5-8

```
// This program averages 3 test scores. It repeats as
// many times as the user wishes.
#include <iostream>
using namespace std;
```

(program continues)

Program 5-8   *(continued)*

```cpp
int main()
{
    int score1, score2, score3;
    double average;
    char again;

    do
    {
        cout << "Enter 3 scores and I will average them: ";
        cin >> score1 >> score2 >> score3;
        average = (score1 + score2 + score3) / 3.0;
        cout << "The average is " << average << ".\n";
        cout << "Do you want to average another set? (Y/N) ";
        cin >> again;
    } while (again == 'Y' || again == 'y');
    return 0;
}
```

Program Output with Example Input Shown in Bold
```
Enter 3 scores and I will average them: 80 90 70 [Enter]
The average is 80.
Do you want to average another set? (Y/N) y [Enter]
Enter 3 scores and I will average them: 60 75 88 [Enter]
The average is 74.333336.
Do you want to average another set? (Y/N) n [Enter]
```

The variable again is set by cin inside the body of the loop. Because the test occurs after the body has executed, it doesn't matter that again isn't initialized.

Notice the use of the || operator in the test expression. Any expression that can be evaluated as true or false may be used to control a loop.

Using do-while with Menus

The do-while loop is a good choice for repeating a menu. Recall Program 4-22, which displays a menu of health club packages. Program 5-9 is a modification of that program, which uses a do-while loop to repeat the program until the user selects item 4 from the menu.

Program 5-9

```cpp
// This program displays a menu and asks the user to make a
// selection. A do-while loop repeats the program until the
// user selects item 4 from the menu.
#include <iostream>
#include <iomanip>
using namespace std;
```

(program continues)

Program 5-9   *(continued)*

```cpp
int main()
{
    int choice, months;
    double charges;

    cout << fixed << showpoint << setprecision(2);
    do
    {
        cout << "\n\t\tHealth Club Membership Menu\n\n";
        cout << "1. Standard Adult Membership\n";
        cout << "2. Child Membership\n";
        cout << "3. Senior Citizen Membership\n";
        cout << "4. Quit the Program\n\n";
        cout << "Enter your choice: ";
        cin >> choice;
        if (choice >= 1 && choice <= 3)
        {
            cout << "For how many months? ";
            cin >> months;
            switch (choice)
            {
                case 1:charges = months * 40.0;
                        break;
                case 2:charges = months * 20.0;
                        break;
                case 3:charges = months * 30.0;
            }
            // Display the monthly charges.
            cout << "The total charges are $";
            cout << charges << endl;
        }
        else if (choice != 4)
        {
            cout << "The valid choices are 1 through 4.\n";
            cout << "Try again.\n";
        }
    } while (choice != 4);
    return 0;
}
```

Program 5-9   *(continued)*

Program Output with Example Input Shown in Bold

```
            Health Club Membership Menu

1.  Standard Adult Membership
2.  Child Membership
3.  Senior Citizen Membership
4.  Quit the Program

Enter your choice: 1 [Enter]
For how many months 12 [Enter]
The total charges are $480.00

            Health Club Membership Menu

1.  Standard Adult Membership
2.  Child Membership
3.  Senior Citizen Membership
4.  Quit the Program

Enter your choice: 4 [Enter]
```

 # Checkpoint   [5.8]

5.5   What will the following program segments display?

A)
```
int count = 10;
do
    cout << "Hello World\n";
while (count++ < 1);
```

B)
```
int v = 0;
do
    cout << v++;
while (v < 5);
```

C)
```
int count = 0, funny = 1, serious = 0, limit = 4;
do
{
    funny++;
    serious += 2;
}
while (count++ < limit);
cout << funny << " " << serious << " ";
cout << count << endl;
```

5.6   Write a program segment with a do-while loop that asks the user to enter a number. The loop should keep a running total of the numbers entered, and stop when the total is greater than 300.

The `for` Loop

The third type of loop in C++ is the `for` loop. It is ideal for situations that require a counter because it has built-in expressions that initialize and update variables. Here is the format of the `for` loop when used to repeat a single statement:

```
for (initialization; test; update)
    statement;
```

The format of the `for` loop when used to repeat a block is:

```
for (initialization; test; update)
{
    statement;
    statement;
    // Place as many statements here
    // as necessary
}
```

There are three expressions inside the parentheses, separated by semicolons. (Notice there is no semicolon after the third expression.) The first expression is the *initialization expression*. It is typically used to initialize a counter or other variable that must have a starting value. This is the first action performed by the loop and it is only done once.

The second expression is the *test expression*. Like the test expression in the `while` and `do-while` loops, it controls the execution of the loop. As long as this expression is true, the body of the `for` loop will repeat. The `for` loop is a pretest loop, so it evaluates the test expression before each iteration.

The third expression is the *update expression*. It executes at the end of each iteration. Typically, it increments a counter or other variable that must be modified in each iteration.

The following program segment is another version of Program 5-3, modified to use the `for` loop instead of the `while` loop. The output is the same as Program 5-3.

```
int num;
cout << "Number     Number Squared\n";
cout << "-------------------------\n";
for (num = 1; num <= 10; num++)
    cout << num << "\t\t" << (num * num) << endl;
```

Figure 5-3 describes the mechanics of the `for` loop.

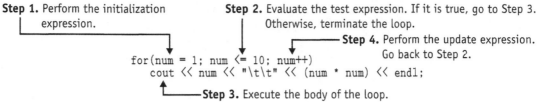

Step 1. Perform the initialization expression.

Step 2. Evaluate the test expression. If it is true, go to Step 3. Otherwise, terminate the loop.

Step 4. Perform the update expression. Go back to Step 2.

```
for(num = 1; num <= 10; num++)
    cout << num << "\t\t" << (num * num) << endl;
```

Step 3. Execute the body of the loop.

Figure 5-3

Note: Because the `for` loop performs a pre-test, it's possible that it will never iterate. Here is an example:

```
for (x = 11; x < 10; x++)
    cout << x << endl;
```

Because the variable `x` is initialized to a value that makes the test expression false from the beginning, this loop terminates as soon as it begins.

WARNING! Be careful not to place a statement in the body of the `for` loop that duplicates the update expression. The following loop, for example, increments `x` twice for each iteration:

```
for (x = 1; x <= 10; x++)
{
    cout << x << (x * x) << endl;
    x++;
}
```

Omitting the `for` Loop's Expressions

The initialization expression may be omitted from inside the `for` loop's parentheses if it has already been performed or no initialization is needed. Here is another look at the `for` loop from the previous program segment with the initialization being performed prior to the loop:

```
int num = 1;
for ( ; num <= 10; num++)
    cout << num << "\t\t" << (num * num) << endl;
```

Note: The semicolon is still required, even though the expression is missing.

You may also omit the update expression if it is being performed elsewhere in the loop or if none is needed. The following `for` loop works just like a `while` loop:

```
int num = 1;
for ( ; num <= 10; )
{
    cout << num << "\t\t" << (num * num) << endl;
    num++;
}
```

You can even go so far as to omit all three expressions from the for loop's parentheses. Be warned, however, that if you leave out the test expression, the loop has no built-in way of terminating. Here is an example:

```
for ( ; ; )
    cout << "Hello World\n";
```

Because this loop has no way of stopping, it will display "Hello World\n" forever (or until something interrupts the program).

Other Forms of the Update Expression

You are not limited to using increment statements in the update expression. Here is a loop that displays all the even numbers from 2 through 100 by adding 2 to its counter:

```
for (number = 2; number <= 100; number += 2)
    cout << number << endl;
```

And here is a loop that counts backward from 10 down to 0:

```
for (number = 10; number >= 0; number--)
    cout << number << endl;
```

The following loop has no formal body. The combined increment operation and cout statement in the update expression perform all the work of each iteration:

```
for (number = 1; number <= 10; cout << number++);
```

Using Initialization and Update Lists

If your loop needs to perform more than one statement as part of the initialization, separate the statements with commas. Program 5-10 is a version of Program 5-5, modified to let the user input sales figures for one week. It initializes two variables in the for loop's initialization.

Program 5-10

```
// This program takes daily sales figures for one week
// and calculates their total.
#include <iostream>
#include <iomanip>
using namespace std;

int main()
{
    const int days = 7;     // Number of days to process.
    int count;
    double total;
```

(program continues)

Program 5-10   *(continued)*

```
    for (count = 1, total = 0.0; count <= days; count++)
    {
        double sales;
        cout << "Enter the sales for day " << count << ": ";
        cin >> sales;
        total += sales;        // Accumulate the running total.
    }
    cout << fixed << showpoint << setprecision(2);
    cout << "The total sales are $" << total << endl;
    return 0;
}
```

Program Output with Example Input Shown in Bold
```
Enter the sales for day 1: 489.32 [Enter]
Enter the sales for day 2: 421.65 [Enter]
Enter the sales for day 3: 497.89 [Enter]
Enter the sales for day 4: 532.37 [Enter]
Enter the sales for day 5: 506.92 [Enter]
Enter the sales for day 6: 489.01 [Enter]
Enter the sales for day 7: 476.55 [Enter]
The total sales are $3413.71
```

In the `for` loop, count is initialized to 1, then `total` is initialized to 0.0. You may place more than one statement in the update expression as well.

```
        double sales;
        for (count = 1, total = 0.0; count <= days; count++, total += sales)
        {
            cout << "Enter the sales for day " << count << ": ";
            cin >> sales;
        }
```

In the update expression of this loop, count is incremented, then the value in `sales` is added to `total` at the end of each iteration. The two statements are separated by a comma.

Connecting multiple statements with commas works well in the initialization and update expressions, but don't try to connect multiple relational expressions this way in the conditional expression. If you wish to perform more than one conditional test, build an expression with the && or || operators, like this:

```
    for (count = 1, total = 0; count <= 10 && total < 500; count++)
    {
            double amount;
            cout << "Enter the amount of purchase #" << count << ": ";
            cin >> amount;
            total += amount;
    }
```

Defining a Variable in the Initialization Expression

Not only may variables be initialized in the initialization expression, but they may be defined there as well. Here is an example:

```cpp
for (int num = 1; num <= 10; num++)
    cout << num << "\t\t" << (num * num) << endl;
```

In this loop, the variable num is both defined and initialized in the initialization expression. It makes sense to define variables that are only used in a loop, like counters, in the loop itself. This makes their purpose clearer.

According to the ANSI standard, when a variable is defined in a for loop's initialization expression, the scope of the variable is limited to the body of the loop. The variable is not visible to statements outside the loop.

 WARNING! Some compilers are not compliant with the ANSI standard regarding this issue. For example, with Microsoft Visual C++ 6.0 the scope of a variable defined in a for loop's initialization expression extends beyond the body of the loop. The variable is visible to all statements in the block of code containing the loop, from the definition down. To allow your code to be compiled with any compiler, you should not define a variable in the initialization expression of a for loop if you plan to use another variable with the same name outside the loop.

Checkpoint [5.8]

5.7   Name the three expressions in a for statement's parentheses.

5.8   What will the following program segments display?

```cpp
A)      for (count = 0; count < 6; count++)
              cout << (count + count);
B)      for (value = -5; value; value++)
              cout << value;
C)      for (x = 5; x <= 14; x += 3)
              cout << x << endl;
        cout << x << endl;
```

5.9   Write a for loop that displays every fifth number, starting at zero, through 100.

5.10   Write a for loop that repeats seven times, asking the user to enter a number. The loop should also calculate the sum of the numbers entered.

5.11   Write a for loop that calculates the total of the following series of numbers:

$$\frac{1}{30} + \frac{2}{29} + \frac{3}{28} + \frac{4}{27} + \ldots \frac{30}{1}$$

5.9 Focus on Software Engineering: *Deciding Which Loop to Use*

> **CONCEPT** Although most repetitive algorithms can be written with any of the three types of loops, each works best in different situations.

Each of C++'s three loops are ideal to use in different situations. Here's a short summary of when each loop should be used:

* The `while` Loop

The `while` loop is a pretest loop. It is ideal in situations where you do not want the loop to iterate if the condition is false from the beginning. It is also ideal if you want to use a sentinel.

* The `do-while` Loop

The `do-while` loop is a posttest loop. It is ideal in situations where you always want the loop to iterate at least once.

* The `for` Loop

The `for` loop is a pretest loop that first executes an initialization expression. In addition, it automatically executes an update expression at the end of each iteration. It is ideal for situations where a counter variable is needed. The `for` loop is primarily used when the exact number of required iterations is known.

5.10 Nested Loops

> **CONCEPT** A loop that is inside another loop is called a *nested loop*.

Nested loops are necessary when a task performs a repetitive operation and that task itself must be repeated. A clock is a good example of something that works like a nested loop. The second hand, minute hand, and hour hand all spin around the face of the clock. The hour hand, however, only makes one revolution for every 12 of the minute hand's revolutions. And it takes 60 revolutions of the second hand for the minute hand to make one revolution. This means that for every complete revolution of the hour hand, the second hand has revolved 720 times.

Here is a program segment with a `for` loop that partially simulates a digital clock. It displays the seconds from 0 to 59:

```
cout << fixed << right;
cout.fill('0');
for (int seconds = 0; seconds < 60; seconds++)
    cout << setw(2) << seconds << endl;
```

Note: The `fill` member function of `cout` changes the fill character, which is a space by default. In the program segment above, the `fill` function causes a zero to be printed in front of all single digit numbers.

We can add a `minutes` variable and nest the loop above inside another loop that cycles through 60 minutes:

```
cout << fixed << right;
cout.fill('0');
for (int minutes = 0; minutes < 60; minutes++)
{
    for (int seconds = 0; seconds < 60; seconds++)
    {
        cout << setw(2) << minutes << ":";
        cout << setw(2) << seconds << endl;
    }
}
```

To make the simulated clock complete, another variable and loop can be added to count the hours:

```
cout << fixed << right;
cout.fill('0');
for (int hours = 0; hours < 24; hours++)
{
    for (int minutes = 0; minutes < 60; minutes++)
    {
        for (int seconds = 0; seconds < 60; seconds++)
        {
            cout << setw(2) << hours << ":";
            cout << setw(2) << minutes << ":";
            cout << setw(2) << seconds << endl;
        }
    }
}
```

The output of the previous program segment follows:

```
00:00:00
00:00:01
00:00:02
        .               (The program will count through each second of 24 hours.)
        .
        .
23:59:59
```

The innermost loop will iterate 60 times for each iteration of the middle loop. The middle loop will iterate 60 times for each iteration of the outermost loop. When the outermost loop has iterated 24 times, the middle loop will have iterated 1,440 times and the innermost loop will have iterated 86,400 times!

The simulated clock example brings up a few points about nested loops:

♦ An inner loop goes through all of its iterations for each iteration of an outer loop.

♦ Inner loops complete their iterations faster than outer loops.

♦ To get the total number of iterations of a nested loop, multiply the number of iterations of all the loops.

Program 5-11 is another test-averaging program. It asks the user for the number of students and the number of test scores per student. A nested inner loops asks for all the test scores for one student, iterating once for each test score. The outer loop iterates once for each student.

Program 5-11

```cpp
// This program averages test scores. It asks the user for the
// number of students and the number of test scores per student.
#include <iostream>
using namespace std;

int main()
{
    int numStudents,        // Number of students
        numTests,           // Number of test per student
        total;              // Accumulator for total scores
    double average;         // Average test score

    cout << "This program averages test scores.\n";
    cout << "For how many students do you have scores? ";
    cin >> numStudents;
    cout << "How many test scores does each student have? ";
    cin >> numTests;
    for (int student = 1; student <= numStudents; student++)
    {
        total = 0;              // Initialize the accumulator.
        for (int test = 1; test <= numTests; test++)
        {
            int score;
            cout << "Enter score " << test << " for ";
            cout << "student " << student << ": ";
            cin >> score;
            total += score;
        }
        average = total / numTests;
        cout << "The average score for student " << student;
        cout << " is " << average << ".\n\n";
    }
    return 0;
}
```

Program 5-11   *(continued)*

Program Output with Example Input Shown in Bold
```
This program averages test scores.
For how many students do you have scores? 2 [Enter]
How many test scores does each student have? 3 [Enter]
Enter score 1 for student 1: 84 [Enter]
Enter score 2 for student 1: 79 [Enter]
Enter score 3 for student 1: 97 [Enter]
The average for student 1 is 86.

Enter score 1 for student 2: 92 [Enter]
Enter score 2 for student 2: 88 [Enter]
Enter score 3 for student 2: 94 [Enter]
The average score for student 2 is 91.
```

5.11   Breaking Out of a Loop

> **CONCEPT**   The break statement causes a loop to terminate early.

WARNING! Use the break statement with great caution. Because it bypasses the loop condition to terminate the loop, it makes code difficult to understand and debug. For this reason, you should avoid using break, when possible. Because it is part of the C++ language, we discuss it briefly in this section.

Sometimes it's necessary to stop a loop before it goes through all its iterations. The break statement, which was used with switch in Chapter 4, can also be placed inside a loop. When it is encountered, the loop stops and the program jumps to the statement immediately following the loop.

The while loop in the following program segment appears to execute 10 times, but the break statement causes it to stop after the fifth iteration.

```cpp
int count = 0;
while (count++ < 10)
{
    cout << count << endl;
    if (count == 5)
        break;
}
```

Using break in a Nested Loop

In a nested loop, the break statement only interrupts the loop it is placed in. The following program segment displays five rows of asterisks on the screen. The outer loop controls the number of rows and the inner loop controls the number of asterisks in each row. The inner loop is designed to display 20 asterisks, but the `break` statement stops it during the eleventh iteration.

```cpp
for (int row = 0; row < 5; row++)
{
    for (int star = 0; star < 20; star++)
    {
        cout << '*';
        if (star == 10)
            break;
    }
    cout << endl;
}
```

The output of the program segment above is:

```
* * * * * * * * * * *
* * * * * * * * * * *
* * * * * * * * * * *
* * * * * * * * * * *
* * * * * * * * * * *
```

5.12   The `continue` Statement

> **CONCEPT**   The `continue` statement causes a loop to stop its current iteration and begin the next one.

 WARNING! As with the `break` statement, use continue with great caution. It makes code difficult to understand and debug. Because it is part of the C++ language, we discuss it briefly in this section.

The `continue` statement causes the current iteration of a loop to end immediately. When `continue` is encountered, all the statements in the body of the loop that appear after it are ignored, and the loop prepares for the next iteration.

In a `while` loop, this means the program jumps to the test expression at the top of the loop. As usual, if the expression is still true, the next iteration begins. In a `do-while` loop, the program jumps to the test expression at the bottom of the loop, which determines if the next iteration will begin. In a `for` loop, `continue` causes the update expression to be executed, and then the test expression to be evaluated.

The following program segment demonstrates the use of `continue` in a `while` loop:

```cpp
int testVal = 0;
while (testVal++ < 10)
{
    if (testVal == 4)
        continue;
    cout << testVal << " ";
}
```

This loop looks like it displays the integers 1 through 10. When testVal is equal to 4, however, the continue statement causes the loop to skip the cout statement and begin the next iteration. The output of the loop is

```
1 2 3 5 6 7 8 9 10
```

Program 5-12 shows a practical application of the continue statement. The program calculates the charges for video rentals where current releases cost $3.50 and all others cost $2.50. If a customer rents several videos, every third one is free. The continue statement is used to skip the part of the loop that calculates the charges for every third video.

Program 5-12

```cpp
// This program calculates the charges for video rentals.
// Every third video is free.
#include <iostream>
#include <iomanip>
using namespace std;

int main()
{
    int videoCount = 1, numVideos;
    double total = 0.0;
    char current;

    cout << "How many videos are being rented? ";
    cin >> numVideos;
    do
    {
        if ((videoCount % 3) == 0)
        {
            cout << "Video #" << videoCount << " is free!\n";
            continue;
        }
        cout << "Is video #" << videoCount;
        cout << " a current release? (Y/N) ";
        cin >> current;
        if (current == 'Y' || current == 'y')
            total += 3.50;
        else
            total += 2.50;
    } while (videoCount++ < numVideos);
    cout << fixed << showpoint << setprecision(2);
    cout << "The total is $" << total;
    return 0;
}
```

Program 5-12 *(continued)*

Program Output with Example Input Shown in Bold
```
How many videos are being rented? 6 [Enter]
Is video #1 a current release? (Y/N) y [Enter]
Is video #2 a current release? (Y/N) n [Enter]
Video #3 is free!
Is video #4 a current release? (Y/N) n [Enter]
Is video #5 a current release? (Y/N) y [Enter]
Video #6 is free!
The total is $12.00
```

5.13 Focus on Software Engineering: *Using Loops for Data Validation*

CONCEPT Loops can be used to create input routines that repeat until acceptable data is entered.

Loops are especially useful for validating input. If an invalid value is entered, a loop can let the user re-enter it as many times as necessary. The following loop asks for a number in the range of 1 through 100:

```
cout << "Enter a number in the range 1 - 100: ";
cin >> number;
while (number < 1 || number > 100)
{
    cout << "ERROR: The value must be in the range 1 - 100: ";
    cin >> number;
}
```

This code first allows the user to enter a number. If the input is valid, the loop will not execute. If the input is not valid, however, the loop will display an error message and require the user to enter another number. The loop will continue to execute until the user enters a valid number.

Program 5-13 calculates the number of soccer teams a youth league may create, based on a given number of players and a maximum number of players per team. The program uses while loops to validate all the user's input.

Program 5-13

```
// This program calculates the number of soccer teams
// that a youth league may create from the number of
// available players. Input validation is demonstrated
// with while loops.
#include <iostream>
using namespace std;
```

(program continues)

Program 5-13 *(continued)*

```cpp
int main()
{
    int players, teamPlayers, numTeams, leftOver;

    // Get the number of players per team.
    cout << "How many players do you wish per team?\n";
    cout << "(Enter a value in the range 9 - 15): ";
    cin >> teamPlayers;
    while (teamPlayers < 9 || teamPlayers > 15) // Validate input.
    {
        cout << "You should have at least 9 but no\n";
        cout << "more than 15 per team.\n";
        cout << "How many players do you wish per team? ";
        cin >> teamPlayers;
    }
    // Get the number of players available.
    cout << "How many players are available? ";
    cin >> players;
    while (players <= 0)   // Validate input.
    {
        cout << "Please enter a positive number: ";
        cin >> players;
    }

    // Perform calculations.
    numTeams = players / teamPlayers;
    leftOver = players % teamPlayers;
    cout << "There will be " << numTeams << " teams with ";
    cout << leftOver << " players left over.\n";
    return 0;
}
```

Program Output with Example Input Shown in Bold
```
How many players do you wish per team?
(Enter a value in the range 9 - 15): 4 [Enter]
You should have at least 9 but no
more than 15 per team.
How many players do you wish per team? 12 [Enter]
How many players are available? -142 [Enter]
Please enter a positive number: 142 [Enter]
There will be 11 teams with 10 players left over.
```

Checkpoint [5.9–5.13]

5.12 Which loop (while, do-while, or for) would be best to use in the following situations?

A) The user must enter a set of exactly 14 numbers.

B) A menu must be displayed for the user to make a selection.

C) A calculation must be made an unknown number of times. (It is possible the calculation will not be made at all.)

D) A series of numbers must be entered by the user, terminated by a sentinel value.

E) A series of values must be entered. The user specifies exactly how many.

5.13 How many times will the value in y be displayed in the following program segment?

```cpp
for (x = 0; x < 20; x++)
{
    for (y = 0; y < 30; y++)
    {
        if (y > 10)
            break;
        cout << y << endl;
    }
}
```

5.14 What will the following program segment display?

```cpp
int x = 0, y = 0;
while (x++ < 5)
{
    if (x == 3)
        continue;
    y += x;
    cout << y << endl;
}
```

5.15 Write an input validation loop that asks the user to enter a number in the range of 10 through 25.

5.16 Write an input validation loop that asks the user to enter Y, y, N, or n.

5.17 Write an input validation loop that asks the user to enter "Yes" or "No".

 See the CaseStudies.pdf file on the accompanying CD for this chapter's case studies.

Review Questions and Exercises

Short Answer

1. Why should you indent the statements in the body of a loop?

2. Describe the difference between pretest loops and posttest loops.

3. Why are the statements in the body of a loop called conditionally-executed statements?

4. What is the difference between the while loop and the do-while loop?

5. Which loop should you use in situations where you wish the loop to repeat until the test expression is false, and the loop should not execute if the test expression is false to begin with?

6. Which loop should you use in situations where you wish the loop to repeat until the test expression is false, but the loop should execute at least one time?

7. Which loop should you use when you know the number of required iterations?

8. Why is it critical that counter variables be properly initialized?

9. Why is it critical that accumulator variables be properly initialized?

10. Why should you be careful not to place a statement in the body of a for loop that changes the value of the loop's counter variable?

Algorithm Workbench

11. Write a while loop that lets the user enter a number. The number should be multiplied by 10, and the result stored in the variable product. The loop should iterate as long as product contains a value less than 100.

12. Write a do-while loop that asks the user to enter two numbers. The numbers should be added and the sum displayed. The user should be asked if he or she wishes to perform the operation again. If so, the loop should repeat; otherwise it should terminate.

13. Write a for loop that displays the following set of numbers:

```
0, 10, 20, 30, 40, 50 . . . 1000
```

14. Write a loop that asks the user to enter a number. The loop should iterate 10 times and keep a running total of the numbers entered.

15. Write a nested loop that displays 10 rows of '#' characters. There should be 15 '#' characters in each row.

16. Convert the following while loop to a do-while loop:

```cpp
int x = 1;
while (x > 0)
{
    cout << "enter a number: ";
    cin >> x;
}
```

17. Convert the following do-while loop to a while loop:

```cpp
char sure;
do
{
    cout << "Are you sure you want to quit? ";
    cin >> sure;
} while (sure != 'Y' && sure != 'N');
```

18. Convert the following while loop to a for loop:

```cpp
int count = 0;
while (count++ < 50)
{
    cout << "count is " << count << endl;
}
```

5

19. Convert the following for loop to a while loop:

```cpp
for (int x = 50; x > 0; x--)
{
    cout << x << " seconds to go.\n";
}
```

True or False

20. T F The operand of the increment and decrement operators can be any valid mathematical expression.

21. T F The cout statement in the following program segment will display 5:
```cpp
int x = 5;
cout << x++;
```

22. T F The cout statement in the following program segment will display 5:
```cpp
int x = 5;
cout << ++x;
```

23. T F The while loop is a pretest loop.

24. T F The do-while loop is a pretest loop.

25. T F The for loop is a posttest loop.

26. T F It is not necessary to initialize counter variables.

27. T F All three of the for loop's expressions may be omitted.

28. T F One limitation of the for loop is that only one variable may be initialized in the initialization expression.

29. T F Variables may be defined inside the body of a loop.

30. T F A variable may be defined in the initialization expression of the for loop.

31. T F In a nested loop, the outer loop executes faster than the inner loop.

32. T F In a nested loop, the inner loop goes through all of its iterations for every single iteration of the outer loop.

33. T F To calculate the total number of iterations of a nested loop, add the number of iterations of all the loops.

34. T F The break statement causes a loop to stop the current iteration and begin the next one.

35. T F The continue statement causes a terminated loop to resume.

36. T F In a nested loop, the break statement only interrupts the loop it is placed in.

Find the Errors

Each of the following program segments has errors. Find as many as you can.

37.
```cpp
int num1 = 0, num2 = 10, result;
num1++;
result = ++(num1 + num2);
cout << num1 << " " << num2 << " " << result;
```

38. This program segment adds two numbers entered by the user.

```
int num1, num2;
char again;
while (again == 'y' || again == 'Y')
    cout << "Enter a number: ";
    cin >> num1;
    cout << "Enter another number: ";
    cin >> num2;
    cout << "Their sum is << (num1 + num2) << endl;
    cout << "Do you want to do this again? ";
    cin >> again;
```

39. This program segment uses a loop to raise a number to a power.

```
int num, bigNum, power, count;
cout << "Enter an integer: ";
cin >> num;
cout << "What power do you want it raised to? ";
cin >> power;
bigNum = num;
while (count++ < power);
    bigNum *= num;
cout << "The result is << bigNum << endl;
```

40. This program segment displays the sum of the numbers 1–100.

```
int count = 1, total;
while (count <= 100)
    total += count;
cout << "The sum of the numbers 1 - 100 is ";
cout << total << endl;
```

Programming Challenges

1. Sum of Numbers

Write a program that asks the user for a positive integer value. The program should use a loop to get the sum of all the integers from 1 up to the number entered. For example, if the user enters 50, the loop will find the sum of 1, 2, 3, 4, ... 50.

Input Validation: Do not accept a negative starting number.

2. Distance Traveled

The distance a vehicle travels can be calculated as follows:

```
distance = speed * time
```

For example, if a train travels 40 miles per hour for 3 hours, the distance traveled is 120 miles.

Write a program that asks the user for the speed of a vehicle (in miles per hour) and how many hours it has traveled. It should then use a loop to display the distance the vehicle has traveled for each hour of that time period. Here is an example of the output:

```
What is the speed of the vehicle in mph? 40
How many hours has it traveled? 3
Hour    Distance Traveled
----------------------------------
  1              40
  2              80
  3              120
```

Input Validation: Do not accept a negative number for speed and do not accept any value less than one for time traveled.

3. Pennies for Pay

Write a program that calculates how much a person would earn over a period of time if his or her salary is one penny the first day, two pennies the second day, and continues to double each day. The program should ask the user for the number of days. Display a table showing how much the salary was for each day, and then show the total pay at the end of the period. The output should be displayed in a dollar amount, not the number of pennies.

Input Validation: Do not accept a number less than one for the number of days worked.

4. Math Tutor

This program started in Problem 11 of Chapter 3, and was modified in Problem 4 of Chapter 4. Modify the program again so it displays a menu allowing the user to select an addition, subtraction, multiplication, or division problem. The final selection on the menu should let the user quit the program. After the user has finished the math problem, the program should display the menu again. This process is repeated until the user chooses to quit the program.

Input Validation: If the user selects an item not on the menu, display an error message and display the menu again.

5. Hotel Occupancy

Write a program that calculates the occupancy rate for a hotel. The program should start by asking the user how many floors the hotel has. A loop should then iterate once for each floor. In each iteration, the loop should ask the user for the number of rooms on the floor and how many of them are occupied. After all the iterations, the program should display how many rooms the hotel has, how many of them are occupied, how many are unoccupied, and the percentage of rooms that are occupied. The percentage may be calculated by dividing the number of rooms occupied by the number of rooms.

 Note: It is traditional that most hotels do not have a thirteenth floor. The loop in this program should skip the entire thirteenth iteration.

Input Validation: Do not accept a value less than one for the number of floors. Do not accept a number less than 10 for the number of rooms on a floor.

6. Average Rainfall

Write a program that uses nested loops to collect data and calculate the average rainfall over a period of years. The program should first ask for the number of years. The outer loop will iterate once for each year. The inner loop will iterate twelve times, once for each month. Each iteration of the inner loop will ask the user for the inches of rainfall for that month.

After all iterations, the program should display the number of months, the total inches of rainfall, and the average rainfall per month for the entire period.

Input Validation: Do not accept a number less than one for the number of years. Do not accept negative numbers for the monthly rainfall.

7. Population

Write a program that will predict the size of a population of organisms. The program should ask the user for the starting number of organisms, their average daily population increase (as a percentage), and the number of days they will multiply. A loop should display the size of the population for each day.

Input Validation: Do not accept a number less than two for the starting size of the population. Do not accept a negative number for average daily population increase. Do not accept a number less than one for the number of days they will multiply.

8. Centigrade to Fahrenheit Table

In Programming Challenge 7 of Chapter 3 you were asked to write a program that converts a centigrade temperature to Fahrenheit. Modify that program so it uses a loop to display a table of the centigrade temperatures 0–20, and their Fahrenheit equivalents.

9. The Greatest and Least of These

Write a program with a loop that lets the user enter a series of integers. The user should enter -99 to signal the end of the series. After all the numbers have been entered, the program should display the largest and smallest numbers entered.

5

10. Payroll Report

Write a program that displays a weekly payroll report. A loop in the program should ask the user for the employee number, gross pay, state tax, federal tax, and FICA withholdings. The loop will terminate when 0 is entered for the employee number. After the data is entered, the program should display totals for gross pay, state tax, federal tax, FICA withholdings, and net pay.

Input Validation: Do not accept negative numbers for any of the items entered. Do not accept values for state, federal, or FICA withholdings that are greater than the gross pay. If the state tax + federal tax + FICA withholdings for any employee are greater than gross pay, print an error message and ask the user to re-enter the data for that employee.

11. Savings Account Balance

Write a program that calculates the balance of a savings account at the end of a period of time. It should ask the user for the annual interest rate, the starting balance, and the number of months that have passed since the account was established. A loop should then iterate once for every month, performing the following:

A)   Ask the user for the amount deposited into the account during the month. (Do not accept negative numbers.) This amount should be added to the balance.

B)   Ask the user for the amount withdrawn from the account during the month. (Do not accept negative numbers.) This amount should be subtracted from the balance.

C)   Calculate the monthly interest. The monthly interest rate is the annual interest rate divided by 12. Multiply the monthly interest rate by the balance, and add the result to the balance.

After the last iteration, the program should display the ending balance, the total amount of deposits, the total amount of withdrawals, and the total interest earned.

 Note: If a negative balance is calculated at any point, a message should be displayed indicating the account has been closed and the loop should terminate.

12. Bar Chart

Write a program that asks the user to enter today's sales for five stores. The program should then display a bar graph comparing each store's sales. Create each bar in the bar graph by displaying a row of asterisks. Each asterisk should represent $100 of sales.

Here is an example of the program's output.

```
Enter today's sales for store 1: 1000 [Enter]
Enter today's sales for store 2: 1200 [Enter]
Enter today's sales for store 3: 1800 [Enter]
Enter today's sales for store 4: 800 [Enter]
Enter today's sales for store 5: 1900 [Enter]

SALES BAR CHART
Store 1: **********
Store 2: ************
Store 3: ******************
Store 4: ********
Store 5: *******************
```

6

Functions

■ Topics in this Chapter

6.1 Focus on Software Engineering: *Modular Programming*

CONCEPT	A program may be broken up into manageable functions.

A function is a collection of statements that performs a specific task. So far you have experienced functions in two ways: (1) you have created a function called `main` in every program you've written, and (2) you have used library functions such as `pow` and `strcmp`. In this chapter you will learn how to create your own functions that can be used like library functions.

One reason to use functions is that they break a program up into small, manageable units. Each unit is a module, programmed as a separate function. Imagine a book that has a thousand pages, but isn't divided into chapters or sections. Trying to find a single topic in the book would be very difficult. Real-world programs can easily have thousands of lines of code, and unless they are modularized, they can be very difficult to modify and maintain.

Another reason to use functions is that they simplify programs. If a specific task is performed in several places in a program, a function can be written once to perform that task, and then be executed anytime it is needed.

6.2 Defining and Calling Functions

> **CONCEPT** A function call is a statement that causes a function to execute. A function definition contains the statements that make up the function.

When creating a function, you must write its *definition*. All function definitions have the following parts:

Return type: A function can send a value to the part of the program that activated it. The return type is the data type of the value that is sent from the function.

Name: You should give each function a descriptive name. In general, the same rules that apply to variable names also apply to function names.

Parameter list: The program can send data into a function. The parameter list is a list of variables that hold the values being passed to the function.

Body: The body of a function is the set of statements that perform the function's operation. They are enclosed in a set of braces.

Figure 6-1 shows the definition of a simple function with the various parts labeled.

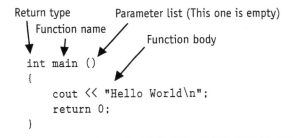

Figure 6-1

 Note: The line in the definition that reads int main() is called the *function header*.

void **Functions**

You already know that a function can return a value. The main function in all of the programs you have seen in this book is declared to return an int value to the operating system. The return 0; statement causes the value 0 to be returned when the main function finishes executing.

It isn't necessary for all functions to return a value, however. Some functions simply perform one or more statements and then terminate. These are called *void functions*. The displayMessage function, shown below, is an example.

```
void displayMessage()
{
    cout << "Hello from the function displayMessage.\n";
}
```

The function's name is displayMessage. This name gives an indication of what the function does: It displays a message. You should always give functions names that reflect their purpose. Notice that the function's return type is void. This means the function does not return a value to the part of the program that executed it. Also notice the function has no return statement. It simply displays a message on the screen and exits.

Calling a Function

A function is executed when it is *called*. Function main is called automatically when a program starts, but all other functions must be executed by *function call* statements. When a function is called, the program branches to that function and executes the statements in its body. Let's look at Program 6-1, which contains two functions: main and displayMessage.

Program 6-1

```
// This program has two functions: main and displayMessage
#include <iostream>
using namespace std;

//******************************************
// Definition of function displayMessage   *
// This function displays a greeting.      *
//******************************************
void displayMessage()
{
    cout << "Hello from the function displayMessage.\n";
}
```

(program continues)

Program 6-1 *(continued)*

```
int main()
{
    cout << "Hello from main.\n";
    displayMessage();
    cout << "Back in function main again.\n";
    return 0;
}
```

Program Output
```
Hello from main.
Hello from the function displayMessage.
Back in function main again.
```

The function `displayMessage` is called by the following line in `main`:

```
displayMessage();
```

This line is the function call. It is simply the name of the function followed by a set of parentheses and a semicolon. Let's compare this with the function header:

Function Header   ⟶   `void displayMessage()`
Function Call   ⟶   `displayMessage();`

The function header is part of the function definition. It declares the function's return type, name, and parameter list. It is not terminated with a semicolon because the definition of the function's body follows it.

The function call is a statement that executes the function, so it is terminated with a semicolon like all other C++ statements. The return type is not listed in the function call, and, if the program is not passing data into the function, the parentheses are left empty.

 Note: Later in this chapter you will see how data can be passed into a function by being listed inside the parentheses.

Even though the program starts executing at `main`, the function `displayMessage` is defined first. This is because the compiler must know the function's return type, the number of parameters, and the type of each parameter before it is called. One way to ensure the compiler will know this information is to place the function definition before all calls to that function. (Later you will see an alternative, and preferred method of accomplishing this.)

 Note: You should always document your functions by writing comments that describe what they do. These comments should appear just before the function definition.

Notice how Program 6-1 flows. It starts, of course, in function main. When the call to display-Message is encountered, the program branches to that function and performs its statements. Once displayMessage has finished executing, the program branches back to function main and resumes with the line that follows the function call. This is illustrated in Figure 6-2.

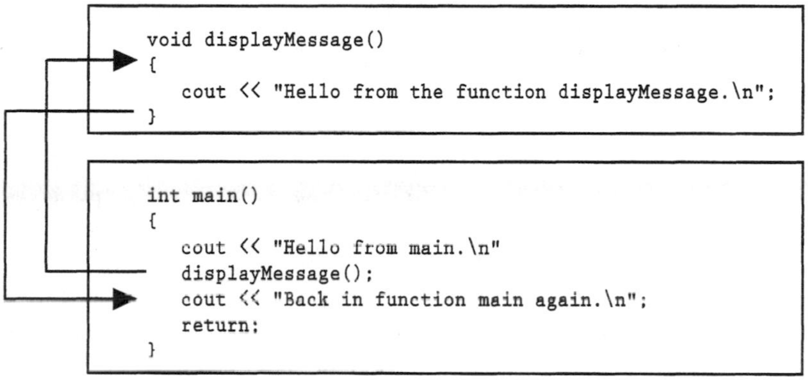

Figure 6-2

Function call statements may be used in control structures like loops, if statements, and switch statements. Program 6-2 places the displayMessage function call inside a loop.

Program 6-2

```cpp
// The function displayMessage is repeatedly called from a loop.
#include <iostream>
using namespace std;

//******************************************
// Definition of function displayMessage   *
// This function displays a greeting.       *
//******************************************

void displayMessage()
{
    cout << "Hello from the function displayMessage.\n";
}

int main()
{
    cout << "Hello from main.\n";
    for (int count = 0; count < 5; count++)
        displayMessage();     // Call displayMessage
    cout << "Back in function main again.\n";
    return 0;
}
```

Program 6-2 *(continued)*

Program Output
```
Hello from main.
Hello from the function displayMessage.
Hello from the function displayMessage.
Hello from the function displayMessage.
Hello from the function displayMessage.
Hello from the function displayMessage.
Back in function main again.
```

It is possible to have many functions and function calls in a program. Program 6-3 has three functions: main, first, and second.

Program 6-3
```cpp
// This program has three functions: main, first, and second.
#include <iostream>
using namespace std;

//*****************************************
// Definition of function first          *
// This function displays a message.     *
//*****************************************

void first()
{
    cout << "I am now inside the function first.\n";
}

//*****************************************
// Definition of function second         *
// This function displays a message.     *
//*****************************************

void second()
{
    cout << "I am now inside the function second.\n";
}

int main()
{
    cout << "I am starting in function main.\n";
    first();   // Call function first
    second();  // Call function second
    cout << "Back in function main again.\n";
    return 0;
}
```

Program 6-3 *(continued)*

Program Output
```
I am starting in function main.
I am now inside the function first.
I am now inside the function second.
Back in function main again.
```

In Program 6-3, function `main` contains a call to `first` and a call to `second`:

```
first();
second();
```

Each call statement causes the program to branch to a function and then back to `main` when the function is finished. Figure 6-3 illustrates the paths taken by the program.

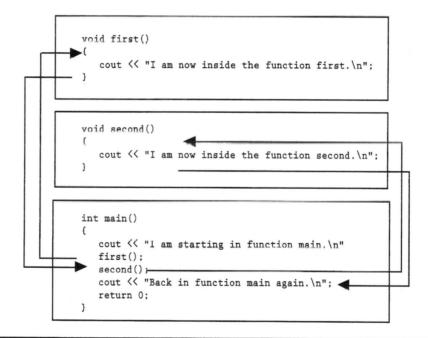

Figure 6-3

Functions may also be called in a hierarchical, or layered fashion. This is demonstrated by Program 6-4, which has three functions: `main`, `deep`, and `deeper`.

Program 6-4

```cpp
// This program has three functions: main, deep, and deeper
#include <iostream>
using namespace std;

//****************************************
// Definition of function deeper          *
// This function displays a message.       *
//****************************************

void deeper()
{
    cout << "I am now inside the function deeper.\n";
}

//****************************************
// Definition of function deep            *
// This function displays a message.       *
//****************************************

void deep()
{
    cout << "I am now inside the function deep.\n";
    deeper();  // Call function deeper
    cout << "Now I am back in deep.\n";
}

int main()
{
    cout << "I am starting in function main.\n";
    deep();    // Call function deep
    cout << "Back in function main again.\n";
    return 0;
}
```

Program Output

```
I am starting in function main.
I am now inside the function deep.
I am now inside the function deeper.
Now I am back in deep.
Back in function main again.
```

In Program 6-4, function main only calls the function deep. In turn, deep calls deeper. The paths taken by the program are shown in Figure 6-4.

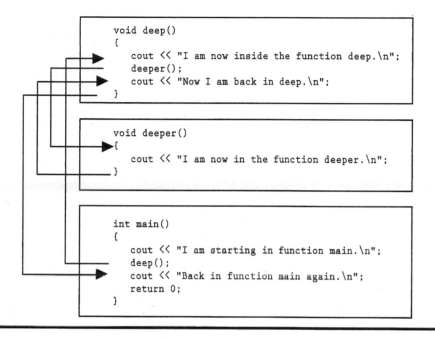

Figure 6-4

⑦ Checkpoint [6.1–6.2]

6.1 Is the following a function header or a function call?

```
calcTotal();
```

6.2 Is the following a function header or a function call?

```
void showResults()
```

6.3 What will the output of the following program be if the user enters 10?

```cpp
#include <iostream>
using namespace std;

void func1()
{
    cout << "Able was I\n";
}

void func2()
{
    cout << "I saw Elba\n";
}
```

```
int main()
{
    int input;
    cout << "Enter a number: ";
    cin >> input;
    if (input < 10)
    {
        func1();
        func2();
    }
    else
    {
        func2();
        func1();
    }
    return 0;
}
```

6.3 Function Prototypes

CONCEPT A function prototype eliminates the need to place a function definition before all calls to the function.

Before the compiler encounters a call to a particular function, it must already know the function's return type, the number of parameters it uses, and the type of each parameter. (You will learn how to use parameters in the next section.)

One way of ensuring that the compiler has this information is to place the function definition before all calls to that function. This was the approach taken in Programs 6-1, 6-2, 6-3, and 6-4. Another method is to declare the function with a *function prototype*. Here is a prototype for the displayMessage function in Program 6-1:

```
void displayMessage();
```

The prototype looks similar to the function header, except there is a semicolon at the end. The statement above tells the compiler that the function displayMessage has a void return type (it doesn't return a value) and uses no parameters.

Note: Function prototypes are also known as *function declarations.*

WARNING! You must either place the function definition or function prototype ahead of all calls to the function. Otherwise the program will not compile.

Function prototypes are usually placed near the top of a program so the compiler will encounter them before any function calls. Program 6-5 is a modification of Program 6-3. The definitions of the functions first and second have been placed after main, and a function prototype has been placed after the using namespace std statement.

Program 6-5

```cpp
// This program has three functions: main, First, and Second.
#include <iostream>
using namespace std;

// Function Prototypes
void first();
void second();

int main()
{
    cout << "I am starting in function main.\n";
    first();   // Call function first
    second();  // Call function second
    cout << "Back in function main again.\n";
    return 0;
}

//***********************************
// Definition of function first.    *
// This function displays a message. *
//***********************************

void first()
{
    cout << "I am now inside the function first.\n";
}

//***********************************
// Definition of function second.   *
// This function displays a message. *
//***********************************

void second()
{
    cout << "I am now inside the function second.\n";
}
```

Program Output

> *(The program's output is the same as the output of Program 6-3.)*

When the compiler is reading Program 6-5, it encounters the calls to the functions `first` and `second` in `main` before it has read the definition of those functions. Because of the function prototypes, however, the compiler already knows the return type and parameter information of `first` and `second`.

 Note: Although some programmers make `main` the last function in the program, many prefer it to be first because it is the program's starting point.

6.4 Sending Data into a Function

CONCEPT When a function is called, the program may send values into the function.

Values that are sent into a function are called *arguments*. You're already familiar with how to use arguments in a function call. In the following statement the function pow is being called and two arguments, 2 and 4, are passed to it:

```
result = pow(2, 4);
```

By using *parameters*, you can design your own functions that accept data this way. A parameter is a special variable that holds a value being passed into a function. Here is the definition of a function that uses a parameter:

```
void displayValue(int num)
{
    cout << "The value is " << num << endl;
}
```

Notice the integer variable definition inside the parentheses (int num). The variable num is a parameter. This enables the function displayValue to accept an integer value as an argument. Program 6-6 is a complete program using this function.

 Note: In this text, the values that are passed into a function are called arguments, and the variables that receive those values are called parameters. There are several variations of these terms in use. Some call the arguments *actual parameters* and call the parameters *formal parameters*. Others use the terms *actual argument* and *formal argument*. Regardless of which set of terms you use, it is important to be consistent.

Program 6-6

```
// This program demonstrates a function with a parameter.
#include <iostream>
using namespace std;

// Function Prototype
void displayValue(int);

int main()
{
    cout << "I am passing 5 to displayValue.\n";
    displayValue(5);  // Call displayValue with argument 5
    cout << "Now I am back in main.\n";
    return 0;
}
```

(program continues)

Program 6-6 *(continued)*

```
//**********************************************************
// Definition of function displayValue.                    *
// It uses an integer parameter whose value is displayed.  *
//**********************************************************

void displayValue(int num)
{
    cout << "The value is " << num << endl;
}
```

Program Output
```
I am passing 5 to displayValue.
The value is 5
Now I am back in main.
```

First, notice the function prototype for `displayValue`:

```
void displayValue(int);
```

It is not necessary to list the name of the parameter variable inside the parentheses. Only its data type is required. The function prototype shown above could optionally have been written as:

```
void displayValue(int num);
```

However, the compiler ignores the name of the parameter variable in the function prototype.

In main, the `displayValue` function is called with the argument 5 inside the parentheses. The number 5 is passed into num, which is `displayValue`'s parameter. This is illustrated in Figure 6-5.

```
                       displayValue(5);


                   void displayValue(int num)
                   {
                       cout << "The value is " << num << endl;
                   }
```

Figure 6-5

Any argument listed inside the parentheses of a function call is copied into the function's parameter variable. In essence, parameter variables are initialized to the value of their corresponding arguments. The following program segment shows the function `displayValue` being called several times with a different argument being passed each time.

```
cout << "I am passing several values to displayValue.\n";
displayValue(5);  // Call displayValue with argument 5
displayValue(10); // Call displayValue with argument 10
displayValue(2);  // Call displayValue with argument 2
displayValue(16); // Call displayValue with argument 16
cout << "Now I am back in main.\n";
```

Program Output

```
I am passing several values to displayValue.
The value is 5
The value is 10
The value is 2
The value is 16
Now I am back in main.
```

Each time the function is called, num takes on a different value. Any expression whose value could normally be assigned to num may be used as an argument. For example, the following function call would pass the value 8 into num:

```
displayValue(3 + 5);
```

If you pass an argument whose type is not the same as the parameter's type, the argument will be promoted or demoted automatically. For instance, the argument in the following function call would be truncated, causing the value 4 to be passed to num:

```
displayValue(4.7);
```

Often, it's useful to pass several arguments into a function. Program 6-7 shows the definition of a function with three parameters.

Program 6-7

```
// This program demonstrates a function with three parameters.
#include <iostream>
using namespace std;

// Function Prototype
void showSum(int, int, int);

int main()
{
    int value1, value2, value3;

    cout << "Enter three integers and I will display ";
    cout << "their sum: ";
    cin >> value1 >> value2 >> value3;
    showSum(value1, value2, value3);    // Call showSum with 3 arguments
    return 0;
}

//***************************************************************
// Definition of function showSum.                             *
// It uses three integer parameters. Their sum is displayed.   *
//***************************************************************

void showSum(int num1, int num2, int num3)
{
    cout << (num1 + num2 + num3) << endl;
}
```

Program 6-7 *(continued)*

Program Output with Example Input Shown in Bold
```
Enter three integers and I will display their sum: 4 8 7 [Enter]
19
```

In the function header for showSum, the parameter list contains three variable definitions separated by commas:

```
void showSum(int num1, int num2, int num3)
```

 WARNING! Each variable must have a data type listed before its name. You can't leave out the data type of any variable in the parameter list. A compiler error would occur if the parameter list were defined as int num1, num2, num3 instead of int num1, int num2, int num3.

In the function call, the variables value1, value2, and value3 are passed as arguments:

```
showSum(value1, value2, value3);
```

Notice the syntax difference between the function header and the function call when passing variables as arguments into parameters. In a function call, you do *not* include the variable's data types inside the parentheses. For example, it would be an error to write this function call as:

```
showSum(int value1, int value2, int value3);      // Wrong!
```

When a function with multiple parameters is called, the arguments are passed to the parameters in order. This is illustrated in Figure 6-6.

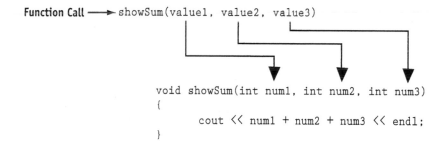

Figure 6-6

The following function call will cause 5 to be passed into the num1 parameter, 10 to be passed into num2, and 15 to be passed into num3:

```
showSum(5, 10, 15);
```

However, the following function call will cause 15 to be passed into the num1 parameter, 5 to be passed into num2, and 10 to be passed into num3:

```
showSum(15, 5, 10);
```

Note: The function prototype must list the data type of each parameter.

Note: Like all variables, parameters have a scope. The scope of a parameter is limited to the body of the function which uses it.

6.5 Passing Data by Value

 CONCEPT When an argument is passed into a parameter, only a copy of the argument's value is passed. Changes to the parameter do not affect the original argument.

As you've seen in this chapter, parameters are special-purpose variables that are defined inside the parentheses of a function definition. They are separate and distinct from the arguments that are listed inside the parentheses of a function call. The values that are stored in the parameter variables are copies of the arguments. Normally, when a parameter's value is changed inside a function it has no affect on the original argument. Program 6-8 demonstrates this concept.

Program 6-8

```cpp
// This program demonstrates that changes to a function parameter
// have no affect on the original argument.
#include <iostream>
using namespace std;

// Function Prototype
void changeThem(int, double);

int main()
{
    int whole = 12;
    double real = 3.5;

    cout << "In main the value of whole is " << whole << endl;
    cout << "and the value of real is " << real << endl;
    changeThem(whole, real);    // Call changeThem with 2 arguments
    cout << "Now back in main again, the value of ";
    cout << "whole is " << whole << endl;
    cout << "and the value of real is " << real << endl;
    return 0;
}
```

(program continues)

Program 6-8 *(continued)*

```
//**************************************************************
// Definition of function changeThem.                         *
// It uses i, an int parameter, and f, a double. The values of *
// i and f are changed and then displayed.                    *
//**************************************************************

void changeThem(int i, double f)
{
    i = 100;
    f = 27.5;
    cout << "In changeThem the value of i is changed to ";
    cout << i << endl;
    cout << "and the value of f is changed to " << f << endl;
}
```

Program Output
```
In main the value of whole is 12
and the value of real is 3.5
In changeThem the value of i is changed to 100
and the value of f is changed to 27.5
Now back in main again, the value of whole is 12
and the value of real is 3.5
```

Even though the parameters i and f are changed in the function changeThem, the arguments whole and real are not modified. The variables i and f only contain copies of whole and real. The changeThem function does not have access to the original arguments. When only a copy of an argument is passed to a function, it is said to be *passed by value*. This is because the function receives a copy of the argument's value, and does not have access to the original argument.

Figure 6-7 illustrates that a parameter variable's storage location in memory is separate from that of the original argument.

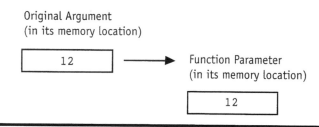

Figure 6-7

 Note: Later in this chapter you will learn ways to give a function access to its original arguments.

6.6 Focus on Software Engineering:
Using Functions in a Menu-Driven Program

CONCEPT Functions are ideal for use in menu-driven programs. When the user selects an item from a menu, the program can call the appropriate function.

In Chapters 4 and 5 you saw a menu-driven program that calculates the charges for a health club membership. Program 6-9 is a *modular* version of that program. A modular program is broken up into functions that perform specific tasks.

Program 6-9

```
// This is a menu-driven program that makes a function call
// for each selection the user makes.
#include <iostream>
#include <iomanip>
using namespace std;

// Function prototypes
void adult(int);
void child(int);
void senior(int);

int main()
{
    int choice, months;
    double charges;

    cout << fixed << showpoint << setprecision(2);
    do
    {
        cout << "\n\t\tHealth Club Membership Menu\n\n";
        cout << "1. Standard Adult Membership\n";
        cout << "2. Child Membership\n";
        cout << "3. Senior Citizen Membership\n";
        cout << "4. Quit the Program\n\n";
        cout << "Enter your choice: ";
        cin >> choice;
        if (choice >= 1 && choice <= 3)
        {
            cout << "For how many months? ";
            cin >> months;
```

(program continues)

Program 6-9 *(continued)*

```cpp
            switch (choice)
            {
                case 1: adult(months);
                        break;
                case 2: child(months);
                        break;
                case 3: senior(months);
            }
        }
        else if (choice != 4)
        {
            cout << "The valid choices are 1 through 4.\n";
            cout << "Try again.\n";
        }
    } while (choice != 4);
    return 0;
}

//*****************************************************************
// Definition of function adult. Uses an integer parameter, mon. *
// mon holds the number of months the membership should be       *
// calculated for. The cost of an adult membership for that      *
// number of months is displayed.                                *
//*****************************************************************

void adult(int mon)
{
    cout << "The total charges are $";
    cout << (mon * 40.0) << endl;
}


//*****************************************************************
// Definition of function child. Uses an integer parameter, mon. *
// mon holds the number of months the membership should be       *
// calculated for. The cost of an adult membership for that      *
// number of months is displayed.                                *
//*****************************************************************

void child(int mon)
{
    cout << "The total charges are $";
    cout << (mon * 20.0) << endl;
}
```

(program continues)

Program 6-9 *(continued)*

```
//************************************************************
// Definition of function senior. Uses an integer parameter, mon. *
// mon holds the number of months the membership should be        *
// calculated for. The cost of an adult membership for that       *
// number of months is displayed.                                 *
//************************************************************

void senior(int mon)
{
    cout << "The total charges are $";
    cout << (mon * 30.0) << endl;
}
```

Program Output with Example Input Shown in Bold

```
          Health Club Membership Menu

1. Standard Adult Membership
2. Child Membership
3. Senior Citizen Membership
4. Quit the Program

Enter your choice: 1 [Enter]
For how many months? 12 [Enter]
The total charges are $480.00

          Health Club Membership Menu

1. Standard Adult Membership
2. Child Membership
3. Senior Citizen Membership
4. Quit the Program

Enter your choice: 4 [Enter]
```

The functions adult, child, and senior each use a parameter named mon. The number of months that the user entered in main is passed as an argument into this parameter. The functions then calculate the appropriate charges for that number of months.

Checkpoint [6.3–6.6]

6.4 Indicate which of the following is the function prototype, the function header, and the function call:

```
void showNum(float num)

void showNum(float);

showNum(45.67);
```

6.5 Write a function named timesTen. The function should have an integer parameter named number. When timesTen is called, it should display the product of number times 10. (Note: just write the function. Do not write a complete program.)

6.6 Write a function prototype for the timesTen function you wrote in question 6.6.

6.7 What is the output of the following program?

```cpp
#include <iostream>
using namespace std;

void func1(double, int); // Function prototype

int main()
{
    int x = 0;
    float y = 1.5;

    cout << x << " " << y << endl;
    func1(y, x);
    cout << x << " " << y << endl;
    return 0;
}

void func1(double a, int b)
{
    cout << a << " " << b << endl;
    a = 0.0;
    b = 10;
    cout << a << " " << b << endl;
}
```

6.7 The return Statement

CONCEPT The return statement causes a function to end immediately.

When the last statement in a function has finished executing, the function terminates and the program returns to the statement following the function call. It's possible, however, to force a function to return before the last statement has been executed. When the return statement is encountered, the function immediately terminates and the program returns. This is demonstrated in Program 6-10. The function divide shows the quotient of arg1 divided by arg2. if arg2 is set to zero, the function returns.

Program 6-10

```cpp
// This program uses a function to perform division. If division
// by zero is detected, the function returns.
#include <iostream>
using namespace std;

// Function prototype.
void divide(double, double);

int main()
{
    double num1, num2;
    cout << "Enter two numbers and I will divide the first\n";
    cout << "number by the second number: ";
    cin >> num1 >> num2;
    divide(num1, num2);
    return 0;
}

//*************************************************************
// Definition of function divide.                            *
// Uses two parameters: arg1 and arg2. The function divides arg1*
// by arg2 and shows the result. If arg2 is zero, however, the *
// function returns.                                          *
//*************************************************************

void divide(double arg1, double arg2)
{
    if (arg2 == 0.0)
    {
        cout << "Sorry, I cannot divide by zero.\n";
        return;
    }
    cout << "The quotient is " << (arg1 / arg2) << endl;
}
```

Program Output with Example Input Shown in Bold
```
Enter two numbers and I will divide the first
number by the second number: 12 0 [Enter]
Sorry, I cannot divide by zero.
```

6.8 Returning a Value from a Function

CONCEPT A function may send a value back to the part of the program that called the function.

You've seen that data may be passed into a function by way of its parameters. Data may also be returned from a function, back to the part of the program that called it.

Although several arguments may be passed into a function, only one value may be returned from it. Think of a function as having multiple communications channels for receiving data (parameters), but only one channel for sending data (the return value). This is illustrated in Figure 6-8.

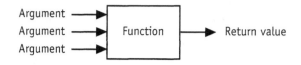

Figure 6-8

 Note: It is possible to return multiple values from a function, but they must be "packaged" in such a way that they are treated as a single value. This is a topic of Chapter 11.

The data type of the return value precedes the function name in the header and the prototype. The following prototype declares a function named square that returns an integer:

```
int square(int);
```

This function square returns an integer and accepts an integer argument. Here is the definition of the function:

```
int square(int number)
{
    return number * number;
}
```

This function only has one line, which is a return statement. When a function returns a value, it must have a return statement. The expression that follows the return key word is evaluated, converted to the data type the function returns, and sent back to the part of the program that called the function. This is demonstrated in Program 6-11.

Program 6-11

```
// This program uses a function that returns a value.
#include <iostream>
using namespace std;

//Function prototype
int square(int);

int main()
{
    int value, result;
    cout << "Enter a number and I will square it: ";
    cin >> value;
    result = square(value);
    cout << value << " squared is " << result << endl;
    return 0;
}
```

(program continues)

Program 6-11 *(continued)*

```
//*******************************************************
// Definition of function square.                       *
// This function accepts an int argument and returns    *
// the square of the argument as an int.                *
//*******************************************************

int square(int number)
{
    return number * number;
}
```

Program Output with Example Input Shown in Bold
```
Enter a number and I will square it: 20 [Enter]
20 squared is 400
```

Here is the line that calls the square function:

```
result = square(value);
```

An expression is something that has a value. If a function returns a value, a call to that function is an expression. The statement above assigns the value returned from square to the variable result. So, when 20 is passed as an argument into square, 20 times 20, or 400, is returned and assigned to result. Figure 6-9 illustrates how data is passed to and returned from the function.

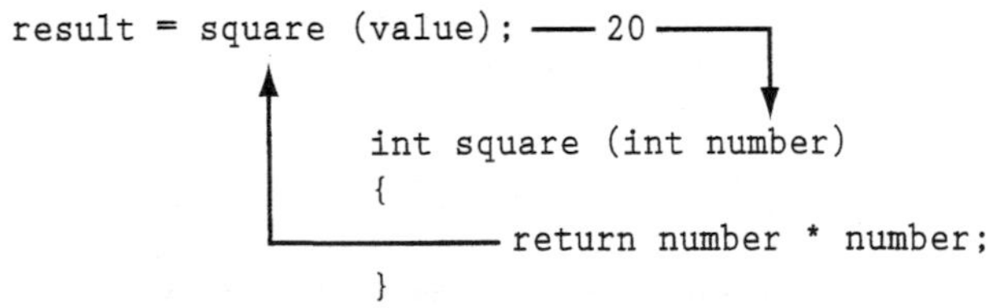

Figure 6-9

Actually, the result variable is unnecessary in Program 6-11. The return value of the square function could have been displayed by the cout object, as shown in the statement here:

```
cout << value << " squared is " << square(value) << endl;
```

Program 6-12 shows a version of the square function that returns a double. The function is used in a mathematical statement that calculates the area of a circle.

Program 6-12

```
// This program uses the return value of the square function
// in a mathematical statement.
#include <iostream>
#include <iomanip>
using namespace std;
```

(program continues)

Program 6-12 *(continued)*

```cpp
// This program uses the return value of the square function
// in a mathematical statement.
#include <iostream>
#include <iomanip>
using namespace std;

//Function prototypes
double getRadius();
double square(double);

int main()
{
    const double PI = 3.14159;
    double rad;

    cout << fixed << showpoint << setprecision(2);
    cout << "This program calculates the area of ";
    cout << "a circle.\n";
    rad = getRadius();
    cout << "The area is " << PI * square(rad) << endl;
    return 0;
}

//***********************************************************
// Definition of function getRadius.                        *
// This function asks the user to enter the radius of       *
// the circle and then returns that number as a double.     *
//***********************************************************

double getRadius()
{
    double radius;

    cout << "Enter the radius of the circle: ";
    cin >> radius;
    return radius;
}

//***********************************************************
// Definition of function square.                           *
// This function accepts a double argument and returns      *
// the square of the argument as a double.                  *
//***********************************************************

double square(double number)
{
    return number * number;
}
```

Program 6-12 *(continued)*

___

Program Output with Example Input Shown in Bold
```
This program calculates the area of a circle.
Enter the radius of the circle: 10 [Enter]
The area is 314.16
```
___

Program 6-12 also uses a function to get the radius of the circle from the user and return that value back to `main`. The function `getRadius` accepts no arguments and returns a `float`.

The `square` function in Program 6-11 returns an `int`, while the one in Program 6-12 returns a `double`. The return type of a function should be the type of the data you wish to return from the function. Likewise, the statement that calls the function should properly handle the return value. For example, if `square` returns a `double` and is used in the following statements, the fractional portion of the return value will be truncated:

```
int result;
result = square(2.7);
```

 Note: When writing the comments for a function that returns a value, document the purpose of the return value and its data type.

Note: If you give a function a return type other than void, you must have a return statement in that function.

6.9 Returning a Boolean Value

CONCEPT Functions may return `true` or `false` values.

Frequently there is a need for a function that tests an argument and returns a `true` or `false` value indicating whether or not a condition exists. For example, in a program that needs to know if numbers are even or odd, a function could be written to return `true` if its argument is even, and return `false` if its argument is odd. Program 6-13 demonstrates such a function.

Program 6-13

___
```
// This program uses a function that returns true or false.
#include <iostream>
using namespace std;

// Function prototype
bool isEven(int);
```

(program continues)
___

Program 6-13 *(continued)*

```cpp
int main()
{
    int val;

    cout << "Enter an integer and I will tell you ";
    cout << "if it is even or odd: ";
    cin >> val;
    if (isEven(val))
        cout << val << " is even.\n";
    else
        cout << val << " is odd.\n";
    return 0;
}

//*****************************************************************
// Definition of function isEven. This function accepts an       *
// integer argument and tests it to be even or odd. The function *
// returns true if the argument is even or false if the argument *
// is odd. The return value is a bool.                           *
//*****************************************************************

bool isEven(int number)
{
    bool status;

    if (number % 2)
        status = false;   // number is odd if there's a remainder.
    else
        status = true;    // Otherwise, the number is even.
    return status;
}
```

Program Output with Example Input Shown in Bold
```
Enter an integer and I will tell you if it is even or odd: 5 [Enter]
5 is odd.
```

The isEven function is called in the following statement:

```cpp
    if (isEven(val))
```

When the if statement executes, isEven is called with val as its argument. If val is even, isEven returns true , otherwise it returns false.

Checkpoint [6.7–6.9]

6.8   How many return values may a function have?

6.9   Write a header for a function named distance. The function should return a double and have two double parameters: rate and time.

6.10   Write a header for a function named days. The function should return an int and have three int parameters: years, months (with the default argument 12), and weeks.

6.11   Write a header for a function named getKey. The function should return a char and use no parameters.

6.12   Write a header for a function named lightYears. The function should return a long and have one long parameter: miles.

6.10 Local and Global Variables

CONCEPT A local variable is defined inside a function and is not accessible outside the function. A global variable is defined outside all functions and is accessible to all functions in its scope.

Local Variables

Just as you've defined variables inside function main, you may also define them inside other functions. Variables defined inside a function are *local* to that function. They are hidden from the statements in other functions, which normally cannot access them. Program 6-14 shows that because the variables defined in a function are hidden, other functions may have separate, distinct variables with the same name.

Program 6-14

```cpp
// This program shows that variables defined in a function
// are hidden from other functions.
#include <iostream>
using namespace std;

void anotherFunction();  // Function prototype

int main()
{
    int num = 1;          // Local variable

    cout << "In main, num is " << num << endl;
    anotherFunction();
    cout << "Back in main, num is " << num << endl;
    return 0;
}
```

(program continues)

Program 6-14 *(continued)*

```
//*******************************************************
// Definition of anotherFunction                        *
// It has a local variable, num, whose initial value    *
// is displayed.                                         *
//*******************************************************

void anotherFunction()
{
    int num = 20;

    cout << "In anotherFunction, num is " << num << endl;
}
```

___

Program Output

```
In main, num is 1
In anotherFunction, num is 20
Back in main, num is 1
```

___

Even though there are two variables named num, the program can only "see" one of them at a time. When the program is executing in main, the num variable defined in main is visible. When anotherFunction is called, however, only variables defined inside it are visible, so the num variable in main is hidden. Figure 6-10 illustrates the closed nature of the two functions. The boxes represent the scope of the variables.

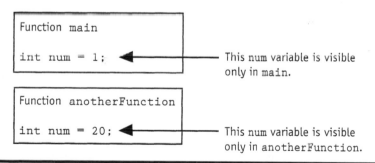

Figure 6-10

___

Global Variables

Although local variables are safely hidden from other functions, they do not provide a convenient way of sharing data. When large amounts of data must be accessible to all the functions in a program, global variables are an easy alternative.

A global variable is any variable defined outside all the functions in a program. The scope of a global variable is the portion of the program from the variable definition to the end. Program 6-15 shows two functions, main and anotherFunction, which access the same global variable, num.

Program 6-15

```cpp
// This program shows that a global variable is visible
// to all the functions that appear in a program after
// the variable's definition.
#include <iostream>
using namespace std;

void anotherFunction();   // Function prototype
int num = 2;              // Global variable

int main()
{
    cout << "In main, num is " << num << endl;
    anotherFunction();
    cout << "Back in main, num is " << num << endl;
    return 0;
}

//*****************************************************
// Definition of anotherFunction                     *
// This function changes the value of the            *
// global variable num.                              *
//*****************************************************

void anotherFunction()
{
    cout << "In anotherFunction, num is " << num << endl;
    num = 50;
    cout << "But, it is now changed to " << num << endl;
}
```

Program Output
```
In main, num is 2
In anotherFunction, num is 2
But, it is now changed to 50
Back in main, num is 50
```

In Program 6-15, num is defined outside of all the functions. Because its definition appears before the definitions of main and anotherFunction, both functions have access to it.

Global Variables Are Initialized to Zero by Default

Unless you explicitly initialize numeric global variables, they are automatically initialized to zero. Global character variables are initialized to NULL.* The variable globalNum in Program 6-16 is never set to any value by a statement, but because it is global, it is automatically set to zero.

---

* The NULL character is stored as ASCII code 0.

Program 6-16

```cpp
// This program has an uninitialized global variable.
#include <iostream>
using namespace std;

int globalNum; // Global variable. Automatically set to zero.

int main()
{
    cout << "globalNum is " << globalNum << endl;
    return 0;
}
```

Program Output
```
globalNum is 0
```

Local and Global Variables with the Same Name

If a function has a local variable with the same name as a global variable, only the local variable can be seen by the function. This is demonstrated by Program 6-17 (with apologies to folks living in Maine).

Program 6-17

```cpp
// This program shows that when a local variable has the
// same name as a global variable, the function only sees
// the local variable.
#include <iostream>
using namespace std;

// Function prototypes
void texas();
void arkansas();

int cows = 10;

int main()
{
    cout << "There are " << cows << " cows in main.\n";
    texas();
    arkansas();
    cout << "Back in main, there are " << cows << " cows.\n";
    return 0;
}
```

(program continues)

Program 6-17 *(continued)*

```cpp
//*******************************************
// Definition of function texas.           *
// The local variable cows is set to 100.  *
//*******************************************

void texas()
{
    int cows = 100;

    cout << "There are " << cows << " cows in texas.\n";
}

//*******************************************
// Definition of function arkansas.        *
// The local variable cows is set to 50.   *
//*******************************************

void arkansas()
{
    int cows = 50;

    cout << "There are " << cows << " cows in arkansas.\n";
}
```

Program Output
```
There are 10 cows in main.
There are 100 cows in texas.
There are 50 cows in arkansas.
Back in main, there are 10 cows.
```

When the program is executing in function main, the global variable cows is visible. In the functions texas and arkansas, however, there are local variables with the name cows. The global variable is not visible when the program is executing in those functions.

Program 6-18 is a simple cash register program that uses global and local variables. The function ringUpSale calculates and displays the price, sales tax, and subtotal for each item being purchased. It has a local variable, tax, which has the same name as a global variable. The tax variable in ringUpSale is used to calculate the sales tax on an item, while the global tax variable is used by main to calculate the total sales tax of the purchase.

Program 6-18

```cpp
// This program has local and global variables. In the function
// ringUpSale, there is a local variable named tax. There is
// also a global variable with the same name.
#include <iostream>
#include <iomanip>
using namespace std;
```

(program continues)

Program 6-18 *(continued)*

```cpp
void ringUpSale(); // Function prototype

// Global Variables
const double TAX_RATE = 0.06;
double tax, sale, total;

int main()
{
    char again;

    cout << fixed << showpoint << setprecision(2);
    do
    {
        ringUpSale();
        cout << "Is there another item to be purchased? ";
        cin >> again;
    } while (again == 'y' || again == 'Y');

    tax = sale * TAX_RATE;
    total = sale + tax;
    cout << "The tax for this sale is " << tax << endl;
    cout << "The total is " << total << endl;
    return 0;
}

//******************************************************************
// Definition of function ringUpSale.                             *
// This function asks for the quantity and unit price of an item. *
// It then calculates and displays the sales tax and subtotal     *
// for those items.                                               *
//******************************************************************

void ringUpSale()
{
    int qty;
    double unitPrice, tax, thisSale, subTotal;

    cout << "Quantity: ";
    cin >> qty;
    cout << "Unit price: ";
    cin >> unitPrice;
    thisSale = qty * unitPrice; // Get the total unit price.
    sale += thisSale;           // Update global variable sale.
    tax = thisSale * taxRate;   // Get sales tax for these items.
    subTotal = thisSale + tax;  // Get subtotal for these items.
    cout << "Price for these items: " << thisSale << endl;
    cout << "Tax for these items: " << tax << endl;
    cout << "SubTotal for these items: " << subTotal << endl;
}
```

Program 6-18   *(continued)*

Program Output with Example Input Shown in Bold
```
Quantity: 2 [Enter]
Unit Price: 20.00 [Enter]
Price for these items: 40.00
Tax for these items: 2.40
SubTotal for these items: 42.40
Is there another item to be purchased? y [Enter]
Quantity: 3 [Enter]
Unit Price: 12.00 [Enter]
Price for these items: 36.00
Tax for these items: 2.16
SubTotal for these items: 38.16
Is there another item to be purchased? n [Enter]
The tax for this sale is 4.56
The total is 80.56
```

 WARNING! Be Careful With Global Variables. It's tempting to make all your variables global, especially when you are first learning to program. After all, you can access them from any function without passing their values as parameters. Although this might make your programs easier to create, most likely it will cause problems later. While debugging your program, if you find that the wrong value is being stored in a global variable, you'll have to track down every statement that accesses it to determine where the bad value is coming from. In a program with thousands of lines, this can be a tedious and time-consuming process.

Also, when two or more functions modify the same variable, you must be very careful that what one function does will not upset the accuracy or correctness of another function. Although global variables make it easy to share data, they require great responsibility of the programmer. Some instructors prefer that you not use them at all.

6.11   Static Local Variables

If a function is called more than once in a program, the values stored in the function's local variables do not persist between function calls. This is because the variables are destroyed when the function terminates and are then re-created when the function starts again. This is shown in Program 6-19.

Program 6-19

```
// This program shows that local variables do not retain
// their values between function calls.
#include <iostream>
using namespace std;
```

(program continues)

Program 6-19 *(continued)*

```cpp
// Function prototype
void showLocal();

int main()
{
    showLocal();
    showLocal();
    return 0;
}

//******************************************************************
// Definition of function showLocal.                              *
// The initial value of localNum, which is 5, is displayed.       *
// The value of localNum is then changed to 99 before the         *
// function returns.                                              *
//******************************************************************

void showLocal()
{
    int localNum = 5;  // Local variable

    cout << "localNum is " << localNum << endl;
    localNum = 99;
}
```

Program Output
```
localNum is 5
localNum is 5
```

Even though the last statement in the showLocal function stores 99 in localNum, the variable is destroyed when the function returns. The next time the function is called, localNum is re-created and initialized to 5 again.

Sometimes it's desirable for a program to "remember" what value is stored in a local variable between function calls. This can be accomplished by making the variable static. Static local variables are not destroyed when a function returns. They exist for the lifetime of the program, even though their scope is only the function in which they are defined. Program 6-20 demonstrates some characteristics of static local variables:

Program 6-20

```cpp
// This program uses a static local variable.
#include <iostream>
using namespace std;

void showStatic(); // Function prototype
```

(program continues)

Program 6-20 *(continued)*

```cpp
int main()
{
    for (int count = 0; count < 5; count++)
        showStatic();
    return 0;
}

//**************************************************************
// Definition of function showStatic.                         *
// statNum is a static local variable. Its value is displayed *
// and then incremented just before the function returns.     *
//**************************************************************

void showStatic()
{
    static int statNum;

    cout << "statNum is " << statNum << endl;
    statNum++;
}
```

Program Output
```
statNum is 0
statNum is 1
statNum is 2
statNum is 3
statNum is 4
```

In Program 6-20, statNum is incremented in the showStatic function, and it retains its value between each function call. Notice that even though statNum is not explicitly initialized, it starts at zero. Like global variables, all static local variables are initialized to zero by default. (Of course, you can provide your own initialization value, if necessary.)

If you do provide an initialization value for a static local variable, the initialization only occurs once. This is because initialization normally happens when the variable is created, and static local variables are only created once during the running of a program. Let's take a look at the output of Program 6-20 when statNum is initialized to 5.

```cpp
void showStatic()
{
    static int statNum = 5;

    cout << "statNum is " << statNum << endl;
    statNum++;
}
```

Program Output
```
statNum is 5
statNum is 6
statNum is 7
statNum is 8
statNum is 9
```

Even though the statement that defines statNum initializes it to 5, the initialization does not happen each time the function is called. If it did, the variable would not be able to retain its value between function calls.

Checkpoint [6.10–6.11]

6.13 What is the difference between a static local variable and a global variable?

6.14 What is the output of the following program?

```cpp
#include <iostream>
using namespace std;

void showVar(); // Function prototype

int main()
{
    for (int count = 0; count < 10; count++)
        showVar();
    return 0;
}

// Definition of function showVar
void showVar()
{
    static int var = 10;

    cout << var << endl;
    var++;
}
```

6.12 Default Arguments

CONCEPT Default arguments are passed to parameters automatically if no argument is provided in the function call.

It's possible to assign *default arguments* to function parameters. A default argument is passed to the parameter when the actual argument is left out of the function call. The default arguments are usually listed in the function prototype. Here is an example:

```cpp
void showArea(double = 20.0, double = 10.0);
```

Default arguments are literal values or constants with an = operator in front of them, appearing after the data types listed in a function prototype. Since parameter names are optional in function prototypes, the example prototype could also be declared as

```
void showArea(double length = 20.0, double width = 10.0);
```

In both example prototypes, the function showArea has two double parameters. The first is assigned the default argument 20.0 and the second is assigned the default argument 10.0. Here is the definition of the function:

```
void showArea(double length, double width)
{
    double area = length * width;
    cout << "The area is " << area << endl;
}
```

The default argument for length is 20.0 and the default argument for width is 10.0. Because both parameters have default arguments, they may optionally be omitted in the function call, as shown here:

```
showArea();
```

In this function call, both default arguments will be passed to the parameters. The parameter length will take the value 20.0 and width will take the value 10.0. The output of the function will be

```
The area is 200
```

The default arguments are only used when the actual arguments are omitted from the function call. In the call below, the first argument is specified, but the second is omitted:

```
showArea(12.0);
```

The value 12.0 will be passed to length, while the default value 10.0 will be passed to width. The output of the function will be

```
The area is 120
```

Of course, all the default arguments may be overridden. In the function call below, arguments are supplied for both parameters:

```
showArea(12.0, 5.5);
```

The output of the function call above will be

```
The area is 66
```

 Note: If a function does not have a prototype, default arguments may be specified in the function header. The showArea function could be defined as follows:

```
void showArea(double length = 20.0, double width = 10.0)
{
    double area = length * width;
    cout << "The area is " << area << endl;
}
```

 WARNING! A function's default arguments should be assigned in the earliest occurrence of the function name. This will usually be the function prototype.

Program 6-21 uses a function that displays asterisks on the screen. Arguments are passed to the function specifying how many columns and rows of asterisks to display. Default arguments are provided to display 1 row of 10 asterisks.

Program 6-21

```
// This program demonstrates default function arguments.
#include <iostream>
using namespace std;

// Function prototype with default arguments
void displayStars(int = 10, int = 1);

int main()
{
    displayStars();            // Use default values for cols and rows.
    cout << endl;
    displayStars(5);           // Use default value for rows.
    cout << endl;
    displayStars(7, 3);        // Use 7 for cols and 3 for rows.
    return 0;
}

//*********************************************************
// Definition of function displayStars.                  *
// The default argument for cols is 10 and for rows is 1.*
// This function displays a square made of asterisks.    *
//*********************************************************

void displayStars(int cols, int rows)
{
    // Nested loop. The outer loop controls the rows
    // and the inner loop controls the columns.
    for (int down = 0; down < rows; down++)
    {
        for (int across = 0; across < cols; across++)
            cout << "*";
        cout << endl;
    }
}
```

Program 6-21   *(continued)*

Program Output
```
*********

*****

*******
*******
*******
```

Although C++'s default arguments are very convenient, they are not totally flexible in their use. When an argument is left out of a function call, all arguments that come after it must be left out as well. In the `displayStars` function in Program 6-21, it is not possible to omit the argument for `cols` without also omitting the argument for `rows`. For example, the following function call would be illegal:

```
displayStars(, 3); // Illegal function call.
```

It's possible for a function to have some parameters with default arguments and some without. For example, in the following function (which displays an employee's gross pay), only the last parameter has a default argument:

```
// Function prototype
void calcPay(int empNum, double payRate, double hours = 40.0);

// Definition of function calcPay
void calcPay(int empNum, double payRate, double hours)
{
    double wages;

    wages = payRate * hours;
    cout << fixed << showpoint << setprecision (2);
    cout << "Gross pay for employee number ";
    cout << empNum << " is " << wages << endl;
}
```

When calling this function, arguments must always be specified for the first two parameters (`empNum` and `payRate`) since they have no default arguments. Here are examples of valid calls:

```
calcPay(769, 15.75);       // Use default arg for 40 hours
calcPay(142, 12.00, 20);   // Specify number of hours
```

When a function uses a mixture of parameters with and without default arguments, the parameters with default arguments must be defined last. In the `calcPay` function, `hours` could not have been defined before either of the other parameters. The following prototypes are illegal:

```
// Illegal prototype
void calcPay(int empNum, double hours = 40.0, double payRate);

// Illegal prototype
void calcPay(double hours = 40.0, int empNum, double payRate);
```

Here is a summary of the important points about default arguments:

◆ The value of a default argument must be a literal value or a named constant.

◆ When an argument is left out of a function call (because it has a default value), all the arguments that come after it must be left out too.

◆ When a function has a mixture of parameters both with and without default arguments, the parameters with default arguments must be declared last.

6.13 Using Reference Variables as Parameters

CONCEPT When used as parameters, reference variables allow a function to access the parameter's original argument. Changes to the parameter are also made to the argument.

Earlier you saw that arguments are normally passed to a function by value, and that the function cannot change the source of the argument. C++ provides a special type of variable called a *reference variable* that, when used as a function parameter, allows access to the original argument.

A reference variable is an alias for another variable. Any changes made to the reference variable are actually performed on the variable for which it is an alias. By using a reference variable as a parameter, a function may change a variable that is defined in another function.

Reference variables are defined like regular variables, except you place an ampersand (&) in front of the name. For example, the following function definition makes the parameter refVar as a reference variable:

```
void doubleNum(int &refVar)
{
    refVar *= 2;
}
```

 Note: The variable refVar is called "a reference to an int."

This function doubles refVar by multiplying it by 2. Since refVar is a reference variable, this action is actually performed on the variable that was passed to the function as an argument. When prototyping a function with a reference variable, be sure to include the ampersand after the data type. Here is the prototype for the doubleNum function:

```
void doubleNum(int &);
```

Note: Some programmers prefer not to put a space between the data type and the ampersand. The following prototype is equivalent to the one on the previous page:

```
void doubleNum(int&);
```

Note: The ampersand must appear in both the prototype and the header of any function that uses a reference variable as a parameter. It does not appear in the function call.

Program 6-22 demonstrates how the doubleNum function works.

Program 6-22

```cpp
// This program uses a reference variable as a function
// parameter.
#include <iostream>
using namespace std;

// Function prototype. The parameter is a reference variable.
void doubleNum(int &);

int main()
{
    int value = 4;

    cout << "In main, value is " << value << endl;
    cout << "Now calling doubleNum..." << endl;
    doubleNum(value);
    cout << "Now back in main. value is " << value << endl;
    return 0;
}

//*********************************************************
// Definition of doubleNum.                              *
// The parameter refVar is a reference variable. The value *
// in refVar is doubled.                                  *
//*********************************************************

void doubleNum (int &refVar)
{
    refVar *= 2;
}
```

Program Output
```
In main, value is 4
Now calling doubleNum...
Now back in main. value is 8
```

The parameter refVar in Program 6-22 "points" to the value variable in function main. When a program works with a reference variable, it is actually working with the variable it references, or points to. This is illustrated in Figure 6-11.

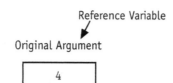

Figure 6-11

Recall that function arguments are normally passed by value, which means a copy of the argument's value is passed into the parameter variable. When a reference parameter is used, it is said that the argument is *passed by reference*.

Program 6-23 is a modification of Program 6-22. The function getNum has been added. The function asks the user to enter a number, which is stored in userNum. userNum is a reference to main's variable value.

Program 6-23

```
// This program uses reference variables as function parameters.
#include <iostream>
using namespace std;

// Function prototypes. Both functions use reference variables
// as parameters
void doubleNum(int &);
void getNum(int &);

int main()
{
    int value;
    getNum(value);
    doubleNum(value);
    cout << "That value doubled is " << value << endl;
    return 0;
}

//**************************************************************
// Definition of getNum.                                      *
// The parameter userNum is a reference variable. The user is *
// asked to enter a number, which is stored in userNum.       *
//**************************************************************
```

(program continues)

Program 6-23 *(continued)*

```cpp
void getNum(int &userNum)
{
    cout << "Enter a number: ";
    cin >> userNum;
}

//*********************************************************
// Definition of doubleNum.                              *
// The parameter refVar is a reference variable. The value *
// in refVar is doubled.                                 *
//*********************************************************

void doubleNum (int &refVar)
{
    refVar *= 2;
}
```

Program Output with Example Input Shown in Bold
```
Enter a number: 12 [Enter]
That value doubled is 24
```

 Note: Only variables may be passed by reference. If you attempt to pass a non-variable argument, such as a literal, constant, or an expression, into a reference parameter, an error will result. Using the `doubleNum` function as an example, the following statements will generate an error.

```cpp
doubleNum(5);                    // Error
doubleNum(userNum + 10);         // Error
```

If a function uses more than one reference variable as a parameter, be sure to place the ampersand before each reference variable name. Here is the prototype and definition for a function that uses four reference variable parameters:

```cpp
// Function prototype with four reference variables
// as parameters.
void addThree(int &, int &, int &, int &);

// Definition of addThree.
// All four parameters are reference variables.
void addThree(int &sum, int &num1, int &num2, int &num3)
{
    cout << "Enter three integer values: ";
    cin >> num1 >> num2 >> num3;
    sum = num1 + num2 + num3;
}
```

WARNING! Don't get carried away with using reference variables as function parameters. Any time you allow a function to alter a variable that's outside the function, you are creating potential debugging problems. Reference variables should only be used as parameters when the situation requires them.

Checkpoint [6.12–6.13]

6.15 What kinds of values may be specified as default arguments?

6.16 Write the prototype and header for a function called `compute`. The function should have three parameters: an `int`, a `float`, and a `long` (not necessarily in that order). The `int` parameter should have a default argument of 5, and the `long` parameter should have a default argument of 65536. The `float` parameter should not have a default argument.

6.17 Write the prototype and header for a function called `calculate`. The function should have three parameters: an `int`, a reference to a `float`, and a `long` (not necessarily in that order.) Only the `int` parameter should have a default argument, which is 47.

6.18 What is the output of the following program?

```cpp
#include <iostream>
using namespace std;

void func1(int = 2, int = 4, int = 6);
void func2(int &, int &, int &);
void func3(int, int, int);

int main()
{
    func1();
    func1(5);
    func1(2,1);
    func1(3,1,5);
    return 0;
}
void func1(int a, int b, int c)
{
    a++; b--; c = a + b;
    func2(a, b, c);
    func3(a, b, c);
}
void func2(int &a, int &b, int &c)
{
    a += 2; b *= 2; c /= 2;
}
void func3(int a, int b, int c)
{
    cout << "a = " << a << ", b = " << b << ", c = " << c << endl;
}
```

6.14 Overloading Functions

> **CONCEPT** Two or more functions may have the same name, as long as their parameter lists are different.

Sometimes you will create two or more functions that perform the same operation, but use a different set of parameters or parameters of different data types. For instance, in Program 6-12 there is a square function that uses an int parameter, and in Program 6-12 there is a square function that uses a double parameter. Both functions do the same thing: return the square of their argument. The only difference is the data type involved in the operation.

If you were to use both these functions in the same program, you could assign a unique name to each one. For example, the function that squares an int might be named squareInt, and the one that squares a double might be named squareDouble. C++, however, allows you to *overload* function names. That means you may assign the same name to multiple functions, as long as their parameter lists are different. Program 6-24 uses both square functions.

Program 6-24

```cpp
// This program uses overloaded functions.
#include <iostream>
#include <iomanip>
using namespace std;

// Function prototypes
int square(int);
double square(double);

int main()
{
    int userInt;
    double userFloat;

    cout << fixed << showpoint << setprecision(2);
    cout << "Enter an integer and a floating-point value: ";
    cin >> userInt >> userFloat;
    cout << "Here are their squares: ";
    cout << square(userInt) << " and " << square(userFloat);
    return 0;
}
```

(program continues)

Program 6-24 *(continued)*

```
//****************************************************************
// Definition of overloaded function square.                    *
// This function uses an int parameter, number. It returns the  *
// square of number as an int.                                  *
//****************************************************************

int square(int number)
{
    return number * number;
}

//****************************************************************
// Definition of overloaded function square.                    *
// This function uses a double parameter, number. It returns the *
// square of number as a double.                                *
//****************************************************************

double square(double number)
{
    return number * number;
}
```

Program Output with Example Input Shown in Bold
```
Enter an integer and a floating-point value: 12 4.2 [Enter]
Here are their squares: 144 and 17.64
```

Here are the headers for the square functions used in Program 6-24:

```
int square(int number)
```

```
double square(double number)
```

In a C++ function call, the function name and the parameter list are both used to identify the function. In Program 6-24, when an `int` argument is passed to `square`, the version of the function that has an `int` parameter is called. Likewise, when a `double` argument is passed to `square`, the version with a `double` parameter is called. Note that the compiler does not consider the return value when determining which overloaded function to call. The following functions could not be used in the same program because their parameter list isn't different.

```
int square(int)
```

```
double square(int)
```

Overloading is also convenient when there are similar functions that use a different number of parameters. For example, consider a program with functions that return the sum of integers. One returns the sum of two integers, another returns the sum of three integers, and yet another returns the sum of four integers. Here are their function headers:

```
int sum(int num1, int num2)

int sum(int num1, int num2, int num3)

int sum(int num1, int num2, int num3, int num4)
```

Because the number of parameters is different in each, they all may be used in the same program. Program 6-25 is an example that uses two functions, each named calcWeeklyPay, to determine an employee's gross weekly pay. One version of the function uses an int and a double parameter, while the other version only uses a double parameter.

Program 6-25

```
// This program demonstrates overloaded functions to calculate
// the gross weekly pay of hourly paid or salaried employees.
#include <iostream>
#include <iomanip>
using namespace std;

// Function prototypes
void getChoice(char &);
double calcWeeklyPay(int, double);
double calcWeeklyPay(double);

int main()
{
    char selection;
    int worked;
    double rate, yearly;

    cout << fixed << showpoint << setprecision(2);
    cout << "Do you want to calculate the weekly pay of\n";
    cout << "(H) an hourly paid employee, or \n";
    cout << "(S) a salaried employee?\n";
    getChoice(selection);
    switch (selection)
    {
        case 'H' :
        case 'h' :  cout << "How many hours were worked? ";
                    cin >> worked;
                    cout << "What is the hour pay rate? ";
                    cin >> rate;
                    cout << "The gross weekly pay is $";
                    cout << calcWeeklyPay(worked, rate) << endl;
                    break;
```

(program continues)

Program 6-25   *(continued)*

```
            case 'S' :
            case 's' :    cout << "What is the annual salary? ";
                          cin >> yearly;
                          cout << "The gross weekly pay is $";
                          cout << calcWeeklyPay(yearly) << endl;
                          break;
    }
    return 0;
}

//*************************************************************
// Definition of function getChoice.                         *
// The parameter letter is a reference to a char.            *
// This function asks the user for an H or an S and returns  *
// the validated input.                                      *
//*************************************************************

void getChoice(char &letter)
{
    cout << "Enter your choice (H or S): ";
    cin >> letter;
    while (letter != 'H' && letter != 'h' &&
        letter != 'S' && letter != 's')
    {
        cout << "Please enter H or S: ";
        cin >> letter;
    }
}

//*************************************************************
// Definition of overloaded function calcWeeklyPay.          *
// This function calculates the gross weekly pay of          *
// an hourly paid employee. The parameter hours holds the    *
// number of hours worked. The parameter payRate holds the   *
// hourly pay rate. The function returns the weekly salary.  *
//*************************************************************

double calcWeeklyPay(int hours, double payRate)
{
    return hours * payRate;
}
```

(program continues)

Program 6-25 *(continued)*

```
//***********************************************************
// Definition of overloaded function calcWeeklyPay.         *
// This function calculates the gross weekly pay of         *
// a salaried employee. The parameter holds the employee's  *
// annual salary. The function returns the weekly salary.   *
//***********************************************************

double calcWeeklyPay(double annSalary)
{
    return annSalary / 52.0;
}
```

Program Output with Example Input Shown in Bold
```
Do you want to calculate the weekly pay of
(H) an hourly paid employee, or
(S) a salaried employee?
Enter your choice (H or S): H [Enter]
How many hours were worked? 40 [Enter]
What is the hour pay rate? 18.50 [Enter]
The gross weekly pay is $740.00
```

Program Output with Example Input Shown in Bold
```
Do you want to calculate the weekly pay of
(H) an hourly paid employee, or
(S) a salaried employee?
Enter your choice (H or S): S [Enter]
What is the annual salary? 68000.00 [Enter]
The gross weekly pay is $1307.69
```

6.15 The `exit()` Function

> **CONCEPT** The `exit()` function causes a program to terminate, regardless of which function or control mechanism is executing.

A C++ program stops executing when the `return` statement in function `main` is encountered. When other functions end, however, the program does not stop. Control of the program goes back to the place immediately following the function call. Sometimes it's convenient or even necessary to terminate a program in a function other than `main`. To accomplish this, the `exit` function is used.

When the `exit` function is called, it causes the program to stop, regardless of which function contains the call. Program 6-26 demonstrates it.

Program 6-26

```cpp
// This program shows how the exit function causes a program
// to stop executing.
#include <iostream>
#include <cstdlib>     // For exit
using namespace std;

void function();       // Function prototype

int main()
{
    function();
    return 0;
}

//***********************************************************
// This function simply demonstrates that exit can be used  *
// to terminate a program from a function other than main.  *
//***********************************************************

void function()
{
    cout << "This program terminates with the exit function.\n";
    cout << "Bye!\n";
    exit(0);
    cout << "This message will never be displayed\n";
    cout << "because the program has already terminated.\n";
}
```

Program Output

```
This program terminates with the exit function.
Bye!
```

To use the `exit` function, be sure to include the `cstdlib` header file. Notice the function takes an integer argument. This argument is the exit code you wish the program to pass back to the computer's operating system. This code is sometimes used outside of the program to indicate whether the program ended successfully or as the result of a failure. In Program 6-26, the exit code zero is passed, which commonly indicates a successful exit. If you are unsure which code to use with the `exit` function, there are two named constants, `EXIT_FAILURE` and `EXIT_SUCCESS`, defined in `cstdlib` for you to use. The constant `EXIT_FAILURE` is defined as the termination code that commonly represents an unsuccessful exit under the current operating system. Here is an example of its use:

```cpp
exit(EXIT_FAILURE);
```

The constant EXIT_SUCCESS is defined as the termination code that commonly represents a successful exit under the current operating system. Here is an example:

```
exit(EXIT_SUCCESS);
```

 Note: Generally, the exit code is only important if you know it will be tested outside the program. If it is not used, just pass zero, or EXIT_SUCCESS.

 ## Checkpoint [6.14–6.16]

6.19 What is the output of the following program?

```cpp
#include <iostream>
using namespace std;

int manip(int, int);
int main ()
{
    int x = 4, y = 7;

    cout << manip(x, y) << endl;
    return 0;
}

int manip(int val1, int val2)
{
    return (val1 + val2) * 2;
}
```

6.20 When completed, the following program skeleton should ask the user for the length and width of a yard, and then display the yard's area. You must write the prototype and the definition of the function calcArea to complete the program.

```cpp
// Program to calculate the area of a rectangular yard.
#include <iostream>
using namespace std;

// Place prototype here for calcArea.

int main()
{
    double length, width, area;
    cout << "This program calculates the area of a\n";
    cout << "rectangular yard. It must know the yard's\n";
    cout << "length and width. How long is the yard? ";
    cin >> length;
    cout << "How wide is the yard? ";
    cin >> width;
    area = calcArea(length, width);
    cout << "The area of the yard is " << area;
    return 0;
}
```

```
double calcArea(double len, double wide)
{
    // You must write this function which is to calculate and return
    // the area of the yard. Simply multiply the length
    // by the width and return the value.
}
```

6.16   Stubs and Drivers

Stubs and *drivers* are very helpful tools for testing and debugging programs that use functions. They allow you to test the individual functions in a program, in isolation from the parts of the program that call the functions.

A *stub* is a dummy function that is called instead of the actual function it represents. It usually displays a test message acknowledging that it was called, and nothing more. For example, if stubs were used in Program 6-9 (the modular health club membership program), they might look like those listed below.

```
// Stub for the adult function.
void adult(int months)
{
    cout << "The function adult was called with " << months;
    cout << " as its argument.\n";
}

// Stub for the child function.
void child(int months)
{
    cout << "The function child was called with " << months;
    cout << " as its argument.\n";
}

// Stub for the senior function.
void senior(int months)
{
    cout << "The function senior was called with " << months;
    cout << " as its argument.\n";
}
```

Below is example output of the program if it were run with the stubs shown above, instead of the actual functions.

```
            Health Club Membership Menu

    1.  Standard Adult Membership
    2.  Child Membership
    3.  Senior Citizen Membership
    4.  Quit the Program

Enter your choice: 1
For how many months? 4
The function adult was called with 4 as its argument.
```

```
              Health Club Membership Menu

        1.  Standard Adult Membership
        2.  Child Membership
        3.  Senior Citizen Membership
        4.  Quit the Program

    Enter your choice: 4
```

As you can see, by replacing an actual function with a stub, you can concentrate your testing efforts on the parts of the program that call the function. Primarily, the stub allows you to determine if your program is calling a function when you expect it to, and confirm that valid values are being passed to the function. If the stub represents a function that returns a value, then the stub should return a test value. This helps you confirm that the return value is being handled properly. When the parts of the program that call a function are debugged to your satisfaction, you can move on to testing and debugging the actual functions themselves. This is where *drivers* become useful.

A driver is a program that tests a function by simply calling it. If the function accepts arguments, the driver passes test data. If the function returns a value, the driver displays the return value on the screen. This allows you to see how the function performs in isolation from the rest of the program it will eventually be part of. For example, let's assume we are using drivers to test the functions in the health club membership program. Program 6-27 is a driver for testing the adult function.

Program 6-27

```cpp
// This program is a driver for testing the adult function.
#include <iostream>
using namespace std;

// Prototype
void adult(int);

int main()
{
    cout << "Calling the adult function with argument 2.\n";
    adult(2);
    cout << "Calling the adult function with argument 10.\n";
    adult(10);
    cout << "Calling the adult function with argument 25.\n";
    adult(25);
    return 0;
}
```

(program continues)

Program 6-27 *(continued)*

```
//********************************************************************
// Definition of function adult. Uses an integer parameter, mon.  *
// mon holds the number of months the membership should be         *
// calculated for. The cost of an adult membership for that many   *
// months is displayed.                                            *
//********************************************************************

void adult(int mon)
{
    cout << "The total charges are $";
    cout << (mon * 40.0) << endl;
}
```

Program Output
```
Calling the adult function with argument 2.
The total charges are $80
Calling the adult function with argument 10.
The total charges are $400
Calling the adult function with argument 25.
The total charges are $1000
```

As shown in the example above, a driver can be used to thoroughly test a function. It can repeatedly call the function with different test values as arguments. When the function performs as desired, it can be placed into the actual program it will be part of.

 See the CaseStudies.pdf file on the accompanying CD for this chapter's case studies.

Review Questions and Exercises

Short Answer

1. Why do local variables lose their values between calls to the function in which they are defined?
2. What is the difference between an argument and a parameter variable?
3. Where do you define parameter variables?
4. If you are writing a function that accepts an argument and you want to make sure the function cannot change the value of the argument, what do you do?
5. When a function accepts multiple arguments, does it matter what order the arguments are passed in?
6. How do you return a value from a function?
7. What is the advantage of breaking your application's code into several small procedures?

8. How would a `static` local variable be useful?

9. Give an example where passing an argument by reference would be useful.

Algorithm Workbench

10. Examine the following function header, then write an example call to the function.

```
void showValue(int quantity)
```

11. The following statement calls a function named `half`. The `half` function returns a value that is half that of the argument. Write the function.

```
result = half(number);
```

12. A program contains the following function.

```
int cube(int num)
{
    return num * num * num;
}
```

Write a statement that passes the value 4 to this function and assigns its return value to the variable `result`.

13. Write a function, named `timesTen`, that accepts an argument. When the function is called, it should display the product of its argument multiplied times 10.

14. A program contains the following function.

```
void display(int arg1, double arg2, char arg3)
{
    cout << "Here are the values: "
         << arg1 << " " << arg2 << " "
         << arg3 << endl;
}
```

Write a statement that calls the procedure and passes the following variables to it:

```
int age;
double income;
char initial;
```

15. Write a function named `getNumber`, which uses a reference parameter variable to accept an integer argument. The function should prompt the user to enter a number in the range of 1 through 100. The input should be validated and stored in the parameter variable.

True or False

16. T F Functions should be given names that reflect their purpose.

17. T F Function headers are terminated with a semicolon.

18. T F Function prototypes are terminated with a semicolon.

19. T   F   If other functions are defined before `main`, the program still starts executing at function `main`.

20. T   F   When a function terminates, it always branches back to `main`, regardless of where it was called from.

21. T   F   Arguments are passed to the function parameters in the order they appear in the function call.

22. T   F   The scope of a parameter is limited to the function which uses it.

23. T   F   Changes to a function parameter always affect the original argument as well.

24. T   F   In a function prototype, the names of the parameter variables may be left out.

25. T   F   Many functions may have local variables with the same name.

26. T   F   Overuse of global variables can lead to problems as programs become larger and more complex.

27. T   F   Static local variables are not destroyed when a function returns.

28. T   F   All static local variables are initialized to –1 by default.

29. T   F   Initialization of static local variables only happens once, regardless of how many times the function in which they are defined is called.

30. T   F   When a function with default arguments is called and an argument is left out, all arguments that come after it must be left out as well.

31. T   F   It is not possible for a function to have some parameters with default arguments and some without.

32. T   F   The `exit` function can only be called from `main`.

33. T   F   A stub is a dummy function that is called instead of the actual function it represents.

Find the Errors

Each of the following functions has errors. Locate as many errors as you can.

34.
```cpp
void total(int value1, value2, value3)
{
    return value1 + value2 + value3;
}
```

35.
```cpp
float average(int value1, int value2, int value3)
{
    float average;

    average = value1 + value2 + value3 / 3;
}
```

36.
```cpp
void area(int length = 30, int width)
{
    return length * width;
}
```

37.
```cpp
void getValue(int value&)
{
    cout << "Enter a value: ";
    cin >> value&;
}
```

38. *(Overloaded functions)*

```cpp
int getValue()
{
    int inputValue;
    cout << "Enter an integer: ";
    cin >> inputValue;
    return inputValue;
}
double getValue()
{
    double inputValue;
    cout << "Enter a floating-point number: ";
    cin >> inputValue;
    return inputValue;
}
```

Programming Challenges

1. Markup

Write a program that asks for the wholesale cost of an item and its markup percentage. (For example, if an item's wholesale cost is $5 and its retail price is $10, the markup is 100 percent).

The program should have a function that accepts the wholesale cost and markup percentage as arguments, and returns the retail price of the item. The retail price should be displayed.

Input Validation: Do not accept negative values for either the wholesale cost of the item or the percent markup.

2. Lowest Score Drop

This program is to calculate the average of a series of test scores, where the lowest score in the series is dropped. It should use the following functions:

◆ getValues should ask for five test scores and store them in variables.

◆ findLowest should determine which of the five scores is the lowest and return that value.

◆ calcAverage should calculate and display the average of the four highest scores.

Input Validation: Do not accept test scores higher than 100 or lower than 0.

3. Winning Division

This program should calculate which division in a company had the greatest sales for a quarter. It should use the following functions:

- ◆ A function should ask the user for and return the quarterly sales figures for the company's Northeast, Southeast, Northwest, and Southwest divisions.

- ◆ A function should determine which division had the highest sales figures.

A message should be displayed indicating the leading division and its sales figures for the quarter.

Input Validation: Do not accept dollar amounts less than $0.00.

4. Days Out

Write a program that calculates the average number of days a company's employees are absent. The program should have the following functions:

- ◆ A function that asks the user for the number of employees in the company. This value should be returned as an `int`. (The function accepts no arguments.)

- ◆ A function that accepts one argument: the number of employees in the company. The function should ask the user to enter the number of days each employee missed during the past year. The total of these days should be returned as an `int`.

- ◆ A function that takes two arguments: the number of employees in the company and the total number of days absent for all employees during the year. The function should return, as a `double`, the average number of days absent. (This function does not perform screen output and does not ask the user for input.)

Input Validation: Do not accept a number less than 1 or for the number of employees. Do not accept a negative number for the days any employee missed.

5. Order Status

The Middletown Wholesale Copper Wire Company sells spools of copper wiring for $100 each. Write a program that displays the status of an order. The program should have a function that asks for the following data:

- ◆ The number of spools ordered.

- ◆ The number of spools in stock.

- ◆ If there are special shipping and handling charges.

(Shipping and handling is normally $10 per spool.) If there are special charges, it should ask for the special charges per spool.

The gathered data should be passed as arguments to another function that displays:

- ◆ The number of spools ready to ship from current stock.

- ◆ The number of spools on backorder (if the number ordered is greater than what is in stock.)

◆ Subtotal of the portion ready to ship (the number of spools ready to ship times $100).

◆ Total shipping and handling charges on the portion ready to ship.

◆ Total of the order ready to ship.

The shipping and handling parameter in the second function should have the default argument 10.00.

> *Input Validation: Do not accept numbers less than 1 for spools ordered. Do not accept a number less than 0 for spools in stock or shipping and handling charges.*

6. Overloaded Hospital

Write a program that computes and displays the charges for a patient's hospital stay. First, the program should ask if the patient was admitted as an in-patient or an out-patient. If the patient was an in-patient, the following data should be entered:

◆ The number of days spent in the hospital

◆ The daily rate

◆ Hospital medication charges

◆ Charges for hospital services (lab tests, etc.)

The program should ask for the following data if the patient was an out-patient:

◆ Charges for hospital services (lab tests, etc.)

◆ Hospital medication charges

The program should use two overloaded functions to calculate the total charges. One of the functions should accept arguments for the in-patient data, while the other function accepts arguments for out-patient information. Both functions should return the total charges.

> *Input Validation: Do not accept negative numbers for any data.*

7. Population

In a population, the birth rate is the percentage increase of the population due to births and the death rate is the percentage decrease of the population due to deaths. Write a program that displays the size of a population for any number of years. The program should ask for the following data:

◆ The starting size of a population

◆ The annual birth rate

◆ The annual death rate

◆ The number of years to display

Write a function that calculates the size of the population for a year. The formula is

```
N = P + BP - DP
```

Where N is the new population size, P is the previous population size, B is the birth rate, and D is the death rate.

Input Validation: Do not accept numbers less than 2 for the starting size. Do not accept negative numbers for birth rate or death rate. Do not accept numbers less than 1 for the number of years.

8. Paint Job Estimator

A painting company has determined that for every 115 square feet of wall space, one gallon of paint and eight hours of labor will be required. The company charges $18.00 per hour for labor. Write a modular program that allows the user to enter the number of rooms that are to be painted and the price of the paint per gallon. It should also ask for the square feet of wall space in each room. It should then display the following data:

 ◆ The number of gallons of paint required

 ◆ The hours of labor required

 ◆ The cost of the paint

 ◆ The labor charges

 ◆ The total cost of the paint job

Input validation: Do not accept a value less than 1 for the number of rooms. Do not accept a value less than $10.00 for the price of paint. Do not accept a negative value for square footage of wall space.

Group Project

9. Travel Expenses

This program should be designed and written by a team of students. Here are some suggestions:

 ◆ One student should design function main, which will call the other functions in the program. The remainder of the functions will be designed by other members of the team.

 ◆ The requirements of the program should be analyzed so each student is given about the same work load.

 ◆ The parameters and return types of each function should be decided in advance.

 ◆ Stubs and drivers should be used to test and debug the program.

 ◆ The program can be implemented either as a multi-file program, or all the functions can be cut and pasted into the main file.

Here is the assignment: Write a program that calculates and displays the total travel expenses of a businessperson on a trip. The program should have functions that ask for and return the following:

◆ The total number of days spent on the trip

◆ The time of departure on the first day of the trip, and the time of arrival back home on the last day of the trip

◆ The amount of any round-trip airfare

◆ The amount of any car rentals

◆ Miles driven, if a private vehicle was used. Calculate the vehicle expense as $0.27 per mile driven

◆ Parking fees (The company allows up to $6 per day. Anything in excess of this must be paid by the employee.)

◆ Taxi fees, if a taxi was used anytime during the trip (The company allows up to $10 per day, for each day a taxi was used. Anything in excess of this must be paid by the employee.)

◆ Conference or seminar registration fees

◆ Hotel expenses (The company allows up to $90 per night for lodging. Anything in excess of this must be paid by the employee.)

◆ The amount of *each* meal eaten. On the first day of the trip, breakfast is allowed as an expense if the time of departure is before 7 a.m. Lunch is allowed if the time of departure is before 12 noon. Dinner is allowed on the first day if the time of departure is before 6 p.m. On the last day of the trip, breakfast is allowed if the time of arrival is after 8 a.m. Lunch is allowed if the time of arrival is after 1 p.m. Dinner is allowed on the last day if the time of arrival is after 7 p.m. The program should only ask for the amounts of allowable meals. (The company allows up to $9 for breakfast, $12 for lunch, and $16 for dinner. Anything in excess of this must be paid by the employee.)

The program should calculate and display the total expenses incurred by the businessperson, the total allowable expenses for the trip, the excess that must be reimbursed by the businessperson, if any, and the amount saved by the businessperson if the expenses were under the total allowed.

Input Validation: Do not accept negative numbers for any dollar amount or for miles driven in a private vehicle. Do not accept numbers less than 1 for the number of days. Only accept valid times for the time of departure and the time of arrival.

7

Arrays

- ## Topics in this Chapter

7.1   Arrays Hold Multiple Values

CONCEPT   An array allows you to store and work with multiple values of the same data type.

The variables you have worked with so far are designed to hold only one value at a time. Each of the variable definitions in Figure 7-1 cause only enough memory to be reserved to hold one value of the specified data type.

```
int count;     Enough memory for 1 int
                      12314

float price;   Enough memory for 1 float
                      56.981

char letter;   Enough memory for 1 char
                        A
```

Figure 7-1

An array works like a variable that can store a group of values, all of the same type. The values are stored together in consecutive memory locations. Here is a definition of an array of integers:

```
int days[6];
```

The name of this array is days. The number inside the brackets is the array's *size declarator*. It indicates the number of *elements*, or values, the array can hold. The days array can store six elements, each one an integer. This is depicted in Figure 7-2.

days array: enough memory for 6 int values

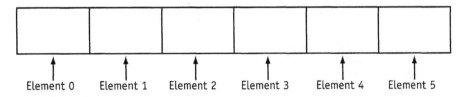

Figure 7-2 Element 0   Element 1   Element 2   Element 3   Element 4   Element 5

An array's size declarator must be a constant integer expression with a value greater than zero. It can be either a literal, as in the example, or a named constant, as shown in the following:

```
const int NUM_DAYS = 6;
int days[NUM_DAYS];

#define ARRAY_SIZE 6
int days[ARRAY_SIZE];
```

Arrays of any data type can be defined. The following are all valid array definitions:

```
float temperatures[100]; // Array of 100 floats
char name[41];           // Array of 41 characters
long units[50];          // Array of 50 long integers
double sizes[1200];      // Array of 1200 doubles
```

Memory Requirements of Arrays

The amount of memory used by an array depends on the array's data type and the number of elements. The hours array, defined here, is an array of six shorts.

```
short hours [6];
```

On a typical PC, a short uses two bytes of memory, so the hours array would occupy 12 bytes. This is shown in Figure 7-3:

hours array: Each element uses 2 bytes

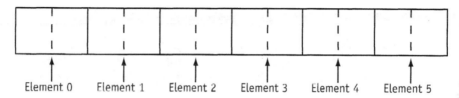

Figure 7-3   Element 0   Element 1   Element 2   Element 3   Element 4   Element 5

The size of an array can be calculated by multiplying the size of an individual element by the number of elements in the array. Table 7-1 shows the sizes of various arrays defined using Borland C++ or Microsoft Visual C++.

Table 7-1

Array Definition	Number of Elements	Size of each Element	Size of the Array
char letters[25];	25	1 byte	25 bytes
short rings[100];	100	2 bytes	200 bytes
int miles[84];	84	4 bytes	336 bytes
float temp[12];	12	4 bytes	48 bytes
double distance[1000];	1000	8 bytes	8000 bytes

7.2 Accessing Array Elements

CONCEPT The individual elements of an array are assigned unique subscripts. These subscripts are used to access the elements.

Even though an entire array has only one name, the elements may be accessed and used as individual variables. This is possible because each element is assigned a number known as a *subscript*. A subscript is used as an index to pinpoint a specific element within an array. The first element is assigned the subscript 0, the second element is assigned 1, and so forth. The six elements in the array hours would have the subscripts 0 through 5. This is shown in Figure 7-4.

Subscripts

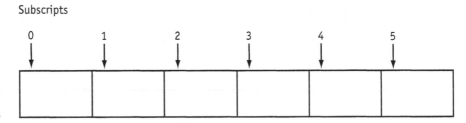

Figure 7-4

 Note: Subscript numbering in C++ always starts at zero. The subscript of the last element in an array is one less than the total number of elements in the array. This means that in the array shown in Figure 7-4, the element hours[6] does not exist. hours[5] is the last element in the array.

Each element in the hours array, when accessed by its subscript, can be used as a short variable. Here is an example of a statement that stores the number 20 in the first element of the array:

```
hours[0] = 20;
```

 Note: The expression hours[0] is pronounced "hours sub zero." You would read this assignment statement as "hours sub zero is assigned twenty."

Figure 7-5 shows the contents of the array hours after the statement assigns 20 to hours[0].

hours[0]	hours[1]	hours[2]	hours[3]	hours[4]	hours[5]
20	?	?	?	?	?

Figure 7-5

 Note: Because values have not been assigned to the other elements of the array, question marks will be used to indicate that the contents of those elements are unknown. If an array is defined globally, all of its elements are initialized to zero by default. Local arrays, however, have no default initialization value.

The following statement stores the integer 30 in hours[3].

```
hours[3] = 30;
```

Figure 7-6 shows the contents of the array after the statement above executes:

hours[0]   hours[1]   hours[2]   hours[3]   hours[4]   hours[5]

| 20 | ? | ? | 30 | ? | ? |

Figure 7-6

Note: Understand the difference between the array size declarator and a subscript. The number inside the brackets of an array definition is the size declarator. The number inside the brackets of an assignment statement or any statement that works with the contents of an array is a subscript.

Inputting and Outputting Array Contents

Array elements may be used with the cin and cout objects like any other variable. The following program segment shows the array hours being used to store and display values entered by the user.

```
const int NUM_EMPLOYEES = 6;
int hours[NUM_EMPLOYEES];

cout << "Enter the hours worked by three employees: ";
cin >> hours[0];
cin >> hours[1];
cin >> hours[2];
cout << "The hours you entered are:";
cout << " " << hours[0];
cout << " " << hours[1];
cout << " " << hours[2] << endl;
```

Program Output with Example Input Shown in Bold
```
Enter the hours worked by three employees: 20 12 40 [Enter]
The hours you entered are: 20 12 40
```

Figure 7-7 shows the contents of the array hours with the values entered by the user in the example output above.

hours[0]   hours[1]   hours[2]

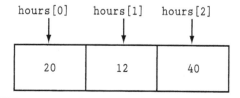

Figure 7-7

Even though the size declarator of an array definition must be a constant or a literal, subscript numbers can be stored in variables. This makes it possible to use a loop to "cycle through" an entire array, performing the same operation on each element. For example, Program 7-1 uses two for loops: one for inputting the values into the array and another for displaying the contents of the array.

Program 7-1

```
// This program asks the user for the number of hours worked
// by each employee. It uses an int array to store the values.
#include <iostream>
using namespace std;

int main()
{
    const int NUM_EMPLOYEES = 6; // Number of employees
    int hours[NUM_EMPLOYEES];    // Each employee's hours
    int count;                   // Loop counter

    // Input the hours worked.
    cout << "Enter the hours worked by " << NUM_EMPLOYEES << " employees: ";
    for (count = 0; count < NUM_EMPLOYEES; count++)
        cin >> hours[count];

    // Display the contents of the array.
    cout << "The hours you entered are:";
    for (count = 0; count < NUM_EMPLOYEES; count++)
        cout << " " << hours[count];
    cout << endl;
    return 0;
}
```

Program Output with Example Input Shown in Bold
```
Enter the hours worked by six employees: 20 12 40 30 30 15 [Enter]
The hours you entered are: 20 12 40 30 30 15
```

Notice in Program 7-1 that a const integer named NUM_EMPLOYEES is defined with the value 6, and used as the size declarator for the hours array. It is also used as the upper limit in the test expressions of the for loops. This is a good practice because it makes the program easier to maintain. If we ever need to change the size of the array, we need only to change the value of the named constant.

Any integer expression may be used as a subscript. Program 7-2 is a more user-friendly version of Program 7-1. The expression count - 1 is used to calculate the subscript of the desired array element.

Program 7-2

```cpp
// This program asks the user for the number of hours worked
// by each employees. It uses an int array to store the values.
#include <iostream>
using namespace std;

int main()
{
    const int NUM_EMPLOYEES = 6; // Number of employees
    short hours[NUM_EMPLOYEES];   // Each employee's hours
    int count;                    // Loop counter

    // Input the hours worked.
    cout << "Enter the hours worked by " << NUM_EMPLOYEES << " employees.\n";
    for (count = 1; count <= NUM_EMPLOYEES; count++)
    {
        cout << "Employee " << count << ": ";
        cin >> hours[count - 1];
    }

    // Display the contents of the array.
    cout << "The hours you entered are\n";
    for (count = 1; count <= NUM_EMPLOYEES; count++)
    {
        cout << "Employee " << count << ": ";
        cout << hours[count - 1] << endl;
    }
    cout << endl;
    return 0;
}
```

Program Output with Example Input Shown in Bold
```
Enter the hours worked by 6 employees.
Employee 1: 20 [Enter]
Employee 2: 12 [Enter]
Employee 3: 40 [Enter]
Employee 4: 30 [Enter]
Employee 5: 30 [Enter]
Employee 6: 15 [Enter]
The hours you entered are
Employee 1: 20
Employee 2: 12
Employee 3: 40
Employee 4: 30
Employee 5: 30
Employee 6: 15
```

7.3 No Bounds Checking in C++

> **CONCEPT** C++ gives you the freedom to store data past an array's boundaries.

One of the reasons for C++'s popularity is the freedom it gives programmers to work with the computer's memory. Many of the safeguards provided by other languages to prevent programs from unsafely accessing memory are absent in C++. For example, C++ does not perform array bounds checking. This means you can write programs with subscripts that go beyond the boundaries of a particular array. Program 7-3 demonstrates this capability.

 WARNING! Think twice before you compile and run Program 7-3. The program will attempt to write to an area of memory outside the array. This is an invalid operation, and will most likely cause the program to crash. Under some operating systems, it could even cause the computer to lock up.

Program 7-3

```
// This program unsafely accesses an area of memory by writing
// values beyond an array's boundary.
// WARNING: If you compile and run this program, it could crash
#include <iostream>
using namespace std;

int main()
{
    int values[3];              // An array of 3 integers.

    cout << "I will store 5 numbers in a 3 element array!\n";
    for (int count = 0; count < 5; count++)
        values[count] = 100;
    cout << "If you see this message, it means the computer\n";
    cout << "has not crashed! Here are the numbers:\n";
    for (int count = 0; count < 5; count++)
        cout << values[count] << endl;
    return 0;
}
```

The values array can hold three integer elements, with the subscripts 0, 1, and 2. The loop, however, stores the number 100 in elements 0, 1, 2, 3, and 4. The elements with subscripts 3 and 4 do not exist, but C++ allows the program to write beyond the boundary of the array, as if those elements were there. Figure 7-8 depicts the way the array is set up in memory when the program first starts to execute, and what happens when the loop writes data beyond the boundary of the array.

You must always make sure that any time values are assigned to array elements, they are written within the array's boundaries.

The Way the `values` Array is Set Up in Memory
(The Outlined Area is the Array)

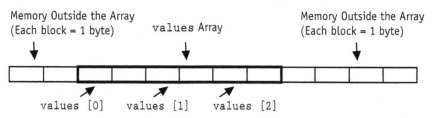

How the Numbers Assigned to the Elements Overflow the Array's Boundaries
(The Shaded Area Is the Section of Memory Written to)

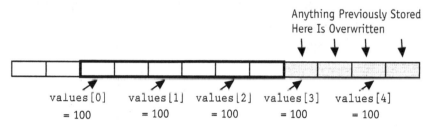

Figure 7-8

Checkpoint [7.1–7.3]

7.1 Define the following arrays:

A) `empNums`, a 100–element array of `int`s

B) `payRates`, a 25–element array of `float`s

C) `miles`, a 14–element array of `long`s

D) `cityName`, a 26–element array of `char`s

E) `lightYears`, a 1,000–element array of `double`s

7.2 What's wrong with the following array definitions?

```
int readings[-1];
float measurements[4.5];
int size;
char name[size];
```

7.3 What would the valid subscript values be in a four-element array of `double`s?

7.4 What is the difference between an array's size declarator and a subscript?

7.5 What is "array bounds checking"? Does C++ perform it?

7.6 What is the output of the following code?

```
int values[5], count;
```

```
for (count = 0; count < 5; count++)
    values[count] = count + 1;
for (count = 0; count < 5; count++)
    cout << values[count] << endl;
```

7.4 Array Initialization

CONCEPT Arrays may be initialized when they are defined.

Writing separate assignment statements for the individual elements of an array can mean a lot of typing, especially for large arrays. For example, consider the following program segment.

```
const int MONTHS = 12;
int days[MONTHS];

days[0] = 31;   // January
days[1] = 28;   // February
days[2] = 31;   // March
days[3] = 30;   // April
days[4] = 31;   // May
days[5] = 30;   // June
days[6] = 31;   // July
days[7] = 31;   // August
days[8] = 30;   // September
days[9] = 31;   // October
days[10] = 30;  // November
days[11] = 31;  // December
```

This program segment uses 12 assignment statements to store the initial values into the array. Fortunately, there is an alternative. Like other variables, C++ allows you to initialize arrays when you define them. The following statement defines the array days and initializes it with the same values established by the set of assignment statements in the program segment:

```
int days[MONTHS] = {31, 28, 31, 30, 31, 30, 31, 31, 30, 31, 30, 31};
```

The series of values inside the braces and separated with commas is called an *initialization list*. These values are stored in the array elements in the order they appear in the list. (The first value, 31, is stored in days[0], the second value, 28, is stored in days[1], and so forth). Figure 7-9 shows the contents of the array after the initialization.

Subscripts

0	1	2	3	4	5	6	7	8	9	10	11
31	28	31	30	31	30	31	31	30	31	30	31

Figure 7-9

Program 7-4 initializes the array at its definition rather than using the separate assignment statements.

Program 7-4

```cpp
// This program displays the number of days in each month.
#include <iostream>
using namespace std;

int main()
{
    const int MONTHS = 12;
    int days[MONTHS] = {31, 28, 31, 30,
                        31, 30, 31, 31,
                        30, 31, 30, 31};
    for (int count = 0; count < MONTHS; count++)
    {
        cout << "Month " << (count + 1) << " has ";
        cout << days[count] << " days.\n";
    }
    return 0;
}
```

Program Output

```
Month 1 has 31 days.
Month 2 has 28 days.
Month 3 has 31 days.
Month 4 has 30 days.
Month 5 has 31 days.
Month 6 has 30 days.
Month 7 has 31 days.
Month 8 has 31 days.
Month 9 has 30 days.
Month 10 has 31 days.
Month 11 has 30 days.
Month 12 has 31 days.
```

Note: Notice that C++ allows you to spread the initialization list across multiple lines. Both of the following array definitions are equivalent:

```cpp
double coins[5] = {0.05, 0.1, 0.25, 0.5, 1.0};
double coins[5] = {0.05,
                   0.1,
                   0.25,
                   0.5,
                   1.0};
```

Program 7-5 shows a character array being initialized with the first 10 letters of the alphabet. The array is then used to display those character's ASCII codes.

Program 7-5

```cpp
// This program uses an array of 10 characters to store the
// first 10 Letters of the alphabet. The ASCII codes of the
// characters are displayed.
#include <iostream>
using namespace std;

int main()
{
    const int NUM_LETTERS = 10;
    char letters[NUM_LETTERS] = {'A', 'B', 'C', 'D', 'E',
                                 'F', 'G', 'H', 'I', 'J'};

    cout << "Character" << "\t" << "ASCII Code\n";
    cout << "---------" << "\t" << "----------\n";
    for (int count = 0; count < NUM_LETTERS; count++)
    {
        cout << letters[count] << "\t\t";
        cout << static_cast<int>(letters[count]) << endl;
    }
    return 0;
}
```

Program Output

```
Character    ASCII Code
---------    ----------
A            65
B            66
C            67
D            68
E            69
F            70
G            71
H            72
I            73
J            74
```

 Note: The initialization list cannot have more values than the array has elements.

Partial Array Initialization

When an array is being initialized, C++ does not require a value for every element. It's possible to only initialize part of an array, such as:

```cpp
int numbers[7] = {1, 2, 4, 8};
```

This definition initializes only the first four elements of a seven-element array, as illustrated in Figure 7-10.

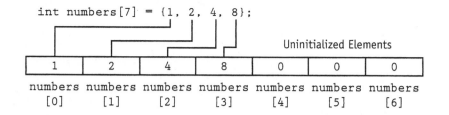

Figure 7-10

It's important to note that if an array is partially initialized, the uninitialized elements will be set to zero. This is true even if the array is defined locally. (If a local array is completely uninitialized, its elements will contain "garbage," like all other local variables.) Program 7-6 shows the contents of the array numbers after it is partially initialized.

Program 7-6

```cpp
// This program has a partially initialized array.
#include <iostream>
using namespace std;

int main()
{
    const int SIZE = 7;
    int numbers[SIZE] = {1, 2, 4, 8}; // Initialize the first 4
                                      // elements.

    cout << "Here are the contents of the array;\n";
    for (int index = 0; index < SIZE; index++)
        cout << numbers[index] << " ";
    return 0;
}
```

Program Output
```
Here are the contents of the array:
1 2 4 8 0 0 0
```

If you leave an element uninitialized, you must leave all the elements that follow it uninitialized as well. C++ does not provide a way to skip elements in the initialization list. For example, the following is *not* legal:

```cpp
int array[6] = {2, 4, , 8, , 12}; // NOT Legal!
```

Implicit Array Sizing

It's possible to define an array without specifying its size, as long as you provide an initialization list. C++ automatically makes the array large enough to hold all the initialization values. For example, the following definition creates an array with five elements:

```cpp
double ratings[] = {1.0, 1.5, 2.0, 2.5, 3.0};
```

Because the size declarator is omitted, C++ counts the number of items in the initialization list and gives the array that many elements.

 Note: You *must* specify an initialization list if you leave out the size declarator. Otherwise, C++ doesn't know how large to make the array.

Initializing with Strings

When initializing a character array with a string, simply enclose the string in quotation marks, as shown here:

```
char name[7] = "Warren";
```

Although there are six characters in the string "Warren," the array must have enough elements to also accommodate the null terminator at the end of the string. It's important to note that anytime a string literal is used in C++, the null terminator is automatically included. That's why name is defined above with seven elements. Figure 7-11 shows the contents of name after the initialization:

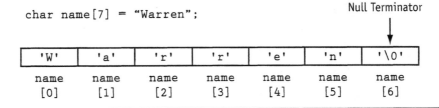

Figure 7-11

 Note: Recall from Chapter 2 that '\0' represents the null terminator. '\0' is an escape sequence that is stored in memory as a single character. Its ASCII code is 0.

The null terminator is not automatically included when an array is initialized with individual characters. It must be included in the initialization list, as shown below:

```
char name[7] = {'W', 'a', 'r', 'r', 'e', 'n', '\0'};
```

Program 7-7 shows two character arrays initialized with strings. The first is initialized with a string literal and the second is initialized with individual characters.

Program 7-7

```
// This program displays the contents of two char arrays.
#include <iostream>
using namespace std;

int main()
{
    char name1[] = "Holly";
    char name2[] = {'W', 'a', 'r', 'r', 'e', 'n', '\0'};
```

(program continues)

Program 7-7   *(continued)*

```
    cout << name1 << endl;
    cout << name2 << endl;
    return 0;
}
```

Program Output
```
Holly
Warren
```

In Program 7-7, notice that the size declarators for each array are left out. The compiler will size the arrays just large enough to hold the values they are initialized with. name1 will have six elements because the string "Holly" has five characters, plus the null terminator. name2 will have seven elements because there are seven characters in the initialization list.

In Chapter 2 you were shown that to display a string stored in a character array, you simply use the stream insertion operator to send the name of the array (without the brackets) to the cout object. It's important to point out that character arrays containing null-terminated strings are the only type of array this technique works with. You cannot display the contents of numeric arrays in this fashion. The following program segment will not display the values stored in qty:

```
int qty[4] = {2, 7, 9, 8};
cout << qty << endl;          // Wrong!
```

7.5   Processing Array Contents

CONCEPT   Individual array elements are processed like any other type of variable.

Processing array elements is no different than processing other variables. For example, the following statement multiplies hours[3] by the variable rate:

```
pay = hours[3] * rate;
```

And the following are examples of pre-increment and post-increment operations on array elements:

```
int score[5] = {7, 8, 9, 10, 11};
++score[2];    // Pre-increment operation on the value in score[2]
score[4]++;    // Post-increment operation on the value in score[4]
```

 Note: When using increment and decrement operators, be careful not to confuse the subscript with the array element. For example, the following statement decrements the variable count, but does nothing to the value in amount[count]:

```
amount[count--];
```

To decrement the value stored in `amount[count]`, use the following statement:

```
amount[count]--;
```

Program 7-8 demonstrates the use of array elements in a simple mathematical statement. A loop steps through each element of the array, using the elements to calculate the gross pay of five employees.

Program 7-8

```cpp
// This program stores, in an array, the hours worked by
// employees who all make the same hourly wage.
#include <iostream>
#include <iomanip>
using namespace std;

int main()
{
    const int NUM_EMPLOYEES = 5;
    int hours[NUM_EMPLOYEES];
    double payrate;

    // Input the hours worked.
    cout << "Enter the hours worked by ";
    cout << NUM_EMPLOYEES << " employees who all\n";
    cout << "earn the same hourly rate.\n";
    for (int index = 0; index < NUM_EMPLOYEES; index++)
    {
        cout << "Employee #" << (index + 1) << ": ";
        cin >> hours[index];
    }

    // Input the hourly rate for all employees.
    cout << "Enter the hourly pay rate for all the employees: ";
    cin >> payrate;

    // Display each employee's gross pay.
    cout << "Here is the gross pay for each employee:\n";
    cout << fixed << showpoint << setprecision(2);
    for (index = 0; index < NUM_EMPLOYEES; index++)
    {
        float grossPay = hours[index] * payrate;
        cout << "Employee #" << (index + 1);
        cout << ": $" << grossPay << endl;
    }
    return 0;
}
```

Program 7-8 *(continued)*

Program Output with Example Input Shown in Bold
```
Enter the hours worked by five employees who all
earn the same hourly rate.
Employee #1: 5 [Enter]
Employee #2: 10 [Enter]
Employee #3: 15 [Enter]
Employee #4: 20 [Enter]
Employee #5: 40 [Enter]
Enter the hourly pay rate for all the employees: 12.75 [Enter]
Here is the gross pay for each employee:
Employee #1: $63.75
Employee #2: $127.50
Employee #3: $191.25
Employee #4: $255.00
Employee #5: $510.00
```

In Program 7-8, the following statement defines the variable grossPay and initializes it with the value of hours[index] times payRate:

```
float grossPay = hours[index] * payRate;
```

Array elements may also be used in relational expressions. For example, the following if statement tests cost[20] to determine if it is less than cost[0]:

```
if (cost[20] < cost[0])
```

And the following statement sets up a while loop to iterate as long as value[place] does not equal 0:

```
while (value[place] != 0)
```

Thou Shall Not Assign

The following statement defines two integer arrays: newValues and oldValues. newValues is uninitialized and oldValues is initialized with 10, 100, 200, and 300:

```
int newValues[4], oldValues[4] = {10, 100, 200, 300};
```

At first glance, it might appear that the following statement assigns the contents of the array oldValues to newValues:

```
newValues = oldValues;      // Wrong!
```

Unfortunately, this statement will not work. The only way to assign one array to another is to assign the individual elements in the arrays. Usually, this is best done with a loop, such as:

```
for (int count = 0; count < 4; count++)
    newValues[count] = oldValues[count];
```

The reason the assignment operator will not work with an entire array at once is complex, but important to understand. Anytime the name of an array is used without brackets and a subscript, *it is seen as the array's beginning memory address.* To illustrate this, consider the definition of the arrays newValues and oldValues above. Figure 7-12 depicts the two arrays in memory.

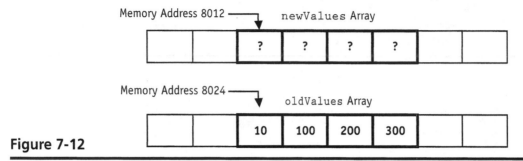

Figure 7-12

In the figure, newValues is shown starting at memory address 8012 and oldValues is shown starting at 8024. (Of course, these are just arbitrary addresses, picked for illustration purposes. In reality the addresses would probably be different.) Table 7-2 shows various expressions that use the names of these arrays, and their values.

Table 7-2

Expression	Value
oldValues[0]	10 (Contents of Element 0 of oldValues)
oldValues[1]	100 (Contents of Element 1 of oldValues)
oldValues[2]	200 (Contents of Element 2 of oldValues)
oldValues[3]	300 (Contents of Element 3 of oldValues)
newValues	8012 (Memory Address of newValues)
oldValues	8024 (Memory Address of oldValues)

Because the name of an array without the brackets and subscript stands for the array's starting memory address, the following statement

```
newValues = oldValues;
```

is interpreted by C++ as

```
8012 = 8024;
```

The statement will not work because you cannot change the starting memory address of an array.

Printing the Contents of an Array

To display the contents of an array, you must use a loop to display the contents of each element. Suppose a program has the following array definition:

```
int array[5] = { 10, 20, 30, 40, 50 };
```

C++ does NOT allow you to display the contents of the array by merely passing the name of the array to cout. For example, the following statement will not do what you might expect:

```
cout << array << endl;      // Wrong!
```

Remember from the previous section that an array name is seen as the array's beginning memory address. When this statement executes, cout will display the array's memory address, not the array's contents. Use a loop to display the contents of each of the array's elements, as follows.

```
for (int count = 0; count < 5; count++)
    cout << array[count] << endl;
```

The only exception to this rule is when you are displaying the contents of a char array that contains a C-string. For example, assume a program has the following code segment:

```
char name[5] = "Ruth";
cout << name << endl;
```

This cout statement displays the string "Ruth" instead of the array's address. This is because the stream insertion operator is designed to behave differently when it receives the address of a char array. When the stream insertion operator receives the address of a char array, it assumes a C-string is stored at that address, and sends the C-string to cout.

 WARNING! Do not pass the name of a char array to cout if the char array does not contain a null-terminated C-string. If you do, cout will display all the characters in memory, starting at the array's address, until it encounters a null terminator.

Summing the Values in a Numeric Array

To sum the values in an array, you must use a loop with an accumulator variable. The loop adds the value in each array element to the accumulator. For example, assume that the following statements appear in a program and that values have been stored in the units array.

```
const int NUM_UNITS = 24;
int units[NUM_UNITS];
```

The following loop adds the values of each element in the array to the total variable. When the code is finished, total will contain the sum of the units array's elements.

```
int total = 0;                 // Initialize accumulator
for (int count = 0; count < NUM_UNITS; count++)
    total += units[count];
```

Note: The first statement in the code segment sets `total` to 0. Recall from Chapter 5 that an accumulator variable must be set to 0 before it is used to keep a running total or the sum will not be correct.

Getting the Average of the Values in a Numeric Array

The first step in calculating the average of all the values in an array is to sum the values. The second step is to divide the sum by the number of elements in the array. Assume that the following statements appear in a program and that values have been stored in the `scores` array.

```cpp
const int NUM_SCORES = 10;
double scores[NUM_SCORES];
```

The following code calculates the average of the values in the `scores` array. When the code completes, the average will be stored in the `average` variable.

```cpp
double total = 0;                   // Initialize accumulator
double average;                     // Will hold the average
for (int count = 0; count < NUM_SCORES; count++)
    total += scores[count];
average = total / NUM_SCORES;
```

Notice that the last statement, which divides `total` by `numScores`, is not inside the loop. This statement should only execute once, after the loop has finished its iterations.

Finding the Highest and Lowest Values in a Numeric Array

The algorithms for finding the highest and lowest values in an array are very similar. First, let's look at code for finding the highest value in an array. Assume that the following code exists in a program, and that values have been stored in the array.

```cpp
const int SIZE = 50;
int numbers[SIZE];
```

The code to find the highest value in the array is as follows.

```cpp
int count;
int highest;

highest = numbers[0];
for (count = 1; count < SIZE; count++)
{
    if (numbers[count] > highest)
        highest = numbers[count];
}
```

First we copy the value in the first array element to the variable `highest`. Then the loop compares all of the remaining array elements, beginning at subscript 1, to the value in `highest`. Each time it finds a value in the array that is greater than highest, it copies that value to highest. When the loop has finished, highest will contain the highest value in the array.

The following code finds the lowest value in the array. As you can see, it is nearly identical to the code for finding the highest value.

```cpp
int count;
int lowest;

lowest = numbers[0];
for (count = 1; count < SIZE; count++)
{
   if (numbers[count] < lowest)
      lowest = numbers[count];
}
```

When the loop has finished, lowest will contain the lowest value in the array.

Program 7-9 demonstrates the algorithms for finding the sum, average, highest, and lowest values in an array.

Program 7-9

```cpp
// This program gets five days of sales data from the user
// and displays the total, average, highest, and lowest amounts.
#include <iostream>
#include <iomanip>
using namespace std;

int main()
{
    const int NUM_DAYS = 5;   // Number of days
    int count;                // Loop counter
    double sales[NUM_DAYS],   // To hold sales amounts
           total = 0,         // Accumulator
           average,           // To hold the average
           highest,           // To hold the highest sales
           lowest;            // To hold the lowest sales


    // Get the sales data.
    cout << "Enter the sales for this week.\n";
    for (count = 0; count < NUM_DAYS; count++)
    {
        cout << "Day " << (count +1) <<": ";
        cin >> sales[count];
    }
```

(program continues)

Program 7-9 *(continued)*

```cpp
    // Calculate the total sales.
    for (count = 0; count < NUM_DAYS; count++)
        total += sales[count];

    // Get the average.
    average = total / NUM_DAYS;

    // Find the highest sales amount.
    highest = sales[0];
    for (count = 1; count < NUM_DAYS; count++)
    {
        if (sales[count] > highest)
            highest = sales[count];
    }

    // Find the lowest sales amount.
    lowest = sales[0];
    for (count = 1; count < NUM_DAYS; count++)
    {
        if (sales[count] < lowest)
            lowest = sales[count];
    }

    // Display the results.
    cout << fixed << showpoint << setprecision(2);
    cout << "The total sales are $" << total << endl;
    cout << "The average sales amount is $" << average << endl;
    cout << "The highest sales amount is $" << highest << endl;
    cout << "The lowest sales amount is $" << lowest << endl;

    return 0;
}
```

Program Output with Example Input Shown in Bold

```
Enter the sales for this week.
Day 1: 2698.72 [Enter]
Day 2: 3757.29 [Enter]
Day 3: 1109.67 [Enter]
Day 4: 2498.65 [Enter]
Day 5: 1489.47 [Enter]
The total sales are $11553.80
The average sales amount is $2310.76
The highest sales amount is $3757.29
The lowest sales amount is $1109.67
```

Working with Arrays and Files

Saving the contents of an array to a file is a straightforward procedure: Use a loop to step through each element of the array, writing its contents to the file. For example, assume a program defines an array with the following statements.

```
const int SIZE = 5;
int values[SIZE] = {10,20,30,40,50};
```

The following code opens a file named values.txt and writes the contents of each element of the values array to the file.

```
ofstream outputFile;

// Open the file.
outputFile.open("values.txt");

// Write the array elements to the file.
for (int count = 0; count < SIZE; count++)
   outputFile << values[count] << endl;

// Close the file.
outputFile.close();
```

The following code demonstrates how to open the values.txt file and read its contents into the values array.

```
ifstream inputFile;
int count = 0;

// Open the file.
inputFile.open("values.txt");

// Read the values into the array.
while(count < SIZE && inputFile >> values[count])
   count++;

// Close the file.
inputFile.close();
return 0;
```

The loop repeats as long as count is less than SIZE and the end of the file has not been encountered. The first part of the while loop's condition, count < SIZE, prevents the loop from writing outside the array boundaries. Recall from Chapter 4 that the && operator performs short-circuit evaluation, so the second part of the while loop's condition, inputFile >> values[count], will be executed only if count is less than SIZE.

7.6 Focus on Software Engineering: *Using Parallel Arrays*

CONCEPT By using the same subscript, you can build relationships between data stored in two or more arrays.

Sometimes it's useful to store related data in two or more arrays. It's especially useful when the related data is of unlike types. For example, Program 7-10 is another variation of the payroll program. It uses two arrays: one to store the hours worked by each employee (as ints), and another to store each employee's hourly pay rate (as floats).

Program 7-10

```cpp
// This program stores, in an array, the hours worked by five
// employees who all make the same hourly wage.
#include <iostream>
#include <iomanip>
using namespace std;

int main()
{
    const int NUM_EMPLOYEES = 5;
    int hours[NUM_EMPLOYEES];          // Holds hours worked
    double payRate[NUM_EMPLOYEES];     // Holds pay rates

    // Input the hours worked.
    cout << "Enter the hours worked by " << NUM_EMPLOYEES;
    cout << " employees and their\n";
    cout << "hourly pay rates.\n";
    for (int index = 0; index < NUM_EMPLOYEES; index++)
    {
        cout << "Hours worked by employee #" << (index+1) << ": ";
        cin >> hours[index];
        cout << "Hourly pay rate for employee #" << (index+1) << ": ";
        cin >> payRate[index];
    }

    // Display each employee's gross pay.
    cout << "Here is the gross pay for each employee:\n";
    cout << fixed << showpoint << setprecision(2);
```

(program continues)

Program 7-10 *(continued)*

```
    for (index = 0; index < NUM_EMPLOYEES; index++)
    {
        double grossPay = hours[index] * payRate[index];
        cout << "Employee #" << (index + 1);
        cout << ": $" << grossPay << endl;
    }
    return 0;
}
```

Program Output with Example Input Shown in Bold
```
Enter the hours worked by five employees and their
hourly pay rates.
Hours worked by employee #1: 10 [Enter]
Hourly pay rate for employee #1: 9.75 [Enter]
Hours worked by employee #2: 15 [Enter]
Hourly pay rate for employee #2: 8.62 [Enter]
Hours worked by employee #3: 20 [Enter]
Hourly pay rate for employee #3: 10.50 [Enter]
Hours worked by employee #4: 40 [Enter]
Hourly pay rate for employee #4: 18.75 [Enter]
Hours worked by employee #5: 40 [Enter]
Hourly pay rate for employee #5: 15.65 [Enter]
Here is the gross pay for each employee:
Employee #1: $97.50
Employee #2: $129.30
Employee #3: $210.00
Employee #4: $750.00
Employee #5: $626.00
```

Notice in the loops the same subscript is used to access both arrays. That's because the data for one employee is stored in the same relative position in each array. For example, the hours worked by employee #1 are stored in hours[0], and the same employee's pay rate is stored in payRate[0]. The subscript relates the data in both arrays.

This concept is illustrated in Figure 7-13.

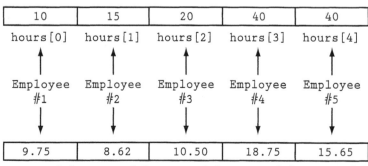

Figure 7-13

Checkpoint [7.4–7.6]

7.7 Define the following arrays:

A) `temps`, a seven-element array of `float`s initialized with the values 14.7, 16.3, 18.43, 21.09, 17.9, 18.76, and 26.7.

B) `alpha`, an eight-element array of `char`s initialized with the values 'J', 'B', 'L', 'A', '*', '$', 'H', and 'M'.

7.8 Are each of the following valid or invalid array definitions? (If a definition is invalid, explain why.)

```
int matrix[5] = {1, 2, 3, 4, 5, 6, 7};
double radii[10] = {3.2, 4.7};
int table[7] = {2, , , 27, , 45, 39};
char codes[] = {'A', 'X', '1', '2', 's'};
int blanks[];
char name[6] = "Joanne";
```

7.9 Given the following array definition:

```
int values[] = {2, 6, 10, 14};
```

What do each of the following display?

```
A) cout << ++values[0];
B) cout << values[1]++;
C) x = 2;
   cout << values[++x];
```

7.10 Given the following array definition:

```
int nums[5] = {1, 2, 3};
```

What will the following statement display?

```
cout << nums[3];
```

7.11 What is the output of the following code? (You may need to use a calculator.)

```
const int SIZE = 6;
int time[SIZE] =   {1, 2, 3, 4, 5},
    speed[SIZE] = {18, 4, 27, 52, 100},
    dist[SIZE];

for (int count = 0; count < SIZE; count++)
     dist[count] = time[count] * speed[count];
for (int count = 0; count < SIZE; count++)
{
   cout << time[count] << " ";
   cout << speed[count] << " ";
   cout << dist[count] << endl;
}
```

7.7 Arrays as Function Arguments

CONCEPT To pass an array as an argument to a function, pass the name of the array.

Quite often you'll want to write functions that process the data in arrays. For example, functions could be written to put values in an array, display an array's contents on the screen, total all of an array's elements, or calculate their average. Usually, such functions accept an array as an argument.

When a single element of an array is passed to a function, it is handled like any other variable. For example, Program 7-11 shows a loop that passes one element of the array `collection` to the function `showValue` each time the loop iterates.

Program 7-11

```cpp
// This program demonstrates that an array element is passed
// to a function like any other variable.
#include <iostream>
using namespace std;

void showValue(int);       // Function prototype

int main()
{
    const int SIZE = 8;
    int collection[SIZE] = {5, 10, 15, 20, 25, 30, 35, 40};

    for (int cycle = 0; cycle < SIZE; cycle++)
        showValue(collection[cycle]);
    return 0;
}

//*********************************************
// Definition of function showValue.          *
// This function accepts an integer argument.  *
// The value of the argument is displayed.      *
//*********************************************

void showValue(int num)
{
    cout << num << " ";
}
```

Program Output
```
5 10 15 20 25 30 35 40
```

Each time showValue is called in this program, a copy of an array element is passed into the parameter variable num. The showValue function simply displays the contents of num, and doesn't work directly with the array element itself. (In other words, the array element is passed by value.)

If the function were written to accept the entire array as an argument, however, the parameter would be set up differently. In the following function definition, the parameter nums is followed by an empty set of brackets. This indicates that the argument will be an array, not a single value.

```cpp
void showValues(int nums[], int size)
{
   for (int index = 0; index < size; index++)
      cout << nums[index] << " ";
   cout << endl;
}
```

The reason there is no size declarator inside the brackets of nums is because nums is not actually an array. It's a special variable that can accept the address of an array. When an entire array is passed to a function, it is not passed by value, but passed by reference. Imagine the CPU time and memory that would be necessary if a copy of a 10,000-element array were created each time it was passed to a function! Instead, only the starting memory address of the array is passed. Program 7-12 shows the function showValues in use.

Program 7-12

```cpp
// This program demonstrates an array being passed to a function.
#include <iostream>
using namespace std;

void showValues(int [], int);   // Function prototype

int main()
{
   const int ARRAY_SIZE = 8;
   int collection[ARRAY_SIZE] = {5, 10, 15, 20, 25, 30, 35, 40};

   showValues(collection, ARRAY_SIZE);
   return 0;
}

//*****************************************************
// Definition of function showValue                  *
// This function accepts an array of integers and    *
// the array's size as its arguments. The contents   *
// of the array are displayed.                        *
//*****************************************************
```

(program continues)

Program 7-12 *(continued)*

```
void showValues(int nums[], int size)
{
    for (int index = 0; index < size; index++)
        cout << nums[index] << " ";
    cout << endl;
}
```

Program Output
5 10 15 20 25 30 35 40

 Note: Notice that in the function prototype, empty brackets appear after the data type of the array parameter. This indicates that showValues accepts the address of an array of integers.

In Program 7-12, the function showValues is called in the following statement:

```
showValues(collection, ARRAY_SIZE);
```

The first argument is the name of the array. Remember, in C++ the name of an array without brackets and a subscript is actually the beginning address of the array. In this function call, the address of the collection array is being passed as the first argument to the function. The second argument is the size of the array.

In the showValues function, the beginning address of the collection array is copied into the nums parameter variable. The nums variable is then used to reference the collection array. Figure 7-14 illustrates the relationship between the collection array and the nums parameter variable. When the contents of nums[0] is displayed, it is actually the contents of collection[0] that appears on the screen.

collection Array of 8 integers

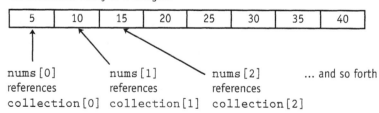

Figure 7-14

 Note: Although nums is not a reference variable, it works like one.

The nums parameter variable in the showValues function can accept the address of any integer array and can be used to reference that array. So, we can use the showValues function to display the contents of any integer array by passing the name of the array and its size as arguments. Program 7-13 uses the function to display the contents of two different arrays.

Program 7-13

```
// This program demonstrates the showValues function being
// used to display the contents of two arrays.
#include <iostream>
using namespace std;

void showValues(int [], int);// Function prototype

int main()
{
    int set1[8] = {5, 10, 15, 20, 25, 30, 35, 40};
    int set2[5] = {2, 4, 6, 8, 10};

    showValues(set1, 8);
    showValues(set2, 5);
    return 0;
}

//****************************************************
// Definition of function showValue.                *
// This function accepts an array of integers and   *
// the array's size as its arguments. The contents  *
// of the array are displayed.                      *
//****************************************************

void showValues(int nums[], int size)
{
    for (int index = 0; index < size; index++)
        cout << nums[index] << " ";
    cout << endl;
}
```

Program Output
```
5 10 15 20 25 30 35 40
2 4 6 8 10
```

Recall from Chapter 6 that when a reference variable is used as a parameter, it gives the function access to the original argument. Any changes made to the reference variable are actually performed on the argument referenced by the variable. Array parameters work very much like reference variables. They give the function direct access to the original array. Any changes made with the array parameter are actually made on the original array used as the argument. The function doubleArray in Program 7-14 uses this capability to double the contents of each element in the array.

Program 7-14

```cpp
// This program uses a function to double the value of
// each element of an array.
#include <iostream>
using namespace std;

// Function prototypes
void doubleArray(int [], int);
void showValues(int [], int);

int main()
{
    const int ARRAY_SIZE = 7;
    int set[ARRAY_SIZE] = {1, 2, 3, 4, 5, 6, 7};

    // Display the initial values.
    cout << "The arrays values are:\n";
    showValues(set, ARRAY_SIZE);

    // Double the values in the array.
    doubleArray(set, ARRAY_SIZE);

    // Display the resulting values.
    cout << "After calling doubleArray the values are:\n";
    showValues(set, ARRAY_SIZE);

    return 0;
}

//*****************************************************
// Definition of function doubleArray                *
// This function doubles the value of each element   *
// in the array passed into nums. The value passed   *
// into size is the number of elements in the array. *
//*****************************************************

void doubleArray(int nums[], int size)
{
    for (int index = 0; index < size; index++)
        nums[index] *= 2;
}
```

(program continues)

Program 7-14 *(continued)*

```
//*************************************************
// Definition of function showValue.             *
// This function accepts an array of integers and *
// the array's size as its arguments. The contents *
// of the array are displayed.                    *
//*************************************************

void showValues(int nums[], int size)
{
    for (int index = 0; index < size; index++)
        cout << nums[index] << " ";
    cout << endl;
}
```

Program Output
```
The arrays values are:
1 2 3 4 5 6 7
After calling doubleArray the values are:
2 4 6 8 10 12 14
```

 WARNING! Like reference variables, array parameters require responsibility. It's important to realize that when an array is passed as an argument, the function has the capability of modifying the original data in the array.

Some Useful Array Functions

Section 7.5 introduced you to algorithms such as summing an array and finding the highest and lowest values in an array. Now we can write general purpose functions that perform those operations. To demonstrate, Program 7-15 follows. This program, which is a modification of Program 7-9, uses the following functions: sumArray, getHighest, and getLowest.

Program 7-15

```
// This program gets five days of sales data from the user
// and displays the total, average, highest, and lowest amounts.
#include <iostream>
#include <iomanip>
using namespace std;

// Function prototypes
double sumArray(double[], int);
double getHighest(double[], int);
double getLowest(double[], int);
```

(program continues)

Program 7-15 *(continued)*

```cpp
int main()
{
   const int NUM_DAYS = 5; // Number of days
   double sales[NUM_DAYS], // To hold sales amounts
          total,           // To hold the total sales
          average,         // To hold the average
          highest,         // To hold the highest sales
          lowest;          // To hold the lowest sales

   // Get the sales data.
   cout << "Enter the sales for this week.\n";
   for (int count = 0; count < NUM_DAYS; count++)
   {
      cout << "Day " << (count +1) <<": ";
      cin >> sales[count];
   }

   // Get the total sales.
   total = sumArray(sales, NUM_DAYS);

   // Calculate the average.
   average = total / NUM_DAYS;

   // Find the highest sales amount.
   highest = getHighest(sales. NUM_DAYS);

   // Find the lowest sales amount.
   lowest = getLowest(sales, NUM_DAYS);

   // Display the results.
   cout << fixed << showpoint << setprecision(2);
   cout << "The total sales are $" << total << endl;
   cout << "The average sales amount is $" << average << endl;
   cout << "The highest sales amount is $" << highest << endl;
   cout << "The lowest sales amount is $" << lowest << endl;

   return 0;
}

//****************************************************
// Definition of sumArray                           *
// This function accepts a double array and its size *
// as arguments. The sum of the array's elements     *
// is returned as an double.                         *
//****************************************************
```

(program continues)

Program 7-15 *(continued)*

```cpp
double sumArray(double array[], int size)
{
    double total = 0; // Accumulator

    for (int count = 0; count < size; count++)
        total += array[count];
    return total;
}

//******************************************************
// Definition of getHighest                           *
// This function accepts a double array and its size   *
// as arguments. The highest value in the array is     *
// returned as an double.                              *
//******************************************************

double getHighest(double array[], int size)
{
    double highest;

    highest = array[0];
    for (int count = 1; count < size; count++)
    {
        if (array[count] > highest)
            highest = array[count];
    }
    return highest;
}

//******************************************************
// Definition of getLowest                            *
// This function accepts a double array and its size   *
// as arguments. The lowest value in the array is      *
// returned as an double.                              *
//******************************************************

double getLowest(double array[], int size)
{
    double lowest;

    lowest = array[0];
    for (int count = 1; count < size; count++)
    {
        if (array[count] < lowest)
            lowest = array[count];
    }
    return lowest;
}
```

Program 7-15 *(continued)*

Program Output with Example Input Shown in Bold
```
Enter the sales for this week.
Day 1: 2698.72 [Enter]
Day 2: 3757.29 [Enter]
Day 3: 1109.67 [Enter]
Day 4: 2498.65 [Enter]
Day 5: 1489.47 [Enter]
The total sales are $11553.80
The average sales amount is $2310.76
The highest sales amount is $3757.29
The lowest sales amount is $1109.67
```

Checkpoint [7.7]

7.12 Given the following array definitions:
```
double array1[4] = {1.2, 3.2, 4.2, 5.2};
double array2[4];
```

will the following statement work? If not, why?

```
array2 = array1;
```

7.13 When an array name is passed to a function, what is actually being passed?

7.14 When used as function arguments, are arrays passed by value?

7.15 What is the output of the following program? (You may need to consult the ASCII table in Appendix A.)
```
#include <iostream>
using namespace std;

// Function prototypes
void fillArray(char [], int);
void showArray(char [], int);

int main ()
{
    char prodCode[8] = {'0', '0', '0', '0', '0', '0', '0', '0'};

    fillArray(prodCode, 8);
    showArray(prodCode, 8);
    return 0;
}

// Definition of function fillArray.
// (Hint: 65 is the ASCII code for 'A')
```

```
void fillArray(char arr[], int size)
{
   char code = 65;

   for (int k = 0; k < size; code++, k++)
      arr[k] = code;
}

// Definition of function showArray.

void showArray(char codes[], int size)
{
   for (int k = 0; k < size; k++)
      cout << codes[k];
   cout << endl;
}
```

7.8 Two-dimensional Arrays

CONCEPT A two-dimensional array is like several identical arrays put together. It is useful for storing multiple sets of data.

An array is useful for storing and working with a set of data. Sometimes, though, it's necessary to work with multiple sets of data. For example, in a grade-averaging program a teacher might record all of one student's test scores in an array of doubles. If the teacher has 30 students, that means she'll need 30 arrays of doubles to record the scores for the entire class. Instead of defining 30 individual arrays, however, it would be better to define a two-dimensional array.

Two-dimensional arrays can hold multiple sets of values. It's best to think of a two-dimensional array as having rows and columns of elements, as shown in Figure 7-15. This figure shows an array of test scores, having three rows and four columns.

	Column 0	Column 1	Column 2	Column 3
Row 0	scores[0] [0]	scores[0] [1]	scores[0] [2]	scores[0] [3]
Row 1	scores[1] [0]	scores[1] [1]	scores[1] [2]	scores[1] [3]
Row 2	scores[2] [0]	scores[2] [1]	scores[2] [2]	scores[2] [3]

Figure 7-15

The array depicted in the figure above has three rows (numbered 0 through 2), and four columns (numbered 0 through 3). There are a total of 12 elements in the array.

To define a two-dimensional array, two size declarators are required: The first one is for the number of rows and the second one is for the number of columns. Here is an example definition of a two-dimensional array with three rows and four columns:

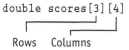

Rows   Columns

The first size declarator specifies the number of rows, and the second size declarator specifies the number of columns. Notice that each number is enclosed in its own set of brackets.

When processing the data in a two-dimensional array, each element has two subscripts: one for its row and another for its column. In the scores array defined above, the elements are referenced as:

The elements in row 0:	The elements in row 1:	The elements in row 2:
scores[0][0]	scores[1][0]	scores[2][0]
scores[0][1]	scores[1][1]	scores[2][1]
scores[0][2]	scores[1][2]	scores[2][2]
scores[0][3]	scores[1][3]	scores[2][3]

The subscripted references are used in a program just like the references to elements in a single dimensional array, except now you use two subscripts. The first subscript represents the row position, and the second subscript represents the column position. For example, the following statement assigns the value 92.25 to the element at row 2, column 1 of the scores array:

```
scores[2][1] = 92.25;
```

And the following statement displays the element at row 0, column 2:

```
cout << scores[0][2];
```

Programs that cycle through each element of a two-dimensional array usually do so with nested loops. Program 7-16 shows an example.

Program 7-16

```
// This program demonstrates a two-dimensional array.
#include <iostream>
#include <iomanip>
using namespace std;

int main()
{
    const int NUM_DIVS = 3;            // Number of divisions
    const int NUM_QTRS = 4;            // Number of quarters
    double sales[NUM_DIVS][NUM_QTRS];  // 2D array, 3 rows and 4 columns.
    double totalSales = 0;             // To hold the total sales.
    int div, qtr;                      // Loop counters.

    cout << "This program will calculate the total sales of\n";
    cout << "all the company's divisions.\n";
    cout << "Enter the following sales data:\n\n";
```

(program continues)

Program 7-16 *(continued)*

```cpp
    // Nested loops to fill the array with quarterly
    // sales figures for each division.
    for (div = 0; div < NUM_DIVS; div++)
    {
        for (qtr = 0; qtr < NUM_QTRS; qtr++)
        {
            cout << "Division " << (div + 1);
            cout << ", Quarter " << (qtr + 1) << ": $";
            cin >> sales[div][qtr];
        }
        cout << endl;          // Print blank line.
    }

    // Nested loops used to add all the elements.
    for (div = 0; div < NUM_DIVS; div++)
    {
        for (qtr = 0; qtr < NUM_QTRS; qtr++)
            totalSales += sales[div][qtr];
    }

    cout << fixed << showpoint << setprecision(2);
    cout << "The total sales for the company are: $";
    cout << totalSales << endl;
    return 0;
}
```

Program Output with Example Input Shown in Bold

```
This program will calculate the total sales of
all the company's divisions.
Enter the following sales data:

Division 1, Quarter 1: $31569.45 [Enter]
Division 1, Quarter 2: $29654.23 [Enter]
Division 1, Quarter 3: $32982.54 [Enter]
Division 1, Quarter 4: $39651.21 [Enter]

Division 2, Quarter 1: $56321.02 [Enter]
Division 2, Quarter 2: $54128.63 [Enter]
Division 2, Quarter 3: $41235.85 [Enter]
Division 2, Quarter 4: $54652.33 [Enter]

Division 3, Quarter 1: $29654.35 [Enter]
Division 3, Quarter 2: $28963.32 [Enter]
Division 3, Quarter 3: $25353.55 [Enter]
Division 3, Quarter 4: $32615.88 [Enter]

The total sales for the company are: $456782.34
```

When initializing a two-dimensional array, it helps to enclose each row's initialization list in a set of braces. Here is an example:

```
int hours[3][2] = {{8, 5}, {7, 9}, {6, 3}};
```

The same definition could also be written as:

```
int hours[3][2] = {{8, 5},
                   {7, 9},
                   {6, 3}};
```

In either case, the values are assigned to hours in the following manner:

```
hours[0][0] is set to 8
hours[0][1] is set to 5
hours[1][0] is set to 7
hours[1][1] is set to 9
hours[2][0] is set to 6
hours[2][1] is set to 3
```

Figure 7-16 illustrates the initialization.

	Column 0	Column 1
Row 0	8	5
Row 1	7	9
Row 2	6	3

Figure 7-16

The extra braces that enclose each row's initialization list are optional. Both of the following statements perform the same initialization:

```
int hours[3][2] = {{8, 5}, {7, 9}, {6, 3}};
int hours[3][2] = {8, 5, 7, 9, 6, 3};
```

Because the extra braces visually separate each row, however, it's a good idea to use them. In addition, the braces give you the ability to leave out initializers within a row without omitting the initializers for the rows that follow it. For instance, look at the following array definition:

```
int table[3][2] = {{1}, {3, 4}, {5}};
```

`table[0][0]` is initialized to 1, `table[1][0]` is initialized to 3, `table[1][1]` is initialized to 4, and `table[2][0]` is initialized to 5. `table[0][1]` and `table[2][1]` are not initialized. Because some of the array elements are initialized, these two initialized elements are automatically set to zero.

Passing Two-dimensional Arrays to Functions

Program 7-17 demonstrates passing a two-dimensional array to a function. When a two-dimensional array is passed to a function, the parameter type must contain a size declarator for the number of columns. Here is the header for the function showArray, from Program 7-17:

```
void showArray(int array[][COLS], int rows)
```

COLS is a global named constant which is set to 4. The function can accept any two-dimensional integer array, as long as it consists of four columns. In the program, the contents of two separate arrays are displayed by the function.

Program 7-17

```cpp
// This program demonstrates accepting a two-dimensional array argument.
#include <iostream>
#include <iomanip>
using namespace std;

const int COLS = 4;         // Number of columns in each array
const int TBL1_ROWS = 3;    // Number of rows in table1
const int TBL2_ROWS = 4;    // Number of rows in table2

void showArray(int [][COLS], int); // Function prototype

int main()
{
   int table1[TBL1_ROWS][COLS] = {{1, 2, 3, 4},
                                  {5, 6, 7, 8},
                                  {9, 10, 11, 12}};
   int table2[TBL2_ROWS][COLS] = {{10, 20, 30, 40},
                                  {50, 60, 70, 80},
                                  {90, 100, 110, 120},
                                  {130, 140, 150, 160}};
   cout << "The contents of table1 are:\n";
   showArray(table1, TBL1_ROWS);
   cout << "The contents of table2 are:\n";
   showArray(table2, TBL2_ROWS);
   return 0;
}
```

(program continues)

Program 7-17 *(continued)*

```
//*******************************************************************
// Function Definition for showArray                               *
// The first argument is a two-dimensional int array with COLS     *
// columns. The second argument, rows, specifies the number of     *
// rows in the array. The function displays the array's contents.  *
//*******************************************************************

void showArray(int array[][COLS], int rows)
{
    for (int x = 0; x < rows; x++)
    {
        for (int y = 0; y < COLS; y++)
        {
            cout << setw(4) << array[x][y] << " ";
        }
        cout << endl;
    }
}
```

Program Output
```
The contents of table1 are:
  1    2    3    4
  5    6    7    8
  9   10   11   12
The contents of table2 are:
 10   20   30   40
 50   60   70   80
 90  100  110  120
130  140  150  160
```

C++ requires the columns to be specified in the function prototype and header because of the way two-dimensional arrays are stored in memory. Onc row follows another, as shown in Figure 7-17.

Figure 7-17

When the compiler generates code for accessing the elements of a two-dimensional array, it needs to know how many bytes separate the rows in memory. The number of columns is a critical factor in this calculation.

Summing All the Elements of a Two-dimensional Array

To sum all the elements of a two-dimensional array, you can use a pair of nested loops to add the contents of each element to an accumulator. The following code shows an example.

```cpp
const int NUM_ROWS = 5;      // Number of rows
const int NUM_COLS = 5;      // Number of columns
int total = 0;               // Accumulator
int numbers[NUM_ROWS][NUM_COLS] = {{2, 7, 9, 6, 4},
                                   {6, 1, 8, 9, 4},
                                   {4, 3, 7, 2, 9},
                                   {9, 9, 0, 3, 1},
                                   {6, 2, 7, 4, 1}};

// Sum the array elements.
for (int row = 0; row < NUM_ROWS; row++)
{
   for (int col = 0; col < NUM_COLS; col++)
      total += numbers[row][col];
}

// Display the sum.
cout << "The total is " << total << endl;
```

Summing the Rows of a Two-dimensional Array

Sometimes you may need to calculate the sum of each row in a two-dimensional array. For example, suppose a two-dimensional array is used to hold a set of test scores for a set of students. Each row in the array is a set of test scores for one student. To get the sum of a student's test scores (perhaps so an average may be calculated), you use a loop to add all the elements in one row. The following code shows an example.

```cpp
const int NUM_STUDENTS = 3;   // Number of students
const int NUM_SCORES = 5;     // Number of test scores
double total;                 // Accumulator is set in the loops
double average;               // To hold each student's average
double scores[NUM_STUDENTS][NUM_SCORES] = {{88, 97, 79, 86, 94},
                                           {86, 91, 78, 79, 84},
                                           {82, 73, 77, 82, 89}};

// Get each student's average score.
for (int row = 0; row < NUM_STUDENTS; row++)
{
   // Set the accumulator.
   total = 0;

   // Sum a row.
   for (int col = 0; col < NUM_SCORES; col++)
      total += scores[row][col];
```

```
      // Get the average
      average = total / NUM_SCORES;

      // Display the average.
      cout << "Score average for student "
           << (row + 1) << " is " << average <<endl;
   }
```

Notice that the total variable, which is used as an accumulator, is set to zero just before the inner loop executes. This is because the inner loop sums the elements of a row and stores the sum in total. Therefore, the total variable must be set to zero before each iteration of the inner loop.

Summing the Columns of a Two-dimensional Array

Sometimes you may need to calculate the sum of each column in a two-dimensional array. In the previous example a two-dimensional array is used to hold a set of test scores for a set of students. Suppose you wish to calculate the class average for each of the test scores. To do this, you calculate the average of each column in the array. This is accomplished with a set of nested loops. The outer loop controls the column subscript and the inner loop controls the row subscript. The inner loop calculates the sum of a column, which is stored in an accumulator. The following code demonstrates.

```
const int NUM_STUDENTS = 3;    // Number of students
const int NUM_SCORES = 5;      // Number of test scores
double total;                  // Accumulator is set in the loops
double average;                // To hold each score's class average
double scores[NUM_STUDENTS][NUM_SCORES] = {{88, 97, 79, 86, 94},
                                           {86, 91, 78, 79, 84},
                                           {82, 73, 77, 82, 89}};

// Get the class average for each score.
for (int col = 0; col < NUM_SCORES; col++)
{
   // Reset the accumulator.
   total = 0;

   // Sum a column
   for (int row = 0; row < NUM_STUDENTS; row++)
      total += scores[row][col];

   // Get the average
   average = total / NUM_STUDENTS;

   // Display the class average.
   cout << "Class average for test " << (col + 1)
        << " is " << average << endl;
}
```

7.9 Arrays of Strings

CONCEPT A two-dimensional array of characters can be used as an array of strings.

Because strings are stored in single dimensional character arrays, an array of strings would be a two-dimensional character array. Figure 7-18 depicts such an array.

```
char scientists[4][9] = {"Galileo",
                         "Kepler",
                         "Newton",
                         "Einstein" };
```

G	a	l	i	l	e	o	\0	
K	e	p	l	e	r	\0		
N	e	w	t	o	n	\0		
E	i	n	s	t	e	i	n	\0

Figure 7-18

The longest string in the array shown above is nine characters (including the null terminator), so the array must have nine columns. The rows with strings of less than nine characters will have unused elements.

Just as the name of an array represents the array's address, a two-dimensional array with only the row subscript represents the address of that row. For instance, in the array defined above, scientists[0] represents the address of row 0, scientists[1] represents the address of row 1, and so forth. The following cout statement will display the string "Einstein" on the screen:

```
cout << scientists[3];
```

Likewise, the following loop will display all the names in the array:

```
for (int count = 0; count < 4; count++)
    cout << scientists[count] << endl;
```

Program 7-18 uses a two-dimensional character array to hold the names of the months and a single dimensional integer array to hold the number of days in each month.

Program 7-18

```cpp
// This program displays the number of days in each month.
#include <iostream>
using namespace std;

int main()
{
    const int NUM_MONTHS = 12;  // The number of months
    const int STRING_SIZE = 10; // Maximum size of each string
    char months[NUM_MONTHS][STRING_SIZE] =
                    { "January", "February", "March",
                      "April", "May", "June",
                      "July", "August", "September",
                      "October", "November", "December" };
    int days[NUM_MONTHS] = {31, 28, 31, 30,
                            31, 30, 31, 31,
                            30, 31, 30, 31};

    for (int count = 0; count < NUM_MONTHS; count++)
    {
        cout << months[count] << " has ";
        cout << days[count] << " days.\n";
    }
    return 0;
}
```

Program Output

```
January has 31 days.
February has 28 days.
March has 31 days.
April has 30 days.
May has 31 days.
June has 30 days.
July has 31 days.
August has 31 days.
September has 30 days.
October has 31 days.
November has 30 days.
December has 31 days.
```

7.10 Arrays with Three or More Dimensions

CONCEPT	C++ does not limit the number of dimensions that an array may have. It is possible to create arrays with multiple dimensions, to model data that occurs in multiple sets.

C++ allows you to create arrays with virtually any number of dimensions. Here is an example of a three-dimensional array definition:

```
double seats[3][5][8];
```

This array can be thought of as three sets of five rows, with each row containing eight elements. The array might be used to store the prices of seats in an auditorium, where there are eight seats in a row, five rows in a section, and a total of three sections.

Figure 7-19 illustrates the concept of a three-dimensional array as "pages" of two-dimensional arrays.

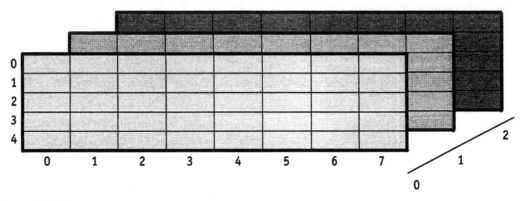

Figure 7-19

Arrays with more than three dimensions are difficult to visualize, but can be useful in some programming problems. For example, in a factory warehouse where cases of widgets are stacked on pallets, an array with four dimensions could be used to store a part number for each widget. The four subscripts of each element could represent the pallet number, case number, row number, and column number of each widget. Similarly, an array with five dimensions could be used if there were multiple warehouses.

 Note: When writing functions that accept multi-dimensional arrays as arguments, all but the first dimension must be explicitly stated in the parameter list.

Checkpoint [7.8–7.12]

7.16 Define a two-dimensional array named `settings` large enough to hold the table of data below. Initialize the array with the values in the table.

12	24	32	21	42
14	67	87	65	90
19	1	24	12	8

7.17 Fill in the table below so it shows the contents of the following array:

```
int table[3][4] = {{2, 3}, {7, 9, 2}, {1}};
```


7.18 Write a function called `displayArray7`. The function should accept a two-dimensional array as an argument and display its contents on the screen. The function should work with any of the following arrays:

```
int hours[5][7];
int stamps[8][7];
int autos[12][7];
int cats[50][7];
```

7.19 A video rental store keeps videos on 50 racks with 10 shelves each. Each shelf holds 25 videos. Define a three-dimensional array large enough to represent the store's storage system.

See the CaseStudies.pdf file on the accompanying CD for this chapter's case studies.

7.11 If You Plan to Continue in Computer Science: *Introduction to the STL* `vector`

CONCEPT The Standard Template Library offers a `vector` data type, which in many ways, is superior to standard arrays

The *Standard Template Library* (STL) is a collection of data types and algorithms that you may use in your programs. These data types and algorithms are *programmer-defined*. They are not part of the C++ language, but were created in addition to the built-in data types. If you plan to continue your studies in the field of computer science, you should become familiar with the STL. This section introduces one of the STL data types. For more information on the STL, see Chapter 16.

 Note: Many older compilers do not support the STL.

The data types that are defined in the STL are commonly called *containers*. They are called containers because they store and organize data. There are two types of containers in the STL: sequence containers and associative containers. A *sequence container* organizes data in a sequential fashion, similar to an array. *Associative containers* organize data with keys, which allow rapid, random access to elements stored in the container.

In this section you will learn to use the `vector` data type, which is a sequence container. A `vector` is like an array in the following ways:

- A `vector` holds a sequence of values, or elements.
- A `vector` stores its elements in contiguous memory locations.
- You can use the array subscript operator [] to read the individual elements in the `vector`.

However, a `vector` offers several advantages over arrays. Here are just a few:

- You do not have to declare the number of elements that the vector will have.
- If you add a value to a vector that is already full, the vector will automatically increase its size to accommodate the new value.
- `vectors` can report the number of elements they contain.

Defining a `vector`

To use vectors in your program, you must include the vector header file with the following statement:

```
#include <vector>
```

 Note: To use the `vector` data type, you must have the `using namespace std;` statement in your program.

Now you are ready to define an actual vector object. The syntax for defining a vector is somewhat different from the syntax used in defining a regular variable or array. Here is an example:

```
vector<int> numbers;
```

This statement defines numbers as a vector of ints. Notice that the data type is enclosed in angled brackets, immediately after the word vector. Because the vector expands in size as you add values to it, there is no need to declare a size. You can define a starting size, if you prefer. Here is an example:

```
vector<int> numbers(10);
```

This statement defines numbers as a vector of 10 ints. This is only a starting size, however. Although the vector has 10 elements, its size will expand if you add more than 10 values to it.

 Note: If you specify a starting size for a vector, the size declarator is enclosed in parentheses, not square brackets.

When you specify a starting size for a vector, you may also specify an initialization value. The initialization value is copied to each element. Here is an example:

```
vector<int> numbers(10, 2);
```

In this statement, numbers is defined as a vector of 10 ints. Each element in numbers is initialized to the value 2.

You may also initialize a vector with the values in another vector. For example, look at the following statement. Assume that set1 is a vector of ints that already has values stored in it.

```
vector<int> set2(set1);
```

After this statement executes, the vector set2 will be a copy of the vector set1.

Table 7-3 summarizes the vector definition procedures we have discussed.

Table 7-3

Definition Format	Description
vector<float> amounts;	Defines amounts as an empty vector of floats.
vector<int> scores(15);	Defines scores as a vector of 15 ints.
vector<char> letters(25, 'A');	Defines letters as a vector of 25 characters. Each element is initialized with 'A'.
vector<double> values2(values1);	Defines values2 as a vector of doubles. All the elements of values1, which is also a vector of doubles, are copied to value2.

Storing and Retrieving Values in a `vector`

To store a value in an element that already exists in a vector, you may use the array subscript operator []. For example, look at Program 7-19.

Program 7-19

```cpp
// This program stores, in two vectors, the hours worked by 5
// employees, and their hourly pay rates.
#include <iostream>
#include <iomanip>
#include <vector>          // Needed to define vectors
using namespace std;

int main()
{
    const int NUM_EMPLOYEES = 5;           // Number of employees
    vector<int> hours(NUM_EMPLOYEES);      // A vector of integers
    vector<double> payRate(NUM_EMPLOYEES); // A vector of doubles
    int index;                             // Loop counter

    // Input the data.
    cout << "Enter the hours worked by " << NUM_EMPLOYEES;
    cout << " employees and their hourly rates.\n";
    for (index = 0; index < NUM_EMPLOYEES; index++)
    {
        cout << "Hours worked by employee #" << (index + 1);
        cout << ": ";
        cin >> hours[index];
        cout << "Hourly pay rate for employee #";
        cout << (index + 1) << ": ";
        cin >> payRate[index];
    }

    // Display each employee's gross pay.
    cout << "\nHere is the gross pay for each employee:\n";
    cout << fixed << showpoint << setprecision(2);
    for (index = 0; index < NUM_EMPLOYEES; index++)
    {
        double grossPay = hours[index] * payRate[index];
        cout << "Employee #" << (index + 1);
        cout << ": $" << grossPay << endl;
    }
    return 0;
}
```

Program 7-19 *(continued)*

Program Output with Example Input Shown in Bold
```
Enter the hours worked by five employees and their
hourly rates.
Hours worked by employee #1: 10 [Enter]
Hourly pay rate for employee #1: 9.75 [Enter]
Hours worked by employee #2: 15 [Enter]
Hourly pay rate for employee #2: 8.62 [Enter]
Hours worked by employee #3: 20 [Enter]
Hourly pay rate for employee #3: 10.50 [Enter]
Hours worked by employee #4: 40 [Enter]
Hourly pay rate for employee #4: 18.75 [Enter]
Hours worked by employee #5: 40 [Enter]
Hourly pay rate for employee #5: 15.65 [Enter]

Here is the gross pay for each employee:
Employee #1: $97.50
Employee #2: $129.30
Employee #3: $210.00
Employee #4: $750.00
Employee #5: $626.00
```

Notice that Program 7-23 uses the following statements to define two vectors.

```
vector<int> hours(NUM_EMPLOYEES);        // A vector of integers
vector<double> payRate(NUM_EMPLOYEES);   // A vector of doubles
```

Both of the vectors are defined with the starting size 5, which is the value of the named constant NUM_EMPLOYEES. The program uses the following loop to store a value in each element of both vectors:

```
for (index = 0; index < NUM_EMPLOYEES; index++)
{
    cout << "Hours worked by employee #" << (index + 1);
    cout << ": ";
    cin >> hours[index];
    cout << "Hourly pay rate for employee #";
```

Because the values entered by the user are being stored in `vector` elements that already exist, the program uses the array subscript operator [], as shown in the following statements:

```
cin >> hours[index];
```

```
cin >> payRate[index];
```

Using the `push_back` Member Function

You cannot use the [] operator to access a vector element that does not exist. To store a value in a vector that does not have a starting size, or is already full, use the push_back member function. The push_back member function accepts a value as an argument, and stores that value after the last element in the vector. (It pushes the value onto the back of the vector.) Here is an example:

```
numbers.push_back(25);
```

Assuming numbers is a vector of ints, this statement stores 25 as the last element. If numbers is full, the statement creates a new, last element, and stores 25 in it. If there are no elements in numbers, this statement creates an element and stores 25 in it.

Program 7-20 is a modification of Program 7-19. This version, however, allows the user to specify the number of employees. The two vectors, hours and payRate, are defined without starting sizes. Because these vectors have no starting elements, the push_back member function is used to store values in the vectors.

Program 7-20

```
// This program stores, in two arrays, the hours worked by five
// employees, and their hourly pay rates.
#include <iostream>
#include <iomanip>
#include <vector>              // Needed to define vectors
using namespace std;

int main()
{
    vector<int> hours;         // hours is an empty vector
    vector<double> payRate;    // payRate is an empty vector
    int numEmployees;          // The number of employees
    int index;                 // Loop counter

    // Get the number of employees.
    cout << "How many employees do you have? ";
    cin >> numEmployees;

    // Input the payroll data.
    cout << "Enter the hours worked by " << numEmployees;
    cout << " employees and their hourly rates.\n";
```

(program continues)

Program 7-20   *(continued)*

```
for (index = 0; index < numEmployees; index++)
{
    int tempHours;    // To hold the number of hours entered
    double tempRate;  // To hold the payrate entered

    cout << "Hours worked by employee #" << (index + 1);
    cout << ": ";
    cin >> tempHours;
    hours.push_back(tempHours);  // Add an element to hours
    cout << "Hourly pay rate for employee #";
    cout << (index + 1) << ": ";
    cin >> tempRate;
    payRate.push_back(tempRate); // Add an element to payRate
}

// Display each employee's gross pay.
cout << "Here is the gross pay for each employee:\n";
cout << fixed << showpoint << setprecision(2);
for (index = 0; index < numEmployees; index++)
{
    double grossPay = hours[index] * payRate[index];
    cout << "Employee #" << (index + 1);
    cout << ": $" << grossPay << endl;
}
return 0;
}
```

Program Output with Example Input Shown in Bold

```
How many employees do you have? 3 [Enter]
Enter the hours worked by three employees and their hourly rates.
Hours worked by employee #1: 40 [Enter]
Hourly pay rate for employee #1: 12.63 [Enter]
Hours worked by employee #2: 25 [Enter]
Hourly pay rate for employee #2: 10.35 [Enter]
Hours worked by employee #3: 45 [Enter]
Hourly pay rate for employee #3: 22.65 [Enter]
Here is the gross pay for each employee:
Employee #1: $505.20
Employee #2: $258.75
Employee #3: $1019.2
```

Notice that in Program 7-20 the second loop, which calculates and displays each employee's gross pay, uses the [] operator to access the elements of the hours and payRate vectors:

```
for (index = 0; index < numEmployees; index++)
{
    double grossPay = hours[index] * payRate[index];
    cout << "Employee #" << (index + 1);
    cout << ": $" << grossPay << endl;
}
```

This is possible because the first loop uses the push_back member function to create the elements in the two vectors.

Determining the Size of a vector

Unlike arrays, vectors can report the number of elements they contain. This is accomplished with the size member function. Here is an example of a statement that uses the size member function:

```
numValues = set.size();
```

In this statement, assume that numValues is an int and set is a vector. After the statement executes, numValues will contain the number of elements in the vector set.

The size member function is especially useful when you are writing functions that accept vectors as arguments. For example, look at the following code for the showValues function:

```
void showValues(vector<int> vect)
{
    for (int count = 0; count < vect.size(); count++)
        cout << vect[count] << endl;
}
```

Because the vector can report its size, this function does not need to accept a second argument indicating the number of elements in the vector. Program 7-21 demonstrates this function.

Program 7-21

```
// This program demonstrates the vector size
// member function.
#include <iostream>
#include <vector>
using namespace std;

// Function prototype
void showValues(vector<int>);
```

(program continues)

Program 7-21 *(continued)*

```
int main()
{
    vector<int> values;

    for (int count = 0; count < 7; count++)
        values.push_back(count * 2);
    showValues(values);
    return 0;
}

//****************************************************
// Definition of function showValues.                *
// This function accepts an int vector as its         *
// argument. The value of each of the vector's        *
// elements is displayed.                             *
//****************************************************

void showValues(vector<int> vect)
{
    for (int count = 0; count < vect.size(); count++)
        cout << vect[count] << endl;
}
```

Program Output

```
0
2
4
6
8
10
12
```

Removing Elements from a `vector`

Use the `pop_back` member function to remove the last element from a `vector`. In the following statement, assume that `collection` is the name of a `vector`.

```
collection.pop_back();
```

This statement removes the last element from the `collection` vector. Program 7-22 demonstrates the function.

Program 7-22

```cpp
// This program demonstrates the vector pop_back member function.
#include <iostream>
#include <vector>
using namespace std;

int main()
{
    vector<int> values;

    // Store values in the vector
    values.push_back(1);
    values.push_back(2);
    values.push_back(3);
    cout << "The size of values is " << values.size() << endl;

    // Remove a value from the vector
    cout << "Popping a value from the vector...\n";
    values.pop_back();
    cout << "The size of values is now " << values.size() << endl;

    // Now remove another value from the vector
    cout << "Popping a value from the vector...\n";
    values.pop_back();
    cout << "The size of values is now " << values.size() << endl;

    // Remove the last value from the vector
    cout << "Popping a value from the vector...\n";
    values.pop_back();
    cout << "The size of values is now " << values.size() << endl;
    return 0;
}
```

Program Output
```
The size of values is 3
Popping a value from the vector...
The size of values is now 2
Popping a value from the vector...
The size of values is now 1
Popping a value from the vector...
The size of values is now 0
```

Clearing a `vector`

To completely clear the contents of a `vector`, use the `clear` member function, as shown in the following statement:

```cpp
numbers.clear();
```

After this statement executes, the `numbers` vector will be cleared of all its elements. Program 7-23 demonstrates the function.

Program 7-23

```
// This program demonstrates the vector clear member function.
#include <iostream>
#include <vector>
using namespace std;

int main()
{
    vector<int> values(100);

    cout << "The values vector has "
         << values.size() << " elements.\n";
    cout << "I will call the clear member function...\n";
    values.clear();
    cout << "Now, the values vector has "
         << values.size() << " elements.\n";
    return 0;
}
```

Program Output
```
The values vector has 100 elements.
I will call the clear member function...
Now, the values vector has 0 elements.
```

Detecting an Empty `vector`

To determine if a vector is empty, use the `empty` member function. The function returns `true` if the vector is empty, and `false` if the vector has elements stored in it. Assuming `set` is a vector, here is an example of its use:

```
if (set.empty())
    cout << "No values in set.\n";
```

Program 7-24 uses a function named `avgVector`, which demonstrates the `empty` member function.

Program 7-24

```
// This program demonstrates the vector's empty member function.
#include <iostream>
#include <vector>
using namespace std;

// Function prototype
double avgVector(vector<int>);
```

(program continues)

Program 7-24 *(continued)*

```cpp
int main()
{
    vector<int> values;
    int numValues;
    double average;

    cout << "How many values do you wish to average? ";
    cin >> numValues;
    for (int count = 0; count < numValues; count++)
    {
        int tempValue;

        cout << "Enter a value: ";
        cin >> tempValue;
        values.push_back(tempValue);
    }
    average = avgVector(values);
    cout << "Average: " << average << endl;
    return 0;
}

//****************************************************************
// Definition of function avgVector.                            *
// This function accepts an int vector as its argument. If      *
// the vector contains values, the function returns the         *
// average of those values. Otherwise, an error message is      *
// displayed and the function returns 0.0.                      *
//****************************************************************

double avgVector(vector<int> vect)
{
    int total = 0;         // accumulator
    double avg;            // average

    if (vect.empty())      // Determine if the vector is empty
    {
        cout << "No values to average.\n";
        avg = 0.0;
    }
    else
    {
        for (int count = 0; count < vect.size(); count++)
            total += vect[count];
        avg = total / vect.size();
    }
    return avg;
}
```

Program 7-24   *(continued)*

Program Output with Example Input Shown in Bold
```
How many values do you wish to average? 5 [Enter]
Enter a value: 12
Enter a value: 18
Enter a value: 3
Enter a value: 7
Enter a value: 9
Average: 9
```

Program Output with Example Input Shown in Bold
```
How many values do you wish to average? 0 [Enter]
No values to average.
Average: 0
```

Summary of vector Member Functions

Table 7-4 provides a summary of the `vector` member function we have discussed, as well as some additional ones.

Table 7-4

Member Function	Description
`at(element)`	Returns the value of the element located at *element* in the vector. *Example:* `x = vect.at(5);` This statement assigns the value of the fifth element of `vect` to `x`.
`capacity()`	Returns the maximum number of elements that may be stored in the vector without additional memory being allocated. (This is not the same value as returned by the size member function). *Example:* `x = vect.capacity();` This statement assigns the capacity of `vect` to `x`.
`clear()`	Clears a vector of all its elements. *Example:* `vect.clear();` This statement removes all the elements from `vect`.

`empty()`	Returns true if the vector is empty. Otherwise, it returns false.
	Example:
	`if (vect.empty())`
	`    cout << "The vector is empty.";`
	This statement displays the message if `vect` is empty.

Table 7-4

pop_back()	Removes the last element from the vector. *Example:* `vect.pop_back();` This statement removes the last element of vect, thus reducing its size by 1.
push_back(*value*)	Stores a value in the last element of the vector. If the vector is full or empty, a new element is created. *Example:* `vect.push_back(7);` This statement stores 7 in the last element of vect.
reverse()	Reverses the order of the elements in the vector (the last element becomes the first element, and the first element becomes the last element.) *Example:* `vect.reverse();` This statement reverses the order of the element in vect.
resize(*elements*, *value*)	Resizes a vector by *elements* elements. Each of the new elements is initialized with the value in *value*. *Example:* `vect.resize(5, 1);` This statement increases the size of vect by five elements. The five new elements are initialized to the value 1.
swap(*vector2*)	Swaps the contents of the vector with the contents of *vector2*. *Example:* `vect1.swap(vect2);` This statement swaps the contents of vect1 and vect2.

 ## Checkpoint [7.13]

7.20 What header file must you #include in order to define vector objects?

7.21 Write a definition statement for a vector named frogs. frogs should be an empty vector of ints.

7.22 Write a definition statement for a vector named lizards. lizards should be a vector of 20 floats.

7.23 Write a definition statement for a vector named toads. toads should be a vector of 100 chars, with each element initialized to 'Z'.

7.24 gators is an empty vector of ints. Write a statement that stores the value 27 in gators.

7.25 snakes is a vector of doubles, with 10 elements. Write a statement that stores the value 12.897 in element 4 of the snakes vector.

Review Questions and Exercises

Short Answer

1. What is the difference between a size declarator and a subscript?

2. Look at the following array definition.

   ```
   int values[10];
   ```

   How many elements does the array have?

   What is the subscript of the first element in the array?

   What is the subscript of the last element in the array?

   Assuming that an int uses 4 bytes of memory, how much memory does the array use?

3. Why should a function that accepts an array as an argument, and processes that array, also accept an argument specifying the array's size?

4. Given the following array definition:

   ```
   int values[5] = { 4, 7, 6, 8, 2 };
   ```

   What does each of the following statements display?

   ```
   cout << values[4] << endl;          _____
   cout << (values[2] + values[3]) << endl;   _____
   cout << ++values[1] << endl;        _____
   ```

5. How do you define an array without providing a size declarator?

6. Look at the following array definition.

   ```
   int numbers[5] = { 1, 2, 3 };
   ```

   What value is stored in numbers[2]?

   What value is stored in numbers[4]?

7. Assuming that array1 and array2 are both arrays, why is it not possible to assign the contents of array2 to array1 with the following statement?

   ```
   array1 = array2;
   ```

8. Assuming that numbers is an array of doubles, will the following statement display the contents of the array?

   ```
   cout << numbers << endl;
   ```

9. Is an array passed to a function by value or by reference?

10. When you pass an array name as an argument to a function, what is actually being passed?

11. How do you establish a parallel relationship between two or more arrays?

12. Look at the following array definition.

```
char day[] = "Tuesday";
```

How many elements are in the day array?

Is the string stored in the day array terminated by a null character?

13. Look at the following array definition.

```
double sales[8][10];
```

How many rows does the array have?

How many columns does the array have?

How many elements does the array have?

Write a statement that stores a number in the last column of the last row in the array.

14. When writing a function that accepts a two-dimensional array as an argument, which size declarator must you provide in the parameter for the array?

15. What advantages does a vector offer over an array?

Algorithm Workbench

16. names is an integer array with 20 elements. Write a for loop that prints each element of the array.

17. The arrays numberArray1 and numberArray2 have 100 elements. Write code that copies the values in numberArray1 to numberArray2.

18. In a program you need to store the identification numbers of 10 employees (as ints) and their weekly gross pay (as doubles).

    a. Define two arrays that may be used in parallel to store the ten employee identification numbers and gross pay amounts.

    b. Write a loop that uses these arrays to print each of the employees' identification number and weekly gross pay.

19. Define a two-dimensional array of integers named grades. It should have 30 rows and 10 columns.

20. In a program you need to store the populations of 12 countries.

    a. Define two arrays that may be used in parallel to store the names of the countries and their populations.

    b. Write a loop that uses these arrays to print each country's name and its population.

21. The following code totals the values in two arrays: numberArray1 and numberArray2. Both arrays have 25 elements. Will the code print the correct sum of values for both arrays? Why or why not?

```
int total = 0;      // Accumulator
int count;          // Loop counter
```

```
// Calculate and display the total of the first array.
for (count = 0; count < 24; count++)
    total += numberArray1[count];
cout << "The total for numberArray1 is " << total << endl;
// Calculate and display the total of the second array.
for (count = 0; count < 24; count++)
    total += numberArray2[count];
cout << "The total for numberArray2 is " << total << endl;
```

22. Write a statement that defines a two-dimensional array to hold three strings. Initialize the array with your first, middle, and last names.

23. Look at the following array definition.

```
int numberArray[9][11];
```

Write a statement that assigns 145 to the first column of the first row of this array.

Write a statement that assigns 18 to the last column of the last row of this array.

24. `values` is a two-dimensional array of `float`s with 10 rows and 20 columns. Write code that sums all the elements in the array and stores the sum in the variable `total`.

25. An application uses a two-dimensional array defined as follows.

```
int days[29][5];
```

Write code that sums each row in the array and displays the results.

Write code that sums each column in the array and displays the results.

True or False

26. T F An array's size declarator can either be a literal, named constant, or variable.

27. T F To calculate the amount of memory used by an array, multiply the number of elements by the number of bytes each element uses.

28. T F The individual elements of an array are accessed and indexed by unique numbers.

29. T F The first element in an array is accessed by the subscript 1.

30. T F The subscript of the last element in a single-dimensional array is one less than the total number of elements in the array.

31. T F The contents of an array element cannot be displayed with `cout`.

32. T F Subscript numbers may be stored in variables.

33. T F You can write programs that use invalid subscripts for an array.

34. T F The values in an initialization list are stored in the array in the order they appear in the list.

35. T F If an array is partially initialized, the uninitialized elements will contain "garbage."

36. T F If you leave an element uninitialized, you do not have to leave all the ones that follow it uninitialized.

37. T F If you leave out the size declarator of an array definition, you do not have to include an initialization list.

38. T F When initializing an array with a string, the null terminator is automatically included.

39. T F When initializing an array with individual characters, the null terminator is automatically included.

40. T F You cannot use the assignment operator to copy one array's contents to another in a single statement.

41. T F When an array name is used without brackets and a subscript, it is seen as the value of the first element in the array.

42. T F When defining a parameter variable to hold a single-dimensional array argument, you do not have to include the size declarator.

43. T F When an array is passed to a function, the function has access to the original array.

44. T F A two-dimensional array is like several identical arrays put together.

45. T F The first size declarator (in the declaration of a two-dimensional array) represents the number of columns. The second size defintion represents the number of rows.

46. T F Two-dimensional arrays may be passed to functions, but the row size must be specified in the definition of the parameter variable.

47. T F A vector is an associative container.

48. T F To use a vector, you must include the vector header file.

49. T F vectors can report the number of elements they contain.

50. T F You can use the [] operator to insert a value into a vector that has no elements.

51. T F If you add a value to a vector that is already full, the vector will automatically increase its size to accommodate the new value.

Find the Error

Each of the following definitions and program segments has errors. Locate as many as you can.

52. ```
int size;
double values[size];
```

53. ```
int collection[-20];
```

54. ```
int hours[3] = 8, 12, 16;
```

55. ```
char name[17] = "George Washington";
```

56. ```
float ratings[];
```
```

57. ```
char greeting[] = {'H', 'e', 'l', 'l', 'o'};
cout << greeting;
```

58. ```
int array1[4], array2[4] = {3, 6, 9, 12};
array1 = array2;
```

59. ```
void showValues(int nums[4][])
{
    for (rows = 0; rows < 4; rows++)
        for (cols = 0; cols < 5; cols++)
            cout << nums[rows][cols];
}
```

## Programming Challenges

### 1. Largest/Smallest Array Values

Write a program that lets the user enter 10 values into an array. The program should then display the largest and smallest values stored in the array.

### 2. Rainfall Statistics

Write a program that lets the user enter the total rainfall for each of 12 months into an array of doubles. The program should calculate and display the total rainfall for the year, the average monthly rainfall, and the months with the highest and lowest amounts.

*Input Validation: Do not accept negative numbers for monthly rainfall figures.*

### 3. Lowercase to Uppercase Converter

Write a program that lets the user enter a string into a character array. The program should then convert all the lowercase letters to uppercase. (If a character is already uppercase, or is not a letter, it should be left alone.) Hint: Consult the ASCII chart in Appendix A. Notice that the lowercase letters are represented by the ASCII codes 97 through 122. If you subtract 32 from any lowercase character's ASCII code, it will yield the ASCII code of the uppercase equivalent.

### 4. Proper Words

Write a function that uses an array parameter to accept a string as its argument. It should convert the first letter of each word in the string to uppercase. If any of the letters are already uppercase, they should be left alone. (See the hint in problem 3 for help on converting lowercase characters to uppercase.) Demonstrate the function in a simple program that asks the user to input a string, passes it to the function, and then displays the string after it has been modified.
```

5. Quarterly Sales Statistics

Write a program that lets the user enter four quarterly sales figures for six divisions of a company. The figures should be stored in a two-dimensional array. Once the figures are entered, the program should display the following data for each quarter:

♦ A list of the sales figures by division

♦ Each division's increase or decrease from the previous quarter (This will not be displayed for the first quarter.)

♦ The total sales for the quarter

♦ The company's increase or decrease from the previous quarter (This will not be displayed for the first quarter.)

♦ The average sales for all divisions that quarter

♦ The division with the highest sales for that quarter

The program should be modular, with functions that calculate the statistics above.

Input Validation: Do not accept negative numbers for sales figures.

6. Payroll

Write a program that uses the following arrays:

♦ empId: an array of seven long integers to hold employee identification numbers. The array should be initialized with the following numbers:

5658845	4520125	7895122	8777541
8451277	1302850	7580489	

♦ hours: an array of seven integers to hold the number of hours worked by each employee

♦ payRate: an array of seven doubles to hold each employee's hourly pay rate

♦ wages: an array of seven doubles to hold each employee's gross wages

The program should relate the data in each array through the subscripts. For example, the number in element 0 of the hours array should be the number of hours worked by the employee whose identification number is stored in element 0 of the empId array. That same employee's pay rate should be stored in element 0 of the payRate array.

The program should display each employee number and ask the user to enter that employee's hours and pay rate. It should then calculate the gross wages for that employee (hours times pay rate), which should be stored in the wages array. After the data has been entered for all the employees, the program should display each employee's identification number and gross wages.

Input Validation: Do not accept negative values for hours or numbers less than 6.00 for pay rate.

7. Driver's License Exam

The local Driver's License Office has asked you to write a program that grades the written portion of the driver's license exam. The exam has 20 multiple choice questions. Here are the correct answers:

1. B	6. A	11. B	16. C
2. D	7. B	12. C	17. C
3. A	8. A	13. D	18. B
4. A	9. C	14. A	19. D
5. C	10. D	15. D	20. A

Your program should store the correct answers shown above in an array. It should ask the user to enter the student's answers for each of the 20 questions, which should be stored in another array. After the student's answers have been entered, the program should display a message indicating whether the student passed or failed the exam. (A student must correctly answer 15 of the 20 questions to pass the exam.) It should then display the total number of correctly answered questions, the total number of incorrectly answered questions, and a list showing the question numbers of the incorrectly answered questions.

Input Validation: Only accept the letters A, B, C, or D as answers.

8. Grade Book

A teacher has five students who have taken four tests. The teacher uses the following grading scale to assign a letter grade to a student, based on the average of his or her four test scores.

Test Score	Letter Grade
90–100	A
80–89	B
70–79	C
60–69	D
0–59	F

Write a program that uses a two-dimensional array of characters to hold the five student names, a single-dimensional array of five characters to hold the five students' letter grades, and five single-dimensional arrays of four `doubles` to hold each student's set of test scores.

The program should allow the user to enter each student's name and his or her four test scores. It should then calculate and display each student's average test score and a letter grade based on the average.

Input validation: Do not accept test scores less than zero or greater than 100.

9. Grade Book Modification

Modify the grade book application in Programming Challenge 8 so it drops each student's lowest score when determining the test score averages and letter grades.

10. Lottery Application

Write a program that simulates a lottery. The program should have an array of five integers named lottery, and should generate a random number in the range of 0 through 9 for each element in the array. The user should enter five digits which should be stored in an integer array named user. The program is to compare the corresponding elements in the two arrays and keep a count of the digits that match. For example, the following shows the lottery array and the user array with sample numbers stored in each. There are two matching digits (elements 2 and 4).

lottery array:

7	4	9	1	3

user array:

4	2	9	7	3

The program should display the random numbers stored in the lottery array and the number of digits matching digits. If all of the digits match, display a message proclaiming the user as a grand prize winner.

11. Number Analysis

The Chapter 7 folder on the Student CD contains a text file named numbers.txt. This file contains 12 random numbers. Write a program that reads the contents of this file into an array, and then displays the following data:

- ◆ The lowest number in the array
- ◆ The highest number in the array
- ◆ The total of the numbers in the array
- ◆ The average of the numbers in the array

12. *vector* Modification

Modify the National Commerce Bank case study presented in Program 7-21 so pin1, pin2, and pin3 are vectors instead of arrays. You must also modify the testPIN function to accept a vector instead of an array.

Group Project

13. Theater Seating

This program should be designed and written by a team of students. Here are some suggestions:

- ◆ One student should design function `main`, which will call the other functions in the program. The remainder of the functions will be designed by other members of the team.

- ◆ The requirements of the program should be analyzed so each student is given about the same work load.

- ◆ The parameters and return types of each function should be decided in advance.

- ◆ The program can be implemented either as a multi-file program, or all the functions can be cut and pasted into the main file.

Here is the assignment: Write a program that can be used by a small theater to sell tickets for performances. The theater's auditorium has 15 rows of seats, with 30 seats in each row. The program should display a screen that shows which seats are available and which are taken. For example, the following screen shows a chart depicting each seat in the theater. Seats that are taken are represented by an * symbol, and seats that are available are represented by a # symbol:

```
                    Seats
          123456789012345678901234567890
Row  1    ***####***####*##########****####
Row  2    ####***************####*******##
Row  3    **####************##########****####
Row  4    **#######***************##******
Row  5    *********######*********##########
Row  6    ################***********####
Row  7    ########***********##############
Row  8    ************##****###############
Row  9    ###########*****###############****
Row 10    ######***************#############
Row 11    #***********################**
Row 12    ################********#########*
Row 13    ####***********########**########
Row 14    ##############################
Row 15    ##############################
```

Here is a list of tasks this program must perform:

- ◆ When the program begins, it should ask the user to enter the seat prices for each row. The prices can be stored in a separate array. (Alternatively, the prices may be read from a file.)

- ◆ Once the prices are entered, the program should display a seating chart similar to the one shown above. The user may enter the row and seat numbers for tickets being sold. Every time a ticket or group of tickets is purchased, the program should display the total ticket prices and update the seating chart.

- The program should keep a total of all ticket sales. The user should be given an option of viewing this amount.
- The program should also give the user an option to see a list of how many seats have been sold, how many seats are available in each row, and how many seats are available in the entire auditorium.

Input Validation: When tickets are being sold, do not accept row or seat numbers that do not exist. When someone requests a particular seat, the program should make sure that seat is available before it is sold.

Pointers

- ## Topics in this Chapter

8.1   Getting the Address of a Variable

CONCEPT   The address operator (&) returns the memory address of a variable.

Every variable is allocated a section of memory large enough to hold a value of the variable's data type. On a PC, for instance, it's common for 1 byte to be allocated for chars, 2 bytes for shorts , 4 bytes for ints, longs, and floats, and 8 bytes for doubles.

Each byte of memory has a unique *address*. A variable's address is the address of the first byte allocated to that variable. Suppose the following variables are defined in a program:

```
char letter;
short number;
float amount;
```

Figure 8-1 illustrates how they might be arranged in memory and shows their addresses.

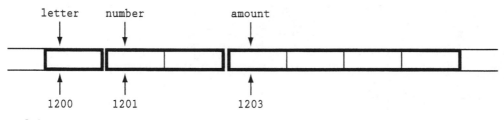

Figure 8-1

In Figure 8-1, the variable `letter` is shown at address 1200, `number` is at address 1201, and `amount` is at address 1203.

 Note: The addresses of the variables shown in Figure 8-1 are arbitrary values used only for illustration purposes.

Getting the address of a variable is accomplished with an operator in C++. When the address operator (&) is placed in front of a variable name, it returns the address of that variable. Here is an expression that returns the address of the variable `amount`:

&amount

And here is a statement that displays the variable's address on the screen:

cout << &amount;

 Note: Do not confuse the address operator with the & symbol used when defining a reference variable.

Program 8-1 demonstrates the use of the address operator to display the address, size, and contents of a variable.

Program 8-1

```cpp
// This program uses the & operator to determine a variable's
// address and the sizeof operator to determine its size.
#include <iostream>
using namespace std;

int main()
{
    int x = 25;

    cout << "The address of x is " << &x << endl;
    cout << "The size of x is " << sizeof(x) << " bytes\n";
    cout << "The value in x is " << x << endl;
    return 0;
}
```

Program 8-1 *(continued)*

Program Output
```
The address of x is 0x8f05
The size of x is 4 bytes
The value in x is 25
```

 Note: The address of the variable x is displayed in hexadecimal. This is the way addresses are normally shown in C++.

8.2 Pointer Variables

CONCEPT *Pointer variables*, which are often just called *pointers*, are designed to hold memory addresses. With pointer variables you can indirectly manipulate data stored in other variables.

Although most students agree that the topic of pointers is one of the more difficult subjects in C++, it is also one of the most important. Many operations are best performed with pointers, and some tasks aren't possible without them. They are very useful for things such as the following:

♦ Working directly with memory locations that regular variables don't give you access to

♦ Working with strings and arrays

♦ Creating new variables in memory while the program is running

♦ Creating arbitrarily-sized lists of values in memory

Pointers are special variables that C++ provides for working with memory addresses. Just like int variables are designed to hold and work with integers, pointer variables are designed to hold and work with addresses.

The definition of a pointer variable looks pretty much like any other definition. Here is an example:

```
int *ptr;
```

The asterisk in front of the variable name indicates that ptr is a pointer variable. The int data type indicates that ptr can be used to hold the address of an integer variable. The definition statement above would read "ptr is a pointer to an int."

 Note: In this defintition, the word int does not mean that ptr is an integer variable. It means that ptr can hold the address of an integer variable. Remember, pointers only hold one kind of value: an address.

Many programmers prefer to define pointers with the asterisk next to the type name, rather than the variable name. For example, the previous definition shown above could be written as:

```
int* ptr;
```

This style of definition might visually reinforce the fact that ptr's data type is not int, but pointer-to-int. Both definition styles are correct.

Program 8-2 demonstrates a very simple usage of a pointer: storing and printing the address of another variable.

Program 8-2

```
// This program stores the address of a variable in a pointer.
#include <iostream>
using namespace std;

int main()
{
    int x = 25;
    int *ptr;

    ptr = &x;    // Store the address of x in ptr
    cout << "The value in x is " << x << endl;
    cout << "The address of x is " << ptr << endl;
    return 0;
}
```

Program Output
```
The value in x is 25
The address of x is 0x7e00
```

In Program 8-2, two variables are defined: x and ptr. The variable x is an int and the variable ptr is a pointer to an int. The variable x is initialized with the value 25. The variable ptr is assigned the address of x with the following statement:

```
ptr = &x;
```

Figure 8-2 illustrates the relationship between ptr and x.

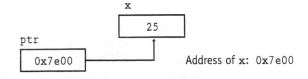

Figure 8-2

As shown in Figure 8-2, x, which is located at memory address 0x7e00, contains the number 25. ptr contains the address 0x7e00. In essence, it "points" to the variable x.

The real benefit of pointers is that they allow you to indirectly access and modify the variable being pointed to. In Program 8-2, for instance, ptr could be used to change the contents of the variable x. This is done with the *indirection operator*, which is an asterisk (*). When the indirection operator is placed in front of a pointer variable name, it *dereferences* the pointer. When you are working with a dereferenced pointer, you are actually working with the value the pointer is pointing to. This is demonstrated in the following program segment.

```
ptr = &x;    // Store the address of x in ptr
cout << "Here is the value in x, printed twice:\n";
cout << x << "   " << *ptr << endl;
*ptr = 100;
cout << "Once again, here is the value in x:\n";
cout << x << "   " << *ptr << endl;
```

Program Output
```
Here is the value in x, printed twice:
25   25
Once again, here is the value in x:
100   100
```

Every time the expression *ptr appears in the program, the program indirectly uses the variable x. The following cout statement displays the value in x twice:

```
cout << x << "   " << *ptr << endl;
```

And the following statement stores 100 in x:

```
*ptr = 100;
```

With the indirection operator, ptr can be used to indirectly access the variable it is pointing to. Program 8-3 demonstrates that pointers can point to different variables.

Program 8-3

```
// This program demonstrates the use of the indirection operator.
#include <iostream>
using namespace std;

int main()
{
    int x = 25, y = 50, z = 75;
    int *ptr;

    cout << "Here are the values of x, y, and z:\n";
    cout << x << "   " << y << "   " << z << endl;
```

(program continues)

Program 8-3 *(continued)*

```
ptr = &x;        // Store the address of x in ptr.
*ptr *= 2;       // Multiply value in x by 2.
ptr = &y;        // Store the address of y in ptr.
*ptr *= 2;       // Multiply value in y by 2.
ptr = &z;        // Store the address of z in ptr.
*ptr *= 2;       // Multiply value in z by 2.
cout << "Once again, here are the values of x, y, and z:\n";
cout << x << "   " << y << "   " << z << endl;
return 0;
}
```

Program Output
```
Here are the values of x, y, and z:
25  50  75
Once again, here are the values of x, y, and z:
50  100  150
```

Note: So far you've seen three different uses of the asterisk in C++:

◆ As the multiplication operator, in statements such as

```
distance = speed * time;
```

◆ In the definition of a pointer variable, such as

```
int *ptr;
```

◆ As the indirection operator, in statements such as

```
*ptr = 100;
```

8.3 The Relationship Between Arrays and Pointers

CONCEPT Array names can be used as constant pointers, and pointers can be used as array names.

You learned earlier that an array name, without brackets and a subscript, actually represents the starting address of the array. This means that an array name is really a pointer. Program 8-5 illustrates this by showing an array name being used with the indirection operator.

Program 8-4

```cpp
// This program shows an array name being dereferenced with the *
// operator.
#include <iostream>
using namespace std;

int main()
{
    short numbers[] = {10, 20, 30, 40, 50};

    cout << "The first element of the array is ";
    cout << *numbers << endl;
    return 0;
}
```

Program Output
```
The first element of the array is 10
```

Because numbers works like a pointer to the starting address of the array, the first element is retrieved when numbers is dereferenced. So how could the entire contents of an array be retrieved using the indirection operator? Remember, array elements are stored together in memory, as illustrated in Figure 8-3.

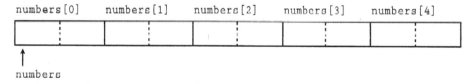

Figure 8-3   numbers

It makes sense that if numbers is the address of numbers[0], values could be added to numbers to get the addresses of the other elements in the array. It's important to know, however, that pointers do not work like regular variables when used in mathematical statements. In C++, when you add a value to a pointer, you are actually adding that value *times the size of the data type being referenced by the pointer*. In other words, if you add one to numbers, you are actually adding 1 * sizeof(short) to numbers. If you add two to numbers, the result is numbers + 2 * sizeof(short), and so forth. On a PC, this means the following are true, because short integers typically use two bytes:

```
*(numbers + 1) is actually *(numbers + 1 * 2)
*(numbers + 2) is actually *(numbers + 2 * 2)
*(numbers + 3) is actually *(numbers + 3 * 2)
```

and so forth.

This automatic conversion means that an element in an array can be retrieved by using its subscript or by adding its subscript to a pointer to the array. If the expression *numbers, which is the same as *(numbers + 0), retrieves the first element in the array, then *(numbers + 1) retrieves the second element. Likewise, *(numbers + 2) retrieves the third element, and so forth. Figure 8-4 shows the equivalence of subscript notation and pointer notation.

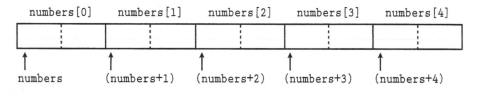

Figure 8-4

 Note: The parentheses are critical when adding values to pointers. The * operator has precedence over the + operator, so the expression *number + 1 is not equivalent to *(number + 1). *number + 1 adds one to the contents of the first element of the array, while *(number + 1) adds one to the address in number, then dereferences it.

Program 8-5 shows the entire contents of the array being accessed, using pointer notation.

Program 8-5

```cpp
// This program processes an array using pointer notation.
#include <iostream>
using namespace std;

int main()
{
   const int SIZE = 5;
   int numbers[SIZE];
   int count;

   cout << "Enter " << SIZE << " numbers: ";
   for (count = 0; count < SIZE; count++)
      cin >> *(numbers + count);
   cout << "Here are the numbers you entered:\n";
   for (count = 0; count < SIZE; count++)
      cout << *(numbers + count)<< " ";
   cout << endl;
   return 0;
}
```

Program Output with Example Input Shown in Bold
```
Enter five numbers: 5 10 15 20 25 [Enter]
Here are the numbers you entered:
5 10 15 20 25
```

When working with arrays, remember the following rule:

array[index] is equivalent to *(array + index)

 WARNING! Remember that C++ performs no bounds checking with arrays. When stepping through an array with a pointer, it's possible to give the pointer an address outside of the array.

To demonstrate just how close the relationship is between array names and pointers, look at Program 8-6. It defines an array of doubles and a double pointer, which is assigned the starting address of the array. Not only is pointer notation then used with the array name, but subscript notation is used with the pointer!

Program 8-6

```cpp
// This program uses subscript notation with a pointer variable and
// pointer notation with an array name.
#include <iostream>
#include <iomanip>
using namespace std;

int main()
{
    const int NUM_COINS = 5;
    double coins[NUM_COINS] = {0.05, 0.1, 0.25, 0.5, 1.0};
    double *doublePtr;    // Pointer to a double
    int count;            // Array index

    doublePtr = coins;    // doublePtr now points to coins array
    cout << setprecision(2);
    cout << "Here are the values in the coins array:\n";
    for (count = 0; count < NUM_COINS; count++)
        cout << doublePtr[count] << " ";
    cout << "\nAnd here they are again:\n";
    for (count = 0; count < NUM_COINS; count++)
        cout << *(coins + count) << " ";
    cout << endl;
    return 0;
}
```

Program Output

```
Here are the values in the coins array:
0.05 0.1 0.25 0.5 1
And here they are again:
0.05 0.1 0.25 0.5 1
```

Notice that the address operator is not needed when an array's address is assigned to a pointer. Because the name of an array is already an address, use of the & operator would be incorrect. You can, however, use the address operator to get the address of an individual element in an array. For instance, &numbers[1] gets the address of numbers[1]. This technique is used in Program 8-7.

Program 8-7

```cpp
// This program uses the address of each element in the array.
#include <iostream>
#include <iomanip>
using namespace std;

int main()
{
   const int NUM_COINS = 5;
   double coins[NUM_COINS] = {0.05, 0.1, 0.25, 0.5, 1.0};
   double *doublePtr; // Pointer to a double
   int count;         // Array index

   cout.precision(2);
   cout << "Here are the values in the coins array:\n";
   for (count = 0; count < NUM_COINS; count++)
   {
      doublePtr = &coins[count];
      cout << *doublePtr << " ";
   }
   cout << endl;
   return 0;
}
```

Program Output
```
Here are the values in the coins array:
0.05 0.1 0.25 0.5 1
```

The only difference between array names and pointer variables is that you cannot change the address an array name points to. For example, given the following definitions:

```cpp
double readings[20], totals[20];
double *dptr;
```

These statements are legal:

```cpp
dptr = readings; // Make dptr point to readings.
dptr = totals;   // Make dptr point to totals.
```

But these are illegal:

```cpp
readings = totals;    // ILLEGAL! Cannot change readings.
totals = fptr;        // ILLEGAL! Cannot change totals.
```

Array names are *pointer constants*. You can't make them point to anything but the array they represent.

8.4 Pointer Arithmetic

CONCEPT Some mathematical operations may be performed on pointers.

The contents of pointer variables may be changed with mathematical statements that perform addition or subtraction. This is demonstrated in Program 8-8. The first loop increments the pointer variable, stepping it through each element of the array. The second loop decrements the pointer, stepping it through the array backward.

Program 8-8

```cpp
// This program uses a pointer to display the contents of an array.
#include <iostream>
using namespace std;

int main()
{
    const int SIZE = 8;
    int set[SIZE] = {5, 10, 15, 20, 25, 30, 35, 40};
    int *nums, index;
    nums = set;
    cout << "The numbers in set are:\n";
    for (index = 0; index < SIZE; index++)
    {
        cout << *nums << " ";
        nums++;
    }
    cout << "\nThe numbers in set backward are:\n";
    for (index = 0; index < SIZE; index++)
    {
        nums--;
        cout << *nums << " ";
    }
    return 0;
}
```

Program Output
```
The numbers in set are:
5 10 15 20 25 30 35 40
The numbers in set backward are:
40 35 30 25 20 15 10 5
```

 Note: Because nums is a pointer to an integer, the increment operator adds the size of one integer to nums, so it points to the next element in the array. Likewise, the decrement operator subtracts the size of one integer from the pointer.

Not all arithmetic operations may be performed on pointers. For example, you cannot multiply or divide a pointer. The following operations are allowable:

- The ++ and -- operators may be used to increment or decrement a pointer variable.

- An integer may be added to or subtracted from a pointer variable. This may be performed with the + and - operators, or the += and -= operators.

- A pointer may be subtracted from another pointer.

8.5   Initializing Pointers

CONCEPT Pointers may be initialized with the address of an existing object.

Remember that a pointer is designed to point to an object of a specific data type. When a pointer is initialized with an address, it must be the address of an object the pointer can point to. For instance, the following definition of pint is legal because myValue is an integer:

```
int myValue;
int *pint = &myValue;
```

The following is also legal because ages is an array of integers:

```
int ages[20];
int *pint = ages;
```

But the following definition of pint is illegal because myFloat is not an int:

```
float myFloat;
int *pint = &myFloat; // Illegal!
```

Pointers may be defined in the same statement as other variables of the same type. The following statement defines an integer variable, myValue, and then defines a pointer, pint, which is initialized with the address of myValue:

```
int myValue, *pint = &myValue;
```

And the following statement defines an array, readings, and a pointer, marker, which is initialized with the address of the first element in the array:

```
double readings[50], *marker = readings;
```

Of course, a pointer can only be initialized with the address of an object that has already been defined. The following is illegal because pint is being initialized with the address of an object that does not exist yet:

```
int *pint = &myValue; // Illegal!
int myValue;
```

 # Checkpoint [8.1–8.5]

8.1 Write a statement that displays the address of the variable count.

8.2 Write the definition statement for a variable fltPtr. The variable should be a pointer to a float.

8.3 List three uses of the * symbol in C++.

8.4 Rewrite the following loop so it uses pointer notation (with the indirection operator) instead of subscript notation.

```
for (int x = 0; x < 100; x++)
    cout << array[x] << endl;
```

8.5 Assume ptr is a pointer to an int, and holds the address 12000. On a system with 4-byte integers, what address will be in ptr after the following statement?

```
ptr += 10;
```

8.6 Are each of the following definitions valid or invalid? If any are invalid, why?

```
A)  int ivar;
    int *iptr = &ivar;
B)  int ivar, *iptr = &ivar;
C)  float fvar;
    int *iptr = &fvar;
D)  int nums[50], *iptr = nums;
E)  int *iptr = &ivar;
    int ivar;
```

8.6 Comparing Pointers

> **CONCEPT** If one address comes before another address in memory, the first address is considered "less than" the second. C++'s relational operators may be used to compare pointer values.

Pointers may be compared by using any of C++'s relational operators:

```
>  <  ==  !=  >=  <=
```

In an array, all the elements are stored in consecutive memory locations, so the address of element 1 is greater than the address of element 0. This is illustrated in Figure 8-5.

An array of five integers

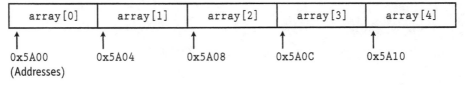

| array[0] | array[1] | array[2] | array[3] | array[4] |

↑ 0x5A00   ↑ 0x5A04   ↑ 0x5A08   ↑ 0x5A0C   ↑ 0x5A10

Figure 8-5 (Addresses)

Because the addresses grow larger for each subsequent element in the array, the following `if` statements are all true:

```
if (&array[1] > &array[0])
if (array < &array[4])
if (array == &array[0])
if (&array[2] != &array[3])
```

Note: Comparing two pointers is not the same as comparing the values the two pointers point to. For example, the following `if` statement compares the addresses stored in the pointer variables `ptr1` and `ptr2`:

```
if (ptr1 < ptr2)
```

The following statement, however, compares the values that `ptr1` and `ptr2` point to:

```
if (*ptr1 < *ptr2)
```

The capability of comparing addresses gives you another way to be sure a pointer does not go beyond the boundaries of an array. Program 8-9 initializes the pointer `nums` with the starting address of the array `set`. `nums` is then stepped through the array `set` until the address it contains is equal to the address of the last element of the array. Then the pointer is stepped backward through the array until it points to the first element.

Program 8-9

```
// This program uses a pointer to display the contents
// of an integer array.
#include <iostream>
using namespace std;
```

(program continues)

Program 8-9 *(continued)*

```cpp
int main()
{
    int set[8] = {5, 10, 15, 20, 25, 30, 35, 40};
    int *nums = set;            // Make nums point to set
    cout << "The numbers in set are:\n";
    cout << *nums << " ";       // Display first element
    while (nums < &set[7])
    {
        nums++;
        cout << *nums << " ";
    }
    cout << "\nThe numbers in set backward are:\n";
    cout << *nums << " ";       // Display first element
    while (nums > set)
    {
        nums--;
        cout << *nums << " ";
    }
    return 0;
}
```

Program Output
```
The numbers in set are:
5 10 15 20 25 30 35 40
The numbers in set backward are:
40 35 30 25 20 15 10 5
```

8.7 Pointers as Function Parameters

CONCEPT A pointer can be used as a function parameter. It gives the function access to the original argument, much like a reference parameter does.

In Chapter 6 you were introduced to the concept of reference variables being used as function parameters. A reference variable acts as an alias to the original variable used as an argument. This gives the function access to the original argument variable, allowing it to change the variable's contents. When a variable is passed into a reference parameter, the argument is said to be passed by reference.

Another way to pass an argument by reference is to use a pointer variable as the parameter. Admittedly, reference variables are much easier to work with than pointers. Reference variables hide all the "mechanics" of dereferencing and indirection. You should still learn to use pointers as function arguments, however, because some tasks, especially when dealing with strings, are best done with pointers.* Also, the C++ library has many functions that use pointers as parameters.

---

* It is also important to learn this technique in case you ever need to write a C program. In C, the only way to pass a variable by reference is to use a pointer.

Here is the definition of a function that uses a pointer parameter:

```
void doubleValue(int *val)
{
    *val *= 2;
}
```

The purpose of this function is to double the variable pointed to by val with the following statement:

```
*val *= 2;
```

When val is dereferenced, the *= operator works on the variable pointed to by val. This statement multiplies the original variable, whose address is stored in val, by two. Of course, when the function is called, the address of the variable that is to be doubled must be used as the argument, not the variable itself. Here is an example of a call to the doubleValue function:

```
doubleValue(&number);
```

This statement uses the address operator (&) to pass the address of number into the val parameter. After the function executes, the contents of number will have been multiplied by two. The use of this function is illustrated in Program 8-10.

Program 8-10

```
// This program uses two functions that accept addresses of
// variables as arguments.
#include <iostream>
using namespace std;

// Function prototypes
void getNumber(int *);
void doubleValue(int *);

int main()
{
    int number;

    getNumber(&number);       // Pass address of number to getNumber
    doubleValue(&number);     // and doubleValue.
    cout << "That value doubled is " << number << endl;
    return 0;
}
```

(program continues)

Program 8-10 *(continued)*

```
//****************************************************************
// Definition of getNumber. The parameter, input, is a pointer. *
// This function asks the user for a number. The value entered   *
// is stored in the variable pointed to by input.                *
//****************************************************************

void getNumber(int *input)
{
    cout << "Enter an integer number: ";
    cin >> *input;
}

//****************************************************************
// Definition of doubleValue. The parameter, val, is a pointer. *
// This function multiplies the variable pointed to by val by    *
// two.                                                          *
//****************************************************************

void doubleValue(int *val)
{
    *val *= 2;
}
```

Program Output with Example Input Shown in Bold
```
Enter an integer number: 10 [Enter]
That value doubled is 20
```

Program 8-10 has two functions that use pointers as parameters. Notice the function prototypes:

```
void getNumber(int *);
void doubleValue(int *);
```

Each one uses the notation int * to indicate the parameter is a pointer to an int. As with all other types of parameters, it isn't necessary to specify the name of the variable in the prototype. The * is required, though.

The getNumber function asks the user to enter an integer value. The following cin statement stores the value entered by the user in memory:

```
cin >> *input;
```

The indirection operator causes the value entered by the user to be stored, not in input, but in the variable pointed to by input.

 WARNING! It's critical that the indirection operator be used in the statement above. Without it, cin would store the value entered by the user in input, as if the value were an address. If this happens, input will no longer point to the num-ber variable in function main. Subsequent use of the pointer will result in errone-ous, if not disastrous results.

When the getNumber function is called, the address of the number variable in function main is passed as the argument. After the function executes, the value entered by the user is stored in number. Next, the doubleValue function is called, with the address of number passed as the argument. This causes number to be multiplied by two.

It's worth noting that pointer variables can be used to accept array addresses as arguments. Either subscript or pointer notation may then be used to work with the contents of the array. This is demonstrated in Program 8-11.

Program 8-11

```cpp
// This program demonstrates that a pointer may be used as a
// parameter to accept the address of an array.
#include <iostream>
#include <iomanip>
using namespace std;

// Function prototypes
void getSales(double *, int);
double totalSales(double *, int);

int main()
{
    const int QTRS = 4;
    double sales[QTRS];

    getSales(sales, QTRS);
    cout << fixed << showpoint << setprecision(2);
    cout << "The total sales for the year are $";
    cout << totalSales(sales, QTRS) << endl;
    return 0;
}

//****************************************************************
// Definition of getSales. This function uses a pointer to accept *
// the address of an array of doubles. The function asks the user *
// user to enter sales figures and stores them in the array.      *
//****************************************************************
void getSales(double *array, int size)
{
    for (int count = 0; count < size; count++)
    {
        cout << "Enter the sales figure for quarter ";
        cout << (count + 1) << ": ";
        cin >> array[count];
    }
}
```

(program continues)

Program 8-11 *(continued)*

```
//*****************************************************************
// Definition of totalSales. This function uses a pointer to      *
// accept the address of an array. The function returns the total *
// of the elements in the array.                                  *
//*****************************************************************
double totalSales(double *array, int size)
{
   double sum = 0.0;

   for (int count = 0; count < size; count++)
   {
      sum += *array;
      array++;
   }
   return sum;
}
```

Program Output with Example Input Shown in Bold
```
Enter the sales figure for quarter 1: 10263.98 [Enter]
Enter the sales figure for quarter 2: 12369.69 [Enter]
Enter the sales figure for quarter 3: 11542.13 [Enter]
Enter the sales figure for quarter 4: 14792.06 [Enter]
The total sales for the year are $48967.86
```

Notice that in the `getSales` function in Program 8-11, even though the parameter `array` is defined as a pointer, subscript notation is used in the `cin` statement:

```
cin >> array[count];
```

In the `totalSales` function, `array` is used with the indirection operator in the following statement:

```
sum += *array;
```

And in the next statement, the address in `array` is incremented to point to the next element:

```
array++;
```

 Note: The two previous statements could be combined into the following statement:

```
sum += *array++;
```

The * operator will first dereference `array`, then the ++ operator will increment the address in `array`.

8.8 Focus on Software Engineering: *Dynamic Memory Allocation*

CONCEPT | Variables may be created and destroyed while a program is running.

As long as you know how many variables you will need during the execution of a program, you can define those variables up front. For example, a program to calculate the area of a rectangle will need three variables: one for the rectangle's length, one for the rectangle's width, and one to hold the area. If you are writing a program to compute the payroll for 30 employees, you'll probably create an array of 30 elements to hold the amount of pay for each person.

But what about those times when you don't know how many variables you need? For instance, suppose you want to write a test-averaging program that will average any number of tests. Obviously the program would be very versatile, but how do you store the individual test scores in memory if you don't know how many variables to define? Quite simply, you allow the program to create its own variables "on the fly." This is called *dynamic memory allocation*, and is only possible through the use of pointers.

To dynamically allocate memory means that a program, while running, asks the computer to set aside a chunk of unused memory large enough to hold a variable of a specific data type. Let's say a program needs to create an integer variable. It will make a request to the computer that it allocate enough bytes to store an `int`. When the computer fills this request, it finds and sets aside a chunk of unused memory large enough for the variable. It then gives the program the starting address of the chunk of memory. The program can only access the newly allocated memory through its address, so a pointer is required to use those bytes.

The way a C++ program requests dynamically allocated memory is through the `new` operator. Assume a program has a pointer to an `int` defined as

```
int *iptr;
```

Here is an example of how this pointer may be used with the `new` operator:

```
iptr = new int;
```

This statement is requesting that the computer allocate enough memory for a new `int` variable. The operand of the new operator is the data type of the variable being created. Once the statement executes, `iptr` will contain the address of the newly allocated memory. This is illustrated in Figure 8-6. A value may be stored in this new variable by dereferencing the pointer:

```
*iptr = 25;
```

Any other operation may be performed on the new variable by simply using the dereferenced pointer. Here are some example statements:

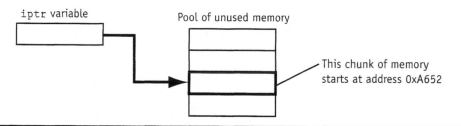

Figure 8-6

```
cout << *iptr;        // Display the contents of the new variable.
cin >> *iptr;         // Let the user input a value.
total += *iptr;       // Use the new variable in a computation.
```

Although the statements above illustrate the use of the new operator, there's little purpose in dynamically allocating a single variable. A more practical use of the new operator is to dynamically create an array. Here is an example of how a 100-element array of integers may be allocated:

```
iptr = new int[100];
```

Once the array is created, the pointer may be used with subscript notation to access it. For instance, the following loop could be used to store the value 1 in each element:

```
for (int count = 0; count < 100; count++)
    iptr[count] = 1;
```

But what if there isn't enough free memory to accommodate the request? What if the program asks for a chunk large enough to hold a 100,000-element array of floats, and that much memory isn't available? When memory cannot be dynamically allocated, C++ throws an exception and terminates the program. *Throwing an exception* means the program signals that an error has occurred. You will learn more about exceptions in chapter 16.

Programs created with older C++ compilers behave differently when memory cannot be dynamically allocated. Under older compilers, the new operator returns the address 0, or NULL when it fails to allocate the requested amount of memory. (NULL is a named constant, defined in the iostream file, which stands for address 0.) A program created with an older compiler should always check to see if the new operator returns NULL, as shown in the following code:

```
iptr = new int[100];
if (iptr == NULL)
{
    cout << "Error allocating memory!\n";
    return;
}
```

 Note: A pointer that contains the address 0 is called a *null pointer.*

The if statement determines whether iptr points to address 0. If it does, then the new operator was unable to allocate enough memory for the array. In this case, an error message is displayed and the return statement terminates the function.

 WARNING! The address 0 is considered an unusable address. Most computers store special operating system data structures in the lower areas of memory. Anytime you use the new operator with an older compiler, you should always test the pointer for the NULL address before you use it.

When a program is finished using a dynamically allocated chunk of memory, it should release it for future use. The delete operator is used to free memory that was allocated with new. Here is an example of how delete is used to free a single variable, pointed to by iptr:

```
delete iptr;
```

If iptr points to a dynamically allocated array, the [] symbol must be placed between delete and iptr:

```
delete [] iptr;
```

 WARNING! Only use pointers with delete that were previously used with new. If you use a pointer with delete that does not reference dynamically allocated memory, unexpected problems could result!

.net Appendix F on the Student CD discusses garbage collection in .NET.

Program 8-12 demonstrates the use of new and delete. It asks for sales figures for any number of days. The figures are stored in a dynamically allocated array, and then totaled and averaged.

Program 8-12

```
// This program totals and averages the sales figures for any
// number of days. The figures are stored in a dynamically
// allocated array.
#include <iostream>
#include <iomanip>
using namespace std;

int main()
{
    double *sales, total = 0, average;
    int numDays, count;
```

(program continues)

Program 8-12 *(continued)*

```cpp
    cout << "How many days of sales figures do you wish ";
    cout << "to process? ";
    cin >> numDays;
    sales = new double[numDays];  // Allocate memory

    // Get the sales figures from the user
    cout << "Enter the sales figures below.\n";
    for (count = 0; count < numDays; count++)
    {
        cout << "Day " << (count + 1) << ": ";
        cin >> sales[count];
    }

    // Calculate the total sales
    for (count = 0; count < numDays; count++)
    {
        total += sales[count];
    }

    // Calculate the average sales per day
    average = total / numDays;

    // Display the results
    cout << fixed << showpoint << setprecision(2);
    cout << "\nTotal Sales: $" << total << endl;
    cout << "Average Sales: $" << average << endl;

    // Free dynamically allocated memory
    delete [] sales;

    return 0;
}
```

Program Output with Example Input Shown in Bold

```
How many days of sales figures do you wish to process? 5 [Enter]
Enter the sales figures below.
Day 1: 898.63 [Enter]
Day 2: 652.32 [Enter]
Day 3: 741.85 [Enter]
Day 4: 852.96 [Enter]
Day 5: 921.37 [Enter]

Total Sales: $4067.13
Average Sales: $813.43
```

8.9 Focus on Software Engineering: *Returning Pointers from Functions*

CONCEPT Functions can return pointers, but you must be sure the object the pointer references still exists.

Like any other data type, functions may return pointers. For example, the following function locates the null terminator in a string and returns a pointer to it.

```
char *findNull(char *str)
{
    char *ptr = str;

    while (*ptr != '\0')
            ptr++;
    return ptr;
}
```

The char * return type in the function header indicates the function returns a pointer to a char:

```
char *findNull(char *str)
```

When writing functions that return pointers, however, you should take care not to create elusive bugs. For instance, see if you can determine what's wrong with the following function.

```
char *getName()
{
    char name[81];
    cout << "Enter your name: ";
    cin.getline(name, 81);
    return name;
}
```

The problem, of course, is that the function returns a pointer to an object that no longer exists. Because name is defined locally, it is destroyed when the function terminates. Attempting to use the pointer will result in erroneous and unpredictable results.

You should only return a pointer from a function if it is

◆ A pointer to an object that was passed into the function as an argument

◆ A pointer to a dynamically allocated object

For instance, the following function is acceptable:

```
char *getName(char *name)
{
    cout << "Enter your name: ";
```

```
        cin.getline(name, 81);
        return name;
}
```

This function accepts a pointer to the memory location where the user's input is to be stored. Because the pointer references a memory location that was valid prior to the function being called, it is safe to return a pointer to the same location. Here is another acceptable function:

```
char *getName()
{
    char *name;

    name = new char[81];
    cout << "Enter your name: ";
    cin.getline(name, 81);
    return name;
}
```

This function uses the new operator to allocate a section of memory. This memory will remain allocated until the delete operator is used or the program ends, so it's safe to return a pointer to it.

 ## Checkpoint [8.6–8.9]

8.7 Assuming array is an array of ints, will each of the following program segments display "True" or "False"?

A) ```
   if (array < &array[1])
        cout << "True";
   else
        cout << "False";
   ```

B) ```
   cout << ((&array[4] < &array[1]) ? "True" : "False");
   ```

C) ```
   if (array != &array[2])
        cout << "True";
   else
        cout << "False";
   ```

8.8 Give an example of the proper way to call the following function:

```
void makeNegative(int *val)
{
  if (*val > 0)
        *val = -(*val);
}
```
```

8.9 Assume `ip` is a pointer to an `int`. Then, write a statement that will dynamically allocate an array of 500 integers and store its address in `ip`. Write a statement that will free the memory allocated in the statement you just wrote.

8.10 What is a null pointer?

 See the CaseStudies.pdf file on the accompanying CD for this chapter's case studies.

Review Questions and Exercises

Short Answer

1. What does the indirection operator do?

2. Look at the following code.

```
int x = 7;
int *iptr = &x;
```

What will be displayed if you send the expression `*iptr` to cout? What happens if you send the expression `ptr` to cout?

3. So far you have learned three different uses for the `*` operator. What are they?

4. What math operations are allowed on pointers?

5. Assuming that `ptr` is a pointer to an `int`, what happens when you add 4 to `ptr`?

6. Look at the following array definition.

```
int numbers[] = { 2, 4, 6, 8, 10 };
```

What will the following statement display?

```
cout << *(numbers + 3) << endl;
```

7. What is the purpose of the `new` operator?

8. What happens when a program uses the `new` operator to allocate a block of memory, but the amount of requested memory isn't available? How do programs written with older compilers handle this?

9. What is the purpose of the `delete` operator?

10. Under what circumstances can you successfully return a pointer from a function?

Algorithm Workbench

11. Look at the following code.

```
double value = 29.7;
double *ptr = &value;
```

Write a cout statement that uses the `ptr` variable to display the contents of the `value` variable.

12. Look at the following array definition.

```
int set[10];
```

Write a statement using pointer notation that stores the value 99 in set[7];

13. Write code that dynamically allocates an array of 20 integers, then uses a loop to allow the user to enter values for each element of the array.

14. Assume that tempNumbers is a pointer that points to a dynamically allocated array. Write code that releases the memory used by the array.

15. Look at the following function definition.

```
void getNumber(int &n)
{
    cout << "Enter a number: ";
    cin >> n;
}
```

In this function, the parameter n is a reference variable. Rewrite the function so that n is a pointer.

True or False

16. T F Each byte of memory is assigned a unique address.

17. T F The * operator is used to get the address of a variable.

18. T F Pointer variables are designed to hold addresses.

19. T F The & symbol is called the indirection operator.

20. T F The & operator dereferences a pointer.

21. T F When the indirection operator is used with a pointer variable, you are actually working with the value the pointer is pointing to.

22. T F Array names cannot be dereferenced with the indirection operator.

23. T F When you add a value to a pointer, you are actually adding that number times the size of the data type referenced by the pointer.

24. T F The address operator is not needed when assigning an array's address to a pointer.

25. T F You can change the address that an array name points to.

26. T F Any mathematical operation, including multiplication and division, may be performed on a pointer.

27. T F Pointers may be compared using the relational operators.

28. T F When used as function parameters, reference variables are much easier to work with than pointers.

29. T F The new operator dynamically allocates memory.

30. T F A pointer variable that has not been initialized is called a null pointer.

31. T F The address 0 is generally considered unusable.

32. T F When using a pointer with the `delete` operator, it is not necessary that the pointer was previously used with the `new` operator.

Find the Error

Each of the following definitions and program segments has errors. Locate as many as you can.

33. `int ptr*;`

34. ```
int x, *ptr;
&x = ptr;
```

35. ```
int values[20], *iptr;
iptr = values;
iptr *= 2;
```

36. ```
int *iptr = &ivalue;
int ivalue;
```

37. ```
int *pint;
new pint;
```

38. ```
int *getNum()
{
    int wholeNum;

    cout << "Enter a number: ";
    cin >> wholeNum;
    return &wholeNum;
}
```

## Programming Challenges

### 1. Array Allocator

Write a function that dynamically allocates an array of integers. The function should accept an integer argument indicating the number of elements to allocate. The function should return a pointer to the array.

### 2. Test Averaging

Write a program that dynamically allocates an array large enough to hold any number of test scores the user wishes to enter. (Use the function you wrote in problem #1). Once all the scores are entered, the array should be passed to a function that sorts them in ascending order. Another function should then be called that calculates the average score. The program should display the sorted list of scores and average, with appropriate headings.

*Input validation: Do not accept negative numbers for test scores.*
```

3. Drop Lowest Score

Modify problem 2 above so the lowest test score is dropped. This score should not be included in the calculation of the average.

 See the CaseStudies.pdf file on the accompanying CD for this chapter's case studies.

4. Case Study Modification #1

Modify Program 8-13 (the United Cause case study program) so it can be used with any set of donations. The program should dynamically allocate the donations array and ask the user to input its values.

5. Case Study Modification #2

Modify Program 8-13 (the United Cause case study program) so the arrptr array is sorted in descending order instead of ascending order.

6. Mode Function

In statistics, the *mode* of a set of values is the value which occurs most often or with the greatest frequency. Write a function that accepts as arguments the following:

A) An array of integers

B) An integer that indicates the number of elements in the array

The function should determine the mode of the array. That is, it should determine which value in the array occurs most often. The mode is the value the function should return. If the array has no mode (none of the values occur more than once), the function should return –1. (Assume the array will always contain non-negative values.)

Demonstrate your pointer prowess by using pointer notation instead of array notation in this function.

7. Median Function

In statistics, when a set of values is sorted in ascending or descending order, its *median* is the middle value. If the set contains an even number of values, the median is the mean, or average of the two middle values. Write a function that accepts as arguments the following:

A) An array of integers

B) An integer that indicates the number of elements in the array

The function should determine the median of the array. This value should be returned as a float. (Assume the values in the array are already sorted.)

Demonstrate your pointer prowess by using pointer notation instead of array notation in this function.

8. Movie Statistics

Write a program that can be used to gather statistical data about the number of movies college students see in a month. The program should perform the following steps:

A) Ask the user how many students were surveyed. An array of integers with this many elements should then be dynamically allocated.

B) Allow the user to enter the number of movies each student saw into the array.

C) Calculate and display the average, median, and mode of the values entered. (Use the functions you wrote in problems 6 and 7 to calculate the median and mode.)

Input Validation: Do not accept negative numbers for input.

9

Characters, Strings, and the `string` Class

■ Topics in this Chapter

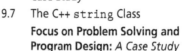

9.1   Character Testing

> **CONCEPT** The C++ library provides several functions for testing characters. To use these functions you must include the `cctype` header file.

The C++ library provides several functions that allow you to test the value of a character. These functions test a single `char` argument and return either `true` or `false`.* For example, the following program segment uses the `isupper` function to determine whether the character passed as an argument is an uppercase letter. If it is, the function returns `true`. Otherwise, it returns `false`.

---

* These functions actually return an `int` value. The return value is nonzero to indicate `true`, or zero to indicate `false`.

```
char letter = 'a';
if (isupper(letter))
    cout << "Letter is uppercase.\n";
else
    cout << "Letter is lowercase.\n";
```

Since the variable `letter`, in this example, contains a lowercase character, `isupper` returns `false`. The `if` statement will cause the message "Letter is lowercase" to be displayed.

Table 9-1 lists several character testing functions. Each of these is implemented in the `cctype` header file, so be sure to include that file when using the functions. To use these functions you must include the `cctype` header file.

Table 9-1

Character Function	Description
isalpha	Returns true (a nonzero number) if the argument is a letter of the alphabet. Returns 0 if the argument is not a letter.
isalnum	Returns true (a nonzero number) if the argument is a letter of the alphabet or a digit. Otherwise it returns 0.
isdigit	Returns true (a nonzero number) if the argument is a digit from 0 through 9. Otherwise it returns 0.
islower	Returns true (a nonzero number) if the argument is a lowercase letter. Otherwise, it returns 0.
isprint	Returns true (a nonzero number) if the argument is a printable character (including a space). Returns 0 otherwise.
ispunct	Returns true (a nonzero number) if the argument is a printable character other than a digit, letter, or space. Returns 0 otherwise.
isupper	Returns true (a nonzero number) if the argument is an uppercase letter. Otherwise, it returns 0.
isspace	Returns true (a nonzero number) if the argument is a whitespace character. Whitespace characters are any of the following: space ' ' vertical tab '\v' newline '\n' tab '\t' Otherwise, it returns 0.

Program 9-1 uses several of the functions shown in Table 9-1. It asks the user to input a character and then displays various messages, depending upon the return value of each function.

Program 9-1

```cpp
// This program demonstrates some of the character testing functions.
#include <iostream>
#include <cctype>
using namespace std;

int main()
{
    char input;

    cout << "Enter any character: ";
    cin.get(input);
    cout << "The character you entered is: " << input << endl;
    if (isalpha(input))
        cout << "That's an alphabetic character.\n";
    if (isdigit(input))
        cout << "That's a numeric digit.\n";
    if (islower(input))
        cout << "The letter you entered is lowercase.\n";
    if (isupper(input))
        cout << "The letter you entered is uppercase.\n";
    if (isspace(input))
        cout << "That's a whitespace character.\n";
    return 0;
}
```

Program Output with Example Input Shown in Bold
```
Enter any character: A [Enter]
The character you entered is: A
That's an alphabetic character.
The letter you entered is uppercase.
```

Program Output With Other Example Input
```
Enter any character: 7 [Enter]
The character you entered is: 7
That's a numeric digit.
```

Program 9-2 shows a more practical application of the character testing functions. It tests a seven-character customer number to determine whether it is in the proper format.

Program 9-2

```cpp
// This program tests a customer number to determine if it is
// in the proper format.
#include <iostream>
#include <cctype>
using namespace std;

const int SIZE 8:
```

(program continues)

Program 9-2 *(continued)*

```cpp
// Function prototype
bool testNum(char []);

int main()
{
    char customer[SIZE];

    cout << "Enter a customer number in the form ";
    cout << "LLLNNNN\n";
    cout << "(LLL = letters and NNNN = numbers): ";
    cin.getline(customer, SIZE);
    if (testNum(customer))
        cout << "That's a valid customer number.\n";
    else
    {
        cout << "That is not the proper format of the ";
        cout << "customer number.\nHere is an example:\n";
        cout << "    ABC1234\n";
    }
    return 0;
}

//***********************************************************
// Definition of function testNum                          *
// This function accepts a character array as its argument *
// and tests its contents for a valid customer number.     *
//***********************************************************

bool testNum(char custNum[])
{
    int count;// Loop counter

    // Test the first three characters for alphabetic letters
    for (count = 0; count < 3; count++)
    {
        if (!isalpha(custNum[count]))
            return false;
    }

    // Test the last four characters for numeric digits
    for (count = 3; count < SIZE-1; count++)
    {
        if (!isdigit(custNum[count]))
            return false;
    }
    return true;
}
```

Program 9-2   *(continued)*

Program Output with Example Input Shown in Bold
```
Enter a customer number in the form LLLNNNN
(LLL = letters and NNNN = numbers): RQS4567 [Enter]
That's a valid customer number.
```

Program Output With Other Example Input Shown in Bold
```
Enter a customer number in the form LLLNNNN
(LLL = letters and NNNN = numbers): AX467T9 [Enter]
That is not the proper format of the customer number.
Here is an example:
  ABC1234
```

In this program, the customer number is expected to consist of three alphabetic letters followed by four numeric digits. The testNum function accepts an array argument and tests the first three characters with the following loop:

```
for (count - 0; count < 3; count++)
{
    if (!isalpha(custNum[count]))
        return 0;
}
```

The isalpha function returns true if its argument is an alphabetic character. The ! operator is used in the if statement to determine whether the tested character is NOT alphabetic. If this is so for any of the first three characters, the function testNum returns 0. Likewise, the next four characters are tested to be numeric digits with the following loop:

```
for (count = 3; count < SIZE-1; count++)
{
    if (!isdigit(custNum[count]))
        return false;
}
```

The isdigit function returns true if its argument is the character representation of any of the digits 0 through 9. Once again, the ! operator is used to determine whether the tested character is *not* a digit. If this is so for any of the last four characters, the function testNum returns false. If the customer number is in the proper format, the function will cycle through both the loops without returning false. In that case, the last line in the function is the return true statement, which indicates the customer number is valid.

9.2 Character Case Conversion

CONCEPT The C++ library offers functions for converting a character to upper- or lowercase.

The C++ library provides two functions, `toupper` and `tolower`, for converting the case of a character. The functions are described in Table 9-2. (These functions are prototyped in the header file `cctype`, so be sure to include it.)

Table 9-2

Function	Description
`toupper`	Returns the uppercase equivalent of its argument.
`tolower`	Returns the lowercase equivalent of its argument.

Each of the functions in Table 9-2 accepts a single character argument. If the argument is a lowercase letter, the `toupper` function returns its uppercase equivalent. For example, the following statement will display the character A on the screen:

```
cout << toupper('a');
```

If the argument is already an uppercase letter, `toupper` returns it unchanged. The following statement causes the character Z to be displayed:

```
cout << toupper('Z');
```

Any nonletter argument passed to `toupper` is returned as it is. Each of the following statements display `toupper`'s argument without any change:

```
cout << toupper('*');   // Displays *
cout << toupper ('&');   // Displays &
cout << toupper('%');   // Displays %
```

`toupper` and `tolower` don't actually cause the character argument to change, they simply return the upper- or lowercase equivalent of the argument. For example, in the following program segment, the variable `letter` is set to the value 'A'. The `tolower` function returns the character 'a', but `letter` still contains 'A'.

```
char letter = 'A';
cout << tolower(letter) << endl;
cout << letter << endl;
```

These statements will cause the following to be displayed:

```
a
A
```

The `toupper` function provides a convenient way to perform a case-insensitive test on user input. Examine the following `do while` loop.

```
do
{
    cout << "Calculate another? (Y or N) ";
    cin >> go;
} while(toupper(go) != 'Y' && toupper(go) != 'N');
```

This loop continues as long as the user does not press 'y', 'Y', 'n', or 'N'. Notice how the `toupper` function converts the user-input, stored in `go`, to uppercase. By doing so, the code need only check the uppercase values 'Y' and 'N'.

Checkpoint   [9.1–9.2]

9.1   Write a statement that will convert the contents of the char variable `big` to lowercase. The converted value should be assigned to the variable `little`.

9.2   Write an `if` statement that will display the word "digit" if the variable ch contains a numeric digit. Otherwise, it should display "Not a digit."

9.3   What is the output of the following statement?

```
cout << toupper(tolower('A'));
```

9.4   Write a loop that asks the user "Do you want to repeat the program or quit? (R/Q)". The loop should repeat until the user has entered an R or Q, (either uppercase or lowercase).

9.3   Review of the Internal Storage of C-Strings

> **CONCEPT**   In C++, a C-string is a sequence of characters stored in consecutive memory locations, terminated by a NULL character.

In this section we will discuss strings, string literals, and C-strings. Although you have previously encountered these terms, make sure you understand what each means and the differences between them.

String is a generic term that describes any consecutive sequence of characters. A word, a sentence, a person's name, and the title of a song are all strings. In a program, a string may be constant or variable in nature, and may be stored in a variety of ways.

A *string literal* or *string constant* is the literal representation of a string in a program. In C++, string literals are enclosed in double quotation marks, such as:

```
"What is your name?"
```

The term *C-string* describes a string whose characters are stored in consecutive memory locations and are followed by a NULL character, or null terminator. Recall that a NULL character or null terminator is a byte holding the ASCII code 0. For example, Figure 9-1 illustrates how the string "Bailey" is stored in memory, as a C-string.

Figure 9-1

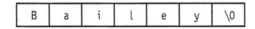

Note: Remember that \0 ("slash zero") is the escape sequence representing the null terminator. It stands for the ASCII code 0.

The purpose of the null terminator is to mark the end of the C-string. Without it, there would be no way for a function to know the length of a C-string argument.

String Literals

A string literal or string constant is enclosed in a set of double-quotation marks (" "). For example, here are five string literals:

```
"Have a nice day."
"What is your name?"
"John Smith"
"Please enter your age:"
"Part Number 45Q1789"
```

All of a program's string literals are stored in memory as C-strings, with the null terminator automatically appended. For example, look at the following program segment.

```
do
{
    cout << "C++ programming is great fun!" << endl;
    cout << "Do you want to see the message again? ";
    cin >> again;
} while (again == 'Y' || again == 'y');
```

The program segment contains two string literals:

```
"C++ programming is great fun!"
"Do you want to see the message again? "
```

Although the strings are not stored in arrays, they are still part of the program's data. The first string occupies 30 bytes of memory (including the null terminator), and the second string occupies 39 bytes. They appear in memory in the following forms:

| C | + | + | | p | r | o | g | r | a | m | m | i | n | g | | i | s | | g | r | e | a | t | | f | u | n | ! | \0 |

| D | o | | y | o | u | | w | a | n | t | | t | o | | s | e | e | | t | h | e | | m | e | s | s | a | g |
| e | | a | g | a | i | n | ? | | \0 |

It's important to realize that a string literal has its own storage location, just like a variable or an array. When a string literal appears in a statement, it's actually its memory address that C++ uses. Look at the following example:

```
cout << "Do you want to see the message again? ";
```

In this statement, the memory address of the string literal "Do you want to see the message again?" is passed to the cout object. cout displays the consecutive characters found at this address. It stops displaying the characters when a null terminator is encountered.

Strings Stored in Arrays

Quite often programs need to accept string input, change the contents of a string, or access a string for performing comparisons. One method of storing nonliteral strings is in character arrays, as C-strings. When defining a character array for holding a C-string, be sure the array is large enough for the null terminator. For example, the following 12-element array can hold a string of no more than 11 characters:

```
char company[12];
```

String input can be performed by the cin object. For example, the following statement allows the user to enter a string (with no whitespace characters) into the company array:

```
cin >> company;
```

Recall from Chapter 7 that an array name with no brackets and no subscript is converted into the beginning address of the array. In the previous statement, company indicates the address in memory where the string is to be stored. Of course, cin has no way of knowing that company only has 12 elements. If the user enters a string of 30 characters, cin will write past the end of the array. This can be prevented by using cin's getline member function. Assume the following array has been defined in a program:

```
char line[80];
```

The following statement uses cin's getline member function to get a line of input (including whitespace characters) and store it in the line array:

```
cin.getline(line, 80);
```

As you will recall from Chapter 3, the first argument tells getline where to store the string input. This statement indicates the starting address of the line array as the storage location for the string. The second argument (80) indicates the maximum length of the string, including the null terminator. cin will read 79 characters, or until the user presses the **[Enter]** key, whichever comes first. cin will automatically append the null terminator to the end of the string.

Once a string is stored in an array, it can be processed using standard subscript notation. For example, Program 9-3 displays a string stored in an array. It uses a loop to display each character in the array until the null terminator is encountered.

Program 9-3

```
// This program displays a string stored in a char array.
#include <iostream>
using namespace std;

int main()
{
   const int SIZE = 80;
   char line[SIZE];
   int count = 0;

   cout << "Enter a sentence of no more than "
        << (SIZE - 1) << " characters:\n";
   cin.getline(line, SIZE);
   cout << "The sentence you entered is:\n";
   while (line[count] != '\0')
   {
      cout << line[count];
      count++;
   }
   return 0;
}
```

Program Output with Example Input Shown in Bold
```
Enter a sentence of no more than 79 characters:
```
C++ is challenging but fun! [Enter]
```
The sentence you entered is:
C++ is challenging but fun!
```

9.4 Library Functions for Working with C-Strings

CONCEPT The C++ library has numerous functions for handling C-strings. These functions perform various tests and manipulations, and require that the cstring header file be included.

Working with C-strings can be tedious. As discussed in Chapter 7, just copying a C-string from one array to another isn't a simple matter. Fortunately, the C++ library provides many functions for manipulating and testing strings. For instance, the following program segment uses the strlen function to determine the length of the string stored in name:

```
char name[50] = "Thomas Edison";
int length;
length = strlen(name);
```

The strlen function accepts a pointer to a C-string as its argument. It returns the length of the string, which is the number of characters up to, but not including, the null terminator. As a result, the variable length will have the number 13 stored in it. The length of a string isn't to be confused with the size of the array holding it. Remember, the only information being passed to strlen is the beginning address of a C-string. It doesn't know where the array ends, so it looks for the null terminator to indicate the end of the string.

 Note: strlen, as well as the other functions discussed in this section, require the cstring header file to be included.

When using a C-string handling function, you must pass one or more C-strings as arguments. This means passing the address of the C-string, which may be accomplished by using any of the following as arguments:

- ◆ The name of the array holding the C-string
- ◆ A pointer variable that holds the address of the C-string
- ◆ A literal string

Anytime a literal string is used as an argument to a function, the address of the literal string is passed. Here is an example of the strlen function being used with such an argument:

```
length = strlen("Thomas Edison");
```

Some functions, such as strcat, require two pointers. The strcat function *concatenates*, or appends one string to another. Here is an example of its use:

```
char string1[13] = "Hello ";
char string2[7] = "World!";
cout << string1 << endl;
cout << string2 << endl;
strcat(string1, string2);
cout << string1 << endl;
```

These statements will cause the following output:

```
Hello
World!
Hello World!
```

The strcat function copies the contents of string2 to the end of string1. In this example, string1 contains the string "Hello " before the call to strcat. After the call, it contains the string "Hello World!". Figure 9-2 shows the contents of both arrays before and after the function call.

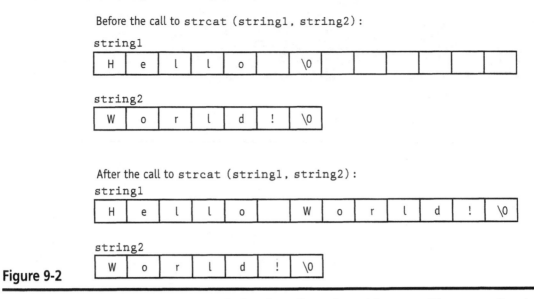

Figure 9-2

Notice the last character in string1 (before the null terminator) is a space. The strcat function doesn't insert a space, so it's the programmer's responsibility to make sure one is already there, if needed. It's also the programmer's responsibility to make sure the array holding string1 is large enough to hold string1 plus string2 plus a null terminator. Here is a program segment that uses the sizeof operator to test an array's size before strcat is called:

```
if (sizeof(string1) >= (strlen(string1) + strlen(string2) + 1))
  strcat(string1, string2);
else
  cout << "String1 is not large enough for both strings.\n";
```

 WARNING! If the array holding the first string isn't large enough to hold both strings, strcat will overflow the boundaries of the array.

Recall from Chapter 7 that one array cannot be assigned to another with the = operator. Each individual element must be assigned, usually inside a loop. The strcpy function can be used to copy one string to another. Here is an example of its use:

```
char name[20];
strcpy(name, "Albert Einstein");
```

The strcpy function's two arguments are C-string addresses. The second C-string is copied to the first C-string, including the null terminator. (The first argument usually references an array.) In this example, the strcpy function will copy the string "Albert Einstein" to the name array.

If anything is already stored in the location referenced by the first argument, it is overwritten, as shown in the following program segment:

```
char string1[10] = "Hello", string2[10] = "World!";
cout << string1 << endl;
cout << string2 << endl;
strcpy(string1, string2);
cout << string1 << endl;
cout << string2 << endl;
```

Here is the output:

```
Hello
World!
World!
World!
```

WARNING! Being true to C++'s nature, strcpy performs no bounds checking. The array specified by the first argument will be overflowed if it isn't large enough to hold the string specified by the second argument.

Table 9-3 summarizes the string handling functions discussed here, as well as others. (All the functions listed require the cstring header file.)

Table 9-3 (See your C++ reference manual for more information on these functions)

Function	Description
strlen	Accepts a C-string or a pointer to a C-string as an argument. Returns the length of the C-string (not including the null terminator. *Example Usage:* len = strlen(name);
strcat	Accepts two C-strings or pointers to two C-strings as arguments. The function appends the contents of the second string to the first C-string. (The first string is altered, the second string is left unchanged.) *Example Usage:* strcat(string1, string2);
strcpy	Accepts two C-strings or pointers to two C-strings as arguments. The function copies the second C-string to the first C-string. The second C-string is left unchanged. *Example Usage:* strcpy(string1, string2);
strncpy	Accepts two C-strings or pointers to two C-strings, and an integer argument. The third argument, an integer, indicates how many characters to copy from the second C-string to the first C-string. If string2 has fewer than *n* characters, string1 is padded with '\0' characters. *Example Usage:* strncpy(string1, string2, n);
strcmp	Accepts two C-strings or pointers to two C-strings arguments. If string1 and string2 are the same, this function returns 0. If string2 is alphabetically greater than string1, it returns a negative number. If string2 is alphabetically less than string1, it returns a positive number. *Example Usage:* if (strcmp(string1, string2))
strstr	Accepts two C-strings or pointers to two C-strings as arguments. Searches for the first occurrence of string2 in string1. If an occurrence of string2 is found, the function returns a pointer to it. Otherwise, it returns a NULL pointer (address 0). *Example Usage:* cout << strstr(string1, string2);

9

The last function in Table 9-3 is strstr, which searches for a string inside of a string. For instance, it could be used to search for the string "seven" inside the larger string "Four score and seven years ago." The function's first argument is the string to be searched, and the second argument is the string to look for. If the function finds the second string inside the first, it returns the address of the occurrence of the second string within the first string. Otherwise it returns the address 0, or the NULL address. Here is an example:

```
char array[] = "Four score and seven years ago";
char *strPtr;
cout << array << endl;
strPtr = strstr(array, "seven");  // search for "seven"
cout << strPtr << endl;
```

In the previously shown program segment, strstr will locate the string "seven" inside the string "Four score and seven years ago." It will return the address of the first character in "seven" which will be stored in the pointer variable strPtr. If run as part of a complete program, this segment will display the following:

```
Four score and seven years ago
seven years ago
```

The strstr function can be useful in any program that must locate data inside one or more strings. Program 9-4 for example, stores a database of product numbers and descriptions in an array of C-strings. It allows the user to look up a product description by entering all or part of its product number.

Program 9-4

```
// This program uses the strstr function to search an array.
#include <iostream>
#include <cstring>       // For strstr
using namespace std;

int main()
{
    const int NUM_PRODS = 5;    // Number of products
    const int LENGTH = 27;      // String length
    char prods[NUM_PRODS][LENGTH] =
                { "TV327 31 inch Television",
                  "CD257 CD Player",
                  "TA677 Answering Machine",
                  "CS109 Car Stereo",
                  "PC955 Personal Computer" };
    char lookUp[LENGTH], *strPtr = NULL;
    int index;
```
(program continues)

Program 9-4 *(continued)*

```
cout << "\tProduct Database\n\n";
cout << "Enter a product number to search for: ";
cin.getline(lookUp, LENGTH);
for (index = 0; index < NUM_PRODS; index++)
{
    strPtr = strstr(prods[index], lookUp);
    if (strPtr != NULL)
        break;
}
if (strPtr == NULL)
    cout << "No matching product was found.\n";
else
    cout << prods[index] << endl;
return 0;
}
```

Program Output with Example Input Shown in Bold
```
        Product Database

Enter a product to search for: CS [Enter]
CS109   Car Stereo
```

Program Output with Other Example Input Shown in Bold
```
        Product Database

Enter a product to search for: AB [Enter]
No matching product was found.
```

In Program 9-4, the for loop cycles through each C-string in the array calling the following statement:

```
    strPtr = strstr(prods[index], lookUp);
```

The strstr function searches the string referenced by prods[index] for the name entered by the user, which is stored in lookUp. If lookUp is found inside prods[index], the function returns its address. In that case, the following if statement causes the for loop to terminate:

```
    if (strPtr != NULL)
        break;
```

Outside the loop, the following if-else statement determines if the string entered by the user was found in the array. If not, it informs the user that no matching product was found. Otherwise, the product number and description are displayed:

```
    if (strPtr == NULL)
        cout << "No matching product was found.\n";
```

```
else
    cout << prods[index] << endl;
```

Checkpoint [9.3–9.4]

9.5 What will the following program segment display?

```
char dog[] = "Fido";
cout << strlen(dog) << endl;
```

9.6 What will the following program segment display?

```
char string1[16] = "Have a ";
char string2[9] = "nice day";
strcat(string1, string2);
cout << string1 << endl;
cout << string2 << endl;
```

9.7 Write a statement that will copy the string "Beethoven" to the array `composer`.

9.8 When complete, the following program skeleton will search for the string "Windy" in the array `place`. If `place` contains "Windy" the program will display the message "Windy found." Otherwise it will display "Windy not found."

```
#include <iostream>
// include any other necessary header files
using namespace std;

int main()
{
    char place[] = "The Windy City";
    // Complete the program. It should search the array place
    // for the string "Windy" and display the message "Windy
    // found" if it finds the string. Otherwise, it should
    // display the message "Windy not found."
    return 0;
}
```

9.5 String/Numeric Conversion Functions

CONCEPT The C++ library provides functions for converting a string representation of a number to a numeric data type and vice versa. These functions require the `cstdlib` header file to be included.

There is a great difference between a number that is stored as a string and one stored as a numeric value. The string "26792" isn't actually a number, but a series of ASCII codes representing the individual digits of the number. It uses six bytes of memory (including the null terminator).

Because it isn't an actual number, it's not possible to perform mathematical operations with it, unless it is first converted to a numeric value.

Several functions exist in the C++ library for converting string representations of numbers into numeric values, and vice-versa. Table 9-4 shows some of these.

Table 9-4 (See your C++ reference manual for more information on these functions)

Function	Description
atoi	Accepts a C-string as an argument. The function converts the C-string to an integer and returns that value. *Example Usage:* num = atoi("4569");
atol	Accepts a C-string as an argument. The function converts the C-string to a long integer and returns that value. *Example Usage:* lnum = atol("500000");
atof	Accepts a C-string as an argument. The function converts the C-string to a double and returns that value. *Example Usage:* fnum = atof("3.14159");
itoa	Converts an integer to a C-string.* The first argument, value, is the integer. The result will be stored at the location pointed to by the second argument, string. The third argument, base, is an integer. It specifies the numbering system that the converted integer should be expressed in. (8 = octal, 10 = decimal, 16 = hexadecimal, etc.). *Example Usage:* itoa(value, string, base);

*The itoa function is not supported by all compilers.

The atoi function converts a string to an integer. It accepts a C-string argument and returns the converted integer value. Here is an example of how to use it:

```
int num;
num = atoi("1000");
```

In these statements, atoi converts the string "1000" into the integer 1000. Once the variable num is assigned this value, it can be used in mathematical operations or any task requiring a numeric value.

 Note: The atoi function as well as the others discussed in this section require that the cstdlib header file be included.

The atol function works just like atoi, except the return value is a long integer. Here is an example:

```
long bigNum;
bigNum = atol("500000");
```

The `atof` function accepts a C-string argument and converts it to a `double`. The numeric `double` value is returned, as shown here:

```
double num;
num = atof("12.67");
```

Although the `atof` function returns a `double`, you can still use it to convert a C-string to a `float`. For example, look at the following code.

```
float x;
x = atof("3.4");
```

The `atof` function converts the string "3.4" to the `double` value 3.4. Because 3.4 is within the range of a `float`, it can be stored in a `float` variable without the loss of data.

 Note: If a string that cannot be converted to a numeric value is passed to any of these functions, the function's behavior is undefined by C++. Many compilers, however, will perform the conversion process until an invalid character is encountered. For example, `atoi("123x5")` might return the integer 123. It is possible that these functions will return 0 if they cannot successfully convert their argument.

The `itoa` function is similar to `atoi`, but it works in reverse. It converts a numeric integer into a string representation of the integer. The `itoa` function accepts three arguments: the integer value to be converted, a pointer to the location in memory where the string is to be stored, and a number that represents the base of the converted value. Here is an example:

```
char numArray[10];
itoa(1200, numArray, 10);
cout << numArray << endl;
```

This program segment converts the integer value 1200 to a string. The string is stored in the array `numArray`. The third argument, 10, means the number should be written in decimal, or base 10 notation. The output of the `cout` statement is

```
1200
```

 WARNING! As always, C++ performs no array bounds checking. Make sure the array whose address is passed to `itoa` is large enough to hold the converted number, including the null terminator.

Now let's look at Program 9-5, which uses a string-to-number conversion function, `atoi`. It allows the user to enter a series of values, or the letters Q or q to quit. The average of the numbers is then calculated and displayed.

Program 9-5

```cpp
// This program demonstrates the strcmp and atoi functions.
#include <iostream>
#include <cctype>          // For tolower
#include <cstring>         // For strcmp
#include <cstdlib>         // For atoi
using namespace std;

int main()
{
    const int SIZE = 20;
    char input[SIZE];
    int total = 0, count = 0;
    double average;

    cout << "This program will average a series of numbers.\n";
    cout << "Enter the first number or Q to quit: ";
    cin.getline(input, SIZE);
    while (tolower(input[0]) != 'q')
    {
        total += atoi(input);    // Keep a running total
        count++;                 // Count the numbers entered
        cout << "Enter the next number or Q to quit: ";
        cin.getline(input, SIZE);
    }
    if (count != 0)
    {
        average = static_cast<double>(total) / count;
        cout << "Average: " << average << endl;
    }
    return 0;
}
```

Program Output with Example Input Shown in Bold
```
This program will average a series of numbers.
Enter the first number or Q to quit: 74 [Enter]
Enter the next number or Q to quit: 98 [Enter]
Enter the next number or Q to quit: 23 [Enter]
Enter the next number or Q to quit: 54 [Enter]
Enter the next number or Q to quit: Q [Enter]
Average: 62.25
```

In the program, the following while statement uses the tolower function to determine whether the first character entered by the user is "q" or "Q".

```cpp
while (tolower(input[0]) != 'q')
```

If the user hasn't entered "Q" or "q" the program uses `atoi` to convert the string in `input` to an integer and adds its value to `total` with the following statement:

```
total += atoi(input);   // Keep a running total
```

The counter is updated and then the user is asked for the next number. When all the numbers are entered, the user terminates the loop by entering "Q" or "q". If one or more numbers are entered, their average is displayed.

Checkpoint [9.5]

9.9   Write a short description of each of the following functions:

```
atoi
atol
atof
itoa
```

9.10   Write a statement that will convert the string "10" to an integer and store the result in the variable num.

9.11   Write a statement that will convert the string "100000" to a `long` and store the result in the variable num.

9.12   Write a statement that will convert the string "7.2389" to a `double` and store the result in the variable num.

9.13   Write a statement that will convert the integer 127 to a string, stored in base-10 notation in the array value.

9.6   Focus on Software Engineering: *Writing Your Own C-String-Handling Functions*

CONCEPT You can design your own specialized functions for manipulating strings.

By being able to pass arrays as arguments, you can write your own functions for processing C-strings. For example, Program 9-6 uses a function to copy a C-string from one array to another.

Program 9-6

```
// This program uses a function to copy a C-string into an array.
#include <iostream>
using namespace std;
```

(program continues)

Program 9-6 *(continued)*

```cpp
void stringCopy(char [], char []);  // Function prototype

int main()
{
    const int LENGTH = 30;
    char first[LENGTH], second[LENGTH];

    cout << "Enter a string with no more than "
         << (LENGTH - 1) << " characters:\n";
    cin.getline(first, LENGTH);
    stringCopy(first, second);
    cout << "The string you entered is:\n" << second << endl;
    return 0;
}

//**********************************************************
// Definition of the stringCopy function.                 *
// This function copies the C-string in string1 to string2.*
//**********************************************************

void stringCopy(char string1[], char string2[])
{
    int index = 0;

    while (string1[index] != '\0')   // Test for null terminator
    {
        string2[index] = string1[index];
        index++;
    }
    string2[index] = '\0';
}
```

Program Output with Example Input Shown in Bold
```
Enter a string with no more than 29 characters:
```
Thank goodness it's Friday! [Enter]
```
The string you entered is:
Thank goodness it's Friday!
```

Notice the function `stringCopy` does not accept an argument indicating the size of the arrays. It simply copies the characters from `string1` into `string2` until it encounters a null terminator in `string1`. When the null terminator is found, the loop has reached the end of the C-string. The last statement in the function assigns a null terminator (the `'\0'` character) to the end of `string2`, so it is properly terminated.

WARNING! Because the stringCopy function doesn't know the size of the second array, it's the programmer's responsibility to make sure the second array is large enough to hold the string in the first array.

Program 9-7 uses another C-string handling function: nameSlice. The program asks the user to enter his or her first and last names, separated by a space. The function searches the string for the space, and replaces it with a null terminator. In effect, this "cuts" the last name off of the string.

Program 9-7

```
// This program uses the function nameSlice to cut the last
// name off of a string that contains the user's first and
// last names.
#include <iostream>
using namespace std;

void nameSlice(char []);          // Function prototype

int main()
{
    const int SIZE=41;
    char name[SIZE];
    cout << "Enter your first and last names, separated ";
    cout << "by a space:\n";
    cin.getline(name, SIZE);
    nameSlice(name);
    cout << "Your first name is: " << name << endl;
    return 0;
}

//******************************************************************
// Definition of function nameSlice. This function accepts a      *
// character array as its argument. It scans the array looking    *
// for a space. When it finds one, it replaces it with a null     *
// terminator.                                                    *
//******************************************************************

void nameSlice(char userName[])
{
    int count = 0;

    while (userName[count] != ' ' && userName[count] != '\0')
        count++;
    if (userName[count] == ' ')
        userName[count] = '\0';
}
```

Program Output with Example Input Shown in Bold
```
Enter your first and last names, separated by a space:
```
Jimmy Jones [Enter]
```
Your first name is: Jimmy
```

The following loop in nameSlice starts at the first character in the array and scans the string searching for either a space or a null terminator:

```
while (userName[count] != ' ' && userName[count] != '\0')
    count++;
```

If the character in userName[count] isn't a space or the null terminator, count is incremented, and the next character is examined. With the example input "Jimmy Jones," the loop finds the space separating "Jimmy" and "Jones" at userName[5]. When the loop stops, count is set to 5. This is illustrated in Figure 9-3.

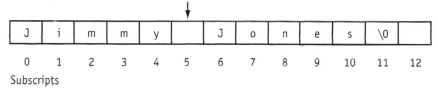

The loop stops when count reaches 5 because userName[5] contains a space

Figure 9-3   Subscripts

 Note: The loop will also stop if it encounters a null terminator. This is so it will not go beyond the boundary of the array if the user didn't enter a space.

Once the loop has finished, userName[count] will either contain a space or a null terminator. If it contains a space, the following if statement replaces it with a null terminator:

```
if (userName[count] == ' ')
    userName[count] = '\0';
```

This is illustrated in Figure 9-4.

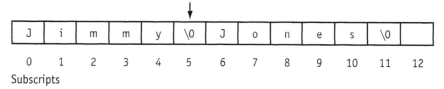

The space is replaced with a null terminator. This now becomes the end of the string

Figure 9-4   Subscripts

The new null terminator now becomes the end of the string.

Using Pointers to Pass C-String Arguments

Pointers are extremely useful for writing functions that process C-strings. If the starting address of a string is passed into a pointer parameter variable, it can be assumed that all the characters, from that address up to the byte that holds the null terminator are part of the string. (It isn't necessary to know the length of the array that holds the string.)

Program 9-8 demonstrates a function, countChars, that uses a pointer to count the number of times a specific character appears in a C-string.

Program 9-8

```
// This program demonstrates a function, countChars, that counts
// the number of times a specific character appears in a string.
#include <iostream>
using namespace std;

int countChars(char *, char);  // Function prototype

int main()
{
    const int SIZE = 51;
    char userString[SIZE], letter;

    cout << "Enter a string (up to 50 characters): ";
    cin.getline(userString, SIZE);
    cout << "Enter a character and I will tell you how many\n";
    cout << "times it appears in the string: ";
    cin >> letter;
    cout << letter << " appears ";
    cout << countChars(userString, letter) << " times.\n";
    return 0;
}

//****************************************************************
// Definition of countChars. The parameter strPtr is a pointer   *
// that points to a string. The parameter Ch is a character that  *
// the function searches for in the string. The function returns  *
// the number of times the character appears in the string.       *
//****************************************************************

int countChars(char *strPtr, char Ch)
{
    int times = 0;

    while (*strPtr != '\0')
    {
        if (*strPtr == Ch)
            times++;
        strPtr++;
    }
    return times;
}
```

Program 9-8 *(continued)*

Program Output with Example Input Shown in Bold
```
Enter a string (up to 50 characters): Starting Out With C++ [Enter]
Enter a character and I will tell you how many
times it appears in the string: t [Enter]
t appears 4 times.
```

In the function `countChars`, `strPtr` points to the C-string that is to be searched and `ch` contains the character to look for. The `while` loop repeats as long the character `strPtr` points to is not the null terminator:

```
while (*strPtr != '\0')
```

Inside the loop, the following `if` statement compares the character that `strPtr` points to with the character in `ch`:

```
if (*strPtr == ch)
```

If the two are equal, the variable `times` is incremented. (`times` keeps a running total of the number of times the character appears.) The last statement in the loop is

```
strPtr++;
```

This statement increments the address in `strPtr`. This causes `strPtr` to point to the next character in the string. Then, the loop starts over. When `strPtr` finally reaches the null terminator, the loop terminates and the function returns the value in `times`.

Checkpoint [9.6]

9.14 What is the output of the following program?

```cpp
#include <iostream>
using namespace std;

// Function Prototype
void mess(char []);

int main()
{
    char stuff[] = "Tom Talbert Tried Trains";

    cout << stuff << endl;
    mess(stuff);
    cout << stuff << endl;
    return 0;
}
```

```
// Definition of function mess
void mess(char str[])
{
    int step = 0;

    while (str[step] != '\0')
    {
        if (str[step] == 'T')
            str[step] = 'D';
        step++;
    }
}
```

 See the CaseStudies.pdf file on the accompanying CD for this chapter's case studies.

9.7 The C++ `string` Class

CONCEPT Standard C++ provides a special data type for storing and working with strings.

C++ provides two ways of storing and working with strings. One method is to store them as C-strings in character array variables. Another way is to store them in `string` class objects. Although `string` class objects are much easier to work with than C-strings, some pre-standard compilers do not support them. Because you are likely to encounter programs in the workplace that use one or the other approach to handling strings, this book teaches both.

What is the `string` Class?

The `string` class is an abstract data type. This means it is not a built-in, primitive data type like int or char. Instead, it is a programmer-defined data type that accompanies the C++ language. It provides many capabilities that make storing and working with strings easy and intuitive.

Using the `string` Class

The first step in using the string class is to #include the `string` header file. This is accomplished with the following preprocessor directive:

```
#include <string>
```

Now you are ready to define a `string` object. Defining a `string` object is similar to defining a variable of a primitive type. For example, the following statement defines a `string` object named movieTitle.

```
string movieTitle;
```

You assign a string value to the movieTitle object with the assignment operator, as shown in the following statement.

```
movieTitle = "Wheels of Fury";
```

The contents of movieTitle is displayed on the screen with the cout object, as shown in the next statement:

```
cout << "My favorite movie is " << movieTitle << endl;
```

Executing the previous three statements within a complete program generates the following output on the screen.

```
My favorite movie is Wheels of Fury
```

As you can see, working with string objects is similar to working with variables of other types. For example, Program 9-9 demonstrates how you can use cin to read a value from the keyboard into a string object.

Program 9-9

```
// This program demonstrates how cin can read a string into
// a string class object.
#include <iostream>
#include <string>
using namespace std;

int main()
{
    string name;

    cout << "What is your name? ";
    cin >> name;
    cout << "Good morning " << name << endl;
    return 0;
}
```

Program Output with Example Input Shown in Bold
```
What is your name? Peggy
Good morning Peggy
```

Reading a Line of Input into a string Object

If you want to read a line of input (with spaces) into a string object, use the getline() function. Here is an example:

```
string name;
cout << "What is your name? ";
getline(cin, name);
```

The `getline()` function's first argument is the name of a stream object you wish to read the input from. The function call above passes the `cin` object to `getline()`, so the function reads a line of input from the keyboard. The second argument is the name of a `string` object. This is where `getline()` stores the input that it reads.

Comparing and Sorting `string` Objects

There is no need to use a function such as `strcmp` to compare `string` objects. You may use the <, >, <=, >=, ==, and != relational operators. For example, assume the following definitions exist in a program:

```
string set1 = "ABC";
string set2 = "XYZ";
```

The object `set1` is considered less than the object `set2` because the characters "ABC" alphabetically precede the characters "XYZ." So, the following `if` statement will cause the message "set1 is less than set2" to be displayed on the screen.

```
if (set1 < set2)
    cout << "set1 is less than set2.\n";
```

Relational operators perform comparisons on `string` objects in a fashion similar to the way the `strcmp` function compares C-strings. One by one, each character in the first operand is compared with the character in the corresponding position in the second operand. If all the characters in both strings match, the two strings are equal. Other relationships can be determined if two characters in corresponding positions do not match. The first operand is less than the second operand if the mismatched character in the first operand is less than its counterpart in the second operand. Likewise, the first operand is greater than the second operand if the mismatched character in the first operand is greater than its counterpart in the second operand.

For example, assume a program has the following definitions:

```
string name1 = "Mary";
string name2 = "Mark";
```

The value in `name1`, "Mary," is greater than the value in `name2`, "Mark." This is because the "y" in "Mary" has a greater ASCII value than the "k" in "Mark."

`string` objects can also be compared to C-strings with relational operators. Assuming `str` is a `string` object, all of the following are valid relational expressions:

```
str > "Joseph"
"Kimberly" < str
str == "William"
```

Program 9-10 demonstrates `string` objects and relational operators.

Program 9-10

```cpp
// This program uses the == operator to compare the string entered
// by the user with the valid stereo part numbers.
#include <iostream>
#include <iomanip>
#include <string>
using namespace std;

int main()
{
    const double APRICE = 249.0, BPRICE = 299.0;
    string partNum;

    cout << "The stereo part numbers are:\n";
    cout << "\tBoom Box, part number S147-29A\n";
    cout << "\tShelf Model, part number S147-29B\n";
    cout << "Enter the part number of the stereo you\n";
    cout << "wish to purchase: ";
    cin >> partNum;
    cout << fixed << showpoint << setprecision(2);

    if (partNum == "S147-29A")
        cout << "The price is $" << APRICE << endl;
    else if (partNum == "S147-29B")
        cout << "The price is $" << BPRICE << endl;
    else
        cout << partNum << " is not a valid part number.\n";
    return 0;
}
```

Program Output with Example Input Shown in Bold
```
The stereo part numbers are:
        Boom Box, part number S147-29A
        Shelf Model, part number S147-29B
Enter the part number of the stereo you
wish to purchase: S147-29A [Enter]
The price is $249.00
```

You may also use relational operators to sort string objects. Program 9-11 demonstrates this.

Program 9-11

```cpp
// This program uses relational operators to alphabetically
// sort two strings entered by the user.
#include <iostream>
#include <string>
using namespace std;
```

(program continues)

Program 9-11 *(continued)*

```cpp
int main ()
{
    string name1, name2;

    cout << "Enter a name (last name first): ";
    getline(cin, name1);
    cout << "Enter another name: ";
    getline(cin, name2);
    cout << "Here are the names sorted alphabetically:\n";
    if (name1 < name2)
        cout << name1 << endl << name2 << endl;
    else if (name1 > name2)
        cout << name2 << endl << name1 << endl;
    else
        cout << "You entered the same name twice!\n";
    return 0;
}
```

Program Output with Example Input Shown in Bold
```
Enter a name (last name first): Smith, Richard [Enter]
Enter another name: Jones, John [Enter]
Here are the names sorted alphabetically:
Jones, John
Smith, Richard
```

Other Ways to Define `string` Objects

There are a variety of ways to initialize a string object when you define it. Table 9-5 shows several example definitions, and describes each. The following program segment demonstrates a `string` object initialized with the string "William Smith."

```cpp
string greeting;
string name("William Smith");

greeting = "Hello ";
cout << greeting << name << endl;
```

The program segment has the following ouput

```
Hello William Smith
```

Notice in the previous program segment the use of the = operator to assign a value to the string object. The `string` class supports several operators, which are described in Table 9-6.

Table 9-5

Definition	Description
`string address;`	Defines an empty `string` object named `address`.
`string name("William Smith");`	Defines a `string` object named `name`, initialized with "William Smith."
`string person1(person2);`	Defines a `string` object named `person1`, which is a copy of `person2`. `person2` may be either a `string` object or character array.
`string set1(set2, 5);`	Defines a `string` object named `set1`, which is initialized to the first five characters in the character array `set2`.
`string lineFull('z', 10);`	Defines a `string` object named `lineFull` initialized with 10 `'z'` characters.
`string firstName(fullName, 0, 7);`	Defines a `string` object named `firstName`, initialized with a substring of the `string fullName`. The substring is seven characters long, beginning at position 0.

Table 9-6

Supported Operator	Description
`>>`	Extracts characters from a stream and inserts them into the `string`. Characters are copied until a whitespace or the end of the string is encountered.
`<<`	Inserts the `string` into a stream.
`=`	Assigns the `string` on the right to the `string` object on the left.
`+=`	Appends a copy of the `string` on the right to the `string` object on the left.
`+`	Returns a `string` that is the concatenation of the two `string` operands.
`[]`	Implements array-subscript notation, as in `name[x]`. A reference to the character in the x position is returned.
Relational Operators	Each of the relational operators are implemented: `<  >  <=  >=  ==  !=`

Program 9-12 demonstrates some of the `string` operators.

Program 9-12

```
// This program demonstrates the C++ string class.
#include <iostream>
#include <string>
using namespace std;

int main ()
{
    string str1, str2, str3;
    str1 = "ABC";
    str2 = "DEF";
    str3 = str1 + str2;
    cout << str1 << endl;
    cout << str2 << endl;
    cout << str3 << endl;
    str3 += "GHI";
    cout << str3 << endl;
    return 0;
}
```

Program Output
```
ABC
DEF
ABCDEF
ABCDEFGHI
```

Using string Class Member Functions

The string class also has member functions. For example, the length member function returns the length of the string stored in the object. The value is returned as an unsigned integer.

Assume the following string object definition exists in a program:

```
string town = "Charleston";
```

The following statement in the same program would assign the value 10 to the variable x.

```
x = town.length();
```

Program 9-13 further demonstrates the length member function.

Program 9-13

```
// This program demonstrates a string
// object's length member function.
#include <iostream>
#include <string>
using namespace std;
```

(program continues)

Program 9-13 *(continued)*

```cpp
int main ()
{
    string town;

    cout << "Where do you live? ";
    cin >> town;
    cout << "Your town's name has " << town.length() ;
    cout << " characters\n";
    return 0;
}
```

Program Output with Example Input
```
Where do you live? Jacksonville
Your town's name has 12 characters
```

The size function returns the length of the string. It is demonstrated in the for loop in Program 10-14.

Program 9-14

```cpp
// This program demonstrates the C++ string class.
#include <iostream>
#include <string>
using namespace std;

int main()
{
    string str1, str2, str3;
    str1 = "ABC";
    str2 = "DEF";
    str3 = str1 + str2;
    for (int x = 0; x < str3.size(); x++)
        cout << str3[x];
    cout << endl;
    if (str1 < str2)
        cout << "str1 is less than str2\n";
    else
        cout << "str1 is not less than str2\n";
    return 0;
}
```

Program Output
```
ABCDEF
str1 is less than str2
```

Table 9-7 lists many of the string class member functions and their overloaded variations.

Table 9-7

Member Function	
Example	**Description**
theString.append(str);	Appends str to theString. str can be a string object or character array.
theString.append(str, x, n);	n number of characters from str, starting at position x, are appended to theString. If theString is too small, the function will copy as many characters as possible.
theString.append(str, n);	The first n characters of the character array str are appended to theString.
theString.append(n, 'z');	Appends n copies of 'z' to theString.
theString.assign(str);	Assigns str to theString. str can be a string object or character array.
theString.assign(str, x, n);	n number of characters from str, starting at position x, are assigned to theString. If theString is too small, the function will copy as many characters as possible.
theString.assign(str, n);	The first n characters of the character array str are assigned to theString.
theString.assign(n, 'z');	Assigns n copies of 'z' to theString.
theString.at(x);	Returns the character at position x in the string.
theString.begin();	Returns an iterator pointing to the first character in the string. (For more information on iterators, see Chapter 15.)
theString.capacity();	Returns the size of the storage allocated for the string.
theString.clear();	Clears the string by deleting all the characters stored in it.
theString.compare(str);	Performs a comparison like the strcmp function (see Chapter 4), with the same return values. str can be a string object or a character array.
theString.compare(x, n, str);	Compares theString and str, starting at position x, and continuing for n characters. The return value is like strcmp. str can be a string object or character array.

(table continues)

Table 9-7 *(continued)*

Member Function

Example	Description
`theString.copy(str, x, n);`	Copies the character array `str` to `theString`, beginning at position `x`, for `n` characters. If `theString` is too small, the function will copy as many characters as possible.
`theString.data();`	Returns a character array containing a null terminated string, as stored in `theString`.
`theString.empty();`	Returns true if `theString` is empty.
`theString.end();`	Returns an iterator pointing to the last character of the string in `theString`. (For more information on iterators, see Chapter 15.)
`theString.erase(x, n);`	Erases `n` characters from `theString`, beginning at position `x`.
`theString.find(str, x);`	Returns the first position at or beyond position `x` where the string `str` is found in `theString`. `str` may be either a `string` object or a character array.
`theString.find('z', x);`	Returns the first position at or beyond position `x` where `'z'` is found in `theString`.
`theString.insert(x, str);`	Inserts a copy of `str` into `theString`, beginning at position `x`, `str` may be either a `string` object or a character array.
`theString.insert(x, n, 'z');`	Inserts `'z'` `n` times into `theString` at position `x`.
`theString.length();`	Returns the length of the string in `theString`.
`theString.replace(x, n, str);`	Replaces the `n` characters in `theString` beginning at position `x` with the characters in string object `str`.
`theString.resize(n, 'z');`	Changes the size of the allocation in `theString` to `n`. If `n` is less than the current size of the string, the string is truncated to `n` characters. If `n` is greater, the string is expanded and `'z'` is appended at the end enough times to fill the new spaces.
`theString.size();`	Returns the length of the string in `theString`.
`theString.substr(x, n);`	Returns a copy of a substring. The substring is `n` characters long and begins at position `x` of `theString`.
`theString.swap(str);`	Swaps the contents of `theString` with `str`.

See the CaseStudies.pdf file on the accompanying CD for this chapter's case studies.

Review Questions and Exercises

Short Answer

1. What header file must you include in a program using character testing functions such as `isalpha` and `isdigit`?

2. What header file must you include in a program using the character conversion functions `toupper` and `tolower`?

3. Assume c is a `char` variable. What value does c hold after each of the following statements execute?

Statement	*Contents of c*
`c = toupper('a');`	_____
`c = toupper('B');`	_____
`c = tolower('D');`	_____
`c = toupper('e');`	_____

4. Look at the following code. What value will be stored in s after the code executes?

   ```
   char name[];
   int s;
   strcpy(name, "Jimmy");
   s = strlen(name);
   ```

5. What header file must you include in a program using string functions such as `strlen` and `strcpy`?

6. What header file must you include in a program using string/numeric conversion functions such as `atoi` and `atof`?

7. What header file must you include in a program using `string` class objects?

8. How do you compare `string` class objects?

Algorithm Workbench

9. The following `if` statement determines whether choice is equal to 'Y' or 'y'.

   ```
   if (choice == 'Y' || choice == 'y')
   ```

   Simplify this statement by using either the `toupper` or `tolower` function.

10. Assume input is a `char` array holding a C-string. Write code that counts the number of elements in the array that contain an alphabetic character.

11. Look at the following array definition.

    ```
    char str[10];
    ```

    Assume that name is also a char array, and it holds a C-string. Write code that copies the contents of name to str if the C-string in name is not too big to fit in str.

12. Look at the following statements.

    ```
    char str[] = "237.89";
    double value;
    ```

    Write a statement that converts the string in str to a double and stores the result in value.

13. Write a function that accepts a pointer to a C-string as its argument. The function should count the number of times the character 'w' occurs in the argument and return that number.

14. Assume that str1 and str2 are string class objects. Write code that displays "They are the same!" if the two objects contain the same string.

True or False

15. T   F   Character testing functions, such as isupper, accept strings as arguments and test each character in the string.

16. T   F   If toupper's argument is already uppercase, it is returned as is, with no changes.

17. T   F   If tolower's argument is already lowercase, it will be inadvertently converted to uppercase.

18. T   F   The strlen function returns the size of the array containing a string.

19. T   F   If the starting address of a string is passed into a pointer parameter, it can be assumed that all the characters, from that address up to the byte that holds the null terminator, are part of the string.

20. T   F   String handling functions accept as arguments pointers to strings (array names or pointer variables), or literal strings.

21. T   F   The strcat function checks to make sure the first string is large enough to hold both strings before performing the concatenation.

22. T   F   The strcpy function will overwrite the contents of its first string argument.

23. T   F   The strcpy function performs no bounds checking on the first argument.

24. T   F   There is no difference between "847" and 847.

Find the Errors

Each of the following programs or program segments has errors. Find as many as you can.

25. ```
    char str[] = "Stop";
    if (isupper(str) == "STOP")
    exit(0);
    ```

26. ```
    char numeric[5];
    int x = 123;
    numeric = atoi(x);
    ```

27. ```
    char string1[] = "Billy";
    char string2[] = " Bob Jones";
    strcat(string1, string2);
    ```

28. ```
    char x = 'a', y = 'a';
    if (strcmp(x, y) == 0)
        exit(0);
    ```

Programming Challenges

1. String Length

Write a function that returns an integer and accepts a pointer to a C-string as an argument. The function should count the number of characters in the string and return that number. Demonstrate the function in a simple program that asks the user to input a string, passes it to the function, and then displays the function's return value.

2. Backward String

Write a function that accepts a pointer to a C-string as an argument and displays its contents backward. For instance, if the string argument is "Gravity" the function should display "ytivarG". Demonstrate the function in a program that asks the user to input a string and then passes it to the function.

3. Word Counter

Write a function that accepts a pointer to a C-string as an argument and returns the number of words contained in the string. For instance, if the string argument is "Four score and seven years ago" the function should return the number 6. Demonstrate the function in a program that asks the user to input a string and then passes it to the function. The number of words in the string should be displayed on the screen. *Optional Exercise:* Write an overloaded version of this function that accepts a string class object as its argument.

4. Average Number of Letters

Modify the program you wrote for problem 3 (Word Counter), so it also displays the average number of letters in each word.

5. Sentence Capitalizer

Write a function that accepts a pointer to a C-string as an argument and capitalizes the first character of each sentence in the string. For instance, if the string argument is "hello. my name is Joe. what is your name?" the function should manipulate the string so it contains "Hello. My name is Joe. What is your name?" Demonstrate the function in a program that asks the user to input a string and then passes it to the function. The modified string should be displayed on the screen. *Optional Exercise:* Write an overloaded version of this function that accepts a string class object as its argument.

6. Vowels and Consonants

Write a function that accepts a pointer to a C-string as its argument. The function should count the number of vowels appearing in the string and return that number.

Write another function that accepts a pointer to a C-string as its argument. This function should count the number of consonants appearing in the string and return that number.

Demonstrate these two functions in a program that performs the following steps:

1. The user is asked to enter a string.

2. The program displays the following menu:
   A) Count the number of vowels in the string
   B) Count the number of consonants in the string
   C) Count both the vowels and consonants in the string
   D) Enter another string
   E) Exit the program

3. The program performs the operation selected by the user and repeats until the user selects E, to exit the program.

7. Name Arranger

Write a program that asks for the user's first, middle, and last names. The names should be stored in three different character arrays. The program should then store, in a fourth array, the name arranged in the following manner: the last name followed by a comma and a space, followed by the first name and a space, followed by the middle name. For example, if the user entered "Carol Lynn Smith", it should store "Smith, Carol Lynn" in the fourth array. Display the contents of the fourth array on the screen.

8. Case Manipulator

Write a program with three functions: upper, lower, and reverse. The upper function should accept a pointer to a C-string as an argument. It should step through each character in the string, converting them to uppercase. The lower function, too, should accept a pointer to a C-string as an argument. It should step through each character in the string, converting them to lowercase. Like upper and lower, reverse should also accept a pointer to a string. As it steps through the string, it should test each character to determine whether it is upper- or lowercase. If a character is uppercase, it should be converted to lowercase. Likewise, if a character is lowercase, it should be converted to uppercase.

Test the functions by asking for a string in function main, then passing it to them in the following order: reverse, lower, and upper.

9. Password Verifier

Imagine you are developing a software package that requires users to enter their own passwords. Your software requires that user's passwords meet the following criteria:

- The password should be at least six characters long.

- The password should contain at least one uppercase and at least one lowercase letter.

- The password should have at least one digit.

Write a program that asks for a password and then verifies that it meets the stated criteria. If it doesn't, the program should display a message telling the user why.

10. Phone Number List

Write a program that has an array of at least 10 string objects that hold people's names and phone numbers. You may make up your own strings, or use the following:

```
"Becky Warren, 678-1223"
"Joe Looney, 586-0097"
"Geri Palmer, 223-8787"
"Lynn Presnell, 887-1212"
"Holly Gaddis, 223-8878"
"Sam Wiggins, 486-0998"
"Bob Kain, 586-8712"
"Tim Haynes, 586-7676"
"Warren Gaddis, 223-9037"
"Jean James, 678-4939"
"Ron Palmer, 486-2783"
```

The program should ask the user to enter a name or partial name to search for in the array. Any entries in the array that match the string entered should be displayed. For example, if the user enters "Palmer" the program should display the following names from the list:

```
Geri Palmer, 223-8787
Ron Palmer, 486-2783
```

11. Check Writer

Write a program that displays a simulated paycheck. The program should ask the user to enter the date, the payee's name, and the amount of the check. It should then display a simulated check with the dollar amount spelled out, as shown here:

```
                                        Date: 11/24/05


Pay to the Order of: John Phillips          $1920.85

One thousand nine hundred twenty and 85 cents
```

Be sure to format the numeric value of the check in fixed-point notation with two decimal places of precision. Be sure the decimal place always displays, even when the number is zero or has no fractional part. Use either C-strings or string class objects in this program.

Input Validation: Do not accept negative dollar amounts, or amounts over $10,000.

10

Structured Data

■ Topics in this Chapter

10.1 Abstract Data Types

> **CONCEPT** Abstract data types (ADTs) are data types created by the programmer. ADTs have their own range (or domain) of data and their own set of operations that may be performed on them.

The term *abstract data type*, or ADT, is very important in computer science and is especially significant in object-oriented programming. This chapter introduces you to the structure, which is one of C++'s mechanisms for creating abstract data types.

Abstraction

An *abstraction* is a general model of something. It is a definition that includes only the general characteristics of an object. For example, the term "dog" is an abstraction. It defines a general type of animal. The term captures the essence of what all dogs are without specifying the detailed characteristics of any particular type of dog. According to *Webster's New Collegiate Dictionary*, a dog is

> a highly variable carnivorous domesticated mammal (*Canis familiaris*) probably descended from the common wolf.

In real life, however, there is no such thing as a mere "dog." There are specific types of dogs, each with their own set of characteristics. There are poodles, cocker spaniels, great danes, rottweillers, and many other breeds. There are small dogs and large dogs. There are gentle dogs and ferocious dogs. They come in all shapes, sizes, and dispositions. A real-life dog is not abstract. It is concrete.

Data Types

C++ has several *primitive data types*, or data types that are defined as a basic part of the language, as shown in Table 10-1.

Table 10-1

bool	int	unsigned long int
char	long int	float
unsigned char	unsigned short int	double
short int	unsigned int	long double

A data type defines what values a variable may hold. Each data type listed in Table 10-1 has its own range of values, such as −32,768 to +32,767 for shorts, and so forth. Data types also define what values a variable may not hold. For example, integer variables may not be used to hold fractional numbers.

In addition to defining a range or domain of values that a variable may hold, data types also define the operations that may be performed on a value. All of the data types listed in Table 10-1 allow the following mathematical and relational operators to be used with them:

```
+, -, *, /, >, <, >=, <=, ==, !=
```

Only the integer data types, however, allow operations with the modulus operator (%). So, a data type defines what values an object may hold and the operations that may be performed on the object.

The primitive data types are abstract in the sense that a data type and an object of that data type are not the same thing. For example, consider the following variable definition:

```
int x = 1, y = 2, z = 3;
```

In the statement above the integer variables x, y, and z are defined. They are three separate instances of the data type int. Each variable has its own characteristics (x is set to 1, y is set to 2, and z is set to 3). In this example, the data type int is the abstraction and the variables x, y, and z are concrete occurrences.

Abstract Data Types

An abstract data type (ADT) is a data type created by the programmer and is composed of one or more primitive data types. The programmer decides what values are acceptable for the data type, as well as what operations may be performed on the data type. In many cases, the programmer designs his or her own specialized operations.

For example, suppose a program is created to simulate a 12-hour clock. The program could contain three ADTs: Hours, Minutes, and Seconds. The range of values for the Hours data type would be the integers 1 through 12. The range of values for the Minutes and Seconds data types would be 0 through 59. If an Hours object is set to 12 and then incremented, it will then take on the value 1. Likewise if a Minutes object or a Seconds object is set to 59 and then incremented, it will take on the value 0.

Abstract data types often combine several values. In the clock program, the Hours, Minutes, and Seconds objects could be combined to form a single Clock object. In this chapter you will learn how to combine variables of primitive data types to form your own data structures, or ADTs.

10.2 Focus on Software Engineering: *Combining Data into Structures*

CONCEPT C++ allows you to group several variables together into a single item known as a structure.

So far you've written programs that keep data in individual variables. If you need to group items together, C++ allows you to create arrays. The limitation of arrays, however, is that all the elements must be of the same data type. Sometimes a relationship exists between items of different types. For example, a payroll system might keep the variables shown in Table 10-2. These variables hold data for a single employee.

All of the variables listed in Table 10-2 are related because they can hold data about the same employee. Their definition statements, though, do not make it clear that they belong together. To create a relationship between variables, C++ gives you the ability to package them together into a *structure*.

Before a structure can be used, it must be declared. Here is the general format of a structure declaration:

Table 10-2

Variable Definition	Data Held
`int empNumber;`	Employee number
`char name[25];`	Employee's name
`double hours;`	Hours worked
`double payRate;`	Hourly pay rate
`double grossPay;`	Gross pay

```
struct tag
{
    variable declaration;
    // ... more declarations
    //     may follow...
};
```

The *tag* is the name of the structure. As you will see later, it's used like a data type name. The variable declarations that appear inside the braces declare *members* of the structure. Here is an example of a structure declaration that holds the payroll data listed in Table 10-2:

```
struct PayRoll
{
    int empNumber;
    char name[25];
    double hours;
    double payRate;
    double grossPay;
};
```

This declaration declares a structure called `PayRoll`. The structure has five members: `empNumber`, `name`, `hours`, `payRate`, and `grossPay`.

 WARNING! Notice that a semicolon is required after the closing brace of the structure declaration.

 Note: In this text we begin the names of structure tags with an uppercase letter. Later you will see the same convention used with unions. This visually differentiates these names from the names of variables.

 Note: The structure declaration shown contains three `float` members, each declared on a separate line. The three could also have been declared on the same line, as

```
struct PayRoll
{
    int empNumber;
```

```
        char name[25];
        double hours, payRate, grossPay;
};
```

Many programmers prefer to place each member declaration on a separate line, however, for increased readability.

It's important to note that the structure declaration in our example does not define a variable. It simply tells the compiler what a PayRoll structure is made of. In essence, it creates a new data type named PayRoll. You can define variables of this type with simple definition statements, just as you would with any other data type. For example, the following statement defines a variable called deptHead:

```
        PayRoll deptHead;
```

The data type of deptHead is the PayRoll structure. The structure tag, PayRoll, is listed before the variable name just as the word int or float would be listed to define variables of those types.

Remember that structure variables are actually made up of other variables known as members. Because deptHead is a PayRoll structure it contains the following members:

```
        empNumber, an int
        name, a 25 element character array
        hours, a double
        payRate, a double
        grossPay, a double
```

Figure 10-1 illustrates this.

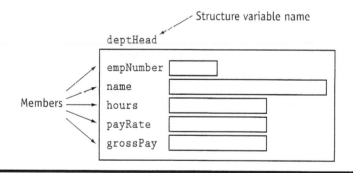

Figure 10-1

Just as it's possible to define multiple int or double variables, it's possible to define multiple structure variables in a program. The following statement defines three PayRoll variables: deptHead, foreman, and associate:

```
        PayRoll deptHead, foreman, associate;
```

Figure 10-2 illustrates the existence of these three variables.

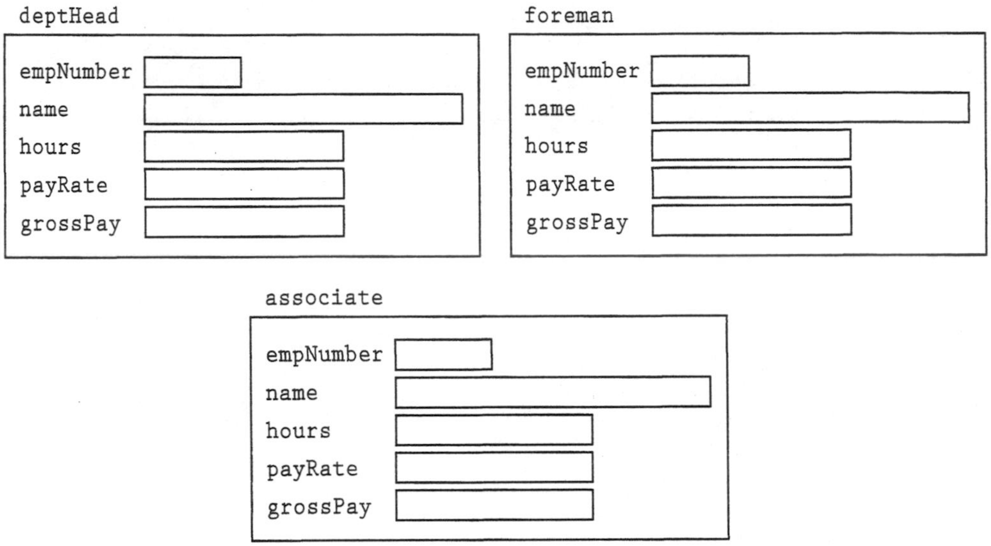

deptHead

empNumber	
name	
hours	
payRate	
grossPay	

foreman

empNumber	
name	
hours	
payRate	
grossPay	

associate

empNumber	
name	
hours	
payRate	
grossPay	

Figure 10-2

Each of the variables defined in this example are separate *instances* of the PayRoll structure and contain their own members. An instance of a structure is a variable that exists in memory. It contains within it all the members described in the structure declaration.

Although the structure variables in the example are separate, each contains members with the same name. (In the next section you'll see how to access these members.) Here are some other examples of structure declarations and variable definitions:

```
struct Time                    struct Date
{                              {
    int hour;                      int day;
    int minutes;                   int month;
    int seconds;                   int year;
};                             };
// Definition of the           // Definition of the structure
// structure variable now.     // variable today.
Time now;                      Date today;
```

In review, there are typically two steps to implementing structures in a program:

◆ Create the structure declaration. This establishes the tag (or name) of the structure and a list of items that are members.

◆ Define variables (or instances) of the structure and use them in the program to hold data.

10.3 Accessing Structure Members

> **CONCEPT** The *dot operator* (.) allows you to access structure members in a program.

C++ provides the dot operator (a period) to access the individual members of a structure. Using our example of deptHead as a PayRoll structure variable, the following statement demonstrates how to access the empNumber member:

```
deptHead.empNumber = 475;
```

In this statement, the number 475 is assigned to the empNumber member of deptHead. The dot operator connects the name of the member variable with the name of the structure variable it belongs to. The following statements assign values to the empNumber members of the deptHead, foreman, and associate structure variables:

```
deptHead.empNumber = 475;
foreman.empNumber = 897;
associate.empNumber = 729;
```

With the dot operator you can use member variables just like regular variables. For example these statements display the contents of deptHead's members:

```
cout << deptHead.empNumber << endl;
cout << deptHead.name << endl;
cout << deptHead.hours << endl;
cout << deptHead.payRate << endl;
cout << deptHead.grossPay << endl;
```

Program 10-1 is a complete program that uses the PayRoll structure.

Program 10-1

```
// This program demonstrates the use of structures.
#include <iostream>
#include <iomanip>
using namespace std;

const int SIZE = 25;

struct PayRoll
{
    int empNumber;      // Employee number
    char name[SIZE];    // Employee's name
    double hours;       // Hours worked
    double payRate;     // Hourly payRate
    double grossPay;    // Gross Pay
};
```

(program continues)

Program 10-1 *(continued)*

```cpp
int main()
{
    PayRoll employee;      // employee is a PayRoll structure

    // Get the employee data.
    cout << "Enter the employee's number: ";
    cin >> employee.empNumber;
    cout << "Enter the employee's name: ";
    cin.ignore();          // To skip the remaining '\n' character
    cin.getline(employee.name, SIZE);
    cout << "How many hours did the employee work? ";
    cin >> employee.hours;
    cout << "What is the employee's hourly pay rate? ";
    cin >> employee.payRate;

    // Calculate the employee's gross pay.
    employee.grossPay = employee.hours * employee.payRate;

    // Display the employee data.
    cout << "Here is the employee's payroll data:\n";
    cout << "Name: " << employee.name << endl;
    cout << "Number: " << employee.empNumber << endl;
    cout << "Hours worked: " << employee.hours << endl;
    cout << "Hourly pay rate: " << employee.payRate << endl;
    cout << fixed << showpoint << setprecision(2);
    cout << "Gross pay: $" << employee.grossPay << endl;
    return 0;
}
```

Program Output with Example Input Shown in Bold

```
Enter the employee's number: 489 [Enter]
Enter the employee's name: Jill Smith [Enter]
How many hours did the employee work? 40 [Enter]
What is the employee's hourly pay rate? 20 [Enter]
Here is the employee's payroll data:
Name: Jill Smith
Number: 489
Hours worked: 40
Hourly pay rate: 20
Gross pay: $800.00
```

Note: Program 10-1 has the following call to `cin`'s ignore member function:

```cpp
cin.ignore();
```

Recall that the `ignore` function causes `cin` to ignore the next character in the input buffer. This is necessary for the `cin.getline` statement to work properly in the program.

Note: The contents of a structure variable cannot be displayed by passing the entire variable to cout. For example, assuming employee is a PayRoll structure variable, the following statement will not work:

```cpp
cout << employee << endl;  // Will not work!
```

Instead, each member must be separately passed to cout.

As you can see from Program 10-1, structure members that are of a primitive data type can be used with cin, cout, mathematical statements, and any operation that can be performed with regular variables. The only difference is that the structure variable name and the dot operator must precede the name of a member. Program 10-2 shows the member of a structure variable being passed to the pow function.

Program 10-2

```cpp
// This program uses a structure to hold geometric data about a circle.
#include <iostream>
#include <cmath>        // For the pow function
#include <iomanip>
using namespace std;

struct Circle
{
    double radius;
    double diameter;
    double area;
};

const double PI = 3.14159;

int main()
{
    Circle c;

    cout << "Enter the diameter of a circle: ";
    cin >> c.diameter;
    c.radius = c.diameter / 2;
    c.area = PI * pow(c.radius, 2.0);
    cout << "The radius and area of the circle are:\n";
    cout << fixed << showpoint << setprecision(2);
    cout << "Radius: " << c.radius << endl;
    cout << "Area: " << c.area << endl;
    return 0;
}
```

Program 10-2 *(continued)*

Program Output with Example Input Shown in Bold
```
Enter the diameter of a circle: 10 [Enter]
The radius and area of the circle are:
Radius: 5
Area: 78.54
```

Comparing Structure Variables

You cannot perform comparison operations directly on structure variables. For example, assume that circle1 and circle2 are Circle structure variables. The following statement will cause an error.

```
if (circle1 == circle2)              // Error!
```

In order to compare two structures, you must compare the individual members, as shown in the following code.

```
if (circle1.radius == circle2.radius &&
    circle1.diameter == circle2.diameter &&
    circle1.area == circle2.area)
```

Strings as Structure Members

When a character array is a structure member, use the same string manipulation techniques with it as you would with any other character array. For example, assume product.description is a character array. The following statement copies into it the string "19-inch television":

```
strcpy(product.description, "19-inch television");
```

Also, assume that product.partNum is a 15-element character array. The following statement reads into it a line of input:

```
cin.getline(product.partNum, 15);
```

Program 10-3 demonstrates the use of a structure containing string data.

Program 10-3

```
// This program uses a structure to hold someone's first,
// middle, and last name.
#include <iostream>
#include <cstring>
using namespace std;

const int LENGTH = 15:
const int FULL_LENGTH = 45;
```

(program continues)

Program 10-3 *(continued)*

```cpp
struct Name
{
    char first[LENGTH];
    char middle[LENGTH];
    char last[FULL_LENGTH];
    char full[FULL_LENGTH];
};

int main()
{
    Name person;

    cout << "Enter your first name: ";
    cin >> person.first;
    cout << "Enter your middle name: ";
    cin >> person.middle;
    cout << "Enter your last name: ";
    cin >> person.last;
    strcpy(person.full, person.first);
    strcat(person.full, " ");
    strcat(person.full, person.middle);
    strcat(person.full, " ");
    strcat(person.full, person.last);
    cout << "\nYour full name is " << person.full << endl;
    return 0;
}
```

Program Output with Example Input Shown in Bold

```
Enter your first name: Josephine [Enter]
Enter your middle name: Yvonne [Enter]
Enter your last name: Smith [Enter]

Your full name is Josephine Yvonne Smith
```

10.4 Initializing a Structure

CONCEPT The members of a structure variable may be initialized with starting values when the structure variable is defined.

A structure variable may be initialized when it is defined, in a fashion similar to the initialization of an array. Assume the following structure declaration exists in a program:

```
struct GeoInfo
{
    char cityName[30];
    char state[3];
    long population;
    int distance;
};
```

A variable may then be defined with an initialization list, as shown in the following:

```
GeoInfo location = {"Asheville", "NC", 50000, 28};
```

This statement defines the variable `location`. The first value in the initialization list is assigned to the first declared member, the second value in the initialization list is assigned to the second member, and so on. The `location` variable is initialized in the folowing manner:

The string "Asheville" is assigned to `location.cityName`
The string "NC" is assigned to `location.state`
50000 is assigned to `location.population`
28 is assigned to `location.distance`

You do not have to provide initializers for all the members of a structure variable. For example, the following statement only initializes the `cityName` member of `location`:

```
GeoInfo location = {"Tampa"};
```

The `state`, `population`, and `distance` members are left uninitialized. The following statement only initializes the `cityName` and `state` members, while leaving `population` and `distance` uninitialized:

```
GeoInfo location = {"Atlanta", "GA"};
```

If you leave a structure member uninitialized, you must leave all the members that follow it uninitialized as well. C++ does not provide a way to skip members in a structure. For example, the following statement, which attempts to skip the initialization of the `population` member, is *not* legal:

```
GeoInfo location = {"Knoxville", "TN", , 90};   // Illegal!
```

Program 10-4 demonstrates the use of partially initialized structure variables.

Program 10-4

```
// This program demonstrates partially initialized
// structure variables
#include <iostream>
#include <iomanip>
using namespace std;

const int LENGTH = 25;
```

(program continues)

Program 10-4 *(continued)*

```cpp
struct EmpPay
{
    char name[LENGTH];
    int empNum;
    double payRate;
    double hours;
    double grossPay;
};

int main()
{
    EmpPay employee1 = {"Betty Ross", 141, 18.75};
    EmpPay employee2 = {"Jill Sandburg", 142, 17.50};

    cout << fixed << showpoint << setprecision(2);
    // Calculate pay for employee1
    cout << "Name: " << employee1.name << endl;
    cout << "Employee Number: " << employee1.empNum << endl;
    cout << "Enter the hours worked by this employee: ";
    cin >> employee1.hours;
    employee1.grossPay = employee1.hours * employee1.payRate;
    cout << "Gross Pay: " << employee1.grossPay << endl << endl;

    // Calculate pay for employee2
    cout << "Name: " << employee2.name << endl;
    cout << "Employee Number: " << employee2.empNum << endl;
    cout << "Enter the hours worked by this employee: ";
    cin >> employee2.hours;
    employee2.grossPay = employee2.hours * employee2.payRate;
    cout << "Gross Pay: " << employee2.grossPay << endl;
    return 0;
}
```

Program Output with Example Input Shown in Bold
```
Name: Betty Ross
Employee Number: 141
Enter the hours worked by this employee: 40 [Enter]
Gross Pay: 750.00

Name: Jill Sandburg
Employee Number: 142
Enter the hours worked by this employee: 20 [Enter]
Gross Pay: 350.00
```

It's important to note that you cannot initialize a structure member in the declaration of the structure. For instance the following declaration is illegal:

```
// Illegal structure declaration
struct GeoInfo
{
    char cityName[30] = "Asheville";    // Error!
    char state[3] = "NC";               // Error!
    long population = 50000;            // Error!
    int distance = 28;                  // Error!
};
```

Remember that a structure declaration doesn't actually create the member variables. It only declares what the structure "looks like." The member variables are created in memory when a structure variable is defined. Because no variables are created by the structure declaration, there's nothing that can be initialized there.

Checkpoint   [10.1–10.4]

10.1   Write a structure declaration to hold the following data about a savings account:

Account Number (15-element character string)
Account Balance (double)
Interest Rate (double)
Average Monthly Balance (double)

10.2   Write a definition statement for a variable of the structure you declared in question 1. Initialize the members with the following data:

Account Number: ACZ42137-B12-7
Account Balance: $4512.59
Interest Rate: 4%
Average Monthly Balance: $4217.07

10.5   Arrays of Structures

CONCEPT	Arrays of structures can simplify some programming tasks.

In Chapter 7 you saw that data can be stored in two or more arrays, with a relationship established between the arrays through their subscripts. Because structures can hold several items of varying data types, a single array of structures can be used in place of several arrays of regular variables.

An array of structures is defined like any other array. Assume the following structure declaration exists in a program:

```cpp
struct BookInfo
{
    char title[50];
    char author[30];
    char publisher[25];
    float price;
};
```

The following statement defines an array, bookList, which has 20 elements. Each element is a BookInfo structure.

```cpp
BookInfo bookList[20];
```

Each element of the array may be accessed through a subscript. For example, bookList[0] is the first structure in the array, bookList[1] is the second, and so forth. To access a member of any element, simply place the dot operator and member name after the subscript. For example, the following expression refers to the title member of bookList[5]:

```cpp
bookList[5].title
```

The following loop steps through the array, displaying the data stored in each element:

```cpp
for (int index = 0; index < 20; index++)
{
    cout << bookList[index].title << endl;
    cout << bookList[index].author << endl;
    cout << bookList[index].publisher << endl;
    cout << bookList[index].price << endl << endl;
}
```

 Note: Because the members title, author, and publisher are also arrays, their individual elements may be accessed as well. The following statement displays the character that is the first element of the title member of bookList[10]:

```cpp
cout << bookList[10].title[0];
```

And the following statement stores the character 't' in the fourth element of the publisher member of bookList[2]:

```cpp
bookList[2].publisher[3] = 't';
```

Program 10-5 calculates and displays payroll data for five employees. It uses a single array of structures.

Program 10-5

```cpp
// This program uses an array of structures.
#include <iostream>
#include <iomanip>
using namespace std;

struct PayInfo
{
   int hours;         // Hours Worked
   double payRate;    // Hourly Pay Rate
};

int main()
{
   const int NUM_WORKERS = 5;    // Number of workers
   PayInfo workers[NUM_WORKERS]; // Array of structures
   int index;                    // Loop counter

   // Get employee pay data.
   cout << "Enter the hours worked by " << NUM_WORKERS
        << " employees and their hourly rates.\n";
   for (index = 0; index < NUM_WORKERS; index++)
   {
      cout << "Hours worked by employee #" << (index + 1);
      cout << ": ";
      cin >> workers[index].hours;
      cout << "Hourly pay rate for employee #";
      cout << (index + 1) << ": ";
      cin >> workers[index].payRate;
   }

   // Display each employee's gross pay.
   cout << "Here is the gross pay for each employee:\n";
   cout << fixed << showpoint << setprecision(2);
   for (index = 0; index < NUM_WORKERS; index++)
   {
      double gross;
      gross = workers[index].hours * workers[index].payRate;
      cout << "Employee #" << (index + 1);
      cout << ": $" << gross << endl;
   }
   return 0;
}
```

Program 10-5 *(continued)*

Program Output with Example Input Shown in Bold
```
Enter the hours worked by 5 employees and their hourly rates.
Hours worked by employee #1: 10 [Enter]
Hourly pay rate for employee #1: 9.75 [Enter]
Hours worked by employee #2: 15 [Enter]
Hourly pay rate for employee #2: 8.62 [Enter]
Hours worked by employee #3: 20 [Enter]
Hourly pay rate for employee #3: 10.50 [Enter]
Hours worked by employee #4: 40 [Enter]
Hourly pay rate for employee #4: 18.75 [Enter]
Hours worked by employee #5: 40 [Enter]
Hourly pay rate for employee #5: 15.65 [Enter]
Here is the gross pay for each employee:
Employee #1: $97.50
Employee #2: $129.30
Employee #3: $210.00
Employee #4: $750.00
Employee #5: $626.00
```

Initializing a Structure Array

To initialize a structure array, simply provide an initialization list for one or more of the elements. For example, the array in Program 10-5 could have been initialized as follows:

```
PayInfo workers[NUM_WORKERS] = {
                            {10, 9.75 },
                            {15, 8.62 },
                            {20, 10.50},
                            {40, 18.75},
                            {40, 15.65}
                          };
```

Like all single-dimensional arrays, you can initialize all or part of the elements in an array of structures, as long as you do not skip elements.

10.6 Focus on Software Engineering: *Nested Structures*

CONCEPT | It's possible for a structure variable to be a member of another structure variable.

Sometimes it's helpful to nest structures inside other structures. For example, consider the following structure declarations:

```
struct Costs
{
    double wholesale;
    double retail;
};
struct Item
{
    char partNum[10];
    char description[25];
    Costs pricing;
};
```

The Costs structure has two members: wholesale and retail, both doubles. Notice that the third member of the Item structure, pricing, is a Costs structure. Assume the variable widget is defined as follows:

```
Item widget;
```

The following statements show examples of accessing members of the pricing variable, which is inside widget:

```
widget.pricing.wholesale = 100.0;
widget.pricing.retail = 150.0;
```

Program 10-6 gives a more elaborate illustration of nested structures.

Program 10-6

```
// This program shows a structure with two nested structure members.
#include <iostream>
using namespace std;

const int ADDR_LENGTH = 50;
const int CITY_LENGTH = 20;
const int STATE_LENGTH = 15;
const int ZIP_LENGTH = 11;
const int NAME_LENGTH = 50;
```

(program continues)

Program 10-6 *(continued)*

```cpp
struct Date
{
   int month;
   int day;
   int year;
};

struct Place
{
   char address[ADDR_LENGTH];
   char city[CITY_LENGTH];
   char state[STATE_LENGTH];
   char zip[ZIP_LENGTH];
};

struct EmpInfo
{
   char name[NAME_LENGTH];
   int empNumber;
   Date birthDate;
   Place residence;
};

int main()
{
   EmpInfo manager;

   // Ask for the manager's name and employee number
   cout << "Enter the manager's name: ";
   cin.getline(manager.name, NAME_LENGTH);
   cout << "Enter the manager's employee number: ";
   cin >> manager.empNumber;

   // Get the manager's birth date
   cout << "Now enter the manager's date of birth.\n";
   cout << "Month (up to 2 digits): ";
   cin >> manager.birthDate.month;
   cout << "Day (up to 2 digits): ";
   cin >> manager.birthDate.day;
   cout << "Year (2 digits): ";
   cin >> manager.birthDate.year;
   cin.get();  // Remove the remaining newline character

   // Get the manager's residence information
   cout << "Enter the manager's street address: ";
   cin.getline(manager.residence.address, ADDR_LENGTH);
   cout << "City: ";
```

(program continues)

Program 10-6 *(continued)*

```
cin.getline(manager.residence.city, CITY_LENGTH);
cout << "State: ";
cin.getline(manager.residence.state, STATE_LENGTH);
cout << "ZIP Code: ";
cin.getline(manager.residence.zip, ZIP_LENGTH);

// Display the information just entered
cout << "\nHere is the manager's information:\n";
cout << manager.name << endl;
cout << "Employee number " << manager.empNumber << endl;
cout << "Date of birth: ";
cout << manager.birthDate.month << "-";
cout << manager.birthDate.day << "-";
cout << manager.birthDate.year << endl;
cout << "Place of residence:\n";
cout << manager.residence.address << endl;
cout << manager.residence.city << ", ";
cout << manager.residence.state << " ";
cout << manager.residence.zip << endl;
return 0;
}
```

Program Output with Example Input Shown in Bold
```
Enter the manager's name: John Smith [Enter]
Enter the manager's employee number: 789 [Enter]
Now enter the manager's date of birth.
Month (up to 2 digits): 10 [Enter]
Day (up to 2 digits): 14 [Enter]
Year (2 digits): 65 [Enter]
Enter the manager's street address: 190 Disk Drive [Enter]
City: Redmond [Enter]
State: WA [Enter]
ZIP Code: 98052 [Enter]

Here is the manager's information:
John Smith
Employee number 789
Date of birth: 10-14-65
Place of residence:
190 Disk Drive
Redmond, WA  98052
```

Checkpoint [10.5–10.6]

For questions 10.3–10.7, assume the Product structure is declared as follows:

```
struct Product
{
    char description[50];    // Product description
    int partNum;             // Part number
    double cost;             // Product cost
};
```

10.3   Write a definition for an array of 100 Product structures. Do not initialize the array.

10.4   Write a loop that will step through the entire array you defined in question 10.3, setting all the product descriptions to a null string, all part numbers to zero, and all costs to zero.

10.5   Write the statements that will store the following data in the first element of the array you defined in question 10.3:

Description: Claw hammer
Part Number: 547
Part Cost: $8.29

10.6   Write a loop that will display the contents of the entire array you created in question 10.3.

10.7   Write a structure declaration called Measurement, with the following members:

miles, an integer
meters, a long integer

10.8   Write a structure declaration called Destination, with the following members:

city, a 35 element character array
distance, a Measurement structure (declared in question 10.7)

Also define a variable of this structure type.

10.9   Write statements that store the following data in the variable you defined in question 10.8:

City: Tupelo
Miles: 375
Meters: 603,375

10.7 Structures as Function Arguments

CONCEPT	Structure variables may be passed as arguments to functions.

Like other variables, the individual members of a structure variable may be used as function arguments. For example, assume the following structure declaration exists in a program:

```
struct Rectangle
{
    double length;
    double width;
    double area;
};
```

Let's say the following function definition exists in the same program:

```
double multiply(double x, double y)
{
    return x * y;
}
```

Assuming that box is a variable of the Rectangle structure type, the following function call will pass box.length into x and box.width into y. The return value will be stored in box.area.

```
box.area = multiply(box.length, box.width);
```

Sometimes it's more convenient to pass an entire structure variable into a function instead of individual members. For example, the following function definition uses a Rectangle structure variable as its parameter:

```
void showRect(Rectangle r)
{
    cout << r.length << endl;
    cout << r.width << endl;
    cout << r.area << endl;
}
```

The following function call passes the box variable into r:

```
showRect(box);
```

Inside the function showRect, r's members contain a copy of box's members. This is illustrated in Figure 10-3.

```
                        showRect(box);
                             └──────────────────────┐
                                                    ▼
                        void showRect(Rectangle r)
                        {
                              cout << r.length << endl;
                              cout << r.width << endl;
                              cout << r.area << endl;
                        }
```

Figure 10-3

Once the function is called, r.length contains a copy of box.length, r.width contains a copy of box.width, and r.area contains a copy of box.area.

Structures, like all variables, are normally passed by value into a function. If a function is to access the members of the original argument, a reference variable may be used as the parameter. Program 10-7 uses two functions that accept structures as arguments. Arguments are passed to the getItem function by reference, and to the showItem function by value.

Program 10-7

```cpp
// This program has functions that accept structure variables
// as arguments.
#include <iostream>
#include <iomanip>
using namespace std;

const int DESC_SIZE = 50;

struct InvItem
{
    int partNum;                    // Part number
    char description[DESC_SIZE];    // Item description
    int onHand;                     // Units on hand
    double price;                   // Unit price
};

// Function Prototypes
void getItem(InvItem&);     // Argument passed by reference
void showItem(InvItem);     // Argument passed by value

int main()
{
    InvItem part;

    getItem(part);
    showItem(part);
    return 0;
}
```

(program continues)

Program 10-7 *(continued)*

```
//************************************************************
// Definition of function getItem. This function uses        *
// a structure reference variable as its parameter. It asks  *
// the user for data to store in the structure.              *
//************************************************************

void getItem(InvItem &p)     // Uses a reference parameter
{
    cout << "Enter the part number: ";
    cin >> p.partNum;
    cout << "Enter the part description: ";
    cin.get();  // Eat the remaining newline character
    cin.getline(p.description, DESC_SIZE);
    cout << "Enter the quantity on hand: ";
    cin >> p.onHand;
    cout << "Enter the unit price: ";
    cin >> p.price;
}

//************************************************************
// Definition of function showItem. This function accepts    *
// an argument of the InvItem structure type. The contents   *
// of the structure are displayed.                           *
//************************************************************

void showItem(InvItem p)
{
    cout << fixed << showpoint << setprecision(2);
    cout << "Part Number: " << p.partNum << endl;
    cout << "Description: " << p.description << endl;
    cout << "Units On Hand: " << p.onHand << endl;
    cout << "Price: $" << p.price << endl;
}
```

Program Output with Example Input Shown in Bold

```
Enter the part number: 800 [Enter]
Enter the part description: Screwdriver [Enter]
Enter the quantity on hand: 135 [Enter]
Enter the unit price: 1.25 [Enter]
Part Number: 800
Description: Screwdriver
Units On Hand: 135
Price: $1.25
```

Notice that the InvItem structure declaration in Program 10-7 appears before both the proto-types and the definitions of the getItem and showItem functions. This is because both functions use an InvItem structure variable as their parameter. The compiler must know what InvItem is before it encounters any definitions for variables of that type. Otherwise, an error will occur.

Constant Reference Parameters

Sometimes structures can be quite large. Passing large structures by value can decrease a pro-gram's performance because a copy of the structure has to be created. When a structure is passed by reference, however, it isn't copied. A reference that points to the original argument is passed instead. So, it's often preferable to pass large objects such as structures by reference.

Of course, the disadvantage of passing an object by reference is that the function has access to the original argument. It can potentially alter the argument's value. This can be prevented, how-ever, by passing the argument as a constant reference. The showItem function from Program 10-7 is shown here, modified to use a constant reference parameter.

```
void showItem(const InvItem &p)
{
    cout << fixed << showpoint << setprecision(2);
    cout << "Part Number: " << p.partNum << endl;
    cout << "Description: " << p.description << endl;
    cout << "Units On Hand: " << p.onHand << endl;
    cout << "Price: $" << p.price << endl;
}
```

This version of the function is more efficient than the original version because the amount of time and memory consumed in the function call is reduced. Because the parameter is defined as a constant, the function cannot accidentally corrupt the value of the argument.

The prototype for this version of the function follows.

```
void showItem(const InvItem&);
```

10.8 Returning a Structure from a Function

CONCEPT A function may return a structure.

Just as functions can be written to return an int, long, double, or other data type, they can also be designed to return a structure. Recall the following structure declaration from Program 10-2:

```
struct Circle
{
    double radius;
    double diameter;
    double area;
};
```

A function, such as the following, could be written to return a variable of the Circle data type:

```
Circle getData()
{
    Circle temp;
    temp.radius = 10.0;
    temp.diameter = 20.0;
    temp.area = 314.159;
    return temp;
}
```

Notice that the function getData has a return data type of Circle. That means the function returns an entire Circle structure when it terminates. The return value can be assigned to any variable that is a Circle structure. The following statement, for example, assigns getData's return value to the Circle structure variable, piePlate:

```
piePlate = getData();
```

After this statement executes, piePlate.radius will be set to 10.0, piePlate.diameter will be set to 20.0, and piePlate.area will be set to 314.159.

When a function returns a structure, it is always necessary for the function to have a local structure variable to hold the member values that are to be returned. In the getData function above, the values for diameter, radius, and area are stored in the local variable temp.

```
temp.radius = 10.0;
temp.diameter = 20.0;
temp.area = 314.159;
```

temp is then returned from the function.

```
return temp;
```

Program 10-8 is a modification of Program 10-2. The function getInfo gets the circle's diameter from the user and calculates the circle's radius. The diameter and radius are stored in a local structure variable, round, which is returned from the function.

Program 10-8

```
// This program uses a function to return a structure. This
// is a modification of Program 10-2.
#include <iostream>
#include <iomanip>
#include <cmath>          // For the pow function
using namespace std;
```

(program continues)

Program 10-8 *(continued)*

```cpp
// Circle structure declaration
struct Circle
{
    double radius;
    double diameter;
    double area;
};

// Function prototype
Circle getInfo();

// Constant definition for pi
const double PI = 3.14159;

int main()
{
    Circle c;

    c = getInfo();
    c.area = PI * pow(c.radius, 2.0);
    cout << "The radius and area of the circle are:\n";
    cout << fixed << setprecision(2);
    cout << "Radius: " << c.radius << endl;
    cout << "Area: " << c.area << endl;
    return 0;
}

//*************************************************************
// Definition of function getInfo. This function uses a      *
// local variable, round, which is a circle structure.       *
// The user enters the diameter of the circle, which is      *
// stored in round.diameter. The function then calculates    *
// the radius, which is stored in round.radius. round is then *
// returned from the function.                               *
//*************************************************************

Circle getInfo()
{
    Circle round;

    cout << "Enter the diameter of a circle: ";
    cin >> round.diameter;
    round.radius = round.diameter / 2;
    return round;
}
```

(program continues)

Program 10-8 *(continued)*

Program Output with Example Input Shown in Bold
```
Enter the diameter of a circle: 10 [Enter]
The radius and area of the circle are:
Radius: 5.00
Area: 78.54
```

 Note: In Chapter 6 you learned that C++ only allows you to return a single value from a function. Structures, however, provide a way around this limitation. Even though a structure may have several members, it is technically a single value. By packaging multiple values inside a structure, you can return as many variables as you need from a function.

10.9   Pointers to Structures

> **CONCEPT** You may take the address of a structure variable and create variables that are pointers to structures.

Defining a variable that is a pointer to a structure is as simple as defining any other pointer variable: The data type is followed by an asterisk and the name of the pointer variable. Here is an example:

```
Circle *cirPtr;
```

This statement defines `cirPtr` as a pointer to a `Circle` structure. Once again, assuming `piePlate` is a `Circle` structure, the following statement stores the address of `piePlate` in the pointer variable `cirPtr`:

```
cirPtr = &piePlate;
```

This is illustrated in Figure 10-4.

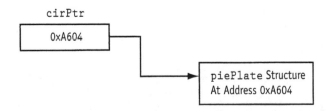

Figure 10-4

Indirectly accessing the members of a structure through a pointer can be clumsy, however, if the indirection operator is used. One might think the following statement would access the radius member of the structure pointed to by cirPtr, but it doesn't:

```
*cirPtr.radius = 10;
```

The dot operator has higher precedence than the indirection operator, so the indirection operator tries to dereference cirPtr.radius, not cirPtr. To dereference the cirPtr pointer, a set of parentheses must be used.

```
(*cirPtr).radius = 10;
```

Because of the awkwardness of this notation, C++ has a special operator for dereferencing structure pointers. It's called the *structure pointer operator*, and it consists of a hyphen (-) followed by the greater-than symbol (>). The previous statement, rewritten with the structure pointer operator, looks like this:

```
cirPtr->radius = 10;
```

The structure pointer operator takes the place of the dot operator in statements using pointers to structures. The operator automatically dereferences the structure pointer on its left. There is no need to enclose the pointer name in parentheses.

 Note: The structure pointer operator is supposed to look like an arrow, thus visually indicating that a "pointer" is being used.

Program 10-9, a modification of Program 10-1, shows a structure pointer being used to dynamically allocate a structure variable.

Program 10-9

```
// This program uses a structure pointer to dynamically allocate
// a structure variable in memory.
#include <iostream>
#include <iomanip>
using namespace std;

const int NAME_SIZE = 25;

struct PayRoll
{
    int empNumber;           // Employee number
    char name[NAME_SIZE];    // Employee's name
    double hours;            // Hours worked
    double payRate;          // Hourly Payrate
    double grossPay;         // Gross Pay
};
```

(program continues)

Program 10-9 *(continued)*

```cpp
int main()
{
    PayRoll *employee;       // pointer to a PayRoll structure

    // Dynamically allocate a struct
    employee = new PayRoll;

    // Get the employee data.
    cout << "Enter the employee's number: ";
    cin >> employee->empNumber;
    cout << "Enter the employee's name: ";
    cin.ignore();  // To skip the remaining '\n' character
    cin.getline(employee->name, NAME_SIZE);
    cout << "How many hours did the employee work? ";
    cin >> employee->hours;
    cout << "What is the employee's hourly pay rate? ";
    cin >> employee->payRate;

    // Calculate the employee's gross pay.
    employee->grossPay = employee->hours * employee->payRate;

    // Display the employee data.
    cout << "Here is the employee's payroll data:\n";
    cout << "name: " << employee->name << endl;
    cout << "Number: " << employee->empNumber << endl;
    cout << "hours worked: " << employee->hours << endl;
    cout << "Hourly Payrate: " << employee->payRate << endl;
    cout << fixed << showpoint << setprecision(2);
    cout << "Gross Pay: $" << employee->grossPay << endl;

    // Free the allocated memory
    delete employee;

    return 0;
}
```

Program Output with Example Input Shown in Bold

```
Enter the employee's number: 489 [Enter]
Enter the employee's name: Jill Smith [Enter]
How many hours did the employee work? 40 [Enter]
What is the employee's hourly pay rate? 20 [Enter]
Here is the employee's payroll data:
Name: Jill Smith
Number: 489
Hours worked: 40
Hourly pay rate: 20
Gross pay: $800.00
```

Pointer variables can also be used as function parameters. Program 10-10 shows that a pointer to a structure may be used as a function parameter, allowing the function to access the members of the original structure argument.

Program 10-10

```cpp
// This program demonstrates a function that uses a
// pointer to a structure variable as a parameter.
#include <iostream>
#include <iomanip>
using namespace std;

const int NAME_LENGTH = 35;

struct Student
{
    char name[NAME_LENGTH];   // Student's name
    int idNum;                // Student ID number
    int creditHours;          // Credit hours enrolled
    double gpa;               // Current GPA
};

void getData(Student *);      // Function prototype

int main()
{
    Student freshman;

    // Get the student data.
    cout << "Enter the following student data:\n";
    getData(&freshman);       // Pass the address of freshman.
    cout << "\nHere is the student data you entered:\n";

    // Now display the data stored in freshman
    cout << setprecision(2);
    cout << "Name: " << freshman.name << endl;
    cout << "ID Number: " << freshman.idNum << endl;
    cout << "Credit Hours: " << freshman.creditHours << endl;
    cout << "GPA: " << freshman.gpa << endl;
    return 0;
}

//*********************************************************
// Definition of function getData. Uses a pointer to a   *
// Student structure variable. The user enters student   *
// data, which is stored in the variable.                *
//*********************************************************
```

(program continues)

Program 10-10   *(continued)*

```
void getData(Student *s)
{
    cout << "Student Name: ";
    cin.getline(s->name, NAME_LENGTH);
    cout << "Student ID Number: ";
    cin >> s->idNum;
    cout << "Credit Hours Enrolled: ";
    cin >> s->creditHours;
    cout << "Current GPA: ";
    cin >> s->gpa;
}
```

Program Output with Example Input Shown in Bold
```
Enter the following student data:
Student Name: Frank Smith [Enter]
Student ID Number: 4876 [Enter]
Credit Hours Enrolled: 12 [Enter]
Current GPA: 3.45 [Enter]

Here is the student data you entered:
Name: Frank Smith
ID Number: 4876
Credit Hours: 12
GPA: 3.45
```

10.10   Focus on Software Engineering: *When to Use . , When to Use ->, and When to Use ***

Sometimes structures contain pointers as members. For example, the following structure declaration has an int pointer member:

```
struct GradeInfo
{
    char name[25];      // Student names
    int *testScores;    // Dynamically allocated array
    double average;     // Test average
};
```

It is important to remember that the structure pointer operator (->) is used to dereference a pointer to a structure, not a pointer that is a member of a structure. If a program dereferences the testScores pointer in this structure, the indirection operator must be used. For example, assuming the following variable has been defined:

```
GradeInfo student1;
```

The following statement will display the value pointed to by the testScores member:

```
cout << *student1.testScores;
```

It is still possible to define a pointer to a structure that contains a pointer member. For instance, the following statement defines stPtr as a pointer to a GradeInfo structure:

```
GradeInfo *stPtr;
```

Assuming stPtr points to a valid GradeInfo variable, the following statement will display the value pointed to by its testScores member:

```
cout << *stPtr->testScores;
```

In this statement, the * operator dereferences stPtr->testScores, while the -> operator dereferences stPtr. It might help to remember that the following expression:

```
stPtr->testScores
```

is equivalent to

```
(*stPtr).testScores
```

So, the expression

```
*stPtr->testScores
```

is the same as

```
*(*stPtr).testScores
```

The awkwardness of this last expression shows the necessity of the -> operator. Table 10-3 lists some expressions using the *, ->, and . operators, and describes what each references.

Table 10-3

Expression	Description
s->m	s is a structure pointer and m is a member. This expression accesses the m member of the structure pointed to by s.
*a.p	a is a structure variable and p, a pointer, is a member. This expression dereferences the value pointed to by p.
(*s).m	s is a structure pointer and m is a member. The * operator dereferences s, causing the expression to access the m member of the structure pointed to by s. This expression is the same as s->m.
*s->p	s is a structure pointer and p, a pointer, is a member of the structure pointed to by s. This expression accesses the value pointed to by p. (The -> operator dereferences s and the * operator dereferences p.)
*(*s).p	s is a structure pointer and p, a pointer, is a member of the structure pointed to by s. This expression accesses the value pointed to by p. (*s) dereferences s and the outermost * operator dereferences p. The expression *s->p is equivalent.

Checkpoint [10.7–10.10]

Assume the following structure declaration exists for questions 10.11–10.16:

```
struct Rectangle
{
    int length;
    int width;
};
```

10.10 Write a function that accepts a `Rectangle` structure as its argument and displays the structure's contents on the screen.

10.11 Write a function that uses a `Rectangle` structure reference variable as its parameter and stores the user's input in the structure's members.

10.12 Write a function that returns a `Rectangle` structure. The function should store the user's input in the members of the structure before returning it.

10.13 Write the definition of a pointer to a `Rectangle` structure.

10.14 Assume `rptr` is a pointer to a `Rectangle` structure. Which of the expressions, A. B, or C, is equivalent to the following expression:

```
rptr->width
```

A) `*rptr.width`
B) `(*rptr).width`
C) `rptr.(*width)`

10.11 Unions

CONCEPT A *union* is like a structure, except all the members occupy the same memory area.

A union, in almost all regards, is just like a structure. The difference is that all the members of a union use the same memory area, so only one member can be used at a time. A union might be used in an application where the program needs to work with two or more values (of different data types), but only needs to use one of the values at a time. Unions conserve memory by storing all their members in the same memory location.

Unions are declared just like structures, except the key word `union` is used instead of `struct`. Here is an example:

```
union PaySource
{
    short hours;
    float sales;
};
```

A union variable of the data type shown above can then be defined as

```
PaySource employee1;
```

The PaySource union variable defined here has two members: hours (a short), and sales (a float). The entire variable will only take up as much memory as the largest member (in this case, a float). The way this variable is stored on a typical PC is illustrated in Figure 10-5.

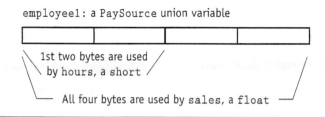

employee1: a PaySource union variable

1st two bytes are used by hours, a short

All four bytes are used by sales, a float

Figure 10-5

As shown in Figure 10-5, the union uses 4 bytes on a typical PC. It can store a short or a float, depending on which member is used. When a value is stored in the sales member, all four bytes are needed to hold the data. When a value is stored in the hours member, however, only the first 2 bytes are used. Obviously, both members can't hold values at the same time. This union is demonstrated in Program 10-11.

Program 10-11

```
// This program demonstrates a union.
#include <iostream>
#include <iomanip>
using namespace std;

union PaySource
{
    int hours;
    double sales;
};

int main()
{
    PaySource employee1;
    char payType;
    double payRate, grossPay;

    cout << fixed << showpoint << setprecision(2);
    cout << "This program calculates either hourly wages or\n";
    cout << "sales commission.\n";
    cout << "Enter H for hourly wages or C for commission: ";
    cin >> payType;
```

(program continues)

Program 10-11 *(continued)*

```
    if (payType == 'H')
    {
        cout << "What is the hourly pay rate? ";
        cin >> payRate;
        cout << "How many hours were worked? ";
        cin >> employee1.hours;
        grossPay = employee1.hours * payRate;
        cout << "Gross pay: $" << grossPay << endl;
    }
    else if (payType == 'C')
    {
        cout << "What are the total sales for this employee? ";
        cin >> employee1.sales;
        grossPay = employee1.sales * 0.10;
        cout << "Gross pay: $" << grossPay << endl;
    }
    else
    {
        cout << payType << " is not a valid selection.\n";
    }
    return 0;
}
```

Program Output with Example Input Shown in Bold
```
This program calculates either hourly wages or
sales commission.
Enter H for hourly wages or C for commission: C [Enter]
What are the total sales for this employee? 5000 [Enter]
Gross pay: $500.00
```

Program Output with Other Example Input Shown in Bold
```
This program calculates either hourly wages or
sales commission.
Enter H for hourly wages or C for commission: H [Enter]
What is the hourly pay rate? 20 [Enter]
How many hours were worked? 40 [Enter]
Gross pay: $800.00
```

Everything else you already know about structures applies to unions. For example, arrays of unions may be defined. A union may be passed as an argument to a function or returned from a function. Pointers to unions may be defined and the members of the union referenced by the pointer can be accessed with the -> operator.

Anonymous Unions

The members of an anonymous union have names, but the union itself has no name. Here is the general format of an anonymous union declaration:

```
union
{
    member declaration;
    ...
};
```

An anonymous union declaration actually creates the member variables in memory, so there is no need to separately define a union variable. Anonymous unions are simple to use because the members may be accessed without the dot operator. Program 10-12, which is a modification of Program 10-11, demonstrates the use of an anonymous union.

Program 10-12

```
// This program demonstrates an anonymous union.
#include <iostream>
#include <iomanip>
using namespace std;

int main()
{
    union   // Anonymous union
    {
        int hours;
        double sales;
    };

    char payType;
    double payRate, grossPay;

    cout << fixed << showpoint << setprecision(2);
    cout << "This program calculates either hourly wages or\n";
    cout << "sales commission.\n";
    cout << "Enter H for hourly wages or C for commission: ";
    cin >> payType;
    if (payType == 'H')
    {
        cout << "What is the hourly pay rate? ";
        cin >> payRate;
        cout << "How many hours were worked? ";
        cin >> hours;    // Anonymous union member
        grossPay = hours * payRate;
        cout << "Gross pay: $" << grossPay << endl;
    }
```

(program continues)

Program 10-12 *(continued)*

```
    else if (payType == 'C')
    {
        cout << "What are the total sales for this employee? ";
        cin >> sales;    // Anonymous union member
        grossPay = sales * 0.10;
        cout << "Gross pay: $" << grossPay << endl;
    }
    else
    {
        cout << payType << " is not a valid selection.\n";
    }
    return 0;
}
```

Program Output with Example Input Shown in Bold
```
This program calculates either hourly wages or
sales commission.
Enter H for hourly wages or C for commission: C [Enter]
What are the total sales for this employee? 12000 [Enter]
Gross pay: $1200.00
```

 Note: Notice the anonymous union in Program 10-12 is declared inside function `main`. If an anonymous union is declared globally (outside all functions), it must be declared static. This means the word `static` must appear before the word `union`.

 See the CaseStudies.pdf file on the accompanying CD for this chapter's case studies.

 # Checkpoint [10.11]

10.15 Declare a union named `ThreeTypes` with the following members:

`letter:`	A character
`whole:`	An integer
`real:`	A double

10.16 Write the definition for an array of 50 of the `ThreeTypes` structures you declared in question 10.15.

10.17 Write a loop that stores the floating point value 2.37 in all the elements of the array you defined in question 10.16.

10.18 Write a loop that stores the character 'A' in all the elements of the array you defined in question 10.16.

10.19 Write a loop that stores the integer 10 in all the elements of the array you defined in question 10.16.

10.12 Enumerated Data Types

CONCEPT An enumerated data type is a programmer-defined data type. It consists of values known as enumerators, which represent integer constants.

Using the enum key word you can create your own data type and specify the values that belong to that type. Such a type is known as an *enumerated data type*. Here is an example of an enumerated data type declaration:

```
enum Day { MONDAY, TUESDAY, WEDNESDAY, THURSDAY, FRIDAY };
```

An enumerated type declaration begins with the key word enum, followed by the name of the type, followed by a list of identifiers inside braces, and is terminated with a semicolon. The example declaration creates an enumerated data type named Day. The identifiers MONDAY, TUESDAY, WEDNESDAY, THURSDAY, and FRIDAY, which are listed inside the braces, are known as *enumerators*. They represent the values that belong to the Day data type. Here is the general format of an enumerated type declaration:

```
enum TypeName { One or more enumerators };
```

Note that the enumerators are not enclosed in quotation marks, therefore they are not strings. Enumerators must be legal C++ identifiers.

Once you have created an enumerated data type in your program, you can define variables of that type. For example, the following statement defines workDay as a variable of the Day type:

```
Day workDay;
```

Because workDay is a variable of the Day data type, we may assign any of the enumerators MONDAY, TUESDAY, WEDNESDAY, THURSDAY, or FRIDAY to it. For example, the following statement assigns the value WEDNESDAY to the workDay variable.

```
Day workDay = WEDNESDAY;
```

So just what are these enumerators MONDAY, TUESDAY, WEDNESDAY, THURSDAY, and FRIDAY? You can think of them as integer named constants. Internally, the compiler assigns integer values to the enumerators, beginning with 0. The enumerator MONDAY is stored in memory as the number 0, TUESDAY is stored in memory as the number 1, WEDNESDAY is stored in memory as the number 2, and so forth. To prove this, look at the following code.

```
cout << MONDAY << endl << TUESDAY << endl
     << WEDNESDAY << endl << THURSDAY << endl
     << FRIDAY << endl;
```

10

This statement will produce the following output:

```
0
1
2
3
4
```

 Note: When making up names for enumerators, it is not required that they be written in all uppercase letters. For example, we could have written the enumerators of the Days type as monday, tuesday, etc. Because they represent constant values, however, many programmers prefer to write them in all uppercase letters. This is strictly a preference of style.

Assigning an Integer to an `enum` Variable

Even though the enumerators of an enumerated data type are stored in memory as integers, you cannot directly assign an integer value to an enum variable. For example, assuming that workDay is a variable of the Day data type previously described, the following assignment statement is illegal.

```
workDay = 3;   // Error!
```

Compiling this statement will produce an error message such as "Cannot convert int to Day." When assigning a value to an enum variable, you should use a valid enumerator. However, if circumstances require that you store an integer value in an enum variable, you can do so by casting the integer. Here is an example:

```
workDay = static_cast<Day>(3);
```

This statement will produce the same results as:

```
workDay = THURSDAY;
```

Assigning an Enumerator to an `int` Variable

Although you cannot directly assign an integer value to an enum variable, you can directly assign an enumerator to an integer variable. For example, the following code will work just fine.

```
enum Day { MONDAY, TUESDAY, WEDNESDAY, THURSDAY, FRIDAY };
int x;
x = THURSDAY;
cout << x << endl;
```

When this code runs it will display 3. You can also assign a variable of an enumerated type to an integer variable, as shown here:

```
Day workDay = FRIDAY;
int x = workDay;
cout << x << endl;
```

When this code runs it will display 4.

Comparing Enumerator Values

Enumerator values can be compared using the relational operators. For example, using the Day data type we have been discussing, the following expression is true.

```
FRIDAY > MONDAY
```

The expression is true because the enumerator FRIDAY is stored in memory as 4 and the enumerator MONDAY is stored as 0. The following code will display the message "Friday is greater than Monday."

```
if (FRIDAY > MONDAY)
    cout << "Friday is greater than Monday.\n";
```

You can also compare enumerator values with integer values. For example, the following code will display the message "Monday is equal to zero."

```
if (MONDAY == 0)
    cout << "Monday is equal to zero.\n";
```

Let's look at a complete program that uses much of what we have learned so far. Program 10-13 uses the Day data type that we have been discussing.

Program 10-13

```cpp
// This program demonstrates an enumerated data type.
#include <iostream>
#include <iomanip>
using namespace std;

enum Day { MONDAY, TUESDAY, WEDNESDAY, THURSDAY, FRIDAY };

int main()
{
    const int NUM_DAYS = 5;    // The number of days
    double sales[NUM_DAYS];     // To hold sales for each day
    double total = 0.0;         // Accumulator
    int index;                  // Loop counter

    // Get the sales for each day.
    for (index = MONDAY; index <= FRIDAY; index++)
    {
        cout << "Enter the sales for day "
             << index << ": ";
        cin >> sales[index];
    }
```

(program continues)

Program 10-13

```
    // Calcualte the total sales.
    for (index = MONDAY; index <= FRIDAY; index++)
        total += sales[index];

    // Display the total.
    cout << "The total sales are $" << setprecision(2)
         << fixed << total << endl;

    return 0;
}
```

Program Output with Example Input Shown in Bold
```
Enter the sales for day 0: 1525.00 [Enter]
Enter the sales for day 1: 1896.50 [Enter]
Enter the sales for day 2: 1975.63 [Enter]
Enter the sales for day 3: 1678.33 [Enter]
Enter the sales for day 4: 1498.52 [Enter]
The total sales are $8573.98
```

Anonymous Enumerated Types

Notice that Program 10-13 does not define a variable of the Day data type. Instead it uses the Day data type's enumerators in the for loops. The counter variable index is initialized to MONDAY (which is 0), and the loop iterates as long as index is less than or equal to FRIDAY (which is 4). When you do not need to define variables of an enumerated type, you can actually make the type anonymous. An *anonymous enumerated type* is simply one that does not have a name. For example, in Program 10-13 we could have declared the enumerated type as:

```
    enum { MONDAY, TUESDAY, WEDNESDAY, THURSDAY, FRIDAY };
```

This declaration still creates the enumerators. We just can't use the data type to define variables because the type does not have a name.

Using Math Operators to Change the Value of an enum Variable

Even though enumerators are really integers, and enum variables really hold integer values, you can run into problems when trying to perform math operations with them. For example, look at the following code.

```
    Day day1, day2;    // Defines two Day variables.
    day1 = TUESDAY;    // Assign TUESDAY to day1.
    day2 = day1 + 1;   // ERROR! This will not work!
```

The third statement causes a problem because the expression day1 + 1 results in the integer value 2. The assignment operator then attempts to assign the integer value 2 to the enum variable day2. Because C++ cannot implicitly convert an int to a Day, an error occurs. You can fix this by using a cast to explicitly convert the result to Day, as shown here:

```
day2 = static_cast<Day>(day1 + 1);   // This works.
```

Using an enum Variable to Step through an Array's Elements

Because enumerators are stored in memory as integers, you can use them as array subscripts. For example, look at the following code.

```
enum Day { MONDAY, TUESDAY, WEDNESDAY, THURSDAY, FRIDAY };
const int NUM_DAYS = 5;
double sales[NUM_DAYS];
sales[MONDAY] = 1525.0;       // Stores 1525.0 in sales[0].
sales[TUESDAY] = 1896.5;      // Stores 1896.5 in sales[1].
sales[WEDNESDAY] = 1975.63;   // Stores 1975.63 in sales[2].
sales[THURSDAY] = 1678.33;    // Stores 1678.33 in sales[3].
sales[FRIDAY] = 1498.52;      // Stores 1498.52 in sales[4].
```

This code stores values in all five elements of the sales array. Because enumerator values can be used as array subscripts, you can use an enum variable in a loop to step through the elements of an array. However, using an enum variable for this purpose is not as straight forward as using an int variable. This is because you cannot use the ++ or -- operators directly on an enum variable. To understand what I mean, first look at the following code taken from Program 10-13:

```
for (index = MONDAY; index <= FRIDAY; index++)
{
   cout << "Enter the sales for day "
        << index << ": ";
   cin >> sales[index];
}
```

In this code, index is an int variable used to step through each element of the array. It is reasonable to expect that we could use a Day variable instead, as shown in the following code.

```
Day workDay;   // Define a Day variable

// ERROR!!! This code will NOT work.
for (workDay = MONDAY; workDay <= FRIDAY; workDay++)
{
   cout << "Enter the sales for day "
        << workDay << ": ";
   cin >> sales[workDay];
}
```

Notice that the for loop's update expression uses the ++ operator to increment workDay. Although this works fine with an int variable, the ++ operator cannot be used with an enum variable. Instead, you must convert workDay++ to an equivalent expression that will work. The expression workDay++ attempts to do the same thing as:

```
workDay = workDay + 1;   // Good idea, but still won't work.
```

However, this still will not work. We have to use a cast to explicitly convert the expression workDay + 1 to the Day data type, like this:

```
workDay = static_cast<Day>(workDay + 1);
```

This is the expression that we must use in the for loop instead of workDay++. The corrected for loop looks like this:

```
for (workDay = MONDAY; workDay <= FRIDAY;
                workDay = static_cast<Day>(workDay + 1))
{
   cout << "Enter the sales for day "
        << workDay << ": ";
   cin >> sales[workDay];
}
```

Program 10-14 is a version of Program 10-13 that is modified to use a Day variable to step through the elements of the sales array.

Program 10-14

```
// This program demonstrates an enumerated data type.
#include <iostream>
#include <iomanip>
using namespace std;

enum Day { MONDAY, TUESDAY, WEDNESDAY, THURSDAY, FRIDAY };

int main()
{
   const int NUM_DAYS = 5;     // The number of days
   double sales[NUM_DAYS];      // To hold sales for each day
   double total = 0.0;          // Accumulator
   Day workDay;                 // Loop counter

   // Get the sales for each day.
   for (workDay = MONDAY; workDay <= FRIDAY;
                        workDay = static_cast<Day>(workDay + 1))
   {
      cout << "Enter the sales for day "
           << workDay << ": ";
      cin >> sales[workDay];
   }
```

(program continues)

Program 10-14

```
// Calcualte the total sales.
for (workDay = MONDAY; workDay <= FRIDAY;
                       workDay = static_cast<Day>(workDay + 1))
    total += sales[workDay];
// Display the total.
cout << "The total sales are $" << setprecision(2)
     << fixed << total << endl;

return 0;
}
```

Program Output with Example Input Shown in Bold

```
Enter the sales for day 0: 1525.00 [Enter]
Enter the sales for day 1: 1896.50 [Enter]
Enter the sales for day 2: 1975.63 [Enter]
Enter the sales for day 3: 1678.33 [Enter]
Enter the sales for day 4: 1498.52 [Enter]
The total sales are $8573.98
```

Using Enumerators to Output Values

As you have already seen, sending an enumerator to cout causes the enumerator's integer value to be displayed. For example, assuming we are using the Day type previously described, the following statement displays 0.

```
cout << MONDAY << endl;
```

If you wish to use the enumerator to display a string such as "Monday," you'll have to write code that produces the desired string. For example, in the following code assume that workDay is a Day variable that has been initialized to some value. The switch statement displays the name of a day, based upon the value of the variable.

```
switch(workDay)
{
    case MONDAY    : cout << "Monday";
                     break;
    case TUESDAY   : cout << "Tuesday";
                     break;
    case WEDNESDAY : cout << "Wednesday";
                     break;
    case THURSDAY  : cout << "Thursday";
                     break;
    case FRIDAY    : cout << "Friday";
}
```

Program 10-15 shows this type of code used in a function. Instead of asking the user to enter the sales for day 0, day 1, and so forth, it displays the names of the days.

Program 10-15

```cpp
// This program demonstrates an enumerated data type.
#include <iostream>
#include <iomanip>
using namespace std;

enum Day { MONDAY, TUESDAY, WEDNESDAY, THURSDAY, FRIDAY };

// Function prototype
void displayDayName(Day);

int main()
{
    const int NUM_DAYS = 5;     // The number of days
    double sales[NUM_DAYS];     // To hold sales for each day
    double total = 0.0;         // Accumulator
    Day workDay;                // Loop counter

    // Get the sales for each day.
    for (workDay = MONDAY; workDay <= FRIDAY;
                      workDay = static_cast<Day>(workDay + 1))
    {
        cout << "Enter the sales for day ";
        displayDayName(workDay);
        cout << ": ";
        cin >> sales[workDay];
    }

    // Calcualte the total sales.
    for (workDay = MONDAY; workDay <= FRIDAY;
                      workDay = static_cast<Day>(workDay + 1))
        total += sales[workDay];

    // Display the total.
    cout << "The total sales are $" << setprecision(2)
         << fixed << total << endl;

    return 0;
}

//*************************************************************
// Definition of the displayDayName function                 *
// This function accepts an argumet of the Day type and      *
// displays the corresponding name of the day.               *
//*************************************************************

void displayDayName(Day d)
{
    switch(d)
    {
        case MONDAY    : cout << "Monday";
                         break;
```

(program continues)

Program 10-15

```
        case TUESDAY   : cout << "Tuesday";
                         break;
        case WEDNESDAY : cout << "Wednesday";
                         break;
        case THURSDAY  : cout << "Thursday";
                         break;
        case FRIDAY    : cout << "Friday";
    }
}
```

Program Output with Example Input Shown in Bold
```
Enter the sales for Monday: 1525.00 [Enter]
Enter the sales for Tuesday: 1896.50 [Enter]
Enter the sales for Wednesday: 1975.63 [Enter]
Enter the sales for Thursday: 1678.33 [Enter]
Enter the sales for Friday: 1498.52 [Enter]
The total sales are $8573.98
```

Specifying Integer Values for Enumerators

By default, the enumerators in an enumerated data type are assigned the integer values 0, 1, 2, and so forth. If this is not appropriate, you can specify the values to be assigned, as in the following example.

```
        enum Water { FREEZING = 32, BOILING = 212 };
```

Program 10-16

```
// This program demonstrates an enumerated data type.
#include <iostream>
#include <iomanip>
using namespace std;

int main()
{
    enum Water { FREEZING = 32, BOILING = 212 };
    int waterTemp; // To hold the water temperature

    cout << "Enter the current water temperature: ";
    cin >> waterTemp;
    if (waterTemp <= FREEZING)
        cout << "The water is frozen.\n";
    else if (waterTemp >= BOILING)
        cout << "The water is boiling.\n";
    else
        cout << "The water is not frozen or boiling.\n";

    return 0;
}
```

Program 10-16

Program Output with Example Input Shown in Bold
```
Enter the current water temperature: 10 [Enter]
The water is frozen.
```

Program Output with Example Input Shown in Bold
```
Enter the current water temperature: 300 [Enter]
The water is boiling.
```

Program Output with Example Input Shown in Bold
```
Enter the current water temperature: 92 [Enter]
The water is not frozen or boiling.
```

If you leave out the value assignment for one or more of the enumerators, it will be assigned a default value. Here is an example:

```
enum Colors { RED, ORANGE, YELLOW = 9, GREEN, BLUE };
```

In this example the enumerator RED will be assigned the value 0, ORANGE will be assigned the value 1, YELLOW will be assigned the value 9, GREEN will be assigned the value 10, and BLUE will be assigned the value 11.

Enumerators Must Be Unique Within the Same Scope

Enumerators are identifiers just like variable names, named constants, and function names. As with all identifiers, they must be unique within the same scope. For example, an error will result if both of the following enumerated types are declared within the same scope. The reason is that ROOSEVELT is declared twice.

```
enum Presidents { MCKINLEY, ROOSEVELT, TAFT };
enum VicePresidents { ROOSEVELT, FAIRBANKS, SHERMAN };   // Error!
```

The following declarations will also cause an error if they appear within the same scope.

```
enum Status { OFF, ON };
const int OFF = 0;        // Error!
```

Declaring the Type and Defining the Variables in One Statement

The follow code uses two lines to declare an enumerated data type and define a variable of the type.

```
enum Car { PORSCHE, FERRARI, JAGUAR };
Car sportsCar;
```

C++ allows you to declare an enumerated data type and define one or more variables of the type in the same statement. The previous code could be combined into the following statement:

```
enum Car { PORSCHE, FERRARI, JAGUAR } sportsCar;
```

The following statement declares the Car data type and defines two variables: myCar and yourCar.

```
enum Car { PORSCHE, FERRARI, JAGUAR } myCar, yourCar;
```

Checkpoint

10.20 Look at the following declaration.

```
enum Flower { ROSE, DAISY, PETUNIA };
```

In memory, what value will be stored for the enumerator ROSE? For DAISY? For PETUNIA?

10.21 What will the following code display?

```
enum { HOBBIT, ELF = 7, DRAGON };
cout << HOBBIT << " " << ELF << " " << DRAGON << endl;
```

10.22 Does the enumerated data type declared in Checkpoint question 10.20 have a name, or is it anonymous?

10.23 What will the following code display?

```
enum Letters { Z, Y, X };
if (Z > X)
    cout << "Z is greater than X.\n";
else
    cout << "Z is not greater than X.\n";
```

10.24 Will the following code cause an error, or will it compile without any errors? If it causes an error, rewrite it so that it compiles.

```
enum Color { RED, GREEN, BLUE };
Color c;
c = 0;
```

10.25 Will the following code cause an error, or will it compile without any errors? If it causes an error, rewrite it so that it compiles.

```
enum Color { RED, GREEN, BLUE };
Color c = RED;
    c++;
```

10

Review Questions and Exercises

Short Answer

1. What is a primitive data type?

2. Does a structure declaration cause a structure variable to be created?

3. Both arrays and structures are capable of storing multiple values. What is the difference between an array and a structure?

4. Look at the following structure declaration.

```
struct Point
{
    int x;
    int y;
};
```

Write statements that

A) Define a `Point` structure variable named `center`
B) Assign 12 to the `x` member of `center`
C) Assign 7 to the `y` member of `center`
D) Display the contents of the `x` and `y` members of `center`

5. Look at the following structure declaration.

```
struct FullName
{
    char lastName[26];
    char middleName[26];
    char firstName[26];
};
```

Write statements that

A) Define a `FullName` structure variable named `info`
B) Assign your last, middle, and first name to the members of the `info` variable
C) Display the contents of the members of the `info` variable

6. Look at the following code.

```
struct PartData
{
    char partName[51];
    int idNumber;
};

PartData inventory[100];
```

Write a statement that displays the contents of the `partName` member of element 49 of the `inventory` array.

7. Look at the following code.

```
struct Town
{
    char townName[51];
    char countyName[51];
    double population;
    double elevation;
};

Town t = { "Canton", "Haywood", 9478 };
```

A) What value is stored in t.townName?
B) What value is stored in t.countyName?
C) What value is stored in t.population?
D) What value is stored in t.elevation?

8. Look at the following code.

```
structure Rectangle
{
    int length;
    int width;
};

Rectangle *r;
```

Write statements that

A) Dynamically allocate a Rectangle structure variable and use r to point to it.
B) Assign 10 to the structure's length member and 14 to the structure's width member.

9. What is the difference between a union and a structure?

10. Look at the following code.

```
union Values
{
    int ivalue;
    double dvalue;
};

Values v;
```

Assuming that an int uses 4 bytes and a double uses 8 bytes, how much memory does the variable v use?

11. What will the following code display?

```
enum { POODLE, BOXER, TERRIER };
cout << POODLE << " " << BOXER << " " << TERRIER << endl;
```

12. Look at the following declaration.

```
enum Person { BILL, JOHN, CLAIRE, BOB};
Person p;
```

Indicate whether each of the following statements or expressions is valid or invalid.

A) p = BOB;
B) p++;
C) BILL > BOB
D) p = 0;
E) int x = BILL;
F) p = static_cast<Person>(3);
G) cout << CLAIRE << endl;

Algorithm Workbench

13. The structure Car is declared as follows:

```
struct Car
{
    char carMake[20];
    char carModel[20];
    int yearModel;
    double cost;
};
```

Write a definition statement that defines a Car structure variable initialized with the following data:

> Make: Ford
> Model: Mustang
> Year Model: 1997
> Cost: $20,000

14. Define an array of 25 of the Car structure variables (the structure is declared in question 13).

15. Define an array of 35 of the Car structure variables. Initialize the first three elements with the following data:

Make	Model	Year	Cost
Ford	Taurus	1997	$21,000
Honda	Accord	1992	$11,000
Lamborghini	Countach	1997	$200,000

16. Write a loop that will step through the array you defined in question 15, displaying the contents of each element.

17. Declare a structure named `TempScale`, with the following members:

    ```
    fahrenheit: a double
    centigrade: a double
    ```

    Next, declare a structure named `Reading`, with the following members:

    ```
    windSpeed: an int
    humidity: a double
    temperature: a TempScale structure variable
    ```

    Next define a `Reading` structure variable.

18. Write statements that will store the following data in the variable you defined in question 17.

    Wind Speed: 37 mph
    Humidity: 32%
    Fahrenheit temperature: 32 degrees
    Centigrade temperature: 0 degrees

19. Write a function called `showReading`. It should accept a `Reading` structure variable (see question 17) as its argument. The function should display the contents of the variable on the screen.

20. Write a function called `findReading`. It should use a `Reading` structure reference variable (see question 17) as its parameter. The function should ask the user to enter values for each member of the structure.

21. Write a function called `getReading`, which returns a `Reading` structure (see question 15). The function should ask the user to enter values for each member of a `Reading` structure, then return the structure.

22. Write a function called `recordReading`. It should use a `Reading` structure pointer variable (see question 17) as its parameter. The function should ask the user to enter values for each member of the structure pointed to by the parameter.

23. Rewrite the following statement using the structure pointer operator:

    ```
    (*rptr).windSpeed = 50;
    ```

24. Rewrite the following statement using the structure pointer operator:

    ```
    *(*strPtr).num = 10;
    ```

25. Write the declaration of a union called `Items` with the following members:

    ```
    alpha       a character
    num         an integer
    bigNum      a long integer
    real        a float
    ```

    Next, write the definition of an `Items` union variable.

26. Write the declaration of an anonymous union with the same members as the union you declared in question 25.

27. Write a statement that stores the number 452 in the num member of the anonymous union you declared in question 26.

28. Look at the following statement.

```
enum Color { RED, ORANGE, GREEN, BLUE };
```

A) What is the name of the data type declared by this statement?
B) What are the enumerators for this type?
C) Write a statement that defines a variable of this type and initializes it with a valid value.

29. A pet store sells dogs, cats, birds, and hamsters. Write a declaration for an anonymous enumerated data type that can represent the types of pets the store sells.

True or False

30. T F A semicolon is required after the closing brace of a structure or union declaration.

31. T F A structure declaration does not define a variable.

32. T F The contents of a structure variable can be displayed by passing the structure variable to the cout object.

33. T F Structure variables may not be initialized.

34. T F In a structure variable's initialization list, you do not have to provide initializers for all the members.

35. T F You may skip members in a structure's initialization list.

36. T F The following expression refers to the element 5 in the array carInfo:

    carInfo.model[5]

37. T F An array of structures may be initialized.

38. T F A structure variable may not be a member of another structure.

39. T F A structure member variable may be passed to a function as an argument.

40. T F An entire structure may not be passed to a function as an argument.

41. T F A function may return a structure.

42. T F When a function returns a structure, it is always necessary for the function to have a local structure variable to hold the member values that are to be returned.

43. T F The indirection operator has higher precedence than the dot operator.

44. T F The structure pointer operator does not automatically dereference the structure pointer on its left.

45. T F In a union, all the members are stored in different memory locations.

46. T F All the members of a union may be used simultaneously.

47. T F You may define arrays of unions.

48. T F You may not define pointers to unions.

49. T F An anonymous union has no name.

50. T F If an anonymous union is defined globally (outside all functions), it must be declared static.

Find the Errors

Each of the following declarations, programs, and program segments has errors. Locate as many as you can.

51.
```cpp
struct Values
{
    char name[30];
    int age;
}
```

52.
```cpp
struct TwoVals
{
    int a, b;
};
int main ()
{
    TwoVals.a = 10;
    TwoVals.b = 20;
    return 0;
}
```

53.
```cpp
#include <iostream>
using namespace std;

struct names
{
    char first[20];
    char last[20];
};
int main ()
{
    names customer = "Smith", "Orley";
    cout << names.first << endl;
    cout << names.last << endl;
    return 0;
}
```

54.
```cpp
struct TwoVals
{
    int a = 5;
    int b = 10;
};

int main()
{
    TwoVals varray[10];

    varray.a[0] = 1;
    return 0;
}
```

55.
```cpp
struct TwoVals
{
    int a;
    int b;
};
TwoVals getVals()
{
    TwoVals.a = TwoVals.b = 0;
}
```

56.
```cpp
#include <iostream>
using namespace std;

union Compound
{
    int x;
    float y;
};

int main()
{
    Compound u;
    u.x = 1000;
    cout << u.y << endl;
    return 0;
}
```

Programming Challenges

1. Corporate Sales Data

Write a program that uses a structure to store the following data on a company division:

> Division name (such as East, West, North, or South)
> First-Quarter Sales
> Second-Quarter Sales
> Third-Quarter Sales
> Fourth-Quarter Sales
> Total Annual Sales
> Average Quarterly Sales

The program should use four variables of this structure. Each variable should represent one of the following corporate divisions: East, West, North, and South. The user should be asked for the four quarters' sales figures for each division. Each division's total and average sales should be calculated and stored in the appropriate member of each structure variable. These figures should then be displayed on the screen.

Input Validation: Do not accept negative numbers for any sales figures.

2. Weather Statistics

Write a program that uses a structure to store the following weather data for a particular month:

> Total rainfall
> High temperature
> Low temperature
> Average temperature

The program should have an array of 12 structures to hold weather data for an entire year. When the program runs, it should ask the user to enter data for each month. (The average temperature should be calculated.) Once the data is entered for all the months, the program should calculate and display the average monthly rainfall, the total rainfall for the year, the highest and lowest temperatures for the year (and the months they occurred in), and the average of all the monthly average temperatures.

Input Validation: Only accept temperatures within the range between −100 and +140 degrees Fahrenheit.

10

3. Soccer Scores

Write a program that stores the following data about a soccer player in a structure:

>Player's name
>Player's number
>Points scored by player

The program should keep an array of 12 of these structures. Each element is for a different player on a team. When the program runs it should ask the user to enter the data for each player. It should then show a table that lists each player's number, name, and points scored. The program should also calculate and display the total points earned by the team. The number and name of the player that has earned the most points should also be displayed.

>*Input Validation: Do not accept negative values for player's numbers or points scored.*

4. Customer Accounts

Write a program that uses a structure to store the following data about a customer account:

>Name
>Address
>City, State, and ZIP
>Telephone number
>Account balance
>Date of last payment

The program should use an array of at least 20 structures. It should let the user enter data into the array, change the contents of any element, and display all the data stored in the array. The program should have a menu-driven user interface.

>*Input Validation: When the data for a new account is entered, be sure the user enters data for all the fields. No negative account balances should be entered.*

5. Search Function for Customer Accounts Program

Add a function to Programming Challenge 4 that allows the user to search the structure array for a particular customer's account. It should accept part of the customer's name as an argument and then search for an account with a name that matches it. All accounts that match should be displayed. If no account matches, a message should be displayed.

6. Speakers' Bureau

Write a program that keeps track of a speakers' bureau. The program should use a structure to store the following data about a speaker:

>Name
>Telephone number
>Speaking topic
>Fee required

The program should use an array of at least 10 structures. It should let the user enter data into the array, change the contents of any element, and display all the data stored in the array. The program should have a menu-driven user interface.

Input Validation: When the data for a new speaker is entered, be sure the user enters data for all the fields. No negative amounts should be entered for a speaker's fee.

7. Search Function for the Speakers' Bureau Program

Add a function to Programming Challenge 6 that allows the user to search for a speaker on a particular topic. It should accept a key word as an argument and then search the array for a structure with that key word in the Speaking Topic field. All structures that match should be displayed. If no structure matches, a message should be displayed.

8. Course Grade

Write a program that uses a structure to store the following data:

Member Name	Description
Name	Student name
Idnum	Student ID number
Tests	Pointer to an array of test scores
Average	Average test score
Grade	Course grade

The program should keep a list of test scores for a group of students. It should ask the user how many tests scores there are to be and how many students there are. It should then dynamically allocate an array of structures. Each structure's `Tests` member should point to a dynamically allocated array which will hold the test scores.

After the arrays have been dynamically allocated, the program should ask for the ID number and all the test scores for each student. The average test score should be calculated and stored in the `average` member of each structure. The course grade should be computed, based on the following grading scale:

Average Test Grade	Course Grade
91–100	A
81–90	B
71–80	C
61–70	D
60 or below	F

The course grade should then be stored in the `Grade` member of each structure. Once all this data is calculated, a table should be displayed on the screen listing each student's name, ID number, average test score, and course grade.

Input Validation: Be sure all the data for each student is entered. Do not accept negative numbers for any test score.

9. Drink Machine Simulator

Write a program that simulates a soft drink machine. The program should use a structure that stores the following data:

Drink name
Drink cost
Number of drinks in machine

The program should create an array of five structures. The elements should be initialized with the following data:

Drink Name	Cost	Number in Machine
Cola	.75	20
Root Beer	.75	20
Lemon-Lime	.75	20
Grape Soda	.80	20
Cream Soda	.80	20

Each time the program runs, it should enter a loop that performs the following steps: A list of drinks is displayed on the screen. The user should be allowed to either quit the program or pick a drink. If the user selects a drink, he or she will next enter the amount of money that is to be inserted into the drink machine. The program should display the amount of change that would be returned and subtract one from the number of that drink left in the machine. If the user selects a drink that has sold out, a message should be displayed. The loop then repeats. When the user chooses to quit the program it should display the total amount of money the machine earned.

Input Validation: When the user enters an amount of money, do not accept negative values, or values greater than $1.00.

10. Inventory Bins

Write a program that simulates inventory bins in a warehouse. Each bin holds a number of the same type of parts. The program should use a structure that keeps the following data:

Description of the part kept in the bin
Number of parts in the bin

The program should have the following functions:

AddParts: a function that accepts as its argument the number of parts being added to a bin. The function increases the bin's part count by this number.

RemoveParts: a function that accepts as its argument the number of parts being removed from a bin. The function decreases the bin's part count by this number.

The program should have an array of 10 bins, initialized with the following data:

Part Description	Number of Parts in the Bin
Valve	10
Bearing	5
Bushing	15
Coupling	21
Flange	7
Gear	5
Gear Housing	5
Vacuum Gripper	25
Cable	18
Rod	12

When the program runs, repeat a loop that performs the following steps: The user should see a list of what each bin holds and how many parts are in each bin. The user can choose to either quit the program or select a bin. When a bin is selected, the user can either add parts to it or remove parts from it. The loop then repeats, showing the updated bin data on the screen.

Input Validation: No bin can hold more than 30 parts, so don't let the user add more than a bin can hold. Also, don't accept negative values for the number of parts being added or removed.

11. Multipurpose Payroll

Write a program that calculates pay for either an hourly paid worker or a salaried worker. Hourly paid workers are paid their hourly pay rate times the number of hours worked. Salaried workers are paid their regular salary plus any bonus they may have earned. The program should declare two structures for the following data:

Hourly Paid:
HoursWorked
HourlyRate

Salaried:
Salary
Bonus

The program should also declare a union with two members. Each member should be a structure variable: one for the hourly paid worker and another for the salaried worker.

The program should ask the user whether he or she is calculating the pay for an hourly paid worker or a salaried worker. Regardless of which the user selects, the appropriate members of the union will be used to store the data that will be used to calculate the pay.

Input Validation: Do not accept negative numbers. Do not accept values greater than 80 for .

11

Advanced File Operations

11.1 File Operations

CONCEPT A file is a collection of data which is usually stored on a computer's disk. Data can be saved to files and then later reused.

Almost all real-world programs use files to store and retrieve data. Here are a few examples of familiar software packages that use files extensively.

◆ **Word Processors:** Word processing programs are used to write letters, memos, reports, and other documents. The documents are then saved in files so they can be edited and reprinted.

◆ **Database Management Systems:** DBMSs are used to create and maintain databases. Databases are files that contain large collections of data, such as payroll records, inventories, sales statistics, and customer records.

◆ **Spreadsheets**: Spreadsheet programs are used to work with numerical data. Numbers and mathematical formulas can be inserted into the rows and columns of the spreadsheet. The spreadsheet can then be saved to a file for use later.

◆ **Compilers**: Compilers translate the source code of a program, which is saved in a file, into an executable file. Throughout the previous chapters of this book you have created many C++ source files and compiled them to executable files.

Chapter 3 introduced you to file operations using the `ifstream` and `ofstream` data types. You saw how to open a file for input with an `ifstream` object, and how to open a file for output with an `ofstream` object. That chapter also explained that the stream extraction operator (>>) may be used with an `ifstream` object to read data from a file, and that the stream insertion operator (<<) may be used with an `ofstream` object to write data to a file. Chapter 4 discussed how to test for errors when a file is opened, and Chapter 5 explained how to use an `ifstream` object's `eof` member function to detect whether the end of a file has been encountered. That chapter also demonstrated techniques for using loops with files.

Chapters 3, 4, and 5 provided enough information for you to write programs that perform simple file operations. This chapter covers more advanced file operations, and focuses primarily on the `fstream` data type. As a review, Table 11-1 compares the `ifstream`, `ofstream`, and `fstream` data types. All of these data types require the `fstream` header file.

Table 11-1   File Stream

Data Type	Description
`ifstream`	Input File Stream. This data type can be used only to read data from files into memory.
`ofstream`	Output File Stream. This data type can be used to create files and write data to them.
`fstream`	File Stream. This data type can be used to create files, write data to them, and read data from them.

Using the `fstream` Data Type

You define an `fstream` object just as you define objects of other data types. The following statement defines an `fstream` object named `dataFile`.

```
fstream dataFile;
```

As with `ifstream` and `ofstream` objects, you use an `fstream` object's `open` method to open a file. An `fstream` object's `open` method requires two arguments, however. The first argument is a string containing the name of the file. The second argument is a file access flag that indicates the mode in which you wish to open the file. Here is an example.

```
dataFile.open("info.txt", ios::out);
```

The first argument in this function call is the name of the file, `info.txt`. The second argument is the file access flag `ios::out`. This tells C++ to open the file in output mode. Output mode allows data to be written to a file. The following statement uses the ios::in access flag to open a file in input mode, which allows data to be read from the file.

```
dataFile.open("info.txt", ios::in);
```

There are many file access flags, as listed in Table 11-2.

Table 11-2

File Access Flag	Meaning
ios::app	Append mode. If the file already exists, its contents are preserved and all output is written to the end of the file. By default, this flag causes the file to be created if it does not exist.
ios::ate	If the file already exists, the program goes directly to the end of it. Output may be written anywhere in the file.
ios::binary	Binary mode. When a file is opened in binary mode, data is written to or read from it in pure binary format. (The default mode is text.)
ios::in	Input mode. Data will be read from the file. If the file does not exist, it will not be created and the open function will fail.
ios::out	Output mode. Data will be written to the file. By default, the file's contents will be deleted if it already exists.
ios::trunc	If the file already exists, its contents will be deleted (truncated). This is the default mode used by ios::out.

Several flags may be used together if they are connected with the | operator. For example, assume dataFile is an fstream object in the following statement:

```
dataFile.open("info.txt", ios::in | ios::out);
```

This statement opens the file info.txt in both input and output modes. This means data may be written to and read from the file.

 Note: When used by itself, the ios::out flag causes the file's contents to be deleted if the file already exists. When used with the ios::in flag, however, the file's existing contents are preserved. If the file does not already exist, it will be created.

The following statement opens the file in such a way that data will only be written to its end:

```
dataFile.open("info.txt", ios::out | ios::app);
```

By using different combinations of access flags, there are many possible modes in which files may be opened.

Program 11-1 uses an `fstream` object to open a file for output, and then writes data to the file.

Program 11-1

```cpp
// This program uses an fstream object to write data to a file.
#include <iostream>
#include <fstream>
using namespace std;

int main()
{
    fstream dataFile;

    cout << "Opening file...\n";
    dataFile.open("demofile.txt", ios::out);   // Open for output.
    cout << "Now writing data to the file.\n";
    dataFile << "Jones\n";                      // Write line 1.
    dataFile << "Smith\n";                      // Write line 2.
    dataFile << "Willis\n";                     // Write line 3.
    dataFile << "Davis\n";                      // Write line 4.
    dataFile.close();                           // Close the file.
    cout << "Done.\n";
    return 0;
}
```

Program Screen Output
```
Opening file...
Now writing data to the file.
Done.
```

Output to File demofile.txt
```
Jones
Smith
Willis
Davis
```

The file output is shown for Program 11-1 the way it would appear if the file contents were displayed on the screen. The \n characters cause each name to appear on a separate line. The actual file contents, however, appear as a stream of characters as shown in Figure 11-1.

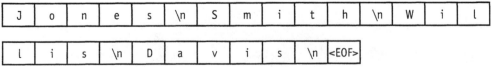

Figure 11-1

As you can see from the figure, \n characters are written to the file along with all the other characters. The characters are added to the file sequentially, in the order they are written by the program. The very last character is an *end-of-file marker*. It is a character that marks the end of the file and is automatically written when the file is closed. (The actual character used to mark the end of a file depends upon the operating system being used. It is always a non-printing character. For example, some systems use control-Z.)

Program 11-2 is a modification of Program 11-1 that further illustrates the sequential nature of files. The file is opened, two names are written to it, and it is closed. The file is then reopened by the program in append mode (with the `ios::app` access flag). When a file is opened in append mode, its contents are preserved and all subsequent output is appended to the file's end. Two more names are added to the file before it is closed and the program terminates.

Program 11-2

```cpp
// This program writes data to a file, closes the file,
// then reopens the file and appends more data.
#include <iostream>
#include <fstream>
using namespace std;

int main()
{
    ofstream dataFile;

    cout << "Opening file...\n";
    dataFile.open("demofile.txt", ios::out);     // Open for output.
    cout << "Now writing data to the file.\n";
    dataFile << "Jones\n";                        // Write line 1.
    dataFile << "Smith\n";                        // Write line 2.
    cout << "Now closing the file.\n";
    dataFile.close();                             // Close the file.

    cout << "Opening the file again...\n";
    dataFile.open("demofile.txt", ios::app);     // Open in append mode.
    cout << "Writing more data to the file.\n";
    dataFile << "Willis\n";                       // Write line 3.
    dataFile << "Davis\n";                        // Write line 4.
    dataFile.close();                             // Close the file.
    cout << "Done.\n";
    return 0;
}
```

Output to File demofile.txt
```
Jones
Smith
Willis
Davis
```

The first time the file is opened, the names are written as shown in Figure 11-2.

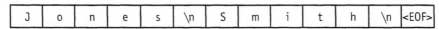

Figure 11-2

The file is closed and an end-of-file character is automatically written. When the file is reopened, the new output is appended to the end of the file, as shown in Figure 11-3.

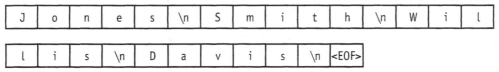

Figure 11-3

 Note: If the `ios::out` flag had been used instead of `ios::app` the second time the file was opened, the file's contents would have been deleted. If this had been the case, the names Jones and Smith would have been erased and the file would only have contained the names Willis and Davis.

File Open Modes with `ifstream` and `ofstream` Objects

The `ifstream` and `ofstream` data types each have a default mode in which they open files. This mode determines the operations that may be performed on the file, and what happens if the file that is being opened already exists. Table 11-3 describes each data type's default open mode.

Table 11-3

File Type	Default Open Mode
`ofstream`	The file is opened for output only. Data may be written to the file, but not read from the file. If the file does not exist, it is created. If the file already exists, its contents are deleted (the file is truncated).
`ifstream`	The file is opened for input only. Data may be read from the file, but not written to it. The file's contents will be read from its beginning. If the file does not exist, the open function fails.

You cannot change the fact that `ifstream` files may only be read from, and `ofstream` files may only be written to. You can, however, vary the way operations are carried out on these files by providing a file access flag as an optional second argument to the open function. The following code shows an example using an `ofstream` object.

```
ofstream outputFile;
outputFile.open("values.txt", ios::app);
```

The `ios::app` flag specifies that data written to the values.txt file should be appended to its existing contents.

Checking for a File's Existence Before Opening It

Sometimes you want to determine whether a file already exists before opening it for output. You can do this by first attempting to open the file for input. If the file does not exist, the open operation will fail. In that case, you can create the file by opening it for output. The following code gives an example.

```
fstream dataFile;
dataFile.open("values.txt", ios::in);
if (dataFile.fail())
{
        // The file does not exist, so create it.
        dataFile.open("values.txt", ios::out);
        //
        // Continue to process the file...
        //
}
else    // The file already exists.
{
        dataFile.close();
        cout << "The file values.txt already exists.\n";
}
```

Opening a File with the File Stream Object Definition Statement

An alternative to using the open member function is to use the file stream object definition statement to open the file. Here is an example:

```
fstream dataFile("names.txt", ios::in | ios::out);
```

This statement defines an `fstream` object named `dataFile` and uses it to open the file names.txt. The file is opened in both input and output modes. This technique eliminates the need to call the open function when your program knows the name and access mode of the file at the time the object is defined. You may also use this technique with `ifstream` and `ofstream` objects, as shown in the following examples.

```
ifstream inputFile("info.txt");
ofstream outputFile("addresses.txt");
ofstream dataFile("customers.txt", ios::app);
```

You may also test for errors after you have opened a file with this technique. The following code shows an example.

```
ifstream inputFile("SalesData.txt");
if (!inputFile)
    cout << "Error opening SalesData.txt.\n";
```

More About File Names

Each operating system has its own rules for naming files. Some systems allow long file names such as:

```
SalesInfoFrom1997
CorpSalesReport
VehicleRegistrations
```

Other systems only allow shorter file names. The older MS-DOS operating system, for example, allows file names of no more than eight characters with an optional three character extension.

Extensions are commonly used with file names. The name and extension are separated by a period, known as a "dot." While the file name identifies the file's purpose, the extension usually identifies the type of data contained in the file. For example, the .txt extension identifies a text file that may be opened with a text editor such as Notepad. The .cpp extension identifies a C++ program. The file name payroll.cpp would identify a payroll program written in C++. Table 11-4 lists other example file names and what type of data they contain.

Table 11-4

File Name and Extension	File Contents
myprog.bas	BASIC program
menu.bat	DOS batch file
install.doc	Microsoft Word document
crunch.exe	Executable file
bob.html	HTML (Hypertext Markup Language) file
3dmodel.java	Java program or applet
vacation.jpg	JPEG image file
invent.obj	Object file
instructions.pdf	Adobe Portable Document Format file
prog1.prj	Borland C++ project file
ansi.sys	System device driver
readme.txt	Text file

Checkpoint [11.1]

11.1   Which file access flag would you use if you want all output to be written to the end of an existing file?

11.2   How do you use more than one file access flag?

11.3   Assuming that `diskInfo` is an `fstream` object, write a statement that opens the file `names.dat` for output.

11.4   Assuming that `diskInfo` is an `fstream` object, write a statement that opens the file `customers.txt` for output, where all output will be written to end of the file.

11.5   Assuming that `diskInfo` is an `fstream` object, write a statement that opens the file `payable.txt` for both input and output.

11.6   Write a statement that defines an `fstream` object named `dataFile` and opens a file named `salesfigures.txt` for input. (Note: The file should be opened with the definition statement, not an `open` function call.)

11.2   File Output Formatting

CONCEPT File output may be formatted in the same way that screen output is formatted.

The same output formatting techniques that are used with `cout`, which are covered in Chapter 3, may also be used with file stream objects. For example, the `setprecision` and `fixed` manipulators may be called to establish the number of digits of precision that floating point values are rounded to. Program 11-3 demonstrates this.

Program 11-3

```
// This program uses the setprecision and fixed
// manipulators to format file output.
#include <iostream>
#include <iomanip>
#include <fstream>
using namespace std;

int main()
{
    fstream dataFile;
    double num = 17.816392;
```

(program continues)

Program 11-3 *(continued)*

```
    dataFile.open("numfile.txt", ios::out); // Open in output mode.

    dataFile << fixed;                       // Format for fixed-point notation.
    dataFile << num << endl;                 // Write the number.

    dataFile << setprecision(4);             // Format for four decimal places.
    dataFile << num << endl;                 // Write the number.

    dataFile << setprecision(3);             // Format for three decimal places.
    dataFile << num << endl;                 // Write the number.

    dataFile << setprecision(2);             // Format for two decimal places.
    dataFile << num << endl;                 // Write the number

    dataFile << setprecision(1);             // Format for one decimal place.
    dataFile << num << endl;                 // Write the number

    cout << "Done.\n";
    dataFile.close();                        // Close the file.
    return 0;
}
```

Contents of File `numfile.txt`
```
17.816392
17.8164
17.816
17.82
17.8
```

Notice the file output is formatted just as cout would format screen output. Program 11-4 shows the setw stream manipulator being used to format file output into columns.

Program 11-4

```
// This program writes three rows of numbers to a file.
#include <iostream>
#include <fstream>
#include <iomanip>
using namespace std;
```

(program continues)

Program 11-4   *(continued)*

```cpp
int main()
{
    const int ROWS = 3; COLS = 3;

    fstream outFile("table.txt", ios::out);
    int nums[ROWS][COLS] = { 2897, 5, 837,
                             34, 7, 1623,
                             390, 3456, 12 };

    // Write the three rows of numbers with each
    // number in a field of eight character spaces.
    for (int row = 0; row < ROWS; row++)
    {
        for (int col = 0; col < COLS; col++)
        {
            outFile << setw(8) << nums[row][col];
        }
        outFile << endl;
    }
    outFile.close();
    cout << "Done.\n";
    return 0;
}
```

Contents of File `table.txt`
```
    2897       5     837
      34       7    1623
     390    3456      12
```

Figure 11-4 shows the way the characters appear in the file.

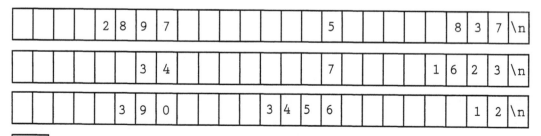

Figure 11-4

11.3 Passing File Stream Objects to Functions

CONCEPT File stream objects may be passed by reference to functions.

When writing actual programs, you'll want to create modularized code for handling file operations. File stream objects may be passed to functions, but they should always be passed by reference. The openFile function shown below uses an fstream reference object parameter:

```cpp
bool openFileIn(fstream &file, char *name)
{
    bool status;

    file.open(name, ios::in);
    if (file.fail())
        status = false;
    else
        status = true;
    return status;
}
```

The internal state of file stream objects changes with most every operation. They should always be passed to functions by reference to ensure internal consistency. Program 11-5 shows an example of how file stream objects may be passed as arguments to functions.

Program 11-5

```cpp
// This program demonstrates how file stream objects may
// be passed by reference to functions.
#include <iostream>
#include <fstream>
using namespace std;

// Function prototypes
bool openFileIn(fstream &, char [51]);
void showContents(fstream &);

int main()
{
    fstream dataFile;

    if (!openFileIn(dataFile,"demofile.txt"))
    {
        cout << "File open error!" << endl;
        return 0;        // Exit the program on error.
    }
```

(program continues)

Program 11-5 *(continued)*

```cpp
    cout << "File opened successfully.\n";
    cout << "Now reading data from the file.\n\n";
    showContents(dataFile);
    dataFile.close();
    cout << "\nDone.\n";
    return 0;
}

//*************************************************************
// Definition of function openFileIn. Accepts a reference    *
// to an fstream object as its argument. The file is opened  *
// for input. The function returns true upon success, false  *
// upon failure.                                             *
//*************************************************************

bool openFileIn(fstream &file, char *name)
{
    bool status;

    file.open(name, ios::in);
    if (file.fail())
        status = false;
    else
        status = true;
    return status;
}

//*************************************************************
// Definition of function showContents. Accepts an fstream   *
// reference as its argument. Uses a loop to read each name  *
// from the file and displays it on the screen.              *
//*************************************************************

void showContents(fstream &file)

{
    char name[81];

    file >> name;
    while (!file.eof())
    {
        cout << name << endl;
        file >> name;
    }
}
```

Program 11-5   *(continued)*

Program Screen Output

```
File opened successfully.
Now reading data from the file.

Jones
Smith
Willis
Davis

Done.
```

11.4   More Detailed Error Testing

CONCEPT | All stream objects have error state bits that indicate the condition of the stream.

All stream objects contain a set of bits that act as flags. These flags indicate the current state of the stream. Table 11-5 lists these bits.

Table 11-5

Bit	Description
ios::eofbit	Set when the end of an input stream is encountered.
ios::failbit	Set when an attempted operation has failed.
ios::hardfail	Set when an unrecoverable error has occurred.
ios::badbit	Set when an invalid operation has been attempted.
ios::goodbit	Set when all the flags above are not set. Indicates the stream is in good condition.

These bits can be tested by the member functions listed in Table 11-6. (You've already learned about the eof() and fail() functions.) One of the functions listed in the table, clear(), can be used to set a status bit.

Table 11-6

Function	Description
eof()	Returns true (nonzero) if the eofbit flag is set, otherwise returns false.
fail()	Returns true (nonzero) if the failbit or hardfail flags are set, otherwise returns false.
bad()	Returns true (nonzero) if the badbit flag is set, otherwise returns false.
good()	Returns true (nonzero) if the goodbit flag is set, otherwise returns false.
clear()	When called with no arguments, clears all the flags listed above. Can also be called with a specific flag as an argument.

The function showState, shown here, accepts a file stream reference as its argument. It shows the state of the file by displaying the return values of the eof(), fail(), bad(), and good() member functions:

```cpp
void showState(fstream &file)
{
    cout << "File Status:\n";
    cout << "   eof bit: " << file.eof() << endl;
    cout << "  fail bit: " << file.fail() << endl;
    cout << "   bad bit: " << file.bad() << endl;
    cout << "  good bit: " << file.good() << endl;
    file.clear(); // Clear any bad bits
}
```

Program 11-6 uses the showState function to display testFile's status after various operations. First, the file is created and the integer value 10 is stored in it. The file is then closed and reopened for input. The integer is read from the file, and then a second read operation is performed. Because there is only one item in the file, the second read operation will result in an error.

Program 11-6

```cpp
// This program demonstrates the return value of the stream
// object error testing member functions.
#include <iostream>
#include <fstream>
using namespace std;

// Function prototype
void showState(fstream &);

int main()
{
    int num = 10;

    fstream testFile("stuff.dat", ios::out);
    if (testFile.fail())
    {
        cout << "ERROR: Cannot open the file.\n";
        return 0;
    }

    cout << "Writing the value " << num << " to the file.\n";
    testFile << num;                    // Write the integer to testFile.
    showState(testFile);
    testFile.close();                   // Close the file
```

(program continues)

Program 11-6 *(continued)*

```
    testFile.open("stuff.dat", ios::in);    // Open for input.
    if (testFile.fail())
    {
        cout << "ERROR: Cannot open the file.\n";
        return 0;
    }

    cout << "Reading from the file.\n";
    testFile >> num;                         // Read the only number in the file.
    cout << "The value " << num << " was read.\n";
    showState(testFile);
    cout << "Forcing a bad read operation.\n";
    testFile >> num;                         // Force an invalid read operation.
    showState(testFile);
    testFile.close();                        // Close the file.
    return 0;
}
//******************************************************************
// Definition of function showState. This function uses            *
// an fstream reference as its parameter. The return values of      *
// the eof(), fail(), bad(), and good() member functions are        *
// displayed. The clear() function is called before the function    *
// returns.                                                         *
//******************************************************************

void showState(fstream &file)
{
    cout << "File Status:\n";
    cout << "  eof bit: " << file.eof() << endl;
    cout << "  fail bit: " << file.fail() << endl;
    cout << "  bad bit: " << file.bad() << endl;
    cout << "  good bit: " << file.good() << endl;
    file.clear();// Clear any bad bits
    return 0;
}
```

Program Output

```
Writing the value 10 to the file.
File Status:
  eof bit: 0
  fail bit: 0
  bad bit: 0
  good bit: 1
Reading from the file.
The value 10 was read.
```

(output continues)

Program 11-6 *(continued)*

```
File Status:
  eof bit: 1
  fail bit: 0
  bad bit: 0
  good bit: 1
Forcing a bad read operation.
File Status:
  eof bit: 1
  fail bit: 1
  bad bit: 0
  good bit: 0
```

11.5 Member Functions for Reading and Writing Files

CONCEPT File stream objects have member functions for more specialized file reading and writing.

If whitespace characters are part of the data in a file, a problem arises when the file is read by the >> operator. Because the operator considers whitespace characters as delimiters, it does not read them. For example, consider the file `murphy.txt`, which contains the following data:

Jayne Murphy
47 Jones Circle
Almond, NC 28702

Figure 11-5 shows the way the data is recorded in the file.

J	a	y	n	e		M	u	r	p	h	y	\n	4	7
	J	o	n	e	s		C	i	r	c	l	e	\n	A
l	m	o	n	d	,		N	C			2	8	7	0
2	\n	<EOF>												

Figure 11-5

The problem that arises from the use of the >> operator is evident in the output of Program 11-7.

Program 11-7

```cpp
// This program demonstrates how the >> operator should not
// be used to read data that contains whitespace characters
// from a file.
#include <iostream>
#include <fstream>
using namespace std;

int main()
{
    const int SIZE = 81;

    fstream nameFile;
    char input[SIZE];

    nameFile.open("murphy.txt", ios::in);
    if (!nameFile)
    {
        cout << "ERROR: Cannot open file.\n";
        return 0;
    }

    // Get input from file.
    nameFile >> input;
    while (!nameFile.eof())
    {
        cout << input;
        nameFile >> input;
    }

    nameFile.close();
    return 0;
}
```

Program Screen Output
```
JayneMurphy47JonesCircleAlmond,NC28702
```

The `getline` Member Function

The problem with Program 11-7 can be solved by using the file stream object's `getline` member function. The function reads a "line" of data, including whitespace characters. Here is an example of the function call:

```
dataFile.getline(str, 81, '\n');
```

The three arguments in this statement are explained as follows

str   This is the name of a character array, or a pointer to a section of memory.
                    The data read from the file will be stored here.

81   This number is one greater than the maximum number of characters to be read. In this example, a maximum of 80 characters will be read.

'\n'   This is a delimiter character of your choice. If this delimiter is encountered, it will cause the function to stop reading before it has read the maximum number of characters. (This argument is optional. If it's left out, '\n' is the default.)

The statement is an instruction to read a line of characters from the file. The function will read until it has read 80 characters or encounters a \n, whichever happens first. The line of characters will be stored in the str array.

Modifying Program 11-7 to use the getline member function changes the way the input file is processed. The getline member function reads whole lines of data from the file.

```cpp
// Get input from file.
nameFile.getline(input, 81);        // Use \n as a delimiter.
while (!nameFile.eof())
{
    cout << input << endl;
    nameFile.getline(input, 81);    // Use \n as a delimiter.
}

nameFile.close();
```

Program Output Using getline
```
Jayne Murphy
47 Jones Circle
Almond, NC 28702
```

Because the third argument of the getline function was left out, its default value is \n. Sometimes you might want to specify another delimiter. For example, consider a file that contains multiple names and addresses, and that is internally formatted in the following manner:

Contents of names2.txt
```
Jayne Murphy$47 Jones Circle$Almond, NC 28702\n$Bobbie Smith$
217 Halifax Drive$Canton, NC 28716\n$Bill Hammet$PO Box 121$
Springfield, NC 28357\n$
```

Think of this file as consisting of three records. A record is a complete set of data about a single item. Also, the records in the file above are made of three fields. The first field is the person's name. The second field is the person's street address or P.O. box number. The third field contains the person's city, state, and ZIP code. Notice that each field ends with a $ character, and each record ends with a \n character. Program 11-8 demonstrates how a getline function can be used to detect the $ characters.

Program 11-8

```cpp
// This file demonstrates the getline function with a user-
// specified delimiter.
#include <iostream>
#include <fstream>
using namespace std;

int main()
{
    const int SIZE = 81;

    fstream dataFile("names2.txt", ios::in);
    char input[SIZE];

    dataFile.getline(input, SIZE, '$');
    while (!dataFile.eof())
    {
        cout << input << endl;
        dataFile.getline(input, SIZE, '$');
    }
    dataFile.close();
    return 0;
}
```

Program Output
```
Jayne Murphy
47 Jones Circle
Almond, NC 28702

Bobbie Smith
217 Halifax Drive
Canton, NC 28716

Bill Hammet
PO Box 121
Springfield, NC 28357
```

Notice that the \n characters, which mark the end of each record, are also part of the output. They cause an extra blank line to be printed on the screen, separating the records.

 Note: When using a printable character, such as $, to delimit data in a file, be sure to select a character that will not actually appear in the data itself. Since it's doubtful that anyone's name or address contains a $ character, it's an acceptable delimiter. If the file contained dollar amounts, however, another delimiter would have been chosen.

The get Member Function

Another useful member function is get. It reads a single character from the file. Here is an example of its usage:

```
inFile.get(ch);
```

In this example, ch is a char variable. A character will be read from the file and stored in ch. Program 11-9 shows the function used in a complete program. The user is asked for the name of a file. The file is opened and the get function is used in a loop to read the file's contents, one character at a time.

Program 11-9

```
// This program asks the user for a file name. The file is
// opened and its contents are displayed on the screen.
#include <iostream>
#include <fstream>
using namespace std;

int main()
{
    const int SIZE = 51;

    fstream file;
    char ch, fileName[SIZE];

    cout << "Enter a file name: ";
    cin >> fileName;

    file.open(fileName, ios::in);
    if (!file)
    {
        cout << fileName << " could not be opened.\n";
        return 0;
    }

    file.get(ch);            // Get a character
    while (!file.eof())
    {
        cout << ch;
        file.get(ch);        // Get another character
    }
    file.close();
    return 0;
}
```

Program 11-9 will display the contents of any file. The get function even reads whitespaces, so all the characters will be shown exactly as they appear in the file.

The put Member Function

The put member function writes a single character to the file. Here is an example of its usage:

```
outFile.put(ch);
```

In this statement, the variable ch is assumed to be a char variable. Its contents will be written to the file associated with the file stream object outFile. Program 11-10 demonstrates the put function.

Program 11-10

```
// This program demonstrates the put member function.
#include <iostream>
#include <fstream>
using namespace std;

int main()
{
    fstream dataFile("sentence.txt", ios::out);
    char ch;

    cout << "Type a sentence and be sure to end it with a ";
    cout << "period.\n";
    cin.get(ch);
    while (ch != '.')
    {
        dataFile.put(ch);
        cin.get(ch);
    }
    dataFile.put(ch);      // Write the period.
    dataFile.close();
    return 0;
}
```

Program Screen Output with Example Input Shown in Bold

Type a sentence and be sure to end it with a period.
I am on my way to becoming a great programmer. [Enter]

Resulting Contents of the File sentence.txt:

I am on my way to becoming a great programmer.

Checkpoint [11.2–11.5]

11.7   Assume the file input.txt contains the following characters:

R	u	n		S	p	o	t		r	u	n	\n	S	e

e		S	p	o	t		r	u	n	\n	<EOF>

What will the following program display on the screen?

```cpp
#include <iostream>
#include <fstream>
using namespace std;

int main()
{
    const int SIZE = 81;

    fstream inFile("input.txt", ios::in);
    char item[SIZE];

    inFile >> item;
    while (!inFile.eof())
    {
        cout << item << endl;
        inFile >> item;
    }
    inFile.close();
    return 0;
}
```

11.8   Describe the difference between reading a file with the >> operator and the getline member function.

11.9   What will be stored in the file out.txt after the following program runs?

```cpp
#include <iostream>
#include <fstream>
#include <iomanip>
using namespace std;

int main()
{
    const int SIZE = 5;

    ofstream outFile("out.txt");
    double nums[SIZE] = {100.279, 1.719, 8.602, 7.777, 5.099};
```

```
outFile << fixed << setprecision(2);
for (int count = 0; count < 5; count++)
{
    outFile << setw(8) << nums[count];
}
outFile.close();
return 0;
}
```

11.6 Focus on Software Engineering: *Working with Multiple Files*

CONCEPT It's possible to have more than one file open at once in a program.

Quite often you will need to have multiple files open at once. In many real-world applications, data about a single item is categorized and written to several different files. For example, a payroll system might keep the following files:

emp.dat — A file that contains the following data about each employee: name, job title, address, telephone number, employee number, and the date hired.

pay.dat — A file that contains the following data about each employee: employee number, hourly pay rate, overtime rate, and number of hours worked in the current pay cycle.

withold.dat — A file that contains the following data about each employee: employee number, dependents, and extra withholdings.

When the system is writing paychecks, you can see that it will need to open each of the files listed above and read data from them. (Notice that each file contains the employee number. This is how the program can locate a specific employee's data.)

In C++, you open multiple files by defining multiple file stream objects. For example, if you need to read from three files, you can define three file stream objects, such as:

```
ifstream file1, file2, file3;
```

Sometimes you will need to open one file for input and another file for output. For example, Program 11-11 asks the user for a file name. The file is opened and read. Each character is converted to uppercase and written to a second file called out.txt. This type of program can be considered a *filter*. Filters read the input of one file, changing the data in some fashion, and write it out to a second file. The second file is a modified version of the first file.

Program 11-11

```cpp
// This program demonstrates reading from one file and writing
// to a second file.
#include <iostream>
#include <fstream>
#include <cctype> // Needed for the toupper function.
using namespace std;

int main()
{
    const int SIZE = 81;

    ifstream inFile;
    ofstream outFile("out.txt");
    char fileName[SIZE], ch;

    cout << "Enter a file name: ";
    cin >> fileName;
    inFile.open(fileName);

    if (!inFile)
    {
        cout << "Cannot open " << fileName << endl;
        return 0;
    }
    inFile.get(ch);                       // Get a character from file 1
    while (!inFile.eof())                 // Test for end of file
    {
        outFile.put(toupper(ch));         // Write uppercase character to file 2
        inFile.get(ch);                   // Get another character from file 1
    }
    inFile.close();
    outFile.close();
    cout << "File conversion done.\n";
    return 0;
}
```

Program Screen Output with Example Input Shown in Bold

```
Enter a file name: hownow.txt [Enter]
File conversion done.
```

Contents of `hownow.txt`

```
how now brown cow.
How Now?
```

Resulting Contents of `out.txt`

```
HOW NOW BROWN COW.
HOW NOW?
```

11.7   Binary Files

CONCEPT   Binary files contain data that is unformatted and not necessarily stored as ASCII text.

All the files you've been working with so far have been text files. That means the data stored in the files has been formatted as ASCII text. Even a number, when stored in a file with the << operator, is converted to text. For example, consider the following program segment:

```
ofstream file("num.dat");
int x = 1297;
file << x;
```

The last statement writes the contents of x to the file. When the number is written, however, it is stored as the characters '1', '2', '9', and '7'. This is illustrated in Figure 11-6.

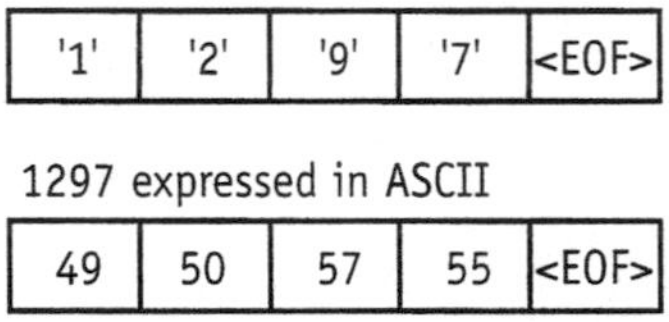

Figure 11-6

The number 1297 isn't stored in memory (in the variable x) in the fashion depicted in the figure above, however. It is formatted as a binary number, occupying two bytes on a typical PC. Figure 11-7 shows how the number is represented in memory, using binary or hexadecimal.

Figure 11-7

The unformatted representation of the number shown in Figure 11-7 is the way the "raw" data is stored in memory. Data can be stored in a file in its pure, binary format. The first step is to open the file in binary mode. This is accomplished by using the ios::binary flag. Here is an example:

```
file.open("stuff.dat", ios::out | ios::binary);
```

Notice the `ios::out` and `ios::binary` flags are joined in the statement with the | operator. This causes the file to be opened in both output and binary modes.

 Note: By default, files are opened in text mode.

The `write` and `read` Member Functions

The file stream object's `write` member function is used to write binary data to a file. The general format of the `write` member function is

```
fileObject.write(address, size);
```

Let's look at the parts of this function call format.

- ◆ *fileObject* is the name of a file stream object.
- ◆ *address* is the starting address of the section of memory that is to be written to the file. This argument is expected to be the address of a `char` (or a pointer to a `char`).
- ◆ *size* is the number of bytes of memory to write. This argument must be an integer value.

For example, the following code uses a file stream object named `file` to write a character to a binary file.

```
char letter = 'A';
file.write(&letter, sizeof(letter));
```

The first argument passed to the `write` function is the address of the `letter` variable. This tells the `write` function where the data that is to be written to the file is located. The second argument is the size of the `letter` variable, which is returned from the `sizeof` operator. This tells the `write` function the number of bytes of data to write to the file. Because the sizes of data types can vary among systems, it is best to use the `sizeof` operator to determine the number of bytes to write. After this function call executes, the contents of the `letter` variable will be written to the binary file associated with the `file` object.

The following code shows another example. This code writes an entire `char` array to a binary file.

```
const int SIZE = 4;
char data[SIZE] = {'A', 'B', 'C', 'D'};
file.write(data, sizeof(data));
```

In this code, the first argument is the name of the `data` array. By passing the name of the array we are passing a pointer to the beginning of the array. Because `data` is an array of `char` values, the name of the array is a pointer to a `char`. The second argument passes the name of the array to the `sizeof` operator. When the name of an array is passed to the `sizeof` operator, the operator returns the number of bytes allocated to the array. After this function call executes, the contents of the `data` array will be written to the binary file associated with the `file` object.

The read member function is used to read binary data from a file into memory. The general format of the read member function is

```
fileObject.read(address, size);
```

Here are the parts of this function call format:

- *fileObject* is the name of a file stream object.
- *address* is the starting address of the section of memory where the data being read from the file is to be stored. This is expected to be the address of a char (or a pointer to a char).
- *size* is the number of bytes of memory to read from the file. This argument must be an integer value.

For example, suppose we want to read a single character from a binary file and store that character in the letter variable. The following code uses a file stream object named file to do just that.

```
char letter;
file.read(&letter, sizeof(letter));
```

The first argument passed to the read function is the address of the letter variable. This tells the read function where to store the value that is read from the file. The second argument is the size of the letter variable. This tells the read function the number of bytes to read from the file. After this function executes, the letter variable will contain a character that was read from the file.

The following code shows another example. This code reads enough data from a binary file to fill an entire char array.

```
char data[4];
file.read(data, sizeof(data));
```

In this code, the first argument is the address of the data array. The second argument is the number of bytes allocated to the array. On a system that uses 1-byte characters, this function will read four bytes from the file and store them in the data array.

Program 11-12 demonstrates writing a char array to a file and then reading the data from the file back into memory.

Program 11-12

```
// This program uses the write and read functions.
#include <iostream>
#include <fstream>
using namespace std;

int main()
{
    const int SIZE = 4;
```

(program continues)

Program 11-12   *(continued)*

```
      fstream file;
      char data[SIZE] = {'A', 'B', 'C', 'D'};

      // Open the file for output in binary mode.
      file.open("test.dat", ios::out | ios::binary);

      // Write the contents of the array to the file.
      cout << "Writing the characters to the file.\n";
      file.write(data, sizeof(data));

      // Close the file.
      file.close();

      // Open the file for input in binary mode.
      file.open("test.dat", ios::in | ios::binary);

      // Read the contents of the file into the array.
      cout << "Now reading the data back into memory.\n";
      file.read(data, sizeof(data));
      // Display the contents of the array.
      for (int count = 0; count < SIZE; count++)
         cout << data[count] << " ";
      cout << endl;

      // Close the file.
      file.close();
      return 0;
}
```

Program Screen Output

```
Writing the characters to the file.
Now reading the data back into memory.
A B C D
```

Writing Data Other Than `char` to Binary Files

Because the write and read member functions expect their first argument to be a pointer to a char, you must use a type cast when writing and reading items that are of other data types. To convert a pointer from one type to another you should use the reinterpret_cast type cast. The general format of the type cast is

```
reinterpret_cast<dataType>(value)
```

where *dataType* is the data type that you are converting to, and *value* is the value that you are converting. For example, the following code uses the type cast to store the address of an int in a char pointer variable.

```
int x = 65;
char *ptr;
ptr = reinterpret_cast<char *>(&x);
```

The following code shows how to use the type cast to pass the address of an integer as the first argument to the write member function.

```
int x = 27;
file.write(reinterpret_cast<char *>(&x), sizeof(x));
```

After the function executes, the contents of the variable x will be written to the binary file associated with the file object. The following code shows an int array being written to a binary file.

```
const int SIZE = 10;
int numbers[SIZE] = {1, 2, 3, 4, 5, 6, 7, 8, 9, 10};
file.write(reinterpret_cast<char *>(numbers), sizeof(numbers));
```

After this function call executes, the contents of the numbers array will be written to the binary file. The following code shows values being read from the file and stored into the numbers array.

```
const int SIZE = 10;
int numbers[SIZE];
file.read(reinterpret_cast<char *>(numbers), sizeof(numbers));
```

Program 11-13 demonstrates writing an int array to a file and then reading the data from the file back into memory.

Program 11-13

```
// This program writes an array of integers to a binary file
// and then reads the data from the file back into the array.
#include <iostream>
#include <fstream>
using namespace std;

int main()
{
    const int SIZE = 10;
    fstream file;
    int numbers[SIZE] = {1, 2, 3, 4, 5, 6, 7, 8, 9, 10};

    // Open the file for output in binary mode.
    file.open("numbers.dat", ios::out | ios::binary);

    // Write the contents of the array to the file.
    cout << "Writing the data to the file.\n";
    file.write(reinterpret_cast<char *>(numbers), sizeof(numbers));

    // Close the file.
    file.close();
```

(program continues)

Program 11-13   *(continued)*

```
// Open the file for input in binary mode.
file.open("numbers.dat", ios::in | ios::binary);

// Read the contents of the file into the array.
cout << "Now reading the data back into memory.\n";
file.read(reinterpret_cast<char *>(numbers), sizeof(numbers));

// Display the contents of the array.
for (int count = 0; count < SIZE; count++)
    cout << numbers[count] << " ";
cout << endl;

// Close the file.
file.close();
return 0;
}
```

Program Screen Output

```
Writing the data to the file.
Now reading the data back into memory.
1 2 3 4 5 6 7 8 9 10
```

11.8   Creating Records with Structures

CONCEPT   Structures may be used to store fixed-length records to a file.

Earlier in this chapter the concept of fields and records was introduced. A field is an individual piece of data pertaining to a single item. A record is made up of fields and is a complete set of data about a single item. For example, a set of fields might be a person's name, age, address, and phone number. Together, all those fields that pertain to one person make up a record.

In C++, structures provide a convenient way to organize data into fields and records. For example, the following code could be used to create a record containing data about a person.

```
const int NAME_SIZE = 51, ADDR_SIZE = 51, PHONE_SIZE = 14;

struct Info
{
    char name[NAME_SIZE];
    int  age;
    char address1[ADDR_SIZE];
    char address2[ADDR_SIZE];
    char phone[PHONE_SIZE];
};
```

Besides providing an organizational structure for data, structures also package data into a single unit. For example, assume the structure variable person is defined as :

```
Info person;
```

Once the members (or fields) of person are filled with data, the entire variable may be written to a file using the write function:

```
file.write(reinterpret_cast<char *>(&person), sizeof(person));
```

The first argument is the address of the person variable. The reinterpret_cast operator is used to convert the address to a char pointer. The second argument is the sizeof operator with person as its argument. This returns the number of bytes used by the person structure. Program 11-14 demonstrates this technique.

 Note: Because structures can contain a mixture of data types, you should always use the ios::binary mode when opening a file to store them.

Program 11-14

```cpp
// This program uses a structure variable to store a record to a file.
#include <iostream>
#include <fstream>
using namespace std;

const int NAME_SIZE = 51, ADDR_SIZE = 51, PHONE_SIZE = 14;

// Declare a structure for the record.
struct Info
{
    char name[NAME_SIZE];
    int  age;
    char address1[ADDR_SIZE];
    char address2[ADDR_SIZE];
    char phone[PHONE_SIZE];
};

int main()
{
    Info person;
    char again;
    fstream people("people.dat", ios::out | ios::binary);

    do
    {
        // Get data about a person.
        cout << "Enter the following data about a "
             << "person:\n";
        cout << "Name: ";
        cin.getline(person.name, NAME_SIZE);
```

(program continues)

Program 11-14   *(continued)*

```cpp
        cout << "Age: ";
        cin >> person.age;
        cin.ignore(); // Skip over the remaining newline.
        cout << "Address line 1: ";
        cin.getline(person.address1, ADDR_SIZE);
        cout << "Address line 2: ";
        cin.getline(person.address2, ADDR_SIZE);
        cout << "Phone: ";
        cin.getline(person.phone, PHONE_SIZE);

        // Write the contents of the person structure to the file.
        people.write(reinterpret_cast<char *>(&person),
                 sizeof(person));

        // Find out whether the user wants to write another record.
        cout << "Do you want to enter another record? ";
        cin >> again;
        cin.ignore(); // Skip over the remaining newline.
    } while (again == 'Y' || again == 'y');
    people.close();
    return 0;
}
```

Program Screen Output with Example Input Shown in Bold

```
Enter the following data about a person:
Name: Charlie Baxter [Enter]
Age: 42 [Enter]
Address line 1: 67 Kennedy Bvd. [Enter]
Address line 2: Perth, SC 38754 [Enter]
Phone: (803)555-1234 [Enter]
Do you want to enter another record? Y [Enter]
Enter the following data about a person:
Name: Merideth Murney [Enter]
Age: 22 [Enter]
Address line 1: 487 Lindsay Lane [Enter]
Address line 2: Hazelwood, NC 28737 [Enter]
Phone: (828)555-9999 [Enter]
Do you want to enter another record? N [Enter]
```

Program 11-14 allows you to build a file by filling the members of the `person` variable, and then writing the variable to the file. Program 11-15 opens the file and reads each record into the `person` variable, then displays the data on the screen.

Program 11-15

```cpp
// This program demonstrates the use of a structure variable to
// read a record of data from a file.
#include <iostream>
#include <fstream>            .
using namespace std;

const int NAME_SIZE = 51, ADDR_SIZE = 51, PHONE_SIZE = 14;

// Declare a structure for the record.
struct Info
{
   char name[NAME_SIZE];
   int age;
   char address1[ADDR_SIZE];
   char address2[ADDR_SIZE];
   char phone[PHONE_SIZE];
};

int main()
{
    Info person;
    char again;
    fstream people;

    // Open the file for input in binary mode.
    people.open("people.dat", ios::in | ios::binary);

    // Test for errors.
    if (!people)
    {
        cout << "Error opening file. Program aborting.\n";
        return 0;
    }

    cout << "Here are the people in the file:\n\n";
    // Read the first record from the file.
    people.read(reinterpret_cast<char *>(&person),
            sizeof(person));

    // While not at the end of the file, display
    // the records.
    while (!people.eof())
    {
        // Display the record.
        cout << "Name: ";
        cout << person.name << endl;
```

(program continues)

Program 11-15 *(continued)*

```
        cout << "Age: ";
        cout << person.age << endl;
        cout << "Address line 1: ";
        cout << person.address1 << endl;
        cout << "Address line 2: ";
        cout << person.address2 << endl;
        cout << "Phone: ";
        cout << person.phone << endl;

        // Wait for the user to press the Enter key.
        cout << "\nPress the Enter key to see the next record.\n";
        cin.get(again);

        // Read the next record from the file.
        people.read(reinterpret_cast<char *>(&person),
                    sizeof(person));
    }

    cout << "That's all the data in the file!\n";
    people.close();
    return 0;
}
```

Program Screen Output (Using the same file created by Program 11-15 as input)

```
Here are the people in the file:

Name: Charlie Baxter
Age: 42
Address line 1: 67 Kennedy Bvd.
Address line 2: Perth, SC   38754
Phone: (803)555-1234

Press the Enter key to see the next record.

Name: Merideth Murney
Age: 22
Address line 1: 487 Lindsay Lane
Address line 2: Hazelwood, NC   28737
Phone: (828)555-9999

Press the Enter key to see the next record.

That's all the data in the file!
```

11.9 Random-Access Files

> **CONCEPT** Random Access means non-sequentially accessing data in a file.

All of the programs created so far in this chapter have performed *sequential file access*. When a file is opened, the position where reading and/or writing will occur is at the file's beginning (unless the `ios::app` mode is used, which causes data to be written to the end of the file). If the file is opened for output, bytes are written to it one after the other. If the file is opened for input, data is read beginning at the first byte. As the reading or writing continues, the file stream object's read/write position advances sequentially through the file's contents.

The problem with sequential file access is that in order to read a specific byte from the file, all the bytes that precede it must be read first. For instance, if a program needs data stored at the hundredth byte of a file, it will have to read the first 99 bytes to reach it. If you've ever listened to a cassette tape player, you understand sequential access. To listen to a song at the end of the tape, you have to listen to all the songs that come before it, or fast-forward over them. There is no way to immediately jump to that particular song.

Although sequential file access is useful in many circumstances, it can slow a program down tremendously. If the file is very large, locating data buried deep inside it can take a long time. Alternatively, C++ allows a program to perform *random file access*. In random file access, a program may immediately jump to any byte in the file without first reading the preceding bytes. The difference between sequential and random file access is like the difference between a cassette tape and a compact disc. When listening to a CD, there is no need to listen to or fast forward over unwanted songs. You simply jump to the track that you want to listen to. This is illustrated in Figure 12-8.

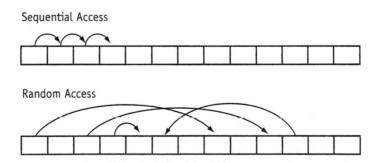

Sequential Access

Random Access

Figure 11-8

The `seekp` and `seekg` Member Functions

File stream objects have two member functions that are used to move the read/write position to any byte in the file. They are `seekp` and `seekg`. The `seekp` function is used with files opened for output and `seekg` is used with files opened for input. (It makes sense if you remember that "p" stands for "put" and "g" stands for "get." seekp is used with files that you put data into, and seekg is used with files you get data out of.)

Here is an example of seekp's usage:

```
file.seekp(20L, ios::beg);
```

The first argument is a long integer representing an offset into the file. This is the number of the byte you wish to move to. In this example, 20L is used. (Remember, the L suffix forces the compiler to treat the number as a long integer.) This statement moves the file's write position to byte number 20. (All numbering starts at 0, so byte number 20 is actually the twenty-first byte.)

The second argument is called the mode, and it designates where to calculate the offset *from*. The flag ios::beg means the offset is calculated from the beginning of the file. Alternatively, the offset can be calculated from the end of the file or the current position in the file. Table 11-7 lists the flags for all three of the random-access modes.

Table 11-7

Mode Flag	Description
ios::beg	The offset is calculated from the beginning of the file.
ios::end	The offset is calculated from the end of the file.
ios::cur	The offset is calculated from the current position.

Table 11-8 shows examples of seekp and seekg using the various mode flags:

Table 11-8

Statement	How It Affects the Read/Write Position
file.seekp(32L, ios::beg);	Sets the write position to the 33rd byte (byte 32) from the beginning of the file.
file.seekp(-10L, ios::end);	Sets the write position to the 10th byte from the end of the file.
file.seekp(120L, ios::cur);	Sets the write position to the 121st byte (byte 120) from the current position.
file.seekg(2L, ios::beg);	Sets the read position to the 3rd byte (byte 2) from the beginning of the file.
file.seekg(-100L, ios::end);	Sets the read position to the 100th byte from the end of the file.
file.seekg(40L, ios::cur);	Sets the read position to the 41st byte (byte 40) from the current position.
file.seekg(0L, ios::end);	Sets the read position to the end of the file.

Notice that some of the examples in Table 11-7 use a negative offset. Negative offsets result in the read or write position being moved backward in the file, while positive offsets result in a forward movement.

Assume the file `letters.txt` contains the following data:

```
abcdefghijklmnopqrstuvwxyz
```

Program 11-16 uses the `seekg` function to jump around to different locations in the file, retrieving a character after each stop.

Program 11-16

```cpp
// This program demonstrates the seekg function.
#include <iostream>
#include <fstream>
using namespace std;

int main()
{
    fstream file("letters.txt", ios::in);
    char ch;

    // Move to byte 5 from the beginnng of the file
    // (the 6th byte) and read the character there.
    file.seekg(5L, ios::beg);
    file.get(ch);
    cout << "Byte 5 from beginning: " << ch << endl;

    // Move to the 10th byte from the end of the file
    // and read the character there.
    file.seekg(-10L, ios::end);
    file.get(ch);
    cout << "10th byte from end: " << ch << endl;

    // Move to byte 3 from the current position
    // (the 4th byte) and read the character there.
    file.seekg(3L, ios::cur);
    file.get(ch);
    cout << "Byte 3 from current: " << ch << endl;

    file.close();
    return 0;
}
```

Program Screen Output
```
Byte 5 from beginning: f
10th byte from end: q
Byte 3 from current: u
```

Program 11-17 shows a more robust example of the seekg function. It opens the people.dat file created by Program 11-14. The file contains two records. Program 11-17 displays record 1 (the second record) first, then displays record 0.

The program has two important functions other than main. The first, byteNum, takes a record number as its argument and returns that record's starting byte. It calculates the record's starting byte by multiplying the record number by the size of the Info structure. This returns the offset of that record from the beginning of the file. The second function, showRec, accepts an Info structure as its argument and displays its contents on the screen.

Program 11-17

```cpp
// This program randomly reads a record of data from a file.
#include <iostream>
#include <fstream>
using namespace std;

const int NAME_SIZE = 51, ADDR_SIZE = 51, PHONE_SIZE = 14;

// Declare a structure for the record.
struct Info
{
   char name[NAME_SIZE];
   int age;
   char address1[ADDR_SIZE];
   char address2[ADDR_SIZE];
   char phone[PHONE_SIZE];
};

// Function Prototypes
long byteNum(int);
void showRec(Info);

int main()
{
   fstream people;
   Info person;

   // Open the file for input in binary mode.
   people.open("people.dat", ios::in | ios::binary);

   // Test for errors.
   if (!people)
   {
      cout << "Error opening file. Program aborting.\n";
      return 0;
   }
```

(program continues)

Program 11-17   *(continued)*

```
    // Read and display record 1 (the second record).
    cout << "Here is record 1:\n";
    people.seekg(byteNum(1), ios::beg);
    people.read(reinterpret_cast<char *>(&person), sizeof(person));
    showRec(person);

    // Read and display record 0 (the first record).
    cout << "\nHere is record 0:\n";
    people.seekg(byteNum(0), ios::beg);
    people.read(reinterpret_cast<char *>(&person), sizeof(person));
    showRec(person);

    // Close the file.
    people.close();
    return 0;
}

//*************************************************************
// Definition of function byteNum. Accepts an integer as     *
// its argument. Returns the byte number in the file of the  *
// record whose number is passed as the argument.            *
//*************************************************************

long byteNum(int recNum)
{
    return sizeof(Info) * recNum;
}

//*************************************************************
// Definition of function showRec. Accepts an Info structure *
// as its argument, and displays the structure's contents.   *
//*************************************************************

void showRec(Info record)
{
    cout << "Name: ";
    cout << record.name << endl;
    cout << "Age: ";
    cout << record.age << endl;
    cout << "Address line 1: ";
    cout << record.address1 << endl;
    cout << "Address line 2: ";
    cout << record.address2 << endl;
    cout << "Phone: ";
    cout << record.phone << endl;
    return 0;
}
```

Program 11-17   *(continued)*

Program Screen Output (Using the same file created by Program 11–19 as input)
```
Here is record 1:
Name: Merideth Murney
Age: 22
Address line 1: 487 Lindsay Lane
Address line 2: Hazelwood, NC   28737
Phone: (828)555-9999

Here is record 0:
Name: Charlie Baxter
Age: 42
Address line 1: 67 Kennedy Bvd.
Address line 2: Perth, SC   38754
Phone: (803)555-1234
```

WARNING! If a program has read to the end of a file, you must call the file stream object's `clear` member function before calling `seekg` or `seekp`. This clears the file stream object's `eof` flag. Otherwise, the `seekg` or `seekp` function will not work.

The `tellp` and `tellg` Member Functions

File stream objects have two more member functions that may be used for random file access: `tellp` and `tellg`. Their purpose is to return, as a long integer, the current byte number of a file's read and write position. As you can guess, `tellp` returns the write position and `tellg` returns the read position. Assuming `pos` is a long integer, here is an example of the functions' usage:

```
pos = outFile.tellp();
pos = inFile.tellg();
```

One application of these functions is to determine the number of bytes that a file contains. The following example demonstrates how to do this using the `tellg` function.

```
file.seekg(0L, ios::end);
numBytes = file.tellg();
cout << "The file has " << numBytes << " bytes.\n";
```

First the `seekg` member function is used to move the read position to the last byte in the file. Then the `tellg` function is used to get the current byte number of the read position.

Program 11-18 demonstrates the `tellg` function. It opens the `letters.txt` file, which was also used in Program 11-16. The file contains the following characters:

```
abcdefghijklmnopqrstuvwxyz
```

Program 11-18

```cpp
// This program demonstrates the tellg function.
#include <iostream>
#include <fstream>
using namespace std;

int main()
{
    long offset, numBytes;
    char ch, again;
    fstream file("letters.txt", ios::in);

    // Determine the number of bytes in the file.
    file.seekg(0L, ios::end);
    numBytes = file.tellg();
    cout << "The file has " << numBytes << " bytes.\n";

    // Go back to the beginning of the file.
    file.seekg(0L, ios::beg);

    do
    {
        // Display the current read position.
        cout << "Currently at position " << file.tellg() << endl;

        // Get a byte number from the user.
        cout << "Enter an offset from the beginning of the file: ";
        cin >> offset;

        // Move the read position to that byte, read the
        // character there, and display it.
        if (offset >= numBytes)            // Past the end of the file?
            cout << "Cannot read past the end of the file.\n";
        else
        {
            file.seekg(offset, ios::beg);
            file.get(ch);
            cout << "Character read: " << ch << endl;
        }

        // Does the user want to try this again?
        cout << "Do it again? ";
        cin >> again;
    } while (again == 'Y' || again == 'y');

    // Close the file.
    file.close();
    return 0;
}
```

Program 11-18 *(continued)*

Program Output with Example Input Shown in Bold
```
The file has 26 bytes.
Currently at position 0
Enter an offset from the beginning of the file: 5 [Enter]
Character read: f
Do it again? y [Enter]
Currently at position 6
Enter an offset from the beginning of the file: 0 [Enter]
Character read: a
Do it again? y [Enter]
Currently at position 1
Enter an offset from the beginning of the file: 26 [Enter]
Cannot read past the end of the file.
Do it again? n [Enter]
```

Rewinding a Sequential-Access File with `seekg`

Sometimes when processing a sequential file it is necessary for a program to read the contents of the file more than one time. For example, suppose a program searches a file for an item specified by the user. The program must open the file, read its contents, and determine if the specified item is in the file. If the user needs to search the file again for another item, the program must read the file's contents again.

One simple approach for reading a file's contents more than once is to close and reopen the file, as shown in the following code example.

```
dataFile.open("file.txt", ios::in);     // Open the file.

//
// Read and process the file's contents.
//

dataFile.close();                       // Close the file.
dataFile.open("file.txt", ios::in);     // Open the file again.

//
// Read and process the file's contents again.
//

dataFile.close();                       // Close the file.
```

Each time the file is reopened, its read position is located at the beginning of the file. The read position is the byte in the file that will be read with the next read operation.

Another approach is to "rewind" the file. This means moving the read position to the beginning of the file without closing and reopening it. This is accomplished with the file stream object's `seekg` member function to move the read position back to the beginning of the file. The following example code demonstrates.

```
dataFile.open("file.txt", ios::in);      // Open the file.

//
// Read and process the file's contents.
//

dataFile.clear();                        // Clear the eof flag.
dataFile.seekg(0L, ios::beg);            // Rewind the read position.

//
// Read and process the file's contents again.
//

dataFile.close();                        // Close the file.
```

Notice that prior to calling the seekg member function, the clear member function is called. As previously mentioned this clears the file object's eof flag and is necessary only if the program has read to the end of the file. This approach eliminates the need to close and reopen the file each time the file's contents are processed.

11.10 Opening a File for Both Input and Output

CONCEPT You may perform input and output on an fstream file without closing it and reopening it.

Sometimes you'll need to perform both input and output on a file without closing and reopening it. For example, consider a program that allows you to search for a record in a file and then make changes to it. A read operation is necessary to copy the data from the file to memory. After the desired changes have been made to the data in memory, a write operation is necessary to replace the old data in the file with the new data in memory.

Such operations are possible with fstream objects. The ios::in and ios::out file access flags may be joined with the | operator, as shown in the following statement.

```
fstream file("data.dat", ios::in | ios::out)
```

The same operation may be accomplished with the open member function:

```
file.open("data.dat", ios::in | ios::out);
```

You may also specify the ios::binary flag if binary data is to be written to the file. Here is an example:

```
file.open("data.dat", ios::in | ios::out | ios::binary);
```

When an fstream file is opened with both the ios::in and ios::out flags, the file's current contents are preserved and the read/write position is initially placed at the beginning of the file. If the file does not exist, it is created.

Programs 11-19, 11-20, and 11-21, demonstrate many of the techniques we have discussed. Program 11-19 sets up a file with five blank inventory records. Each record is a structure with members for holding a part description, quantity on hand, and price. Program 11-20 displays the contents of the file on the screen. Program 11-21 opens the file in both input and output modes, and allows the user to change the contents of a specific record.

Program 11-19

```cpp
// This program sets up a file of blank inventory records.
#include <iostream>
#include <fstream>
using namespace std;

const int DESC_SIZE = 31, NUM_RECORDS = 5;

// Declaration of InventoryItem structure
struct InventoryItem
{
   char desc[DESC_SIZE];
   int qty;
   double price;
};

int main()
{
   fstream inventory("Inventory.dat", ios::out | ios::binary);
   InventoryItem record = { "", 0, 0.0 };

   // Write the blank records
   for (int count = 0; count < NUM_RECORDS; count++)
   {
      cout << "Now writing record " << count << endl;
      inventory.write(reinterpret_cast<char *>(&record),
                  sizeof(record));
   }

   // Close the file.
   inventory.close();
   return 0;
}
```

Program Screen Output

```
Now writing record 0
Now writing record 1
Now writing record 2
Now writing record 3
Now writing record 4
```

Program 11-20 simply displays the contents of the inventory file on the screen. It can be used to verify that Program 11-19 successfully created the blank records, and that Program 11-21 correctly modified the designated record.

Program 11-20

```cpp
// This program displays the contents of the inventory file.
#include <iostream>
#include <fstream>
using namespace std;

const int DESC_SIZE = 31;

// Declaration of InventoryItem structure
struct InventoryItem
{
    char desc[DESC_SIZE];
    int qty;
    double price;
};

int main()
{
    fstream inventory("Inventory.dat", ios::in | ios::binary);
    InventoryItem record = { "", 0, 0.0 };

    // Now read and display the records
    inventory.read(reinterpret_cast<char *>(&record),
                sizeof(record));
    while (!inventory.eof())
    {
        cout << "Description: ";
        cout << record.desc << endl;
        cout << "Quantity: ";
        cout << record.qty << endl;
        cout << "Price: ";
        cout << record.price << endl << endl;
        inventory.read(reinterpret_cast<char *>(&record), sizeof(record));
    }

    // Close the file.
    inventory.close();
    return 0;
}
```

Here is the screen output of Program 11-20 if it is run immediately after Program 11-19 sets up the file of blank records.

Program Screen Output

```
Description:
Quantity: 0
Price: 0.0

Description:
Quantity: 0
Price: 0.0

Description:
Quantity: 0
Price: 0.0

Description:
Quantity: 0
Price: 0.0

Description:
Quantity: 0
Price: 0.0
```

Program 11-21 allows the user to change the contents of an individual record in the inventory file.

Program 11-21

```cpp
// This program allows the user to edit a specific record.
#include <iostream>
#include <fstream>
using namespace std;

const int DESC_SIZE = 31;

// Declaration of InventoryItem structure
struct InventoryItem
{
    char desc[DESC_SIZE];
    int qty;
    double price;
};

int main()
{
    fstream inventory("Inventory.dat", ios::in | ios::out | ios::binary);
    InventoryItem record;
    long recNum;
```

(program continues)

Program 11-21   *(continued)*

```
// Get the record number of the desired record.
cout << "Which record do you want to edit? ";
cin >> recNum;

// Move to the record and read it.
inventory.seekg(recNum * sizeof(record), ios::beg);
inventory.read(reinterpret_cast<char *>(&record),
          sizeof(record));

// Display the record contents.
cout << "Description: ";
cout << record.desc << endl;
cout << "Quantity: ";
cout << record.qty << endl;
cout << "Price: ";
cout << record.price << endl;
// Get the new record data.
cout << "Enter the new data:\n";
cout << "Description: ";
cin.ignore();
cin.getline(record.desc, DESC_SIZE);
cout << "Quantity: ";
cin >> record.qty;
cout << "Price: ";
cin >> record.price;

// Move back to the beginning of this record's position.
inventory.seekp(recNum * sizeof(record), ios::beg);

// Write the new record over the current record.
inventory.write(reinterpret_cast<char *>(&record),
            sizeof(record));

// Close the file.
inventory.close();
return 0;
}
```

Program Screen Output with Example Input Shown in Bold

```
Which record do you want to edit? 2 [Enter]
Description:
Quantity: 0
Price: 0.0
Enter the new data:
Description: Wrench [Enter]
Quantity: 10 [Enter]
Price: 4.67 [Enter]
```

Checkpoint [11.9–11.10]

11.10 Describe the difference between the seekg and the seekp functions.

11.11 Describe the difference between the tellg and the tellp functions.

11.12 What is the number of the first byte in a file?

11.13 Briefly describe what each of the following statements do:

```
file.seekp(100L, ios::beg);
file.seekp(-10L, ios::end);
file.seekg(-25L, ios::cur);
file.seekg(30L, ios::cur);
```

11.14 Describe the mode that each of the following statements cause a file to be opened in:

```
file.open("info.dat", ios::in | ios::out);
file.open("info.dat", ios::in | ios::app);
file.open("info.dat", ios::in | ios::out | ios::ate);
file.open("info.dat", ios::in | ios::out | ios::binary);
```

 See the CaseStudies.pdf file on the accompanying CD for this chapter's case studies.

Review Questions and Exercises

Short Answer

1. What capability does the fstream data type provide that the ifstream and ofstream data types do not?

2. Which file access flag do you use to open a file when you want all output written to the end of the file's existing contents?

3. Assume that the file data.txt already exists, and the following statement executes. What happens to the file?

   ```
   fstream file("data.txt", ios::out);
   ```

4. How do you combine multiple file access flags when opening a file?

5. Should file stream objects be passed to functions by value or by reference? Why?

6. Under what circumstances is a file stream object's ios::hardfail bit set? What member function reports the state of this bit?

7. Under what circumstances is a file stream object's ios::eofbit bit set? What member function reports the state of this bit?

8. Under what circumstances is a file stream object's ios::badbit bit set? What member function reports the state of this bit?

9. How do you read the contents of a text file that contains whitespace characters as part of its data?

10. What arguments do you pass to a file stream object's `write` member function?

11. What arguments do you pass to a file stream object's `read` member function?

12. What type cast do you use to convert a pointer from one type to another?

13. What is the difference between the `seekg` and `seekp` member functions?

14. How do you get the byte number of a file's current `read` position? How do you get the byte number of a file's current write position?

15. If a program has read to the end of a file, what must you do before using either the `seekg` or `seekp` member functions?

16. How do you determine the number of bytes that a file contains?

17. How do you rewind a sequential-access file?

Algorithm Workbench

18. Write a statement that defines a file stream object named `places`. The object will be used for both output and input.

19. Write two statements that use a file stream object named `people` to open a file named people.dat. (Show how to open the file with a member function and at the definition of the file stream object.) The file should be opened for output.

20. Write two statements that use a file stream object named `pets` to open a file named pets.dat. (Show how to open the file with a member function and at the definition of the file stream object.) The file should be opened for input.

21. Write two statements that use a file stream object named `places` to open a file named places.dat. (Show how to open the file with a member function and at the definition of the file stream object.) The file should be opened for both input and output.

22. Write a program segment that defines a file stream object named `employees`. The file should be opened for both input and output (in binary mode). If the file fails to open, the program segment should display an error message.

23. Write code that opens the file data.txt for both input and output, but first determines if the file exists. If the file does not exist, the code should create it, then open it for both input and output.

24. Write code that determines the number of bytes contained in the file associated with the file stream object `dataFile`.

25. The `infoFile` file stream object is used to sequentially access data. The program has already read to the end of the file. Write code that rewinds the file.

True or False

26. T F Different operating systems have different rules for naming files.

27. T F `fstream` objects are only capable of performing file output operations.

28. T F `ofstream` objects, by default, delete the contents of a file if it already exists when opened.

29. T F `ifstream` objects, by default, create a file if it doesn't exist when opened.

30. T F Several file access flags may be joined by using the | operator.

31. T F A file may be opened in the definition of the file stream object.

32. T F If a file is opened in the definition of the file stream object, no mode flags may be specified.

33. T F A file stream object's `fail` member function may be used to determine if the file was successfully opened.

34. T F The same output formatting techniques used with `cout` may also be used with file stream objects.

35. T F The `>>` operator expects data to be delimited by whitespace characters.

36. T F The `getline` member function can be used to read text that contains whitespaces.

37. T F It is not possible to have more than one file open at once in a program.

38. T F Binary files contain unformatted data, not necessarily stored as text.

39. T F Binary is the default mode in which files are opened.

40. T F The `tellp` member function tells a file stream object which byte to move its write position to.

41. T F It is possible to open a file for both input and output.

Find the Error

Each of the following programs or program segments has errors. Find as many as you can.

42.
```cpp
fstream file(ios::in | ios::out);
file.open("info.dat");
if (!file)
{
    cout << "Could not open file.\n";
}
```

43.
```cpp
fstream dataFile("info.dat", ios:in | ios:binary);
int x = 5;
dataFile << x;
```

44.
```cpp
fstream dataFile("info.dat", ios:in);
char line[81];
dataFile.getline(line);
```

45.
```cpp
fstream dataFile("info.dat", ios:in);
char stuff[81] = "abcdefghijklmnopqrstuvwxyz";
dataFile.put(stuff);
```

46.
```cpp
fstream inFile("info.dat", ios:in);
int x;
inFile.seekp(5);
inFile >> x;
```

Programming Challenges

1. Head Program

Write a program that asks the user for the name of a file. The program should display the first 10 lines of the file on the screen (the "head" of the file). If the file has fewer than 10 lines, the entire file should be displayed, with a message indicating the entire file has been displayed.

 Note: Using an editor, you should create a simple text file that can be used to test this program.

2. File Display Program

Write a program that asks the user for the name of a file. The program should display the contents of the file on the screen. If the file's contents won't fit on a single screen, the program should display 24 lines of output at a time, and then pause. Each time the program pauses, it should wait for the user to strike a key before the next 24 lines are displayed.

 Note: Using an editor, you should create a simple text file that can be used to test this program.

3. Tail Program

Write a program that asks the user for the name of a file. The program should display the last 10 lines of the file on the screen (the "tail" of the file). If the file has less than 10 lines, the entire file should be displayed, with a message indicating the entire file has been displayed.

 Note: Using an editor, you should create a simple text file that can be used to test this program.

4. Line Numbers

(This assignment could be done as a modification of the program in problem 2.) Write a program that asks the user for the name of a file. The program should display the contents of the file on the screen. Each line of screen output should be preceded with a line number, followed by a colon. The line numbering should start at 1. Here is an example:

```
1:George Rolland
2:127 Academy Street
3:Brasstown, NC  28706
```

If the file's contents won't fit on a single screen, the program should display 24 lines of output at a time, and then pause. Each time the program pauses, it should wait for the user to strike a key before the next 24 lines are displayed.

 Note: Using an editor, you should create a simple text file that can be used to test this program.

5. String Search

Write a program that asks the user for a file name and a string to search for. The program should search the file for every occurrence of a specified string. When the string is found, the line that contains it should be displayed. After all the occurrences have been located, the program should report the number of times the string appeared in the file.

 Note: Using an editor, you should create a simple text file that can be used to test this program.

6. Sentence Filter

Write a program that asks the user for two file names. The first file will be opened for input and the second file will be opened for output. (It will be assumed that the first file contains sentences that end with a period.) The program will read the contents of the first file, change all the letters to lowercase except the first letter of each sentence, which should be made uppercase. The revised contents should be stored in the second file.

 Note: Using an editor, you should create a simple text file that can be used to test this program.

7. File Encryption Filter

File encryption is the science of writing the contents of a file in a secret code. Your encryption program should work like a filter, reading the contents of one file, modifying the data into a code, and then writing the coded contents out to a second file. The second file will be a version of the first file, but written in a secret code.

Although there are complex encryption techniques, you should come up with a simple one of your own. For example, you could read the first file one character at a time, and add 10 to the ASCII code of each character before it is written to the second file.

8. File Decryption Filter

Write a program that decrypts the file produced by the program in Programming Challenge 7. The decryption program should read the contents of the coded file, restore the data to its original state, and write it to another file.

9. Corporate Sales Data Output

Write a program that uses a structure to store the following data on a company division:

> Division name (such as East, West, North, or South)
> Quarter (1, 2, 3, or 4)
> Quarterly Sales

The user should be asked for the four quarters' sales figures for the East, West, North, and South divisions. The data for each quarter for each division should be written to a file.

Input Validation: Do not accept negative numbers for any sales figures.

10. Corporate Sales Data Input

Write a program that reads the data in the file created by the program in Programming Challenge 9. The program should calculate and display the following figures:

- Total corporate sales for each quarter
- Total yearly sales for each division
- Total yearly corporate sales
- Average quarterly sales for the divisions
- The highest and lowest quarters for the corporation

11. Inventory Program

Write a program that uses a structure to store the following inventory data in a file:

> Item description
> Quantity on hand
> Wholesale cost
> Retail cost
> Date added to inventory

The program should have a menu that allows the user to perform the following tasks:

- Add new records to the file.
- Display any record in the file.
- Change any record in the file.

    Input Validation: The program should not accept quantities, or wholesale or retail costs less than 0. The program should not accept dates that the programmer determines are unreasonable.

12. Inventory Screen Report

Write a program that reads the data in the file created by the program in Programming Challenge 11. The program should calculate and display the following data:

- The total wholesale value of the inventory
- The total retail value of the inventory
- The total quantity of all items in the inventory

Group Project

14. Customer Accounts

This program should be designed and written by a team of students. Here are some suggestions:

- ◆ One student should design function `main`, which will call other program functions. The remainder of the functions will be designed by other members of the team.

- ◆ The requirements of the program should be analyzed so each student is given about the same workload.

Write a program that uses a structure to store the following data about a customer account:

> Name
> Address
> City, State, and ZIP
> Telephone number
> Account Balance
> Date of last payment

The structure should be used to store customer account records in a file. The program should have a menu that lets the user perform the following operations:

- ◆ Enter new records into the file.

- ◆ Search for a particular customer's record and display it.

- ◆ Search for a particular customer's record and delete it.

- ◆ Search for a particular customer's record and change it.

- ◆ Display the contents of the entire file.

> *Input Validation: When the data for a new account is entered, be sure the user enters data for all the fields. No negative account balances should be entered.*

12

Introduction to Classes

■ Topics in this Chapter

12.1 Procedural and Object-Oriented Programming

CONCEPT Procedural programming is a method of writing software. It is a programming practice centered on the procedures or actions that take place in a program. Object-oriented programming is centered around the object. Objects are created from abstract data types that encapsulate data and functions together.

There are two common programming methods in practice today: procedural programming and object-oriented programming (or OOP). Up to this chapter, you have learned to write procedural programs.

In a procedural program, you typically have data stored in a collection of variables and/or structures, coupled with a set of functions that perform operations on the data. The data and the functions are separate entities. For example, in a program that works with the geometry of a rectangle you might have the variables in Table 12-1:

Table 12-1

Variable Definition	Description
`double width;`	Holds the rectangle's width
`double length;`	Holds the rectangle's length

In addition to the variables listed in Table 12-1, you might also have the functions listed in Table 12-2:

Table 12-2

Function Name	Description
`setData()`	Stores values in `width` and `length`
`displayWidth()`	Displays the rectangle's width
`displayLength()`	Displays the rectangle's length
`displayArea()`	Displays the rectangle's area

Usually, variables and data structures are passed to the functions that perform the desired operations. As you can see, procedural programming is centered around functions.

The Limitations of Procedural Programming

Even though the most important part of a program is the data and the way the data is organized, the procedural paradigm keeps programmers focused on the functions, or routines, that make up a program. Often this leads to problems such as these:

◆ *Programs with excessive global data*
   The developers of large procedural programs sometimes resort to storing their primary data in global variables and structures. This is so that all the functions have convenient access to critical data. This public accessibility, however, opens the door for a programmer to write code that accidentally destroys or corrupts vital data.

♦ *Complex and convoluted programs*
Even though a program that is highly modularized (broken into many logical functions) is preferable to one that isn't, there's a limit to the number of functions a person is capable of comprehending. It's common for real-world programs to have hundreds of functions that interact in a multitude of ways. If a new programmer without intimate knowledge of the code is brought into the project, he or she may have difficulty understanding the program.

♦ *Programs that are difficult to modify and extend*
When a program reaches a certain level of complexity, it becomes difficult to modify its code and understand how the modification will impact other parts of the program. Often, there is a delicate dependency between two or more functions. When a programmer alters one function, he or she might unknowingly affect other functions in adverse ways.

What Is Object-Oriented Programming?

Just as procedural programming is centered around functions, object-oriented programming is centered around the *object*, which packages together both the data and the functions that operate on the data.

Earlier you learned that variables represent storage locations in the computer's memory. A program may use variables to store data of primitive types, such as ints, floats, doubles, and others. Then you created your own abstract data types by declaring structures. A structure is like a "compound" variable because it is made of several data elements. Nevertheless, it still represents a storage location in the computer's memory. Now you will learn about classes, which are very similar to structures. Classes usually have not only member variables, but member functions as well. The member functions and member variables are packaged together into a single unit.* Conceptually, however, the idea of a variable as a storage location in memory doesn't quite describe an entity that is made of both data and functions. Such an entity is more appropriately called an *object*. Just as procedural programming is centered around functions, object-oriented programming is centered around objects.

Figure 12-1 shows a representation of a Rectangle object that encapsulates the data and functions needed to work with rectangles:

In the object-oriented approach, the variables and functions are all members of the Rectangle object. They are bound together in a single unit. When an operation is to be performed, such as calculating the area of the rectangle, a *message* is passed to the object telling it to perform the getArea function. Because getArea is a member of the Rectangle object, there is no need to pass copies of the width and length variables to it. They are all members of the same object, so the function has immediate access to them.

---

* Technically, an object is an instance of a class. The class has member functions that may operate on the object's member variables.

```
┌─────────────────────────────────────────┐
│ Member Variables                         │
│       double width;                      │
│       double length;                     │
├─────────────────────────────────────────┤
│ Member Functions                         │
│       void setWidth(double w)            │
│       { ... function code ...}           │
│                                          │
│       void setLength(double len)         │
│       { ... function code ...}           │
│                                          │
│       double  getWidth()                 │
│       { ... function code ...}           │
│                                          │
│       double  getLength()                │
│       { ... function code ...}           │
│                                          │
│       double  getArea()                  │
│       { ... function code ...}           │
│                                          │
└─────────────────────────────────────────┘
```

Figure 12-1

 Note: In OOP terminology, an object's member variables are often called its *attributes* and its member functions are sometimes referred to as its *behaviors* or *methods*.

Not only do objects have associated data and functions, they also have the ability to restrict other parts of the program from accessing their member variables and inner workings. This is known as *data hiding*. Data hiding is an important part of object-oriented programming because it allows the creation of objects whose critical data is protected from accidental corruption. It also allows an algorithm's complexity to be hidden from the world outside the object. The only data and functions that are accessible are those necessary to use the object for its intended purpose. These publicly-available members form an interface for using the object. This is illustrated in Figure 12-2.

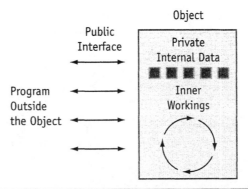

Figure 12-2

An everyday example of object-oriented technology is the automobile. It has a rather simple interface that consists of an ignition switch, steering wheel, gas pedal, brake pedal, and a stick-shift for changing gears. Vehicles with manual transmissions also provide a clutch pedal. If you want to drive an automobile (to become its user), you only have to learn to operate these elements of its interface. To start the motor, you simply turn the key in the ignition switch. What happens internally is irrelevant to the user. If you want to steer the auto to the left, you rotate the steering wheel left. The movements of all the linkages connecting the steering wheel to the front tires occur transparently.

Because automobiles have simple user interfaces, they can be driven by people who have no mechanical knowledge. This is good for the makers of automobiles because it means more people are likely to become customers. It's good for the users of automobiles because it lessens the chance that accidental damage will occur during some simple operation, like starting the motor.

These are also valid concerns in software development. A real-world program is rarely written by only one person. Even the programs you created so far weren't written entirely by you. If you incorporated C++ library functions, or objects like cin and cout, you used code written by someone else. In the world of professional software development, programmers commonly work in teams, buy and sell their code, and collaborate on projects. With OOP, programmers can create objects with powerful engines tucked away "under the hood," but simple interfaces that safeguard the object's algorithms and may be learned quickly.

How Are Objects Used?

Objects are created from programmer-defined abstract data types. Typically, programmers create two types of objects: general-purpose and application-specific.

General-Purpose Objects

General-purpose objects may be used in a variety of applications. They are commonly designed for purposes such as

◆ creating data types that are improvements on C++'s built-in data types.

◆ creating data types that are missing from C++. For instance, an object could be designed to process currencies or dates as if they were built-in data types.

◆ creating objects that perform commonly needed tasks, such as input validation and screen output in a graphical user interface.

Application-Specific Objects

Application-specific objects, as their name suggests, are data types created for a specific application. These objects afford the benefits of OOP to the processing of specific types of data. For example, the Westside Hardware Company might have an inventory program that uses objects specifically designed to process their inventory records.

Although objects like these are very useful in their respective applications, they cannot be used for general purposes. For example, the Westside Hardware Company's inventory object wouldn't be needed in a program that averages student test scores.

12.2 Introduction to Classes

> **CONCEPT** In C++, the class is the construct primarily used to create objects.

A *class* is similar to a structure. It is a data type defined by the programmer, consisting of variables and functions. Here is the general format of a class declaration:

```
class ClassName
{
    declaration;
    // ... more declarations
    // may follow...
};
```

The declaration statements inside a class declaration are for the variables and functions that are members of that class. For example, the following code declares a class named `Rectangle` with two member variables: `width` and `length`.

```
class Rectangle
{
    double width;
    double length;
};                          // Don't forget the semicolon.
```

There is a problem with this class, however. Unlike structures, the members of a class are *private* by default. Private class members cannot be accessed by programming statements outside the class. So, no statements outside this `Rectangle` class can access the `width` and `length` members.

Recall from our earlier discussion on object-oriented programming that an object can perform data hiding, which means that critical data stored inside the object is protected from code outside the object. In C++, a class's private members are hidden, and can be accessed only by functions that are members of the same class. A class's *public* members may be accessed by code outside the class.

Access Specifiers

C++ provides the key words `private` and `public` which you may use in class declarations. These key words are known as *access specifiers* because they specify how class members may be accessed. The following is the general format of a class declaration that uses the `private` and `public` access specifiers.

```
class ClassName
{
private:
// Declarations of private
// members appear here.
```

```
public:
        // Declarations of public
        // members appear here.
};
```

Notice that the access specifiers are followed by a colon (:), and then followed by one or more member declarations. In this general format, the `private` access specifier is used first. All of the declarations that follow it, up to the `public` access specifier, are for private members. Then, all of the declarations that follow the `public` access specifier are for public members.

Public Member Functions

To allow access to a class's private member variables, you create public member functions that work with the private member variables. For example, consider the `Rectangle` class. To allow access to a `Rectangle` object's `width` and `length` member variables, we will add the member functions listed in Table 12-3.

Table 12-3

Member Function	Description
setWidth	This function accepts an argument which is assigned to the `width` member variable.
setLength	This function accepts an argument which is assigned to the `length` member variable.
getWidth	This function returns the value stored in the `width` member variable.
getLength	This function returns the value stored in the `length` member variable.
getArea	This function returns the product of the `width` member variable multiplied by the `length` member variable. This value is the area of the rectangle.

 Appendix D on the Student CD shows how to diagram a class using UML.

For the moment we will not actually define the functions described in Table 12-3. We leave that for later. For now we will only include declarations, or prototypes, for the functions in the class declaration:

```
class Rectangle
{
    private:
        double width;
        double length;
    public:
        void setWidth(double);
        void setLength(double);
        double getWidth();
        double getLength();
        double getArea();
};
```

In this declaration, the member variables `width` and `length` are declared as `private`, which means they can be accessed only by the class's member functions. The member functions, however, are declared as `public`, which means they can be called from statements outside the class. If code outside the class needs to store a width or a length in a `Rectangle` object, it must do so by calling the object's `setWidth` or `setLength` member functions. Likewise, if code outside the class needs to retrieve a width or length stored in a `Rectangle` object, it must do so with the object's `getWidth` or `getLength` member functions. These public functions provide an interface for code outside the class to use `Rectangle` objects.

 Note: Even though the default access of a class is private, it's still a good idea to use the `private` key word to explicitly declare private members. This clearly documents the access specification of all the members of the class.

There is no rule requiring you to declare private members before public members. The `Rectangle` class could be declared as follows:

```
class Rectangle
{
    public:
        void setWidth(double);
        void setLength(double);
        double getWidth();
        double getLength();
        double getArea();
    private:
        double width;
        double length;
};
```

In addition, it is not required that all members of the same access specification be declared in the same place. Here is yet another declaration of the `Rectangle` class.

```
class Rectangle
{
    private:
        double width;
    public:
        void setWidth(double);
        void setLength(double);
        double getWidth();
        double getLength();
        double getArea();
    private:
        double length;

};
```

Although C++ gives you freedom in arranging class member declarations, you should adopt a consistent standard. Most programmers choose to group member declarations of the same access specification together.

 Note: Notice in our example that the first character of the class name is written in uppercase. This is not required, but serves as a visual reminder that the class name is not a variable name.

Defining Member Functions

The Rectangle class declaration contains declarations or prototypes for five member functions: setWidth, setLength, getWidth, getLength, and getArea. The definitions of these functions are written outside the class declaration:

```
//***************************************************************
// setWidth assigns its argument to the private member width. *
//***************************************************************

void Rectangle::setWidth(double w)
{
    width = w;
}



//***************************************************************
// setLength assigns its argument to the private member length. *
//***************************************************************

void Rectangle::setLength(double len)
{
    length = len;
}

//***************************************************************
// getWidth returns the value in the private member width.    *
//***************************************************************

double Rectangle::getWidth()
{
    return width;
}

//***************************************************************
// getLength returns the value in the private member length. *
//***************************************************************
```

```
double Rectangle::getLength()
{
    return length;
}

//*********************************************************
// getArea returns the product of width times length.   *
//*********************************************************

double Rectangle::getArea()
{
    return width * length;
}
```

In each function definition, the following precedes the name of each function:

```
Rectangle::
```

The two colons are called the *scope resolution operator*. When `Rectangle::` appears before the name of a function in a function header, it identifies the function as a member of the `Rectangle` class.

Here is the general format of the function header of any member function defined outside the declaration of a class:

> *⟨ReturnType⟩ ⟨ClassName⟩::⟨functionName⟩ (ParameterList)*

 WARNING! Remember, the class name and scope resolution operator extends the name of the function. They must appear after the return type and immediately before the function name in the function header. The following would be incorrect:

```
Rectangle::double getArea() //Incorrect!
```

In addition, if you leave the class name and scope resolution operator out of a member function's header, the function will not become a member of the class.

```
double getArea() // Not a member of the Rectangle class!
```

12.3 Defining an Instance of a Class

CONCEPT Class objects must be defined after the class is declared.

Like structure variables, class objects are not created in memory until they are defined. This is because a class declaration by itself does not create an object, but is merely the description of an object. It is similar to the blueprint for a house. The blueprint itself is not a house, but is a detailed description of a house. When we use the blueprint to build an actual house, we could say we are building an instance of the house described by the blueprint. If we so desire, we can build several identical houses from the same blueprint. Each house is a separate instance of the house described by the blueprint. This idea is illustrated in Figure 12-3.

Blueprint that describes a house.

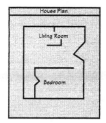

Instances of the house described by the blueprint.

Figure 12-3

A class declaration serves a similar purpose. We can use it to create one or more objects, which are instances of the class.

Class objects are created with simple definition statements, just like variables. For example, the following statement defines box as an object of the Rectangle class:

```
Rectangle box;
```

Defining a class object is called the *instantiation* of a class. In this statement, box is an *instance* of the Rectangle class.

Accessing an Object's Members

The members of a class object are accessed just like the members of a structure: with the dot operator. For example, the following statement calls the setWidth member function of the box object, passing 12.7 as an argument.

```
box.setWidth(12.7);
```

Here are other examples of statements that call the member functions of the box object:

```
box.setLength(4.8);              // Set length to 4.8.
x = box.getWidth();              // Assign box's width to x.
cout << box.getLength();         // Display box's length.
cout << box.getArea();           // Display box's area.
```

 Note: Notice that the member functions can access member variables of the same object without using the dot operator. The functions are able to access `width`, and `length` without any extra notation.

A Class Demonstration Program

Program 12-1 is a complete program that demonstrates the `Rectangle` class.

Program 12-1

```
// This program demonstrates a simple class.
#include <iostream>
using namespace std;

// Rectangle class declaration.
class Rectangle
{
    private:
        double width;
        double length;
    public:
        void setWidth(double);
        void setLength(double);
        double getWidth();
        double getLength();
        double getArea();
};

//************************************************************
// setWidth assigns its argument to the private member width. *
//************************************************************

void Rectangle::setWidth(double w)
{
    width = w;
}
```

(program continues)

Program 12-1 *(continued)*

```
//************************************************************
// setLength assigns its argument to the private member length. *
//************************************************************

void Rectangle::setLength(double len)
{
    length = len;
}

//************************************************************
// getWidth returns the value in the private member width.   *
//************************************************************

double Rectangle::getWidth()
{
    return width;
}

//************************************************************
// getLength returns the value in the private member length. *
//************************************************************

double Rectangle::getLength()
{
    return length;
}

//************************************************************
// getArea returns the product of width times length.    *
//************************************************************

double Rectangle::getArea()
{
    return width * length;
}

//************************************************************
// Function main                                          *
//************************************************************

int main()
{
    Rectangle box;          // Define an instance of the class.
    double rectWidth,       // Local variable for width.
           rectLength;      // Local variable for length.
```

(program continues)

Program 12-1 *(continued)*

```
    // Get the rectangle's width and length from the user.
    cout << "This program will calculate the area of a\n";
    cout << "rectangle. What is the width? ";
    cin >> rectWidth;
    cout << "What is the length? ";
    cin >> rectLength;

    // Store the width and length of the rectangle
    // in the box object.
    box.setWidth(rectWidth);
    box.setLength(rectLength);

    // Display the rectangle's data.
    cout << "Here is the rectangle's data:\n";
    cout << "Width: " << box.getWidth() << endl;
    cout << "Length: " << box.getLength() << endl;
    cout << "Area: " << box.getArea() << endl;
    return 0;
}
```

Program Output with Example Input Shown in Bold
```
This program will calculate the area of a
rectangle. What is the width? 10 [Enter]
What is the length? 5 [Enter]
Here is the rectangle's data:
Width: 10
Length: 5
Area: 50
```

Pointers to Objects

A pointer to a class object can also be defined. The following statement defines the pointer boxPtr:

```
    Rectangle *boxPtr;
```

Assuming box is an object of the Rectangle class, boxPtr can be made to point to it with the following statement:

```
    boxPtr = &box;
```

The boxPtr pointer can then be used to call box's member functions by using the -> operator. The following statements show examples.

```
    boxPtr->setWidth(12.5);          // Set width to 12.5.
    boxPtr->setLength(4.8);          // Set length to 4.8.
    x = boxPtr->getWidth();          // Assign the width to x.
    cout << boxPtr->getLength();     // Display the length.
    cout << boxPtr->getArea();       // Display the area.
```

Checkpoint [12.1–12.3]

12.1 TRUE or FALSE: You must declare all private members of a class before the public members.

12.2 Which of the following shows the correct use of the scope resolution operator in a member function definition?

A) `InvItem::void setOnHand(int units)`

B) `void InvItem::setOnHand(int units)`

12.3 An object's private member variables are accessed from outside the object by

A) public member functions

B) any function

C) the dot operator

D) the scope resolution operator

12.4 Assuming that `soap` is an instance of the `InvItem` class, which of the following is a valid call to the `setOnHand` member function?

A) `setOnHand(20);`

B) `soap::setOnHand(20);`

C) `soap.setOnHand(20);`

D) `soap:setOnHand(20);`

12.5 Complete the following code skeleton to declare a class named `Date`. The class should contain variables and functions to store and retrieve a date in the form 4/2/03.

```
class Date
{
    private:

    public:

}
```

12.4 Why Have Private Members?

CONCEPT In object-oriented programming, an object should protect its important data by making it private and providing a public interface to access that data.

You might be questioning the rationale behind making the member variables in the Rectangle class private. You might also be questioning why member functions were defined for such simple tasks as setting variables and getting their contents. After all, if the member variables were declared as public, the member functions wouldn't be needed.

As mentioned earlier in this chapter, classes usually have variables and functions that are meant only to be used internally. They are not intended to be accessed by statements outside the class. This protects critical data from being accidentally modified or used in a way that might adversely affect the behavior of the object. When a member variable is declared as private, the only way for an application to store values in the variable is through a public member function. Likewise, the only way for an application to retrieve the contents of a private member variable is through a public member function. In essence, the public members become an interface to the object. They are the only members that may be accessed by any application that uses the object.

In the Rectangle class, the member variables length and width might be considered critical. Therefore, they are declared as private and an interface is constructed with the public member functions.

The public member functions can be written to filter out invalid data. For example, look at the following version of the setWidth member function.

```
bool Rectangle::setWidth(double w)
{
    bool status;      // Flag variable.

    if (w < 0)
    {
        width = 0.0;
        status = false;
    }
    else
    {
        width = w;
        status = true;
    }
    return status;
}
```

Appendix D on the Student CD shows how to denote private and public members in UML.

Notice that this function returns a bool value. When a negative number is passed to this function, it sets the flag variable status to false and then assigns 0.0 to the width member variable. Otherwise, the value passed to the function is assigned to the width member variable and the status variable is set to true. The function returns the value of the status variable, which indicates whether the operation was carried out. The following code demonstrates how a member function is called.

```cpp
if (!box.setWidth(rectWidth))
        cout << "Invalid value for width.\n";
```

The setLength member function could be written in a similar fashion, as shown here.

```cpp
bool Rectangle::setLength(double len)
{
    bool status;        // Flag variable.

    if (len < 0)
    {
        length = 0.0;
        status = false;
    }
    else
    {
        length = len;
        status = true;
    }
    return status;
}
```

A member function that stores a value in a private member variable is sometimes referred to as a *set function* because it sets the value of the variable. A member function that retrieves a value from a private member variable is sometimes referred to as a *get function* because it gets the value of the member variable. When designing classes, it is a common practice to make all member variables private, and to provide public set and get member functions for accessing those variables.

12.5 Focus on Software Engineering: *Some Design Considerations*

CONCEPT Usually class declarations are stored in their own header files. Member function definitions are stored in their own .cpp files.

In Program 12-1, the class declaration, member function definitions, and application program are all stored in one file. A more conventional way of designing C++ programs is to store class declarations and member function definitions in their own separate files. Typically, program components are stored in the following fashion:

◆ Class declarations are stored in their own header files. A header file that contains a class declaration is called a *class specification* file. The name of the class specification file is usually the same as the name of the class, with a .h extension. For example, the Rectangle class would be declared in the file rectangle.h.

◆ The member function definitions for a class are stored in a separate .cpp file which is called the *class implementation* file. The file usually has the same name as the class, with the .cpp extension. For example the Rectangle class's member functions would be defined in the file rectangle.cpp.

◆ Any program that uses the class should #include the class's header file. The class's .cpp file (that which contains the member function definitions) should be compiled and linked with the main program. This process can be automated with a project or make utility.

Program 12-2 organizes the code by storing the class declaration and member function definitions in their own files.

 Note: The #ifndef directive shown in the next program is called an *include guard*, and allows the program to be conditionally compiled. This prevents a header file from accidentally being included more than once.

In the Rectangle.h file, the #ifndef directive checks for the existence of a constant, RECTANGLE_H. if the constant has not been defined, it is immediately defined and the file is included. If the constant has been defined, everything between the #ifndef and #endif directives is skipped.

Program 12-2

***Contents of* Rectangle.h**
```
// Specification file for the Rectangle class.
#ifndef RECTANGLE_H
#define RECTANGLE_H

// Rectangle class declaration.

class Rectangle
{
    private:
        double width;
        double length;
    public:
        bool setWidth(double);
        bool setLength(double);
        double getWidth();
        double getLength();
        double getArea();
};

#endif
```

(program continues)

Program 12-2 *(continued)*

Contents of `Rectangle.cpp`

```cpp
// Implementation file for the Rectangle class.
#include "Rectangle.h"

//*****************************************************************
// setWidth sets the value of the member variable width. If the  *
// argument is negative, it assigns 0.0 to width and returns     *
// false. If the argument is non-negative, it assigns it to      *
// width and returns true.                                       *
//*****************************************************************

bool Rectangle::setWidth(double w)
{
    bool status;        // Flag variable

    if (w < 0)
    {
        width = 0.0;
        status = false;
    }
    else
    {
        width = w;
        status = true;
    }
    return status;
}


//*****************************************************************
// setLength sets the value of the member variable length. If the *
// argument is negative, it assigns 0.0 to length and returns     *
// false.  If the argument is non-negative, it assigns it to      *
// length and returns true.                                       *
//*****************************************************************

bool Rectangle::setLength(double len)
{
    bool status;        // Flag variable.

    if (len < 0)
    {
        length = 0.0;
        status = false;
    }
```

(program continues)

Program 12-2 *(continued)*

```
    else
    {
        length = len;
        status = true;
    }
    return status;
}

//*************************************************************
// getWidth returns the value in the private member width.   *
//*************************************************************

double Rectangle::getWidth()
{
    return width;
}
//*************************************************************
// getLength returns the value in the private member length. *
//*************************************************************

double Rectangle::getLength()
{
    return length;
}

//*************************************************************
// getArea returns the product of width times length.    *
//*************************************************************

double Rectangle::getArea()
{
    return width * length;
}
```

Contents of the main program, `Pr12-2.cpp`

```
// This program uses the Rectangle class's specification
// and implementation files.
#include <iostream>
#include "Rectangle.h"    // Contains the class declaration.
using namespace std;

int main()
{
    Rectangle box;        // Define an instance of the class.
    double rectWidth,     // Local varibale for width.
        rectLength;       // Local variable for length.
```

(program continues)

Program 12-2 *(continued)*

```
// Get the rectangle's width and length from the user.
cout << "This program will calculate the area of a\n";
cout << "rectangle. What is the width? ";
cin >> rectWidth;
cout << "What is the length? ";
cin >> rectLength;

if (!box.setWidth(rectWidth))          // Store the width.
    cout << "Invalid value for width.\n";
else if (!box.setLength(rectLength))   // Store the length.
    cout << "Invalid value for length.\n";

else
{
    // Display the rectangle's data.
    cout << "Here is the rectangle's data:\n";
    cout << "Width: " << box.getWidth() << endl;
    cout << "Length: " << box.getLength() << endl;
    cout << "Area: " << box.getArea() << endl;
}
    return 0;
}
```

Notice that Program 12-2 uses the following #include directive to include the contents of the Rectangle.h header file:

```
#include "Rectangle.h"
```

The name of the header file is enclosed in double-quote characters (" ") instead of angled brackets (< >). When you are including a C++ system header file, such as iostream, you enclose the name of the file in angled brackets. This indicates that the file is located in the compiler's *include file directory*. The include file directory is the directory or folder where all of the standard C++ header files are located. When you are including a header file that you have written, such as a class specification file, you enclose the name of the file in double-quote characters. This indicates that the file is located in the current project directory.

Table 12-4 summarizes how the different files of Program 12-2 are organized and compiled on a typical Windows computer.

Performing I/O in a Class Object

Another important class design issue is the use of cin and cout in member functions. Notice that none of the Rectangle class's member functions use cin or cout. This is so anyone who writes a program that uses the Rectangle class will not be locked into the way the class performs input or

Table 12-4

`Rectangle.h`	Contains the declaration of the `Rectangle` class. This file is included by `Rectangle.cpp` and `Pr12-2.cpp`.
`Rectangle.cpp`	Contains the `Rectangle` class's member function definitions. This file is compiled to an object file such as `Rectangle.obj`.
`Pr12-2.cpp`	Contains function `main`. This file is compiled to an object file, such as `Pr12-2.obj`, which is linked with `Rectangle.cpp`'s object file to form an executable file.
	`Rectangle.cpp` is compiled and `Rectangle.obj` is created.
	`Pr12-2.cpp` is compiled and `Pr12-2.obj` is created.
	`Pr12-2.obj` and `Rectangle.obj` are linked to make the executable file `Pr12-2.exe`.

output. Unless a class is specifically designed to perform I/O, operations like user input and output are best left to the person designing the application. Classes should provide member functions for retrieving any important data without displaying them on the screen. Likewise, they should provide member functions that store data into private member variables without using `cin`.

Note: There are instances where it is appropriate for a class to perform I/O. For example, a class might be designed to display a menu on the screen and get the user's selection. Another example is a class designed to handle a program's file I/O. Classes that hold and manipulate data, however, should not be tied to any particular I/O routines. This will make them more versatile.

12.6 Focus on Software Engineering: *Using Private Member Functions*

CONCEPT A private member function may only be called from a function that is a member of the same class.

Sometimes a class will contain one or more member functions necessary for internal processing, but not useful to the program outside the class. In some cases a class may contain member functions that initialize member variables or destroy their contents. Those functions should not be accessible by an external part of program because they may be called at the wrong time. In these cases, the member functions should be declared as `private`. When a member function is declared as `private`, it may only be called internally.

For example, consider the following `TestGrade` class. This class holds a numeric test score in the range of 0 through 100 and determines a letter grade for the test.

```
// TestGrade class declaration.

class TestGrade
{
private:
    double score;                      // Holds the numeric score.
    char letterGrade;                  // Holds the letter grade.
    void determineLetterGrade();       // Determines the letter grade.
public:
    bool setScore(double);             // Sets the numeric score.
    double getScore();                 // Returns the numeric score.
    char getLetterGrade();             // Returns the letter grade.
};
```

Notice that the class has three private members: score, which is a double variable, letterGrade, which is a char variable, and determineLetterGrade, which is a function. Because determine-LetterGrade is a private member function, it can be called only by statements in functions that are also members of the TestGrade class. Here is the code for the determineLetterGrade function.

```
void TestGrade::determineLetterGrade()
{
    if (score >= 90 && score <= 100)
        letterGrade = 'A';
    else if (score >= 80 && score < 90)
        letterGrade = 'B';
    else if (score >= 70 && score < 80)
        letterGrade = 'C';
    else if (score >= 60 && score < 70)
        letterGrade = 'D';
    else
        letterGrade = 'F';
}
```

Although this function doesn't do anything destructive, it makes sense that this function should execute automatically when the score variable is set. The function is called by the public member function setScore, which follows.

```
bool TestGrade::setScore(double s)
{
    bool status;                // Flag variable.

    if (s < 0 || s > 100)
    {
        score = 0.0;
        status = false;
    }
    else
    {
```

```
            score = s;
            determineLetterGrade();
            status = true;
        }

        return status;
    }
```

Program 12-3 demonstrates this class.

Program 12-3

Contents of `TestGrade.h`

```
// Specification file for the TestGrade class.

#ifndef TESTGRADE_H
#define TESTGRADE_H

// TestGrade class declaration.

class TestGrade
{
private:
    double score;                  // Holds the numeric score.
    char letterGrade;              // Holds the letter grade.
    void determineLetterGrade();   // Determines the letter grade.
public:
    bool setScore(double);         // Sets the numeric score.
    double getScore();             // Returns the numeric score.
    char getLetterGrade();         // Returns the letter grade.
};

#endif
```

Contents of `TestGrade.cpp`

```
// Implementation file for the TestGrade class.
#include "TestGrade.h"

//*********************************************************
// The determineLetterGrade function is a private member.*
// It determines the letter grade, which is based on      *
// the numeric score. The letter grade is stored in       *
// the letterGrade member variable.                       *
//*********************************************************
```

(program continues)

Program 12-3 *(continued)*

```cpp
void TestGrade::determineLetterGrade()
{
    if (score >= 90 && score <= 100)
        letterGrade = 'A';
    else if (score >= 80 && score < 90)
        letterGrade = 'B';
    else if (score >= 70 && score < 80)
        letterGrade = 'C';
    else if (score >= 60 && score < 70)
        letterGrade = 'D';
    else
        letterGrade = 'F';
}

//*****************************************************
// The setScore function sets the value of the score  *
// member variable. If the argument is outside the    *
// range of 0 through 100, score is set to 0.0 and    *
// the function returns false. If the argument is a   *
// valid test score, it is assigned to score and the  *
// function returns true.                             *
//*****************************************************

bool TestGrade::setScore(double s)
{
    bool status;        // Flag variable.

    if (s < 0 || s > 100)
    {
        score = 0.0;
        status = false;
    }

    else
    {
        score = s;
        determineLetterGrade();
        status = true;
    }

    return status;
}
```

(program continues)

Program 12-3 *(continued)*

```
//*****************************************************
// The getScore function returns the value in the     *
// score member variable.                             *
//*****************************************************

double TestGrade::getScore()
{
    return score;
}

//*****************************************************
// The getLetterGrade function returns the value in   *
// the letterGrade member variable.                   *
//*****************************************************

char TestGrade::getLetterGrade()
{
    return letterGrade;
}
```

Contents of the main program, `Pr12-3.cpp`
```
// This program demonstrates a class with a private member function.
#include <iostream>
#include "TestGrade.h"
using namespace std;

int main()
{
    double examScore;
    TestGrade finalExam;

    // Get the exam score from the user.
    cout << "Enter your final exam numeric score: ";
    cin >> examScore;

    if (!finalExam.setScore(examScore))
        cout << "That is not a valid exam score.\n";
    else
    {
        cout << "Your numeric score is: ";
        cout << finalExam.getScore() << endl;
        cout << "Your letter grade is: ";
        cout << finalExam.getLetterGrade() << endl;
    }
    return 0;
}
```

Program 12-3 *(continued)*

Program Output with Example Input Shown in Bold
```
Enter your final exam numeric score: 87.6 [Enter]
Your numeric score is: 87.6
Your letter grade is: B
```

12.7 Inline Member Functions

CONCEPT When the body of a member function is written inside a class declaration, it is declared inline.

When the body of a member function is small, it is usually more convenient to place the function's definition, instead of its prototype, in the class declaration. For example, in the Rectangle class the member functions getWidth, getLength, and getArea each have only one statement. The class could easily be declared as follows:

```
// Rectangle class declaration.

class Rectangle
{
    private:
        double width;
        double length;
    public:
        bool setWidth(double);
        bool setLength(double);
        double getWidth()
                { return width; }
        double getLength()
                { return length; }
        double getArea()
                { return width * length; }
};
```

When a member function is defined in the declaration of a class, it is called an *inline function*. Notice that because the function definitions are part of the class, there is no need to use the scope resolution operator and class name in the function header.

Notice that the getWidth, getLength, and getArea functions are declared inline, but the setWidth and setLength functions are not. They still must be defined outside the class declaration.

Inline Functions and Performance

A lot goes on "behind the scenes" each time a function is called. A number of special items, such as the function's return address in the program and the values of arguments, are stored in a section of memory called the *stack*. In addition, local variables are created and a location is reserved for the function's return value. All this overhead, which sets the stage for a function call, takes precious CPU time. Although the time needed is minuscule, it can add up if a function is called many times, as in a loop.

Inline functions are compiled differently than other functions. In the executable code, inline functions aren't "called" in the conventional sense. In a process known as *inline expansion*, the compiler replaces the call to an inline function with the code of the function itself. This means that the overhead needed for a conventional function call isn't necessary for an inline function, and can result in improved performance.* Because the inline function's code can appear multiple times in the executable program, however, the size of the program can increase.†

Checkpoint [12.4–12.7]

12.6 Assume the following class components exist in a program:

BasePay class declaration
BasePay member function definitions
Overtime class declaration
Overtime member function definitions

In what files would you store each of these components?

12.7 What is the advantage of using a private member function?

12.8 What is the disadvantage of using a private member function?

12.9 What is an inline member function?

---

* Because inline functions cause code to increase in size, they can decrease performance on systems that use paging.
† Writing a function inline is a request to the compiler. The compiler will ignore the request if inline expansion is not possible or practical.

12.8 Constructors

CONCEPT A constructor is a member function that is automatically called when a class object is created.

A constructor is a member function that has the same name as the class. It is automatically called when the object is created in memory, or instantiated. It is helpful to think of constructors as initialization routines. They are very useful for initializing member variables or performing other setup operations.

To illustrate how constructors work, look at this Demo class declaration:

```cpp
class Demo
{
public:
    Demo(); // Constructor
};

Demo::Demo()
{
    cout << "Welcome to the constructor!\n";
}
```

The class Demo only has one member: a function also named Demo. This function is the constructor. When a class object is defined, the function Demo is automatically called. This is illustrated in Program 12-4.

 Appendix D on the Student CD shows how to represent a contructor in UML.

Program 12-4

```cpp
// This program demonstrates a constructor.
#include <iostream>
using namespace std;

// Demo class declaration.

class Demo
{
public:
    Demo();            // Constructor
};

Demo::Demo()
{
    cout << "Welcome to the constructor!\n";
}
```

(program continues)

Program 12-4 *(continued)*

```
//*****************************************
// Function main.                          *
//*****************************************

int main()
{
    Demo demoObj;      // Define a Demo object;

    cout << "This program demonstrates an object\n";
    cout << "with a constructor.\n";
    return 0;
}
```

Program Output
```
Welcome to the constructor!
This program demonstrates an object
with a constructor.
```

Notice that the constructor's function header looks different than that of a regular member function. There is no return type—not even void. This is because constructors are not executed by explicit function calls and cannot return a value. The function header of a constructor's external definition takes the following form:

<*ClassName*>::<*ClassName*> (*ParameterList*)

In Program 12-4, demoObject's constructor executes automatically when the object is defined. Because the object is defined before the cout statements in function main, the constructor displays its message first. Program 12-5 further illustrates when a constructor executes. The object demoObject is defined between two cout statements.

 Note: When a constructor does not have to accept arguments, it is called a *default constructor*. Like regular functions, constructors may accept arguments, have default arguments, be declared inline, and be overloaded. (You will see examples of these later in this chapter.)

Program 12-6 shows a more practical use of a constructor: to dynamically allocate memory. The InventoryItem class holds simple data about an item in an inventory. A description of the item is stored in the dynamically allocated array description, and the number of units on hand is stored in Units. The constructor allocates memory for the description array, enough for 51 characters. (Notice that the constructor is inline.)

Program 12-5

```cpp
// This program demonstrates a constructor.
#include <iostream>
using namespace std;

// Demo class declaration.

class Demo
{
public:
    Demo();     // Constructor
};

Demo::Demo()
{
    cout << "Welcome to the constructor!\n";
}

//****************************************
// Function main.                        *
//****************************************

int main()
{
    cout << "This is displayed before the object is created\n\n";
    Demo demoObject;// Define a Demo object.
    cout << "\nThis is displayed after the object is created.\n";
    return 0;
}
```

Program Output
```
This is displayed before the object is created

Welcome to the constructor!

This is displayed after the object is created.
```

 Note: The class in Program 12-6 allocates memory, but does not free it when it is no longer needed. In the next section we will add the capability of automatically freeing the allocated memory when the object goes out of existence.

Program 12-6

```cpp
// This program shows a class constructor dynamically allocating memory.
#include <iostream>
#include <cstring>
using namespace std;

const int DEFAULT_SIZE = 51;

// InventoryItem class declaration.

class InventoryItem
{
    private:
        char *description;
        int units;
    public:
        InventoryItem()
            { description = new char [DEFAULT_SIZE]; }
        void setDescription(char *d)
            { strcpy(description, d); }
        void setUnits(int u)
            { units = u; }
        const char *getDescription()
            { return description; }
        int getUnits()
            { return units; }
};

//*******************************************
// Function main.                           *
//*******************************************

int main()
{
    InventoryItem stock;

    stock.setDescription("Wrench");
    stock.setUnits(20);
    cout << "Item Description: " << stock.getDescription() << endl;
    cout << "Units on hand: " << stock.getUnits() << endl;
    return 0;
}
```

Program Output
```
Item Description: Wrench
Units on hand: 20
```

Note: In Program 12-7, the `getDescription` member function returns a `const char` pointer. This is a security measure. It prevents any code that calls the function from changing the string that the return value points to.

Constructors and Dynamically Allocated Class Objects

Class objects themselves may be dynamically allocated in memory. For example, assume the following pointer is defined in a program:

```
InventoryItem *objectPtr;
```

This code defines `objectPtr` as an `InventoryItem` pointer. It can hold the address of any `InventoryItem` object. It may also be used to dynamically allocate an `InventoryItem` object, as shown in the following code.

```
objectPtr = new InventoryItem;
```

When the `InventoryItem` object is created in memory by the new operator, its constructor is automatically executed.

12.9 Destructors

CONCEPT A destructor is a member function that is automatically called when an object is destroyed.

Destructors are member functions with the same name as the class, preceded by a tilde character (~). For example, the destructor for the `Rectangle` class would be named ~`Rectangle`.

Destructors are automatically called when an object is destroyed. In the same way that constructors set things up when an object is created, destructors perform shutdown procedures when the object goes out of existence. For example, a common use of destructors is to free memory that was dynamically allocated by the class object.

Program 12-7 shows a simple class with a constructor and a destructor. It illustrates when, during the program's execution, each is called.

Program 12-7

```cpp
// This program demonstrates a destructor.
#include <iostream>
using namespace std;

class Demo
{
public:
    Demo();        // Constructor
    ~Demo();       // Destructor
};
```

(program continues)

Program 12-7 *(continued)*

```cpp
Demo::Demo()
{
    cout << "Welcome to the constructor!\n";
}

Demo::~Demo()
{
    cout << "The destructor is now running.\n";
}

//***********************************************
// Function main.                               *
//***********************************************

int main()
{
    Demo demoObject;      // Define a demo object;

    cout << "This program demonstrates an object\n";
    cout << "with a constructor and destructor.\n";
    return 0;
}
```

Program Output
```
Welcome to the constructor!
This program demonstrates an object
with a constructor and destructor.
The destructor is now running.
```

In Program 12-7, the InventoryItem class has a constructor that allocates memory, but doesn't free the memory when it is no longer needed. The class has been modified in Program 12-9 with the addition of a destructor that frees the allocated memory. Notice that the destructor is written inline.

Program 12-8

```cpp
// This program demonstrates a class with a destructor.
#include <iostream>
#include <cstring>
using namespace std;
```

(program continues)

Program 12-8 *(continued)*

```cpp
const int DEFAULT_SIZE = 51;

// InventoryItem class declaration.

class InventoryItem
{
   private:
      char *description;
      int units;
   public:
      InventoryItem()          // Constructor
         { description = new char [DEFAULT_SIZE]; }
      ~InventoryItem()          // Destructor
         { delete [] description; }
      void setDescription(char *d)
         { strcpy(description, d); }
      void setUnits(int u)
         { units = u; }
      const char *getDescription()
         { return description; }
      int getUnits()
         { return units; }
};

//*********************************************
// Function main.                             *
//*********************************************

int main()
{
   InventoryItem stock;

   stock.setDescription("Wrench");
   stock.setUnits(20);
   cout << "Item Description: " << stock.getDescription() << endl;
   cout << "Units on hand: " << stock.getUnits() << endl;
   return 0;
}
```

Program Output
```
Item Description: Wrench
Units on hand: 20
```

Destructors and Dynamically Allocated Class Objects

If a class object has been dynamically allocated by the new operator, its memory should be released when the object is no longer needed. For example, in the following code objectPtr is a pointer to a dynamically allocated InventoryItem class object.

```
InventoryItem *objectPtr;      // Define an InventoryItem pointer.
objectPtr = new InventoryItem; // Dynamically create an InventoryItem object.
```

The following statement shows the delete operator being used to destroy the dynamically created object.

```
delete objectPtr;
```

When the object pointed to by objectPtr is destroyed, its destructor is automatically called.

In addition to the fact that destructors are automatically called when an object is destroyed, the following points should be mentioned:

- ◆ Like constructors, destructors have no return type.

- ◆ Destructors cannot accept arguments, so they never have a parameter list.

12.10 Constructors That Accept Arguments

CONCEPT Data can be passed as arguments to an object's constructor.

Often data must be passed to a constructor in order for the object to be properly initialized. For example, consider the Sale class declared here. It is a simple class designed to calculate the total of a retail sale.

```
class Sale
{
private:
    double taxRate;
    double total;
public:
    Sale(double rate)          // Constructor
        { taxRate = rate; }
    double getTaxRate()
        { return taxRate; }
    void calcSale(double cost)
        { total = cost + (cost * taxRate); }
    double getTotal()
        { return total; }
};
```

The constructor's purpose is to establish the sales tax rate. The member variable taxRate is used by the calcSale function to compute the total of the sale. The constructor accepts an argument, which is stored in the taxRate member variable. Because the constructor is automatically called when the object is created, the argument is passed to it as part of the object definition. Here is an example:

```
Sale cashier(0.06);
```

This statement defines `cashier` as an instance of the `Sale` class. The constructor is called with the value 0.06 passed as its argument. As with all function calls, the argument is copied into the constructor's parameter variable. The contents of the parameter is then assigned by the constructor to the member variable `taxRate`. Program 12-9 shows the class in use.

Program 12-9

Contents of `Sale.h`
```
// Specification file for the Sale class.
#ifndef SALE_H
#define SALE_H

class Sale
{
private:
    double taxRate;
    double total;
public:
    Sale(double rate)        // Constructor
        { taxRate = rate; }
    double getTaxRate()
        { return taxRate; }
    void calcSale(double cost)
        { total = cost + (cost * taxRate); }
    double getTotal()
        { return total; }
};

#endif
```

Contents of main program, `Pr12-9.cpp`
```
// This program demonstrates passing an argument to a constructor.
#include <iostream>
#include <iomanip>
#include "Sale.h"
using namespace std;

int main()
{
    Sale cashier(0.06);       // 6% sales tax rate
    double amount;
```

(program continues)

Program 12-9 *(continued)*

```
    cout << fixed << showpoint << setprecision(2);
    cout << "Enter the amount of the sale: ";
    cin >> amount;
    cashier.calcSale(amount);
    cout << "The total of the sale is $";
    cout << cashier.getTotal() << endl;
    return 0;
}
```

Program Output with Example Input Shown in Bold
```
Enter the amount of the sale: 125.00 [Enter]
The total of the sale is $132.50
```

Constructors may also have default arguments. Recall from Chapter 6 that default arguments are passed to parameters automatically if no argument is provided in the function call. The default value is listed in the parameter list of the function prototype or definition. Here is the Sale class, with its constructor modified to accept a default argument:

```
class Sale
{
private:
    double taxRate;
    double total;
public:
    Sale(double rate = 0.05)       // Constructor with default argument
        { taxRate = rate; }
    double getTaxRate()
        { return taxRate; }
    void calcSale(double cost)
        { total = cost + (cost * taxRate); }
    double getTotal()
        { return total; }
};
```

If an object of the Sale class is defined with no argument passed to the constructor, the constructor will be called with the default argument 0.05. This is demonstrated in Program 12-10.

Program 12-10

Contents of *Sale2.h*
```
// Specification file for the Sale class.
#ifndef SALE_H
#define SALE_H
```

(program continues)

Program 12-10 *(continued)*

```cpp
class Sale
{
private:
    double taxRate;
    double total;
public:
    Sale(double rate = 0.05)        // Constructor with default argument
        { taxRate = rate; }
    double getTaxRate()
        { return taxRate; }
    void calcSale(double cost)
        { total = cost + (cost * taxRate); }
    double getTotal()
        { return total; }
};

#endif
```

Contents of main program, Pr13-10.cpp

```cpp
// This program demonstrates a constructor with a default argument.
#include <iostream>
#include <iomanip>
#include "Sale2.h"
using namespace std;

int main()
{
    Sale cashier1;              // Use default sales tax rate
    Sale cashier2(0.06);        // Use 6% sales tax rate
    double amount;

    // Get the amount of the sale from the user.
    cout << fixed << showpoint << setprecision(2);
    cout << "Enter the amount of the sale: ";
    cin >> amount;

    // Pass the amount to each class object.
    cashier1.calcSale(amount);
    cashier2.calcSale(amount);

    // Display the total as calculated by cashier1,
    // using the 5% default tax rate.
    cout << "With a 0.05 sales tax rate, the total\n";
    cout << "of the sale is $";
    cout << cashier1.getTotal() << endl;
```

(program continues)

Program 12-10 *(continued)*

```
    // Display the total as calculated by cashier2,
    // using a 6% tax rate.
    cout << "With a 0.06 sales tax rate, the total\n";
    cout << "of the sale is $";
    cout << cashier2.getTotal() << endl;
    return 0;
}
```

Program Output with Example Input Shown in Bold
```
Enter the amount of the sale: 125.00 [Enter]
With a 0.05 sales tax rate, the total
of the sale is $131.25
With a 0.06 sales tax rate, the total
of the sale is $132.50
```

 Note: It was mentioned earlier that when a constructor doesn't have to accept arguments, it's called a *default constructor*. If a constructor has default arguments for all its parameters, it can be called with no explicit arguments. It, then, becomes the default constructor.

 ## Checkpoint [12.8-12.10]

12.10 Briefly describe the purpose of a constructor.

12.11 Briefly describe the purpose of a destructor.

12.12 A member function that is never declared with a return data type, but that may have arguments is

    A) The constructor
    B) The destructor
    C) Both the constructor and the destructor
    D) Neither the constructor nor the destructor

12.13 Destructor function names always start with

    A) A number
    B) Tilde character (~)
    C) A data type name
    D) None of the above

12.14 A constructor that requires no arguments is called

    A) A default constructor
    B) An overloaded constructor
    C) A null constructor
    D) None of the above

12.15 TRUE or FALSE: Constructors are never declared with a return data type.

12.16 TRUE or FALSE: Destructors are never declared with a return type.

12.17 TRUE or FALSE: Destructors may take any number of arguments.

12.11   Focus on Software Engineering: *Input Validation Objects*

CONCEPT   This section shows how classes may be designed to validate user input.

As mentioned earlier in this chapter, one application of OOP is to design general-purpose objects that may be used by a variety of applications. An example of such an object is one that performs input validation. For example, assume a program displays a menu that allows the user to select items A, B, C, or D. The program should validate any character entered by the user and only accept one of these four letters. In C++, a class can be designed to handle this type of input validation and then be used in many programs.

The `CharRange` Input Validation Class

Now we will examine the `CharRange` class. An object of the `CharRange` class allows the user to enter a character, then it validates that the character is within a specified range of characters. When the user enters a character outside the designated range, the object displays a user-defined error message and waits for the user to re-enter the character. The code for the class is shown here.

Contents of *Chrange.h*
```
// Specification file for the CharRange class.
#ifndef CHRANGE_H
#define CHRANGE_H

class CharRange
{
private:
    char input;        // To hold the user input
    char lower;        // Lowest valid character
    char upper;        // Highest valid character
    char *errMsg;      // Pointer to user-defined error message
public:
    CharRange(char, char, const char *);
    ~CharRange()
        { delete errMsg; }
```

```cpp
        void setLower(char ch)
            { lower = ch; }
        void setUpper(char ch)
            { upper = ch; }
        char getLower()
            { return lower; }
        char getUpper()
            { return upper; }
        char getChar();
    };

#endif
```

Contents of `Chrange.cpp`

```cpp
// Implementation file for the CharRange class.
#include <iostream>
#include <cstring>    // For strlen and strcpy
#include <cctype>     // For toupper
#include "Chrange.h"
using namespace std;

//*********************************************************
// CharRange constructor. Parameters low and high hold    *
// the lower and upper characters in the range. str       *
// points to a C-string that is an error message to       *
// display when a character outside the range is entered.  *
//*********************************************************

CharRange::CharRange(char low, char high, const char *str)
{
    // Set the lower and upper characters.
    lower = toupper(low);
    upper = toupper(high);

    // Allocate memory for the user-defined error message.
    errMsg = new char[strlen(str) + 1];

    // Copy the user-defined error message to errMsg.
    strcpy(errMsg, str);
}
```

```
//***************************************************************
// getChar member function. This function reads a character   *
// from the keyboard. If the character is less than the       *
// the contents of lower, or greater than the contents of     *
// upper (both private members or the CharRange class), the   *
// error message stored in the errMsg member is displayed,    *
// and another character is read. If the character is within  *
// the range, it is returned from the function.               *
//***************************************************************

char CharRange::getChar()
{
    // Get a character from the keyboard and
    // store it in input.
    cin.get(input);
    cin.ignore();

    // Convert input to uppercase.
    input = toupper(input);

    // If the character is outside the range, display
    // the error message and get another character.
    while (input < lower || input > upper)
    {
        cout << errMsg;
        cin.get(input);
        cin.ignore();
        input = toupper(input);
    }

    // Return the valid character.
    return input;
}
```

Let's look at the class's member functions. The constructor establishes the range of valid characters:

```
CharRange::CharRange(char low, char high, const char *str)
{
    // Set the lower and upper characters.
    lower = toupper(low);
    upper = toupper(high);

    // Allocate memory for the user-defined error message.
    errMsg = new char[strlen(str) + 1];

    // Copy the user-defined error message to errMsg.
    strcpy(errMsg, str);
}
```

The parameters low and high specify the lowest and highest characters in the range of valid characters. For example, if 'X' were passed into low and 'Z' were passed into high, the valid range of characters would X, Y, and Z. The toupper function is used to get the uppercase equivalents of the values in these parameters, which are copied into the private members lower and upper.

The parameter str is a pointer to a char. This parameter points to a user-defined error message that is to be displayed when the user enters an invalid character. The constructor uses the new operator to allocate enough memory to hold the string that str points to, and then copies the string to the allocated memory. The member variable errMsg points to the error message.

Here's an example of how to define an object of the CharRange class:

```
CharRange input('A', 'D', "Enter a character in the range A - D");
```

This statement creates a CharRange object named input. The object allows the user to enter a character in the range A through D (valid characters are A, B, C, and D). If the user enters a character outside this range, the user-defined error message "Enter a character in the range A–D" is displayed and the user is allowed to re-enter the character.

The user input is gathered by the getChar member function:

```cpp
char CharRange::getChar()
{
    // Get a character from the keyboard and
    // store it in input.
    cin.get(input);
    cin.ignore();

    // Convert input to uppercase.
    input = toupper(input);

    // If the character is outside the range, display
    // the error message and get another character.
    while (input < lower || input > upper)
    {
        cout << errMsg;
        cin.get(input);
        cin.ignore();
        input = toupper(input);
    }

    // Return the valid character.
    return input;
}
```

This function reads a character from the keyboard, converts it to uppercase, and validates it. If the character is outside the range specified by the lower and upper variables, the user-defined error message is displayed another character is read.

Note: As mentioned before, you do not always want to use `cin` and `cout` statements in a class's member functions. This, however, is a class that is specifically designed to perform input and output.

Program 12-11 is a simple program that demonstrates the CharRange class. (The CharRange class will be used again in other programs.)

Program 12-11

```cpp
// This program demonstrates the CharRange class.
#include <iostream>
#include "Chrange.h"       // Remember to compile & link Chrange.cpp
using namespace std;

// Error message to be displayed when the user
// enters an invalid character.
const char *msg = "Only enter J, K, L, M, or N: ";

int main()
{
    char ch;                // To hold user input

    // Create an object to check for characters
    // in the range J - N.
    CharRange input('J', 'N', msg);

    cout << "Enter any of the characters J, K, L, M, or N.\n";
    cout << "Entering N will stop this program.\n";
    ch = input.getChar();
    while (ch != 'N')
    {
        cout << "You entered " << ch << endl;
        ch = input.getChar();
    }

    return 0;
}
```

Program Output with Example Input Shown in Bold
```
Enter any of the characters J, K, L, M, or N.
Entering N will stop this program.
```
j [Enter]
```
You entered J
```
k [Enter]
```
You entered K
```
q [Enter]
```
Only enter J, K, L, M, or N: n [Enter]
```

12.12 Overloading Constructors

CONCEPT | More than one constructor may be defined for a class.

Recall from Chapter 6 that when two or more functions share the same name, the function name is said to be overloaded. Multiple functions with the same name may exist in a C++ program, as long as their parameter lists are different.

A class's member functions may be overloaded, including the constructor. One constructor might take an integer argument, for example, while another constructor takes a double. There could even be a third constructor taking two integers. As long as each constructor takes a different list of parameters, the compiler can tell them apart. The InventoryItem class appears here with three constructors:

Contents of *InventoryItem.h*

```
// Specification file for the InventoryItem class.
#ifndef INVENTORYITEM_H
#define INVENTORYITEM_H
#include <cstring>    // Needed for strlen and strcpy

const int DEFAULT_SIZE = 51;

// InventoryItem class declaration.
class InventoryItem
{
   private:
      char *description;
      int units;
   public:
      InventoryItem()                   // Constructor #1
         { description = new char [DEFAULT_SIZE]; }

      InventoryItem(char *desc)         // Constructor #2
         { description = new char [strlen(desc) + 1];
           strcpy(description, desc); }

      InventoryItem(char *desc, int u) // Constructor #3
         { description = new char [strlen(desc) + 1];
           strcpy(description, desc);
           units = u;}

      ~InventoryItem()                  // Destructor
         { delete [] description; }

      void setDescription(char *d)
         { strcpy(description, d); }
```

```
            void setUnits(int u)
               { units = u; }

            const char *getDescription()
               { return description; }

            int getUnits()
               { return units; }
     };
     #endif
```

  Appendix D on the Student CD shows how to represent overloaded constructors in UML.

The first constructor takes no arguments, so it is the default constructor. It sets the description pointer to the address of a dynamically allocated block of memory large enough to hold 51 characters.

The second constructor takes an argument, desc, which is a char pointer. This allows the description of an item to be passed as a C-string argument. This constructor uses the strlen function to get the length of the string that desc points to. A block of memory large enough to hold the string plus a null terminator is allocated and the description pointer is set to its address. The string is then copied to description with the strcpy function.

The third constructor allows an item description and a number of units to be passed as arguments. It has two parameters: desc, a char pointer, and u, an int. As with the second constructor, memory is allocated for description and the string pointed to by the desc parameter is copied to it. The value passed to the u parameter is assigned to units.

Program 12-12 demonstrates the class.

Program 12-12

```
// This program demonstrates a class with overloaded constructors.
#include <iostream>
#include "InventoryItem.h"
using namespace std;

int main()
{
    InventoryItem item1;                // Call the default constructor.
    InventoryItem item2("Wrench");      // Set description.
    InventoryItem item3("Pliers", 10);  // Set description and units.

    // Set the descritption and units for item1.
    item1.setDescription("Hammer");
    item1.setUnits(12);

    // Set the units for item2.
    item2.setUnits(17);
```

(program continues)

Program 12-12 *(continued)*

```
cout << "The following items are in inventory:\n";
// Display the data for item 1.
cout << "Description: " << item1.getDescription() << "\t\t";
cout << "Units on Hand: " << item1.getUnits() << endl;

// Display the data for item 2.
cout << "Description: " << item2.getDescription() << "\t\t";
cout << "Units on Hand: " << item2.getUnits() << endl;

// Display the data for item 3.
cout << "Description: " << item3.getDescription() << "\t\t";
cout << "Units on Hand: " << item3.getUnits() << endl;
return 0;
}
```

Program Output
```
The following items are in inventory:
Description: Hammer            Units on Hand: 12
Description: Wrench            Units on Hand: 17
Description: Pliers            Units on Hand: 10
```

12.13 Only One Default Constructor and One Destructor

When an object is defined without an argument list for its constructor, the compiler automatically calls the default constructor. For this reason, a class may have only one default constructor. If there were more than one constructor that could be called without an argument, the compiler would not know which one to call by default.

Remember, a constructor whose parameters all have a default argument is considered a default constructor. It would be an error to create a constructor that accepts no parameters along with another constructor that has default arguments for all its parameters. In such a case the compiler would not be able to resolve which constructor to execute.

Classes may also only have one destructor. Because destructors take no arguments, the compiler has no way to distinguish different destructors.

12.14 Arrays of Objects

CONCEPT You may define and work with arrays of class objects.

Like any other data type in C++, you can define arrays of class objects. An array of `InventoryItem` objects could be created to represent a business's inventory records. Here is an example of such a definition:

```
InventoryItem inventory[40];
```

This statement defines an array of 40 `InventoryItem` objects. The name of the array is `inventory`, and the default constructor is called for each object in the array.

If you wish to define an array of objects and call a constructor that requires arguments, you must specify the arguments for each object individually in an initializer list. Here is an example:

```
InventoryItem inventory[3] = {"Hammer", "Wrench", "Pliers"};
```

The compiler treats each item in the initializer list as an argument for an array element's constructor. Recall that the second constructor in the `InventoryItem` class declaration takes the item description as an argument. So, this statement defines an array of three objects and calls that constructor for each object. The constructor for `inventory[0]` is called with "Hammer" as its argument, the constructor for `inventory[1]` is called with "Wrench" as its argument, and the constructor for `inventory[2]` is called with "Pliers" as its argument.

 WARNING! If the class does not have a default constructor you must provide an initializer for each object in the array.

If a constructor requires more than one argument, the initializer must take the form of a function call. For example, look at the following definition statement.

```
InventoryItem inventory[3] = { InventoryItem("Hammer", 12),
                               InventoryItem("Wrench", 17),
                               InventoryItem("Pliers", 10) };
```

This statement calls the third constructor in the `InventoryItem` class declaration for each object in the `inventory` array.

It isn't necessary to call the same constructor for each object in an array. For example, look at the following statement.

```
InventoryItem inventory[3] = { "Hammer",
                               InventoryItem("Wrench", 17),
                               "Pliers"};
```

This statement calls the second constructor for `inventory[0]` and `inventory[2]`, and calls the third constructor for `inventory[1]`.

If you do not provide an initializer for all of the objects in an array, the default constructor will be called for each object that does not have an initializer. For example, the following statement defines an array of three objects, but only provides initializers for the first two. The default constructor is called for the third object.

```
InventoryItem inventory[3] = { "Hammer",
                               InventoryItem("Wrench", 17) };
```

In summary, if you use an initializer list for class object arrays, there are three things to remember:

◆ If there is no default constructor you must furnish an initializer for each object in the array.

◆ If there are fewer initializers in the list than objects in the array, the default constructor will be called for all the remaining objects.

◆ If a constructor requires more than one argument, the initializer takes the form of a constructor function call.

Accessing Members of Objects in an Array

Objects in an array are accessed with subscripts, just like any other data type in an array. For example, to call the setUnits member function of inventory[2], the following statement could be used:

```
inventory[2].setUnits(30);
```

This statement sets the units variable of inventory[2] to the value 30. Program 12-13 shows an array of InventoryItem objects being used in a complete program.

Program 12-13

```cpp
// This program demonstrates an array of class objects.
#include <iostream>
#include <iomanip>
#include "InventoryItem.h"
using namespace std;

int main()
{
    const int NUM_ITEMS = 5;
    InventoryItem inventory[NUM_ITEMS] = { InventoryItem("Hammer", 12),
                                    InventoryItem("Wrench", 17),
                                    InventoryItem("Pliers", 10),
                                    InventoryItem("Ratchet", 14),
                                    InventoryItem("Screwdriver", 22)};

    cout << "Inventory Item\t\tUnits On Hand\n";
    cout << "------------------------------------\n";

    for (int i = 0; i < NUM_ITEMS; i++)
    {
        cout << setw(14) << inventory[i].getDescription();
        cout << setw(18) << inventory[i].getUnits() << endl;
    }

    return 0;
}
```

Program 12-13 *(continued)*

Program Output

```
Inventory Item          Units On Hand
- - - - - - - - - - - - - - - - - - - - - - - - - - - -
          Hammer            12
          Wrench            17
          Pliers            10
         Ratchet            14
     Screwdriver            22
```

 ## Checkpoint [12.11–12.14]

12.18 What will the following program display on the screen?

```cpp
#include <iostream>
using namespace std;

class Package
{
private:
    int value;
public:
    Package()
        { value = 7; cout << value << endl; }
    Package(int v)
        { value = v; cout << value << endl; }
    ~Package()
        { cout << value << endl; }
};

int main()
{
    Package obj1(4);
    Package obj2();
    Package obj3(2);
    return 0;
}
```

 See the CaseStudies.pdf file on the accompanying CD for this chapter's case studies.

12.15 Focus on Object-Oriented Programming: *Creating an Abstract Array Data Type*

CONCEPT The absence of array bounds checking in C++ is a source of potential hazard for many programmers. In this section we examine a simple integer list class that provides bounds checking.

One of the benefits of object-oriented programming is the ability to create abstract data types that are improvements on built-in data types. As you know, arrays provide no bounds checking in C++. You can, however, create a class that has array-like characteristics and performs bounds checking. For example, look at the following IntList class.

Contents of *IntList.h*

```cpp
// Specification file for the the IntList class.
#ifndef INTLIST_H
#define INTLIST_H

class IntList
{
private:
    int *list;              // Pointer to the array.
    int numElements;        // Number of elements.
    bool isValid(int);      // Validates subscripts.
public:
    IntList(int);           // Constructor
    ~IntList();             // Destructor
    bool set(int, int);     // Sets an element to a value.
    bool get(int, int&);    // Returns an element.
};

#endif
```

Contents of *IntList.cpp*

```cpp
// Implementation file for the IntList class.
#include "IntList.h"

//***********************************
// Constructor.                     *
// Each element in the list is      *
// set to zero.                     *
//***********************************
```

```
IntList::IntList(int size)
{
    list = new int[size];
    numElements = size;
    for (int ndx = 0; ndx < size; ndx++)
        list[ndx] = 0;
}

//************************************
// Destructor.                       *
// Releases the memory allocated for *
// the array.                        *
//************************************

IntList::~IntList()
{
    delete [] list;
}

//**********************************************
// isValid member function.                    *
// This private member functon returns true    *
// if the argument is a valid subscript into   *
// the list. It returns false otherwise, and   *
// displays an error message.                  *
//**********************************************

bool IntList::isValid(int element)
{
    bool status;

    if (element < 0 || element >= numElements)
        status = false;
    else
        status = true;
    return status;
}

//**********************************************
// set member function.                        *
// Stores a value in a specific element        *
// of the list. If the value passed to         *
// element is a valid subscript, the           *
// function returns true. Otherwise, it        *
// returns false.                              *
//**********************************************
```

```cpp
bool IntList::set(int element, int value)
{
    bool status;

    if (isValid(element))
    {
        list[element] = value;
        status = true;
    }
    else
        status = false;
    return status;
}

//********************************************************
// get member function.                                 *
// Retrieves the value stored in the element            *
// specified by the argument element. If the            *
// element is a valid subscript, the retrieved          *
// value is stored in value and the function            *
// returns true. If element is an invalid subscript,    *
// the function returns false.                          *
//********************************************************

bool IntList::get(int element, int &value)
{
    bool status;

    if (isValid(element))
    {
        value = list[element];
        status = true;
    }
    else
        status = false;
    return status;
}
```

The IntList class allows you to store and retrieve numbers in a dynamically-allocated array of integers. Here is a synopsis of the members.

list   A pointer to an int. This member points to the dynamically-allocated array of integers.

numElements   An integer that holds the number of elements in the dynamically-allocated array.

isValid   This function validates a subscript into the array. It accepts a subscript value as an argument, and returns boolean `true` if the subscript is in the range 0 through numElements - 1. If the value is outside that range, boolean `false` is returned.

Constructor   The class constructor accepts an `int` argument that is the number of elements to allocate for the array. The array is allocated and each element is set to zero.

set   The `set` member function sets a specific element of the `list` array to a value. The first argument is the element subscript, and the second argument is the value to be stored in that element. The function uses `isValid` to validate the subscript. If an invalid subscript is passed to the function, no value is stored in the array and boolean `false` is returned. The function stores the value in the array and returns boolean `true` if the subscript is valid.

get   The `get` member function retrieves a value from a specific element in the `list` array. The first argument is the subscript of the element whose value is to be retrieved. The function uses `isValid` to validate the subscript. If the subscript is valid, the value is copied into the second argument (which is passed to a reference variable), and boolean `true` is returned. If the subscript is invalid, no value is retrieved from the array and boolean `false` is returned.

Program 12-14 demonstrates the class. A loop uses the `set` member to fill the array with nines and prints an asterisk on the screen each time a 9 is successfully stored. Then another loop uses the `get` member to retrieve the values from the array and prints them on the screen. Finally, a statement uses the `set` member to demonstrate the subscript validation by attempting to store a value in element 50.

Program 12-14

```
// This program demonstrates the IntList class.
#include <iostream>
#include "IntList.h"
using namespace std;

int main()
{
    const int SIZE = 20;
    IntList numbers(SIZE);
    int val, x;
```

(program continues)

Program 12-14 *(continued)*

```cpp
    // Store nines in the list and display
    // an asterisk each time a 9 is
    // successfully stored.
    for (x = 0; x < SIZE; x++)
    {
        if (numbers.set(x, 9))
            cout << "* ";
        else
            cout << "Error setting element " << x << endl;
    }
    cout << endl;

    // Display the nines.
    for (x = 0; x < SIZE; x++)
    {
        if (numbers.get(x, val))
            cout << val << " ";
        else
            cout << "Error getting element " << x << endl;
    }
    cout << endl;

    // Attempt to store a value outside
    // the list's bounds.
    if (numbers.set(50, 9))
        cout << "Element 50 successfully set.\n";
    else
        cout << "Error setting element 50." << endl;

    return 0;
}
```

Program Output
```
* * * * * * * * * * * * * * * * * * * *
9 9 9 9 9 9 9 9 9 9 9 9 9 9 9 9 9 9 9 9
Error setting element 50.
```

12.16 Focus on Object-Oriented Programming: *Extending the Abstract Array Data Type*

In the previous section we demonstrated the IntList class, which behaves like an integer array, with the added ability of performing bounds checking. In this section we continue our development of the IntList class by adding the following member functions:

linearSearch   A function that performs a linear search on the array for a specified value. If the value is found in the array, its subscript is returned. If the value is not found in the array, −1 is returned.

binarySearch   A function that performs a binary search on the array for a specified value. If the value is found in the array, its subscript is returned. If the value is not found in the array, –1 is returned.

bubbleSort   A function that uses the bubble sort algorithm to sort the array in ascending order.

selectionSort A function that uses the selection sort algorithm to sort the array in ascending order.

The member functions are implemented as simple modifications of the algorithms presented in Appendix Q on the accompanying CD. The class specification is shown here.

Contents of `IntList2.h`

```cpp
// Specification file for the IntList class.
#ifndef INTLIST_H
#define INTLIST_H

class IntList
{
private:
    int *list;                // Pointer to the array.
    int numElements;          // Number of elements.
    bool isValid(int);        // Validates subscripts.
public:
    IntList(int);             // Constructor
    ~IntList();               // Destructor
    bool set(int, int);       // Sets an element to a value.
    bool get(int, int&);      // Returns an element.
    int linearSearch(int);    // Performs a linear search.
    int binarySearch(int);    // Performs a binary search.
    void bubbleSort();        // Performs a bubble sort.
    void selectionSort();     // Performs a selection sort.
};

#endif
```

The code for the new member functions follows. These are stored in `IntList2.cpp`.

```cpp
//****************************************************
// linearSearch member function.                    *
// performs a linear search on the list for value.  *
// If value is found, its array subscript is returned. *
// Otherwise, -1 is returned indicating the value was *
// not in the array.                                 *
//****************************************************

int IntList::linearSearch(int value)
{
    int status = -1;
```

```
    for (int i = 0; i < numElements; i++)
    {
        if (list[i] == value)
        {
            status =  i;
            break;
        }
    }
    return status;
}

//**********************************************************
// binarySearch member function.                           *
// Performs a binary search on the list for value.         *
// If the value is found, its array subscript is returned. *
// Otherwise, -1 is returned indicating the value was not  *
// in the array.                                           *
//**********************************************************

int IntList::binarySearch(int value)
{
    int first = 0,                      // First element
        last = numElements - 1,         // Last element
        middle,                         // Mid-point of search
        position = -1;                  // Position of search value
    bool found = false;                 // Flag

    // First, sort the list.
    selectionSort();
    while (!found && first <= last)
    {
        middle = (first + last) / 2;    // Calculate mid-point
        if (list[middle] == value)      // If value is found at mid-point
        {
            found = true;
            position = middle;
        }
        else if (list[middle] > value)  // If value is in lower half
            last = middle - 1;
        else
            first = middle + 1;         // If value is in upper half
    }
    return position;
}

//*********************************************
// bubbleSort member function.                *
// Performs an ascending order                *
// bubble sort on list.                       *
//*********************************************
```

```cpp
void IntList::bubbleSort()
{
    int swap, temp;

    do
    {
        swap = 0;
        for (int i = 0; i < (numElements - 1); i++)
        {
                if (list[i] > list[i + 1])
                {
                        temp = list[i];
                        list[i] = list[i + 1];
                        list[i + 1] = temp;
                        swap = 1;
                }
        }
    } while (swap != 0);
}

//*******************************************
// selectionSort member function.          *
// Performs an ascending                    *
// order selection sort on list.           *
//*******************************************

void IntList::selectionSort()
{
    int startScan, minIndex, minValue;

    for (startScan = 0; startScan < (numElements - 1); startScan++)
    {
        minIndex = startScan;
        minValue = list[startScan];
        for(int i = startScan + 1; i < numElements; i++)
        {
                if (list[i] < minValue)
                {
                        minValue = list[i];
                        minIndex = i;
                }
        }
        list[minIndex] = list[startScan];
        list[startScan] = minValue;
    }
}
```

Program 12-15 demonstrates the class's selection sort capability by storing 20 random numbers in the array, displaying them, sorting them, and then displaying them again.

Program 12-15

```
// This program demonstrates the IntList's
// selection sort capability.
#include <iostream>
#include <cstdlib>// For rand
#include "IntList2.h"
using namespace std;

int main()
{
    const int SIZE = 20;
    IntList numbers(SIZE);
    int val, x;

    // Store random numbers in the list.
    for (x = 0; x < SIZE; x++)
    {
        if (!numbers.set(x, rand()))
        {
            cout << "Error storing a value at element "
                << x << endl;
        }
    }

    // Display the numbers
    for (x = 0; x < SIZE; x++)
    {
        if (numbers.get(x, val))
            cout << val << endl;
    }

    cout << "Press ENTER to continue...";
    cin.get();

    // Sort the numbers using selectionSort
    numbers.selectionSort();

    // Display the numbers
    cout << "Here are the sorted values:\n";
    for (x = 0; x < SIZE; x++)
    {
        if (numbers.get(x, val))
            cout << val << endl;
    }
    cout << endl;

    return 0;
}
```

Program 12-15

Program Output
```
41
18467
6334
26500
19169
15724
11478
29358
26962
24464
5705
28145
23281
16827
9961
491
2995
11942
4827
5436
Press ENTER to continue...
Here are the sorted values:
41
491
2995
4827
5436
5705
6334
9961
11478
11942
15724
16827
18467
19169
23281
24464
26500
26962
28145
29358
```

Program 12-16 demonstrates the class's binary search algorithm. As in the previous program, 20 random numbers are generated and stored in the array. The program displays a list of the numbers and asks the user to pick one. The binarySearch function is then used to find that number's subscript position in the sorted array.

Program 12-16

```
// This program demonstrates the IntList's
// binary search capability.
#include <iostream>
#include <cstdlib>// For rand
#include "IntList2.h"
using namespace std;

int main()
{
    const int SIZE=20;
    IntList numbers(SIZE);
    int val, x, searchResults;

    // Store random numbers in the list.
    for (x = 0; x < SIZE; x++)
    {
        if (!numbers.set(x, rand()))
        {
            cout << "Error storing a value at element "
                << x << endl;
        }
    }

    // Display the numbers
    for (x = 0; x < SIZE; x++)
    {
        if (numbers.get(x, val))
            cout << val << endl;
    }

    // Get a value to search for.
    cout << "Enter one of the numbers shown above: ";
    cin >> val;

    // Search for the value.
    cout << "Searching...\n";
    searchResults = numbers.binarySearch(val);

    // Display the results.
    if (searchResults == -1)
        cout << "That value was not found in the array.\n";
    else
    {
        cout << "After the array was sorted, that value\n";
        cout << "is found at subscript " << searchResults << endl;
    }

    return 0;
}
```

Program 12-16

Program Output with Example Input Shown in Bold

```
41
18467
6334
26500
19169
15724
11478
29358
26962
24464
5705
28145
23281
16827
9961
491
2995
11942
4827
5436
Enter one of the numbers shown above: 5705 [Enter]
Searching...
After the array was sorted, that value
is found at subscript 5
```

12.17 If You Plan to Continue in Computer Science: *An Object-Oriented System Development Primer*

CONCEPT Object-oriented systems are developed through two processes: object-oriented analysis and object-oriented design. After reviewing the basics of object-oriented programming, this section briefly discusses each process.

Object Basics

Before discussing specific object-oriented development activities, we must understand the basic object-oriented concepts. In addition, we must be able to differentiate the object-oriented approach from the procedural approach.

Procedural Programming vs. Object-Oriented Programming

There are primarily two methods of programming in use today: *procedural*, and *object-oriented*. The earliest programming languages were procedural. This means that a program is made of one or more *procedures*. A procedure is a set of programming language statements that are executed by the computer, one after the other. The statements might gather input from the user, manipulate data stored in the computer's memory, and perform calculations or any other operation necessary to complete its task. For example, suppose we want the computer to calculate someone's gross pay. Here is a list of things the computer should do:

1. Display a message on the screen asking "How many hours did you work?"

2. Allow the user to enter the number of hours worked. Once the user enters a number, store it in memory.

3. Display a message on the screen asking "How much do you get paid per hour?"

4. Allow the user to enter their hourly pay rate. Once the user enters a number, store it in memory.

5. Once both the number of hours worked, and the hourly pay rate are entered, multiply the two numbers and store the result in memory.

6. Display a message on the screen that tells the amount of money earned. The message must include the result of the calculation performed in step 5.

If the algorithm's six steps are performed in order, one after the other, it will succeed in calculating and displaying the user's gross pay.

Procedural programming was the standard when users were interacting with text-based computer terminals. For example, Figure 12-4 illustrates the screen of an older MS-DOS computer running a program that performs the pay-calculating algorithm. The user has entered the numbers shown in bold.

```
How many hours did you work? 10
How much are you paid per hour? 15
You have earned $150.00
C>_
```

Figure 12-4

In text-based environments using procedural programs, the user responds to the program. Modern operating systems, however, such as Windows 9x, Windows NT, and Windows 2000 use a graphical user interface, or *GUI* (pronounced "gooey"). Although GUIs have made programs friendlier and easier to interact with, they have not simplified the task of programming. GUIs make it necessary for the programmer to create a variety of on-screen elements such as windows, dialog boxes, buttons, menus, and other items. Furthermore, the programmer must write statements that handle the user's interactions with these on-screen elements, in any order they might occur. No longer does the user respond to the program, but the program responds to the user.

This has helped influence the shift from procedural programming to object-oriented programming. Whereas procedural programming is centered on creating procedures, object-oriented programming is centered on creating *objects*. An object is a programming entity that contains data and actions. The data contained in an object is known as the object's *attributes*. The actions, or behaviors, that an object performs are known as the object's *methods*. The object is, conceptually, a self-contained unit consisting of data (attributes) and actions (methods).

Object-oriented programming (OOP) has revolutionized GUI software development. For instance, in a GUI environment, the pay-calculating program might appear as the window shown in Figure 12-5.

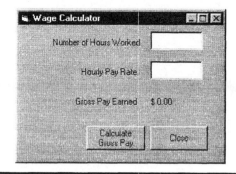

Figure 12-5

This window can be thought of as an object. It contains other objects as well, such as text input boxes, and command buttons. Each object has attributes that determine the object's appearance. For example, look at the command buttons. One has the caption "Calculate Gross Pay" and the other reads "Close". These captions, as well as the buttons' sizes and positions, are attributes of the command button objects. Objects can also hold data that has been entered by the user. For example, one of the text input boxes allows the user to enter the number of hours worked. When this data is entered, it is stored as an attribute of the text input box.

The objects also have actions, or methods. For example, when the user clicks the "Calculate Gross Pay" button with the mouse, one would expect the program to display the amount of gross pay. The "Calculate Gross Pay" button performs this action.

The Benefits of OOP in Non-GUI Environments

The complexity of GUI software development was not the first difficult challenge that procedural programmers faced. Long before Windows and other GUIs, programmers were wrestling with the problems of code/data separation. In procedural programming, there is a distinct separation between data and program code. Data is kept in variables of specific data types, as well as programmer-defined data structures. The program code passes the data to modules that are designed to receive and manipulate it. But, what happens if the format of the data is altered? Quite often, a program's specifications change, resulting in redesigned data structures, changed data types, and additional variables being added to the program. When the structure of the data changes, the modules that operate on the data must also be changed to accept the new format. This results in added work for programmers and a greater opportunity for bugs to appear in the code.

OOP addresses the problem of code/data separation through *encapsulation* and *data hiding*. Encapsulation refers to the combining of data and procedures into a single object. Data hiding refers to an object's ability to hide its data from code that is outside the object. When an object's data is hidden, it can only be accessed through the object's procedures, so an object's procedures provide an interface for programming statements outside the object to access the object's data. This means that programming statements outside the object do not need to know about the type or internal structure of an object's data. They only need to know how to interact with the object's procedures. When a programmer changes the type or structure of an object's internal data, he or she also modifies the object's procedures that provide the interface to the data.

Component Reusability

Another trend in software development that has encouraged the use of OOP is *component reusability*. A component is a software object that performs a specific, well-defined operation or that provides a particular service. The component is not a stand-alone program, but can be used by programs that need the component's service. For example, Sharon is a programmer who has developed a component for rendering 3D images. She is a math whiz and knows a lot about computer graphics, so her component is coded to perform all the necessary 3D mathematical operations and handle the computer's video hardware. Tom, who is writing a program for an architectural firm, needs his application to display 3D images of buildings. Because he is working under a tight deadline, and does not possess a great deal of knowledge about computer graphics, he can use Sharon's component to perform the 3D rendering (for a small fee, of course!).

Component reusability and object-oriented programming technology set the stage for large-scale computer applications to become systems of unique collaborating entities (components).

An Everyday Example of an Object

Think of your alarm clock as an object. It has the following attributes:

- ◆ The current second (a value in the range of 0–59)
- ◆ The current minute (a value in the range of 0–59)
- ◆ The current hour (a value in the range of 1–12)
- ◆ The time the alarm is set for (a valid hour and minute)
- ◆ Whether the alarm is on or off ("on" or "off")

As you can see, the attributes are merely data values that define the alarm clock's "state." The alarm clock also has the following methods:

- ◆ Increment the current second
- ◆ Increment the current minute
- ◆ Increment the current hour
- ◆ Sound alarm
- ◆ Set time
- ◆ Set alarm time

◆ Turn alarm on

◆ Turn alarm off

The methods are all actions that the clock performs. Each method manipulates one or more of the attributes. For example, every second the "Increment the current second" method executes. This changes the value of the current second attribute. If the current second attribute is set to 59 when this method executes, the method is programmed to reset the current second to 0, and then cause the "Increment current minute" method to execute. This method adds 1 to the current minute, unless it is set to 59. In that case, it resets the current minute to 0 and causes the "Increment current hour" method to execute. (It might also be noted that the "Increment current minute" method compares the new time to the alarm time. If the two times match, and the alarm is turned on, the "Sound alarm" method is executed.)

The methods described in the previous paragraph are part of the alarm clock object's private, internal workings. External entities (such as yourself) do not have direct access to the alarm clock's attributes, but these methods do. The object is designed to execute these methods automatically and hide the details from you, the user. These methods, along with the object's attributes, are part of the alarm clock's *private persona*.

Some of the alarm clock's methods are publicly available to you, however. For example, the "Set time" method allows you to set the alarm clock's time. You activate the method by pressing a set of buttons on top of the clock. By using another set of buttons, you can activate the "Set alarm time" method. In addition, another button allows you to execute the "Turn alarm on" and "Turn alarm off" methods. These methods are part of the alarm clock's *public persona*. They define an interface that external entities may use to interact with the object.

Classes and Objects

Specifically, you have learned to create C++ classes in this chapter. In general terms, a *class* is a type, or category of object. A class specifies the attributes and methods that objects of that class posses. A class is not an object, however. An object is a specific instance of a class.

For example, Jessica is an entomologist (someone who studies insects) and enjoys writing computer programs. She designs a program to catalog different types of insects. In the program, she creates a class named Insect, which specifies variables and methods for holding and manipulating data common to all types of insects. The Insect class is not an object, but a data type that specific objects may be created from. Next, she defines a housefly object, which is an instance of the Insect class. The housefly object is an entity that occupies computer memory and stores data about houseflies. It contains the attributes and methods specified by the Insect class.

Object Relationships

Special relationships may exist among objects. The possible relationships may be formally stated as

◆ Access

◆ Ownership

◆ Inheritance

Informally, these three relationships may be described as

◆ Uses a

◆ Has a

◆ Is a

The access relationship

The first relationship, access, allows an object to modify the attributes of another object. Normally, an object has private attributes, which are not accessible to parts of the program outside the object. An access relationship between two objects means that one object has access to the other object's private attributes. When this relationship exists, it can be said that one object *uses* the other. This type of relationship is discussed further in Chapter 13.

The ownership relationship

The second relationship, ownership, means that one object is an attribute of another object. For example, a human resources system might have an object that represents an employee. That object might have, as an attribute, another object that holds the employee's name. It can be said that the employee object has a name object. In OOP terminology, this type of relationship is known as a *whole-part hierarchy*, or *composition*. This is also discussed in Chapter 13.

The inheritance relationship

The third type of relationship is inheritance. Sometimes an object class is based on another class. This means that one class is a specialized case of the other. For example, consider a program that uses classes representing cars, trucks, and jet planes. Although those three types of objects in the real world are very different, they have some common characteristics: They are all modes of transportation, and they all carry some number of passengers. So, each of the three classes could be based on a Vehicle class that has the attributes and behaviors common to all of the classes. This is illustrated in Figure 12-6.

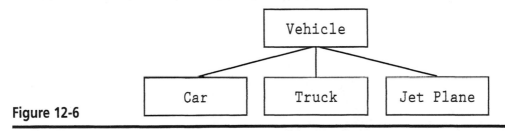

Figure 12-6

In OOP terminology, the Vehicle class is the *base class*. The Car, Truck, and Jet Plane classes are *derived classes*. All of the attributes and behaviors of the Vehicle class are inherited by the Car, Truck, and Jet Plane classes. The relationship implies that a Car is a Vehicle, a Truck is a Vehicle, and a Jet Plane is a Vehicle. Inheritance is discussed in detail in Chapter 14.

In addition to inheriting the attributes and behaviors of the base class, derived classes add their own. For example, the `Car` class might have attributes and behaviors that set and indicate whether it is a sedan or coupe, and the type of engine it has. The `Truck` class might have attributes and behaviors that set and indicate the maximum amount of weight it can carry, and the number of miles it can travel between refueling. The `Jet Plane` class might have attributes and behaviors that set and indicate the plane's altitude and heading. These added components make the derived classes more specialized than the base class. For that reason, this type of relationship is often called a *generalization/specialization hierarchy*.

Messages

We have established the fact that objects have methods, which are behaviors. But how do we make an object perform a behavior? Quite simply, we send the object a *message*, requesting that it execute a particular named method. In C++, messages are actually member function calls. For example, suppose a program has a class named `Shape`, which has a public member function named `calcArea`. The program defines an instance of the `Shape` class named `square`, and contains the following statement:

```
square.calcArea();
```

This statement sends the `calcArea` message to the `square` object.

Polymorphism

The term *polymorphism* means the ability to take many forms. In an object-oriented system, polymorphism means that the same message may be sent to two or more objects, but each object might behave differently. For example, suppose a program uses three classes: `Snail`, `Spider`, and `Cheetah`. All of these classes are derived from another class named `Animal`. Each of the derived classes has a method named `calcSpeed`, which reports the animal's speed. The `Snail` class's `calcSpeed` method reports speed expressed in inches per hour. The `Spider` class's `calcSpeed` method, however, behaves differently. It reports speed in feet per hour. The `Cheetah` class's `calcSpeed` method behaves in yet another way: It reports speed in miles per hour. Because each specialized class has its own unique requirements, it provides a specialized version of the `calcSpeed` method.

Developing an Object-Oriented System

Object-oriented systems development generally consists of two phases: object-oriented analysis, and object-oriented design. A *systems analyst* usually conducts these phases. This section briefly discusses the analyst's activities in each phase.

Object-Oriented Analysis

During object-oriented analysis, the analyst creates a logical design of the system. The logical design specifies what the system is to do, but does not specify how the system should do it. In general, the object-oriented analysis phase consists of the following steps:

1. Examine the problem domain and model the system from within the context of that perspective.

First, you should understand the nature of the problem you are trying to solve. This involves examining the following parameters:

- ◆ The significant events that are part of the problem.
- ◆ The internal parties that will interact with the system.
- ◆ The external parties that will interact with the system.
- ◆ The inputs and outputs required by the system.

Once you have identified the system's major events, internal and external parties, inputs, and outputs, you can create a model. The *Unified Modeling Language* (*UML*) is a tool that is widely used to graphically depict and document system designs. UML specifies a number of diagrams for modeling the various parts of a system. One such diagram is the *use case diagram*. A use case diagram shows the sequence of steps that take place in performing a task and identifies the parties (actors) involved in the task.

2. Identify objects (entities) that exist within the boundaries of the system.

In order to determine which classes will appear in a program, the analyst should think of the real-world objects and data elements that are present in the problem. One popular method of discovering the objects within a problem is to write a description of the problem with its major events and parties, then identify all the nouns in the description. Each noun is candidate to become a class. Here are examples of items that may be candidates for classes:

- ◆ The result of a business event, such as a customer order
- ◆ Physical objects, such as vehicles, machines, or manufactured products
- ◆ Record keeping items, such as customer histories and payroll records
- ◆ Any role played by a human (employee, client, teacher, student, and so forth)

In object-oriented analysis, classes are first modeled with a *class diagram*. The class diagram, which is another UML tool, shows all the classes involved in a use case.

3. Identify the necessary object relationships and interactions for the system.

The next step is to identify the relationships that exist between and among the classes. You identify these relationships by looking for the natural associations that exist between the objects. Once identified, you can add the appropriate relationship to the class diagram.

4. Understand that there is no "right" solution to these tasks.

For each problem, there may be many solutions. The role of the analyst is to understand the problem and design a system that efficiently solves it or improves the existing process.

Object-Oriented Design

During object-oriented design, the analyst determines how the objects and system requirements identified in the analysis phase will be implemented. It usually involves the following activities:

1. Determine the correct hierarchical relationship between objects in the system.

In this step, the analyst determines how to implement the object relationships identified in the analysis phase, and verifies that those relationships are correct. If the relationships are not correct, the models produced during the analysis phase are modified.

2. Determine the correct ownership of the attributes and behaviors in the individual object-to-object interactions.

When relationships exist between classes, especially the inheritance relationship, a "spectrum" of classes emerges. The analyst must carefully consider which class in the spectrum is the appropriate owner of each attribute and method.

3. Implement and test the object/system interaction.

Finally, the analyst (or a programmer/developer) implements the design using an object-oriented programming language. The language must support the features specified in the object-oriented design. In addition, the system's interactions with the operating system and the user interface are implemented. The system is then tested and further refined.

Design Issues

The analyst must address many reusability and design issues that impact the complexity and efficiency of an object-oriented system. Among them are the following:

- ◆ Are the classes too specific in design to be used generically, or too general in design to be used without modification or extension?

- ◆ To change a class's capabilities, should the class be modified, or should a child class be designed as a specialization? If the class is to be modified, will the changes create unwanted side effects because of other relationships that exist?

- ◆ Is the definition of a class such that objects of the class can stand on their own in multiple scenarios?

- ◆ Is there an overuse of inheritance or specialization? Inheritance can be taken to an extreme, where one class is the child of another class, which is the child of another class, and so on. Excessive generalization/specialization relationships might be necessary in some cases, but they can result in overly complex systems.

- ◆ Does it make sense to implement an entity as an object? Are there other data structures that make more sense?

Review Questions and Exercises

Short Answer

1. What is the difference between a class and an instance of the class?

2. What is the difference between the following `Person` structure and `Person` class?

```
struct Person
{
    char name[51];
    int age;
};

class Person
{
    char name[51];
    int age;
};
```

3. What is the default access specification of class members?

4. Look at the following function header for a member function.

```
void Circle::getRadius()
```

   What is the name of the function?

   What class is the function a member of?

5. A contractor uses a blueprint to build a set of identical houses. Are classes analogous to the blueprint or the houses?

6. What is a `set` function? What is a `get` function?

7. Is it a good idea to make member variables private? Why or why not?

8. Why should you avoid writing statements in a class member function that use `cout` or `cin`? Is there ever an exception to this?

9. Under what circumstances should a member function be private?

10. What is a constructor? What is a destructor?

11. What is a default constructor? Is it possible to have more than one default constructor?

12. Is it possible to have more than one constructor? Is it possible to have more than one destructor?

13. If a class object is dynamically allocated in memory, does its constructor execute? If so, when?

14. When defining an array of class objects, how do you pass arguments to the constructor for each object in the array?

Algorithm Workbench

15. Write a class declaration named `Circle` with a private member variable named `radius`. Write set and get functions to access the `radius` variable, and a function named `getArea` that returns the area of the circle. The area is calculated as:

    ```
    3.14159 * radius * radius
    ```

16. Add a default constructor to the `Circle` class in question 15. The constructor should initialize the radius member to 0.

17. Add an overloaded constructor to the `Circle` class in question 16. The constructor should accept an argument and assign its value to the `radius` member variable.

18. Write a statement that defines an array of five objects of the `Circle` class in question 17. Let the default constructor execute for each element of the array.

19. Write a statement that defines an array of five objects of the `Circle` class in question 18. Pass the following arguments to the elements' constructor: 12, 7, 9, 14, and 8.

20. Write a `for` loop that displays the radius and area of the circles represented by the array you defined in question 19.

True or False

21. T   F   Private members must be declared before public members.
22. T   F   Class members are private by default.
23. T   F   Members of a `struct` are private by default.
24. T   F   Classes and structures in C++ are very similar.
25. T   F   All private members of a class must be declared together.
26. T   F   All public members of a class must be declared together.
27. T   F   Pointers to class objects may be defined.
28. T   F   Unless you are designing a class specifically to perform I/O, you should avoid `cin`, `cout`, or other I/O statements in the class's member functions.
29. T   F   A private member function may be called from a statement outside the class, as long as the statement is in the same program as the class declaration.
30. T   F   Constructors do not have to have the same name as the class.
31. T   F   Constructors may not have a return type.
32. T   F   Constructors cannot take arguments.
33. T   F   Destructors cannot take arguments.
34. T   F   Destructors may return a value.
35. T   F   Constructors may have default arguments.
36. T   F   Member functions may be overloaded.

37. T   F   Constructors may not be overloaded.

38. T   F   A class may not have a constructor with no parameter list, and a constructor whose arguments all have default values.

39. T   F   A class may only have one destructor.

40. T   F   When an array of objects is defined, the constructor is only called for the first element.

Find the Errors

Each of the following class declarations or programs contain errors. Find as many as possible.

41.
```cpp
class Circle:
{
private
    double centerX;
    double centerY;
    double radius;
public
    setCenter(double, double);
    setRadius(double);
}
```

42.
```cpp
#include <iostream>
using namespace std;

class DumbBell;
{
    int weight;
public:
    void setWeight(int);
};
void setWeight(int W)
{
    weight = w;
}

int main()
{
    DumBell bar;

    DumbBell(200);
    cout << "The weight is " << bar.weight << endl;
    return 0;
}
```

Programming Challenges

1. Date

Design a class called Date. The class should store a date in three integers: month, day, and year. There should be member functions to print the date in the following forms:

12/25/05
December 25, 2005
25 December 2005

Demonstrate the class by writing a complete program implementing it.

Input Validation: Do not accept values for the day greater than 31 or less than 1. Do not accept values for the month greater than 12 or less than 1.

2. Inventory Class

Design an Inventory class that can hold information and calculate data for items in a retail store's inventory. The class should have the following *private* member variables:

Variable Name	Description
itemNumber	an int that holds the items item number.
quantity	an int for holding the quantity of the items on-hand.
cost	a double for holding the wholesale per-unit cost of the item
totalCost	a double for holding the total inventory cost of the item (calculated as quantity times cost).

The class should have the following *public* member functions:

Demonstrate the class in a driver program.

Input Validation: Do not accept negative values for item number, quantity, or cost.

3. Widget Factory

Design a class for a widget manufacturing plant. Assuming that 10 widgets may be produced each hour, the class object will calculate how many days it will take to produce any number of widgets. (The plant operates two shifts of eight hours each per day.) Write a program that asks the user for the number of widgets that have been ordered and then displays the number of days it will take to produce them.

Input Validation: Do not accept negative values for the number of widgets ordered.

Member Function	Description
Default Constructor	sets all the member variables to 0.
Constructor #2	accepts an item's number, cost, and quantity as arguments. The function should copy these values to the appropriate member variables and then call the setTotalCost function.
setItemNumber	accepts an integer argument that is copied to the itemNumber member variable.
setQuantity	accepts an integer argument that is copied to the quantity member variable.
setCost	accepts a double argument that is copied to the cost member variable.
setTotalCost	calculates the total inventory cost for the item (quantity times cost) and stores the result in totalCost.
getItemNumber	returns the value in itemNumber.
getQuantity	returns the value in quantity.
getCost	returns the value in cost.
getTotalCost	returns the value in totalCost.

4. Population

In a population, the birth rate and death rate are calculated as follows:

Birth Rate = Number of Births ÷ Population
Death Rate = Number of Deaths ÷ Population

For example, in a population of 100,000 that has 8,000 births and 6,000 deaths per year, the birth rate and death rate are:

Birth Rate = 8,000 ÷ 100,000 = 0.08
Death Rate = 6,000 ÷ 100,000 = 0.06

Design a Population class that stores a population, number of births, and number of deaths for a period of time. Member functions should return the birth rate and death rate. Implement the class in a program.

Input Validation: Do not accept population figures less than 1, or birth or death numbers less than 0.

5. Number Array Class

Design a class that has an array of floating-point numbers. The constructor should accept an integer argument and dynamically allocate the array to hold that many numbers. The destructor should free the memory held by the array. In addition, there should be member functions to perform the following operations:

- ◆ Store a number in any element of the array
- ◆ Retrieve a number from any element of the array
- ◆ Return the highest value stored in the array
- ◆ Return the lowest value stored in the array
- ◆ Return the average of all the numbers stored in the array

Demonstrate the class in a program.

6. Payroll

Design a `PayRoll` class that has data members for an employee's hourly pay rate, number of hours worked, and total pay for the week. Write a program with an array of seven `PayRoll` objects. The program should ask the user for the number of hours each employee has worked and will then display the amount of gross pay each has earned.

Input Validation: Do not accept values greater than 60 for the number of hours worked.

7. Mortgage Payment

Design a class that will determine the monthly payment on a home mortgage. The monthly payment with interest compounded monthly can be calculated as follows:

$$\text{Payment} = \frac{\text{Loan} \times \dfrac{\text{Rate}}{12} \times \text{Term}}{\text{Term} - 1}$$

where

$$\text{Term} = \left(1 + \frac{\text{Rate}}{12}\right)^{12 \times \text{Years}}$$

Payment = the monthly payment
Loan = the dollar amount of the loan
Rate = the annual interest rate
Years = the number of years of the loan

The class should have member functions for setting the loan amount, interest rate, and number of years of the loan. It should also have member functions for returning the monthly payment amount and the total amount paid to the bank at the end of the loan period. Implement the class in a complete program.

Input Validation: Do not accept negative numbers for any of the loan values.

8. Cash Register

Design a CashRegister class that can be used with the InventoryItem class discussed in this chapter. The CashRegister class should perform the following:

1. Ask the user for the item and quantity being purchased.
2. Get the item's cost from the InventoryItem object.
3. Add a 30% profit to the cost to get the item's unit price.
4. Multiply the unit price times the quantity being purchased to get the purchase subtotal.
5. Compute a 6% sales tax on the subtotal to get the purchase total.
6. Display the purchase subtotal, tax, and total on the screen.
7. Subtract the quantity being purchased from the onHand variable of the InventoryItem class object.

Implement both classes in a complete program. Feel free to modify the InventoryItem class in any way necessary.

Input Validation: Do not accept a negative value for the quantity of items being purchased.

Group Project

9. Patient Fees

This program should be designed and written by a team of students. Here are some suggestions:

- ◆ One or more students may work on a single class.
- ◆ The requirements of the program should be analyzed so each student is given about the same workload.
- ◆ The parameters and return types of each function and class member function should be decided in advance.
- ◆ The program will be best implemented as a multi-file program.

You are to write a program that computes a patient's bill for a hospital stay. The different components of the program are:

The PatientAccount Object
The Surgery Object

The Pharmacy object
The main program

- The PatientAccount class will keep a total of the patient's charges. It will also keep track of the number of days spent in the hospital. The group must decide on the hospital's daily rate.

- The Surgery class will have stored within it the charges for at least five types of surgery. It can update the charges variable of the PatientAccount class.

- The Pharmacy class will have stored within it the price of at least five types of medication. It can update the charges variable of the PatientAccount class.

- The student who designs the main program will design a menu that allows the user to enter a type of surgery and a type of medication, and check the patient out of the hospital. When the patient checks out, the total charges should be displayed.

13

More About Classes

13.1 Instance and Static Members

CONCEPT Each instance of a class has its own copies of the class's instance variables. If a member variable is declared static, however, all instances of that class have access to that variable. If a member function is declared static, it may be called without any instances of the class being defined.

Instance Variables

Each class object (an instance of a class) has its own copy of the class's member variables. An object's member variables are separate and distinct from the member variables of other objects of the same class. For example, recall that the Rectangle class discussed in Chapter 12 has two member variables: width and length. Suppose that we define two objects of the Rectangle class and set their width and length member variables as shown in the following code.

```
Rectangle box1, box2;

// Set the width and length for box1.
box1.setWidth(5);
box1.setLength(10);
```

```
// Set the width and length for box2.
box2.setWidth(500);
box2.setLength(1000);
```

This code creates box1 and box2, which are two distinct objects. Each has its own width and length member variables, as illustrated in Figure 13-1.

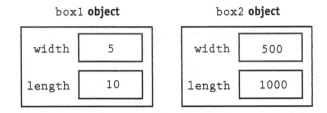

box1 object   **box2 object**

| width | 5 | | width | 500 |
| length | 10 | | length | 1000 |

Figure 13-1

When the getWidth member function is called, it returns the value stored in the calling object's width member variable. For example, the following statement displays 5 500.

```
cout << box1.getWidth() << " " << box2.getWidth() << endl;
```

In object-oriented programming, member variables such as the Rectangle class's width and length members are known as *instance variables*. They are called instance variables because each instance of the class has its own copies of the variables.

Static Member Variables

It is possible to create a member variable that is shared by all the objects of the same class. To create such a member variable, simply place the key word static in front of the variable declaration, then place a definition for the variable outside of the class. For example, look at the following declaration for the StaticDemo class.

```
class StaticDemo
{
private:
    int instanceVariable;          // Instance variable
    static int staticVariable;     // Static variable
public:
    void setInstanceVariable(int n)
        { instanceVariable = n; }

    void setStaticVariable(int n)
        { staticVariable = n; }

    int getInstanceVariable()
        { return instanceVariable; }
```

```
        int getStaticVariable()
            { return staticVariable; }
};

    // Definition of the static member variable, written outside the class.
    int StaticDemo::staticVariable;
```

This class declares two integer member variables: instanceVariable and staticVariable. The staticVariable member is declared static. Notice that a definition statement for the static variable appears outside of the class declaration. The external definition statement is required, and causes the variable to be created in memory.

When a program creates instances of the StaticDemo class, all of the instances share this static member variable. When one class object stores a value in staticVariable, that same value will appear to all the other StaticDemo objects. For example, assume the following statements appear in a program.

```
    StaticDemo demo1, demo2;

    // Use demo1 to store values in the instanceVariable
    // and staticVariable members.
    demo1.setInstanceVariable(1);
    demo1.setStaticVariable(5);

    // Use demo2 to store a value in the instanceVariable
    // member, but do not store a value in staticVariable.
    demo2.setInstanceVariable(100);

    // Display the values in the demo1's member variables.
    cout << "demo1's members are "
        << demo1.getInstanceVariable() << " and "
        << demo1.getStaticVariable() << endl;

    // Display the values in the demo2's member variables,
    // including staticVariable.
    cout << "demo2's members are "
        << demo2.getInstanceVariable() << " and "
        << demo2.getStaticVariable() << endl;
```

The cout statements in this code will display:

```
    demo1's members are 1 and 5
    demo2's members are 100 and 5
```

The value 5 was stored in staticVariable by the demo1 object. Because demo1 and demo2 share the staticVariable member, the value 5 shows up in both objects. This is illustrated by Figure 13-2.

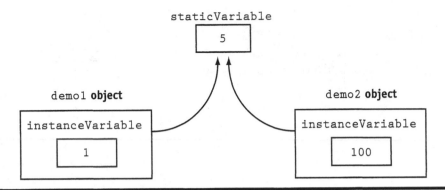

Figure 13-2

A more practical use of a static member variable is demonstrated in Program 13-1. The Budget class is used to gather the budget requests for all the divisions of a company. The class uses a static member, corpBudget, to hold the amount of the overall corporate budget. When the member function addBudget is called, its argument is added to the current contents of corpBudget. By the time the program is finished, corpBudget will contain the total of all the values placed there by all the Budget class objects.

Program 13-1

Contents of *Budget.h*

```
// Specification file for the Budget class
#ifndef BUDGET_H
#define BUDGET_H

// Budget class declaration
class Budget
{
private:
    static double corpBudget;   // Static member
    double divisionBudget;      // Instance member
public:
    Budget()
        { divisionBudget = 0; }

    void addBudget(double b)
        { divisionBudget += b;
          corpBudget += b; }

    double getDivisionBudget()
        { return divisionBudget; }
```

(program continues)

Program 13-1 *(continued)*

```cpp
double getCorpBudget()
     { return corpBudget; }
};

double Budget::corpBudget = 0;   // Static member

#endif
```

Contents of main program, `Pr13-1.cpp`

```cpp
// This program demonstrates a static class member variable.
#include <iostream>
#include <iomanip>
#include "Budget.h"
using namespace std;

int main()
{
    int count;                      // Loop counter
    const int NUM_DIVISIONS = 4;    // Number of divisions
    Budget divisions[NUM_DIVISIONS]; // Array of Budget objects

    // Get the budget requests for each division.
    for (count = 0; count < NUM_DIVISIONS; count++)
    {
        double budgetAmount;
        cout << "Enter the budget request for division ";
        cout << (count + 1) << ": ";
        cin >> budgetAmount;
        divisions[count].addBudget(budgetAmount);
    }

    // Display the budget requests and the corporate budget.
    cout << fixed << showpoint << setprecision(2);
    cout << "\nHere are the division budget requests:\n";
    for (count = 0; count < NUM_DIVISIONS; count++)
    {
        cout << "\tDivision " << (count + 1) << "\t$ ";
        cout << divisions[count].getDivisionBudget() << endl;
    }
    cout << "\tTotal Budget Requests:\t$ ";
    cout << divisions[0].getCorpBudget() << endl;

    return 0;
}
```

Program 13-1 *(continued)*

Program Output with Example Input Shown in Bold
```
Enter the budget request for division 1: 100000 [Enter]
Enter the budget request for division 2: 200000 [Enter]
Enter the budget request for division 3: 300000 [Enter]
Enter the budget request for division 4: 400000 [Enter]

Here are the division budget requests:
    Division 1      $ 100000.00
    Division 2      $ 200000.00
    Division 3      $ 300000.00
    Division 4      $ 400000.00
    Total Budget Requests:    $ 1000000.00
```

Static Member Functions

It is possible to declare a static member function by placing the `static` key word in the function's prototype. Here is the general form:

```
static <ReturnType> <FunctionName> (<ParameterTypeList>);
```

A function that is a static member of a class cannot access any non-static member data in its class. With this limitation in mind, you might wonder what purpose static member functions serve. The following two points are important for understanding their usefulness:

♦ Even though static member variables are declared in a class, they are actually defined outside the class declaration. The lifetime of a class's static member variable is the lifetime of the program. This means that a class's static member variables come into existence before any instances of the class are created.

♦ The static member functions of a class are callable before any instances of the class are created. This means that the static member functions of a class can access the class's static member variables *before* any instances of the class are defined in memory. This gives you the ability to create very specialized setup routines for class objects.

Program 13-2, a modification of Program 13-1, demonstrates this. It asks the user to enter the main office's budget request before any division requests are entered. The `Budget` class has been modified to include a static member function named `mainOffice`. This function adds its argument to the static `corpBudget` variable, and is called before any instances of the `Budget` class are defined.

Program 13-2

Contents of `Budget2.h`
```
// Specification file for the Budget class
#ifndef BUDGET_H
#define BUDGET_H
```

(program continues)

Program 13-2 *(continued)*

```cpp
// Budget class declaration
class Budget
{
private:
    static double corpBudget;       // Static member variable
    double divisionBudget;          // Instance member variable
public:
    Budget()
        { divisionBudget = 0; }

    void addBudget(double b)
        { divisionBudget += b;
          corpBudget += b; }

    double getDivisionBudget()
        { return divisionBudget; }

    double getCorpBudget()
        { return corpBudget; }

    static void mainOffice(double);// Static member function
};

#endif
```

Contents of `Budget2.cpp`
```cpp
// Implementation file for budget class
#include "Budget2.h"

double Budget::corpBudget = 0;      // Definition of static member variable

//**********************************************************
// Definition of static member function mainOffice.        *
// This function adds the main office's budget request to   *
// the corpBudget variable.                                 *
//**********************************************************

void Budget::mainOffice(double moffice)
{
    corpBudget += moffice;
}
```

Contents of main program, `Pr13-2.cpp`
```cpp
// This program demonstrates a static member function.
#include <iostream>
#include <iomanip>
#include "Budget2.h"
using namespace std;
```
(program continues)

Program 13-2 *(continued)*

```cpp
int main()
{
    int count;                      // Loop counter
    double mainOfficeRequest;       // Main office budget request
    const int NUM_DIVISIONS = 4;    // Number of divisions

    // Get the main office's budget request.
    // Note that no instances of the Budget class have been defined.
    cout << "Enter the main office's budget request: ";
    cin >> mainOfficeRequest;
    Budget::mainOffice(mainOfficeRequest);

    Budget divisions[NUM_DIVISIONS]; // An array of Budget objects.

    // Get the budget requests for each division.
    for (count = 0; count < NUM_DIVISIONS; count++)
    {
        double budgetAmount;
        cout << "Enter the budget request for division ";
        cout << (count + 1) << ": ";
        cin >> budgetAmount;
        divisions[count].addBudget(budgetAmount);
    }

    // Display the budget requests and the corporate budget.
    cout << fixed << showpoint << setprecision(2);
    cout << "\nHere are the division budget requests:\n";
    for (count = 0; count < NUM_DIVISIONS; count++)
    {
        cout << "\tDivision " << (count + 1) << "\t$ ";
        cout << divisions[count].getDivisionBudget() << endl;
    }
    cout << "\tTotal Budget Requests:\t$ ";
    cout << divisions[0].getCorpBudget() << endl;

    return 0;
}
```

Program Output with Example Input Shown in Bold

```
Enter the main office's budget request: 100000 [Enter]
Enter the budget request for division 1: 100000 [Enter]
Enter the budget request for division 2: 200000 [Enter]
Enter the budget request for division 3: 300000 [Enter]
Enter the budget request for division 4: 400000 [Enter]

Here are the division budget requests:
    Division 1    $ 100000.00
    Division 2    $ 200000.00
    Division 3    $ 300000.00
    Division 4    $ 400000.00
    Total Requests (including main office): $ 1100000.00
```

Notice the statement that calls the static function `mainOffice`:

```
Budget::mainOffice(amount);
```

Calls to static member functions do not use the regular notation of connecting the function name to an object name with the dot operator. Instead, static member functions are called by connecting the function name to the class name with the scope resolution operator.

 Note: If an instance of a class with a static member function exists, the static member function can be called with the class object name and the dot operator, just like any other member function.

13.2 Friends of Classes

CONCEPT A friend is a function or class that is not a member of a class, but has access to the private members of the class.

Private members are hidden from all parts of the program outside the class, and accessing them requires a call to a public member function. Sometimes you will want to create an exception to that rule. A *friend* function is a function that is not part of a class, but that has access to the class's private members. In other words, a friend function is treated as if it were a member of the class. A friend function can be a regular stand-alone function, or it can be a member of another class. (In fact, an entire class can be declared a friend of another class.)

In order for a function or class to become a friend of another class, it must be declared as such by the class granting it access. Classes keep a "list" of their friends, and only the external functions or classes whose names appears in the list are granted access. A function is declared a friend by placing the key word `friend` in front of a prototype of the function. Here is the general format:

```
friend <ReturnType> <FunctionName> (<ParameterTypeList>);
```

In the following declaration of the `Budget` class, the `addBudget` function of another class, `AuxiliaryOffice` has been declared a friend:

```
class Budget
{
private:
    static double corpBudget;      // Static member variable
    double divisionBudget;         // Instance member variable
public:
    Budget()
        { divisionBudget = 0; }
```

```
void addBudget(double b)
   { divisionBudget += b;
     corpBudget += divisionBudget; }

double getDivisionBudget()
   { return divisionBudget; }

double getCorpBudget()
   { return corpBudget; }

static void mainOffice(double);        // Static member function

friend void AuxiliaryOffice::addBudget(float, Budget &);
};
```

Let's assume another class, `AuxiliaryOffice`, represents a division's auxiliary office, perhaps in another country. The auxiliary office makes a separate budget request, which must be added to the overall corporate budget. The friend declaration of the `AuxiliaryOffice::addBudget` function tells the compiler that the function is to be granted access to `Budget`'s private members. Notice the function takes two arguments: a `double` and a reference object of the `Budget` class. The `Budget` class object that is to be modified by the function is passed to it, by reference, as an argument. Here is the declaration of the `AuxiliaryOffice` class:

```
class AuxiliaryOffice
{
private:
    float auxBudget;
public:
    AuxiliaryOffice()
        { auxBudget = 0; }
    double getDivisionBudget()
        { return auxBudget; }
    void addBudget(double, Budget &);
};
```

And here is the definition of the `AuxiliaryOffice` class's `addBudget` member function:

```
void AuxiliaryOffice::addBudget(double b, Budget &div)
{
    auxBudget += b;
    div.corpBudget += b;
}
```

The parameter `div`, a reference to a `Budget` class object, is used in the following statement:

```
div.corpBudget += b;
```

This statement adds the parameter b to `div.corpBudget`. Program 13-3 demonstrates the classes.

Program 13-3

Contents of `Auxil.h`
```
// Specification file for the AuxiliaryOffice class
#ifndef AUXIL_H
#define AUXIL_H

class Budget;   // Forward declaration of Budget class

// Aux class declaration

class AuxiliaryOffice
{
private:
    double auxBudget;
public:
    AuxiliaryOffice()
        { auxBudget = 0; }
    double getDivisionBudget()
        { return auxBudget; }
    void addBudget(double, Budget &);
};

#endif
```

Contents of `Auxil.cpp`
```
// Implementation file for the AuxiliaryOffice class
#include "Auxil.h"
#include "Budget3.h"

//*************************************************************
// Definition of member function mainOffice.                 *
// This function is declared a friend by the Budget class.    *
// It adds the value of argument b to the static corpBudget   *
// member variable of the Budget class.                       *
//*************************************************************

void AuxiliaryOffice::addBudget(double b, Budget &div)
{
    auxBudget += b;
    div.corpBudget += b;
}
```

Program 13-3 *(continued)*

Contents of *Budget3.h*
```cpp
// Specification file for the Budget class
#ifndef BUDGET_H
#define BUDGET_H
#include "Auxil.h"

// Budget class declaration
class Budget
{
private:
   static double corpBudget;  // Static member variable
   double divisionBudget;     // Instance member variable
public:
   Budget()
      { divisionBudget = 0; }

   void addBudget(double b)
      { divisionBudget += b;
        corpBudget += b; }

   double getDivisionBudget()
      { return divisionBudget; }

   double getCorpBudget()
      { return corpBudget; }

   static void mainOffice(double);  // Static member function

   friend void AuxiliaryOffice::addBudget(double, Budget &);
};
#endif
```

Contents of *Budget3.cpp*
```cpp
// Implementation file for budget class
#include "Budget3.h"

double Budget::corpBudget = 0;  // Definition of static member variable

//************************************************************
// Definition of static member function mainOffice.         *
// This function adds the main office's budget request to   *
// the corpBudget variable.                                 *
//************************************************************

void Budget::mainOffice(double moffice)
{
    corpBudget += moffice;
}
```

Program 13-3 *(continued)*

Contents of main program, `Pr13-3.cpp`

```cpp
// This program demonstrates a static member function.
#include <iostream>
#include <iomanip>
#include "Budget3.h"
using namespace std;

int main()
{
   int count;                      // Loop counter
   double mainOfficeRequest;       // Main office budget request
   const int NUM_DIVISIONS = 4;    // Number of divisions

   // Get the main office's budget request.
   cout << "Enter the main office's budget request: ";
   cin >> mainOfficeRequest;
   Budget::mainOffice(mainOfficeRequest);

   Budget divisions[NUM_DIVISIONS]; // An array of Budget objects.
   AuxiliaryOffice auxOffices[4];   // An array of AuxiliaryOffice

   // Get the budget requests for each division
   // and their auxiliary offices.
   for (count = 0; count < NUM_DIVISIONS; count++)
   {
      double budgetAmount;
      // Get the request for the division office.
      cout << "Enter the budget request for division ";
      cout << (count + 1) << ": ";
      cin >> budgetAmount;
      divisions[count].addBudget(budgetAmount);

      // Get the request for the auxiliary office.
      cout << "Enter the budget request for that division's\n";
      cout << "auxiliary office: ";
      cin >> budgetAmount;
      auxOffices[count].addBudget(budgetAmount, divisions[count]);
   }

   // Display the budget requests and the corporate budget.
   cout << fixed << showpoint << setprecision(2);
   cout << "\nHere are the division budget requests:\n";
```

(program continues)

Program 13-3 *(continued)*

```
for (count = 0; count < NUM_DIVISIONS; count++)
   {
      cout << "\tDivision " << (count + 1) << "\t\t$";
      cout << divisions[count].getDivisionBudget() << endl;
      cout << "\tAuxiliary office:\t$";
      cout << auxOffices[count].getDivisionBudget() << endl << endl;
   }
   cout << "Total Budget Requests:\t$ ";
   cout << divisions[0].getCorpBudget() << endl;
   return 0;
}
```

Program Output with Example Input Shown in Bold

Enter the main office's budget request: **100000 [Enter]**
Enter the budget request for division 1: **100000 [Enter]**
Enter the budget request for that division's
auxiliary office: **50000 [Enter]**
Enter the budget request for division 2: **200000 [Enter]**
Enter the budget request for that division's
auxiliary office: **40000 [Enter]**
Enter the budget request for division 3: **300000 [Enter]**
Enter the budget request for that division's
auxiliary office: **70000 [Enter]**
Enter the budget request for division 4: **400000 [Enter]**
Enter the budget request for that division's
auxiliary office: **65000 [Enter]**

Here are the division budget requests:
        Division 1 $100000.00
        Auxiliary office: $50000.00

        Division 2 $200000.00
        Auxiliary office: $40000.00

        Division 3 $300000.00
        Auxiliary office: $70000.00

        Division 4 $400000.00
        Auxiliary office: $65000.00

Total Budget Requests: $ 1325000.00

Notice the `Auxil.h` file contains the following line:

```
class Budget;  // Forward declaration of Budget class
```

The line above is a *forward declaration* of the `Budget` class. It's necessary because the compiler will see the `Budget` class mentioned in the declaration of the `addBudget` member function, shown below:

```
void addBudget(double, Budget &);
```

Because the compiler is processing this file before it processes the `budget.h` file, it will not know that `Budget` is a class. The forward declaration tells the compiler that a class named `Budget` will be declared later in the program.

 Note: As mentioned before, it is possible to make an entire class a friend of another class. The `Budget` class could make the `AuxiliaryOffice` class its friend with the following declaration:

```
friend class AuxiliaryOffice;
```

This may not be a good idea, however. Every member function of `AuxiliaryOffice` (including ones that may be added later) would have access to the private members of `Budget`. The best practice is to declare as friends only those functions that must have access to the private members of the class.

 ## Checkpoint [13.1–13.2]

13.1   What is the difference between a regular member variable and a static member variable?

13.2   Static member variables are declared inside the class declaration. Where are static member variables defined?

13.3   Does a static member variable come into existence in memory before, at the same time as, or after any instances of its class?

13.4   What limitation does a static member function have?

13.5   What action is possible with a static member function that isn't possible with a regular member function?

13.6   If class X declares function f as a friend, does function f become a member of class X?

13.7   Class Y is a friend of class X, which means the member functions of class Y have access to the private members of class X. Does the friend key word appear in class Y's declaration or in class X's declaration?

13.3 Memberwise Assignment

> **CONCEPT** The = operator may be used to assign one object to another, or to initialize one object with another object's data. By default, each member of one object is copied to its counterpart in the other object.

Like other variables (except arrays), objects may be assigned to each other using the = operator. As an example, consider Program 13-4 which uses a `Rectangle` class similar to the one discussed in Chapter 12:

Program 13-4

```cpp
// This program demonstrates memberwise assignment.
#include <iostream>
using namespace std;

// Rectangle class declaration
class Rectangle
{
    private:
        double width;
        double length;
    public:
        void setWidth(double w)
            { width = w; }

        void setLength(double len)
            { length = len; }

        double getWidth()
            { return width; }

        double getLength()
            { return length; }

        double getArea()
            { return width * length; }
};

int main()
{
    Rectangle box1, box2;// Define two Rectangle objects.

    // Set the width and length for box1.
    box1.setWidth(10);
    box1.setLength(20);
```

(program continues)

Program 13-4 *(continued)*

```
    // Assign the members of box1 to box2.
    box2 = box1;

    // Display the contents of box2.
    cout << "box2's width is " << box2.getWidth() << endl;
    cout << "box2's length is " << box2.getLength() << endl;

    return 0;
}
```

Program Output
```
box2's width is 10
box2's length is 20
```

As you can see, the following statement copies the width and length variables of box1 directly into the width and length variables of box2:

```
    box2 = box1;
```

Memberwise assignment also occurs when one object is initialized with another object's values. Remember the difference between assignment and initialization: assignment occurs between two objects that already exist, and initialization happens to an object being created. Consider the following program segment:

```
    Rectangle box1;          // Define box1.
    box1.setWidth(100);      // Set box1's width.
    box1.setLength(50);      // Set box1's length.
    Rectangle box2 = box1;   // Define box2, initialize with box1's values
```

The fourth statement defines a Rectangle object, box2, and initializes it to the values stored in box1. Because memberwise assignment takes place, the box2 object will contain the exact same values as the box1 object.

13.4 Copy Constructors

CONCEPT A copy constructor is a special constructor, called whenever a new object is created and initialized with another object's data.

Most of the time, the default memberwise assignment behavior in C++ is perfectly acceptable. There are instances, however, where memberwise assignment cannot be used. For example, consider the following class:

```
#include <cstring>

class PersonInfo
{
private:
    char *name;
    int age;
public:
    PersonInfo(char *n, int a)
        { name = new char[strlen(n) + 1];
          strcpy(name, n);
          age = a; }

    ~PersonInfo()
        { delete [] name; }

    char *getName()
        { return name; }

    int getAge()
        { return age; }
};
```

A potential problem with this class above lies in the fact that one of its members, name, is a pointer. The constructor performs a critical operation with the pointer: it dynamically allocates a section of memory and copies a string to it. For instance, the following statement creates a personInfo object named person1, whose name member references dynamically allocated memory holding the string "Maria Jones-Tucker":

```
PersonInfo person1("Maria Jones-Tucker", 25);
```

This is depicted in Figure 13-3.

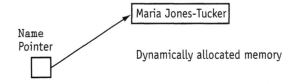

Figure 13-3

Consider what happens when another PersonInfo object is created and initialized with the person1 object, as in the following statement:

```
PersonInfo person2 = person1;
```

In the statement above, person2's constructor isn't called. Instead, memberwise assignment takes place, copying each of person1's member variables into person2. This means that a separate section of memory is not allocated for person2's name member. It simply gets a copy of the address stored in person1's name member. Both pointers will point to the same address, as depicted in Figure 13-4.

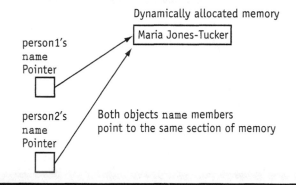

Figure 13-4

In this situation, either object can manipulate the string, causing the changes to show up in the other object. Likewise, one object can be destroyed, causing its destructor to be called, which frees the allocated memory. The remaining object's name pointer would still reference this section of memory, although it should no longer be used.

The solution to this problem is to create a *copy constructor* for the object. A copy constructor is a special constructor that's called when an object is initialized with another object's data. It has the same form as other constructors, except it has a reference parameter of the same class type as the object itself. For example, here is a copy constructor for the PersonInfo class:

```
PersonInfo(PersonInfo &obj)
   { name = new char[strlen(obj.name) + 1];
     strcpy(name, obj.name);
     age = obj.age; }
```

When the = operator is used to initialize a PersonInfo object with the contents of another PersonInfo object, the copy constructor is called. The PersonInfo object that appears on the right side of the = operator is passed as an argument to the copy constructor. For example, look at the following statement:

```
PersonInfo person1("Molly McBride", 27);
PersonInfo person2 = person1;
```

In this code, the person1 object is passed as an argument to the person2 object's copy constructor.

 Note: C++ requires that a copy constructor's parameter be a reference object.

As you can see from studying the copy constructor's code, person2's name member will properly reference its own dynamically allocated memory. There will be no danger of person1 inadvertently destroying or corrupting person2's data. The complete class listing is shown here.

```cpp
#include <cstring>

class PersonInfo
{
private:
    char *name;
    int age;
public:
    PersonInfo(char *n, int a)          // Constructor
        { name = new char[strlen(n) + 1];
          strcpy(name, n);
          age = a; }

    PersonInfo(PersonInfo &obj)         // Copy constructor
    { name = new char[strlen(obj.name) + 1];
        strcpy(name, obj.name);
        age = obj.age; }

    ~PersonInfo()
        { delete [] name; }

    char *getName()
        { return name; }

    int getAge()
        { return age; }
};
```

Copy Constructors and Function Parameters

When a class object is passed by value as an argument to a function, it is passed to a parameter that is also a class object, and the copy constructor of the function's parameter is called. Remember, a non-reference class object is used as a function parameter it is created when the function is called, and it is initialized with the argument's value.

This is why C++ requires the parameter of a copy constructor to be a reference object. If an object were passed to the copy constructor by value, the copy constructor would create a copy of the argument and store it in the parameter object. When the parameter object is created, its copy constructor will be called, thus causing another parameter object to be created. This process will continue indefinitely (or at least until the available memory fills up, causing the program to halt).

To prevent the copy constructor from calling itself an infinite number of times, C++ requires its parameter to be a reference object.

Using `const` Parameters

Because copy constructors are required to use reference parameters, they have access to their argument's data. Since the purpose of a copy constructor is to make a copy of the argument, there is no reason the constructor should modify the argument's data. With this in mind, it's a good idea to make copy constructors' parameters constant by specifying the const key word in the parameter list. Here is an example:

```
PersonInfo(const PersonInfo &obj)
    { name = new char[strlen(obj.name) + 1];
      strcpy(name, obj.name);
      age = obj.age; }
```

The const key word ensures that the function cannot change the contents of the parameter. This will prevent you from inadvertently writing code that corrupts data.

The Default Copy Constructor

Although you may not realize it, you have seen the action of a copy constructor before. If a class doesn't have a copy constructor, C++ creates a *default copy constructor* for it. The default copy constructor performs the memberwise assignment discussed in the previous section.

Checkpoint [13.3–13.4]

13.8 Briefly describe what is meant by memberwise assignment.

13.9 Describe two instances when memberwise assignment occurs.

13.10 Describe a situation in which memberwise assignment should not be used.

13.11 When is a copy constructor called?

13.12 How does the compiler know that a member function is a copy constructor?

13.13 What action is performed by a class's default copy constructor?

13.5 Operator Overloading

CONCEPT C++ allows you to redefine how standard operators work when used with class objects.

C++ provides many operators to manipulate data of the primitive data types. However, what if you wish to use an operator to manipulate class objects? For example, assume that a class named Date exists, and objects of the Date class hold the month, day, and year in member variables. Suppose the Date class has a member function named add. The add member function adds a number of days to the date, and adjusts the member variables if the date goes to another month or year. For example, the following statement adds five days to the date stored in the today object:

```
today.add(5);
```

Although it might be obvious that the statement is adding five days to the date stored in today, the use of an operator might be more intuitive. For example, look at the following statement:

```
today += 5;
```

This statement uses the standard += operator to add 5 to today. This behavior does not happen automatically, however. The += operator must be *overloaded* for this action to occur. In this section, you will learn to overload many of C++'s operators to perform specialized operations on class objects.

 Note: You have already experienced the behavior of an overloaded operator. The / operator performs two types of division: floating point and integer. If one of the / operator's operands is a floating point type, the result will be a floating point value. If both of the / operator's operands are integers, however, a different behavior occurs: the result is an integer and any fractional part is thrown away.

Overloading the = Operator

Although copy constructors solve the initialization problems inherent with objects containing pointer members, they do not work with simple assignment statements. Copy constructors are just that—constructors. They are only invoked when an object is created. Statements like the following still perform memberwise assignment:

```
person2 = person1;
```

In order to change the way the assignment operator works, it must be overloaded. Operator overloading permits you to redefine an existing operator's behavior when used with a class object.

C++ allows a class to have special member functions called *operator functions*. If you wish to redefine the way a particular operator works with an object, you define a function for that operator. The Operator function is then executed any time the operator is used with an object of that class. For example, the following version of the PersonInfo class overloads the = operator:

```
#include <cstring>

class PersonInfo
{
private:
    char *name;
    int age;
public:
    PersonInfo(char *n, int a)        // Constructor
        { name = new char[strlen(n) + 1];
          strcpy(name, n);
          age = a; }
```

```
PersonInfo(PersonInfo &obj)          // Copy constructor
{ name = new char[strlen(obj.name) + 1];
    strcpy(name, obj.name);
    age = obj.age; }

~PersonInfo()
    { delete [] name; }

char *getName()
    { return name; }

int getAge()
    { return age; }

void operator=(const PersonInfo &right)
{ delete [] name;
    name = new char[strlen(right.name) + 1];
    strcpy(name, right.name);
    age = right.age; }
};
```

Let's examine the operator function to understand how it works. First look at the function header:

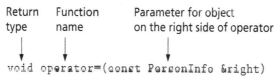

Return type   Function name   Parameter for object on the right side of operator

void operator=(const PersonInfo &right)

The name of the function is `operator=`. This specifies that the function overloads the = operator. Because it is a member of the PersonInfo class, this function will be called only when an assignment statement executes where the object on the left side of the = operator is a PersonInfo object.

 Note: You can, if you choose, put spaces around the operator symbol. For instance, the function header above could also read:

```
void operator = (const PersonInfo &right)
```

The function has one parameter: a constant reference object named `right`. This parameter references the object on the right side of the operator. For example, when the statement below is executed, `right` will reference the person1 object:

```
person2 = person1;
```

 Note: It is not required for the parameter of an operator function be a reference object. The PersonInfo example declares `right` as a const reference for the following reasons:

- ◆ It was declared as a reference for efficiency purposes. This prevents the compiler from making a copy of the object being passed into the function.

- ◆ It was declared constant so the function will not accidentally change the contents of the argument.

Note: In the example, the parameter was named `right` simply to illustrate that it references the object on the right side of the operator. You can name the parameter anything you wish. It will always take the object on the operator's right as its argument.

In learning the mechanics of operator overloading, it might be helpful to think of the statement above as the following function call:

```
person2.operator=(person1);
```

In this statement you can see exactly what is going on in the function call. The `person1` object is being passed to the function's parameter, `right`. Inside the function, the values in `right`'s members are used to initialize `person2`. Notice that the `operator=` function has access to the `right` parameter's private members. Because the `operator=` function is a member of the `PersonInfo` class, it has access to the private members of any `PersonInfo` object that is passed into it.

Note: C++ allows operator functions to be called with regular function call notation, or by using the operator symbol.

Program 13-5 demonstrates the `PersonInfo` class with its overloaded assignment operator.

Program 13-5

```
// This program demonstrates the overloaded = operator.
#include <iostream>
#include <cstring>
using namespace std;

class PersonInfo
{
private:
    char *name;
    int age;
public:
    PersonInfo(char *n, int a)    // Constructor
        { name = new char[strlen(n) + 1];
          strcpy(name, n);
          age = a; }
```

(program continues)

Program 13-5 *(continued)*

```cpp
    PersonInfo(PersonInfo &obj)  // Copy constructor
    { name = new char[strlen(obj.name) + 1];
      strcpy(name, obj.name);
      age = obj.age; }

    ~PersonInfo()
       { delete [] name; }

    char *getName()
       { return name; }

    int getAge()
       { return age; }

    void operator=(const PersonInfo &right)
       { delete [] name;
         name = new char[strlen(right.name) + 1];
         strcpy(name, right.name);
         age = right.age; }
};

int main()
{
    PersonInfo jim("Jim Young", 27),    // Initialize jim
               bob("Bob Faraday", 32),  // Initialize bob
               clone = jim;             // Initialize clone with jim

    // Display the conents of the jim object.
    cout << "The jim Object contains: " << jim.getName();
    cout << ", " << jim.getAge() << endl;

    // Display the contents of the bob object.
    cout << "The bob Object contains: " << bob.getName();
    cout << ", " << bob.getAge() << endl;

    // Display the contents of the clone object.
    cout << "The clone Object contains: " << clone.getName();
    cout << ", " << clone.getAge() << endl << endl;

    // Assign bob to clone.
    cout << "Now the clone will change to bob and ";
    cout << "bob will change to jim.\n\n";
    clone = bob;           // Call overloaded = operator
    bob = jim;             // Call overloaded = operator
```

(program continues)

Program 13-5 *(continued)*

```
    // Display the contents of the jim object.
    cout << "The jim Object contains: " << jim.getName();
    cout << ", " << jim.getAge() << endl;

    // Display the contents of the bob object.
    cout << "The bob Object contains: " << bob.getName();
    cout << ", " << bob.getAge() << endl;

    // Display the contents of the clone object.
    cout << "The clone Object contains: " << clone.getName();
    cout << ", " << clone.getAge() << endl;

    return 0;
}
```

Program Output
```
The jim Object contains: Jim Young, 27
The bob Object contains: Bob Faraday, 32
The clone Object contains: Jim Young, 27

Now the clone will change to bob and bob will change to jim.

The jim Object contains: Jim Young, 27
The bob Object contains: Jim Young, 27
The clone Object contains: Bob Faraday, 32
```

The = Operator's Return Value

There is only one problem with the overloaded = operator shown in Program 13-5: it has a void return type. C++'s built-in = operator allows multiple assignment statements such as:

```
    a = b = c;
```

In this statement, the expression b = c causes c to be assigned to b and then returns the value of c. The return value is then stored in a. If a class object's overloaded = operator is to function this way, it too must have a valid return type.

For example, the PersonInfo class's operator= function could be written as:

```
    const PersonInfo operator=(const PersonInfo &right)
            { delete [] name;
              name = new char[strlen(right.name) + 1];
              strcpy(name, right.name);
              age = right.age;
              return *this;
            }
```

The data type of the operator function specifies that a const PersonInfo object is returned. Look at the last statement in the function:

```
return *this;
```

This statement returns the value of a dereferenced pointer: this. But what is this? Read on.

The this Pointer

The this pointer is a special built-in pointer that is available to a class's member functions. It always points to the instance of the class making the function call. For example, if person1 and person2 are both PersonInfo objects, the following statement causes the getName function to operate on person1:

```
cout << person1.getName() << endl;
```

Likewise, the following statement causes getName to operate on person2:

```
cout << person2.getName() << endl;
```

When getName is operating on person1, the this pointer is pointing to person1. When getName is operating on person2, this is pointing to person2. The this pointer always points to the object that a member function is called from.

 Note: The this pointer is passed as a hidden argument to all non-static member functions.

The overloaded = operator function is demonstrated by the statement clone = bob = jim in Program 13-6.

Program 13-6

```
// This program demonstrates the overloaded = operator
// with a return value.
#include <iostream>
#include <cstring>
using namespace std;

class PersonInfo
{
private:
    char *name;
    int age;
```

(program continues)

Program 13-6 *(continued)*

```cpp
public:
    PersonInfo(char *n, int a)        // Constructor
        { name = new char[strlen(n) + 1];
          strcpy(name, n);
          age = a; }

    PersonInfo(PersonInfo &obj)       // Copy constructor
    { name = new char[strlen(obj.name) + 1];
      strcpy(name, obj.name);
      age = obj.age; }

    ~PersonInfo()
        { delete [] name; }

    char *getName()
        { return name; }

    int getAge()
        { return age; }

    const PersonInfo operator=(const PersonInfo &right)
        { delete [] name;
          name = new char[strlen(right.name) + 1];
          strcpy(name, right.name);
          age = right.age;
          return *this;}
};

int main()
{
    PersonInfo jim("Jim Young", 27),    // Initialize jim
               bob("Bob Faraday", 32),  // Initialize bob
               clone = jim;             // Initialize clone with jim

    // Display the conents of the jim object.
    cout << "The jim Object contains: " << jim.getName();
    cout << ", " << jim.getAge() << endl;

    // Display the contents of the bob object.
    cout << "The bob Object contains: " << bob.getName();
    cout << ", " << bob.getAge() << endl;

    // Display the contents of the clone object.
    cout << "The clone Object contains: " << clone.getName();
    cout << ", " << clone.getAge() << endl << endl;
```

(program continues)

Program 13-6 *(continued)*

```
    // Assign jim to bob and clone.
    cout << "Now the clone and bob will change to jim.\n\n";
    clone = bob = jim;          // Call overloaded = operator

    // Display the contents of the jim object.
    cout << "The jim Object contains: " << jim.getName();
    cout << ", " << jim.getAge() << endl;

    // Display the contents of the bob object.
    cout << "The bob Object contains: " << bob.getName();
    cout << ", " << bob.getAge() << endl;

    // Display the contents of the clone object.
    cout << "The clone Object contains: " << clone.getName();
    cout << ", " << clone.getAge() << endl;

    return 0;
}
```

Program Output

```
The jim Object contains: Jim Young, 27
The bob Object contains: Bob Faraday, 32
The clone Object contains: Jim Young, 27

Now the clone and bob will change to jim.

The jim Object contains: Jim Young, 27
The bob Object contains: Jim Young, 27
The clone Object contains: Jim Young, 27
```

Some General Issues of Operator Overloading

Now that you have had a taste of operator overloading, let's look at some of the general issues involved in this programming technique.

First, you can change an operator's entire meaning, if that's what you wish to do. There is nothing to prevent you from changing the = symbol from an assignment operator to a "display" operator. For instance, the following class does just that:

```
class Weird
{
private:
    int value;
public:
    Weird(int v)
        {value = v; }
    void operator=(const weird &right)
        { cout << right.value << endl; }
};
```

Although the `operator=` function in the `Weird` class overloads the assignment operator, the function doesn't perform an assignment. Instead, it displays the contents of `right.value`. Consider the following program segment:

```
Weird a(5), b(10);
a = b;
```

Although the statement `a = b` looks like an assignment statement, it actually causes the contents of b's `value` member to be displayed on the screen:

```
10
```

Another operator overloading issue is that you cannot change the number of operands taken by an operator. The = symbol must always be a binary operator. Likewise, ++ and - - must always be unary operators.

The last issue is that although you may overload most of the C++ operators, you cannot overload all of them. Table 13-1 shows all of the C++ operators that may be overloaded.

Table 13-1

+	-	*	/	%	^	&	|	~	!	=	<
>	+=	-=	*=	/=	%=	^=	&=	|=	<<	>>	>>=
<<=	==	!=	<=	>=	&&	||	++	- -	->*	,	->
[]	()	new	delete								

 Note: Some of the operators in Table 13-1 are beyond the scope of this book and are not covered.

The only operators that cannot be overloaded are:

```
?:    .    .*    ::    sizeof
```

Overloading Math Operators

Many classes would benefit not only from an overloaded assignment operator, but also from overloaded math operators. To illustrate this, consider the `FeetInches` class shown in the following two files.

Contents of *FeetInches.h*
```
// Specification file for the FeetInches class
#ifndef FEETINCHES_H
#define FEETINCHES_H

// The FeetInches class holds distances or measurements
// expressed in feet and inches.
```

```cpp
class FeetInches
{
private:
    int feet;
    int inches;
    void simplify();      // Defined in feetinch.cpp
public:
    FeetInches(int f = 0, int i = 0)
        { feet = f;
          inches = i;
          simplify(); }

    void setFeet(int f)
        { feet = f; }

    void setInches(int i)
        { inches = i;
          simplify(); }

    int getFeet()
        { return feet; }

    int getInches()
        { return inches; }
};

#endif
```

Contents of FeetInches.cpp

```cpp
// Implementation file for the FeetInches class
#include <cstdlib>           // Needed for abs()
#include "FeetInches.h"

//*************************************************************
// Definition of member function simplify. This function      *
// checks for values in the inches member greater than        *
// twelve or less than zero. If such a value is found,         *
// the numbers in feet and inches are adjusted to conform      *
// to a standard feet & inches expression. For example,        *
// 3 feet 14 inches would be adjusted to 4 feet 2 inches and   *
// 5 feet -2 inches would be adjusted to 4 feet 10 inches.     *
//*************************************************************

void FeetInches::simplify()
{
    if (inches >= 12)
    {
        feet += (inches / 12);
        inches = inches % 12;
    }
```

```
        else if (inches < 0)
        {
            feet -= ((abs(inches) / 12) + 1);
            inches = 12 - (abs(inches) % 12);
        }
    }
```

The `FeetInches` class is designed to hold distances or measurements expressed in feet and inches. It consists of six member functions:

- ♦ A constructor that allows the feet and inches members to be set. The default values for these members is zero.
- ♦ A `setFeet` function for storing a value in the feet member.
- ♦ A `setInches` function for storing a value in the inches member.
- ♦ A `getFeet` function for returning the value in the feet member.
- ♦ A `getInches` function for returning the value in the inches member.
- ♦ A `simplify` function for normalizing the values held in feet and inches. This function adjusts any set of values where the inches member is greater than 12 or less than 0. For example, 3 feet 14 inches would be adjusted to read 4 feet 2 inches, and 5 feet –3 inches would be adjusted to read 4 feet 9 inches.

 Note: The `simplify` function uses the standard library function `abs()` to get the absolute value of the inches member. The `abs()` function requires that `cstdlib` be included.

An enhancement of this class would be the ability to use standard math operators in such a way that one `FeetInches` object could be added to or subtracted from another. For example, assume the `length1` and `length2` objects are defined and initialized as follows:

```
FeetInches length1(3, 5), length2(6, 3);
```

`length1` is holding the value 3 feet 5 inches, and `length2` is holding the value 6 feet 3 inches. Imagine being able to add these two objects in a statement like:

```
length3 = length1 + length2;
```

Wouldn't it be useful if the statement above resulted in `length3` being set to 9 feet 8 inches? That behavior is possible if the + operator is overloaded. Here's the member function that overloads the + operator for the `FeetInches` class:

```
FeetInches FeetInches::operator+(const FeetInches &right)
{
    FeetInches temp;
    temp.inches = inches + right.inches;
```

```
        temp.feet = feet + right.feet;
        temp.simplify();
        return temp;
}
```

This function is called anytime the + operator is used with two FeetInches objects. Just like the overloaded = operator we defined in the previous section, this function has one parameter: a constant reference object named right. This parameter references the object on the right side of the operator. For example, when the statement below is executed, right will reference the length2 object:

```
length3 = length1 + length2;
```

As before, it might be helpful to think of the statement above as the following function call:

```
length3 = length1.operator+(length2);
```

The length2 object is being passed to the function's parameter, right. When the function finishes, it will return a FeetInches object to length3. Now let's see what is happening inside the function. First, notice that a FeetInches object named temp is defined locally:

```
FeetInches temp;
```

This object is a temporary location for holding the results of the addition. Next, there is a statement that adds inches to right.inches and stores the result in temp.inches:

```
temp.inches = inches + right.inches;
```

The inches variable is a member of length1, the object making the function call. It is the object on the left side of the operator. right.inches references the inches member of length2. The next statement is very similar. It adds feet to right.feet and stores the result in temp.feet:

```
temp.feet = feet + right.feet;
```

At this point in the function, temp contains the sum of the feet and inches members of both objects in the expression. The next step is to adjust the values so they conform to a normal value expressed in feet and inches. This is accomplished by calling temp.simplify():

```
temp.simplify();
```

The last step is to return the value stored in temp:

```
return temp;
```

In the statement length3 = length1 + length2, the return statement in the operator function causes the values stored in temp to be returned to the length3 object.

Program 13-7 shows the FeetInches class expanded, not only with the + operator overloaded, but the - operator as well. The program also demonstrates the overloaded operators.

Program 13-7

Contents of `FeetInches2.h`
```
// Specification file for the FeetInches class
#ifndef FEETINCHES_H
#define FEETINCHES_H

// The FeetInches class holds distances or measurements
// expressed in feet and inches.

class FeetInches
{
private:
    int feet;
    int inches;
    void simplify();
public:
    FeetInches(int f = 0, int i = 0)
        { feet = f;
          inches = i;
          simplify(); }

    void setFeet(int f)
        { feet = f; }

    void setInches(int i)
        { inches = i;
          simplify(); }

    int getFeet()
        { return feet; }

    int getInches()
        { return inches; }

    FeetInches operator + (const FeetInches &); // Overloaded +
    FeetInches operator - (const FeetInches &); // Overloaded -
};

#endif
```

Contents of `FeetInches2.cpp`
```
// Implementation file for the FeetInches class
#include <cstdlib>  // Needed for abs()
#include "FeetInches2.h"

//**************************************************************
// Definition of member function simplify. This function      *
// checks for values in the inches member greater than         *
```

(program continues)

Program 13-7 *(continued)*

```
// 12 or less than zero. If such a value is found,        *
// the numbers in feet and inches are adjusted to conform *
// to a standard feet & inches expression. For example,   *
// 3 feet 14 inches would be adjusted to 4 feet 2 inches and *
// 5 feet -2 inches would be adjusted to 4 feet 10 inches. *
//**********************************************************

void FeetInches::simplify()
{
    if (inches >= 12)
    {
        feet += (inches / 12);
        inches = inches % 12;
    }
    else if (inches < 0)
    {
        feet -= ((abs(inches) / 12) + 1);
        inches = 12 - (abs(inches) % 12);
    }
}


//**********************************************
// Overloaded binary + operator.              *
//**********************************************

FeetInches FeetInches::operator + (const FeetInches &right)
{
    FeetInches temp;

    temp.inches = inches + right.inches;
    temp.feet = feet + right.feet;
    temp.simplify();
    return temp;
}


//**********************************************
// Overloaded binary - operator.              *
//**********************************************

FeetInches FeetInches::operator - (const FeetInches &right)
{
    FeetInches temp;

    temp.inches = inches - right.inches;
    temp.feet = feet - right.feet;
    temp.simplify();
    return temp;
}
```

Program 13-7 *(continued)*

Contents of the main program file, `Pr13-7.cpp`

```cpp
// This program demonstrates the FeetInches class's overloaded
// + and - operators.
#include <iostream>
#include "FeetInches2.h"
using namespace std;

int main()
{
    FeetInches first, second, third;// Three FeetInches objects
    int f, i;                 // To hold user input

    // Get a distance from the user.
    cout << "Enter a distance in feet and inches: ";
    cin >> f >> i;

    // Store the distance in the first object.
    first.setFeet(f);
    first.setInches(i);

    // Get another distance from the user.
    cout << "Enter another distance in feet and inches: ";
    cin >> f >> i;

    // Store the distance in second.
    second.setFeet(f);
    second.setInches(i);

    // Assign first + second to third.
    third = first + second;

    // Display the result.
    cout << "first + second = ";
    cout << third.getFeet() << " feet, ";
    cout << third.getInches() << " inches.\n";

    // Assign first - second to third.
    third = first - second;

    // Display the result.
    cout << "first - second = ";
    cout << third.getFeet() << " feet, ";
    cout << third.getInches() << " inches.\n";

    return 0;
}
```

Program 13-7   *(continued)*

Program Output with Example Input Shown in Bold
```
Enter a distance in feet and inches: 6 5 [Enter]
Enter another distance in feet and inches: 3 10 [Enter]
first + second = 10 feet, 3 inches.
first - second = 2 feet, 7 inches.
```

Overloading the Prefix ++ Operator

Unary operators, such as ++ and −−, are overloaded in a fashion similar to the way binary operators are implemented. Because unary operators only affect the object making the operator function call, however, there is no need for a parameter. For example, let's say you wish to have a prefix increment operator for the FeetInches class. Assume the FeetInches object distance is set to the values 7 feet and 5 inches. A ++ operator function could be designed to increment the object's inches member. The following statement would cause distance to have the value 7 feet 6 inches:

```
++distance;
```

The following function overloads the prefix ++ operator to work in this fashion:

```
FeetInches FeetInches::operator++()
{
    ++inches;
    simplify();
    return *this;
}
```

This function first increments the object's inches member. The simplify() function is called and then the dereferenced this pointer is returned. This allows the operator to perform properly in statements like this:

```
distance2 = ++distance1;
```

Remember, the statement above is equivalent to

```
distance2 = distance1.operator++();
```

Overloading the Postfix ++ Operator

Overloading the postfix ++ operator is only slightly different than overloading the prefix version. Here is the function that overloads the postfix operator with the FeetInches class:

```
FeetInches FeetInches::operator++(int)
{
    FeetInches temp(feet, inches);
    inches++;
    simplify();
    return temp;
}
```

The first difference you will notice is the use of a *dummy parameter*. The word int in the function's parentheses establishes a nameless integer parameter. When C++ sees this parameter in an operator function, it knows the function is designed to be used in postfix mode. The second difference is the use of a temporary local variable, the temp object. temp is initialized with the feet and inches values of the object making the function call. temp, therefore is a copy of the object being incremented, but before the increment takes place. After inches is incremented and the simplify function is called, the contents of temp is returned. This causes the postfix operator to behave correctly in a statement like this:

```
distance2 = distance1++;
```

Program 13-8 demonstrates the class implemented with both prefix and postfix ++ operators. Add the following function prototypes to the specification file, FeetInches3.h, for the FeetInches class.

```
FeetInches operator ++ ();        // Prefix ++
FeetInches operator ++ (int);     // Postfix ++
```

Add the following member function definitions to the implementation file, FeetInches3.cpp, for the FeetInches class.

```
//*************************************************************
// Overloaded prefix ++ operator. Causes the inches member to *
// be incremented. Returns the incremented object.            *
//*************************************************************

FeetInches FeetInches::operator++()
{
    ++inches;
    simplify();
    return *this;
}

//*************************************************************
// Overloaded postfix ++ operator. Causes the inches member to *
// be incremented. Returns the value of the object before the  *
// increment.                                                  *
//*************************************************************

FeetInches FeetInches::operator++(int)
{
    FeetInches temp(feet, inches);

    inches++;
    simplify();
    return temp;
}
```

Program 13-8

Contents of the main program file, `Pr13-8.cpp`

```cpp
// This program demonstrates the FeetInches class' overloaded
// prefix and postfix ++ operators.
#include <iostream>
#include "FeetInches3.h"
using namespace std;

int main()
{
    FeetInches first, second(1, 5); // Define two objects.
    int count;                      // Loop counter

    // Use the prefix ++ operator.
    cout << "Demonstrating prefix ++ operator.\n";
    for (count = 0; count < 12; count++)
    {
        first = ++second;
        cout << "first: " << first.getFeet() << " feet, ";
        cout << first.getInches() << " inches. ";
        cout << "second: " << second.getFeet() << " feet, ";
        cout << second.getInches() << " inches.\n";
    }

    // Use the postfix ++ operator.
    cout << "\nDemonstrating postfix ++ operator.\n";
    for (count = 0; count < 12; count++)
    {
        first = second++;
        cout << "first: " << first.getFeet() << " feet, ";
        cout << first.getInches() << " inches. ";
        cout << "second: " << second.getFeet() << " feet, ";
        cout << second.getInches() << " inches.\n";
    }

    return 0;
}
```

Program Output

```
Demonstrating prefix ++ operator.
first: 1 feet 6 inches. second: 1 feet 6 inches.
first: 1 feet 7 inches. second: 1 feet 7 inches.
first: 1 feet 8 inches. second: 1 feet 8 inches.
first: 1 feet 9 inches. second: 1 feet 9 inches.
first: 1 feet 10 inches. second: 1 feet 10 inches.
first: 1 feet 11 inches. second: 1 feet 11 inches.
first: 2 feet 0 inches. second: 2 feet 0 inches.
first: 2 feet 1 inches. second: 2 feet 1 inches.
first: 2 feet 2 inches. second: 2 feet 2 inches.
first: 2 feet 3 inches. second: 2 feet 3 inches.
```

(output continues)

Program 13-8 *(continued)*

```
first: 2 feet 4 inches. second: 2 feet 4 inches.
first: 2 feet 5 inches. second: 2 feet 5 inches.
Demonstrating postfix ++ operator.
first: 2 feet 5 inches. second: 2 feet 6 inches.
first: 2 feet 6 inches. second: 2 feet 7 inches.
first: 2 feet 7 inches. second: 2 feet 8 inches.
first: 2 feet 8 inches. second: 2 feet 9 inches.
first: 2 feet 9 inches. second: 2 feet 10 inches.
first: 2 feet 10 inches. second: 2 feet 11 inches.
first: 2 feet 11 inches. second: 3 feet 0 inches.
first: 3 feet 0 inches. second: 3 feet 1 inches.
first: 3 feet 1 inches. second: 3 feet 2 inches.
first: 3 feet 2 inches. second: 3 feet 3 inches.
first: 3 feet 3 inches. second: 3 feet 4 inches.
first: 3 feet 4 inches. second: 3 feet 5 inches.
```

 Checkpoint   [13.5]

13.14 Assume there is a class named Pet. Write the prototype for a member function of Pet that overloads the = operator.

13.15 Assume that dog and cat are instances of the Pet class, which has overloaded the = operator. Rewrite the following statement so it appears in function call notation instead of operator notation:

dog = cat;

13.16 What is the disadvantage of an overloaded = operator returning void?

13.17 Describe the purpose of the this pointer.

13.18 The this pointer is automatically passed to what type of functions?

13.19 Assume there is a class named Animal, which overloads the = and + operators. In the following statement, assume cat, tiger, and wildcat are all instances of the Animal class:

wildcat = cat + tiger;

Of the three objects, wildcat, cat, or tiger, which is calling the operator+ function? Which object is passed as an argument into the function?

13.20 What does the use of a dummy parameter in a unary operator function indicate to the compiler?

Overloading Relational Operators

In addition to the assignment and math operators, relational operators may also be overloaded. This capability allows classes to be compared in statements that use relational expressions such as:

```
if (distance1 < distance2)
{
    ... code ...
}
```

Overloaded relational operators are implemented like other binary operators. The only difference is that a relational operator function should always return a `true` or `false` value. Here is the function for overloading the > operator to work with the `FeetInches` class:

```
bool FeetInches::operator > (const FeetInches &right)
{
    bool status;

    if (feet > right.feet)
        status = true;
    else if (feet == right.feet && inches > right.inches)
        status = true;
    else
        status = false;

    return status;
}
```

As you can see, the function compares the `feet` member (and if necessary, the `inches` member) with that of the parameter. If the calling object contains a value greater than that of the parameter, `true` is returned. Otherwise, `false` is returned.

Program 13-9 shows the `FeetInches` class modified to overload the >, <, and == operators. Add the following member function prototypes to the specification file, `FeetInches4.h`, for the `FeetInches` class.

```
bool operator > (const FeetInches &);          // Overloaded >
bool operator < (const FeetInches &);          // Overloaded <
bool operator == (const FeetInches &);         // Overloaded ==
```

Add the following member function definitions to the implementation file, FeetInches4.cpp, for the FeetInches class.

```
//*************************************************************
// Overloaded > operator. Returns true if the current object *
// is set to a value greater than that of right.             *
//*************************************************************

bool FeetInches::operator > (const FeetInches &right)
{
    bool status;

    if (feet > right.feet)
        status = true;
    else if (feet == right.feet && inches > right.inches)
        status = true;
```

```cpp
        else
            status = false;

        return status;
    }

    //**************************************************************
    // Overloaded < operator. Returns true if the current object *
    // is set to a value less than that of right.                *
    //**************************************************************

    bool FeetInches::operator < (const FeetInches &right)
    {
        bool status;

        if (feet < right.feet)
            status = true;
        else if (feet == right.feet && inches < right.inches)
            status = true;
        else
            status = false;

        return status;
    }

    //**************************************************************
    // Overloaded == operator. Returns true if the current object *
    // is set to a value equal to that of right.                 *
    //**************************************************************

    bool FeetInches::operator == (const FeetInches &right)
    {
        bool status;

        if (feet == right.feet && inches == right.inches)
            status = true;
        else
            status = false;

        return status;
    }
```

Program 13-9

Contents of the main program file, `Pr13-9.cpp`

```cpp
// This program demonstrates the FeetInches class's overloaded
// relational operators.
#include <iostream>
#include "FeetInches4.h"
using namespace std;
```

(program continues)

Program 13-9 *(continued)*

```cpp
int main()
{
    FeetInches first, second, third;    // Define three objects.
    int f, i;                           // To hold user input.

    // Get a distance from the user.
    cout << "Enter a distance in feet and inches: ";
    cin >> f >> i;

    // Store the distance in first.
    first.setFeet(f);
    first.setInches(i);

    // Get another distance.
    cout << "Enter another distance in feet and inches: ";
    cin >> f >> i;

    // Store the distance in second.
    second.setFeet(f);
    second.setInches(i);

    // Compare the two objects.
    if (first == second)
        cout << "first is equal to second.\n";
    if (first > second)
        cout << "first is greater than second.\n";
    if (first < second)
        cout << "first is less than second.\n";

    return 0;
}
```

Program Output with Example Input Shown in Bold
```
Enter a distance in feet and inches: 6 5 [Enter]
Enter another distance in feet and inches: 3 10 [Enter]
first is greater than second.
```

Program Output with Other Example Input Shown in Bold
```
Enter a distance in feet and inches: 5 5 [Enter]
Enter another distance in feet and inches: 5 5 [Enter]
first is equal to second.
```

Program Output with Other Example Input Shown in Bold
```
Enter a distance in feet and inches: 3 4 [Enter]
Enter another distance in feet and inches: 3 7 [Enter]
first is less than second.
```

Overloading the << and >> Operators

Overloading the math and relational operators gives you the ability to write those types of expressions with class objects just as naturally as with integers, floats, and other built-in data types. If an object's primary data members are private, however, you still have to make explicit member function calls to send their values to `cout`. For example, assume `distance` is a `FeetInches` object. The following statements display its internal values:

```
cout << distance.getFeet() << " feet, ";
cout << distance.getInches() << "inches";
```

It is also necessary to explicitly call member functions to set a `FeetInches` object's data. For instance, the following statements set the `distance` object to user-specified values:

```
cout << "Enter a value in feet: ";
cin >> f;
distance.setFeet(f);
cout << "Enter a value in inches: ";
cin >> i;
distance.setInches(i);
```

By overloading the stream insertion operator (`<<`), you could send the `distance` object to `cout`, as shown in the following code, and have the screen output automatically formatted in the correct way.

```
cout << distance;
```

Likewise, by overloading the stream extraction operator (`>>`), the `distance` object could take values directly from `cin`, as shown here.

```
cin >> distance;
```

Overloading these operators is done in a slightly different way, however, than overloading other operators. These operators are actually part of the `ostream` and `istream` classes defined in the C++ runtime library. (The `cout` and `cin` objects are instances of `ostream` and `istream`.) You must write operator functions to overload the `ostream` version of `<<` and the `istream` version of `>>`, so they work directly with a class such as `FeetInches`. For example, the following operator function will overload the `<<` operator to format and display the contents of a `FeetInches` object:

```
ostream &operator << (ostream &strm, const FeetInches &obj)
{
    strm << obj.feet << " feet, " << obj.inches << " inches";
    return strm;
}
```

Notice the function has two parameters: an `ostream` reference object and a `const FeetInches` reference object. The `ostream` parameter will be a reference to the actual `ostream` object on the left side of the `<<` operator. The second parameter is a reference to a `FeetInches` object. This parameter will reference the object on the right side of the << operator. This function tells C++ how to handle any expression that has the following form:

```
ostream-object << FeetInches-object
```

So, when C++ encounters the following statement, it will call the overloaded `operator<<` function:

```
cout << distance;
```

Notice that the function's return type is `ostream &`. This means that the function returns a reference to an `ostream` object. When the `return strm;` statement executes, it doesn't return a copy of `strm`, but a reference to it. This allows you to chain together several expressions using the overloaded << operator, such as:

```
cout << distance1 << " " << distance2 << endl;
```

Here is the function that overloads the stream extraction operator to work with the `FeetInches` class:

```cpp
istream &operator >> (istream &strm, FeetInches &obj)
{
    // Prompt the user for the feet.
    cout << "Feet: ";
    strm >> obj.feet;

    // Prompt the user for the inches.
    cout << "Inches: ";
    strm >> obj.inches;

    // Normalize the values.
    obj.simplify();

    return strm;
}
```

The same principles hold true for this operator. It tells C++ how to handle any expression in the following form:

```
istream-object >> FeetInches-object
```

Once again, the function returns a reference to an `istream` object so several of these expressions may be chained together.

You have probably realized that neither of these functions are quite ready to work, though. Both functions attempt to directly access the `FeetInches` object's private members. Because the functions aren't themselves members of the `FeetInches` class, they don't have this type of access. The next step is to make the operator functions friends of `FeetInches`. This is shown in the following listing of the `FeetInches` class declaration.

Note: Some compilers require you to prototype the >> and << operator functions outside the class. For this reason, we have added the following statements to the FeetInches5.h class specification file.

```
class FeetInches;          // Forward Declaration

// Function Prototypes for Overloaded Stream Operators
ostream &operator << (ostream &, const FeetInches &);
istream &operator >> (istream &, FeetInches &);
```

Contents of *FeetInches5.h*

```
// Specification file for the FeetInches class
#ifndef FEETINCHES_H
#define FEETINCHES_H

#include <iostream>
using namespace std;

class FeetInches;     // Forward Declaration

// Function Prototypes for Overloaded Stream Operators
ostream &operator << (ostream &, FeetInches &);
istream &operator >> (istream &, FeetInches &);

// The FeetInches class holds distances or measurements
// expressed in feet and inches.

class FeetInches
{
private:
    int feet;
    int inches;
    void simplify();
public:
    FeetInches(int f = 0, int i = 0)
        { feet = f;
          inches = i;
          simplify(); }

    void setFeet(int f)
        { feet = f; }

    void setInches(int i)
        { inches = i;
          simplify(); }

    int getFeet()
        { return feet; }
```

```
        int getInches()
            { return inches; }

        FeetInches operator + (const FeetInches &);    // Overloaded +
        FeetInches operator - (const FeetInches &);    // Overloaded -
        FeetInches operator ++ ();                     // Prefix ++
        FeetInches operator ++ (int);                  // Postfix ++
        bool operator > (const FeetInches &);          // Overloaded >
        bool operator < (const FeetInches &);          // Overloaded <
        bool operator == (const FeetInches &);         // Overloaded ==
        friend ostream &operator << (ostream &, const FeetInches &);
        friend istream &operator >> (istream &, FeetInches &);
};

#endif
```

The last two lines in the class declaration tell C++ to make the overloaded << and >> operator functions friends of the FeetInches class:

```
friend ostream &operator<<(ostream &, const FeetInches &);
friend istream &operator>>(istream &, FeetInches &);
```

These statements give the operator functions direct access to the FeetInches class's private members. Add the following member function definitions to the implementation file, FeetInches5.cpp, for the FeetInches class.

```
//*********************************************************
// Overloaded << operator. Gives cout the ability to      *
// directly display FeetInches objects.                   *
//*********************************************************

ostream &operator<<(ostream &strm, FeetInches &obj)
{
    strm << obj.feet << " feet, " << obj.inches << " inches";
    return strm;
}

//*********************************************************
// Overloaded >> operator. Gives cin the ability to       *
// store user input directly into FeetInches objects.     *
//*********************************************************

istream &operator >> (istream &strm, FeetInches &obj)
{
    // Prompt the user for the feet.
    cout << "Feet: ";
    strm >> obj.feet;

    // Prompt the user for the inches.
    cout << "Inches: ";
    strm >> obj.inches;
```

```
        // Normalize the values.
        obj.simplify();

        return strm;
    }
```

Program 13-10 demonstrates how the overloaded operators work.

Program 13-10

```
// This program demonstrates the << and >> operators,
// overloaded to work with the FeetInches class.
#include <iostream>
#include "FeetInches5.h"
using namespace std;

int main()
{
    FeetInches first, second;        // Define two objects.

    cout << "Enter a distance in feet and inches.\n";
    cin >> first;
    cout << "Enter another distance in feet and inches.\n";
    cin >> second;
    cout << "The values you entered are:\n";
    cout << first << " and " << second << endl;
    return 0;
}
```

Program Output with Example Input Shown in Bold
```
Enter a distance in feet and inches.
Feet: 6 [Enter]
Inches: 5 [Enter]
Enter another distance in feet and inches.
Feet: 3 [Enter]
Inches: 10 [Enter]
The values you entered are:
6 feet, 5 inches and 3 feet, 10 inches
```

Overloading the [] Operator

In addition to the traditional operators, C++ allows you to change the way the [] symbols work. This gives you the ability of writing classes that have array-like behaviors. For example, the string class overloads the [] operator so you can access the individual characters stored in string class objects. Assume the following definition exists in a program:

```
string name = "William";
```

The first character in the string, 'W,' is stored at name[0], so the following statement will display W on the screen.

```
cout << name[0];
```

You can use the overloaded [] operator to create an array class, like the following one. The class behaves like a regular array, but performs the bounds-checking that C++ lacks.

```cpp
class IntArray
{
private:
    int *aptr;
    int arraySize;
    void subscriptError();          // Handles invalid subscripts.
public:
    IntArray(int);                  // Constructor
    IntArray(const IntArray &);     // Copy constructor
    ~IntArray();                    // Destructor
    int size()
        { return arraySize; }
    int &operator[](const int &);   // Overloaded [] operator
};
```

Before focusing on the overloaded operator, let's look at the constructors and the destructor. The code for the first constructor is:

```cpp
IntArray::IntArray(int s)
{
    arraySize = s;
    aptr = new int [s];
    for (int count = 0; count < arraySize; count++)
        *(aptr + count) = 0;
}
```

When an instance of the class is defined, the number of elements the array is to have is passed into the constructor's parameter, s. This value is copied to the arraySize member, and then used to dynamically allocate enough memory for the array. The constructor's final step is to store zeros in all of the array's elements:

```cpp
    for (int count = 0; count < arraySize; count++)
        *(aptr + count) = 0;
```

The class also has a copy constructor, which is used when a class object is initialized with another object's data:

```cpp
IntArray::IntArray(const IntArray &obj)
{
    arraySize = obj.arraySize;
    aptr = new int [arraySize];
    for(int count = 0; count < arraySize; count++)
        *(aptr + count) = *(obj.aptr + count);
}
```

A reference to the initializing object is passed into the parameter obj. Once the memory is successfully allocated for the array, the constructor copies all the values in obj's array into the calling object's array.

The destructor simply frees the memory allocated by the class's constructors. First, however, it checks the value in arraySize to be sure the array has at least one element:

```
IntArray::~IntArray()
{
    if (arraySize > 0)
        delete [] aptr;
}
```

The [] operator is overloaded similarly to other operators. Here is the definition of the operator[] function for the IntArray class:

```
int &IntArray::operator[](const int &sub)
{
    if (sub < 0 || sub >= arraySize)
        subscriptError();
    return aptr[sub];
}
```

The operator[] function can have only a single parameter. The one shown uses a constant reference to an integer. This parameter holds the value placed inside the brackets in an expression. For example, if table is an IntArray object, the number 12 will be passed into the sub parameter in the following statement:

```
cout << table[12];
```

Inside the function, the value in the sub parameter is tested by the following if statement:

```
if (sub < 0 || sub >= arraySize)
    subscriptError();
```

This statement determines whether sub is within the range of the array's subscripts. If sub is less than 0 or greater than or equal to arraySize, it's not a valid subscript, so the subscriptError function is called. If sub is within range, the function uses it as an offset into the array, and returns a reference to the value stored at that location.

One critically important aspect of the function above is its return type. It's crucial that the function not simply return an integer, but a *reference* to an integer. The reason for this is that expressions such as the following must be possible:

```
table[5] = 27;
```

Remember, the built-in = operator requires the object on its left to be an lvalue. An lvalue must represent a modifiable memory location, such as a variable. The integer return value of a function is not an lvalue. If the operator[] function merely returns an integer, it cannot be used to create expressions placed on the left side of an assignment operator.

A reference to an integer, however, is an lvalue. If the operator[] function returns a reference, it can be used to create expressions like the following:

```
table[7] = 52;
```

In this statement, the operator [] function is called with 7 being passed as its argument. Assuming 7 is within range, the function returns a reference to the integer stored at (aptr + 7). In essence, the statement above is equivalent to:

```
*(aptr + 7) = 52;
```

Because the operator [] function returns actual integers stored in the array, it is not necessary for math or relational operators to be overloaded. Even the stream operators << and >> will work just as they are with the IntArray class.

Here is the complete listing of IntArray.h and IntArray.cpp:

Contents of *IntArray.h*

```cpp
// Specification file for the IntArray class
#ifndef INTARRAY_H
#define INTARRAY_H

class IntArray
{
private:
    int *aptr;
    int arraySize;
    void subscriptError();          // Handles invalid subscripts.
public:
    IntArray(int);                  // Constructor
    IntArray(const IntArray &);     // Copy constructor
    ~IntArray();                    // Destructor
    int size()
        { return arraySize; }
    int &operator[](const int &);   // Overloaded [] operator
};

#endif
```

Contents of *IntArray.cpp*

```cpp
#include <iostream>
#include <cstdlib>                  // For the exit function
#include "IntArray.h"
using namespace std;

//*********************************************************
// Constructor for IntArray class. Sets the size of the  *
// array and allocates memory for it.                    *
//*********************************************************

IntArray::IntArray(int s)
{
    arraySize = s;
    aptr = new int [s];
    for (int count = 0; count < arraySize; count++)
        *(aptr + count) = 0;
}
```

```
//********************************************************
// Copy Constructor for IntArray class.                 *
//********************************************************

IntArray::IntArray(const IntArray &obj)
{
    arraySize = obj.arraySize;
    aptr = new int [arraySize];
    for(int count = 0; count < arraySize; count++)
        *(aptr + count) = *(obj.aptr + count);
}

//********************************************************
// Destructor for IntArray class.                       *
//********************************************************

IntArray::~IntArray()
{
    if (arraySize > 0)
        delete [] aptr;
}



//************************************************************
// subscriptError function. Displays an error message and   *
// terminates the program when a subscript is out of range. *
//************************************************************

void IntArray::subscriptError()
{
    cout << "ERROR: Subscript out of range.\n";
    exit(0);
}

//********************************************************
// Overloaded [] operator. The argument is a subscript. *
// This function returns a reference to the element     *
// in the array indexed by the subscript.               *
//********************************************************

int &IntArray::operator[](const int &sub)
{
    if (sub < 0 || sub > arraySize)
        subscriptError();
    return aptr[sub];
}
```

Program 13-11 demonstrates how the class works.

Program 13-11

```cpp
// This program demonstrates an overloaded [] operator.
#include <iostream>
#include "IntArray.h"
using namespace std;

int main()
{
    const int SIZE = 10;
    IntArray table(SIZE);            // Define an IntArray with 10 elements.

    // Store values in the array.
    for (int x = 0; x < SIZE; x++)
        table[x] = (x * 2);

    // Display the values in the array.
    for (x = 0; x < SIZE; x++)
        cout << table[x] << " ";
    cout << endl;

    // Use the standard + operator on array elements.
    for (x = 0; x < SIZE; x++)
        table[x] = table[x] + 5;

    // Display the values in the array.
    for (x = 0; x < SIZE; x++)
        cout << table[x] << " ";
    cout << endl;

    // Use the standard ++ operator on array elements.
    for (x = 0; x < SIZE; x++)
        table[x]++;

    // Display the values in the array.
    for (x = 0; x < SIZE; x++)
        cout << table[x] << " ";
    cout << endl;

    return 0;
}
```

Program Output

```
0 2 4 6 8 10 12 14 16 18
5 7 9 11 13 15 17 19 21 23
6 8 10 12 14 16 18 20 22 24
```

Program 13-12 demonstrates the IntArray class's bounds-checking capability.

Program 13-12

```
#include <iostream>
#include "IntArray.h"
using namespace std;

int main()
{
   const int SIZE = 10;
   IntArray table(SIZE);

   // Store values in the array.
   for (int x = 0; x < SIZE; x++)
      table[x] = x;
   // Display the values in the array.
   for (x = 0; x < SIZE; x++)
      cout << table[x] << " ";
   cout << endl;
   cout << "Now attempting to use an invalid subscript.\n";
   table[SIZE + 1] = 0;
   return 0;
}
```

Program Output
```
0 1 2 3 4 5 6 7 8 9
Now attempting to use an invalid subscript.
ERROR: Subscript out of range.
```

Checkpoint   [13.5]

13.21 Describe the values that should be returned from functions that overload relational operators.

13.22 What is the advantage of overloading the << and >> operators?

13.23 What type of object should an overloaded << operator function return?

13.24 What type of object should an overloaded >> operator function return?

13.25 If an overloaded << or >> operator accesses a private member of a class, what must be done in that class's declaration?

13.26 Assume the class NumList has overloaded the [] operator. In the expression below, list1 is an instance of the NumList class:

   list1[25]

Rewrite the expression above to explicitly call the function that overloads the [] operator.

13.6   Object Conversion

CONCEPT Special operator functions may be written to convert a class object to any other type.

As you've already seen, operator functions allow classes to work more like built-in data types. Another capability that operator functions can give classes is automatic type conversion.

Data type conversion happens "behind the scenes" with the built-in data types. For instance, suppose a program uses the following variables:

```
int i;
double d;
```

The statement below automatically converts the value in i to a floating-point number and stores it in d:

```
d = i;
```

Likewise, the following statement converts the value in t to an integer (truncating the fractional part) and stores it in i:

```
i = d;
```

The same functionality can also be given to class objects. For example, assuming distance is a FeetInches object and d is a double, the following statement would conveniently convert distance's value into a floating-point number and store it in d, if FeetInches is properly written:

```
d = distance;
```

To be able to use a statement such as this, an operator function must be written to perform the conversion. Here is an operator function for converting a FeetInches object to a float:

```
FeetInches::operator double()
{
    double temp = feet;

    temp += (inches / 12.0);
    return temp;
}
```

This function contains an algorithm that will calculate the decimal equivalent of a feet and inches measurement. For example, the value 4 feet 6 inches will be converted to 4.5. This value is stored in the local variable temp.

 Note: No return type is specified in the function header. Because the function is a FeetInches-to-double conversion function, it will always return a double. Also, because the function takes no arguments, there are no parameters.

Program 13-13 demonstrates the FeetInches class with both a float and an int conversion function. (Note that the int conversion function simply returns the feet member, thus "truncating" the inches value.) The updated class files are also listed.

Program 13-13

Contents of *FeetInches6.h*

```
// Specification file for the FeetInches class
#ifndef FEETINCHES_H
#define FEETINCHES_H

#include <iostream>
using namespace std;

class FeetInches;            // Forward Declaration

// Function Prototypes for Overloaded Stream Operators
ostream &operator << (ostream &, FeetInches &);
istream &operator >> (istream &, FeetInches &);

// The FeetInches class holds distances or measurements
// expressed in feet and inches.

class FeetInches
{
private:
    int feet;
    int inches;
    void simplify();
public:
    FeetInches(int f = 0, int i = 0)
        { feet = f;
          inches = i;
          simplify(); }

    void setFeet(int f)
        { feet = f; }

    void setInches(int i)
        { inches = i;
          simplify(); }

    int getFeet()
        { return feet; }

    int getInches()
        { return inches; }
```

(program continues)

Program 13-13 *(continued)*

```
    FeetInches operator + (const FeetInches &);    // Overloaded +
    FeetInches operator - (const FeetInches &);    // Overloaded -
    FeetInches operator ++ ();                     // Prefix ++
    FeetInches operator ++ (int);                  // Postfix ++
    bool operator > (const FeetInches &);          // Overloaded >
    bool operator < (const FeetInches &);          // Overloaded <
    bool operator == (const FeetInches &);         // Overloaded ==
    friend ostream &operator << (ostream &, const FeetInches &);
    friend istream &operator >> (istream &, FeetInches &);
    operator double();
    operator int()
        { return feet; }
};

#endif
```

Contents of `FeetInches6.cpp`

```
// Implementation file for the FeetInches class
#include <cstdlib>  // Needed for abs()
#include "FeetInches6.h"

//**************************************************************
// Definition of member function simplify. This function      *
// checks for values in the inches member greater than        *
// twelve or less than zero. If such a value is found,         *
// the numbers in feet and inches are adjusted to conform     *
// to a standard feet & inches expression. For example,       *
// 3 feet 14 inches would be adjusted to 4 feet 2 inches and  *
// 5 feet -2 inches would be adjusted to 4 feet 10 inches.    *
//**************************************************************

void FeetInches::simplify()
{
    if (inches >= 12)
    {
        feet += (inches / 12);
        inches = inches % 12;
    }
    else if (inches < 0)
    {
        feet -= ((abs(inches) / 12) + 1);
        inches = 12 - (abs(inches) % 12);
    }
}
```

(program continues)

Program 13-13 *(continued)*

```
//***********************************************
// Overloaded binary + operator.              *
//***********************************************

FeetInches FeetInches::operator + (const FeetInches &right)
{
    FeetInches temp;

    temp.inches = inches + right.inches;
    temp.feet = feet + right.feet;
    temp.simplify();
    return temp;
}



//***********************************************
// Overloaded binary - operator.              *
//***********************************************

FeetInches FeetInches::operator - (const FeetInches &right)
{
    FeetInches temp;

    temp.inches = inches - right.inches;
    temp.feet = feet - right.feet;
    temp.simplify();
    return temp;
}

//*************************************************************
// Overloaded prefix ++ operator. Causes the inches member to *
// be incremented. Returns the incremented object.            *
//*************************************************************

FeetInches FeetInches::operator ++ ()
{
    ++inches;
    simplify();
    return *this;
}

//*************************************************************
// Overloaded postfix ++ operator. Causes the inches member to *
// be incremented. Returns the value of the object before the  *
// increment.                                                  *
//*************************************************************
```

(program continues)

Program 13-13 *(continued)*

```cpp
FeetInches FeetInches::operator ++ (int)
{
    FeetInches temp(feet, inches);

    inches++;
    simplify();
    return temp;
}

//*************************************************************
// Overloaded > operator. Returns true if the current object *
// is set to a value greater than that of right.             *
//*************************************************************

bool FeetInches::operator > (const FeetInches &right)
{
    bool status;

    if (feet > right.feet)
        status = true;
    else if (feet == right.feet && inches > right.inches)
        status = true;
    else
        status = false;

    return status;
}

//*************************************************************
// Overloaded < operator. Returns true if the current object *
// is set to a value less than that of right.                *
//*************************************************************

bool FeetInches::operator < (const FeetInches &right)
{
    bool status;

    if (feet < right.feet)
        status = true;
    else if (feet == right.feet && inches < right.inches)
        status = true;
    else
        status = false;

    return status;
}
```

(program continues)

Program 13-13 *(continued)*

```cpp
//***************************************************************
// Overloaded == operator. Returns true if the current object *
// is set to a value equal to that of right.                   *
//***************************************************************

bool FeetInches::operator == (const FeetInches &right)
{
    bool status;

    if (feet == right.feet && inches == right.inches)
        status = true;
    else
        status = false;

    return status;
}

//*************************************************************
// Overloaded << operator. Gives cout the ability to         *
// directly display FeetInches objects.                      *
//*************************************************************

ostream &operator<<(ostream &strm, const FeetInches &obj)
{
    strm << obj.feet << " feet, " << obj.inches << " inches";
    return strm;
}

//*************************************************************
// Overloaded >> operator. Gives cin the ability to          *
// store user input directly into FeetInches objects.        *
//*************************************************************

istream &operator >> (istream &strm, FeetInches &obj)
{
    // Prompt the user for the feet.
    cout << "Feet: ";
    strm >> obj.feet;

    // Prompt the user for the inches.
    cout << "Inches: ";
    strm >> obj.inches;

    // Normalize the values.
    obj.simplify();

    return strm;
}
```

(program continues)

Program 13-13 *(continued)*

```cpp
//****************************************************************
// Conversion function to convert a FeetInches object           *
// to a double.                                                  *
//****************************************************************

FeetInches::operator double()
{
    double temp = feet;

    temp += (inches / 12.0);
    return temp;
}
```

Contents of the main program file, Pr13-13.cpp
```cpp
// This program demonstrates the the FeetInches class's
// conversion functions.
#include <iostream>
#include "FeetInches6.h"
using namespace std;

int main()
{
    FeetInches distance;
    double d;
    int i;

    // Get a distance from the user.
    cout << "Enter a distance in feet and inches:\n";
    cin >> distance;

    // Convert the distance object to a double.
    d = distance;

    // Convert the distance object to an int.
    i = distance;

    // Display the values.
    cout << "The value " << distance;
    cout << " is equivalent to " << d << " feet\n";
    cout << "or " << i << " feet, rounded down.\n";

    return 0;
}
```

Program 13-13 *(continued)*

___

Program Output with Example Input Shown in Bold
```
Enter a distance in feet and inches:
Feet: 8 [Enter]
Inches: 6 [Enter]
The value 8 feet, 6 inches is equivalent to 8.5 feet
or 8 feet, rounded down.
```
___

 ## Checkpoint [13.6]

13.27 When overloading a binary operator such as + or –, what object is passed into the operator function's parameter?

13.28 Explain why overloaded prefix and postfix ++ and -- operator functions should return a value.

13.29 How does C++ tell the difference between an overloaded prefix and postfix ++ or -- operator function?

13.30 Write member functions of the `FeetInches` class that overload the prefix and postfix -- operators. Demonstrate the functions in a simple program similar to Program 13-13.

 See the CaseStudies.pdf file on the accompanying CD for this chapter's case studies.

13.7 Object Composition

CONCEPT	Object composition occurs when a class contains an instance of another class.

In Chapter 11 you learned that structures can be nested inside other structures. This leads to the creation of structures with instances of other structures as members. The same technique is possible with classes. Making an instance of one class the member of another class is called *object composition*.

Object composition is useful for creating a "has a" relationship between classes. For example, look at the following `Customer` class. It has several instances of the `MyString` and `Account` classes (discussed in the CaseStudies.pdf file on the accompanying CD) as members.

 Appendix D on the Student CD shows how to represent object composition in UML.

Contents of `Customer.h`
```
#include "Account.h"
#include "MyString.h"

class Customer
{
```

```
        public:
            MyString name;
            MyString address;
            MyString city;
            MyString state;
            MyString ZIP;
            Account savings;
            Account checking;
            Customer(char *n, char *a, char *c, char *s, char *z)
                { name = n; address = a; city = c; state = s; zip = z; }
    };
```

The relationship between the different objects that make up this class can be described as follows:

 ◆ the customer has a name,

 ◆ the customer has an address,

 ◆ the customer has a city,

 ◆ the customer has a state,

 ◆ the customer has a ZIP code,

 ◆ the customer has a savings account, and

 ◆ the customer has a checking account.

Program 13-14 demonstrates this class.

Program 13-14

```
// This program demonstrates the Customer class
// which is composed of the Account class and the
// MyString class.
#include <iostream>
#include <iomanip>
#include "Customer.h"
using namespace std;

int main()
{
    // Define a Customer class object.
    Customer smith("Smith, John", "127 Pine View Drive",
                   "Brassville", "NC", "28801");

    // Store data in the smith object.
    smith.savings.makeDeposit(1000);
    smith.checking.makeDeposit(500);
    smith.savings.calcInterest();
    smith.checking.calcInterest();
```

(program continues)

Program 13-14 *(continued)*

```
// Display the data.
cout << fixed << showpoint << setprecision(2);
cout << "Customer Name: " << smith.name << endl;
cout << "Address: " << smith.address << endl;
cout << "City: " << smith.city << endl;
cout << "State: " << smith.state << endl;
cout << "ZIP: " << smith.zip << endl;
cout << "Savings Account Balance: ";
cout << smith.savings.getBalance() << endl;
cout << "Interest earned from savings: ";
cout << smith.savings.getInterest() << endl;
cout << "Checking Accout Balance: ";
cout << smith.checking.getBalance() << endl;
cout << "Interest earned from checking: ";
cout << smith.checking.getInterest() << endl;

return 0;
}
```

Program Output
```
Customer Name: Smith, John
Address: 127 Pine View Drive
City: Brassville
State: NC
ZIP: 28801
Savings Account Balance: 1045.00
Interest earned from savings: 45.00
Checking Account Balance: 522.50
Interest earned from checking: 22.50
```

Checkpoint   [13.7]

13.31   What are the benefits of having operator functions that perform object conversion?

13.32   Why are no return types listed in the prototypes or headers of operator functions that perform data type conversion?

13.33   Assume there is a class named BlackBox. Write the header for a member function that converts a BlackBox object to an int.

13.34   Assume there are two classes, Big and Small. The Big class has, as a member, an instance of the Small class. Write a sentence that describes the relationship between the two classes.

Review Questions and Exercises

Short Answer

1. Describe the difference between an instance member variable and a static member variable.
2. Assume that a class named `Numbers` has the following static member function declaration:

   ```
   static void showTotal();
   ```

   Write a statement that calls the `showTotal` function.
3. A static member variable is declared in a class. Where is the static member variable defined?
4. What is a `friend` function?
5. Why is it not always a good idea to make an entire class a friend of another class?
6. What is memberwise assignment?
7. When is a copy constructor called?
8. How can the compiler determine if a constructor is a copy constructor?
9. Describe a situation where memberwise assignment is not desirable.
10. Why must the parameter of a copy constructor be a reference?
11. What is a default copy constructor?
12. Why would a programmer want to overload operators rather than use regular member functions to perform similar operations?
13. What is passed to the parameter of a class's `operator=` function?
14. Why shouldn't a class's overloaded = operator be implemented with a `void` operator function?
15. How does the compiler know whether an overloaded ++ operator should be used in prefix or postfix mode?
16. What is the `this` pointer?
17. What type of value should be returned from an overloaded relational operator function?
18. The class `Stuff` has both a copy constructor and an overloaded = operator. Assume that `blob` and `clump` are both instances of the `Stuff` class. For each statement below, indicate whether the copy constructor or the overloaded = operator will be called.

    ```
    Stuff blob = clump;
    clump = blob;
    blob.operator=(clump);
    showValues(blob);    // Blob is passed by value.
    ```
19. Explain the programming steps necessary to make a class's member variable static.
20. Explain the programming steps necessary to make a class's member function static.

21. Consider the following class declaration:

```
class Thing
{
private:
    int x;
    int y;
    static int z;
public:
    Thing()
        { x = y = z; }
    static void putThing(int a)
        { z = a; }
};
```

Assume a program containing the class declaration defines three Thing objects with the following statement:

```
Thing one, two, three;
```

How many separate instances of the x member exist?

How many separate instances of the y member exist?

How many separate instances of the z member exist?

What value will be stored in the x and y members of each object?

Write a statement that will call the PutThing member function *before* the objects above are defined.

22. Describe the difference between making a class a member of another class (object composition), and making a class a friend of another class.

23. What is the purpose of a forward declaration of a class?

24. Explain why memberwise assignment can cause problems with a class that contains a pointer member.

25. Why is a class's copy constructor called when an object of that class is passed by value into a function.

Algorithm Workbench

26. Assume a class named Bird exists. Write the header for a member function that overloads the = operator for that class.

27. Assume a class named Dollars exists. Write the headers for member functions that overload the prefix and postfix ++ operators for that class.

28. Assume a class named Yen exists. Write the header for a member function that overloads the < operator for that class.

29. Assume a class named Length exists. Write the header for a member function that overloads cout's << operator for that class.

30. Assume a class named `Collection` exists. Write the header for a member function that over-loads the [] operator for that class.

True or False

31. T F   Static member variables cannot be accessed by non-static member functions.
32. T F   Static member variables are defined outside their class declaration.
33. T F   A static member function may refer to non-static member variables of the same class, but only after an instance of the class has been defined.
34. T F   When a function is declared a `friend` by a class, it becomes a member of that class.
35. T F   A friend function has access to the private members of the class declaring it a `friend`.
36. T F   An entire class may be declared a `friend` of another class.
37. T F   In order for a function or class to become a friend of another class, it must be declared as such by the class granting it access.
38. T F   If a class has a pointer as a member, it's a good idea to also have a copy constructor.
39. T F   You cannot use the – operator to assign one object's values to another object, unless you overload the operator.
40. T F   If a class doesn't have a copy constructor, the compiler generates a default copy constructor for it.
41. T F   If a class has a copy constructor, and an object of that class is passed by value into a function, the function's parameter will *not* call its copy constructor.
42. T F   The `this` pointer is passed to static member functions.
43. T F   All functions that overload unary operators must have a dummy parameter.
44. T F   For an object to perform automatic type conversion, an operator function must be written.
45. T F   It is possible to have an instance of one class as a member of another class.

Find the Error

Each of the following class declarations has errors. Locate as many as you can.

46.
```cpp
class Circle
{
    private:
        double diameter;
        int centerX;
        int centerY;
    public:
        Circle(double d, int x, int y)
            { diameter = d; centerX = x; centerY = y;    }
```

```
                // Overloaded = operator
                void Circle=(Circle &right)
                    { diameter = right.diameter;
                      centerX = right.centerX;
                      centerY = right.centerY; }

                ... Other member functions follow ...
                };
```

47. ```
    class Box
    {
        private:
            double width;
            double length;
            double height;
        public:
            Box(double w, l, h)
                { width = w; length = l; height = h; }
            // Overloaded prefix ++ operator
            void operator++()
                {  ++width; ++length; }
            // Overloaded postfix ++ operator
            void operator++()
                {  width++; length++; }

        ... Other member functions follow ...
    };
    ```

Programming Challenges

1. NumDays Class

Design a class called NumDays. The class's purpose is to store a value that represents a number of work hours and convert it to a number of days. For example, eight hours would be converted to one day, 12 hours would be converted to 1.5 days, and 18 hours would be converted to 2.25 days. The class should have a constructor that accepts a number of hours, as well as member functions for storing and retrieving the hours and days. The class should also have the following overloaded operators:

+   *Addition operator.* When two NumDays objects are added together, the overloaded + operator should return the sum of the two object's hours member.

-   *Subtraction operator.* When one NumDays object is subtracted from another, the overloaded - operator should return the difference of the two object's hours member.

++ *Prefix and postfix increment operators.* These operators should increment the number of hours stored in the object. When incremented, the number of days should be automatically re-calculated.
    ```

-- *Prefix and postfix decrement operators.* These operators should decrement the number of hours stored in the object. When decremented, the number of days should be automatically re-calculated.

2. Time Off

 Note: This assignment assumes you have already completed Programming Challenge 1.

Design a class named `TimeOff`. The purpose of the class is to track an employee's sick leave, vacation, and unpaid time off. It should have, as members, the following instances of the `NumDays` class described in Programming Challenge 1:

maxSickDays	A NumDays object that records the maximum number of days of sick leave the employee may take.
sickTaken	A NumDays object that records the number of days of sick leave the employee has already taken.
maxVacation	A NumDays object that records the maximum number of days of paid vacation the employee may take.
vacTaken	A NumDays object that records the number of days of paid vacation the employee has already taken.
maxUnpaid	A NumDays object that records the maximum number of days of unpaid vacation the employee may take.
unpaidTaken	A NumDays object that records the number of days of unpaid leave the employee has taken.

Additionally, the class should have members for holding the employee's name and identification number. It should have an appropriate constructor and member functions for storing and retrieving data in any of the member objects.

Input Validation: Company policy states that an employee may not accumulate more than 240 hours of paid vacation. The class should not allow the maxVacation object to store a value greater than this amount.

3. Personnel Report

 Note: This assignment assumes you have already completed Programming Challenges 1 and 2.

Write a program that uses an instance of the `TimeOff` class you designed in Programming Challenge 2. The program should ask the user to enter the number of months an employee has worked for the company. It should then use the `TimeOff` object to calculate and display the employee's maximum number of sick leave and vacation days. Employees earn 12 hours of vacation leave and eight hours of sick leave per month.

4. Month class

Design a class named `Month`. The class should have the following private members:

- ◆ `name`   A `MyString` object (from the `MyString` class presented in this chapter) as a member. The `name` object should hold the name of a month, such as "January," "February," etc.

- ◆ `monthNumber`   An integer variable that holds the number of the month. For example, January would be 1, February would be 2, etc. Valid values for this variable are 1 through 12.

In addition, provide the following member functions:

- ◆ A default constructor that sets `monthNumber` to 1 and `name` to "January."

- ◆ A constructor that accepts the name of the month as an argument. It should set `name` to the value passed as the argument and set `monthNumber` to the correct value.

- ◆ A constructor that accepts the number of the month as an argument. It should set `monthNumber` to the value passed as the argument and set `name` to the correct month name.

- ◆ Appropriate set and get functions for the `name` and `monthNumber` member variables.

- ◆ Prefix and postfix overloaded `++` operator functions that increment `monthNumber` and set `name` to the name of next month. If `monthNumber` is set to 12 when these functions execute, they should set `monthNumber` to 1 and `name` to "January."

- ◆ Prefix and postfix overloaded `--` operator functions that decrement `monthNumber` and set `name` to the name of previous month. If `monthNumber` is set to 1 when these functions execute, they should set `monthNumber` to 12 and `name` to "December."

Also, you should overload `cout`'s `<<` operator and `cin`'s `>>` operator to work with the `Month` class. Demonstrate the class in a program.

5. Date Class Modification

Modify the `Date` class in Programming Challenge 1 of Chapter 12. The new version should have the following overloaded operators:

`++` ***Prefix and postfix increment operators.*** These operators should increment the object's day member.

`--` ***Prefix and postfix decrement operators.*** These operators should decrement the object's day member.

- *Subtraction operator.* If one Date object is subtracted from another, the operator should give the number of days between the two dates. For example, if April 10, 2005 is subtracted from April 18, 2005, the result will be 8.

<< cout*'s stream insertion operator.* This operator should cause the date to be displayed in the form

    April 18, 2005

>> cin*'s stream extraction operator.* This operator should prompt the user for a date to be stored in a Date object.

The class should detect the following conditions and handle them accordingly:

◆ When a date is set to the last day of the month and incremented, it should become the first day of the following month.

◆ When a date is set to December 31 and incremented, it should become January 1 of the following year.

◆ When a day is set to the first day of the month and decremented, it should become the last day of the previous month.

◆ When a date is set to January 1 and decremented, it should become December 31 of the previous year.

Demonstrate the class's capabilities in a simple program.

Input Validation: The overloaded >> operator should not accept invalid dates. For example, the date 13/45/04 should not be accepted.

6. FeetInches Modification

Modify the FeetInches class discussed in this chapter (stored in FeetInches6.h and FeetInches6.cpp), so it overloads the following operators:

    <=
    >=
    !=

Demonstrate the class's capabilities in a simple program.

7. Corporate Sales

A corporation has six divisions, each responsible for sales to different geographic locations. Design a DivSales class that keeps sales data for a division, with the following members:

◆ An array with four elements for holding four quarters of sales figures for the division.

◆ A private static variable for holding the total corporate sales for all divisions for the entire year.

◆ A member function that takes four arguments, each assumed to be the sales for a quarter. The value of the arguments should be copied into the array that holds the sales data. The total of the four arguments should be added to the static variable that holds the total yearly corporate sales.

◆ A function that takes an integer argument within the range of 0–3. The argument is to be used as a subscript into the division quarterly sales array. The function should return the value of the array element with that subscript.

Write a program that creates an array of six DivSales objects. The program should ask the user to enter the sales for four quarters for each division. After the data is entered, the program should display a table showing the division sales for each quarter. The program should then display the total corporate sales for the year.

Input Validation: Only accept positive values for quarterly sales figures.

14

Inheritance, Polymorphism, and Virtual Functions

- ### Topics in this Chapter

14.1 What Is Inheritance?

CONCEPT Inheritance allows a new class to be based on an existing class. The new class inherits all the member variables and functions (except the constructors and destructor) of the class it is based on.

Generalization and Specialization

In the real world you can find many objects that are specialized versions of other more general objects. For example, the term "insect" describes a very general type of creature with numerous characteristics. Because grasshoppers and bumble bees are insects, they have all the general characteristics of an insect. In addition, they have special characteristics of their own. For example, the grasshopper has its jumping ability, and the bumble bee has its stinger. Grasshoppers and bumble bees are specialized versions of an insect.

Inheritance and the "is a" Relationship

When one object is a specialized version of another object, there is an *"is a" relationship* between them. For example, a grasshopper *is an* insect. Here are a few other examples of the "is a" relationship.

- ◆ A poodle *is a* dog.
- ◆ A car *is a* vehicle.
- ◆ A flower *is a* plant.
- ◆ A rectangle *is a* shape.
- ◆ A football player *is an* athlete.

When an "is a" relationship exists between classes, it means that the specialized class has all of the characteristics of the general class, plus additional characteristics that make it special. In object-oriented programming, *inheritance* is used to create an "is a" relationship between classes.

Inheritance involves a base class and a derived class. The *base class* is the general class and the *derived class* is the specialized class. The derived class is based on, or derived from, the base class. You can think of the base class as the parent and the derived class as the child. This is illustrated in Figure 14-1.

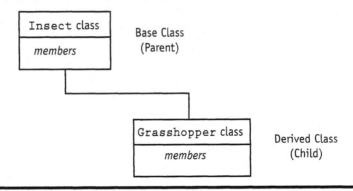

Figure 14-1

The derived class inherits the member variables and member functions of the base class without any of them being rewritten. Furthermore, new member variables and functions may be added to the derived class to make it more specialized than the base class.

Let's look at an example of how inheritance can be used. Most teachers assign various graded activities for their students to complete. A graded activity can consist of a numeric score such as 70, 85, 90, and so on, and a letter grade such as A, B, C, D or F. The following `GradedActivity` class is designed to hold the numeric score and letter grade of a graded activity. When a numeric score is stored by the class, it automatically determines the letter grade.

```
class GradedActivity
{
private:
        char letter;            // To hold the letter grade
        double score;           // To hold the numeric score
        void determineGrade();  // Determines the letter grade
public:
        void setScore(double s)
            { score = s;
              determineGrade();}
```

```
        double getScore()
           { return score; }

        char getLetter()
           { return letter; }
};
```

Here is the definition of the determineGrade member function:

```
void GradedActivity::determineGrade()
{
        if (score >= 90)
           letter = 'A';
        else if (score >= 80)
           letter = 'B';
        else if (score >= 70)
           letter = 'C';
        else if (score >= 60)
           letter = 'D';
        else
           letter = 'F';
}
```

 Appendix D on the Student CD shows how to represent inheritance in UML.

The setScore function stores a numeric score in the score member variable, then calls the determineGrade member function. The determineGrade function assigns a letter grade to the letter member variable.

This class represents the general characteristics of a student's graded activity. There are many different types of graded activities, however, such as quizzes, midterm and final exams, lab reports, essays, and so on. Because the numeric scores might be determined differently for each of these graded activities, we can create derived classes to handle each one. For example, the following FinalExam class is derived from the GradedActivity class. It has member variables for the number of questions on the exam (numQuestions), the number of points each question is worth (pointsEach), and the number of questions missed by the student (numMissed).

```
class FinalExam : public GradedActivity
{
private:
        int numQuestions;      // Number of questions
        double pointsEach;     // Points for each question
        int numMissed;         // Number of questions missed
public:
        // Constructor
        FinalExam(int n)       // Parameter n is the number of questions
           { numQuestions = n;
             pointsEach = 100.0 / n; }
```

```
            double getPointsEach()
                { return pointsEach; }

            void setNumMissed(int);

            int getNumMissed()
                { return numMissed; }
    };
```

The only new notation in this class declaration is in the first line, which reads:

```
    class FinalExam : public GradedActivity
```

This line indicates the name of the class being declared and the name of the base class it is derived from. `FinalExam` is the name of the class being declared and `GradedActivity` is the name of the base class.

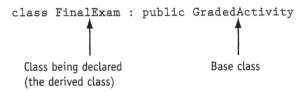

The word `public`, which precedes the name of the base class, is the *base class access specification*. It specifies how the derived class is allowed to access the members of the base class. Although the next section discusses this topic in more detail, let's see how it works in this example: The `GradedActivity` class has both private members and public members. The `public` base class access specification allows code in the `FinalExam` class to access any of the `GradedActivity` class's public members. It also specifies that all public members of `GradedActivity` are inherited as public members of `FinalExam`. This is illustrated in Figure 14-2.

Notice that the private members of the base class (the variables `letter` and `score` and the function `determineGrade`) are not accessible to the derived class. They are still inherited by the derived class, but because they are `private` members of the base class, only member functions of the base class may access them. They are truly private to the base class. Because the functions `setScore`, `getScore`, and `getLetter` are public members of the base class, they also become public members of the derived class.

Here is the code for the `FinalExam` constructor:

```
    FinalExam(int n)         // Parameter n is the number of questions.
            { numQuestions = n;
              pointsEach = 100.0 / n; }
```

This constructor has a parameter, n, which is the number of questions on the test. It assigns n to `numQuestions`, then calculates and assigns the number of points each question is worth to

The individual class declarations contain their own members.

```
class GradedActivity

Private Members:
    char letter;
    double score;
    void determineGrade();

Public Members:
    void setScore(double);
    double getScore();
    char getLetter();
```

```
class FinalExam

Private Members:
    int numQuestions;
    double pointsEach;
    int numMissed;

Public Members:
    FinalExam(int);
    double getPointsEach();
    void setNumMissed();
    int getNumMissed();
```

When the FinalExam class is derived from the GradedActivity class, the FinalExam class appears to have the following members.

```
class FinalExam : public GradedActivity

Private Members:
    int numQuestions;
    double pointsEach;
    int numMissed;

Public Members:
    FinalExam(int);
    double getPointsEach();
    void setNumMissed();
    int getNumMissed();
    void setScore(double);
    double getScore();
    char getLetter();
```

Figure 14-2

pointsEach. The getPointsEach function returns the value in pointsEach, and the getNumMissed function returns the value in numMissed.

Here is the definition of the setNumMissed member function:

```
void FinalExam::setNumMissed(int n)
{
    double numericScore;

    numMissed = n;
    numericScore = 100.0 - (n * pointsEach);
    setScore(numericScore);
}
```

The function's parameter, n, holds the number of questions that the student missed. This value is assigned to numMissed and then used to calculate the numeric score. The last statement calls the setScore function, which is a member of the GradedActivity class. Because FinalExam is derived from GradedActivity, the setScore function is an inherited member of FinalExam.

Program 14-1 shows the GradedActivity and FinalExam classes in use. The GradedActivity class is declared in GradedActivity.h and its member function determineGrade is defined in GradedActivity.cpp. The FinalExam class is declared in FinalExam.h and its constructor is defined in FinalExam.cpp.

Program 14-1

Contents of GradedActivity.h

```cpp
// Specification file for the GradedActivity class
#ifndef GRADEDACTIVITY_H
#define GRADEDACTIVITY_H

// GradedActivity class declaration

class GradedActivity
{
private:
    char letter;            // To hold the letter grade
    double score;           // To hold the numeric score
    void determineGrade();  // Determines the letter grade
public:
    void setScore(double s)
        { score = s;
          determineGrade();}

    double getScore()
        { return score; }

    char getLetter()
        { return letter; }
};

#endif
```

Contents of GradedActivity.cpp

```cpp
// Implementation file for the GradedActivity class
#include "GradedActivity.h"

//********************************************************
// Member function GradedActivity::determineGrade        *
//********************************************************
```

(program continues)

Program 14-1 *(continued)*

```
void GradedActivity::determineGrade()
{
    if (score >= 90)
        letter = 'A';
    else if (score >= 80)
        letter = 'B';
    else if (score >= 70)
        letter = 'C';
    else if (score >= 60)
        letter = 'D';
    else
        letter = 'F';
}
```

Contents of *FinalExam.h*

```
// Specification file for the FinalExam class
#ifndef FINALEXAM_H
#define FINALEXAM_H

#include "GradedActivity.h"

class FinalExam : public GradedActivity
{
private:
    int numQuestions;      // Number of questions
    double pointsEach;     // Points for each question
    int numMissed;         // Number of questions missed
public:
    // Constructor
    FinalExam(int n)       // Parameter n is the number of questions.
        { numQuestions = n;
          pointsEach = 100.0 / n; }

    double getPointsEach()
        { return pointsEach; }

    void setNumMissed(int);

    int getNumMissed()
        { return numMissed; }
};

#endif
```

Program 14-1 *(continued)*

Contents of `FinalExam.cpp`
```
// Implementation file for the FinalExam class
#include "FinalExam.h"

//********************************************************
// Member function FinalExam::setNumMissed              *
// This function accepts the number of questions missed *
// as its argument. It then calculates the numeric score*
// and calls the inherited setScore member function.    *
//********************************************************

void FinalExam::setNumMissed(int n)
{
    double numericScore;

    numMissed = n;
    numericScore = 100.0 - (n * pointsEach);
    setScore(numericScore);
}
```

Contents of the main program file, `Pr14-1.cpp`
```
// This program demonstrates a base class and a derived class
#include <iostream>
#include <iomanip>
#include "FinalExam.h"
using namespace std;

int main()
{
    int questions, missed;

    // Get the number of questions on the final exam.
    cout << "How many questions are on the final exam? ";
    cin >> questions;

    // Define a FinalExam object.
    FinalExam test(questions);

    // Get the number of questions the student missed.
    cout << "How many questions did the student miss? ";
    cin >> missed;

    // Send the number of questions missed to the test object.
    test.setNumMissed(missed);
```

(program continues)

Program 14-1 *(continued)*

```
    // Display the test results.
    cout << setprecision(2);
    cout << "\nEach question counts " << test.getPointsEach()
         << " points.\n";
    cout << "The exam score is " << test.getScore() << endl;
    cout << "The exam grade is " << test.getLetter() << endl;

    return 0;
}
```

Program Output with Example Input Shown in Bold
```
How many questions are on the final exam? 20
How many questions did the student miss? 3

Each question counts 5 points.
The exam score is 85
The exam grade is B
```

Notice in the following lines that the public member functions of the GradedActivity class may be directly called by the test object:

```
    cout << "The exam score is " << test.getScore() << endl;
    cout << "The exam grade is " << test.getLetter() << endl;
```

The getScore and getLetter functions are inherited as public members of the FinalExam class, so they may be accessed as any other public member.

Inheritance does not work in reverse. It is not possible for a base class to call a member function of a derived class. For example, the following classes will not compile in a program because the BadBase constructor attempts to call a function in its derived class:

```
    class BadBase
    {
        private:
            int x;
        public:
            BadBase() { x = getVal(); }      // Error!
    };

    class Derived : public BadBase
    {
        private:
            int y;
        public:
            Derived(int z) { y = z; }
            int getVal() { return y; }
    };
```

Checkpoint [14.1]

14.1 Here is the first line of a class declaration. Circle the name of the base class:

```
class Truck : public Vehicle
```

14.2 Circle the name of the derived class in the following declaration line:

```
class Truck : public Vehicle
```

14.3 Suppose a program has the following class declarations:

```
class Shape
{
private:
    double area;
public:
    void setArea(double a)
        { area = a; }

    double getArea()
        { return area; }
};

class Circle : public Shape
{
private:
    double radius;
public:
    void setRadius(double r)
        { radius = r;
          setArea(3.14 * r * r); }

    double getRadius()
        { return radius; }
};
```

Answer the following questions concerning these classes :

A) When an object of the Circle class is created, what are its private members?

B) When an object of the Circle class is created, what are its public members?

C) What members of the Shape class are not accessible to member functions of the Circle class?

14.2 Protected Members and Class Access

CONCEPT	Protected members of a base class are like private members, but they may be accessed by derived classes. The base class access specification determines how base class members are inherited by the derived class.

 Appendix D on the Student CD shows how to represent protected members in UML.

Until now you have used two access specifications within a class: private and public. C++ provides a third access specification, protected. Protected members of a base class are like private members, except they may be accessed by functions in a derived class. To the rest of the program, however, protected members are inaccessible.

Program 14-2 is a modification of Program 14-1. The private members of the GradedActivity class have been made protected. A new member function, adjustScore, has been added to the FinalExam class. This function directly accesses the score variable, and makes a call to the determineGrade function. If the contents of the score variable has a fractional part of .5 or greater, the function rounds score up to the next whole number.

Program 14-2

Contents of *GradedActivity2.h*

```cpp
// Specification file for the GradedActivity class
#ifndef GRADEDACTIVITY_H
#define GRADEDACTIVITY_H

// GradedActivity class declaration

class GradedActivity
{
protected:
    char letter;              // To hold the letter grade
    double score;             // To hold the numeric score
    void determineGrade();    // Determines the letter grade
public:
    void setScore(double s)
        { score = s;
          determineGrade();}

    double getScore()
        { return score; }

    char getLetter()
        { return letter; }
};

#endif
```

Program 14-2 *(continued)*

Contents of `GradedActivity2.cpp`
```
// Implementation file for the GradedActivity class
#include "GradedActivity2.h"

//*********************************************************
// Member function GradedActivity::determineGrade       *
//*********************************************************

void GradedActivity::determineGrade()
{
    if (score >= 90)
        letter = 'A';
    else if (score >= 80)
        letter = 'B';
    else if (score >= 70)
        letter = 'C';
    else if (score >= 60)
        letter = 'D';
    else
        letter = 'F';
}
```

Contents of `FinalExam2.h`
```
// Specification file for the FinalExam class
#ifndef FINALEXAM_H
#define FINALEXAM_H

#include "GradedActivity2.h"

class FinalExam : public GradedActivity
{
private:
    int numQuestions;      // Number of questions
    double pointsEach;     // Points for each question
    int numMissed;         // Number of questions missed
public:
    // Constructor
    FinalExam(int n)       // Parameter n is the number of questions.
        { numQuestions = n;
          pointsEach = 100.0 / n; }

    double getPointsEach()
        { return pointsEach; }

    void setNumMissed(int);
```

(program continues)

Program 14-2 *(continued)*

```cpp
    int getNumMissed()
        { return numMissed; }

    void adjustScore();
};

#endif
```

Contents of `FinalExam2.cpp`
```cpp
// Implementation file for the FinalExam class
#include "FinalExam2.h"

//********************************************************
// Member function FinalExam::setNumMissed             *
// This function accepts the number of questions missed *
// as its argument. It then calculates the numeric score *
// and calls the inherited setScore member function.    *
//********************************************************

void FinalExam::setNumMissed(int n)
{
    double numericScore;

    numMissed = n;
    numericScore = 100.0 - (n * pointsEach);
    setScore(numericScore);
}


//*********************************************************************
// Definition of Test::adjustScore. If score is within 0.5 points *
// of the next whole point, it rounds the score up and            *
// recalculates the letter grade.                                 *
//*********************************************************************

void FinalExam::adjustScore()
{
    double fraction = score - static_cast<int>(score);

    if (fraction >= 0.5)
    {
        score += (1.0 - fraction);
        determineGrade();
    }
}
```

(program continues)

Program 14-2 *(continued)*

Contents of the main program file, `Pr14-2.cpp`

```cpp
// This program demonstrates a base class and a derived class
#include <iostream>
#include <iomanip>
#include "FinalExam2.h"
using namespace std;

int main()
{
    int questions, missed;

    // Get the number of questions on the final exam.
    cout << "How many questions are on the final exam? ";
    cin >> questions;

    // Define a FinalExam object.
    FinalExam test(questions);

    // Get the number of questions the student missed.
    cout << "How many questions did the student miss? ";
    cin >> missed;

    // Send the number of questions missed to the test object.
    test.setNumMissed(missed);

    // Display the unadjusted test results.
    cout << fixed << setprecision(2);
    cout << "\nEach question counts " << test.getPointsEach()
         << " points.\n";
    cout << "The unadjusted score is " << test.getScore() << endl;
    cout << "The unadjusted grade is " << test.getLetter() << endl;

    // Display the adjusted test results.
    test.adjustScore();
    cout << "The adjusted score is " << test.getScore() << endl;
    cout << "The adjusted grade is " << test.getLetter() << endl;

    return 0;
}
```

Program Output with Example Input Shown in Bold
```
How many questions are on the final exam? 16 [Enter]
How many questions did the student miss? 5 [Enter]

Each question counts 6.25 points.
The unadjusted score is 68.75
The unadjusted grade is D
The adjusted score is 69.00
The adjusted grade is D
```

Now look closer at the base class access specification. The first line of the FinalExam class declaration reads:

```
class FinalExam : public GradedActivity
```

The declaration gives the public access specification to the base class, GradedActivity. Base class access specification may be public, private, or protected. Be careful not to confuse base class access specification with member access specification. Member access specification determines whether a class member is accessible to statements outside the class. Base class access specification determines how base class members are inherited by the derived class.

Table 14-1 summarizes how base class specification affects the way the way base class members appear in the derived class.

Table 14-1

Base Class Access Specification	How Members of the Base Class Appear in the Derived Class
private	• Private members of the base class are inaccessible to the derived class.
	• Protected members of the base class become private members of the derived class.
	• Public members of the base class become private members the derived class.
protected	• Private members of the base class are inaccessible to the derived class.
	• Protected members of the base class become protected members of the derived class.
	• Public members of the base class become protected members of the derived class.
public	• Private members of the base class are inaccessible to the derived class.
	• Protected members of the base class become protected members of the derived class.
	• Public members of the base class become public members of the derived class.

As you can see from Table 14-1, class access specification gives you a great deal of flexibility in determining how base class members will appear in the derived class. Think of a base class's access specification as a filter that base class members must pass through when becoming inherited members of a derived class. This is illustrated in Figure 14-3.

 Note: If the base class access specification is left out of a declaration, the default access specification is private. For example, in the following declaration, Grade is declared as a private base class:

```
class Test : Grade
```

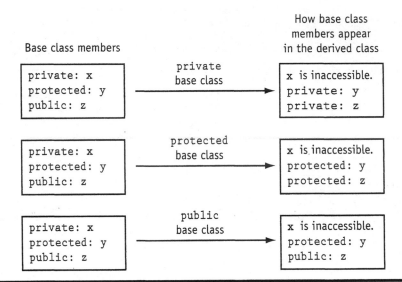

Figure 14-3

 Checkpoint [14.2]

14.4   What is the difference between private members and protected members?

14.5   What is the difference between member access specification and class access specification?

14.6   Suppose a program has the following class declaration:

```
// Declaration of CheckPoint class.
class CheckPoint
{
    private:
      int a;
    protected:
      int b;
      int c;
      void setA(int x) { a = x;}
    public:
      void setB(int y) { b = y;}
      void setC(int z) { c = z;}
};
```

Answer the following questions regarding the class:

A)   Suppose another class, Quiz, is derived from the CheckPoint class. Here is the first line of its declaration:

```
        class Quiz : private CheckPoint
```

Indicate whether each member of the CheckPoint class is private, protected, public, or inaccessible:

```
a
b
c
setA
setB
setC
```

B) Suppose the Quiz class, derived from the CheckPoint class, is declared as

```
class Quiz : protected Checkpoint
```

Indicate whether each member of the CheckPoint class is private, protected, public, or inaccessible:

```
a
b
c
setA
setB
setC
```

C) Suppose the Quiz class, derived from the CheckPoint class, is declared as:

```
class Quiz : public Checkpoint
```

Indicate whether each member of the CheckPoint class is private, protected, public, or inaccessible:

```
a
b
c
setA
setB
setC
```

D) Suppose the Quiz class, derived from the CheckPoint class, is declared as:

```
class Quiz : Checkpoint
```

Is the CheckPoint class a private, public, or protected base class?

14.3 Constructors and Destructors

CONCEPT The base class's constructor is called before the derived class's constructor. The destructors are called in reverse order, with the derived class's destructor being called first.

In inheritance, the base class constructor is called before the derived class constructor. Destructors are called in reverse order. Program 14-3 shows a simple set of demonstration classes, each with a default constructor and a destructor. The `DerivedClass` class is derived from the `BaseClass` class. Messages are displayed by the constructors and destructors to demonstrate when each is called.

Program 14-3

```
// This program demonstrates the order in which base and
// derived class constructors and destructors are called.
#include <iostream>
using namespace std;

//*******************************
// BaseClass declaration        *
//*******************************

class BaseClass
{
public:
    BaseClass()  // Constructor
        { cout << "This is the BaseClass constructor.\n"; }

    ~BaseClass() // Destructor
        { cout << "This is the BaseClass destructor.\n"; }
};

//*******************************
// DerivedClass declaration     *
//*******************************

class DerivedClass : public BaseClass
{
public:
    DerivedClass()  // Constructor
        { cout << "This is the DerivedClass constructor.\n"; }

    ~DerivedClass()  // Destructor
        { cout << "This is the DerivedClass destructor.\n"; }
};
```

(program continues)

Program 14-3   *(continued)*

```
int main()
{
    cout << "We will now define a DerivedClass object.\n";

    DerivedClass object;

    cout << "The program is now going to end.\n";
    return 0;
}
```

Program Output
```
We will now define a DerivedClass object.
This is the BaseClass constructor.
This is the DerivedClass constructor.
The program is now going to end.
This is the DerivedClass destructor.
This is the BaseClass destructor.
```

Passing Arguments to Base Class Constructors

In Program 14-3, both the base class and derived class have default constructors, which are called automatically. But what if the base class's constructor takes arguments? What if there is more than one constructor in the base class? The answer to these questions is to let the derived class constructor pass arguments to the base class constructor. For example, consider the following class:

```
class Rectangle
{
private:
    double width;
    double length;
public:
    Rectangle()                     // Default constructor
        { width = 0.0;
          length = 0.0; }

    Rectangle(double w, double len) // Constructor
        { width = w;
          length = len; }

    double getWidth()
        { return width; }

    double getLength()
        { return length; }

    double getArea()
        { return width * length; }
};
```

This class is designed to hold data about a rectangle. It specifies two constructors. The default constructor simply initializes the member variables `width` and `length` to 0.0. The second constructor takes two arguments, which are assigned to `width` and `length`. Now let's look at a class that is derived from the `Rectangle` class:

```cpp
class Cube : public Rectangle
{
protected:
    double height;
    double volume;
public:
    // Derived class constructor
    Cube(double w, double len, double h) : Rectangle(w, len)
        { height = h;
          volume = getArea() * h; }

    double getHeight()
        { return height; }

    double getVolume()
        { return volume; }
};
```

The `Cube` class is designed to hold data about cubes, which not only have a length and width, but a height and volume as well. Look at the first line of the `Cube` class constructor:

```cpp
Cube(double w, double len, double h) : Rectangle(w, len)
```

Notice the added notation in the header of the constructor. A colon is placed after the parameter list for the derived class constructor, followed by a function call to the base class constructor. This is illustrated here:

```cpp
Cube(double w, double len, double h) : Rectangle(w, len)
```

Derived class constructor　　　　　　Call to base class constructor

The general format of this type of declaration is

<ClassName>::<ClassName>(ParameterList) : <BaseClassName>(ArgumentList)

This notation not only causes arguments to be passed to the base class constructor, but also determines which base class constructor to call if there is more than one.

You only write this notation in the definition of a constructor, not in a prototype. In this example, the derived class constructor is written inline (inside the class declaration), so the notation that contains the call to the base class constructor appears there. If the constructor were defined outside the class, the notation would appear in the function header. For example, the Cube class could appear as follows.

```
class Cube : public Rectangle
{
protected:
        double height;
        double volume;
public:
        Cube(double, double, double);   // Constructor

        double getHeight()
            { return height; }

        double getVolume()
            { return volume; }
};

//****************************************
// Definition of Cube class constructor *
//****************************************

Cube::Cube(double w, double len, double h) : Rectangle(w, len)
{
height = h;
volume = getArea() * h;
}
```

The base class constructor is still executed before the derived class constructor. The Cube constructor accepts arguments for the parameters w, len, and h. The values that are passed to w and len are subsequently passed as arguments to the Rectangle constructor. When the Rectangle constructor finishes, the Cube constructor is then executed.

Any literal value or variable that is in scope may be used as an argument to the derived class constructor. Usually, one or more of the arguments passed to the derived class constructor are, in turn, passed to the base class constructor. The values that may be used as base class constructor arguments are:

- ◆ Derived class constructor parameters

- ◆ Literal values

- ◆ Global variables that are accessible to the file containing the derived class constructor definition

- ◆ Expressions involving any of these items

Program 14-4 shows the Rectangle and Cube classes in use.

Program 14-4

Contents of `Rectangle.h`

```
// Specification file for the Rectangle class.
#ifndef RECTANGLE_H
#define RECTANGLE_H

class Rectangle
{
    private:
        double width;
        double length;
    public:
        Rectangle()        // Default constructor
            { width = 0.0;
              length = 0.0; }

        Rectangle(double w, double len)// Constructor
            { width = w;
              length = len; }

        double getWidth()
            { return width; }

        double getLength()
            { return length; }

        double getArea()
            { return width * length; }
};

#endif
```

Contents of `Cube.h`

```
// Specification file for the Cube class.
#ifndef CUBE_H
#define CUBE_H
#include "Rectangle.h"

class Cube : public Rectangle
{
protected:
    double height;
    double volume;
public:
    // Derived class constructor
    Cube(double w, double len, double h) : Rectangle(w, len)
        { height = h;
          volume = getArea() * h; }
```

(program continues)

Program 14-4 *(continued)*

```cpp
    double getHeight()
        { return height; }

    double getVolume()
        { return volume; }
};

#endif
```

Contents of the main program file, Pr14-4.cpp

```cpp
// This program demonstrates passing arguments to a base
// class constructor.
#include <iostream>
#include "Cube.h"
using namespace std;

int main()
{
    double cubeWidth, cubeLength, cubeHeight;

    // Get the width, length, and height of
    // the cube from the user.
    cout << "Enter the dimensions of a Cube:\n";
    cout << "Width: ";
    cin >> cubeWidth;
    cout << "Length: ";
    cin >> cubeLength;
    cout << "Height: ";
    cin >> cubeHeight;

    // Define a Cube object and use the dimensions
    // entered by the user.
    Cube myCube(cubeWidth, cubeLength, cubeHeight);

    // Display the Cube object's properties.
    cout << "Here are the Cube's properties:\n";
    cout << "Width: " << myCube.getWidth() << endl;
    cout << "Length: " << myCube.getLength() << endl;
    cout << "Height: " << myCube.getHeight() << endl;
    cout << "Base area: " << myCube.getArea() << endl;
    cout << "Volume: " << myCube.getVolume() << endl;

    return 0;
}
```

(program continues)

Program 14-4 *(continued)*

Program Output with Example Input Shown in Bold
```
Enter the dimensions of a Cube:
Width: 10 [Enter]
Length: 15 [Enter]
Height: 12 [Enter]
Here are the Cube's properties:
Width: 10
Length: 15
Height: 12
Base area: 150
Volume: 1800
```

 Note: If the base class has no default constructor then the derived class must have a constructor which calls one of the base class constructors.

 ## Checkpoint [14.3]

14.7 What will the following program display?

```cpp
#include <iostream>
using namespace std;

class Sky
{
public:
    Sky()
        { cout << "Entering the sky.\n"; }
    Sky(char *color)
        { cout << "The sky is " << color << endl; }
    ~Sky()
        { cout << "Leaving the sky.\n"; }
};

class Ground : public Sky
{
public:
    Ground()
        { cout << "Entering the Ground.\n"; }
    Ground(char *c1, char *c2) : Sky(c1)
        { cout << "The ground is " << c2 << endl; }
    ~Ground()
        { cout << "Leaving the Ground.\n"; }
};

int main()
{
    Ground object;
    return 0;
}
```

14.4 Redefining Base Class Functions

CONCEPT A base class member function may be redefined in a derived class.

Inheritance is commonly used to extend a class or give it additional capabilities. Sometimes it may be helpful to overload a base class function with a function of the same name in the derived class. For example, recall the GradedActivity class that was presented earlier in this chapter:

```cpp
class GradedActivity
{
protected:
    char letter;              // To hold the letter grade
    double score;             // To hold the numeric score
    void determineGrade();    // Determines the letter grade
public:
    void setScore(double s)
        { score = s;
          determineGrade();}

    double getScore()
        { return score; }

    char getLetter()
        { return letter; }
};

//*******************************************************
// Member function GradedActivity::determineGrade        *
//*******************************************************

void GradedActivity::determineGrade()
{
    if (score >= 90)
        letter = 'A';
    else if (score >= 80)
        letter = 'B';
    else if (score >= 70)
        letter = 'C';
    else if (score >= 60)
        letter = 'D';
    else
        letter = 'F';
}
```

This class holds a numeric score and determines a letter grade based on that score. The setScore member function stores a value in score, then calls the determineGrade member function to determine the letter grade.

Suppose a teacher wants to "curve" a numeric score before the letter grade is determined. For example, Dr. Harrison determines that in order to curve the grades in her class she must multiply each student's score by a certain percentage. This gives an adjusted score which is used to determine the letter grade.

The following CurvedActivity class is derived from the GradedActivity class. It multiplies the numeric score by a percentage, and passes that value as an argument to the base class's setScore function.

```cpp
class CurvedActivity : public GradedActivity
{
protected:
    double rawScore;        // Unadjusted score
    double percentage;      // Curve percentage
public:
    void setScore(double s)
        { rawScore = s;
          GradedActivity::setScore(rawScore * percentage); }

    void setPercentage(double c)
        { percentage = c; }

    double getPercentage()
        { return percentage; }

    double getRawScore()
        { return rawScore; }

};
```

This CurvedActivity class has the following member variables:

- ◆ rawScore   This variable holds the student's unadjusted score.
- ◆ percentage   This variable holds the value that the unadjusted score must be multiplied by to get the curved score.

It also has the following member functions:

- ◆ setScore   This function accepts an argument which is the student's unadjusted score. The function stores the argument in the rawScore variable, then passes rawScore * percentage as an argument to the base class's setScore function.
- ◆ setPercentage   This function stores a value in the percentage variable.
- ◆ getPercentage   This function returns the value in the percentage variable.
- ◆ getRawScore   This function returns the value in the rawScore variable.

Note: Although we are not using the `CurvedActivity` class as a base class, it still has a protected member section. This is because we might want to use the `CurvedActivity` class itself as a base class, as you will see in the next section.

Notice that the `CurvedActivity` class has a `setScore` member function. This function has the same name as one of the base class member functions. When a derived class's member function has the same name as a base class member function, it is said that the derived class function *redefines* the base class function. When an object of the derived class calls the function, it calls the derived class's version of the function.

There is a distinction between redefining a function and overloading a function. An overloaded function is one with the same name as one or more other functions, but with a different parameter list. The compiler uses the arguments passed to the function to tell which version to call. Overloading can take place with regular functions that are not members of a class. Overloading can also take place inside a class when two or more member functions *of the same class* have the same name. These member functions must have different parameter lists for the compiler to tell them apart in function calls.

Redefining happens when a derived class has a function with the same name as a base class function. The parameter lists of the two functions can be the same because the derived class function is always called by objects of the derived class type.

Let's continue our look at the `CurvedActivity` class. Here is the `setScore` member function:

```
void setScore(float s)
   { rawScore = s;
     GradedActivity::setScore(rawScore * percentage); }
```

This function accepts an argument, which should be the student's unadjusted numeric score, into the parameter `s`. This value is stored in the `rawScore` variable. Then the following statement is executed:

```
GradedActivity::setScore(rawScore * percentage);
```

This statement calls the base class's version of the `setScore` function with the expression `rawScore * percentage` passed as an argument. Notice that the name of the base class and the scope resolution operator precedes the name of the function. This specifies that the base class's version of the `setScore` function is being called. A derived class function may call a base class function of the same name using this notation, which takes this form:

```
<BaseClassName>::<functionName>(ArgumentList);
```

Program 14-5 uses the `GradedActivity` class from Program 14-2 with the `CurrentActivity` class.

Program 14-5

Contents of *CurvedActivity.h*

```cpp
// Specification file for the CurvedActivity class
#ifndef CURVEDACTIVITY_H
#define CURVEDACTIVITY_H
#include "GradedActivity2.h"

// CurvedActivity class declaration

class CurvedActivity : public GradedActivity
{
protected:
    double rawScore;      // Unadjusted score
    double percentage;    // Curve percentage
public:
    void setScore(double s)
        { rawScore = s;
          GradedActivity::setScore(rawScore * percentage); }

    void setPercentage(double c)
        { percentage = c; }

    double getPercentage()
        { return percentage; }

    double getRawScore()
        { return rawScore; }

};

#endif
```

Contents of the main program file, *Pr14-5.cpp*

```cpp
// This program demonstrates a class that redefines
// a base class function.
#include <iostream>
#include <iomanip>
#include "CurvedActivity.h"
using namespace std;

int main()
{
    CurvedActivity exam;
    double numericScore, percentage;

    // Get the unadjusted score.
    cout << "Enter the student's raw numeric score: ";
    cin >> numericScore;
```

(program continues)

Program 14-5 *(continued)*

```
    // Get the curve percentage.
    cout << "Enter the curve percentage for this student: ";
    cin >> percentage;

    // Send the values to the exam object.
    exam.setPercentage(percentage);
    exam.setScore(numericScore);

    // Display the grade data.
    cout << fixed << setprecision(2);
    cout << "The raw score is " << exam.getRawScore() << endl;
    cout << "The curved score is " << exam.getScore() << endl;
    cout << "The curved grade is " << exam.getLetter() << endl;

    return 0;
}
```

Program Output with Example Input Shown in Bold
```
Enter the student's raw numeric score: 87 [Enter]
Enter the curve percentage for this student: 1.06 [Enter]
The raw score is 87.00
The curved score is 92.22
The curved grade is A
```

It is important to note that even though a derived class may redefine a function in the base class, objects that are defined of the base class type still call the base class version of the function. This is demonstrated in Program 14-6.

Program 14-6

```
// This program demonstrates that when a derived class function
// overrides a base class function, objects of the base class
// still call the base class version of the function.
#include <iostream>
using namespace std;

class BaseClass
{
public:
    void showMessage()
        { cout << "This is the Base class.\n"; }
};
```

(program continues)

Program 14-6 *(continued)*

```cpp
class DerivedClass : public BaseClass
{
public:
    void showMessage()
        { cout << "This is the Derived class.\n"; }
};

int main()
{
    BaseClass b;
    DerivedClass d;

    b.showMessage();
    d.showMessage();

    return 0;
}
```

Program Output
```
This is the Base class.
This is the Derived class.
```

In Program 14-6, a class named BaseClass is declared with a member function named show-Message. A class named DerivedClass is then declared, also with a showMessage member function. As their names imply, DerivedClass is derived from BaseClass. Two objects, b and d are defined in function main. The object b is a BaseClass object and d is a DerivedClass object. When b is used to call the showMessage function, it is the BaseClass version that is executed. Likewise, when d is used to call showMessage, the DerivedClass version is used.

14.5 Polymorphism and Virtual Member Functions

CONCEPT | A virtual member function in a base class expects to be overridden in a derived class.

The term *polymorphism* means the ability to take many forms. It occurs when member functions in a class hierarchy behave differently, depending on which object performed the call. You have already learned how to redefine functions in inherited classes. Simply redefining a base class function, however, does not create true polymorphic behavior. For example, consider the following situation:

◆ A base class has member functions named doCalc() and calc(). The calc() function calls the doCalc() function.

◆ A derived class redefines the doCalc() function, but not the calc() function.

In this situation, a problem arises when an object of the derived class calls the inherited function calc(). When calc() calls doCalc(), it is the base class version of doCalc() that gets executed, not the redefined version. This is illustrated in Figure 14-4.

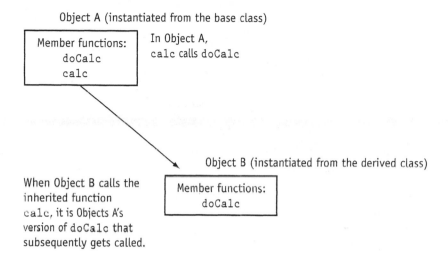

Figure 14-4

For example, consider the following PassFailActivity class, which is derived from the GradedActivity class. The class is intended to determine a letter grade of 'P' for passing, or 'F' for failing.

Contents of *PassFailActivity.h*

```
// Specification file for the GradedActivity class
// NOTE: This class incorrectly uses a redefined member function.
#ifndef PASSFAILACTIVITY_H
#define PASSFAILACTIVITY_H
#include "GradedActivity2.h"

// PassFailActivity class declaration

class PassFailActivity : public GradedActivity
{
protected:
    double passingScore;        // Minimum passing score.
    void determineGrade();      // Redefined function
public:
    void setPassingScore(double s)
        { passingScore = s; }

    double getPassingScore()
        { return passingScore; }
};

#endif
```

Contents of `PassFailActivity.cpp`

```cpp
// Implementation file for the PassFailActivity class
#include "PassFailActivity.h"

//*********************************************************
// Member function PassFailActivity::determineGrade      *
// Will this function get called by the base class's      *
// setScore function?                                      *
//*********************************************************

void PassFailActivity::determineGrade()
{
    if (score >= passingScore)
        letter = 'P';
    else
        letter = 'F';
}
```

This class has a member variable, `passingScore`, which is the minimum score that a student must make to get a grade of 'P'. The `setPassingScore` function sets this variable, and `getPassingScore` returns the value in this variable. Notice that this class redefines the `determineGrade` function. Its version of the function only assigns the grades 'P' or 'F'.

Recall that the `determineGrade` function is called from the `setScore` function, which is a member of the `GradedActivity` class. Will the `setScore` function call the base class version of the function or the derived class version? Program 14-7 shows us.

Program 14-7

```cpp
// This program demonstrates a derived class that redefines
// a base class function. Will the redefined function be called?
#include <iostream>
#include <iomanip>
#include "PassFailActivity.h"
using namespace std;

int main()
{
    PassFailActivity exam;
    double numericScore, minPassingScore;

    // Get the minimum passing score.
    cout << "Enter the minimum passing score for this test: ";
    cin >> minPassingScore;

    // Get student's score.
    cout << "Enter the student's numeric score: ";
    cin >> numericScore;
```

(program continues)

Program 14-7 *(continued)*

```
    // Send the values to the exam object.
    exam.setPassingScore(minPassingScore);
    exam.setScore(numericScore);

    // Display the grade data.
    cout << fixed << setprecision(2);
    cout << "The minimum passing score is "
        << exam.getPassingScore() << endl;
    cout << "The numeric score is " << exam.getScore() << endl;
    cout << "The grade is " << exam.getLetter() << endl;

    return 0;
}
```

Program Output with Example Input Shown in Bold
```
Enter the minimum passing score for this test: 60 [Enter]
Enter the student's numeric score: 75 [Enter]
The minimum passing score is 60.00
The numeric score is 75.00
The grade is C
```

Although the student is supposed to receive a grade of 'P', this program assigned a grade of 'C'. Because the setScore function is a member of the base class, it calls the base class's version of the determineGrade function. For a numeric score of 75, the base class's version of the determineGrade function sets the letter grade to 'C'.

This behavior happens because C++ decides at compile time which version of the determineGrade function to execute when it encounters a call to the function. Because the call to determineGrade is in the setScore function, it binds the call to the version of the function that resides in the same class as setScore. This is called *static binding*.

To remedy this, the determineGrade function can be made *virtual*. A *virtual function* is a member function that expects to be redefined in a derived class. The compiler performs *dynamic binding* on virtual functions. This means that C++ determines at run time which function to call, depending on the type of the object responsible for the call. If a GradedActivity object is responsible for the call, C++ will execute the GradedActivity::determineGrade function. If a PassFailActivity object is responsible for the call, C++ will execute the PassFailActivity::determineGrade function.

Virtual functions are declared by placing the key word virtual before the return type in the base class's function declaration, such as:

```
virtual void determineGrade();
```

 Note: You only place the virtual key word in the function's declaration or prototype. If the function is defined outside the class, you do not place the virtual key word in the function header.

This declaration tells the compiler to expect determineGrade to be redefined in a derived class. The compiler does not bind calls to the function with the actual function itself. Instead, it allows the program to bind calls, at runtime, to the version of the function that belongs to the same class as the object responsible for the call. Program 14-8 is identical to Program 14-7, except it uses a corrected version of the GradedActivity and PassFailActivity classes, where the determineGrade function is declared virtual.

Program 14-8

Contents of *GradedActivity3.h*

```
// Specification file for the GradedActivity class
#ifndef GRADEDACTIVITY_H
#define GRADEDACTIVITY_H

// GradedActivity class declaration

class GradedActivity
{
protected:
    char letter;                    // To hold the letter grade
    double score;                   // To hold the numeric score
    virtual void determineGrade();  // Determines letter grade
public:
    void setScore(double s)
        { score = s;
          determineGrade();}

    double getScore()
        { return score; }

    char getLetter()
        { return letter; }
};

#endif
```

Contents of *GradedActivity3.cpp*

```
// Implementation file for the GradedActivity class
#include "GradedActivity3.h"

//*************************************************************
// Virtual Member function GradedActivity::determineGrade *
//*************************************************************
```

(program continues)

Program 14-8 *(continued)*

```cpp
void GradedActivity::determineGrade()
{
    if (score >= 90)
        letter = 'A';
    else if (score >= 80)
        letter = 'B';
    else if (score >= 70)
        letter = 'C';
    else if (score >= 60)
        letter = 'D';
    else
        letter = 'F';
}
```

Contents of *PassFailActivity2.h*

```cpp
// Specification file for the GradedActivity class
// NOTE: This class correctly uses a redefined
// member function.
#ifndef PASSFAILACTIVITY_H
#define PASSFAILACTIVITY_H

#include "GradedActivity3.h"

// PassFailActivity class declaration

class PassFailActivity : public GradedActivity
{
protected:
    double passingScore;              // Minimum passing score.
    virtual void determineGrade();    // Redefined function
public:
    void setPassingScore(double s)
        { passingScore = s; }

    double getPassingScore()
        { return passingScore; }
};

#endif
```

(program continues)

Program 14-8 *(continued)*

Contents of `PassFailActivity2.cpp`

```cpp
// Implementation file for the PassFailActivity class
#include "PassFailActivity2.h"

//*********************************************************
// Member function PassFailActivity::determineGrade      *
//*********************************************************

void PassFailActivity::determineGrade()
{
    if (score >= passingScore)
        letter = 'P';
    else
        letter = 'F';
}
```

Contents of the main program file, `Pr14-8.cpp`

```cpp
// This program demonstrates a derived class that redefines
// a base class function.
#include <iostream>
#include <iomanip>
#include "PassFailActivity2.h"
using namespace std;

int main()
{
    PassFailActivity exam;
    double numericScore, minPassingScore;

    // Get the minimum passing score.
    cout << "Enter the minimum passing score for this test: ";
    cin >> minPassingScore;

    // Get student's score.
    cout << "Enter the student's numeric score: ";
    cin >> numericScore;

    // Send the values to the exam object.
    exam.setPassingScore(minPassingScore);
    exam.setScore(numericScore);

    // Display the grade data.
    cout << fixed << setprecision(2);
    cout << "The minimum passing score is "
         << exam.getPassingScore() << endl;
    cout << "The numeric score is " << exam.getScore() << endl;
    cout << "The grade is " << exam.getLetter() << endl;

    return 0;
}
```

Program 14-8 *(continued)*

Program Output with Example Input Shown in Bold
```
Enter the minimum passing score for this test: 60 [Enter]
Enter the student's numeric score: 75 [Enter]
The minimum passing score is 60.00
The numeric score is 75.00
The grade is P
```

This program correctly assigns the grade 'P' for a score of 75. The virtual `PassFailActivity::` `determineGrade` function is called because a `PassFailActivity` object is responsible for the call.

 Note: The `determineGrade` function is declared with the `virtual` key word in both the `GradedActivity` and `PassFailActivity` classes. It is only necessary that the function be declared virtual in the base class, however. When a derived class redefines a base class's virtual function, the derived class's function automatically becomes virtual as well. It is still a good idea to use the `virtual` key word in the derived class, however, for documentation purposes.

When a class redefines a virtual function, it is said that the class *overrides* the function. The difference between overriding and redefining base class functions is that overridden functions are dynamically bound, and redefined functions are statically bound. Only virtual functions can be overridden.

14.6   Abstract Base Classes and Pure Virtual Functions

CONCEPT An abstract base class cannot be instantiated, but other classes are derived from it. A pure virtual function is a virtual member function of a base class that must be overridden. When a class contains a pure virtual function as a member, that class becomes an abstract base class.

Sometimes it is helpful to begin a class hierarchy with an *abstract base class*. An abstract base class is not instantiated itself, but serves as a base class for other classes. The abstract base class represents the generic, or abstract form of all the classes that are derived from it.

For example, consider a factory that manufactures airplanes. The factory does not make a generic airplane, but makes three specific types of planes: two different models of prop-driven planes, and one commuter jet model. The computer software that catalogs the planes might use an abstract base class called `Airplane`. That class has members representing the common characteristics of all airplanes. In addition, it has classes for each of the three specific airplane models the factory manufactures. These classes have members representing the unique characteristics of each type of plane. The base class, `Airplane`, is never instantiated, but is used to derive the other classes.

A class becomes an abstract base class when one or more of its member functions is a *pure virtual function*. A pure virtual function is a virtual member function declared in a manner similar to the following:

```
virtual void showInfo() = 0;
```

The = 0 notation indicates that showInfo is a pure virtual function. Pure virtual functions have no body, or definition, in the base class. They must be overridden in derived classes. Additionally, the presence of a pure virtual function in a class prevents a program from instantiating the class. The compiler will generate an error if you attempt to define an object of an abstract base class.

For example, look at the following abstract base class Student. It holds data common to all students, but does not hold all the data needed for students of specific majors.

Contents of Student.h

```
// Specification file for the Student class
#ifndef STUDENT_H
#define STUDENT_H
#include <cstring>          // For strcpy

class Student
{
protected:
    char name[51];          // Student name
    char id[21];            // Student ID
    int yearAdmitted;       // Year student was admitted
    int hoursCompleted;     // Semester hours completed
public:
    Student()                        // Constructor
        { name[0] = '\0'; id[0] = '\0';
          yearAdmitted = 0; hoursCompleted = 0; }

    void setName(char *n)
        { strcpy(name, n); }

    void setID(char *i)
        { strcpy(id, i); }

    void setYearAdmitted(int y)
        { yearAdmitted = y; }

    virtual void setHours() = 0;    // Pure virtual function
    virtual void showInfo() = 0;    // Pure virtual function
};

#endif
```

The Student class contains members for storing a student's name, ID number, year admitted, and number of hours completed. It also has member functions for setting values in the name, id, and yearAdmitted members. Two pure virtual functions are also declared: setHours and showInfo.

These pure virtual functions must be overridden in classes derived from the Student class. They were made pure virtual functions because this class is intended to be the base for classes that represent students of specific majors. For example, a CsStudent class might hold the data for a computer science student, and a BiologyStudent class might hold the data for a Biology student. Computer Science students must take courses in different disciplines than those taken by Biology students. It stands to reason that the CsStudent class will calculate the number of hours taken in a different manner than the BiologyStudent class, and each will have different types of information to display.

Let's look at an example of the CsStudent class.

Contents of *CsStudent.h*

```
// Specification file for the CsStudent class
#ifndef CSSTUDENT_H
#define CSSTUDENT_H
#include "Student.h"

class CsStudent : public Student
{
private:
    int mathHours;       // Hours of math taken
    int csHours;         // Hours of computer science taken
    int genEdHours;      // Hours of general education taken
public:
    void setMathHours(int mh)
        { mathHours = mh; }

    void setCsHours(int csh)
        { csHours = csh; }

    void setGenEdHours(int geh)
        { genEdHours = geh; }

    void setHours()
        { hoursCompleted = genEdHours + mathHours + csHours; }

    void showInfo();     // Defined in CsStudent.cpp
};

#endif
```

Contents of `CsStudent.cpp`

```
// Implementation file for the CsStudent class
#include <iostream>
#include "CsStudent.h"
using namespace std;

//****************************************************
// Definition of the CsStudent::showInfo function   *
// This function displays the student information    *
// for a computer science student.                   *
//****************************************************

void CsStudent::showInfo()
{
    cout << "Name: " << name << endl;
    cout << "Student ID: " << id << endl;
    cout << "Year admitted: " << yearAdmitted << endl;
    cout << "Summary of hours completed:\n";
    cout << "\tGeneral Education: " << genEdHours << endl;
    cout << "\tMath: " << mathHours << endl;
    cout << "\tComputer Science: " << csHours << endl << endl;
    cout << "\tTotal Hours Completed: " << hoursCompleted << endl;
}
```

The `CsStudent` class, which is derived from the `Student` class, has member variables and functions for holding and setting the number of hours completed in math, computer science, and general education. In addition it overrides the `setHours` and `showInfo` functions.

Program 14-9 demonstrates the `Student` and `CsStudent` classes.

Program 14-9

```
// This program demonstrates the CsStudent class, which is
// derived from the abstract base class, Student.
#include <iostream>
#include "CsStudent.h"
using namespace std;

int main()
{
    CsStudent student1;
    const int SIZE = 51;
    char chInput[SIZE];     // Input buffer for entering C-strings.
    int intInput;           // Input buffer for entering integers.

    cout << "Enter the following student information:\n";
    // Set the student's name.
    cout << "Name: ";
    cin.getline(chInput, SIZE);
    student1.setName(chInput);
```

(program continues)

Program 14-9 *(continued)*

```
    // Set the student's ID number.
    cout << "Student ID: ";
    cin.getline(chInput, SIZE);
    student1.setID(chInput);

    // Set the year admitted.
    cout << "Year admitted: ";
    cin >> intInput;
    student1.setYearAdmitted(intInput);

    // Set the # of general ed hours completed.
    cout << "Number of general ed hours completed: ";
    cin >> intInput;
    student1.setGenEdHours(intInput);

    // Set the # of math hours completed.
    cout << "Number of math hours completed: ";
    cin >> intInput;
    student1.setMathHours(intInput);

    // Set the # of computer science hours completed.
    cout << "Number of computer science hours completed: ";
    cin >> intInput;
    student1.setCsHours(intInput);

    // Total the hours entered.
    student1.setHours();

    // Display the information provided.
    cout << "\nSTUDENT INFORMATION\n";
    student1.showInfo();
    return 0;
}
```

Program Output with Example Input Shown in Bold
```
Enter the following student information:
Name: Marty Stamey
Student ID: 167W98337
Year admitted: 2005
Number of general ed hours completed: 12
Number of math hours completed: 9
Number of computer science hours completed: 18
```

(output continues)

Program 14-9   *(continued)*

```
STUDENT INFORMATION
Name: Marty Stamey
Student ID: 167W98337
Year admitted: 2005
Summary of hours completed:
        General Education: 12
        Math: 9
        Computer Science: 18

        Total Hours Completed: 39
```

Remember the following points about abstract base classes and pure virtual functions:

- ◆ When a class contains a pure virtual function, it is an abstract base class.

- ◆ Pure virtual functions are declared with the = 0 notation.

- ◆ Abstract base classes cannot be instantiated.

- ◆ Pure virtual functions have no body, or definition, in the base class.

- ◆ Pure virtual functions *must* be overridden in derived classes in order for them to become nonabstract.

14.7   Base Class Pointers

 CONCEPT Pointers to a base class may be assigned the address of a derived class object. The pointer, however, will ignore any non-virtual overrides the derived class performs.

Pointers to base class objects exhibit behavior that is worth briefly discussing. Here are two important points to remember:

- ◆ A pointer to a base class object may point to an object that is derived from the base class.

- ◆ If the derived class overrides any members of the base class, however, the base class pointer will access objects of the base class.

This is shown in Program 14-10.

Program 14-10

```
// This program demonstrates the behavior of a base class pointer
// when it is pointing to a derived class that overrides members
// of the base class.
#include <iostream>
using namespace std;
```

(program continues)

Program 14-10 *(continued)*

```
class Base
{
    public:
        void show()
            { cout << "This is from the Base class.\n"; }
};

class Derived : public Base
{
    public:
        void show()
            { cout << "This is from the Derived class.\n"; }
};

int main()
{
    Base *bptr;
    Derived dobject;

    bptr = &dobject;
    bptr->show();              //Base class pointer, ignores override.
    return 0;
}
```

Program Output
```
This is from the Base class
```

Because dobject is derived from the Base class, a Base class pointer, such as bptr, may point to it. When bptr is used to call the show function, however, it ignores the fact that dobject has its own version of the function. bptr causes the Base class's show function to execute.

This type of behavior can be altered by the use of virtual functions. If the show function had been declared virtual in the Base class, bptr would have executed the Derived class version.

 ## Checkpoint [14.4–14.7]

14.8   Explain the difference between overloading a function and redefining a function.

14.9   Explain the difference between static binding and dynamic binding.

14.10 Are virtual functions statically bound or dynamically bound?

14.11 What will the following program display?

```
#include <iostream.>
using namespace std;
```

```
class First
{
protected:
    int a;
public:
    First(int x = 1)
        { a = x; }

    virtual void twist()
        { a *= 2; }

    int getVal()
        { twist(); return a; }
};

class Second : public First
{
private:
    int b;
public:
    Second(int y = 5)
        { b = y; }
    virtual void twist()
        { b *= 10; }
};

int main()
{
    First object1;
    Second object2;

    cout << object1.getVal() << endl;
    cout << object2.getVal() << endl;
    return 0;
}
```

14.12 What will the following program display?

```
#include <iostream>
using namespace std;

class Base
{
protected:
    int baseVar;
public:
    Base(int val = 2)
        { baseVar = val; }
```

```
        int getVar()
            { return baseVar; }
};

class Derived : public Base
{
private:
    int derivedVar;
public:
    Derived(int val = 100)
        { derivedVar = val; }
    int getVar()
        { return derivedVar; }
};

int main()
{
    Base *optr;
    Derived object;

    optr = &object;
    cout << optr->getVar() << endl;
    return 0;
}
```

14.8 Classes Derived from Derived Classes

CONCEPT A base class can also be derived from another class.

Sometimes it is desirable to establish a chain of inheritance in which one class is derived from a second class, which in turn is derived from a third class. Figure 14-5 illustrates this. In some programs, this chaining of classes goes on for many layers.

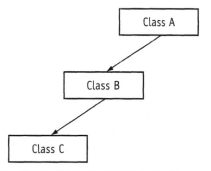

Figure 14-5

In Figure 14-5, class C inherits all of class B's members, including the ones class B inherited from class A. Of course, each class's access specification determines which members are accessible. Let's look at an example of how to create such a chain of inheritance.

In a previous section we discussed the `PassFailActivity` class, which is derived from the `GradedActivity` class. The `PassFailActivity` class determines whether a student's grade is 'P' for passing or 'F' for failing, based on a numeric score. Suppose we wish to extend this class with another more specialized class. For example, the following `PassFailExam` class determines a passing or failing grade for an exam. It has member variables for the number of questions on the exam (`numQuestions`), the number of points each question is worth (`pointsEach`), and the number of questions missed by the student (`numMissed`).

Contents of *PassFailExam.h*

```
// Specification for the PassFailExam class, which
// is derived from the PassFailActivity class
#ifndef PASSFAILEXAM_H
#define PASSFAILEXAM_H
#include "PassFailActivity2.h"

class PassFailExam : public PassFailActivity
{
protected:
    int numQuestions;      // Number of questions
    double pointsEach;     // Points for each question
    int numMissed;         // Number of questions missed
public:
    // Constructor
    PassFailExam(int n)    // Parameter n is the number of questions
        { numQuestions = n;
          pointsEach = 100.0 / n; }

    double getPointsEach()
        { return pointsEach; }

    void setNumMissed(int);

    int getNumMissed()
        { return numMissed; }
};

#endif
```

Contents of *PassFailExam.cpp*

```
// Implementation file for the PassFailExam class
#include "PassFailExam.h"
```

```
//*********************************************************
// Member function PassFailExam::setNumMissed            *
// This function accepts the number of questions missed  *
// as its argument. It then calculates the numeric score *
// and calls the inherited setScore member function.     *
//*********************************************************

void PassFailExam::setNumMissed(int n)
{
    double numericScore;

    numMissed = n;
    numericScore = 100.0 - (n * pointsEach);
    setScore(numericScore);
}
```

Notice that this class is derived from the PassFailActivity class, which is derived from the GradedActivity class. The class hierarchy is shown in Figure 14-6.

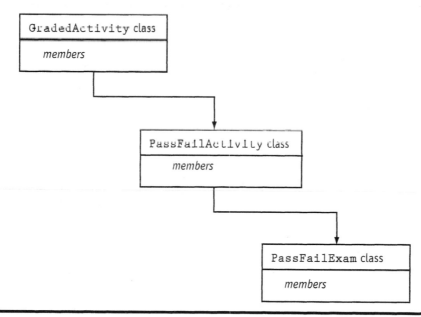

Figure 14-6

The PassFailExam class inherits all of PassFailActivity's members, including the ones that PassFailActivity inherited from GradedActivity. Because the public base class access specification is used, all of the protected members of PassFailActivity become protected members of PassFailExam, and all of the public members of PassFailActivity become public members of PassFailExam. Table 14-2 lists all of the member variables of the PassFailExam class, and Table 14-3 lists all the member functions. These include the members that were inherited from the base classes.

Table 14-2

Member Variable of the PassFailExam class	Access	Inherited?
numQuestions	protected	No
pointsEach	protected	No
numMissed	protected	No
passingScore	protected	Yes, from PassFailActivity
letter	protected	Yes, from PassFailActivity, which inherited it from GradedActivity
score	protected	Yes, from PassFailActivity, which inherited it from GradedActivity

Table 14-3

Member Function of the PassFailExam class	Access	Inherited?
Constructor	public	No
getPointsEach	public	No
setNumMissed	public	No
getNumMissed	public	No
determineGrade	protected	Yes, from PassFailActivity (This is a virtual function, overriding the GradedActivity version.)
setPassingScore	public	Yes, from PassFailActivity
getPassingScore	public	Yes, from PassFailActivity
setScore	public	Yes, from PassFailActivity, which inherited it from GradedActivity
getScore	public	Yes, from PassFailActivity, which inherited it from GradedActivity
getLetter	public	Yes, from PassFailActivity, which inherited it from GradedActivity

This class is demonstrated in Program 14-11.

Program 14-11

```cpp
// This program demonstrates a derived class that is
// derived from another class
#include <iostream>
#include "PassFailExam.h"
using namespace std;

int main()
{
    int numQuestions,       // To hold the number of exam questions
        questionsMissed;    // To hold the number of missed questions
    double minPassingScore; // To hold the minimum passing score

    // Get the number of questions on the exam.
    cout << "How many questions does the exam have? ";
    cin >> numQuestions;

    // Define a PassFailExam object for the exam.
    PassFailExam exam(numQuestions);

    // Get the minimum passing grade.
    cout << "What is the minimum passing score? ";
    cin >> minPassingScore;
    exam.setPassingScore(minPassingScore);

    // Get the number of questions missed by the student.
    cout << "How many questions did the student miss? ";
    cin >> questionsMissed;

    // Pass the number of missed questions to the exam object.
    exam.setNumMissed(questionsMissed);

    // Display the numeric score and grade.
    cout << "Minimum passing score: " << exam.getPassingScore()
         << endl;
    cout << "Exam score: " << exam.getScore() << endl;
    cout << "Grade: " << exam.getLetter() << endl;

    return 0;
}
```

Program Output with Example Input Shown in Bold
```
How many questions does the exam have? 100 [Enter]
What is the minimum passing score? 60 [Enter]
How many questions did the student miss? 25 [Enter]
Minimum passing score: 60
Exam score: 75
Grade: P
```

14.9 Multiple Inheritance

CONCEPT Multiple inheritance is when a derived class has two or more base classes.

In the previous section you saw how a class may be derived from a second class that is itself derived from a third class. The series of classes establishes a chain of inheritance. In such a scheme, you might be tempted to think of the lowest class in the chain as having multiple base classes. A base class, however, should be thought of as the class that another class is directly derived from. Even though there may be several classes in a chain, each class (below the topmost class) only has one base class.

Another way of combining classes is through multiple inheritance. *Multiple inheritance* is when a class has two or more base classes. This is illustrated in Figure 14-7.

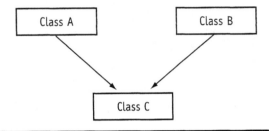

Figure 14-7

In Figure 14-7, class C is directly derived from classes A and B, and inherits the members of both. Neither class A nor B, however, inherits members from the other. Their members are only passed down to class C. Let's look at an example of multiple inheritance. Consider the two classes declared here:

Contents of `Date.h`
```
// Specification file for the Date class
#ifndef DATE_H
#define DATE_H

class Date
{
protected:
    int day;
    int month;
    int year;
public:
    Date(int d, int m, int y)
        { day = d; month = m; year = y; }
```

```
        int getDay()
            { return day; }

        int getMonth()
            { return month; }

        int getYear()
            { return year; }
    };

    #endif
```

Contents of *Time.h*

```
    // Specification file for the Time class
    #ifndef TIME_H
    #define TIME_H

    class Time
    {
    protected:
        int hour;
        int min;
        int sec;
    public:
        Time(int h, int m, int s)
            { hour = h; min = m; sec = s; }

        int getHour()
            { return hour; }

        int getMin()
            { return min; }

        int getSec()
            { return sec; }
    };

    #endif
```

These classes are designed to hold integers that represent the date and time. They both can be used as base classes for a third class we will call DateTime:

Contents of *DateTime.h*

```
    // Specification file for the DateTime class
    #ifndef DATETIME_H
    #define DATETIME_H

    #include "Date.h"
    #include "Time.h"
```

```cpp
class DateTime : public Date, public Time
{
protected:
    char dateTimeString[20];
public:
    DateTime(int, int, int, int, int, int);    // Constructor

    const char *getDateTime()
    { return dateTimeString; }
};

#endif
```

The first line in the `DateTime` declaration reads

```cpp
class DateTime : public Date, public Time
```

Notice there are two base classes listed, separated by a *comma*. Each base class has its own access specification. The general format of the first line of a class declaration with multiple base classes is

```
class <DerivedClassName> : <AccessSpecification> <BaseClassName>,
<AccessSpecification> <BaseClassName> [, ...]
```

The notation in the square brackets indicates that the list of base classes with their access specifications may be repeated. (It is possible to have several base classes.)

Now look at `DateTime`'s constructor:

Contents of `DateTime.cpp`

```cpp
// Implementation file for the DateTime class
#include <cstring>      // For strcpy and strcat
#include <cstdlib>      // For itoa
#include "DateTime.h"

DateTime::DateTime(int dy, int mon, int yr, int hr, int mt, int sc) :
    Date(dy, mon, yr), Time(hr, mt, sc)
{
    char temp[10]; // Temporary work area for itoa()

    // Store the date in dateTimeString, in the form MM/DD/YY
    strcpy(dateTimeString, itoa(getMonth(), temp, 10));
    strcat(dateTimeString, "/");
    strcat(dateTimeString, itoa(getDay(), temp, 10));
    strcat(dateTimeString, "/");
    strcat(dateTimeString, itoa(getYear(), temp, 10));
    strcat(dateTimeString, " ");

    // Store the time in dateTimeString, in the form HH:MM:SS
    strcat(dateTimeString, itoa(getHour(), temp, 10));
    strcat(dateTimeString, ":");
```

```
        strcat(dateTimeString, itoa(getMin(), temp, 10));
        strcat(dateTimeString, ":");
        strcat(dateTimeString, itoa(getSec(), temp, 10));
    }
```

The function header of the constructor contains notation that is used to pass arguments to the constructors of the base classes:

```
DateTime(int dy, int mon, int yr, int hr, int mt, int sc) :
    Date(dy, mon, yr), Time(hr, mt, sc)
```

After the DateTime constructor's parameter list comes a colon, followed by a list of calls to the Date and Time constructors. The calls are separated by a comma. When using multiple inheritance, the general format of a derived class's constructor's header is

> *⟨DerivedClassName⟩(ParameterList) : ⟨BaseClassName⟩(ArgumentList),*
> *⟨ BaseClassName ⟩(ArgumentList)[, ...]*

The order that the base class constructor calls appear in the list does not matter. They are always called in the order of inheritance. That is, they are always called in the order they are listed in the first line of the class declaration. Because Date is listed before Time in the DateTime class declaration, Date's constructor will always be called first. If the classes use destructors, they are always called in reverse order of inheritance.

Program 14-12 shows the Date, Time, and DateTime classes in use.

Program 14-12

```
// This program demonstrates a class with multiple inheritance.
#include <iostream>
#include "DateTime.h"
using namespace std;

int main()
{
    // Define a DateTime object and initialize it
    // with the date 2/4/60 and the time 5:32:27.
    DateTime pastDay(2, 4, 60, 5, 32, 27);

    // Display the date and time.
    cout << pastDay.getDateTime() << endl;
    return 0;
}
```

Program Output
```
4/2/60 5:32:27
```

Note: It should be noted that multiple inheritance opens the opportunity for a derived class to have ambiguous members. That is, two base classes may have member variables or functions of the same name. In situations like these, the derived class should always redefine or override the member functions. Calls to the member functions of the appropriate base class can be performed within the derived class using the scope resolution operator, ::, after the appropriate base class. The derived class can also access the ambiguously named member variables of the correct base class using the scope resolution operator. If these steps aren't taken, the compiler will generate an error when it can't tell which member is being accessed.

 ## Checkpoint [14.8–14.9]

14.13 Does the following diagram depict multiple inheritance or a chain of inheritance?

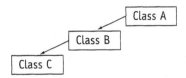

14.14 Does the following diagram depict multiple inheritance or a chain of inheritance?

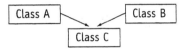

14.15 Examine the following classes. The table lists the variables that are members of the `Third` class (some are inherited). Complete the table by filling in the access specification each member will have in the `Third` class. Write "inaccessible" if a member is inaccessible to the `Third` class.

```
class First
{
    private:
        int a;
    protected:
        double b;
    public:
        long c;
};

class Second : protected First
{
    private:
        int d;
    protected:
        double e;
```

```
    public:
        long f;
};

class Third : public Second
{
    private:
        int g;
    protected:
        double h;
    public:
        long i;
};
```

Member Variable	Access Specification in Third class
a	
b	
c	
d	
e	
f	
g	
h	
i	

14.16 Examine the following class declarations:

```
class Van
{
protected:
    int passengers;
public:
    Van(int p)
    { passengers = p; }
};

class FourByFour
{
```

```
protected:
    double cargoWeight;
public:
    FourByFour(float w)
        { cargoWeight = w; }
};
```

Write the declaration of a class named `SportUtility`. The class should be derived from both the `Van` and `FourByFour` classes above. (This should be a case of multiple inheritance, where both `Van` and `FourByFour` are base classes.)

Review Questions and Exercises

Short Answer

1. What is an "is a" relationship?

2. A program uses two classes: `Dog` and `Poodle`. Which class is the base class and which is the derived class?

3. How does base class access specification differ from class member access specification?

4. What is the difference between a protected class member and a private class member?

5. Can a derived class ever directly access the private members of its base class?

6. Which constructor is called first, that of the derived class or the base class?

7. What is the difference between redefining a base class function and overriding a base class function?

8. When does static binding take place? When does dynamic binding take place?

9. What is an abstract base class?

10. A program has a class `Potato`, which is derived from the class `Vegetable`, which is derived from the class `Food`. Is this an example of multiple inheritance? Why or why not?

11. What base class is named in the line below?

    ```
    class Pet : public Dog
    ```

12. What derived class is named in the line below?

    ```
    class Pet : public Dog
    ```

13. What is the class access specification of the base class named below?

    ```
    class Pet : public Dog
    ```

14. What is the class access specification of the base class named below?

    ```
    class Pet : Fish
    ```

15. Protected members of a base class are like _____ members, except they may be accessed by derived classes.

16. Complete the table below by filling in private, protected, public, or inaccessible in the right-hand column:

In a private base class, this base class MEMBER access specification...	...becomes this access specification in the derived class.
private	
protected	
public	

17. Complete the table below by filling in private, protected, public, or inaccessible in the right-hand column:

In a protected base class, this base class MEMBER access specification...	...becomes this access specification in the derived class.
private	
protected	
public	

18. Complete the table below by filling in private, protected, public, or inaccessible in the right-hand column:

In a public base class, this base class MEMBER access specification...	...becomes this access specification in the derived class.
private	
protected	
public	

Algorithm Workbench

19. Write the first line of the declaration for a `Poodle` class. The class should be derived from the `Dog` class with public base class access.

20. Write the first line of the declaration for a `SoundSystem` class. Use multiple inheritance to base the class on the `CDplayer` class, the `Tuner` class, and the `CassettePlayer` class. Use public base class access in all cases.

21. Suppose a class named `Tiger` is derived from both the `Felis` class and the `Carnivore` class. Here is the first line of the `Tiger` class declaration:

```
class Tiger : public Felis, public Carnivore
```

Here is the function header for the Tiger constructor:

`Tiger(int x, int y) : Carnivore(x), Felis(y)`

Which base class constructor is called first, `Carnivore` or `Felis`?

22. Write the declaration for class B. The class's members should be:

♦ `m`, an integer. This variable should not be accessible to code outside the class or to any class derived from class B.

♦ `n`, an integer. This variable should not be accessible to code outside the class, but should be accessible to any class derived from class B.

♦ `setM`, `getM`, `setN`, and `getN`. These are the set and get functions for the member variables `m` and `n`. These functions should be accessible to code outside the class.

♦ `calc`, a public virtual member function which returns the value of `m` times `n`.

Next write the declaration for class D, which is derived from class B. The class's members should be:

♦ `q`, a `float`. This variable should not be accessible to code outside the class but should be accessible to any class derived from class D.

♦ `r`, a `float`. This variable should not be accessible to code outside the class, but should be accessible to any class derived from class D.

♦ `setQ`, `getQ`, `setR`, and `getR`. These are the set and get functions for the member variables `q` and `r`. These functions should be accessible to code outside the class.

♦ `calc`, a public member function which overrides the base class `calc` function. This function should return the value of `q` times `r`.

True or False

23. T F   The base class's access specification affects the way base class member functions may access base class member variables.

24. T F   The base class's access specification affects the way the derived class member functions may access base class member variables and functions.

25. T F   Private members of a private base class become inaccessible to the derived class.

26. T F   Public members of a private base class become private members of the derived class.

27. T F   Protected members of a private base class become public members of the derived class.

28. T F   Public members of a protected base class become private members of the derived class.

29. T F   Private members of a protected base class become inaccessible to the derived class.

30. T F   Protected members of a public base class become public members of the derived class.

31. T F   The base class constructor is called after the derived class constructor.

32. T F   The base class destructor is called after the derived class destructor.

33. T F   It isn't possible for a base class to have more than one constructor.

34. T F   Arguments are passed to the base class constructor by the derived class constructor.

35. T F   A member function of a derived class may not have the same name as a member function of the base class.

36. T F   Pointers to a base class may be assigned the address of a derived class object.

37. T F   A base class may not be derived from another class.

Find the Errors

Each of the class declarations and/or member function definitions below has errors. Find as many as you can.

38.
```cpp
class Car, public Vehicle
{
    public:
        Car();
        ~Car();
    protected:
        int passengers;
}
```

39.
```cpp
class Truck, public : Vehicle, protected
{
    private:
        double cargoWeight;
    public:
        Truck();
        ~Truck();
};
```

40.
```cpp
class Table : public Furniture
{
    protected:
        int numSeats;
    public:
        Table(int n)  : Furniture(numSeats)
            { numSeats = n; }
        ~Table();
};
```

14

Programming Challenges

1. Time Format

In Program 14-12, the file `Time.h` contains a `Time` class. Design a class called `MilTime` that is derived from the `Time` class. The `MilTime` class should convert time in military (24-hour) format to the standard time format used by the `Time` class. The class should have the following member variables:

milHours:	Contains the hour in 24 hour format. For example, 1:00 pm would be stored as 1300 hours, and 4:30 pm would be stored as 1630 hours.
milSeconds:	Contains the seconds in standard format.

The class should have the following member functions:

Constructor:	The constructor should accept arguments for the hour and seconds, in military format. The time should then be converted to standard time and stored in the `hours`, `min`, and `sec` variables of the `Time` class.
setTime:	Accepts arguments to be stored in the milHour and `milSeconds` variables. The time should then be converted to standard time and stored in the `hours`, `min`, and `sec` variables of the `Time` class.
getHour:	Returns the hour in military format.
getStandHr:	Returns the hour in standard format.

Demonstrate the class in a program that asks the user to enter the time in military format. The program should then display the time in both military and standard format.

Input Validation: The `MilTime` *class should not accept hours greater than 2359, or less than 0. It should not accept seconds greater than 59 or less than 0.*

2. Employee Information

Design a base class named `Employee`. The class should keep the following information in member variables:

Employee name

Social security number, in the format XXX-XX-XXXX, where each X is a digit within the range 0–9.

Employee number, in the format XXX–L, where each X is a digit within the range 0–9, and the L is a letter within the range A–M.

Hire date

Add a constructor, destructor, and other appropriate member functions to the class. The constructor should dynamically allocate enough memory to hold the employee's name, and the destructor should free the unused memory.

Next, design a class named EmployeePay. This class should be derived from the Employee class. It should keep the following information in member variables:

Annual pay, Monthly pay, Dependents (the number of dependents the employee claims).

Demonstrate the class in a program that asks the user to enter sample data, and then displays it on the screen.

Input Validation: Only accept valid social security numbers (with no alphabetic characters) and valid employee numbers (as described above). Do not accept negative values for annual pay or the number of dependents.

3. Hourly Pay

Design a class called HourlyPay, derived from the EmployeePay class you designed in assignment 2 above. The HourlyPay class should store the following information in member variables:

Hourly pay rate
Overtime pay rate
Number of hours worked

Demonstrate the class in a program that asks the user to enter sample data and then displays it on the screen.

Input Validation: Do not accept values over 30 or negative values for the hourly pay rate. Do not accept values over 45 or negative values for the overtime pay rate. Do not accept values over 60 for hours worked.

4. Time Clock

Design a class named TimeClock. The class should be derived from the MilTime class you designed in Programming Challenge 1. The class should allow the programmer to pass two times to it: starting time and ending time. The class should have a member function that returns the amount of time elapsed between the two times. For example, if the starting time is 900 hours (9:00 am), and the ending time is 1300 hours (1:00 pm), the elapsed time is 4 hours.

Input Validation: The class should not accept hours greater than 2359 or less than 0.

5. Paycheck

Write a program that uses the classes you designed in Programming Challenges 3 and 4. The program should ask for sample data for the employee information and the starting and ending work times, and then calculate the employee's pay. Display the information on the screen.

6. Essay Class

Design an Essay class that is derived from the GradedActivity class presented in this chapter. The Essay class should determine the grade a student receives on an essay. The student's essay score can be up to 100, and is determined in the following manner:

◆ Grammer: 30 points

◆ Spelling: 20 points

◆ Correct length: 20 points

◆ Content: 30 points

Demonstrate the class in a simple program.

7. PersonData and CustomerData Classes

Design a class named PersonData with the following member variables:

◆ lastName

◆ firstName

◆ address

◆ city

◆ state

◆ zip

◆ phone

Write the appropriate set and get functions for these member variables.

Next, design a class named CustomerData, which is derived from the PersonData class. The CustomerData class should have the following member variables:

◆ customerNumber

◆ mailingList

The customerNumber variable will be used to hold a unique integer for each customer. The mailingList should be a bool. It will be set to true if the customer wishes to be on a mailing list, or false if the customer does not wish to be on a mailing list. Write appropriate set and get functions for these member variables. Demonstrate an object of the CustomerData class in a simple program.

8. PreferredCustomer Class

A retail store has a preferred customer plan where customers may earn discounts on all their purchases. The amount of a customer's discount is determined by the amount of the customer's cumulative purchases in the store.

◆ When a preferred customer spends $500, he or she gets a 5% discount on all future purchases.

- When a preferred customer spends $1,000, he or she gets a 6% discount on all future purchases.

- When a preferred customer spends $1,500, he or she gets a 7% discount on all future purchases.

- When a preferred customer spends $2,000 or more, he or she gets a 10% discount on all future purchases.

Design a class named `PreferredCustomer`, which is derived from the `CustomerData` class you created in Programming Challenge 7. The `PreferredCustomer` class should have the following member variables:

- `purchasesAmount` (a double)
- `discountLevel` (a double)

The `purchasesAmount` variable holds the total of a customer's purchases to date. The `discountLevel` variable should be set to the correct discount percentage, according to the store's preferred customer plan. Write appropriate member functions for this class and demonstrate it in a simple program.

9. Student Information

Design a class called `StudentInfo`. It should have member variables for the following information:

```
Student name
Student ID number (12 characters)
Major (Computer Science, Business, etc.)
```

Write appropriate member functions to store and retrieve information in the member variables above. The constructor should dynamically allocate enough memory to hold the student's name. The destructor should free the memory.

Design another class called `StudentGradeInfo`. This class should be derived from the `StudentInfo` class. It should have member variables for the following information:

```
Test grades (The class should hold 10 test grades)

Test average
```

Write appropriate member functions to store and retrieve information in the member variables above.

Demonstrate the classes above in a program that defines an array of `StudentGradeInfo` objects. The user should enter the test grades for each student, and the program should display each student's average.

Input Validation: Do not accept test scores less than zero or greater than 100 (the teacher doesn't give extra credit!)

10. Products and Services

This assignment is based on Programming Challenge 7 in Chapter 13, which asked you to design a DivSales class. Design another class named SalesType, which is derived from the DivSales class. The SalesType class should have the two following member variables:

products: a four-element array for holding the quarterly figures for product sales.

services: a four-element array for holding the quarterly figures for sales of services.

The sum of each quarter's product and service sales is the total sales of the division for the quarter. (In other words, products[0] + services[0] = the division's total sales for the first quarter.)

Modify the program you wrote in Chapter 13 so it asks the user to enter the product and service sales for each division. The program should still display each division's total sales for each quarter and the total corporate sales for the year.

Input Validation: Do not accept negative values for any sales figures.

11. Pure Abstract Base Class Project

Define a pure abstract base class called BasicShape. The BasicShape class should have the following members:

Private Member Variable:

area, a double used to hold the shape's area.

Public Member Functions:

getArea. This function should return the value in the member variable area.

calcArea. This function should be a pure virtual function.

Next, define a class named Circle. It should be derived from the BasicShape class. It should have the following members:

Private Member Variables:

centerX, a long integer used to hold the x coordinate of the circle's center.

centerY, a long integer used to hold the y coordinate of the circle's center.

radius, a double used to hold the circle's radius.

Public Member Functions:

constructor–accepts values for centerX, centerY, and radius. Should call the overridden calcArea function described below.

getCenterX–returns the value in centerX.

getCenterY–returns the value in centerY.

calcArea–calculates the area of the circle (area = 3.14159 * radius * radius) and stores the result in the inherited member area.

Next, define a class named Rectangle. It should be derived from the BasicShape class. It should have the following members:

Private Member Variables:

width, a long integer used to hold the width of the rectangle.

length, a long integer used to hold the length of the rectangle.

Public Member Functions:

constructor–accepts values for width and length. Should call the overridden calcArea function described below.

getWidth–returns the value in width.

getLength–returns the value in length.

calcArea–calculates the area of the rectangle (area = length * width) and stores the result in the inherited member area.

After you have created these classes, create a driver program that defines a Circle object and a Rectangle object. Demonstrate that each object properly calculates and reports its area.

Group Project

12. Bank Accounts

This program should be designed and written by a team of students. Here are some suggestions:

- ◆ One or more students may work on a single class.
- ◆ The requirements of the program should be analyzed so each student is given about the same work load.

◆ The parameters and return types of each function and class member function should be decided in advance.

◆ The program will be best implemented as a multi-file program.

Design a generic class to hold the following information about a bank account:

Balance

Number of deposits this month

Number of withdrawals

Annual interest rate

Monthly service charges

The class should have the following member functions:

Constructor:	Accepts arguments for the balance and annual interest rate.
deposit:	A virtual function that accepts an argument for the amount of the deposit. The function should add the argument to the account balance. It should also increment the variable holding the number of deposits.
withdraw:	A virtual function that accepts an argument for the amount of the withdrawal. The function should subtract the argument from the balance. It should also increment the variable holding the number of withdrawals.
calcInt:	A virtual function that updates the balance by calculating the monthly interest earned by the account, and adding this interest to the balance. This is performed by the following formulas:

$$\text{Monthly Interest Rate} = (\text{Annual Interest Rate} / 12)$$
$$\text{Monthly Interest} = \text{Balance} * \text{Monthly Interest Rate}$$
$$\text{Balance} = \text{Balance} + \text{Monthly Interest}$$

monthlyProc:	A virtual function that subtracts the monthly service charges from the balance, calls the calcInt function, and then sets the variables that hold the number of withdrawals, number of deposits, and monthly service charges to zero.

Next, design a savings account class, derived from the generic account class. The savings account class should have the following additional member:

status (to represent an active or inactive account)

If the balance of a savings account falls below $25, it becomes inactive. (The status member could be a flag variable.) No more withdrawals may be made until the balance is raised above $25, at which time the account becomes active again. The savings account class should have the following member functions:

withdraw: A function that checks to see if the account is inactive before a withdrawal is made. (No withdrawal will be allowed if the account is not active.) A withdrawal is then made by calling the base class version of the function.

deposit: A function that checks to see if the account is inactive before a deposit is made. If the account is inactive and the deposit brings the balance above $25, the account becomes active again. The deposit is then made by calling the base class version of the function.

monthlyProc: Before the base class function is called, this function checks the number of withdrawals. If the number of withdrawals for the month is more than 4, a service charge of $1 for each withdrawal above 4 is added to the base class variable that holds the monthly service charges. (Don't forget to check the account balance after the service charge is taken. If the balance falls below $25, the account becomes inactive.)

Next, design a checking account class, also derived from the generic account class. It should have the following member functions:

withdraw: Before the base class function is called, this function will determine if a withdrawal (a check written) will cause the balance to go below $0. If the balance goes below $0, a service charge of $15 will be taken from the account. (The withdrawal will not be made.) If there isn't enough in the account to pay the service charge, the balance will become negative and the customer will owe the negative amount to the bank.

monthlyProc: Before the base class function is called, this function adds the monthly fee of $5 plus $0.10 per withdrawal (check written) to the base class variable that holds the monthly service charges.

Write a complete program that demonstrates these classes by asking the user to enter the amounts of deposits and withdrawals for a savings account and checking account. The program should display statistics for the month, including beginning balance, total amount of deposits, total amount of withdrawals, service charges, and the ending balance.

 Note: You may need to add more member variables and functions to the classes than those listed above.

Appendices on the CD

The following appendices are on the accompanying *C++ Programmer's Handbook* CD:

Appendix A: ASCII Chart   Lists the ASCII and Extended ASCII characters and their codes.

Appendix B: Operator Precedence   Lists the C++ operators and their precedence.

Appendix C: Introduction to Flowcharting   A brief introduction to flowcharting, which discusses sequence, selection, case, repetition, and module structures.

Appendix D: Enumerated Data Types   Shows how to use the `enum` statement to create a programmer-defined enumerated data type.

Appendix E: Namespaces   This appendix explains namespaces and their purpose. Examples showing how to define a namespace and access its members are given.

Appendix F: Creating a Boolean Data Type   This appendix is for students using older compilers that do not support the `bool` data type. It shows how to create a programmer-defined `bool` data type that works like the standard `bool` data type.

Appendix G: Passing Command Line Arguments   Discusses how to write a C++ program that accepts arguments from the command line. This appendix will be useful to students working in a command line environment, such Unix, Linux, or the Windows MS-DOS prompt console.

Appendix H: Header File and Function Reference   This appendix provides a reference for the C++ library functions and header files discussed in the book.

Appendix I: Binary Numbers and Bitwise Operations   A guide to the C++ bitwise operators, as well as a tutorial on the internal storage of integers.

Appendix J: Multi-Source File Programs   Provides a tutorial on creating programs that consist of multiple source files. Function header files, class specification files, and class implementation files are discussed.

Appendix K: Introduction to Microsoft Visual C++ 6.0   A tutorial on how to start a project in Microsoft Visual C++ 6.0, compile a program, save source files, and more.

Appendix L: Introduction to Borland C++ Builder 5   A tutorial on how to start a Borland C++ Builder 5 project, compile a program, save source files, and more.

Appendix M: Introduction to Microsoft Visual C++ .NET   This appendix shows the student how to start a project, compile and run, save, and reopen files. It also explains how to set up a multi file project.

Appendix N: Stream Member Functions for Formatting   Discusses stream member functions for formatting, such as `setf`.

Appendix O: Linked Lists   This appendix covers linked list operations such as creating a linked list, appending a node, traversing the list, searching for a node, inserting a node, deleting a node, and destroying the list.

Appendix P: Recursion   Recursion is defined and demonstrated. This appendix discusses recursive applications and demonstrates a recursive factorial function.

Appendix Q: Searching and Sorting Arrays   This appendix discusses the basics of sorting arrays and searching for data stored in them. It covers the bubble sort, selection sort, linear search, and binary search algorithms.

Appendix R: Answers to Checkpoints

Appendix S: Solutions to Odd Numbered Review Questions

Index